LEGAL REFORM AND ADMINISTRATIVE DETENTION POWERS IN CHINA

Using a new conceptual framework, the author examines the processes of legal reform in post-socialist China. Drawing on Bourdieu's concept of the 'field', the increasingly complex and contested processes of legal reform are analysed in relation to police powers.

The impact of China's post-1978 legal reforms on police powers is examined through a detailed analysis of three administrative detention powers: detention for education of prostitutes; coercive drug rehabilitation; and re-education through labour. The debate surrounding the abolition in 1996 of detention for investigation (also known as shelter and investigation) is also considered. Despite over twenty years of legal reform, police powers remain poorly defined by law and subject to minimal legal constraint. They continue to be seriously and systematically abused. However, there has been both systematic and occasionally dramatic reform of these powers. This book considers the processes which have made these legal changes possible.

SARAH BIDDULPH is Associate Director (China) of the Asian Law Centre at the University of Melbourne, where she has established the Law School's Chinese law programme.

CAMBRIDGE STUDIES IN LAW AND SOCIETY

Cambridge Studies in Law and Society aims to publish the best scholarly work on legal discourse and practice in its social and institutional contexts, combining theoretical insights and empirical research.

The fields that it covers are: studies of law in action; the sociology of law; the anthropology of law; cultural studies of law; including the role of legal discourses in social formations; law and economics; law and politics; and studies of governance. The books consider all forms of legal discourse across societies, rather than being limited to lawyers' discourses alone.

The series editors come from a range of disciplines: academic law; socio-legal studies; sociology; and anthropology. All have been actively involved in teaching and writing about law in context.

Books in the Series

The Politics of Truth and Reconciliation in South Africa
Legitimizing the Post-Apartheid State
Richard A. Wilson

Modernism and the Grounds of Law
Peter Fitzpatrick

Unemployment and Government
Genealogies of the Social
William Walters

Autonomy and Ethnicity
Negotiating Competing Claims in Multi-Ethnic States
Yash Ghai

Constituting Democracy
Law, Globalism and South Africa's Political Reconstruction
Heinz Klug

The New World Trade Organization Agreements
Globalizing Law through Services and Intellectual Property
Christopher Arup

The Ritual of Rights in Japan
Law, Society, and Health Policy
Eric A. Feldman

The Invention of the Passport
Surveillance, Citizenship and the State
John Torpey

Governing Morals
A Social History of Moral Regulation
Alan Hunt

The Colonies of Law
Colonialism, Zionism and Law in Early Mandate Palestine
Ronen Shamir

Law and Nature
David Delaney

Social Citizenship and Workfare in the United States and Western Europe
The Paradox of Inclusion
Joel F. Handler

Law, Anthropology and the Constitution of the Social
Making Persons and Things
Edited by Alain Pottage and Martha Mundy

Judicial Review and Bureaucratic Impact
International and Interdisciplinary Perspectives
Edited by Marc Hertagh and Simon Halliday

Immigrants at the Margins
Law, Race, and Exclusion in Southern Europe
Kitty Calavita

Lawyers and Regulation
The Politics of the Administrative Process
Patrick Schmidt

Law and Globalization from Below
Toward a Cosmopolitan Legality
Edited by Boaventura de Sousa Santos and Cesar A. Rodriguez-Garavito

Public Accountability
Designs, Dilemmas and Experiences
Edited by Michael W. Dowdle

Law, Violence and Sovereignty Among West Bank Palestinians
Tobias Kelly

Law and Society in Vietnam
The Transition from Socialism in Comparative Perspective
Mark Sidel

Legal Reform and Administrative Detention Powers in China
Sarah Biddulph

LEGAL REFORM AND ADMINISTRATIVE DETENTION POWERS IN CHINA

Sarah Biddulph

CAMBRIDGE
UNIVERSITY PRESS

CAMBRIDGE UNIVERSITY PRESS
Cambridge, New York, Melbourne, Madrid, Cape Town, Singapore, São Paulo, Delhi

Cambridge University Press
The Edinburgh Building, Cambridge CB2 8RU, UK

Published in the United States of America by Cambridge University Press, New York

www.cambridge.org
Information on this title: www.cambridge.org/9780521869409

First published 2007

Printed in the United Kingdom at the University Press, Cambridge

A catalogue record for this publication is available from the British Library

ISBN-13 978-0-521-86940-9 hardback

For David

CONTENTS

PREFACE

This book started its life in 1994 when I was sitting in a library in China and came across some handbooks of police regulations that had been misfiled. These handbooks opened the door to research on an area that has taken me twelve years to complete. Throughout the extended period of this project, I have accumulated many debts to a large number of people who have helped and supported me in different ways.

My friends in China have helped me find documents and material; discussed ideas and laws; and aided my understanding of the changing organisation and culture of power, which, from the outside, often appears incomprehensible. I thank them especially because many had real doubts about the advisability of a project on police detention powers, but nevertheless assisted me however they could.

Mal Smith was a friend and mentor for many years. He encouraged me to start this project and to complete it. He is sorely missed. This work was submitted as a PhD thesis at the University of Melbourne in 2004. I owe a great debt of gratitude to my supervisors Michael Dutton and Pip Nicholson. They did more to assist me with this project than supervisors should humanly be asked. Without their comments, criticisms, advice and unswerving support, this project would not be what it is now. All errors of course are mine. My thanks to Jenny Morgan, Richard Mitchell, Tim Lindsey, Sean Cooney, Lisa Stearns and Carol Jones who, along with Michael Dutton, Pip Nicholson, Cheryl Saunders and Lawrence Maher, read and commented on parts or all of this book. Comments and suggestions provided by my two thesis examiners and by the referees for this book have been of great help in focussing my thinking on a number of issues and have assisted me as I finalised the manuscript.

My friends and colleagues in the Law School at the University of Melbourne have been constantly supportive of me and interested in this project, for which I am deeply grateful. Thanks too to Kathryn Taylor and Kerstin Steiner, who helped me produce the final version, and Ingrid Landau, who, with her sister Rose, carefully read the final draft of this book and checked references for me.

My parents have supported me unswervingly throughout this project. My mother read drafts and gave me endless encouragement; my father took ownership of the thesis when it got too heavy.

Finally, my special thanks to David. He has supported and encouraged, cajoled and advised. His support kept me going to the end.

An earlier version of my discussion of the abolition of detention for investigation in chapter 9 was published in 'Mapping Legal Change in the Context of Reforms to Chinese Police Powers' in John Gillespie and Pip Nicholson eds. (2005), *Asian Socialism and Legal Change: The Dynamics of Vietnamese and Chinese Reform*, 212–38. Many thanks to Maree Tait and Asia Pacific Press at the Australian National University for allowing me to use portions of that article in this book.

Some comments on the sources used in this book are warranted. When I started this research, the regulations, rules and other documents which form the basis of this work were not publicly available. The regulatory infrastructure of administrative detention is contained in a wide range of documents, including those issued by various organs of the Chinese Communist Party, documents issued jointly by Party organs and the State Council, State Council administrative regulations, ministerial and local rules and documents and speeches records of meetings. A significant proportion of these are of restricted circulation. I relied heavily on the annual collection of regulations, rules and normative documents compiled by the legal division of the Ministry of Public Security entitled *Public Security Law Enforcement Manual* (*Gong'an Jiguan Zhifa Shouce* 公安机关执法手册) which changed its name to *Necessary Knowledge for Law Enforcement by Public Security Organs* (*Gong'an Jiguan Zhifa Xuzhi* 公安机关执法须知) from 1998. The volume for the year 2004 was the last available at the time this manuscript was completed.

Starting from the late 1990s a wider range of documents and commentary has become publicly available, though information on this topic remains limited. I have also had access to some materials which are unpublished or which I have obtained as photocopies. I have satisfied myself that these materials are what they purport to be, but as they are confidential, I am not able to give more complete references to them. Where I have used these documents, I have set out their publication details as photocopy materials. Access to this range of material gives a unique opportunity to trace in detail the documentary account of the development, reform and efforts to supervise administrative detention powers. I have used national statistics where possible, though in some areas, such as my discussions of enforcement rates in respect of prostitution and drug addiction, statistics are only available for certain provinces and cities. I have used these rather than none at all, especially where they illustrate increased rates of enforcement during law and order campaigns. Unfortunately, some material to which I would have liked to have referred, including comprehensive statistics compiled by the Ministry of Public Security ('MPS'), is classified at a higher level of secrecy than the documents accessible to me.

Unless otherwise stated, translations of Chinese materials are my own. I am grateful to Shi Chenxia for her assistance in checking the Chinese translations in the index of legislation and the glossary of terms at the time my PhD was submitted. Translations of titles of legal materials, Party documents and speeches are set out in Appendix 1, the index of legislation.

ABBREVIATIONS

ALL	Administrative Litigation Law 1989
ALL Interpretation	SPC, Interpretation on Several Questions on the Enforcement of the 'PRC Administrative Litigation Law' 1999
APL	Administrative Punishments Law 1996
ARL	Administrative Review Law 1999
ARR	Administrative Review Regulations 1990
CASS	Chinese Academy of Social Sciences
CCP ('Party')	Chinese Communist Party
CCPCC	Central Committee of the Chinese Communist Party
CMPO	Comprehensive Management of Public Order
CPL	Criminal Procedure Law 1996
CPPCC	Chinese People's Political Consultative Conference
Drugs Decision	NPCSC, Decision on the Prohibition of Drugs 1990
Five Major Cities Meeting	CCPCC approving and issuing the Central Political-Legal Committee Summary of the Public Order Meeting of the Five Major Cities of Beijing, Tianjin, Shanghai, Guangzhou and Wuhan 1981
KMT	Guomindang
MoJ	Ministry of Justice
MPS	Ministry of Public Security
NPC	National People's Congress
NPCSC	Standing Committee of the National People's Congress
PPL	People's Police Law
PRC (also 'China')	People's Republic of China
Prostitution Decision	NPCSC, Decision on Strictly Prohibiting Prostitution and Using Prostitutes 1991

RETL	Re-education through Labour
SAPL	Security Administrative Punishments Law 2006
SAPR	Security Administrative Punishments Regulations 1986
SPC	Supreme People's Court
SPP	Supreme People's Procuratorate
STDs	Sexually transmitted diseases
Supervision Law	NPCSC, PRC Supervision Law of the Standing Committees of Congresses at Each Level 2006
Temporary Measures	MPS, Temporary Measures on Re-education through Labour 1982
USA	United States of America
USSR	Union of Soviet Socialist Republics

PART ONE

INTRODUCTION AND CONCEPTUAL FRAMEWORK

CHAPTER ONE

THE PROBLEMS OF LEGAL REFORM OF POLICE ADMINISTRATIVE DETENTION POWERS

1 INTRODUCTION

This book examines the impact of rebuilding the Chinese legal system since 1978 on the administrative detention powers of the Chinese public security organs (*gong'an jiguan* 公安机关, also referred to in this book as the 'police').[1] The regulation and exercise of police administrative detention powers have arguably been amongst the most problematic areas in the programme of rebuilding China's legal system in the reform era.[2] Until recently, the process of reconstructing the legal system appeared to have limited impact on the definition and exercise of these powers. This has been so for at least two reasons.

First, administrative detention powers are exercised alongside the state's criminal justice powers to target conduct considered to be socially disruptive, to maintain public order, social stability and, ultimately, political stability.[3] Consequently, there has been a high degree of political sensitivity surrounding these powers. Deng Xiaoping repeatedly asserted that success of the economic modernisation programme

[1] The categories of forces falling within the definition of the people's police (*renmin jingcha* 人民警察) are set out in the *PRC People's Police Law* 1995 ('PPL') at art. 2. They include: the public security organs (*gong'an jiguan* 公安机关), the state security organs (*guojia anquan jiguan* 国家安全机关), the police in prisons (*jianyu* 监狱) and RETL management organs (*laodong jiaoyang guanli jiguan* 劳动教养管理机关) and the judicial police (*sifa jingcha* 司法警察) of the people's courts and people's procuratorates. In this book all references to 'the police' are to the public security organs.

[2] By 'reform era', I refer to the period following the Decision of the Third Plenum of the 11th Central Committee of the Chinese Communist Party ('CCPCC') in December 1978 to embark on a programme of economic reform and modernisation and to reconstruct the legal system.

[3] Petracca and Mong, 1990: 1101–2.

was premised on order and stability,[4] a demand reiterated by Jiang Zemin.[5] The maintenance of social control since the introduction of the economic modernisation policy in December 1978 has been so important that it has led sociologist Borge Bakken to comment that the policy of social control itself 'has been one of the crucial pillars of reform'.[6]

In recent years, problems of social disorder have worsened along with the deepening of inequities arising out of economic reform. The importance to the state of maintaining social order, control and stability has, if anything, heightened. The programme to promote the construction of a 'Harmonious Society' launched in February 2005 articulates a broad-ranging plan to address these problems of social inequality and conflict, with the slogan 'democracy, rule of law, equity, justice, sincerity, amity and vitality'.[7] A key focus of the Harmonious Society policy is to protect social stability and order.

Secondly, the slow pace of reform of administrative detention powers is partly because these powers are concentrated in the hands of the public security organs.[8] It is only in the reform era that the Chinese police have become a police force as understood in the Western sense of being a law enforcement agency, that is, a security force responsible for the management of public order and crime control.[9] Prior to 1979 it was more a revolutionary force than a force for law and order. In a socialist state such as China,[10] the public security organs remain

[4] Deng Xiaoping, *The Present Situation and the Tasks Before Us*, 16 January 1980; see also Zhang, Qiong, 2002: 38–9. In a speech in 1987, Deng Xiaoping said 'China is a backward country. If it is to become a developed, modernised country, there must be political stability, strict discipline and good public order, without those we can accomplish nothing': Deng Xiaoping, *The Two Basic Elements in China's Policies*, 4 July 1987; von Senger, 2000: 53.

[5] Jiang Zemin, *Hold High the Great Banner of Deng Xiaoping Theory for an All-round Advancement of the Cause of Building Socialism with Chinese Characteristics into the 21st Century*, 12 September 1997, 26; Lo, 1997: 483–5.

[6] Bakken, 2000: 6. As a consequence, committees of the Chinese Communist Party (the 'Party' or the 'CCP'), in particular the Political-Legal Committee (*Zhengfa Weiyuanhui* 政法委员会), have continued to be directly involved in the formation and implementation of social order policies and in aspects of law and order enforcement: discussed in chapters 4 and 7.

[7] The programme to construct a Harmonious Society was first set out by Hu Jintao at a meeting at the Party School of senior Party and government leaders at provincial and ministerial level on 19 February 2005. Hu is Party Secretary, President and Head of the Central Military Commission. The elements of an harmonious society are '*minzhu fazhi, gongping zhengyi, chengxin youai, chongman huoli, anding youxu, renyu ziran hexie xiangchu de shehui*' (民主法治, 公平正义, 诚信友爱, 充满活力, 安定有序, 人与自然和谐相处的社会): Hu, 20 February 2005.

[8] Discussed in chapters 3 to 6.

[9] Dutton, 2000: 61; Fu, 1994: 280–2.

[10] In this book I have adopted the definition of the state used by Heng in a discussion of the Vietnamese state, in which the state 'is defined broadly as the political authority that runs the country in an institutionalized structure of party and government organs': Heng, 2001:

one of the main forces to buttress the power of the Chinese Communist Party ('CCP' or 'Party') and to enforce its policies.[11] The public security continues to be a particularly powerful organ and central to the state's monopoly on coercion.[12]

Despite this mixture of political sensitivity and concentration of power in the hands of the police, factors that appear to militate against the legal reform of these powers, I demonstrate in this book that there has been both systematic and occasionally dramatic reform of these powers. I consider the processes which have made legal change possible.

2 THE ADMINISTRATIVE DETENTION POWERS

2.1 Introduction

In this book, I focus on three administrative detention powers: detention for education (*shourong jiaoyu* 收容教育); coercive drug rehabilitation (*qiangzhi jiedu* 强制戒毒); and re-education through labour (*laodong jiaoyang* 劳动教养, 'RETL').[13] These powers are imposed primarily by the

214. This definition includes the exercise of power of the CCP as well as the organs of state exercising legislative, executive and adjudicative power. This definition is further refined with reference to the division drawn by Pitman Potter between the 'regime' and its 'subjects'. The 'regime' constitutes the elite at central and provincial level and is defined in contrast to those 'who either have no participation in the exercise of political rule, or whose participation is wholly passive without opportunity for meaningful input': Potter, 1994b: 327.

11 McCormick, 1990: 1–26, arguing China should be characterised as a Leninist state and describing the basic aspects of Leninist political organisation as being 'the central institution is a political party with a broad and formalized ideological agenda that penetrates most aspects of society' (at 87). As a result, the state is dominated by a central party which is 'not just a ruling class but a ruling institution', and 'pre-empts autonomous social or political organisation' (at 87). The Party maintains an extensive organisation whose tasks include supervision of economic, political and social organisation which is buttressed by an extensive police network. The bureaucratic elite is also the political elite and the Party, through the government, has a preponderant role in economic affairs. Hamrin and Zhao, 1995: Introduction, xxv–xxviii, discussing the different models used to describe the transformation of Leninist states including: bureaucratic authoritarianism; communist neo-traditionalism; fragmented authoritarianism; and state corporatism. They conclude that the system in the Deng Xiaoping era (to the late 1980s) more closely resembled a bureaucratic authoritarian system. It is 'bureaucratic' in that the Party 'attempts to incorporate all social organisations within the party-state structure'. It is authoritarian in that the central party state retains 'ultimate, unlimited authority': at xxv-xxvi. They acknowledge that concepts from other theories also have explanatory value in respect of different aspects of the party state structure and operation.

12 Professor Lubman argues that 'police-administered sanctions express the dominance of the criminal process by the police at all times before legal reform began in 1978, except when it became a target of the Cultural Revolution': Lubman, 1999: 80. He argues that police dominance of the criminal justice process has continued into the reform era and is facilitated by the use of administrative forms of detention outside the formal criminal justice system: at 163–4, 168–70. See also McCormick, 1990: 104–14.

13 An alternate translation is rehabilitation through labour: Cohen, 1968: 21; Clarke, 1985: 1899.

Chinese public security organs in the execution of their public order (*zhi'an* 治安) responsibilities.[14] They are framed broadly to target people seen as posing a threat to social order, undermining the ethical life of society and harming the overall modernisation programme. This group includes prostitutes, drug addicts and people who dissent or commit misdemeanours, but whose acts are considered not to be sufficiently serious to warrant a criminal sanction.[15]

Administrative detention powers have been the subject of sustained criticism, both domestically and by international human rights groups. There is good justification for these criticisms. Lawyers and human rights groups have documented severe and chronic abuses of police powers and of administrative detention powers in particular.[16] Despite some legal reform, these powers remain discretionary and largely legally unconstrained.

By focussing on these three controversial powers – detention for education of prostitutes and clients of prostitutes, coercive drug rehabilitation and RETL – I have necessarily omitted other important administrative detention powers exercised by the police. For example, I do not look in any detail at powers such as administrative detention (*xingzheng juliu* 行政拘留) under the *Security Administrative Punishments Law*, detention for questioning (*liuzhi panwen* 留置盘问), detention for training of juvenile offenders (*shourong jiaoyang* 收容教养) in work-study schools[17] or confinement in asylums. The latter topic has been dealt with elsewhere in an excellent and detailed report.[18] The powers of detention for investigation (*shourong shencha* 收容审查)[19] and detention for repatriation (*shourong qiansong* 收容遣送), having been abolished, are considered only in passing. This book does not examine in detail criminal coercive powers exercised under the *Criminal Procedure Law*.

14 Hui, 1991: 100–2. 15 I discuss these powers in detail in chapters 5 and 6.

16 Cohen, 1993; Thornton, 1995; Fenwick, 2001, examining the use of forced labour; Human Rights in China, 2001b; Amnesty International, 1991, containing a detailed analysis of the legal basis for detention for investigation as well as documenting abuses; Amnesty International, 1997: 21–3;Wu, 1992: 81–107; Hung, 2003a; Human Rights in China, 2001b: 1–4, providing a short history of development of RETL and the documents forming its primary legal basis. A more general discussion can be found in Amnesty International, 1992; Amnesty International, 1996; Amnesty International, 1997; Human Rights Delegation to China, 1991; Human Rights in China, 1999; Human Rights in China, 2001b. Epstein, 1992: 13 discusses detention for repatriation briefly, as well as other detention powers such as detention for investigation and RETL in his general discussion of justice in China.

17 Discussed in Curran and Cook, 1993. 18 Munro, 2000.

19 Also translated as 'sheltering for examination' (Hsia and Zeldin, 1992); 'shelter and investigation' (Hecht, 1996: 21–2; Epstein and Wong, 1996: 480; Chen, Jianfu, 1999a: 201–6); and 'sheltering for examination' (Wong, 1996: 367).

2.2 Recent history

Although a range of detention powers was used for minor offenders prior to 1949,[20] the immediate origins of these police detention powers can be traced back to the early days of the establishment of the People's Republic of China ('PRC').[21] Professor Cohen refers to the use of these powers in the period 1949–53 as the '"administrative" roundups of petty thieves, gamblers, opium addicts, whores, pimps, vagrants and other dregs of the old society' where the police 'subjected them to "non-criminal" reform measures during the course of long confinement'.[22]

At this time, a range of powers was included within a category Cohen labelled 'formal administrative sanctions' exercised by the police.[23] Within this category, he lists sanctions imposed under the 1957 *Security Administrative Punishments Regulations* ('SAPR'),[24] supervised production[25] and RETL.[26] In addition to the group of powers discussed by Cohen, other police-imposed administrative detention powers extant in the 1950s and 1960s included detention of prostitutes in Women's Labour Training Centres,[27] Anti-Smoking Rehabilitation Centres for opium addicts[28] and detention for investigation for the detention and repatriation of transients.[29]

Since the 1970s, the social order problems that had, according to official accounts, been brought under control or eradicated[30] have

20 Dikotter *et al.*, 2002: 331–3, discussing detention of opium addicts in the Republican period; Dikotter, 2002: 78–80, discussing detention in police custody for a broad range of minor offences, in poorhouses for vagrants and in madhouses for those considered insane; Sommer, 2000: chapter 7, discussing criminalisation of prostitution in the late Qing under Yongzhen Emperor.

21 The origin of these powers is discussed in chapter 3.

22 Cohen, 1966: 477; Cohen, 1968: 10; Wong, 2002: 294, citing Cohen, includes administrative powers of the police within the populist (or informal) model of justice.

23 Cohen, 1968: 20–1, distinguishing 'formal administrative sanctions', which were exercised by the police, from 'informal administrative sanctions', which were exercised by power elites, work units and the masses during the Anti-Rightist Movement and Cultural Revolution, such as criticism, self-criticism and struggle sessions.

24 Cohen, 1968: 20. Whilst Professor Cohen translates '*Tiaoli*' as 'Act', in this book I adopt the more commonly used translation of '*Tiaoli*' as 'Regulation'.

25 Cohen, 1968: 21, also referred to as controlled production and supervised production.

26 Cohen, 1968: 21.

27 Henriot, 1995: 477, refers to them as *funü laodong jiaoyang suo*. These centres are also referred to as Women's Production Education and Fostering Institutes: Dutton, 2005: 152; and Huang, 1994: 119.

28 Central People's Government, *Circular on Strict Prohibition of Opium and Drug Taking*, 24 February 1950, art. 7.

29 Detention for investigation was split into two powers in 1975: detention for investigation and detention for repatriation.

30 For example, Mou, 1996: 192–3 in respect of prostitution; Zhang, Qiuhan, 1993: 11 in respect of drug addiction.

re-emerged. The powers to detain prostitutes and drug addicts that had officially fallen into desuetude because they were no longer needed have quietly been resurrected. As I discuss in chapter 6, those detention powers such as RETL that had remained extant have been adapted and expanded to meet changing social order problems.

2.3 Legal characterisation

The public security organs currently exercise a range of powers whose legal classifications are divided into criminal and administrative jurisdictions.[31] Powers exercised by the police under the criminal jurisdiction are enumerated in the *PRC Criminal Procedure Law* ('*CPL*').[32] The exercise of these powers is subject to supervision by the People's Procuratorate.[33] The People's Courts have sole jurisdiction to convict a person of a criminal offence.[34]

Administrative powers by contrast, are exercised, usually independently, by the police to sanction minor breaches of the law.[35] Whilst unlawful, the sanctioned conduct is not considered to be sufficiently serious to warrant prosecution under the *Criminal Law*.[36] The detention powers that are the focus of this book fall within the scope of the administrative powers of the police[37] and are regulated by administrative law and procedure, which is discussed in chapters 7 and 8.

In practice, however, these powers fall at the intersection of the categories of criminal and administrative law.[38] For example, detention for investigation, whilst officially categorised as an administrative power,

[31] He, 1991: 1–3, discussing the distinction between criminal, administrative and civil punishments.

[32] The two primary codes concerning criminal justice are the *Criminal Law of the PRC*, which first took effect on 1 January 1980 and was substantially amended in 1997, and the *Criminal Procedure Law of the PRC* ('*CPL*'), which first took effect on 1 January 1980 was substantially amended in 1996. References to the *Criminal Law* and *CPL*, unless otherwise stated, refer to the amended versions of these laws.

[33] *CPL*, art. 8. [34] *CPL*, art. 12.

[35] Police powers in respect of administrative and other infringements are set out in chapter 2 of the *PPL* 1995 as well as in *sui generis* legislation covering particular powers.

[36] The *Criminal Law* sets out at art. 13 the categories of acts enumerated in the criminal law that 'are crimes if according to the law they should be criminally punished'. It then makes the proviso, 'however, if the circumstances are clearly minor and the harm is not great, they are not deemed to be crimes'.

[37] Although this distinction between criminal and administrative powers is less familiar in common law jurisdictions, the coexistence in the police force of criminal investigation powers with a broad range of administrative powers related to social welfare and public order is more common in continental systems, especially those of Germany and France: Funk, 1995: 70; Monjardet, 1995: 49–50; Gramckow, 1995; Thomaneck, 1985.

[38] Liu, 2003.

was in fact used by the police as a substitute for more restrictive criminal coercive powers including criminal detention.[39] One use of RETL has been to detain for further investigation those for whom the police have insufficient evidence to obtain approval to arrest.

The legal form of administrative detention powers raises questions about the ways in which pursuit of social control has influenced the form of legal regulation in this area. The legal forms of detention for education and coercive drug rehabilitation are particularly interesting as their use was revived throughout the late 1970s and early 1980s after the decision was made to rebuild China's legal system. Although RETL was not officially abolished, during the Cultural Revolution its use diminished to the point where a conscious decision needed to be made in the late 1970s to revive it. We cannot just conclude that they are remnants from the pre-reform era, as these powers have been re-established at the same time as the rebuilding of the legal system was underway.

As the Chinese state intensifies its efforts to establish a system of law-based governance, the continuing existence of a wide range of administrative detention powers which are poorly defined by law and almost completely unconstrained by legal supervision mechanisms presents us with a number of uncomfortable questions. Does legal reform extend to administrative detention powers? If it does, how do we explain or justify the existence and legal form of these powers? If it does not, then why not? What are the possibilities for reform of these powers?

Before turning to the three detention powers that are the focus of this book, it is useful briefly to anticipate an example of legal reform I refer to in chapter 9. It is the story of abolition of one of the most controversial police detention powers, detention for investigation. This example illustrates both the possibilities and limits of legal reform. It also suggests the growing importance of law as a forum for debates about the structure and limits of police powers: issues central to this book.

[39] To avoid the inconvenience of the legal procedures required for other powers, detention for investigation was used instead of administrative detention, criminal detention or arrest and became a substitute for criminal arrest and investigation procedures: Li and Liu, 1992: 181. Detention for investigation was also used to avoid the time limits for criminal detention, to extend the investigation period or to punish those who had committed unlawful acts: Zhang and Zhang, 1991: 268.

3 LEGAL REFORM OF ADMINISTRATIVE DETENTION POWERS: THE DEMISE OF DETENTION FOR INVESTIGATION AND THE ISSUES IN THIS BOOK

Like the other detention powers considered in this book, detention for investigation developed out of efforts of the CCP to restore social order after it took power in 1949. In December 1957, the Central Committee of the CCP (the 'CCPCC') and the State Council instructed that unauthorised rural migrants and beggars be taken into detention in order to repatriate them. Troublemakers were to be subject to criminal sanction or RETL.[40] In response to the social upheaval caused by the Great Leap Forward and the resulting famine,[41] in 1961 the CCPCC approved formal creation of stations for the detention and repatriation of rural migrants who had 'blindly floated' (*mangmu liudong* 盲目流动) to the cities and for the investigation of suspected criminal or counter-revolutionary offences.[42] At this time, the power was officially described as one 'primarily to rescue, educate and help settle down people who had floated to the city as beggars and to protect social order'.[43]

Towards the end of the Cultural Revolution in 1975, the use of detention for the investigation of suspected criminal conduct by transients was administratively separated from the detention for repatriation of unauthorised rural migrants.[44] Detention for investigation centres were operated by the police and detention for repatriation by the civil administration organs.[45] The use of detention for investigation expanded dramatically in 1983 when the Party launched the first campaign of the Hard Strike against serious crime.[46]

[40] CCPCC, State Council jointly issuing the *Directive on Preventing the Blind Outflow of the Rural Population*, 18 December 1957; Zhang, Qingwu, 1990: 35.

[41] Spence, 1990: 583. [42] Fan and Xiao, 1991: 142–3; Cui, 1993b: 90–1.

[43] Wang, Jiancheng, 1992: 179.

[44] Fan and Xiao, 1991: 143; State Council approving and issuing MPS, Ministry of Railways, *Report of the National Conference on the Work of Public Order on Railways* in July 1975; MPS *Notice on Doing a Good Job of Ferreting Out Floating Criminals During the New Year and Spring Festival Period*, December 1975.

[45] Fan and Xiao, 1991: 143.

[46] Fan and Xiao, 1991: 143; Cui, 1993b: 92. The Hard Strike against Serious Crime (*Yanli Daji Yanzhong Xingshi Fanzui* 严厉打击严重刑事犯罪) has been commonly abbreviated as '*Yanda*' (严打) or 'Hard Strike': Tanner, Harold, 1999; Tanner, 1994: 12–16. In this book, I adopt Tanner's translation of the term 'Hard Strike'. Tanner, 2000 translates the term as 'Stern Blows' and Bakken, 2000 adopts the translation 'Severe Blows'. The term 'Hard Strike' has been used in two related though distinct contexts. The first is as a proper noun. In chapter 4, I discuss those views, arguing that there have been three 'Hard Strikes' in the reform era: 1983, 1996 and 2001. The second use of the term is descriptive of the style of enforcement, concerted action to strike hard and fast and to punish targeted activities severely and quickly, which is not limited to the three 'Hard Strikes'. The first use is rendered 'Hard Strike'. The second, in lower case, is rendered hard strike.

After this time, detention for investigation became a tool used by the police to detain for interrogation a wide range of people suspected of committing crime. The time limits for detention for investigation were considerably longer than the criminal detention power in the 1979 *CPL*.[47] Not surprisingly, the power was used as a substitute for criminal detention and investigation and for a range of other purposes.[48]

My examination of other administrative detention powers in this book shows that there are many commonalities in the pattern of their development. That is, the use of the powers has changed to address current problems of crime and social order and expanded as an adjunct to the implementation of periodic law and order campaigns. The documentary basis of these powers primarily comprises documents issued by a range of Party and administrative organs, many of them by the CCPCC and the Ministry of Public Security ('MPS'). Another similarity is the serious abuse of these powers which led to a public outcry and to high-level political concern at failures to control these abuses. In chapter 9, I document the debates that started in the 1980s about how detention for investigation could be reformed and, if it could not be reformed, about its abolition.

The most significant point is that the public face of the politically sensitive debate about reforming detention for investigation was conducted in terms of the lawfulness of the power and the developing legal framework governing the state's sanctioning powers. The MPS sought to obtain legal support for detention for investigation by drafting legislation to be passed by the Standing Committee of the National People's Congress ('NPCSC').[49] The MPS and its supporters argued that retention of detention for investigation as an administrative power was both necessary and not inconsistent with either the criminal law regime

[47] Under the 1979 *CPL*, art. 48, the police could only detain a person for three days prior to making an application for arrest to the procuratorate, with a possible extension of up to four days. The procuratorate was required to respond within three days. The total possible time for criminal detention was thus ten days. The initial period of detention for investigation, on the other hand, was one month, with possible extensions approved by higher-level public security organs of up to a total of three months: MPS, *Notice on Strictly Controlling the Use of Detention for Investigation Measures*, 31 July 1985, art. 3.

[48] Liu and Liu, 1992: 181; Zhang and Zhang, 1991: 268; Zhang, Xu, 1993: 20, suggesting that between 80 and 90 per cent of people convicted of criminal offences were first detained under this power. MPS, *Notice Strictly Prohibiting Public Security Organs from Interfering in Economic Disputes and Illegally Seizing People*, 25 April 1992, criticising and prohibiting detention by the police of one party to a contract dispute and demanding payment of the amount in dispute to secure their release.

[49] Gao, 1990: 20.

or the constitutional protection of freedom of the person.[50] When it became clear that the arguments in favour of abolition of the power had been successful, the MPS focussed its attention on reconstituting as much of the original power as possible in the amended *CPL* of 1996.[51]

The example of the abolition of detention for investigation suggests that the process of reconstructing the legal system does impact on the ways in which police power is organised and justified, even though the changes in the end did not result in a dramatic reduction of the powers of the public security organs to detain and interrogate criminal suspects. It suggests that the legal forum is one in which the public security organs are actively engaged to negotiate, define and justify their powers. The vigour of the debate about abolition of detention for investigation, conducted in the legal arena, suggests it was possible for a range of voices to be heard. The preferred view of the public security organs in this case did not prevail.

The story of detention for investigation raises a broader question, namely, what impact does the development of the legal system have on other detention powers? The recent controversy over questions of the legality and subsequent abolition of detention for investigation suggests that legal principle has expanded to cover powers which had previously been on the periphery of law or even beyond its purview. My study of the process of legal change as it relates to three police administrative detention powers builds upon the hypothesis that legal change is a dynamic process, driven by the imperative to structure and rationalise state power in legal terms, but that the ways in which this is achieved are contested and may not be uniform across different state sectors.

4 QUESTIONS AND HYPOTHESIS

Whilst legal reform has proceeded at an astonishing rate, most scholars acknowledge that the criminal justice and administrative sanctioning systems have failed to reform to the same extent as other areas of Chinese law.[52] How do we capture the complexity and inconsistencies

[50] *Constitution*, art. 37; Li and Liu, 1992: 183; Jiang and Zhan, 1994: 95–6.
[51] Discussed in chapter 9.
[52] Lubman, 1995: 2; Clarke, 1995; Lubman, 1999: 85–7; Chiu, 1992; Leng and Chiu, 1985; Amnesty International, 1991; Amnesty International, 1992; Dobinson, 2002; Hecht, 1996; Turack, 1999; Amnesty International, 1996; Human Rights in China, 2001b.

in the process of rebuilding the legal system? Viewed as a process of transition to some form of rule of law[53] or to modernity,[54] the continued existence and use of administrative detention powers appear to stand out as a remnant, a symbol of the incompleteness or partial failure of this process of reform to date. Some suggest that police administrative detention powers and the campaign style of law enforcement contain

53 Peerenboom, 2002c: 525, for example, concludes that the Chinese legal system is in transition to, but has not yet achieved, a formalist rule of law, though he argues it is no longer apposite to characterise the Chinese legal system as one of rule by law. Peerenboom draws a distinction between 'thick' (substantive) and 'thin' (formalist) versions of the rule of law and discusses different versions of the thick theories of the rule of law that take account of different political conceptions of a 'just socio-political order': Peerenboom, 2002c: 486. At 510, he distinguishes a 'thin' or formalist version of the rule of law from rule by law on the grounds that the 'former entails meaningful legal limits on the government actors'. However, the distinction between rule by law and rule of law is drawn differently by other scholars such as Orts, 2001: 94, who defines rule by law in a manner equating to Peerenboom's 'thin' rule of law as 'the use of legal rules in order to assure the uniformity and regularity of an existing legal system'. Orts, 2001: 94 defines the rule of law as referring 'to a normative and political theory of the relationship of legal institutions and the political state that includes, but is not limited to, a theory of limited government through some form of constitutional separation between the judiciary and other state powers', equating to Peerenboom's 'thick' theory of the rule of law. Lubman, 1999: 34–5 analyses legal change in terms of a formalist conception of the rule of law. See also Epstein, 1994; Peerenboom, 2002a; Keith, 1994; Keith and Lin, 2001; Li, Linda Chelan, 2000; Orts, 2001; Peerenboom, 1999. One difficulty with the use of rule of law to judge China's legal transformation lies in the contests over the definition and meaning of the rule of law, even in those countries purporting to have the rule of law: Allars, 1997: 40–9; Rosenfeld, 2001: 1308; Radin, 1989: 781; Clark, 1999: 28, recognising that the meaning of rule of law has changed over time. The divergence in conceptions of the rule of law and the differing conceptions of the relationship of the citizen to the state which these versions of the rule of law embody are further illustrated by the difference between the concept of Rechsstaat, or rational institutionalisation of state power by law: Freckmann and Wegerich, 1999: 59–60, the positive obligations of the 'constitutional state as the legal guarantor of fundamental rights' in France: Rosenfeld, 2001: 1329 and Anglo-American versions of the rule of law that emphasise a negative view of law as 'a buffer between the interests of the state and those of its citizens'; and which emphasise the role of the judiciary in protecting citizens' interests: Rosenfeld, 2001: 1333. Craig, 1997: 467 distinguishes formalist from substantive versions of the rule of law on the basis that the former is concerned with the manner in which law is promulgated, clarity of the norm and the 'temporal' aspects of the law, whilst the latter is concerned in addition with the content of the law, whether it protects rights and so 'good'. In applying the standard of rule of law to China, see generally, Liang, 1989, discussing the significance of historical differences between Western and Chinese understandings of the meanings and function of law. Epstein, 1994 draws a distinction between instrumental forms of law and legal legitimation. Clarke, 2003: 95–100 criticises as teleological analyses that view the development of the Chinese legal system in terms of how far away it is from a rule of law ideal.

54 Tanner, Harold, 1999: 182, 186, using Weber's work as a standard against which to judge modernity and more particularly, interpretations of Weber by US sociologists such as Talcott Parsons that give Weber's consideration of the conditions for the emergence of modern capitalism universal application. Parsons argues that societal evolution and modernisation depends upon the development of a general legal system, which comprises an 'integrated system of universalistic norms': Parsons, 1964: 351, 357. Parsons' expanded application of Weber's work is also discussed in Friedman, 1969b: 20–1.

remnants from the Maoist era.[55] Others see them as illustrative of the incomplete transformation of the Chinese legal system to the rule of law.[56]

Similarly, since 1978, the police have been gradually transforming themselves into a more professional and autonomous force with their own institutional interests.[57] However, the process of modernisation of the police force has been incomplete. Winkler suggests that the Chinese police have become an 'institutional hybrid', continuing to use Maoist strategies of mass campaigns and the retention of 'such mainstream Stalinist institutions as labour camps', at the same time as 'groping toward more modern forms of police work . . . based on legal institutions and professional training'.[58] In the case of administrative detention, Dutton and Lee have concluded that the continuing reliance on administrative detention powers shows the partial nature of professionalisation of the police force to date. They argue that there is a crisis in policing brought about by social change and that the weakening of established modes of social control has prevented the introduction of more comprehensive methods of maintaining social order.[59]

Despite the slowness and unevenness of reform, my hypothesis in analysing the impact of legal reform on police administrative detention powers is that legal reform *is* having an impact on administrative detention powers.

This hypothesis and approach raise three questions, each of which is addressed in this book. These inquiries are substantive and theoretical.

The first question is substantive: what are the continuities and discontinuities between administrative detention in the pre-reform and

[55] Winkler, 1999: 16–17; Lubman, 1999: 169–71, discussing non-judicial sanctioning systems and the problem these pose for the creation of a legal order. Wong, 2002 quotes directly from Cohen's discussion of the use of administrative detention in the 1950s by referring to contemporary problems of policing as continuing to include 'populist' modes of justice including 'administrative roundups' and contrasting this with more formal, regularised and legalised structures and processes of policing.

[56] Peerenboom, 2002a: 8–9, evaluating whether reforms in the criminal justice system represent development toward the rule of law; Dobinson, 2002: 56, finding reforms to the *Criminal Law* have not significantly advanced the rule of law; Chu, 2000: 157–8, 206, concluding that reforms to the *CPL* have had an impact on the behaviour of law enforcement officials and promoted aspects of the rule of law. Potter, 1999: 680–3; Lubman, 1999: 71, 85–7; Clarke and Feinerman, 1995; Tanner, Harold, 1999: 193–4; Dobinson, 2002: 56; Chen, Jianfu, 1999a: 167–96, highlighting the use of criminal law as an instrument of social and political control.

[57] Fu, 1994: 277; Ward and Bracey, 1985; Bracey, 1989; Brewer, 1988: 211–12; Tanner, Harold, 1999: 32–5; Dutton, 2000: 69–70. The professional nature of policing and the technical expertise required to carry out policing functions have also been used as an argument to bolster the powers and independence of the police forces in many Western countries: Dixon, 1997: 6–7.

[58] Winkler, 1999: 16–17.

[59] Dutton and Lee, 1993: 330–4; Dutton, 1995a: 435–8.

reform eras? In order to examine this question, I draw on Dutton's argument that administrative detention powers are both a revival and an adaptation of the techniques used around the time of the founding of the PRC. Dutton and Lee argue that in the reform era, policing techniques such as household registration, which depended for their efficacy upon a static population, lost efficacy.[60] Continuing reliance on the use of administrative sanctions and 'Hard Strikes' have been ways in which the police have sought to deal with the changing problems of crime and public order during the period of economic reform.[61] According to this explanation, abusive practices, whilst structural in nature, are not ideologically driven and do not derive from the authoritarian nature of the state as much as they are the practical consequences of the use of campaign-style policing which encourages use of 'flexible forms of detention' and 'encourages . . . a flexible approach to law'.[62] Dutton argues that today the use of these techniques of policing are technical and pragmatic rather than political in nature.[63] Drawing on Deleuze, he calls this process of redeployment of old forms for new purposes 'repetition with a difference'.[64]

The second set of questions builds upon the first by asking the extent to which, if at all, the programme of legal reform has reached administrative detention. Studies examining administrative detention powers point out that these powers continue to be poorly defined by law, allow the police uncontrolled discretion and are subject to systematic abuse. In order to examine the extent to which legal reform has impacted on administrative detention powers, I pose a series of questions.

To what extent does law structure police powers relating to administrative detention? Are administrative detention powers increasingly defined in legal as opposed to political and administrative terms? If so, in what ways and to what extent is this process of legalisation occurring? To what extent, and if so, in what ways, have the developing principles of administrative law been applied to regularise police administrative detention powers by defining law-making and interpretation powers, limiting administrative discretion and supervising enforcement practice? To address these questions, I examine the legal reforms to administrative detention powers. I also consider the impact

[60] Dutton and Lee, 1993: 330–4. See also Ma, 1997: 131–2; Yu and Zhang, 1999: 259–60.
[61] Dutton, 1992b; Dutton, 1992a; Dutton and Lee, 1993; Dutton, 1995a; Wong, 1996: 373–7 in relation to the changing use of detention for investigation in the 1980s.
[62] Dutton and Lee, 1993: 332; Dutton and Xu, 1998: 315.
[63] Dutton, 1992b: 218–19. [64] Dutton, 1995a: 418–21.

of developments in the broader legal regulatory environment in which these powers are defined and exercised, primarily in the area of administrative law.

These two areas of substantive inquiry pose a third question with which this book is concerned, which is theoretical and methodological in nature. That is: what does the examination of the extent and nature of change reveal about the processes of legal change and the constraints upon it? Commentators suggest that development of the legal regulatory framework in different functional systems,[65] such as security,[66] is not commensurate with legal developments in other functional systems such as, for example, the economy and finance.[67] Legal reforms in different sectors may thus 'be out of synchrony and in conflict with each other'.[68] What conceptual tools can be employed to understand this differential process of legal change?

As I indicated above, there are a number of paradigms within which this change or lack of change may be evaluated. Analyses of the legal form of administrative detention powers have been framed in terms of the shift between formalisation and informalisation of the administration of justice and as a question of whether legal reform reveals some move toward the rule of law. Analyses of police reforms consider the extent of police modernisation and professionalisation. As I discuss in chapter 2, analyses framed in terms of the rule of law have been given added impetus since adoption of the programme of rule according to law by the CCP in 1996. Viewed within this paradigm, administrative detention powers may be adjudged an area of failure in the transition to the rule of law. The reasons for these conclusions are not seriously in dispute. Applying a formalist or 'thin' standard of the rule of law in the Chinese context,[69] Randall Peerenboom argues that a system of rule of law requires that the law and legal system be able 'to impose meaningful restraints on the state and individual members of the ruling elite'.[70] As my analysis of the detention powers in this book will show, these

[65] The bureaucracy is organised into functional systems called *xitong* (系统) which are headed by a 'leadership small group' (*lingdao xiaozu* 领导小组) responsible for policy-making. Yan lists the Foreign Affairs, Finance and Economics, Propaganda, Political-Legal and the Central Military Commission as functional systems; Yan, 1995: 4. Lieberthal includes Party Affairs and Organisation and Personnel as separate *xitong*. Whilst these are Party organisations, the borderline between Party and state organisation is blurred: Lieberthal, 1995: 194–5.

[66] Yan, 1995: 4, lists security as part of the political-legal *xitong* which is in charge of police, judicial and state security affairs.

[67] Within the Finance and Economics *xitong*. [68] Winkler, 1999: 3.

[69] See discussion of the different interpretations of the rule of law above at notes 53 and 54.

[70] Peerenboom, 2002a: 8.

powers remain a flexible tool for the exercise of police power which continues to be defined primarily by administrative and policy documents. It would be difficult to sustain an argument that the legal regulation of administrative detention imposes any meaningful restraints on the police at present.

If we step aside for a moment from an analysis whose central question is one of transition to a particular point, it is possible to reformulate the question to one which focusses more attention on the processes than on the outcomes of reform. Such an approach does not deny the importance of the outcomes or substantive content of rule of law, or that all systems, including those claiming the label of rule of law, are, to an extent, instrumental. An examination of the processes of reform enables attention to be refocussed on how the principles, inconsistencies and complexities in law are produced. The outcomes of reform are thus not predetermined, as the processes of legal change are themselves dynamic and contested. Processes and outcomes, however, are linked and one outcome of these contests over production of the law may be to strengthen and increase the legitimacy of the legal system.

I explore the notion that legal change is a dynamic process involving the interplay between the state's agenda to strengthen the role of law as the primary mode of governance and the particular historical, policy and institutional contexts in which this programme of rebuilding the legal system is given concrete form. I examine the context in which and processes by which administrative detention powers have developed and are enforced, the role of policy, the specific institutional characteristics of the police and their relationship with other organs of state in shaping both the structure of powers and enforcement practice.[71] Such an approach seeks to avoid decontextualised 'grand theory' by embedding its consideration of the legal reform of administrative detention powers in their historical and institutional context and within the policy imperative of ensuring social order and stability.[72] Such an approach

71 Hawkins, 1986: 1179–80, arguing that analyses of decision-making should take into account the context within which policies are developed and decision-making takes place, in preference to adopting a rational-legal approach which assumes that decision-making is merely an application of rules. See also Galligan, 1990: 4–5.

72 Alford, 1986, discussing the need to avoid 'grand theory' when carrying out research on systems different from our own. Wright Mills, 1959: 23, describing 'grand theory' as a 'systematic theory of the nature of man and society' and criticising it as 'all too readily becom[ing] an elaborate and arid formalism'. Alford, 1986: 945–6, citing Skinner, 1985: 3, describing Wright Mills' view of grand theory as 'the belief that the primary goal of the social disciplines should be that of seeking to construct a systematic theory of the nature of man and society'. See also Lubman,

recognises that neither the state nor the police themselves are a monolithic entity with a single view.[73]

5 CONCEPTUAL FRAMEWORK: LEGAL REFORM AND INSTITUTION BUILDING AS A CONTESTED PROCESS

The starting point for mapping the processes of legal change is the empirical view of law as an 'aspect of society'.[74] It takes the view that '[l]aw and the social context in which it operates must be inspected together'.[75] This view emphasises the ways in which law and legal culture are embedded in broader social structures including history, politics, state and possibly non-state institutions.[76]

To invoke Professor Alford:

> legal doctrine cannot be understood simply as written, in isolation from other social phenomena. Implicit in this is the idea that law is contested and dynamic, even in our own legal system [the author is referring to the USA] and others that we might be inclined to think of as already largely 'developed'.[77]

Whilst conceived as embedded in broader social and political frameworks, I explore the extent to which the Chinese legal system is becoming conceptually distinct from them.[78] Rather than assume the continuation of a Leninist instrumental model under which the central Party elites entirely control policy and law-making and enforcement,[79]

1991: 301–2, warning of the dangers of studying current reforms without taking into account its pre-reform antecedents and practices, and at 323–8, against uncritically applying a Western conceptual framework and assumptions to examine aspects of the Chinese legal system.

73 Fu, 1998: 45, suggests that each of the state organs involved in the criminal justice process each 'jealously [guard] their power' and will act both to protect their own power and attack the power of other organs in order to ensure an equilibrium is maintained between them.

74 Cotterrell, 1995: 25–8, discussing empirical legal theory and contrasting it with normative legal theory. See also his idea of law as 'institutionalised doctrine': at 4. Legal doctrine, he argues, is shaped by 'pre-existing patterns of power' (at 8), as well as the practical and institutional contexts in which law is developed and used (at 4).

75 Moore, 1978: 55.

76 See Friedman, 1969b: 18, 54–6; Friedman, 1969a; Reimann, 2002: 677, discussing these issues in relation to comparative law scholarship.

77 Alford, 2000: 56.

78 Tucker, 1984: 258–66, discusses different views of law, from law being completely determined by its political and social context, to law being completely autonomous from external forces where the forces for legal change occur solely from within the legal system itself. He labels them 'reductionists' and 'autonomists' approaches, respectively. Balbus, 1977: 571 refers to the corresponding approaches as 'instrumentalist' or 'reductionist', and 'formalist'.

79 Discussed at note 11 above.

I explore the possibility that the process of rule and norm-making relating to administrative detention is becoming more contested and negotiated.[80]

Conceptualisation of law as a semi-autonomous forum in which interested actors contest the development of legal norms, but which remains heavily influenced by state political power, is suggestive of what Pierre Bourdieu has called the 'juridical field'.[81] In this book, I instead use the term 'legal field'. I draw on the concept of the legal field to provide a conceptual framework within which to examine my hypothesis that the form and content of the legal regulatory regime governing police administrative detention powers is *produced* as the result of interactions between different actors within the legal field and the interaction between the legal and other fields.[82] This conceptual framework contends that these contests are historically structured and that they take place within the bounds of the existing political structure of state, even though they are not completely dominated by the Party state.[83]

In an era where there are many forces on legal systems for change, the legal field facilitates a focus on the active nature of appropriation[84] of historical models and ideas as well as foreign ideas and institutions.[85] An approach focussing on legal change as an ongoing process means that the outcomes of these contests may not necessarily be consistent between subfields of the legal field, such as, for example, the legal regulation of social order and the legal regulation of the economic sphere.

The legal field provides an alternative analytical tool to that which measures legal change as a process of transition from Leninist instrumentalism to the rule of law, or which views the processes of

80 See Chapter 2 at section 2.4.

81 Bourdieu, 1987. I prefer to use an alternate term 'legal field' which is also used by Trubek *et al.*, 1994, and which contains less implication of the centrality of the courts.

82 Bourdieu, 1987.

83 The concept of the legal field and its application to the Chinese context is discussed in chapter 2.

84 Legrand, 2001: 61–2 argues in respect of legal transplants that the meaning of a legal rule is culturally constructed and invested with a local meaning. He argues that foreign rules are 'domesticated' by the local interpretive community. This process of interpretation is itself a contested process and so the meaning of rules is negotiated and is the 'result of divergent and conflicting interests in society': at 64.

85 There is a vast literature that examines the conditions that influence the success of 'transplants' of foreign legal rules and institutions into different national legal systems. See, for example, Kahn-Freund, 1974; Teubner, 1998; Mattei, 1997; Gillespie, 2002; Nelken, 2001; Potter, 2003c.

modernisation and globalisation as inexorably leading to a convergence between national legal systems.[86]

My final question is: how does the use of the legal field as an analytical construct illuminate our understanding of the processes of legal change of police administrative detention powers?

6 ORGANISATION OF THIS BOOK

Chapter 2 develops further the concept of the legal field and tests its applicability as a theoretical framework for the study of the process of legal change in contemporary China. I adapt the concept of the legal field to take account of the non-liberal nature of the Chinese polity. Within the bounds of the Party policy of law-based governance, I consider the evidence suggesting emergence of an increasing space within which differing positions may be adopted about the proper interpretation and implementation of this policy. I argue that the change of Party line to downgrade class struggle has made emergence of this space possible.[87]

Although views are not unanimous, there are indications that policy and law have become institutionally more distinct. Reasons include: the greater diversity and technical complexity of matters regulated by law; strengthening legal institutions; emergence of legal professionals such as lawyers and the legal academy, all of whom have divergent interests in and relationships to law; as well as the increasing use of law by non-state actors. I raise the possibility that the MPS, too, has an incentive to assert itself as an actor in the legal arena as its politically dominant position vis-à-vis other law enforcement agencies weakens.[88] This chapter concludes that, whilst instrumental uses of law in respect of the state's coercive powers remain particularly strong, the conditions exist for law to obtain a degree of autonomy from direct political control. In this environment, the legal field provides a useful framework for examining legal change.

[86] Advocated, for example, by Seita, 1997; discussed by Peerenboom, 2002c: 533; Peerenboom, 1999: 345. Scholars such as Li Buyun suggest that 'there is an increasingly substantive congruence in western and Chinese concepts of the rule of law' but view this convergence in more limited terms by adding the proviso that China should not 'copy indiscriminately each others' experience without paying due attention to legitimate indigenous differences'. Li Buyun's comments referred to in Keith and Lin, 2001: 37.

[87] Discussed in more detail in chapters 4 and 7.

[88] Fu, 1994: 280.

In chapters 3 to 6, I examine the development and uses of administrative detention through a social order policy lens. This examination reveals that administrative detention remains embedded in and forms an integral part of the Party and state's programmes for maintenance of social control and punishment of crime.

Chapter 3 traces the construction of a comprehensive array of social order strategies and powers in the 1950s and 1960s, which included a range of administrative detention powers. I place an examination of the evolution of these administrative detention powers and the pre-reform paradigms of social control in the context of the political environment that diverged sharply from that of the reform era.

In chapter 4 I examine the social order context within which administrative detention powers have developed in the reform era. Whilst contemporary social order policy has drawn on pre-reform strategies, I consider how they have been remade in the changed political and social environment in which they are now employed. A constant is the continuation of direct involvement of the Party in formulation and implementation of social order policy, particularly in the conduct of hard strikes.

I examine the factors that have led to increasing reliance by the police on administrative detention and the strengthening association of administrative detention with the punitive power of the state. Factors include both the weakening of localised community social control and crime-prevention mechanisms and the continuing reliance on hard strike strategies for the serious punishment of crime. I consider the implications of continuing Party involvement in social order policy and the demand for flexibility in enforcement on the prospects for legalisation and regularisation of administrative detention.

I conclude that there are several indicators suggesting that the force for legalisation of administrative detention powers is strengthening. The first is that the closed political nature of social order policy is becoming more open. Debates in the area of social order policy, such as those questioning the continuing efficacy of the hard strike as a strategy for dealing with contemporary problems of crime, indicate there is increasing space for debate and for differing positions to be taken about how to pursue the objectives of social order and crime control. The second is the increasing emphasis placed upon justifying social order policy and 'Hard Strikes' in legal terms and ensuring their congruence with the policy of governance according to law. Both these factors indicate that the centrality of policy in the contemporary uses of administrative detention is not necessarily a barrier to legalisation and regularisation of administrative detention powers.

Chapter 5 examines two detention powers, detention for education of prostitutes and coercive drug rehabilitation, since the beginning of the reform period. It traces the reinvigoration of these powers in the reform era to deal with acts characterised as socially harmful. This chapter traces the way in which development and expansion of these powers has been intertwined with social order policy and the political-legal organs that direct it, and has been particularly linked to 'Hard Strikes'. A corollary has been that, until recently, the legal definition of these powers has imposed negligible substantive or procedural constraints upon the police in the exercise of these detention powers. Although it may be argued that there has been formalistic compliance with the requirement to legalise the powers, they remain primarily defined by policy and administrative instruments.

Despite the limited legalisation of these powers, I conclude that the contemporary context within which detention is imposed in respect of prostitution and drug addiction diverges from that of the pre-reform era. Contemporary social order strategies are now distanced from pre-reform strategies which depended heavily on community-based, ideologically driven techniques of mass mobilisation to eliminate prostitution and drug addiction and to transform the offender. Now, detention of prostitutes and drug addicts forms a component of a more pragmatic and punitive policing regime in which the fine rather than transformation of the offender is the preferred course of action.

Chapter 6 deals with the development and contemporary uses of RETL. It examines the expansion of the scope of targets in the reform era to cover an increasingly broad range of socially disruptive activities in addition to those committing political errors. I trace the numerous documents that give this power a highly fragmented legal basis and that preserve the flexibility of the police both in the identification of targets and procedures for decision-making in the imposition of RETL. Like detention of prostitutes and drug addicts, in the reform era, RETL has developed in ways that reflect the priorities of social order policy and as one of the flexible tools for implementing hard strikes.

Unlike detention of prostitutes and drug addicts, RETL has been subject to intense public and international scrutiny and criticism because of its lack of a comprehensive legislative basis and its abuse. The MPS itself acknowledges that the procedures by which the police determine to send a person to RETL are among the most seriously abused areas of police work.[89] The MPS has responded recently by imposing some procedural guidelines to limit the flexibility of this aspect of decision-making. This move is indicative of the MPS's pragmatic use of law to address abuse and its sensitivity to legally framed criticisms that the definition of RETL is inconsistent with the requirements of governance according to law.

In chapters 7, 8 and 9 the focus changes to examine administrative detention from the point of view of reconstruction of the legal system. As demonstrated in chapters 3 to 6, both the development and uses of administrative detention powers continue to be primarily defined in accordance with the needs of policies of social control and the punishment of crime. From this perspective the degree of legalisation and regularisation of these powers appears slight. Nevertheless, I argue that recent reforms in the legislative framework governing the exercise of power by the police have started to impinge upon administrative detention in a number of different ways. Law now increasingly provides both the forum and the vocabulary in which debates about the reform and restructuring of administrative detention are conducted. This conclusion is illustrated in chapter 9.

Chapter 7 starts by examining Party leadership, both organisational and ideological, over the police and over social order enforcement policy. I contend that the nature and forms of Party leadership over the police is the starting point for any consideration of legalisation of the police force and police powers, as leadership of the Party remains a fundamental tenet of policing. This chapter shows how Party policies both frame and promote reforms such as legalisation and regularisation of police structure and powers.

Chapter 7 considers how the state's programme of rule according to law and 'administration according to law' (*yifa xingzheng* 依法行政) is promoting the reconstitution of the structure and powers of the police in legal rather than political terms. It discusses developments in the area of administrative law that set increasingly comprehensive parameters within which police administrative detention powers must be justified and exercised. Whilst chapters 5 and 6 conclude that the legal definition of administrative detention powers remains weak and that law places limited practical constraints on the use of administrative detention, the reforms discussed in chapter 7 suggest that the regulatory basis

89 See discussion in chapters 6 and 9.

of these powers is increasingly at odds with the broader legal principles of administrative law that are now being articulated.

Far from concluding that the MPS is able to ignore the broader developments in the law, chapter 7 documents the MPS's active engagement in the processes of determining the legal principles governing police power, administrative detention and the balance between empowerment and constraint. The highly contested nature of debates about law and legal principle in which a range of different positions are adopted illustrates the emergence of a legal field which provides an increasingly important forum in which the law governing police power is determined.

Chapter 8 explores efforts to regularise the exercise of police power through an array of overlapping supervision powers exercised by the Party, the MPS, congresses, local governments and courts. An examination of these supervision powers reveals that the standards for supervision and imposition of individual liability upon decision-makers are increasingly defined in legal terms. In a manner similar to the dynamics of legal change discussed in chapter 7, my examination of the different forms of supervision over police decision-making illustrates the diversity of individual and institutional interests in exercising supervision power, including efforts by the MPS to strengthen its vertical controls over local policing. I conclude that the expansion of legal norms and the different institutional interests at play in strengthening different supervision mechanisms are indicative of the operation of a legal field.

At the same time as noting the expansion of concepts of lawfulness and procedural fairness as standards for judging police decision-making, I also conclude that the force of the field, especially to influence individual decision-making, remains weak. Continuing problems of abuse of police detention power show that the expansion of supervision using the criteria of lawfulness has not led inevitably to an improvement in the lawfulness of police decision-making. Severe limitations on the capacity of these forms of supervision to exercise effective control over imposition of detention by the local police remain.

In chapter 9, I examine the ways in which the programme of governance according to law has caught up with administrative detention through an analysis of the debates about abolition of detention for investigation and about more wide-ranging reforms of administrative detention. Considering the ongoing debate about reform or abolition of RETL which is being conducted in legal terms, I argue that the legitimation of this power depends upon finding ways to make RETL appear to be compatible with the developing legal framework governing the exercise of the state's coercive power. Further, I consider the evidence suggesting that legal legitimation of police administrative detention powers as a whole has become an issue requiring resolution. Viewed as a contested process, there is a range of possible outcomes. One is the proposal that seeks to place these powers within a coherent, legally justifiable, but potentially illiberal, conceptual framework based on an adaptation of the Western concept of 'security defence'.

In chapter 10, I conclude that police administrative detention powers continue to form an integral and distinctive part of social order policy which facilitates flexibility in dealing with changing problems of social order. Although it is possible to trace growing legalisation and regularisation of police power, it has occurred unevenly and has done little in practice to constrain the scope of administrative detention, either in theory or practice. However, in both the recent developments in administrative law and the debates surrounding reform or abolition of administrative detention powers, I argue that it is possible to discern a growing space within which there may be debate about how the basic objectives of legalisation of governance in areas touching on social order are to be given concrete form.

I conclude that the concept of the legal field, by focussing on the processes of legal reform, helps to explain the growing force of law and the increasing dynamism of the forces at play in the ongoing production of legal norms that affect administrative detention powers. It also enables an explanation of the continuing weakness of law to impose normative standards on police conduct. The growing force of law helps to explain the necessity for the MPS to be able to justify its powers in legal terms and to make these powers consistent with the legal environment in which they are located. Failure to do so runs the risk of abolition of these powers.

CHAPTER TWO

THE LEGAL FIELD AND THE PROCESS OF LEGAL REFORM SINCE 1978

1 INTRODUCTION

This book posits the legal field as a conceptual framework through which to inquire into the growing force of law in ordering Chinese administrative detention powers and to frame my questions about the processes of legal change.

This chapter sets out Bourdieu's concept of the juridical field and considers how this idea may be applied to an examination of legal change in China. It considers the literature on Chinese legal reforms which suggest that conditions now exist for the emergence of such a field. In particular, I consider the literature examining the extent to which the state's instrumental uses of law have either changed or weakened and conclude that, whilst instrumental uses of law remain pronounced, the Party no longer controls all uses and interpretations of law. In the reform era, the increasing range and complexity of matters regulated by law has enabled a greater number of actors and institutions to participate in developing legal norms and theory and to use law for their own ends. Within the bounds of Party policy, this pluralisation of interests in and uses of law has created a greater scope for these actors to adopt diverging positions in relation to the law.[1]

Bourdieu suggests the juridical field is neither completely determined by state and political power, nor completely autonomous from it.[2] The

[1] Dezalay and Garth, 2001, in a different context use Bourdieu's term 'Palace Wars' to describe these competitions.
[2] Bourdieu, 1987: 814.

juridical field constitutes a metaphorical space where a range of different self-interested legal actors compete over the production and interpretation of the law,[3] where these competitions are themselves historically and politically structured. Such a concept requires adjustment when considering legal change in China. I have first adopted Trubek *et al.*'s terminology of the 'legal field' rather than the 'juridical field'. The former term has broader connotations and avoids the implication of the centrality of the courts in the legal system, which would be an error when considering the Chinese legal system.[4] More importantly, the concept of the legal field must be reconceived in a way that takes account of the non-liberal structure of the Chinese polity, which constrains diversity of interest and position to within the organisational structures of state and the current bounds of political orthodoxy.

Proposing the existence of a relatively autonomous legal field in a state where legal, political and administrative institutions remain strongly interrelated is by no means uncontroversial. Many scholars consider that criminal justice and social order are areas where the least reform has taken place and where the CCP has retained strong instrumental controls over law-making and enforcement.[5] The purpose of questioning whether a legal field is emerging in China is to focus the inquiry on the extent to which, if at all, a set of legal dispositions and values is emerging that is distinct from, though not necessarily antithetical to, the political power of the Party and state.

2 LEGAL REFORM AND INSTITUTION BUILDING AS A CONTESTED PROCESS: THE LEGAL FIELD

2.1 The concept of the legal field[6]

Bourdieu developed a concept of society as comprising a 'series of interrelated yet semi-autonomous fields, each of which has a distinct structure'.[7] The status and degree of autonomy of each of the fields can change. These fields may be divided into subfields, each of which has its own particular logic and rules.[8] Such a conception of society views

[3] Bourdieu, 1987: 816, 817, which defines the language in which conflicts are expressed.
[4] Trubek *et al.*, 1994.
[5] Lubman, 1999: 71, 135. For a similar analysis see: Lubman, 1995: 2; Potter, 1999; Clarke, 1985; Clarke and Feinerman, 1995; Tanner, Harold, 1999: 193–4.
[6] An earlier, abbreviated version of this section is to be found in Biddulph, 2005: 214–16.
[7] Trubek *et al.*, 1994: 414. [8] Bourdieu and Wacquant, 1992: 104.

law as one field which has a range of relations to other social fields. The legal field has particularly close connections to the state and the field of power. The field itself is described as 'an area of structured, socially patterned activity or "practice" in this case (i.e. the legal field) disciplinarily and professionally defined'[9] and a 'network . . . of objective relations between positions'.[10]

The metaphor of the legal field provides a way of considering legal change that focusses our attention both on the relationships between law and other social fields, institutions and actors, and on the internal functioning of the field and the conflicts and contests through which legal norms and a legal order are produced. The logic and rules of the legal field are structured through competitions between legal actors. Such a view rejects an assumption that these rules simply exist or evolve because of some immutable process of development.[11]

The internal dynamic of the legal field is shaped around its own specific sets of behaviours, values and assumptions.[12] It is a space in which different legal actors struggle or compete to 'appropriate the specific products',[13] or stakes, of the field: money, status, power[14] and what Bourdieu describes as the 'right to determine the law',[15] It is a space in which struggles for legitimation take place.[16] These ongoing struggles constitute the field.[17]

Bourdieu draws an analogy between the field and a 'game', such as a game of tennis.[18] In this field, the players compete with each other for the stakes of the game. To enter, they must learn the rules and how to play the game. To play, they must all concur in their belief that both the game itself and the stakes of the game are worth competing for and vie with each other on the basis of the 'rules of the

[9] Terdiman, 1987: 805–6. [10] Bourdieu and Wacquant, 1992: 97.

[11] Bourdieu and Wacquant, 1992: 104.

[12] Terdiman, 1987: 806 suggests that this might informally be referred to as a 'legal culture'. I prefer not to adopt this characterisation as it fails to address the extensive literature and divergent views on what constitutes legal culture. Bourdieu and Wacquant, 1992: 97, state that the logic of the field is '*specific and irreducible* to those that regulate other fields'.

[13] Bourdieu and Wacquant, 1992: 102.

[14] Trubek *et al.*, 1994: 414. These are described by Bourdieu as economic, social, cultural, symbolic and juridical capital: Bourdieu, 1987: 816–17. Juridical capital is the capacity to define the language in which conflicts are expressed. Bourdieu and Wacquant, 1992: 98–9; Johnston and Percy-Smith, 2003: 323, describe social capital as encompassing personal relationships and the benefits available to individuals as a result of participation in social groups.

[15] Bourdieu, 1987: 816, 817. Although these actors are self-interested, this definition suggests that the self-interest is not necessarily narrowly defined. Bourdieu, 1990: 108, argues it should not be understood as rational and conscious self-interest.

[16] Swartz, 1997: 122–3. [17] Bourdieu, 1987: 818.

[18] Bourdieu and Wacquant, 1992: 98.

game'.[19] The contests between legal actors are thus limited by those allowed by the rules of the game.

Bourdieu states:

> The social practices of the law are in fact the product of the functioning of a 'field' whose specific logic is determined by two factors: on the one hand, by the specific power relations which give it its structure and which order the competitive struggles (or more precisely the conflicts over competence) that occur within it; and on the other hand, by the internal logic of juridical functioning which constantly constrains the range of possible actions and, thereby, limits the realm of specifically juridical solutions.[20]

Actors share a legal 'habitus', which is the shared practices, views, values and dispositions of actors. Terdiman describes habitus as the 'habitual ways of understanding, judging and acting'.[21] Through the concept of habitus, Bourdieu provides a means of explaining the existence of the agency[22] of actors that is at the same time structured and constrained by the objective structures of society.[23] The habitus of the legal field is derived from factors such as legal education and professional practice and experience[24] that have been structured and constrained by objective forces such as political and administrative power and which 'encode basic structural constraints'.[25]

Legal actors compete over competence and status with the result that a hierarchy is created amongst them.[26] This conflict, according to Bourdieu, is to determine which actors are authorised to make legitimate interpretations of legal texts and legal practice.[27] Such a hierarchy is susceptible to change over time.[28] Changes in this hierarchy

19 Bourdieu and Wacquant, 1992: 98. Bourdieu uses the term 'illusio', to designate that each of the actors has their own 'interest' in the game and that they accept the stakes as valuable: Bourdieu and Wacquant, 1992: 116–17.

20 Bourdieu, 1987: 816.

21 Terdiman, 1987, at 811, explains the term habitus as: 'the habitual, patterned ways of understanding, judging and acting which arise from our particular position as members of one or several social "fields", and from our particular trajectory in the social structure'.

22 I use the term agency to refer to the capacity of individuals to 'understand and control their own actions' that is a form of individual autonomy and choice. Webb *et al.*, 2002: ix.

23 Webb *et al.*, 2002: 33–5. 24 Bourdieu, 1987: 833. 25 Trubek *et al.*, 1994: 414.

26 Bourdieu, 1987: 817–28, 850; Terdiman, 1987: 808.

27 Bourdieu, 1987: 818; Terdiman, 1987: 808–9. Terdiman explains Bourdieu's use of the term 'text' as encompassing 'not only the written record (in the law, for example, legislation, judicial decisions, briefs, and commentary), but also the structured behaviours and customary procedures characteristic of the field, which have much the same regularity, and are the subjects of much the same interpretive competitions, as the written texts themselves'.

28 Bourdieu, 1987: 821.

of privilege and authority often reflect the changing political status of different groups.[29] Although some actors may dominate the field and 'are in a position to make it function to their own advantage . . . they must always contend with the resistance, the claims, the contention, political or otherwise, of the dominated'.[30]

In China, the process of reconstructing the legal system is slightly over twenty years old, and so it is premature to assert the existence of a highly differentiated set of rules, behaviours, values and assumptions specific to the legal field and its actors. It is possible, though, to identify the evolution or emergence of identifiably legal habitus, rules and stakes of the game. As a consequence, in this book my focus is upon both the dynamic of the field itself and the interrelationship between the legal field and other fields, especially those of politics and policing which had, until recently, controlled the definitions and uses of administrative detention powers. The police force, for example, is a significant player in both the legal and the political field.

2.2 The boundaries of the field

The boundaries of the field are themselves porous and constantly negotiated.[31] According to Bourdieu, the borders of the field are one of the 'stakes of the struggles' that take place within the field.[32] The competitions between legal actors help to define the scope of the legal field.[33] These struggles between legal actors do not challenge the field but serve to reaffirm and strengthen it.[34] Bourdieu's argument suggests that the actors within the legal field are 'engaged in a struggle with those outside the field to gain and sustain acceptance for their conception of law's relation to the social whole and of the law's internal organisation'.[35]

The use of specialised legal language[36] and reasoning are mechanisms by which the legal field is defined and outsiders are excluded. The specialised language of law requires that disputes be reconstructed in legal terms and that they be resolved in accordance with the 'rules and conventions of the field itself'.[37] Conflicts between parties, to be resolved legally, must first be redefined, or as Bourdieu puts it, retranslated, in legal terms and then must be submitted for resolution in accordance with legal rules and procedures.[38] The expansion of the field takes

[29] Bourdieu, 1987: 850. [30] Bourdieu and Wacquant, 1992: 102.
[31] Trubek *et al.*, 1994: 414. [32] Bourdieu and Wacquant, 1992: 100, 104.
[33] Terdiman, 1987: 808. [34] Trubek *et al.*, 1994: 414. [35] Terdiman, 1987: 809.
[36] Bourdieu, 1987: 828–9. [37] Bourdieu, 1987: 831. [38] Bourdieu, 1987: 832.

place as the result of 'appropriative constitution' of matters that were previously defined and exercised in a non-legal way but which are redefined in legal terms and brought within the legal field.[39]

The force of the legal field suggested in Bourdieu's analysis is enhanced by the expansion of state law to regulate a growing range of activities. The increasing prevalence of state law has been noted by other socio-legal scholars as a feature of developed capitalist states and of modernity.[40] In China, law had to be reconstructed after its annihilation during the Cultural Revolution. The expansion of state law has occurred intentionally as part of the modernisation programme adopted at the Third Plenum of the 11th CCPCC in 1978.[41] The decision of the CCPCC to adopt the programme of 'socialist modernisation construction'[42] at that time had economic reform as its central focus[43] and included a decision to rebuild the legal system.[44] Construction of a socialist legal system has been characterised as being of central importance, not only for establishing a socialist market economy but also for social order and political stability.[45]

The Party's programme of reconstructing the legal system was further elevated in importance in 1996, as one eminent Chinese legal scholar has suggested, to the 'same theoretical level as the socialist market economy'[46] with adoption of the slogans 'Use law to rule the country,

39 Bourdieu, 1987: 835–6.

40 Hunt, 1993: 12–13; Cotterrell, 1992: 288–9; Hunt and Wickham, 1994, at 48, discuss the concept of 'juridification' employed by Foucault in the following terms: 'Confronted by the rise of the new disciplines, that are themselves exterior to law, the response of law is to seek to control or "recode" them in the form of law.'

41 *Communique of the Third Plenary Session of the 11th* CCPCC, CCP Central Committee, 1978: 6–16. Much of the groundwork for these decisions was agreed at a preparatory work meeting convened between 10 November and 15 December 1978 approving the programme set out in Deng Xiaoping's speech, *Emancipate the Mind, Seek Truth from Facts and Unite as One in looking to the Future*, discussed in Gai, 2001: 249–50, 256–7. See also Fan and Yao, 1998: 116–21; Baum, 1986: 69; Peerenboom, 1999: 321, 330.

42 (*Shehuizhuyi xiandaihua jianshe.*) Gai, 2001: 249–50; Benshu Bianxie Zu, 2001: 146; Lieberthal, 1995: 133; Baum, 1994: 63–4. White, 1998: Preface, xxi, suggests that the reform process in some areas predated this decision.

43 Also labelled 'material civilisation' (*wuzhi wenming* 物质文明). Benshu Bianxie Zu, 2001: 155; Baum, 1994: 94–7, 143–4; Potter, 1995a: 156–7, discussing the central role played by the state in economic reform.

44 Using the rubric 'legal system construction' (*fazhi jianshe* 法制建设): Deng, 1978.

45 Wang, 1995: 79.

46 Keith and Lin, 2001: 35, attributing this assertion to Professor Li Buyun, one of China's leading legal scholars. The decision to establish a 'socialist market economy with Chinese characteristics' was adopted at the 14th CCP Congress held on 12–18 December 1992, discussed in Gai, 2001: 299–300.

protect the long term peace and good order of the state'[47] and 'ruling the country according to law is the basic programme by which the Party leads the people in ruling the country'.[48] Keith and Lin cite arguments put forward by Chinese scholars supporting an emphasis upon the concept of rule of law (*fazhi* 法治) as it 'forms part of the progress from a traditional to a modern society'.[49]

Bourdieu's analysis suggests that expansion of legal norms to regulate an ever-increasing sphere of activities in China occurs as the result of conscious state policy, and also as the result of the growing force of the legal field. In China, the legal field has expanded and the status of law increased as a result of state sponsorship. The field also constitutes a space in which there is a dynamic interchange between actors who, in seeking to extend their own influence and status and to legitimate their powers by defining them in legal terms, strengthen and expand the field itself.

2.3 Relative autonomy of the legal field

Bourdieu argues that the legal field is relatively autonomous:[50] that is, it is neither entirely self-referential or closed,[51] nor is it entirely instrumental (a tool to serve the interests of dominant groups or the

47 (*Yifa zhiguo, baozhan guojia changzhi jiu'an.*) Jiang Zemin, 'Hold High the Great Banner of Deng Xiaoping Theory for an All-round Advancement of the Cause of Building Socialism with Chinese Characteristics into the 21st Century', 12 September 1997, report delivered at the 15th National Congress of the CCP (in English); Gao, 1998: 1; Liu, 1996: 1.

48 Zhu, Rongji, 1999: 2. This programme was incorporated into the *Constitution* in March 1999, amending art. 5 by adding: 'The People's Republic of China governs the country according to law and makes it a socialist rule of law country.' The proper translation of the last phrase is contested. An alternate interpretation could be 'makes it a socialist country ruled by law'. This is the translation used in the English version of Jiang Zemin's speech, *Hold High the Great Banner of Deng Xiaoping Theory for an All-round Advancement of the Cause of Building Socialism with Chinese Characteristics into the 21st Century*, 12 September 1997, in the *Beijing Review*. Keith and Lin, 2001: 33, prefer an alternate translation: 'socialist rule of law state'. The bases for different translations is discussed in Brugger and Reglar, 1994: 177–81.

49 Keith and Lin, 2001: 33, citing Qiao Keyu. Ronald Keith argues that the earlier academic debates over 'rule of man' versus 'rule of law' were also, in fact, a debate about 'transition of Chinese legal culture from tradition to modernity'. See also Keith, 1994: 39.

50 Bourdieu, 1987: 815; Bourdieu and Wacquant, 1992: 97. This conception of relative autonomy is distinct from the Marxist concept of relative autonomy which, in relation to the state, is based upon the relative autonomy of the state and its institutions from control by the dominant classes, see Miliband, 1985 and, in relation to law, the commodity form of law arguing that the relative autonomy of law from individual actors is required by the logic of the capitalist system, see Balbus, 1977; Tucker, 1984: 267–75.

51 In contrast to the concept of autopoiesis in the systems theory of Niklas Luhmann which Bourdieu distinguishes from his theory of the field. Bourdieu and Wacquant, 1992: 103–4. The limits to applicability of autopoietic theory in East Asian states is discussed in Cooney *et al.*, 2002b: 249–55.

state).[52] The autonomy of the legal field from state power exists to the extent that it is organised around its own particular internal protocols and values.[53]

The legal field is instrumental as it 'functions in close relation [principally] with the exercise . . . of power controlled by the State'.[54] It is centred in the 'national state and the normative order originating from state law'.[55] Bourdieu argues that the legal field has less autonomy than other fields such as the artistic, literary or scientific fields, with its hierarchy and structure closely tied to that of the economic, social and political fields,[56] because of its role in social ordering.[57]

In particular, because of its role in ordering social relations and legitimating the state's vision of order,[58] law is embedded in and permeated by state power. The field of power is conceived as distinct from other fields such as law and the state, or government bureaucracy, which have their own institutions, actors, practices and values. The field of power has been described as 'a metaphor for the ways in which fields actually conduct themselves'.[59] Power is not separate from but operates in fields such as law and the state. Power is especially concentrated in the state because the state has been able to concentrate in itself both economic and physical force, which enables it to concentrate in itself cultural capital[60] and then authority.[61]

According to Bourdieu, changes external to the legal field, especially those in the political field, directly impact on the legal field. Conversely, the internal conflicts within the legal field directly reflect factors external to the legal field.[62] Trubek *et al.* argue that one of the underlying tensions of the legal field is the coexistence of the strong influence of the political, social and economic fields, on the one hand, with the appearance of autonomy of the legal field from them, on the other.[63]

52 Bourdieu, 1987: 814. Contrasting Cotterrell, 1992: 116; Collins, 1984: 23, discussing economist interpretations of Marxist theory where law merely reflects the economic base.
53 Terdiman, 1987: 806.
54 Terdiman, 1987: 807; Bourdieu, 1987: 850, discussing the close relationship between the legal and political field.
55 Trubek *et al.*, 1994: 418.
56 Trubek *et al.*, 1994: 421; Terdiman, 1987: 808.
57 Bourdieu, 1987: 850.
58 Bourdieu, 1987: 838.
59 Webb *et al.*, 2002: 86.
60 Webb *et al.*, 2002: x, a value that is associated with 'culturally authorised tastes, consumption patterns, attributes, skills and awards'.
61 Webb *et al.*, 2002: 92.
62 Bourdieu, 1987: 850; Dezalay and Garth, 2001: 243, in the context of legal transplants argue that 'Developments in the fields of power help to determine the value of particular exports and imports in relation to each other' and more generally to allocate value to legal theories and products.
63 Trubek *et al.*, 1994: 421.

Law's close connections to other social spheres and especially to the political ordering of the state have been discussed by legal scholars from a range of different viewpoints.[64] One example of this literature is the considerations by comparative lawyers of the conditions for the reception of foreign legal concepts and institutions into the legal systems of different countries, commonly referred to as 'legal transplants'. The literature on legal transplants is also interested in examining the ways in which law's connections to society and political power impact on processes of legal change. Arguably this reasoning extends beyond the reception of foreign laws and institutions and is also relevant to analysing the fate of changes to laws and legal institutions initiated and developed domestically.[65]

In his consideration of legal transplants, Otto Kahn-Freund argues that there are 'degrees of transferability'[66] of legal rules and institutions from one system to another. In his view, there is a range of 'environmental determinants'[67] of law including geographical, economic, cultural, social and political determinants that influence the extent to which a foreign legal rule or institution is transferable. He identifies political factors as being of primary importance, suggesting that economic, cultural and social factors have greatly decreased in importance.[68] The extent to which particular institutions or rules are transferable will be influenced, he argues, by the degree to which they reflect the arrangements of power in the donor country and the extent to which those arrangements of power comport with the ways in which power is distributed in the recipient country.[69] He describes political factors as including: the ideological basis of government, that is, whether the country is communist or democratic; the distribution within the state of decision-making power between the judiciary and administrative organs and policy-making power; and the role of 'organised interests'.[70] Cooney *et al.* acknowledge the importance of politics but question the extent to which politics is necessarily the dominant factor in determining the fate of a legal transplant, or in influencing the ways in which law reforms

[64] In the context of systems theory, Teubner, 1998, discusses the differing relationship between law and other social spheres in terms of the 'tightness' and 'looseness' of the connections.

[65] In the context of labour law in Indonesia, see Lindsey and Masduki, 2002; Cooney *et al.*, 2002a: 10. In relation to the study of legal history as comparative law, see Roebuck, 1992: 124, 140.

[66] Kahn-Freund, 1974: 6.

[67] Kahn-Freund, 1974: 11.

[68] Kahn-Freund, 1974: 8–9.

[69] Kahn-Freund, 1974: 11–13.

[70] Kahn-Freund, 1974: 11–12. He defines organised interests broadly to include those representing economic interests, as well as other cultural, religious and social interests.

will operate in practice in East Asian countries.[71] Other studies discuss the differing connections between law, politics and other social systems and the importance of each of these to the reception of foreign laws and institutions and, by extension, to the processes of legal change. These include traditional legal ideologies, informal regulatory systems,[72] dominant patterns of law,[73] legal culture[74] and the ways in which the transplanted law impacts on institutional interest groups and the balance of power between different domestic institutions.[75]

In China, the existence of a semi-autonomous legal field depends upon being able to distinguish law from policy and then being able to point to institutional differentiation between law and political power. These issues are considered below.

2.4 Legal production and legitimation

The legal field is conceived as a site of legal production which is dynamic and without a predictable trajectory, but which is, at the same time, structured. Bourdieu argues that '[T]he power of law is special' as it extends beyond actors in the legal field.[76] The competitions within the legal field extend beyond the right to 'determine the law'[77] and its internal divisions and hierarchies,[78] to a broader legitimating function of 'maintaining the symbolic order'.[79]

The language of law brings certain categories and social groups into existence by naming them in a way that is both socially accepted and endorsed by the state.[80] These symbolic acts of naming only have power to the extent that they reflect pre-existing divisions and structures of society and so the representations and structures of the legal field are themselves structured in ways which are historically constituted.[81]

The force of the legal field, Bourdieu argues, lies in its capacity 'to impose an official representation of the social world which sustains the

[71] Cooney *et al.*, 2002a: 12. [72] Cooney *et al.*, 2002b: 263–4.

[73] Drawing from Weber's argument that domination could be legitimated by law, charisma or tradition, Mattei, 1997, at 12–19, distinguishes three dominant patterns of law that may coexist within one national legal regime: rule of professional law, political law or traditional law. These patterns of law are based on the different social norms that Mattei asserts affect individual behaviour, 'politics, law and philosophical or religious tradition': Mattei, 1997, at 12.

[74] Van Hoecke and Warrington, 1998; Nelken, 1995, discussing different views of legal culture. Dezalay and Garth, 2001: 241–2, discussing the ambiguity of the term and criticising the uses of legal culture to push 'global capitalism US style'. Hintzen, 1999: 169–71, discussing the influence on implementation of law in China of law's cultural context.

[75] Gillespie, 2002: 645–6. [76] Bourdieu, 1987: 843–4. [77] Bourdieu, 1987: 817.

[78] Bourdieu, 1987: 850. [79] Bourdieu, 1987: 852.

[80] Terdiman, 1987: 809. [81] Bourdieu, 1987: 839.

world view of the dominant and favours their interests',[82] but which at the same time constructs those representations as being of universal application and so 'normal'.[83] Law is of particular significance he argues, as: '[L]aw consecrates the established order by consecrating the vision of that order which is held by the State.'[84] Practices that differ from this representation of 'normalcy' become deviant or abnormal.[85]

2.5 Bourdieu's uses of Weber's view of legal domination and legitimation

The capacity of law to legitimate the established political order[86] lies in its appearance of impartiality, neutrality and universality,[87] which is necessary to obtain social consent to the exercise of that power.[88] Bourdieu employs Weber's notion of formal rationality[89] that premises the capacity of law to legitimate the exercise of power on the application of a body of rules that appear to be neutral, impartial and independent of the specific conflict being resolved.[90] Formalisation, systematisation and codification of the law,[91] Bourdieu asserts, give specific legal decisions 'symbolic effectiveness'[92] such that a pronouncement is legitimated simply by the act of stating it. The social consent thus produced in turn contributes to the stability of the legal field itself.[93]

According to Bourdieu, the perceived impartiality and universality of law creates a '*chain of legitimation*' which legitimates the specific decision-making of the 'police officer and the prison guard'. The act of the police officer in carrying out the powers of enforcement is removed 'from the category of arbitrary violence'[94] by this chain of legitimation as the act seems to be an application of a law that is autonomous and universal, as opposed to an arbitrary, unprincipled act. Acts of legal interpretation also pass as autonomous, neutral and universal[95] as they

[82] Bourdieu, 1987: 847–8. In this respect Bourdieu's views bear some resemblance to the logic of Marxist instrumentalist analysis of law as representing the interest of the dominant classes: Collins, 1984: 27–30.
[83] Bourdieu, 1987: 845–6. [84] Bourdieu, 1987: 838.
[85] Bourdieu, 1987: 846. [86] Bourdieu, 1987: 852.
[87] Terdiman, 1987: 809. This view is consistent with some Marxist interpretations of the ideological role of law in legitimating the exercise of state power: Collins, 1984: 50–2, by portraying the 'apparently universal quality' of law that 'presents law as the embodiment of the interests of the community as a whole': Hunt, 1993: 18.
[88] Terdiman, 1987: 810; Epstein, 1994. Epstein considers whether Chinese law reforms are such that law may now serve an ideological function to legitimate the exercise of state power.
[89] Bourdieu, 1987: 825, 845. [90] Bourdieu, 1987: 830. [91] Bourdieu, 1987: 844.
[92] Bourdieu, 1987: 828. [93] Terdiman, 1987: 810. [94] Bourdieu, 1987: 824.
[95] Bourdieu, 1987: 819–20.

are framed as an application of the law, rather than an interpretation or creation of the law.[96]

Weber's analysis of the relationship between modern law, the rise of capitalism and political development in nineteenth-century Germany has been influential in informing contemporary thinking about the relationship between law and modernisation in developing countries.[97] Of particular influence has been the work of Talcott Parsons, which extends the application of Webers' work. Parsons argues that a number of 'evolutionary universals' including a formally rational bureaucracy and legal system are necessary for modernisation generally.[98] A number of scholars have used this application of Weber's ideas of rationality to evaluate China's legal reforms in the areas of economic law,[99] criminal law[100] and police reforms.[101] Not all adopt this analysis unreservedly, though the concept of formal rationality has been influential in many analyses of Chinese legal and political developments.[102]

Because of these differing applications of Weber, Bourdieu's arguments about the legitimating function of rationality in the legal field should be read in light of the critiques of the application or misapplication of Weber's sociological insights in East Asian and other developing countries. The first critique is that the forms of rationality found in Leninist and socialist states may not be equated with the form of

96 Bourdieu, 1987: 823.

97 Trubek, 1972; Jones, 1994. See also, generally, Unger, 1976; Mattei, 1997.

98 Parsons, 1964; Friedman, 1969b: 20, discussing Parsons' view that a modern, rational legal system is necessary for development.

99 Chen Jianfu has concluded that Chinese scholars are now able to assert that the type of legal system necessary for establishment of a market economy is '"rational" law in the sense defined by Max Weber'. Chen, Jianfu, 1999b: 76, implying that this rationality is formal; and see Chen, 2000: 36.

100 Tanner, Harold, 1999: 182, ' . . . we shall first consider what the characteristics of a modern criminal justice system should be . . . Our definition of legal modernity is derived from the work of Max Weber.'

101 Wong asserts that the ranking system 'regularised, rationalised and legalised the police along Weberian lines' and continues that 'a modern Weberian bureaucracy was in the making, public security being restructured according to functional needs and based on a rational division of labour principle'. Wong, 2002: 294.

102 Harding, 1987: 184, describing the transformation of political legitimacy to be based on rational-legal rather than charismatic authority; Chen, Jianfu, 1999b: 76, describing acceptance that rational law in the Weberian sense is required for the operation of a socialist market economy; Shen, 2000: 32–5, discussing the applicability of formal justice in China and at 35–7, considering its weaknesses; Epstein, 1994: 22–9; Yan, 1996: 200–1, as an example of the use made by Chinese scholars of Weber's concepts of formal and substantive rationality.

rationality envisaged by Weber.[103] McCormick points out that, since adopting the reform policy, China 'has sought to rationalise, legalise and institutionalise the structures of the state and party',[104] but at the same time continues to be organised in ways which emphasise patrimonial organisation, involving personalised and *ad hoc* decision-making.[105]

The second critique is of linking economic reform, legal development and political liberalisation. In the 1990s, following the collapse of socialist systems in the USSR and Eastern Europe and with the progress of globalisation,[106] the rule of law has again increasingly been portrayed as necessary for the modernisation of these transitional countries.[107] There has been a renewed interest in ideas about the need for the rule of law as part of modernisation.[108] One commentator notes that the concept of rule of law has been embraced with enthusiasm since the collapse of socialist regimes in Eastern Europe and Russia.[109]

Legitimation of the exercise of state power has been portrayed as a central function of legal systems in modern states.[110] Tamanaha comments that:

> No-one says that the rule of law is an elixir for all ills. But many apparently believe that it is a fundamental component of any successful recipe for political and economic stability and progress, as well as a standard by which to evaluate government legitimacy.[111]

The use of Weber's work to link economic development with increasing societal autonomy and eventual political liberalisation through development of the rule of law which is used to restrain arbitrary exercise of state power and to protect development of civil society[112] has been

[103] McCormick, 1990: 82. [104] McCormick, 1990: 75. [105] McCormick, 1990: 63–4.

[106] Friedman, 2001: 347, asserts that globalisation is primarily of trade and human capital. At 349 he cites as a definition of globalisation: 'The invasive influence of cultural, political, and economic models, which are born in the countries of the first world . . . and are progressively imposed on a great many other nations.'

[107] Chibundu, 1999: 79, comments that the rule of law, free markets and democracy are the triad of concepts that have been used to explain the ascendancy of the West and used as the 'prescription for the laggards of the emerging (or "transitional") and underdeveloped countries of the former communist and Third World Societies'.

[108] Peerenboom, 2002a: 151.

[109] Taiwo, 1999: 151, who engages in a critical examination of this phenomenon.

[110] Weber, 1954; Rosenfeld, 2001: 1307–9. [111] Tamanaha, 2003, 5.

[112] The concept of civil society, briefly, involves the creation of a public sphere between that of the individual or family and the state. The public sphere comprises organisations of self-interested individuals who form associations to achieve a common political purpose. Cohen and Arato

strongly criticised.[113] Even in the West, Weber's analysis has not been without sustained critique.[114]

In 1972, Trubek analysed how the law and development movement conceived a causal link between modern law,[115] which resembles Weber's model of a rational legal system,[116] and economic and political development.[117] Trubek argues that this is an unjustified extrapolation of Weber's analysis of the conditions in which modern capitalism arose in nineteenth-century Germany. In the absence of economic development based on free markets, Trubek asserts that Weber's work cannot be used to support this causal link between economic and legal modernisation.[118] Jones concludes that the distinctive characteristics of Chinese capitalism suggest that economic reform and the development of capitalism is not necessarily dependent upon establishment of the rule of law that is rational and formal in nature,[119] nor upon civil and political freedoms.[120]

These analyses have considered the ways in which East Asian states have used the rule of law as a technique to ensure the success of their

use the concept of civil society to model transition from 'authoritarian socialist party-states' toward liberal democracy: Cohen and Arato, 1992: 15–18. Bonnin *et al*. distinguish increasing social autonomy gained by groups and individuals in authoritarian states such as China as resulting from the 'widening cracks in the official power structure' in contrast with civil society in which there is 'clear-cut institutionalisation of non-official institutions'. The authors suggest that the question should be looked at as one of degrees of autonomy: Bonnin and Chevrier, 1996: 171. Brook and Frolic, 1997: 3–16, discuss whether economic reform has enabled the growth of an autonomous public sphere in China. Cao, 1997: 546–50, 557–8, criticising the application of this model of modernisation to developing countries.

113 Jayasuriya, 1999: 1, discussing the challenge posed by East Asian states including China to the 'conventional wisdom that there are necessary causal connections between markets liberal politics, and the rule of law'.

114 Balbus, 1977: 576, arguing that Weber's concepts of formality and generality and autonomy of law define differences based on social class 'out of political existence'. Cotterrell, 1983: 83, arguing that no legal system can be formally rational to the exclusion of social values and norms; Cotterrell, 1992: 161–2, documenting discussions that changes in society and the forms of its regulation have changed significantly from those of Weber's time Jones, 1994: 200, suggesting that Weber's notion of modernity was a concept limited to its own time.

115 Trubek, 1972: 5–6, listing characteristics of modern law as being that: the modern state depends on rules to maintain social order, law is an instrument to achieve social goals, law is rational, sets out universal principles and is applied uniformly by specialised agencies, law is relatively autonomous and is backed up by the organisational force of the state.

116 Trubek, 1972: 13.

117 Trubek, 1972: 6–8, in respect of economic development, 8–9, in respect of political development. Peerenboom, 2005, argues there is a correlation between economic development and the rule of law, though does not go so far as to assert there is a causal link.

118 Trubek, 1972: 15. 119 Jones, 1994.

120 Jones, 1994: 211–12, discussing Hong Kong, but also referring to China.

economic modernisation programmes and to legitimate their rule, but have emphasised that there is no necessary connection between legal institutions and political liberalisation.[121] In a consideration of legal reforms in Hong Kong in the 1960s and 1970s, Jones suggests that the introduction of the rule of law was used as a means to deal with the crisis of legitimacy of the colonial administration at that time.[122] Instead of facilitating the development of democracy, she argues, the rule of law was very successfully used to avoid political liberalism.[123]

These critiques suggest that any links between legal rationality, capitalism and the rise of liberal democracy are historically specific.[124] Whilst it is clear that the Chinese state intends law to play an important legitimating role, it would be unsafe to assume a causal link between economic reform, legal rationality and democracy in China.

These critiques have several implications for this study. The first is that Bourdieu's use of Weber's concepts of formal rationality as legitimating state power should not be read to encompass a view that reforms promoting legal rationality are necessarily linked to political liberalisation. Indeed, Bourdieu himself explicitly rejects such universalist interpretations.[125] The second is to re-emphasise Bourdieu's concept of legal production and change as being at odds with the idea of some transhistoric transition toward capitalism and the rule of law. A consequence of his conception of the operation of fields is to emphasise the contested nature of the processes through which law is developed and interpreted and to conclude that the direction of change does not have a predetermined trajectory.

3 ADAPTING THE CONCEPT OF THE LEGAL FIELD TO THE CHINESE CONTEXT

3.1 The emergence of the legal field

Bourdieu's concept of the legal field has been developed initially in the context of Western liberal societies such as France and the USA and so he speaks of the legal field operating in 'highly differentiated societies'.[126] Bourdieu suggests that the limits of the field are approached

[121] Jones, 1999; Jayasuriya, 1999: 13, 16–17. [122] Jones, 1999: 46–8, 50–1.
[123] Jones, 1999: 56–9. [124] Trubek, 1972: 15; Jones, 1994: 200; Jayasuriya, 1999: 1–27.
[125] Bourdieu, 1990: 106.
[126] Bourdieu and Wacquant, 1992: 97; Cotterrell, 1992: 168–9, citing studies by Parsons, Teubner and Luhmann discussing the high levels of differentiation between economic, legal, scientific and political subsystems arising out of the complexity of modern societies. Autopoietic systems

when one actor completely dominates a field and crushes all resistance from other dominated actors and all movements 'go from the top-down'.[127] At that instrumentalist end of the spectrum law becomes 'an instrument of domination'.[128]

It is thus necessary to consider the ways in which the concept of the field can be applied to an analysis of legal change in China where the instrumental uses of law remain pronounced.[129] The process of reconstructing the legal system has, from the outset, been initiated and directed by China's political elites to serve a number of important functions including: the facilitation of economic modernisation and limited political reform;[130] the prevention of a repetition of the arbitrary exercise of power and abuses that had occurred in particular during the Cultural Revolution;[131] and the regularisation of the exercise of state power.[132] The operation of the legal field must also be reconceptualised within the dominant Chinese form of governance which Potter has labelled 'patrimonial sovereignty',[133] where 'political leaders and administrative agencies have responsibility *for* society but are not responsible to it' (emphasis in original).[134] However, as reform progresses, there is increasingly evidence to suggest that the Party elites no longer exercise complete domination over legal production and that a distinctively legal discourse is emerging, discussed below. A Chinese political scientist, Pei, for example, has suggested that in some areas, the CCP no longer controls all uses and meanings of law.[135]

I argue that Bourdieu's concept of the legal field should not be read narrowly to be relevant only in systems where there is a liberal

of Luhmann and Teubner's theory see law as a discrete, self-referential system of communication. It is an 'autonomous, differentiated subsystem within society': Tamanaha, 2000: 308. Teubner's work, however, does not assert complete closure or self-referentiality in law but a 'tendency toward' autonomy; Cotterrell, 1995: 106. Nelken has queried the usefulness of autopoiesis to describe legal change in less developed countries as it 'presupposes a high level of modern sub-system differentiation' which does not in fact exist: Nelken, 2001: 20. On this point, see also Cooney and Mitchell, 2002: 251.

127 Bourdieu and Wacquant, 1992: 102. 128 Bourdieu, 1987: 814. 129 Chen, 2000: 31–2.

130 Harding, 1987: 178–9, discussing the expansion of participation in the electoral process at both local and central levels and through workers' congresses in work units.

131 von Senger, 2000: 52.

132 Harding, 1987: 174–8; Deng, 1978: 157; Jones, 1994: 206, 208; Potter, 1994b: 325; Li, 1996: 42.

133 Potter, 2003c: 124–5, describes patrimonial sovereignty as '[d]rawing on traditional norms of Confucian patrimonialism combined with ideals of revolutionary leadership associated with Marxism-Leninism and Maoism, regulatory culture in China tends to emphasise a dynamic by which governance is pursued by a sovereign political authority that remains largely immune to challenge'.

134 Potter, 2003c: 125. 135 Pei, 1995.

democratic form of political organisation. On the contrary, I suggest that a modified version of Bourdieu's concept of the field is especially useful in analysing legal change in countries such as China that are engaged in programmes of market economy reform and legal system reconstruction.

Bourdieu's ideas have already been applied in contexts outside the liberal democratic state. Although expressing contradictory views about the applicability of the legal field outside liberal democracies,[136] Trubek *et al.* have considered the effects of globalisation on the 'legal fields of the developing world (including Eastern Europe and the former Soviet Union)'[137] and Asian states including China.[138] Bourdieu's concept of the field has been used to challenge a view of Chinese political culture as fixed and monolithic and instead to analyse its dynamic and contested nature.[139]

I use the concept of the legal field to examine whether it is possible to trace the *emergence* of such a contested space. Bourdieu suggests that the degree of autonomy of the legal field from the field of power is low,[140] but also contemplates that the level of autonomy itself may change. He notes: '[T]he more autonomous the field . . . the more it is capable of imposing its specific logic.'[141] The distinctive practice or logic of the field directs an inquiry into the extent to which it is possible to identify the emergence of legal language, patterns of legal reasoning and legal practice that are distinct from political discourses. Bourdieu's analysis focusses our attention on the extent to which different institutions and groups compete in a self-interested way over the production and uses of law.[142] In seeking to identify legal actors in China, I explore the

[136] Trubek *et al.*, 1994: 420–1, asserting that both the idea of the rule of law and the legal field 'which asserts the autonomy of the law, only makes sense in certain types of society', that is, liberal societies. They adopt a liberal form of reasoning to argue that in plural societies where there is an absence of 'any shared social vision or widely accepted ideology' to justify the hierarchical orderings of society, 'the idea of a neutral sphere of law provides legitimation for what would otherwise be seen as the unjustifiable exercise of power by dominant groups in society'.

[137] Trubek *et al.*, 1994: 475.

[138] Trubek *et al.*, 1994: 478–81. In the same article, Trubek *et al.* adopt a position which appears to contradict their initial claim that the legal field is only apposite in liberal societies, by examining legal fields in states in South America and Asia, including China, which they group under the title of the 'periphery'. Dezalay and Garth, 2001, discussing the role of legal actors in a range of legal reforms in Argentina, Chile and Mexico.

[139] McCormick and Kelly, 1994: 804.

[140] Bourdieu, 1987: 850.

[141] Bourdieu and Wacquant, 1992: 105.

[142] Bourdieu, 1990: 108, distinguishes rational and conscious pursuit of self-interest from his notion of habitus in which actors act in a strategic way out of a 'sense of the game'. It is an 'intentionality without intention'.

possibility that the emergence of the field and its actors may first describe a pluralisation of interests and positions within the state administrative and political hierarchy and only gradually expand to accommodate non-state actors or actors, such as lawyers, who are becoming institutionally distinct from the state.

Although this may appear to be a use of Bourdieu's concepts in circumstances he may not have anticipated, I am encouraged by the concluding words of Loic Wacquant to his preface to *An Invitation to Reflective Sociology* where he states:

> Therefore an invitation to think with Bourdieu is of necessity an invitation to think beyond Bourdieu, and against him whenever required. This book will have reached its objective, then, if it serves as an instrument of work that readers adapt for purposes of their own concrete analyses. Which means that they should not be afraid, as Foucault intimated of Nietzsche's thought, 'to use it, to deform it, to make it groan and protest' [references omitted].[143]

4 THE CHANGING NATURE OF LEGAL INSTRUMENTALISM: PLURALISATION FROM WITHIN

The Third Plenum of the 11th CCPCC which convened between 18 and 22 December 1978 adopted a new political line.[144] This political line determined that the main contradiction was now 'the contradiction between increasing material and cultural needs of the people and backward social production'.[145] It resolved that the contradiction between the bourgeoisie and the proletariat was no longer central and to move away from the 'leftist' mistakes pursued under Mao Zedong by negating 'class struggle as the key link' and the theory of 'continuous revolution under the dictatorship of the proletariat' as the core policies of socialism.[146] This decision marked a decisive shift in the overall programme of the CCP to 'socialist modernisation

[143] Bourdieu and Wacquant, 1992: xiv.

[144] Set out in the *Communique of the Third Plenary Session of the 11th CCPCC*: CCP Central Committee, 1978: 6–16.

[145] As cited in von Senger, 2000: 48–9. This decision adopted the resolution of the 8th CCP Congress in 1956 and ended the 'two line struggle' (between modernisation and class struggle) that had ensued since then. See also discussion in Brady, 1981: 15.

[146] Gai, 2001: 249–50, 256–7. These judgments were later adopted as formal policy in the *Resolution on Certain Questions in the History of Our Party Since the Founding of the People's Republic of China* adopted by the Sixth Plenary Session of the 11th CCPCC on 27 June 1981.

construction'[147] focussing on economic reform.[148] In his speech to the preparatory meeting for the Third Plenum of the 11th CCPCC, Deng Xiaoping argued that socialist democracy must be 'institutionalised and written into law'.[149] In this speech Deng set out the blueprint for subsequent legal reform: 'that there must be laws to go by, laws must be observed and strictly enforced and breaches of the law must be pursued'.[150]

4.1 Revolutionary and bureaucratic justice between 1949 and 1979

Prior to 1978, scholars argue that the administration of justice in the PRC involved the interrelationship between informal, or 'societal', modes of justice and more formal, bureaucratic, or 'jural', modes of justice.[151] According to Leng and Chiu, the informal mode of justice is characterised by 'socially approved norms and values', politically socialised and 'enforced by extra-judicial apparatuses consisting of administrative agencies and social organizations'.[152] This mode of justice emphasised revolutionary mass-line justice and relied heavily upon mass mobilisational tactics of campaigns of suppression against class enemies and revolutionary transformation of society based on notions of class struggle.[153] Formal modes of justice reflect a preference for entrenchment of a bureaucratic and institutionalised form of

[147] Gai, 2001: 249–50; Benshu Bianxie Zu, 2001: 146; Lieberthal, 1995: 133; White, 1998: preface.

[148] Benshu Bianxie Zu, 2001: 155; Baum, 1994: 94–7, 143–4; Potter, 1995a: 156–7, discussing the central role played by the state in economic reform.

[149] Deng, 1978: 157.

[150] Deng, 1978: 158, *youfa keyi, youfa biyi, zhifa biyan, weifa bijiu* 有法可依, 有法必依, 执法必严, 违法必究. (English translation not rendered according to this text). Restated in the *Communique of the Third Plenary Session of the 11th* CCPCC (in English): CCP Central Committee, 1978: 14.

[151] Leng and Chiu, 1985: 7; Cohen, 1966: 477–88; Brady, 1981; Brady, 1982; Brugger and Reglar, 1994; Baum, 1986; Dreyer, 1996: 163–87; Lubman, 1999: 71–87, providing a comprehensive description of the process of formalisation and informalisation of the legal process in the area of criminal law between 1949 and 1978. Professor Lubman labels the different approaches to the administration of criminal justice in these periods as 'mobilisation' and 'bureaucratisation'. Victor Li also suggests two models of law used by the Communist Party to exercise social control, which he describes as 'internal' and 'external'. Li, 1970: 72–3, at 73, discusses the external model which draws from positive norms from the West and legalist attitudes of law to 'provide a clear and rationalised system of government and administration' to strengthen central control. At 73–4, Li describes the 'internal' model as one that emphasises internal transformation of citizens through education and the internalisation of social norms which he associates with Confucian notions of morality. The term 'Legalist' refers to the theory of law developed by the Legalist philosophers (*fajia*) in the fourth and third centuries BC: see Liu, Yongping, 1998: 173–200.

[152] Leng and Chiu, 1985: 7.

[153] Leng and Chiu, 1985: 7; Brady, 1981; Brady, 1982.

justice and codified laws enforced by a 'regular judicial hierarchy'.[154] They have been linked to periods of consolidation and state building, favouring codified laws, stability and predictability in administration as bases for social order.[155]

The use by the police of an array of administrative detention powers in the pre-reform era has been associated with informal or 'societal' modes of justice.[156] Lubman juxtaposes these administratively imposed sanctions with the formal, or jural, model of justice which emphasises the operation of regularised, court-centred sanctioning systems.[157]

4.2 Socialist legality

Reconstruction of the legal system since 1978 reflects the decision to embrace institutionalised forms of justice and to implement a model of socialist legality in line with Marxist-Leninist views of law.[158] Yu Xingzhong argues that this process of rule-making has been driven by a pragmatic desire to establish a comprehensive infrastructure to underpin economic construction and which reflects current needs and the 'new actuality'.[159] He describes the elements of pragmatism as comprising an emphasis on instrumental aspects of the law, a view of law as deriving from and reflecting objectively determined reality, law-serving policy and the failure to treat individual rights seriously.[160]

The ideological justification for economic reform and the use of market mechanisms, that China was in the 'primary stage of socialism', was adopted at the Party's 13th Congress held between 25 October and 1 November 1987.[161] Socialist legality, according to this theory, should also develop through stages. In the primary stage of socialism, the task of law was to facilitate development of the market economy,[162] to assist maintaining public order and to eliminate political threats.[163]

Baum has argued by analogy to the different forms of socialist legality in the USSR, that the post-1978 form of socialist legality in China is a form of 'controlled pluralism'. Under such a model, the state is relatively tolerant and legalistic but the Party remains the political and spiritual

[154] Leng and Chiu, 1985: 7. [155] Brady, 1981: 16.

[156] Leng and Chiu, 1985: 7; Brady, 1981: 14–18; Brady, 1982: 55–69.

[157] Lubman, 1999: 72–9. See also Clarke, 1985: 1899–1902; Wong, 2002: 294.

[158] Preamble to the 1982 *Constitution* specifies adherence to the Four Cardinal Principles of: leadership of the Communist Party; adherence to the socialist road; adherence to Marxism-Leninism and Mao Zedong Thought; and adherence to the people's democratic dictatorship. Baum, 1986; Brugger and Reglar, 1994: 206–9; Dreyer, 1996: 163–87.

[159] Yu, 1989: 45–6. [160] Yu, 1989: 39–40. [161] Fan and Yao, 1998: 38; Baum, 1994: 219–20.

[162] Shih, 1996: 640. [163] Shen, 2000: 25.

leader of the nation.[164] This model of instrumentalist socialist legality contemplates a downgrading of class struggle and a move toward a more institutionalised and regularised system of justice, but not autonomy of the legal system from political leadership. Whilst law remains an instrument for implementing Party policy, the policy priorities and objectives that law serves have changed from serving as a tool of dictatorship and suppression of class enemies to serving the more complex ends of economic reform.[165]

4.3 The changing nature of legal instrumentalism in the period of economic reform

The economist Marxist-Leninist view of law is that, as part of the superstructure, law lacks autonomy from the economic base, and exists as an instrument of politics. This approach is to view law as a 'flexible tool of social engineering'.[166] The application of these principles in the PRC has been to prefer legislation to be 'general and flexible', enabling legislation to be amenable to changes in the economic base, changes in experience, and to be implemented flexibly in accordance with the differing local situations throughout China and changes in central policy from time to time.[167]

Leninist forms of instrumentalism have emphasised the need for legal flexibility to facilitate the use of law as a tool for the violent suppression of the bourgeoisie and the suppression of other class enemies.[168] As discussed in section 4.1 above, the uses and form of law varied in the pre-reform era depending on the needs of class struggle and as the regime's emphasis changed between governance and revolution.[169] With adoption of the programme of economic modernisation and the need for greater technical complexity in the law, it is possible to trace changes in the form of socialist legality in China. Of the differing interpretations of these developments, one that usefully describes these changes, is that of 'statist instrumentalism' that is employed by developing authoritarian regimes.[170] Under the model of statist instrumentalism, Trubek argues

[164] Baum, 1986: 94–5; Tanner, Harold, 1999: 26–8, identifies different types of socialist legality in the USSR.

[165] Baum, 1986: 94–5; Shen, 2000: 25; Lo, 1997: 480, 483–4; Shih, 1996: 642–3.

[166] Hazard, 1969: 6, 69. [167] Chen, 1988: 198–200.

[168] Berman, 1963: 32, in relation to uses of law in the USSR between 1917 and 1921.

[169] Potter, 2003b: 79.

[170] Trubek, 1972: 5, asserting that the legal systems of all modern states are instrumental in nature, in which law is seen as 'an instrument through which a variety of possible social goals can be achieved'. Trubek, 1972: 39–40, drawing a distinction between 'pluralist instrumentalism' of

that authoritarian regimes 'seek control of the legal order' and retain law as a 'purposive instrument'. This form of statist instrumentalism enables depoliticisation of the political and social problems that arise as a result of economic reform policies by redefining them in technical, legal terms. This process of redefinition thus removes the political significance these issues might otherwise have had. Treated as technical, legal problems, legal elites with technical expertise are thus empowered to resolve these problems according to law. However, Trubek points out that in order to retain control of the apparatus of law, the regime needs to co-opt these legal elites.[171]

Statist and instrumental uses of law in China, according to Jayasuriya, have been a way both of depoliticising economic activity and of preserving limits on individual autonomy and autonomy in the public sphere.[172] Jones discusses a similarly instrumental use of law by the state, in which law is used as a way of introducing a '[r]ational legal administration' which enables the state to legitimate itself, extend its reach and achieve capitalist transformation.[173]

With the progress of economic reform, the meaning and content of socialist legality has continued to change. In the economic sphere, Chen Jianfu asserts that the decision to establish a 'socialist market economy' by the 14th National Congress of the CCP in October 1992 removed the requirement to justify reforms as socialist: that is, the requirement of ideological correctness. He argues that this has resulted in renewed emphasis on law embodying principles of equality, individual rights, universality and rationality.[174] Lo concludes that the dynamic of economic reform has led increasingly to a depoliticisation of the legal system.[175] Other scholars have also concluded that the policy to create a socialist market economy and the official line that 'a market economy is an economy governed by law' have underpinned strengthening of the legal system.[176]

liberal democratic regimes in which policy goals are 'determined by a more open, representative and competitive process' and 'statist instrumentalism' of authoritarian regimes which 'looks exclusively to the bureaucratic-administrative entities of the state'.

171 Trubek, 1972: 35–9, describing statist instrumentalism as 'permitting some line between state and society' but 'they tolerate only a very limited degree of pluralism'.

172 Jayasuriya, 1999: 15. 173 Jones, 1999: 64.

174 Chen, Jianfu, 1999b: 73–6; Chen, 2000: 35–6.

175 Lo, 1997: 480.

176 Wang Jiafu discussed this in his lecture to the CCPCC entitled *Issues in Constructing a Legal System for a Socialist Market Economy*. Lubman, 1995: 12; Chen, Jianfu, 1999b: 74; Chen, Albert, 1999: 126; Keith and Lin, 2001: 18–19. Keith and Lin attribute to Wang Jiafu the first use of the slogan 'the socialist market economy is a rule of law economy': Keith and Lin,

In theory, reforms to legal regulation of economic activities authorise individuals to enter into binding economic relations on the basis of generally applicable legal norms.[177] Increased formalisation of the legal system can be discerned in the gradual substitution of rules issued by executive order with laws passed by the legislative organs according to specified procedures.[178] The expansion of legal norms, or legalisation of the mechanisms for governing economic activity, increasingly regulates the vertical linkages between the state and economic actors and at the same time has facilitated the growth of horizontal linkages between economic actors.[179] Lo concludes that as a consequence of economic reform, the nature and function of law has changed. Law has acquired functions that can no longer be understood as being purely determined by class. The most important roles of law now, he argues, are in regulating society and promoting economic reform.[180]

Corresponding to the increasingly regulatory role of law, views about the proper form of law have changed. Shih points out that many now prefer legal clarity and stability over legal elasticity as a way of regularising developments in the economy and preventing abuse of power and corruption.[181] Increasingly it is seen as appropriate for law to play a role in regularising and supervising state power in terms of authorising state action,[182] imposing procedural requirements on the exercise of power[183] and establishing mechanisms for supervision and accountability for exercises of that power.[184] Chinese administrative law scholars assert that administrative law increasingly embodies principles of equality, openness, fairness, justice and rationality.[185]

In the area of criminal justice, however, the path of reform is arguably more complicated and contains more inconsistent trends than legal

2001: 35. See also Hintzen, 1999: 168, arguing that the party state now limits itself to using macro-economic economic management by legal and financial means.

177 Feinerman, 1994: 228–36. 178 Fan and Xin, 1998: 10.

179 Clarke, 1991: 3, in relation to the role that contract has played in the decentralisation of economic activity. Lubman, 1995: 3, in respect of the expansion of legal codes in a broad range of areas. At 12–13, discussing law as a process of protecting voluntary economic arrangements. Peerenboom, 2002a: 192–9, discusses the weakening of state and party control over different sectors of the Chinese economy.

180 Lo, 1997: 480, 483–4. 181 Shih, 1996: 642–3. 182 Jiang, Mingan, 1998: 13–15.

183 Wang, Xixin, 1998: 260–1, arguing that legislation of mandatory procedural requirements may be one method to achieve fairness and stability in the law, at a time when rapid social and economic transition makes achievement of stability in substantive legal norms difficult.

184 Jiang, Mingan, 1998: 7–9, 17.

185 Jiang, Mingan, 1998: 9; Ma, 1999: 1, discussing the principles underpinning the 1999 *Administrative Review Law* ('ARL').

reform in the economic sphere. Institutionalisation of the state's coercive powers in legal form was seen as one indicator of the move toward instituting socialist legality.[186] In 1979 the National People's Congress ('NPC') passed the *Criminal Law* and the *Criminal Procedure Law* ('*CPL*'). At the time these laws were described by Peng Zhen, then the chair of the NPCSC, as important components in the construction of a socialist legal system and representing a legislative step toward entrenching a more formal model of criminal justice.[187]

However, Party control over the operation of the criminal justice system has remained strong.[188] Particularly since 1983, there have been periodic retreats from formality to reuse of campaign-style enforcement practices with the ongoing reliance on the law enforcement strategy of launching campaigns of 'Hard Strikes'[189] and to strengthen direct Party control over law enforcement practice.[190] Not only was the law amended to facilitate the 1983 'Hard Strike',[191] but targets were viewed as enemies of the people.[192] Commentators agree that such a practice undermines compliance with legally specified procedures and the legally specified separation of the function of state enforcement agencies and leads to widespread abuse of law and extra legal conduct.[193] Lubman concludes that the continuing use of campaigns of 'Hard Strikes' against crime 'demonstrates that the leadership remains committed to the

186 Leng and Chiu, 1985; Cohen, 1966; Brady, 1983; Brady, 1981; Brady, 1982; Lubman, 1999: 71–80; Tanner, Harold, 1999: 25–9.

187 Peng, 1991a: 368, 372.

188 Potter argues that ongoing references to the legal system as comprising the police, procuratorate and courts (*gongjianfa* 公检法) suggests that the primary purpose of the legal system remains 'about criminal law enforcement in pursuit of social control': Potter, 1999: 680–1. Lubman, 1999: 71–2, arguing that the criminal justice system has remained heavily influenced by its pre-reform institutional background.

189 Dutton, 1992b: 217–18.

190 Tanner, 2000: 98–115; and Tanner, Harold, 1999: 85–92, discussing the decision-making process leading to the launch of the 1983 'Hard Strike'.

191 *Decision of the NPCSC Regarding the Severe Punishment of Criminal Elements who Seriously Endanger Public Security*, 2 September 1983 (in English and Chinese); *Decision of the NPCSC Regarding the Procedure for Rapid Adjudication of Cases Involving Criminal Elements who Seriously Endanger Public Security*, 2 September 1983 (in English and Chinese).

192 Tanner, Harold, 1999: 91.

193 Tanner, 1995: 296–7; Bakken, 1993: 50; Dutton and Lee, 1993: 332; Turack, 1999: 50–2; Boxer, 1999, Lubman, 1999: 163–4; Clarke, 1985; Clarke, 1995; Conner, 2000: 153, citing campaigns as one of the factors involved in continuing torture of suspects by the police to obtain a confession. Forster, 1985, in relation to the hard strike against economic crime and corruption in 1982. Dowdle, 1999: 296, argues that the requirement for hard strikes according to law (*yifa yanda* 依法严打) is now carried out as a supplement to the law rather than a surrogate and that uneven enforcement practices are not unknown in the West.

instrumental use of law and to techniques of mobilisation associated with the mass-line'.[194]

Substantial amendments were made to the *CPL* in 1996 and the *Criminal Law* in 1997 to regularise the criminal justice system.[195] Amendments to the *CPL* have sought to define more clearly the jurisdictional boundaries between the courts, procuratorate and police in the criminal justice process.[196] The reforms to the *Criminal Law* provide a more detailed legal regulatory framework for the administration of criminal justice[197] and remove overtly political references such as Marxism, Leninism and Mao Zedong Thought from the statement of the law's purpose.[198] They also removed provisions identified with the persistent influence of class struggle such as the offence of counter-revolution[199] and the principle of analogy.[200]

Keith and Lin assert that the reforms to these laws represent 'a symbolic break with tradition which had accentuated flexibility to deal with the political necessities of class struggle, counterrevolution and social control'.[201] They argue that these reforms recognise the role of law in 'maintaining social security, stability and progress, in the state's macro-adjustment of the market economy *and in the effective protection of citizen's lawful rights and interests*' (emphasis in original).[202] Some commentators express a degree of optimism that

194 Lubman, 1999: 71, 135; for a similar analysis see Lubman, 1995: 2.

195 Potter, 1999: 681–2, conceding that these reforms may have gone some way toward protecting the common criminal, though perhaps not those charged with political offences.

196 Hecht, 1996: 19–60, pointing to developments in this regard, but commenting that there remain shortcomings in these reforms. Also Lubman, 1999: 162–7; Chu, 2000: 165–86.

197 Potter, 1999: 682; Hecht, 1996: 8–9.

198 *Criminal Law*, art. 1. Hu and Li, 1997: 1. In relation to the *CPL*, retention of the statement that the guiding ideology of criminal procedure is Marxism, Leninism and Mao Zedong Thought was considered inappropriate in a legal code, as neither the *Civil Procedure Law* nor the *ALL* contained such a statement. The legal document where it was appropriate was the *Constitution* alone. Also Chen, Jianfu, 1999a: 98.

199 *Criminal Law 1979*, Specific Provisions, chapter 1. The offence of counter-revolution had been seen as continuing recognition and implementation by the legal system of class struggle (Xiao, 1996: 98–9) was replaced with the offence of harming state security. Whilst not narrower in scope than counter-revolution, the offence is now framed in more political neutral terms. Dobinson, 2002: 24–6, in relation to depoliticisation of the *Criminal Law*.

200 The principle of analogy, under which a person could be punished for an action that is not itself a criminal offence, by punishing it according to the most closely analogous provision, was not included in the new *Criminal Law*. *Criminal Law 1979*, art. 79; Potter, 1999: 682. The principle of analogy has been identified as an embodiment of the principle of legal flexibility (Hazard, 1969: 72–6) and has been linked to earlier laws concerned with the punishment of counter-revolutionary crime: Tanner, Harold, 1999: 17; Lubman, 1999: 160–2.

201 Keith and Lin, 2001: 41.

202 Keith and Lin, 2001: 40–1, citing Chen Zexian, and at 178–9. However, they subsequently modified this view in light of the treatment of the Falun Gong: Keith and Lin, 2003.

reforms, although incomplete, may tend to promote procedural justice,[203] though acknowledge the difficulty in implementing them in practice.[204]

In the area of the criminal justice system and enforcement, to a greater extent than in the area of regulation of economic relations, socialist legality emphasises the role of law in empowering state action and continues to include contradictory elements of formality and informality in the law. Even in this area, arguments have emerged that law has a role in protecting citizens' rights against infringement. As this book will reveal, these contradictory elements are even more pronounced in the regulation of administrative detention, but that, of itself, does not preclude the argument that a legal field is evolving.

4.4 Ruling the country according to law and pluralisation from within

The adoption by the CCP of the programme of ruling the country according to law marked renewed emphasis upon the centrality of law to the socialist modernisation programme[205] and its role in promoting social stability during a time of rapid transition.[206] Whether this formulation should be seen as advocating the 'rule of law' and the extent to which law imposes 'meaningful limitations on arbitrary acts of the state and Party'[207] is hotly debated.[208]

The ongoing processes of pluralisation of both law and society indicates that, despite continuing instrumental uses of law, there are expanding spaces within Party orthodoxy for competing positions to be developed and advocated. Scholars have pointed to a weakening of the comprehensive and direct Party controls over society[209] and the increasingly complex and plural relationship between state and society.[210] Bonnin argues that in authoritarian states such as China,

[203] Hecht, 1996; Chu, 2000; Huang, 1998; Huang, 1998; Tanner, Harold, 1999: 191–3, Tanner expressing cautious optimism about the effects the reforms in 1997 and 1996, respectively, to the *Criminal Law* and *CPL* will have to strengthen procedural justice and reduce arbitrary and abusive acts, but points to improved training and funding of state organs as necessary as well to effect substantive changes in the operation of the criminal justice system.

[204] Hecht, 1996; Human Rights in China, 2001a.

[205] Hintzen, 1999: 186; Shih, 1999: 52, 98. [206] Keith and Lin, 2001: 34.

[207] Peerenboom, 1999: 320–1; and a similar formulation in Peerenboom, 2002a: 23.

[208] Keith, 1994; Keith and Lin, 2001; Orts, 2001: 69; Peerenboom, 1999; Peerenboom, 2002a; Peerenboom, 2002c, taking an optimistic view.

[209] Walder, 1995: Introductory chapter, describing how economic reforms have led to political decline. Burns, 1999, discussing the process of adaptation by the Party to changed situations brought about by economic reform.

[210] Gu, 1998; Guo, 2000.

increasing social autonomy gained by groups and individuals is the result of the 'widening cracks in the official power structure' rather than the emergence of civil society in which there is 'clear-cut institutionalisation of non-official institutions'.[211]

Gu develops a model of 'plural institutionalism' to describe the diversity of groups and interests within both the state and social groupings, and the differing forms of interrelationship between them. He examines the ways in which groups of intellectuals created a public space which is not directly controlled by the Party-state but which at the same time is 'structured and refracted by party-state centred institutions'.[212] These studies suggest that questions of autonomy should not be framed in terms of a dichotomous relationship between the Party-state and society or the Party and law, but as an inquiry into the differential links between and amongst different groups.

Scholars point to the evolution of an increasingly complex relationship between law and legal institutions and the Party.[213] From the 1980s, legal academics from universities across China and from intellectual organisations established by the state, such as the Law Research Institute of the Chinese Academy of Social Sciences ('CASS'), have had direct input into the drafting of legislation and the legal theory supporting the programme to rebuild the legal system.[214] In some cases specialist academic drafting groups have been formed under the aegis of the NPCSC to draft important legislation, such as the amendments to the *CPL*,[215] the 1999 *Contract Law*[216] and the 1997 amendments to the *Criminal Law*.[217]

Intellectuals have also had direct input into the formulation of the Party's programme to rule the country according to law. One example was in 1996 when senior Party leaders attended a series of lectures

[211] Bonnin and Chevrier, 1996: 170–1; Bonnin and Chevrier, 1996: 159–62, discussing the blurring in the 1980s of the boundaries between establishment intellectuals acting within the state structure and non-state intellectuals with an autonomous social base.

[212] Gu, 1998.

[213] For example, Shih, 1999: 115, who, after reviewing different academic views on human rights, concludes that the state no longer exercises absolute control over the academic community. White, 1998: 354, arguing that lawyers would choose to frame arguments touching on human rights issues in legal rather than political terms.

[214] Bonnin and Chevrier, 1996: 156–7, discussing generally the increase in officials seeking advice from experts, including legal experts, during the 1980s.

[215] Hecht, 1996: 14–18.

[216] Potter, 2000: 198, discusses the appointment of a drafting Small Group comprising senior professors from CASS and from a number of universities.

[217] Ye, 2000: 208, listing the academics and state agencies involved in the drafting process.

given by legal scholars on various legal topics.[218] The programme of ruling the country according to law which was later adopted by the CCPCC was developed and discussed in books of essays written by and for the Law Research Institute of CASS.[219] Keith and Lin documented the growing jurisprudence, the aim of which is to invest specific meanings and principles into the concept of 'a socialist rule of law country' and to emphasise the role of law in defining and protecting rights and interests.[220]

Within state agencies such as the MPS, research institutes have been established to provide policy input on issues of interest to the MPS, though the views of these research institutes are no longer entirely representative of the views of the MPS.[221] Tanner argues that there is a 'growing personal and professional autonomy' amongst members of these think tanks.[222] Within the courts, Hawes concludes that the increasing willingness of judges to express dissenting opinions shows that law reform is not merely centrally imposed but locally initiated as well.[223]

Studies by scholars including Tanner and Dowdle trace the progressive strengthening of the NPC and the NPCSC.[224] They argue that the increasing institutional autonomy of these organs and the decentralisation of policy-making power from the central political elite may be a precursor to the development toward a more plural legal system.[225]

Similarly, recent reforms have sought to strengthen the professional standards of judges, procurators and lawyers.[226] Xin Chunying argues that the programme of economic reform has led to a diminution in the involvement of administrative agencies of state in particularistic management by way of administrative directive and in settling disputes.[227] As a result, from the early 1990s, there has been increasingly strong popular demand for courts to play a larger role in the resolution of disputes between individuals and legal entities and a corresponding demand for

[218] Including international trade law; the World Trade Organization and foreign related law; and the legal system for a socialist market economy. Reproduced in Sifa Bu Fazhi Xuanquan Si, 1995. People's Daily Report, 9 February 1996, reproduced in Liu *et al.*, 1996: 1–5.

[219] Wang *et al.*, 1996. [220] Keith and Lin, 2001: 1.

[221] Tanner, 2002: 562–3, discussing the emergence of 'third generation' think tanks and the four think tanks established under the MPS.

[222] Tanner, 2002: 572. [223] Hawes, 2003: 2.

[224] Tanner, Murray Scot, 1999: 51–71; Dowdle, 1997: 13–18; Dowdle, 1999: 293–5.

[225] Tanner, Murray Scot, 1999: 232–9; Dowdle, 1997: 18–20; also see Pei, 1995.

[226] *PRC Lawyers Law* sets out criteria for permission to practice. Similarly, qualifications for procurators and judges were set out in the *PRC Procurators Law* 1995 and the *PRC Judges Law* 1995, respectively.

[227] Xin, 2002: 87.

judicial reform as expectations grow that the courts should deliver some form of justice.[228]

Despite the generally acknowledged weakness of the court system,[229] some have traced evidence of institutional strengthening in the Supreme People's Court ('SPC')[230] and a commitment to the strengthening of the nation's courts as a whole. An official programme of judicial reform was announced by Jiang Zemin at the 15th National Congress of the CCP in 1997 for 'promoting judicial reform and providing systematic guarantees for judicial organs to exercise independently and fairly the adjudicatory power and prosecutorial power'.[231] This is the first time that the Party has explicitly called for judicial reform in public.[232] In 1999, the SPC outlined a five-year reform agenda.[233] It is a broad institution-building project, designed to improve the professionalism of personnel, to institute procedural reforms and to crack down on corruption. Other scholars trace the growing professionalism of lawyers as an aspect of the strengthening of legal actors.[234] Whilst the autonomy of lawyers in many areas remains limited, there have been a number of highly public confrontations between lawyers, local governments and the police as lawyers seek to represent clients who have come into conflict with state authorities.[235]

Both Pei and Tanner have proposed that the political consequence of increasing institutional autonomy, especially the decentralisation of policy-making, is increasing pluralism and the breakdown of the centralised power of the CCP.[236] The complex relationship between

[228] Xin, 2002: 85–7.

[229] Clarke, 1996; Dicks, 1995; Peerenboom, 2001: 214–18. [230] Finder, 1993: 222–3.

[231] Jiang Zemin, *Hold High the Great Banner of Deng Xiaoping Theory for an All-round Advancement of the Cause of Building Socialism with Chinese Characteristics into the 21st Century*, 12 September 1997, at 26.

[232] Xin, 2002: 88.

[233] See discussion of the implementation of this programme in the Supreme People's Work Report to the NPC delivered at the third session of the Ninth NPC on 10 March 2000. See also Xin, 2002: 85.

[234] Alford, 1995; Fu, 1998; Lubman, 1999; Lubman, 2000; Lubman, 1995. But for a detailed analysis of the failure of state agencies in practice to give effect to lawyers' capacity to meet with a criminal defendant, see Human Rights in China, 2001a; Orts, 2001: 65–7. In relation to development of legal aid in China, see Liebman, 1999; Lee, 2000; White, 1998: 347–9; and Peerenboom, 2002b: 132.

[235] Buckley, 2006

[236] One argument about the significance of these reforms is that the strengthening of these institutions will have a gradual but inexorable effect on the political structure of the state. Pei argues that as the process of reform is 'path dependent', once certain patterns of institutional and bureaucratic power become entrenched, the process of decentralisation of policy-making power and democratisation of the political and legal system becomes inevitable: Pei, 1995; Pei, 1997, tracing this process in relation to administrative litigation. Tanner, Murray Scot, 1999,

the centre and provinces and increasing importance of local level institutions, such as local people's congresses,[237] further complicates law-making and enforcement. Studies point to the increasing number of state and individual actors who have vested interests in using law for their own objectives, thus reducing the capacity of the CCP elites to control the uses and meanings law.[238] One example of this is the capacity to challenge the lawfulness of state action under the *Administrative Litigation Law* ('*ALL*'). Although it is acknowledged that the *ALL* is of limited effectiveness in many respects, of note has been the increasing use of this legal mechanism by powerful enterprises and interested individuals to challenge acts of administrative agencies.[239]

We are left with a view of a legal arena in which an array of different institutional and individual positions and agendas compete. There are still political limitations on the scope of these competitions, though the outer boundaries of political orthodoxy have expanded since adoption by the Party of the key programmes of economic reform and governance according to law. This analysis indicates that the basic condition for emergence of a legal field – that law is not purely a state apparatus – now exists.

5 ACTORS

One way in which the boundary of the legal field is constituted is by the exclusion of lay people without professional qualifications[240] who must rely on the provision of legal services.[241]

Within this privileged group of legal actors, Bourdieu identifies a range of positions within the field whose views are both complementary and in competition with each other.[242] Reflecting the structure of the French legal system, he points at one end to law professors who are concerned with interpretations of law that provide an overarching conceptual coherence in the law, as well as in teaching these rules in 'normalised and formalised forms'.[243] At the other end of the spectrum,

discussing the growing structural independence of the NPC is cautiously optimistic about its growing autonomy.

237 Young, 2002.

238 Peerenboom, 2001: 196–7; Fu, 1994: 285–6, in relation to efforts by the police to use law to protect themselves against pressures at the local level to perform non-policing work.

239 Finder, 1989: 28; Pei, 1997: 859; Potter, 1994a: 288.

240 Bourdieu, 1987: 828. The state sets conditions for allocation of the professional qualifications that enable entry into the legal field which in turn enables enforcement in the name of the state of legally defined views of justice. Bourdieu, 1987: 838.

241 Bourdieu, 1987: 835. 242 Bourdieu, 1987: 824. 243 Bourdieu, 1987: 821.

he places practitioners such as judges who must apply these principles in specific cases and lawyers who use their expertise to serve the interests of their clients.[244] Trubek *et al.* suggest several different positions in the legal field: legal practitioners,[245] law appliers,[246] guardians of legal doctrine,[247] legal educators[248] and moral regulators.[249]

The impact which these actors may have on the production of legal norms has been described by McBarnet in her study of the ways in which lawyers in Britain use the law. She concludes that lawyers do not just:

> translate factual disputes into clearcut legal terms but that they also 'work *on the law*', to interpret it, to seek loopholes in it, *to make the law fit the facts* of the client's activities and interests. Lawyers are not just translators but transformers and transcenders of the law. What is more they are legal entrepreneurs, routinely 'making law' by establishing legal practice [emphasis in original].[250]

In China, an equivalent range of actors or legal entrepreneurs may be identified with both the opportunity and motivation to influence the ongoing production of legal rules and practice, including legislators, judges, law academics, lawyers, administrative officials authorised to issue binding interpretations of law, legal professional associations, such as the All China Lawyer's Association, and justice departments with power to issue and revoke lawyers' licences.

Of particular relevance to the regulation of administrative detention powers, I argue that police are actors in the legal field, contesting and interacting with other actors in the field. The idea of the police force as having its own institutional culture and interests has been examined extensively in relation to Western policing[251] and is pertinent to an examination of the Chinese police. Goldsmith adopts the concept of

[244] Bourdieu, 1987: 821.
[245] Such as lawyers who provide a range of legal services: Trubek *et al.*, 1994: 416.
[246] Those who make 'authoritative interpretations of legal norms in concrete situations', including judges, arbitrators and administrative officials: Trubek *et al.*, 1994: 416.
[247] Trubek *et al.*, 1994: 416–17, including academics in the continental tradition or judges in the US tradition.
[248] Trubek *et al.*, 1994: 417, those who 'socialise entrants into the habitus of the field including both educators as well as workplaces'.
[249] Trubek *et al.*, 1994: 417, those responsible for policing the conduct of actors such as accrediting bodies, disciplinary organs and workplaces.
[250] McBarnet, 1984: 233.
[251] Dixon, 1997: 6–7, discusses the use by police forces of ideas of police professionalism as a strategy for building and preserving institutional autonomy. Other examples centre around discussions of distinctive 'police culture'. Chan, 1996, discussing the Australian police as constituting a 'field' and the manner in which police exercise their broad discretionary powers. Goldstein, 1960; Lustgarten, 1986: 10–11, 15–16.

the police as constituting a 'semi-autonomous social field' to explore the relationship between police culture and law enforcement.[252] As a semi-autonomous social field, the police have their own distinct legal culture, which is subordinated to and influenced by the state's legal order, but which at the same time influences the state's legal order.[253] The field of policing intersects with the legal field, so that at times their role in the process of legal change is within the legal field, at other times outside it. Seen in this way, the public security organs are neither a monolith nor a simple agent of the state but play a distinctive and self-interested role in the competitions surrounding definitions of their role in policing social order and the production of legal norms.

Bourdieu suggests that the differing relative power between different groups of legal actors might assist in explaining differences between the legal fields in different countries, especially the degree of formalisation and rationalisation of national legal traditions such as the 'Romano-Germanic and the Anglo-American traditions'.[254] He adds that the differing levels of political power of differing groups might also explain the relatively high status of the legal field itself within 'the broader field of power'.[255]

6 CONCLUSION: THE LEGAL FIELD AND THE PROBLEM OF ADMINISTRATIVE DETENTION

The literature on development of the Chinese legal system since 1978 indicates that the ongoing process of socialist modernisation has led not only to the growing importance of law as a mode of governance but also to changes in the form and content of law. Law remains an instrument to implement the Party line, though the model of statist instrumentalism would suggest that in the area of economic regulation these objectives are now better met through formulation of generally applicable legal norms, the conversion of economic and social problems from political into technical legal issues and legal regularisation of state power. The image of law as purely an instrument of the Party must also be reconfigured to take into account evidence of the growing pluralisation of interests and institutions both within and outside the Party and state in respect of law.

[252] Goldsmith, 1990: 92–4.
[253] Goldsmith, 1990; for discussion of the operation of the semi-autonomous social field in other areas, see also Fitzpatrick, 1983; Moore, 1978: 55–81.
[254] Bourdieu, 1987: 822. [255] Bourdieu, 1987: 823.

The complexities of reform are demonstrated in the criminal justice system which continues to retain elements of informality, flexibility and direct Party control at the same time as legislation has been passed to increase formalisation and regularisation. As this book reveals, this complex mixture of formality and informality, direct Party involvement and increasing legal regularisation of the definition and exercise of police powers is pronounced in respect of police administrative detention powers.

Within this environment, the concept of the legal field serves as a productive point of reference in examining the processes of legal change as they relate to administrative detention. It enables a consideration of the complexities of the process of legal reform and the specific social, historical and political contexts within which these reforms take place whilst still taking account of their dynamic and contested nature. It avoids the constraints imposed by characterising the legal system in terms of a dichotomy between autonomy and Party control.

PART TWO

SOCIAL ORDER AND ADMINISTRATIVE DETENTION

CHAPTER THREE

HISTORICAL ANTECEDENTS: THE 1950S AND ADMINISTRATIVE DETENTION

1 INTRODUCTION

From the late 1940s the CCP grappled with the problems of consolidating and institutionalising its political power and restoring order. The public order situation in newly liberated cities was described as generally 'chaotic'.[1] From its efforts to deal with this chaotic situation at the same time as working to entrench its political power, the Party state evolved a comprehensive social order strategy in which administrative detention played an important role. In the official imagination at least, this social order strategy was so successful that the period between 1952 and 1960 was idealised as a time of 'peace and prosperity'.[2]

The ways in which the tasks of establishing political and social order were eventually achieved continue to influence approaches to the maintenance of social order today. They comprised strategies of education and reform, the use of administrative measures and the exercise of dictatorship, that is, the severe punishment of crime and political offences.

The political environment in which the comprehensive programme to manage social order developed in the late 1970s was different from that of the 1950s. The social and economic situation in which it was implemented was also radically altered. However, the contemporary public order programme draws on a similar mix of elements as those attributed to the 1950s and Mao Zedong: education and reform, the use of administrative measures and the severe punishment of crime.

[1] Xi and Yu, 1996:170 (*luan* 乱). [2] Yu, 1993: 39 (*taiping shengshi* 太平盛世).

This chapter is not a history of administrative detention powers and so does not seek to provide a comprehensive coverage of the political and legal developments in the 1950s surrounding the deployment of these powers. Its task is more limited. It is to provide an historical context for the study of the contemporary structure and function of administrative detention powers. The 1980s saw the revival and invigoration of a range of administrative detention powers which on the surface look very similar to their 1950s counterparts, but which in many respects have become very different from them. It is thus necessary to look at social order policy and administrative detention powers in the 1950s in order to see how they were used at that time and to see more clearly what shadow they might have cast over the present.

2 DEVELOPING APPROACHES TO DEALING WITH SOCIAL DISORDER AND THE POLITICALLY SUSPECT

As the CCP asserted control over China's cities, it was confronted with a number of social order problems, characterised as the 'filth and mire left over from the old society'.[3] Two major groups of targets were identified. The first was counter-revolutionaries, which included remnant Guomindang ('KMT') troops and supporters, secret societies, criminal gangs and bandits.[4] Problems of bandits, criminal gangs and politically motivated crime were particularly acute, especially in the cities in the period immediately following the establishment of the PRC. This period was classified as the first 'high tide' of crime. The second group of offenders was those committing the 'remnant crimes that were prevalent from the old society', such as growing, selling and using narcotic drugs; gambling; prostitution; and kidnapping and selling women and children.[5] A large transient population, vagrants, drug addicts and abandoned children also seriously undermined social order.[6]

At the same time as addressing these problems, the newly established Ministry of Public Security under the leadership of Luo Ruiqing

[3] Huang and Zhang, 1996: 252 (*wuni zhuoshui* 污泥浊水).

[4] Xi and Yu, 1996: 244, estimating there were 1 million KMT soldiers, 2 million bandits, 600,000 spies and 600,000 backbone elements of reactionary, anti-Party organisations.

[5] Yu, 1993: 38–9, referring to these groups of crime as the 'two manys'.

[6] Henriot, 1995: 473, citing estimates of 120,000 before 1949; Xi and Yu, 1996: 253, indicating that the number of transients was a cause of serious instability and crime.

struggled with its own organisational problems: lack of politically reliable and well-trained personnel and a shortage of officers.[7] In these circumstances, a number of strategies were adopted and then adapted as the social order and political environment changed. They included registration, use of different forms of administrative detention and control, campaigns of suppression and the imposition of criminal sanctions, and reliance on mass mobilisation and mass-line organisations in waging campaigns and policing local order.

2.1 Registration and control of the politically suspect and the Campaign to Suppress Counter-revolutionaries

As soon as public security organs were established in different areas, the task of household registration commenced.[8] In June 1948, the Northeast Public Security Central Office issued the *Measures on Temporary Management of Household Registration* with the intention of identifying those 'suspected of being counter-revolutionaries, committing unlawful acts or harming social order'.[9] From January 1949, the CCPCC instructed that counter-revolutionaries, including remnant KMT troops and supporters, secret societies and spies, register within a limited period with the public security organs. One set of figures asserts that from 1950 to 1951, 110,000 such people were registered nationwide.[10] 'Hidden counter-revolutionaries' and some KMT troops were detained.[11]

As the household registration system was implemented across China, these suspect groups, later referred to as the 'focal population' (*zhongdian renkou* 重点人口) were targeted for special management and surveillance. Similar measures were developed to manage special types of enterprise, such as seals cutting, printing, brothels, public entertainment

[7] Dutton, 2005: 143–9; Xi and Yu, 1996: 178–83.

[8] Xi and Yu, 1996: 171–2. Wang, 2005: 43–4, asserting that the CCP simply took over existing household registers maintained by the KMT. Wang notes that Luo Ruiqing identified establishment of the household registration system as a major task in his address to the first national public security conference in 1950: at 44. Dutton, 1992c: 230–1, argues that whilst contemporary use of household registration derives its historical antecedents from community security pacts (*baojia*) used in Imperial China, it cannot be viewed as a direct inheritance as it was also influenced by Soviet models of registration and based on a different societal model than Imperial China.

[9] Xi and Yu, 1996: 171.

[10] Huang and Zhang, 1996: 252–3, report that in a three-month period in Beijing 3,533 spies and 3,243 backbone members of reactionary organisations were registered, and nationwide between 1950 and Spring 1951, 110,000 were registered.

[11] Yu, 1992: 3 (*jizhong chabu* 集中插捕); Xi and Yu, 1996: 166–7.

venues and hotels, which it was feared might be susceptible to misuse by counter-revolutionaries or criminals.[12]

The CCP's policy at the time was that only the small number of people who had committed really serious crimes were to be arrested. Those who failed to register or who, after registration, continued 'reactionary' activities, were to be arrested, interrogated and punished.[13] By early 1950 this policy of leniency came into question.[14] The Minister of Public Security, Luo Ruiqing, criticised the techniques of 'summonsing for education', 'short-term detention', and 'detention in trade schools' as ineffective and called for severe punishment to be imposed, including the death sentence for serious and repeat offenders.[15] As the policy of leniency fell into disfavour, surveillance of the politically suspect by community leaders and groups, schools and work units was stepped up.[16]

In October 1950 the CCPCC issued the *Directive on Suppression of Counter-revolutionary Activities*, launching the political campaign against counter-revolutionaries and reactionaries. The *Directive* called for the severe punishment and suppression of bandits, local tyrants, spies, backbone elements of reactionary parties and groups and leaders of secret societies.[17] The campaign was conducted in three stages, ending in late 1953.[18] The launch of the Campaign to Suppress Counter-revolutionaries led to a dramatic increase in the number of people arrested or detained, many of whom were identified from the registers held by the public security organs.[19]

From the launch of the campaign, a number of groups were identified as targets for sanction, and were required to labour and to be subject to

[12] Xi and Yu, 1996: 171–2. In August 1950 the Ministry of Public Security ('MPS') issued the *(Draft) Temporary Measures on the Management of the Special Population*. These were followed in July 1951 by the *Temporary Regulations on Management of Urban Household Registration*. Both these regulations confirmed the public order functions of the household registration system. Yu, 2002: 15–16.

[13] Huang, 1994: 115–16

[14] On 18 March 1950 the Central Committee issued the *Directive on Suppression of Counter-revolutionary Activity*, requiring that leniency not be shown to certain groups. (This is not the same document as the document of the same name issued on 10 October 1950.)

[15] Huang and Zhang, 1996: 255–6. [16] Xi and Yu, 1996: 167.

[17] Yu, 1992: 4. Dutton, 2005: 169–71, argues that the Campaign to Suppress Counter-revolutionaries was in preparation for a year before its public announcement on 10 October 1950 and that the information gathered by the public security organs through registration was used in implementing this campaign.

[18] Yu, 1992: 5.

[19] Dutton, 2005: 167, noting that the numbers of those arrested increased eightfold between October 1950 and 1952. As to the use made of public security registers, see Wang, 2005: 44, 104.

political education in order to transform themselves into new people. If the matter was serious, then they should be given a criminal punishment and sent to reform through labour. Where the matter was not sufficiently serious to warrant imposition of reform through labour, they were to be sent to a period of control (*guanzhi* 管制).[20]

Control was a measure imposed by the public security organs for mass supervision of people who were allowed to remain out of custody. As a result of increased enforcement under the Campaign to Suppress Counter-revolutionaries, prisons did not have sufficient capacity to contain the number of people arrested, so differential measures were adopted depending on the seriousness of the offending conduct. Control was conducted by local communities, schools and work units. Some groups were sent to the countryside to labour under the control of the masses.[21]

A number of groups were identified as targets for control and forced labour. Such groups included anti-Party elements,[22] landlords and rich peasants[23] and counter-revolutionary and bad elements.[24] The *Directive on Suppression of Counter-revolutionary Activities* directed that 'those ordinary spies and low-level members of reactionary groups whose crimes are not serious and have expressed a willingness to repent can be placed immediately under control and the supervision of them strengthened'.[25]

Those who had committed wrongs that were not sufficiently serious to warrant criminal imprisonment or control were subject to administrative control, or organised into work teams to labour under the supervision of the masses.[26] These groups included landlords and

[20] Yu, 1992: 5.

[21] Dutton, 2005: 167–8, pointing to 1951 as the beginning of extensive use of the system of control. Yu, 1992: 402, suggesting that control was in use from 1950. In October 1951 Luo Ruiqing instructed that certain groups, such as people over the age of sixty who would otherwise be sentenced to between five and eight years' imprisonment should be sent to the countryside under the control of the masses. Huang and Zhang, 1996: 271.

[22] Central Committee Approving and Issuing Central Ministry of Public Security, *Report on the Meeting of National Public Security Conference*, 28 November 1950.

[23] Central Committee East China Division, *Directive on Implementing '(Draft) Regulation on Control and Reform of Landlords after Land Reform*' 18 June 1951.

[24] Yu, 1992: 13

[25] The same instruction was included in the Central Ministry of Public Security, *Report of the National Public Security Meeting*, approved and issued by the Central Committee on 28 October 1950, reproduced in Zhonggong Zhongyang Wenxian Yanjiu Shi, 1992a: 441–6 at 444.

[26] Yu, 1992: 5.

rich peasants with the capacity to labour and those released from reform through labour or control who were forced to labour under the supervision of the masses.[27] Politically suspect people cleansed from the mid and lower ranks of the Party, government and army were to be gathered up for training, investigation and sent to work in departments where it was thought they could not do any harm.[28]

The legal status of control was unclear, both as to whether it was a minor criminal sanction or administrative in nature and as to the legal authorisation of its use. Jerome Cohen concludes that control was a criminal sanction and that forced labour was administrative.[29] Dutton characterises control as administrative.[30] Yu indicates that the courts were given power to impose control from 1956, but that it was not formally included as a criminal punishment until the passage of the *PRC Criminal Law* in 1979.[31]

On 27 June 1952, the Administrative Council approved the *Temporary Measures on Control of Counter-revolutionary Elements* which were then issued by the Ministry of Public Security on 17 July 1952, providing a formal regulatory basis for the imposition of control. These temporary measures authorised public security organs to impose control of a period of less than three years, which could be extended where necessary.[32] Where a person continued their criminal or counter-revolutionary behaviour, the period of control could be extended, or the person arrested.[33] The time limits could be shortened where the person was well behaved, performed meritorious service and had demonstrated they were reformed.[34]

Alongside conducting the Campaign to Suppress Counter-revolutionaries, the public security organs were required to preserve social order and to address issues of drug trafficking and addiction, prostitution and vagrancy.[35] Some groups involved in these activities were also subject to registration and some, including prostitutes,

[27] Yu, 1992: 13. In relation to landlords and rich peasants, see CCPCC, *Directive on the Question of Labour, Production and Employment of Landlords in Areas where Land Reform is Already Complete*, 10 May 1951; Central Committee East China, *Division Directive on Implementing '(Draft) Regulation on Control and Reform of Landlords after Land Reform'*, 18 June 1951. Chen, 2003: 82–3 points to this as the origin of the system of forced labour (*qiangzhi laodong* 强制劳动).

[28] CCPCC, *Directive on the Problem of Cleaning up the Mid-levels and Internal Levels*, 21 May 1951.

[29] Cohen, 1968: 275–95. [30] Dutton, 2005: 168.

[31] Yu, 1992: 402–3. [32] Article 6. [33] Article 7.

[34] Article 8. [35] Yu, 1993: 39; Xi and Yu, 1996: 169.

drug addicts, 'unrepentant' gamblers,[36] vagrants,[37] petty thieves and pickpockets,[38] to periods of detention.

A number of enduring characteristics of enforcement practice can be identified from the conduct of the Campaign to Suppress Counter-revolutionaries. The first was the use made of information included in police registers to identify targets. The second was the complementary use of administrative and criminal measures to deal with transgressions of lesser and greater degrees of severity, respectively. Dutton traces the emergence of the complementary use of administrative and criminal measures to 1950 when control of prisons was transferred from the Ministry of Justice to the Ministry of Public Security, thus giving the public security organs control over both criminal and administrative detention facilities.[39]

Another feature of enforcement practices during the conduct of campaigns can be seen in the instruction in the *Directive on Suppression of Counter-revolutionary Activities* to strengthen the leadership of Party committees over the 'important weapons of the peoples' democratic dictatorship', the courts, procuratorate and public security organs. The courts, procuratorate and public security organs were instructed to co-ordinate their work to achieve the objectives of the campaign. As I discuss in the next chapter, these features continue to be seen in the conduct of anti-crime campaigns in the reform era.

Another enduring practice that emerged in the 1950s is reliance on community organisations in implementing social order programmes. As Dutton also argues, in order to increase supervision of politically suspect groups and to carry out the social order protection work required by the Campaign to Suppress Counter-revolutionaries, the public security organs were forced to increase their reliance on different community organisations. From this increasingly institutionalised relationship he

[36] Yu, 1992: 8, who were detained to be educated and reformed in detention for education (*shourong jiaoyang* 收容教养), together with heads of gambling syndicates.

[37] Yu, 1992: 8, who were taken into labour production education centres (*laodong shengchan jiaoyang suo* 劳动生产教养所) and into New Person Learn a Trade Camps (*xinren xiyi chang* 新人习艺场) so that they could learn a trade and the habit of work in order to be transformed into 'useful timer for socialist construction'. Cohen, 1968: 244–8, reproducing the Ministry of the Interior, *Instructions Relating to the Work of Placement and Reform of City Vagrants*, 11 July 1956, suggesting that in the detention of vagrants, no form of coercion should be used and they should not be treated as if they have committed a criminal offence.

[38] Cohen, 1968: 240–4, excerpting an unpublished report by L.C.B. Gower referring to visits to Loafer's Camps and Prostitutes' Camps in April 1956.

[39] Dutton, 2005: 168.

points to development of the 'mass line of policing' where the police work closely with and rely upon mass line organisations.[40] The 'mass line' has remained at the core of policing social order since the early 1950s.

2.2 Conceptual structure: antagonistic and non-antagonistic contradictions

The politics and strategies of the pre-reform period to attack crime, political opponents and socially disruptive behaviour were underpinned by the distinction drawn between 'enemies' and the 'people'.[41] Mao Zedong, in his speech *On the People's Democratic Dictatorship* in June 1949, set out the tasks of state agencies in suppressing class enemies:

> The state apparatus, including the army, the police and the courts, is the instrument by which one class oppresses another. It is an instrument for the oppression of antagonistic classes; it is violence and not 'benevolence'.[42]

This orientation to the 'enemy' was later clearly articulated and implemented in the distinction drawn between antagonistic and non-antagonistic contradictions in Mao Zedong's speech *On the Correct Handling of Contradictions among the People*.[43] Mao's theory of contradictions has been influential in shaping policing policy and structuring powers used to deal with transgression. A recent book on criminal policy edited by Xiao Yang identifies Mao Zedong's Theory of Contradictions as both defining crime and social order problems and determining responses to them.[44]

The theory of contradictions requires a distinction to be drawn between contradictions between the people and the enemy, which are antagonistic contradictions, and contradictions amongst the people, which are non-antagonistic contradictions. Non-antagonistic contradictions between the people are classified as non-fundamental. They may be handled through correcting what is characterised as mistaken views through criticism, education and struggle with a view to

[40] Dutton, 2005: 160–1.

[41] Dutton, 2005, traces the ways in which the distinction between 'friend' and 'enemy' underpinned both pre-reform politics and, in particular, the organisation and policies of the Chinese police. See especially at 23–70.

[42] Mao, 1977: 418.

[43] Mao, 1937a; Mao, 1937b; Mao Zedong, *On the Correct Handling of Contradictions among the People*, 27 February 1957, reproduced in Mao, 1972 (in English).

[44] Xiao, 1996: 90, 94. Xiao, at the time, was the Minister of Justice.

re-establishing unity, and through the use of coercive administrative measures. Antagonistic contradictions involve what is characterised as 'fundamental' contradictions of interests in which one class suppresses another. Unity is impossible. Although the two types of contradiction are considered to be of a fundamentally different nature, if not handled properly, it is possible in certain circumstances for non-antagonistic contradictions to take on the characteristics of antagonistic contradictions.[45]

In his speech *On the Correct Handling of Contradictions among the People*, Mao Zedong distinguished between methods for handling different contradictions:

> The only way to settle questions of an ideological nature or controversial issues among the people is by the democratic method, the method of discussion, of criticism, of persuasion and education, and not by the method of coercion and repression . . .

In addition to education and persuasion, Mao advocated the use of administrative measures for day-to-day management and to resolve contradictions amongst the people:

> Administrative orders and the method of persuasion and education complement each other in resolving contradictions among the people. Even administrative regulations or the maintenance of public order must be accompanied by persuasion and education, for in many cases regulations alone will not work . . .[46]

To resolve antagonistic contradictions, Mao advocated the exercise of dictatorship:

> What is this dictatorship for? Its first function is to suppress the country's reactionary class and parties and the exploiters who resist the socialist revolution, to suppress all those who undermine socialist construction; that is to say, to resolve contradictions between the enemy and us . . . in order to protect the social order and the interests of the vast [number of] people, it is also necessary to put dictatorship into effect over robbers, swindlers, murderer-arsonists, hooligan groups, and all kinds of bad elements who seriously undermine social order . . .[47]

[45] Xiao, 1996: 94–5; Lubman, 1967: 1301–6.

[46] Mao, 1972: 52–3 (in English). A slightly different translation of excerpts from this speech are contained in Cohen, 1968: 83–8 at 86–7.

[47] Excerpt from Mao Zedong's speech, *On the Correct Handling of Contradictions among the People*, 27 February 1957 (in English), reproduced in Cohen, 1968: 83–8 at 85.

In the pre-reform era, mass political campaigns were one of the primary tools for the suppression of class enemies. They relied on techniques of mass mobilisation and concentration of the strength of state organs in co-operation with the masses to attack critical problems.[48] The violent struggles waged in mass political campaigns of the Maoist era were intended both to motivate the people and to defeat enemies.[49] Mao Zedong advocated conducting political campaigns by launching a 'tidal wave' against the 'high tide of crime'[50] and 'gathering superior troops to wage a war of annihilation' against the enemies.[51] Campaigns, though violent and punitive, were intended to transform the social and political environment, 'to break down the normal bureaucratic control over issues so as to attack them head on'.[52] In its political and ideological form, the campaign was essentially a device antithetical to law and the operation of a legal system. It was a tool of mass mobilisation and of revolution designed to circumvent ordinary bureaucratic processes.[53]

3 STRATEGIES TO ELIMINATE PROSTITUTION IN THE 1950S

3.1 Banning prostitution

Prostitution was labelled a 'semi-feudal, semi-colonial evil phenomenon of old China's cities'[54] that was to be eradicated after the CCP established control. Prostitution was very extensive throughout China, with a reported 800 brothels in Shanghai and 500 in Tianjin alone shortly before establishment of the PRC.[55]

The process of prohibiting prostitution began after control was asserted in cities.[56] As Elaine Jeffreys correctly points out, it was public or visible prostitution, such as prostitution conducted in brothels and on the street, that was readily identified and attacked.[57] An

[48] Wang, Mingxin, 1993: 181–2; Lieberthal, 1995: 67.
[49] Lieberthal, 1995, 60–77, discusses the important features of Mao Zedong Thought and the policies implemented on the basis of Mao Zedong Thought. These included following the mass line, periodic waging of political campaigns and conduct of the struggle to overturn established patterns of social relationships and conventions.
[50] Dutton and Lee, 1993: 321–2. [51] Wang, Mingxin, 1993: 180–1.
[52] Lieberthal, 1995: 66. [53] Lieberthal, 1995: 66–7.
[54] Huang, 1994: 119. [55] Ma, Weigang, 1993b: 7.
[56] Shen, 1990: 56, reporting that in Dalian in 1946 prostitutes were detained for education, those working in dance halls were registered and the dance halls closed. Shen also notes a similar process occurring in Harbin in 1948, where prostitutes were sent to other areas to work.
[57] Jeffreys, 2004: 103.

additional incentive for focussing on brothels was that they were seen as sites fostering other harmful social activities such as drug use, gambling, kidnapping and selling women, as well as 'colluding with bandits and harbouring counter-revolutionaries'.[58]

Although there was a unified policy to eradicate prostitution, achieving it in practice was much more complex. Specific strategies were formulated by the local government and Party organs in light of local conditions. These strategies fell into two groupings. The first, where there were adequate resources and the social situation was fairly stable, was to carry out a sudden strike of co-ordinated action in which brothels were raided and closed overnight. This approach was used in Beijing.[59] The second strategy was the registration, restriction and gradual closure of brothels over a comparatively long period of time, an approach used in cities such as Tianjin, Taiyuan, Wuhan and Shanghai. The police in most medium and large cities chose to minimise anticipated social dislocation and hardship that would be caused by the loss of employment and income derived from prostitution-related activities if brothels were closed suddenly. By taking the more gradual approach of restricting and limiting prostitution, authorities had more time to improve their control over public order whilst lessening the ultimate economic impact of brothel closures.[60]

(i) Beijing

In May 1949 the mayor of Beijing, Ye Jianying, directed that the public security organs, together with the Women's Federation and the Civil Affairs Bureau, carry out investigations into prostitution in Beijing to determine what action should be taken. The Committee to Handle Prostitution was established to oversee this investigation, headed by the Party Secretary, Peng Zhen.[61] As part of the preparatory work, the police registered and compiled detailed dossiers on brothels, brothel owners, prostitutes and clients of prostitutes, so that they could be subject to differential treatment.[62]

In September, the Committee to Handle Prostitution submitted its recommendation to the municipal Party Committee and government

[58] Huang and Zhang, 1996: 258.
[59] Ma, Weigang, 1993b: 10. Beijing was called Beiping at that time.
[60] Xi and Yu, 1996: 253–4; Ma, 1994: 56; Ma, Weigang, 1993b: 8.
[61] Ma, Weigang, 1993b: 81–3; Shen, 1990: 56–7; Xi and Yu, 1996: 253–4.
[62] Ma, Weigang, 1993b: 10.

that all brothels be closed in a consolidated strike.[63] At a meeting of heads and deputy heads of government departments of Beijing on 12 November 1949, Luo Ruiqing, then head of Beijing Bureau of Public Security, urged that decisive action be taken to close brothels and punish brothel owners. Plans were made to carry out this strike.[64]

After listening to the report by the public security bureau on 20 November, Peng Zhen reportedly went himself to investigate prostitution in the most notorious areas of Beijing, visiting the eight alleyways outside Qianmen. He was reportedly shocked to find young child-prostitutes in brothels he visited.[65] At 5 p.m. on 21 November, the Beijing Second People's Congress met to pass a resolution to take a range of actions including closure of all brothels.[66] According to police accounts, within twelve hours of the resolution being passed, starting from 5.30 p.m., a concerted action was taken to close all brothels and detain prostitutes. By 5 a.m. the next morning, 2,400 police and officials had closed 224 brothels and, in their words, 'liberated' 1,268 prostitutes, who were sent to eight detention centres for education.[67] Pimps and brothel owners were sentenced to terms of imprisonment, with two being sentenced to death. The example of Beijing was widely publicised. It was used to trumpet the great success of the regime in eradicating vice, as well as to give a warning to those involved in prostitution of what might follow throughout the rest of the country.[68]

(ii) Shanghai

An example of the second, more gradual approach to the eradication of prostitution is Shanghai. In Shanghai, the public security organs sought to identify, restrict and control brothels and prostitution. The police required brothels and prostitutes to register in June 1949 and again in October 1949.[69] Prostitutes were required to be tested for sexually transmitted diseases ('STDs').[70] The public security organs also pressurised brothel owners by requiring them to obtain a special permit subject to restrictive conditions limiting the scope

[63] Ma, 1994: 57; *(Draft) Measures on Dealing with Prostitution in Beiping City*, 26 September 1949.
[64] Huang, 1994: 119; Ma, Weigang, 1993b: 83–4. [65] Ma, Weigang, 1993b: 84–6.
[66] Ma, 1994: 57; *Resolution on Closing Brothels* passed by the Second People's Congress on 21 November 1949,
[67] Dutton, 2005: 152 and Ma, Weigang, 1993b: 11, put the number of prostitutes detained as 1,288, though at 87 Ma asserts the number is 1,268. Xi and Yu, 1996: 254; Ma, 1994: 57, giving similar, though not identical, figures.
[68] Ma, Weigang, 1993b: 11. [69] Ma, Weigang, 1993b: 20–1. [70] Ma, 1994: 56.

of operation and the prostitutes permitted to have customers. Brothels were subject to periodic searches.[71] Extensive propaganda about the 'vile and exploitative' nature of prostitution was used to raise public consciousness and indignation. Prostitutes were encouraged to change their consciousness and become 'new people'. On the basis of this propaganda, denunciation meetings were also organised where prostitutes publicly denounced people including brothel owners and pimps.[72]

The police sought to restrict demand for prostitution by adopting a policy of 'causing trouble for clients of prostitutes'. They required brothel owners to provide a daily list of clients, including their name, address, age and place of work. Police would then contact the workplace of government officials, students and workers on these lists requesting that appropriate measures be taken and efforts made to educate them. Fear of exposure and embarrassment was sufficient to deter many people. By using these tactics, the police reported that they were able to reduce substantially the number of brothels. In October 1949, the number of brothels in Shanghai was 525; by the end of 1950 it was 156 and by the end of the Campaign to Suppress Counter-revolutionaries in November 1951 it was seventy-two. Similar tactics in Tianjin were successful in reducing the number of brothels by 213 by January 1950.[73]

In most areas of China, action to ban prostitution did not commence immediately because of other more pressing social order problems.[74] In Shanghai, action to ban prostitution and forcibly close brothels started in 1951.[75] In other regions, sweeps to close brothels were taken by local governments between 1950 and 1954.[76]

71 Ma, 1994: 56–57; Xi and Yu, 1996: 253–4. 72 Ma, Weigang, 1993b: 10.

73 Ma, Weigang, 1993b: 9–10, 21 (*Mafan piaoke* 麻烦嫖客).

74 Yu, 1993: 38, asserting that there were 513,461 criminal cases at the peak of the first high tide of crime between Spring and Autumn 1950, and 40,000 cadres and citizens were killed by counter-revolutionary elements. In Shanghai between 1950 and 1953, 33,000 people were convicted of criminal offences. See also Henriot, 1995: 473.

75 Henriot, 1995: 474–6, noting that this first sweep did not eradicate either prostitution or brothels and so further sweeps were made in 1952 and 1953.

76 Shen, 1990: 57, reporting that similar actions were taken in cities and provinces throughout China, including Tianjin in 1949, Guangdong in 1951, Henan and Wuhan in 1952 and Lanzhou in 1950. Ma, 1994: 57, asserting that the majority of sweeps to close brothels took place between 1951 and 1953. Yu, 1992: 8, stating that actions to close brothels commenced in 1950 and continued for three years. Yu, 1993: 39, noting that at the time of these sweeps, arrangements were also made for the prostitutes 'to get married and start a new life'.

3.2 Detaining prostitutes

As part of the programme to eradicate prostitution, centres were established to detain prostitutes for education and reform.[77] In Beijing, prostitutes were initially detained during the consolidated strike on the evening of 21 November 1949.[78]

An illustration of the ways in which detention was used as one of a range of strategies to eradicate prostitution can be seen from the case of Shanghai. In Shanghai, the municipal government authorised establishment of a small detention centre in November 1949. Its capacity was insufficient to detain all unregistered prostitutes, who were the primary targets at that time, so the police targeted for detention those without a home and those living on the streets. By November 1951 more than 400 such prostitutes had been detained.[79]

By late 1951, the measures taken to restrict brothels and stabilise social order described above had reached the point where the Shanghai Party Committee decided it was time to take more decisive action to close brothels, as well as to prohibit both street and hidden prostitution (*anchang* 暗娼). Prostitution was pronounced illegal. The public security organs notified brothels and their prostitutes of this decision and gave them a week to 'take another path'. It was decided that the targets for prostitute detention were those whose main occupation was prostitution, who had been prostituting for over a year, who sought clients on the street or in public places or who had a record with the police for several offences. People committing more serious prostitution-related offences such as pimps, brothel owners and people who bullied prostitutes or coerced women to prostitute would be subject to more severe punishment by being sent to reform through labour or being charged with other criminal offences.

In Shanghai, concerted action was taken on the evening of 25 November 1951 to close brothels still in business and to detain the prostitutes in them, as well as unregistered prostitutes. In this action, seventy-two brothels were closed, seventy-four people were later convicted by a court of criminal offences, 260 were sent to reform through

77 There is some difference between authors as to the naming of these centres. Shen, 1990: 57, refers to the detention centres in Beijing as *jiaoyang yuan* (教养院); Henriot, 1995, refers to the centre established in Shanghai as the Women's Labour Training Centre (*Funü Laodong Jiaoyangsuo* 妇女劳动教养所). Dutton, 2005: 152 and Huang, 1994: 119, refer to these centres as Women's Production, Education and Fostering Institutes (*Funü Shengchan Jiaoyangyuan* 妇女生产教养院).

78 Ma, Weigang, 1993b: 89.

79 Ma, Weigang, 1993b: 21–4.

labour and 513 prostitutes were sent to prostitute detention centres.[80] Further such actions were taken in 1952.[81]

After the public security organs had closed brothels and dealt with public prostitutes, attention was then turned to hidden prostitution and the detention for reform of this type of prostitute.[82] Detection was more difficult. In Shanghai police reported that hidden prostitutes were detained whenever they were discovered.[83]

Detention centres were intended to test for and treat illness, especially STDs; to give the detainees new skills such as literacy; to teach inmates to work to support themselves; and to transform their consciousness so that they would break with their past.[84] A high proportion of detainees required treatment for STDs. For example, of the 1,303 prostitutes in detention in Beijing in 1950, 1,259 reportedly had a sexually transmitted disease.[85]

The authorities also made arrangements for detainees after their release, placing them in work, or in the care of families or spouses. As part of their broad social order responsibilities, resident committees were responsible for uncovering and reforming prostitutes in their localities.[86] In Shanghai, after release, many former prostitutes were placed in the custody of their families, or marriages were arranged. Some were returned to their home towns in the countryside; some were assigned to work in factories in the city; and others, especially those who were unmarried, were sent to work on state farms in remote provinces such as Xinjiang, Gansu or Ningxia.[87] Reports indicated that these detention centres continued operation until around 1956.[88]

Despite propaganda to the contrary, the task of reform in these centres met with resistance from the inmates, who were not universally overjoyed at being liberated from their 'oppression'.[89] Henriot reports that prostitution in Shanghai was only finally eradicated in 1958 because

80 Ma, Weigang, 1993b: 21–4. Slightly disparate statistics are given in these accounts. Ma's report is unclear about the number of prostitutes detained. Yu, 1993: 39, asserts there were 513, but also asserts that 234 people were convicted of committing a crime which differs from Ma's account.

81 Huang and Zhang, 1996: 260.

82 Ma, Weigang, 1993b: 12.

83 Ma, Weigang, 1993b: 25.

84 Henriot, 1995: 477–80; Herschatter, 1997: 310.

85 Ma, Weigang, 1993b: 7.

86 Pan, 2004: 35.

87 Herschatter, 1997: 318–19; Henriot, 1995: 482–4, calling the latter option exile.

88 Ma, 1994: 58.

89 Ma, Weigang, 1993b: 90–2, describing management of the 'students' after detention in Beijing's Women's Production Education and Fostering Institutes. Herschatter, 1997: 312–13; Henriot, 1995: 478–9.

local resident committees made it impossible for a woman to prostitute without being discovered and reported.[90]

Subsequent propaganda has extolled the effectiveness of the strategies to eliminate prostitution and the usefulness of prostitute detention and re-education as a 'glorious page written in the world history of prohibiting prostitution'.[91] Other accounts indicate that eradication of prostitution was neither straightforward nor quickly achieved. Henriot and Herschatter's studies suggest that efforts to eliminate prostitution took much longer and were much more difficult than the propaganda generally acknowledges. Prostitution may never have been completely eradicated. An indication that prostitution continued after its official eradication is that prostitutes making their living from prostitution were included within the targets for re-education through labour from 1957.[92] Although efforts were also made to attack hidden prostitution, it is not clear how successful these efforts were, or against precisely what forms of hidden prostitution official attention was directed.

The police relied heavily on propaganda to mobilise mass participation in their efforts both to identify and eradicate prostitution and on the close co-operation of local community organisations.[93] In the end, the so-called 'success' of the campaigns to eradicate prostitution relied heavily upon the effectiveness of local methods of surveillance and control exercised by resident committees; the ability of the state at that time to control unwanted population movements; and to make arrangements for prostitute's lives and work after they were released from detention.

4 STRATEGIES TO ELIMINATE DRUG ADDICTION IN THE 1950S

Prior to 1949, the CCP took steps to control the sale and use of drugs in the areas it controlled.[94] After taking power, it took action to deal with the extensive problems of drug use, first in areas where drug addiction

[90] Henriot, 1995: 475–6; Herschatter, 1997, also asserting that prostitution in Shanghai was eradicated by 1958. Dutton, 2005: 155, asserting that prostitution was eradicated by 1956. Xin, 1993: 94, putting the less probable argument that prostitution was eradicated in 1953.
[91] Mou, 1996: 192–3. [92] See discussion below. [93] Ma, Weigang, 1993b: 12–13.
[94] Zhao and Yu, 2000: 16–17, referring, for example, to acts in 1939, where the CCP criminalised drug-related activities and took action to deal with drug addiction. Guo and Li, 2000: 62–3. The primary focus at this time was on opium and its derivatives, morphine and heroin.

was particularly acute, then nationwide.[95] Estimates in Guizhou shortly before liberation were that 21 per cent of the population smoked opium. In Yunnan Province it was 12.5 per cent of the population. An estimated 4.4 per cent or 20 million people nationwide were drug users.[96]

On 24 February 1950, the Central People's Government issued instructions that concerted action be taken to eliminate drug use in the *Circular on Strict Prohibition of Opium and Drug Taking*. Complementary local regulations were passed by the military control committees in different regions.[97] The *Circular* outlawed the growing, manufacturing, transporting and trafficking of drugs. The public security organs were given responsibility for targeting and punishing transportation of and trafficking in drugs.[98]

At first, a lenient approach was taken to dealing with drug addiction. Article 6 of the *Circular on Strict Prohibition of Opium and Drug Taking* required registration of drug users by the public security organs at city level and by the people's government at township and village level. These people were required to give up their habit within a fixed period and to hand over their equipment for drug use. Only those who either did not register or did not give up drugs within the designated time limits were to be subject to punishment. The *Circular* provided for the establishment of Anti-smoking and Anti-drug Committees under the local government, comprising representatives from government, police and local organisations.[99] The committees were given some latitude to adopt strategies that reflected the local situation.[100] The *Circular* also provided for the establishment of anti-smoking rehabilitation centres (*jieyansuo* 戒烟所) to be run by the local health department in cities where there was 'marked drug use'.[101]

Throughout the country many people involved in drug transportation and trafficking were arrested and punished. However, by autumn of 1950 there was increasing criticism that the approach taken to date was

[95] Zhao and Yu, 2000: 17. [96] Shao, 2004: 285–6.

[97] Zhao and Yu, 2000: 17, 129. Local legislation included South-west Military Commission, *Implementing Measures on Strictly Prohibiting Opium Smoking*, 31 July 1950; Inner Mongolia Autonomous Region People's Government, *Inner Mongolia Autonomous Region Implementing Measures on Strictly Prohibiting Opium Smoking*, April 1951; and North-East People's Government, *Order on Strictly Prohibiting Opium Smoking and other Drugs*, February 1952. Also Ke, 1990: 25; Ma, Weigang, 1993a: 55, listing similar regulations passed by the Military Commissions of other military regions, including the Central South, East China, North-East, and the North-West military commissions.

[98] Ma, Weigang, 1993b: 3. [99] (*Jinyan Jindu Weiyuanhui* 禁烟禁毒委员会).

[100] *Circular on Strict Prohibition of Opium and Drug Taking*, art. 2. Ma, Weigang, 1993b: 2.

[101] *Circular on Strict Prohibition of Opium and Drug Taking*, art. 7.

overly lenient. In a number of cases in early and mid-1950, it became clear that drug trafficking was being used to fund armed struggle against the Communist regime and for KMT military operations.[102] Evidence of these connections lent weight to calls to end lenient treatment of drug offenders. Calls were made to 'correct the phenomenon of handling drug dealers too leniently' and to stop substituting fines for criminal punishments.[103] A circular issued by the Internal Affairs Ministry on 12 September 1950, the *Directive on Implementing the Work of Strict Prohibition of Drug Taking*, criticised this overly lenient approach.[104] Complementary measures issued by the Supreme People's Court in November 1950 also urged the courts to treat drug offences seriously and not to substitute fines for imprisonment.[105]

The campaigns against drug use and drug-related offences more broadly became intertwined with campaigns to suppress bandits and warlords during the Campaign to Suppress Counter-revolutionaries[106] and so the campaigns targeting drug manufacture, transport and dealing were waged with much greater severity from late 1950.[107] Despite increasing severity of punishments and increased enforcement, police reported that the 1950 campaign did not fundamentally resolve the drug problem.[108]

Internal investigations of Party and government officials as part of the Three Anti and Five Anti campaigns revealed that a number of officials were involved in a range of drug-related criminal offences, some with links to counter-revolutionaries and overseas drug cartels.[109] In March and April 1952, a Suppression of Drugs Office was established to carry out investigations.[110] On 15 April 1952, the CCPCC issued the *Directive on Eradication of the Circulation of Drugs* which concluded that the drug problem remained severe despite eradication efforts to date. It directed that a nationwide mass campaign be waged against drug crimes

102 Shao, 2004: 297–305. In relation to the use by the KMT of revenues from drug sales both before and after liberation, see Shen, 1991: 56–7; Ma, Weigang, 1993a: 55; Dutton, 2005: 159.

103 Ma, Weigang, 1993a: 55–6.

104 Guo and Li, 2000: 72; Ma, Weigang, 1993b: 3.

105 Ma, Weigang, 1993b: 3.

106 Ma, Weigang, 1993a: 55.

107 Xia, 2001: 9.

108 Ma, Weigang, 1993a: 55–6, cites the Ministry of Internal Affairs, *Directive on Implementing the Work of Strict Prohibition of Drug Taking*, 12 September 1950 and the SPC, *Measures on Resolutely Abolishing Specialist and Commercial Fines in Handling Drug Criminals*, November 1950.

109 Ma, Weigang, 1993b: 4; Dutton, 2005: 159. The Three Anti Campaign was against waste, corruption and bureaucratism. The Five Anti Campaign was against corruption, tax evasion, stealing state property, cheating on state contracts and stealing state economic secrets; Lieberthal, 1995: 92.

110 (*Sudu Bangongshi* 肃毒办公室); Yu, 1992: 7.

and drug use. Drug users were to be subject to detention for coercive rehabilitation.[111]

On 21 May the Central People's Government issued the *Circular on Suppressing Opium and Drug Smoking*, directing each level of people's government to organise a mass mobilisation to wage an anti-drugs campaign as part of the Three Anti and Five Anti campaigns.[112] In June it determined that the Ministry of Public Security ('MPS') should be responsible for organising the nationwide campaign. The MPS's report recommended that drug offences involving criminal gangs and counter-revolutionaries be severely punished and that the campaign be carried out in three waves. On 30 July the CCPCC formally approved the MPS report.[113] In early August, the MPS convened a National Drug Prohibition Work Meeting to plan the concerted action focussing on 1,202 specially designated areas where the drug problem was particularly serious.[114] Following this meeting, the CCPCC and the MPS launched the first wave of the campaign, which was immediately followed by the second and third waves.[115]

Local Anti-smoking Anti-drug Committees carried out education as well as acting to suppress drug manufacture, transport and use.[116] Funds were expended both to provide welfare relief to impoverished drug addicts and for the manufacture of medicines for curing drug addiction.[117]

Mass mobilisation and education around the elimination of drugs was conducted in the form of a range of large and small-scale meetings organised by the trade unions, the Communist Youth League, the Women's Federation and a range of other social groups.[118] In cities throughout the country, the public security organs organised mass rallies. At one such rally in Beijing on 1 September, attended by 40,000 people, people who had committed serious crimes were arrested and sentenced. At some rallies, drug users who had failed to register were

[111] Ke, 1990: 24–5; Shen, 1991: 57; Ma, Weigang, 1993a: 56. Shen and Ma assert that the anti-drug campaign was waged at that time in order to take advantage of the mass mobilisation and the organisational structures that had been put in place for the purpose of the Three Anti and Five Anti campaigns.

[112] *Wei Chajin Yapian Yandu de Tongling*, referred to in Shao, 2004: 310–11.

[113] Shao, 2004: 311–12; Xi and Yu, 1996: 255; Liu and Yuan, 1997: 32.

[114] (*Quanguo Jindu Gongzuo Huiyi* 全国禁毒工作会议). Yu, 1992: 7; Shao, 2004: 312; Ma, Weigang, 1993b: 5.

[115] Ma, Weigang, 1993a: 56; Shao, 2004: 312.

[116] Guo and Li, 2000: 72–3; Brady, 1981: 18, discussing community action in respect of drug addicts from 1950.

[117] Ma, Weigang, 1993a: 57.

[118] Ma, Weigang, 1993b: 5.

also arrested. This tactic was used to scare many drug users who had refused to register, or had registered using false names, into coming forward voluntarily to register.[119] Ma asserts that as a result of such tactics, 340,000 people presented themselves to their local police station to register and confess their crimes. People were also encouraged to inform on drug offenders, including their own family members. Ma, citing incomplete statistics, asserts that 1.31 million letters of accusation were written, accusing over 220,000 people of drug-related offences.[120]

Despite the large number of people punished, the legal basis for imposition of punishments remained poorly specified by law. As with the actions against prostitution, the law followed the investigation, reporting, decision-making and even in some cases the implementation of the decisions to attack drug use and trafficking. In early November 1952, the Minister of Public Security, Luo Ruiqing, prepared draft *PRC Regulations on the Punishment of Drug Offenders* which set out punishments for different types of drug-related offences. In late November, the Central People's Government decided that the *Regulations* should be approved and implemented by local public security organs, but should only be used internally and not published.[121]

In December 1952 Luo Ruiqing made a concluding report to the CCPCC and to Mao Zedong on the conduct of the anti-drugs campaign. On 18 December the CCPCC issued Luo Ruiqing's 'Concluding Report on the Nationwide Campaign to Eradicate Drugs', marking an end to the campaign.[122] During the campaign, police commentators assert that 345,463 drug users were registered, 82,056 people were arrested, 880 were executed and the balance punished with life imprisonment, fixed-term imprisonment, reform through labour or control, with a small number released.[123] Two authors claim that over the three-year period from October 1949 to November 1952, 20 million drug users were cured of their habit.[124]

119 Shao, 2004: 312–13. 120 Ma, Weigang, 1993b: 5.

121 *PRC Regulations on Punishment of Drug Crimes*, referred to in Shao, 2004: 321 and Ma, Weigang, 1993b: 6.

122 Ma, Weigang, 1993b: 6–7.

123 Shao, 2004: 312. Similar figures are provided by Zhang, Qiuhan, 1993: 11; Guo and Li, 2000: 72. Slightly different figures are given by Xi and Yu, 1996: 255, asserting that during the July to November 1952 campaign, 35,000 people were arrested, 880 people were handled for serious drug crimes and 3,996,056 *liang* of opium seized. Yu, 1993: 38–9, concurs with the number of drug addicts registered, and asserts that 36,000 serious drug users were arrested.

124 Shao, 2004: 322; Zhao and Yu, 2000: 137; Ma, Weigang, 1993a: 57. Ma's estimate is lower, asserting that over 10 million drug addicts were cured over a three-year period.

Subsequent propaganda has extolled the effectiveness of these campaigns as 'a glorious page written in the history of our country's struggle to prohibit drugs'.[125] Despite this propaganda, it appears that the problem of drug use and addiction was never completely eliminated[126] and the use of detention to rehabilitate drug users never entirely ended. In 1973, for example, the State Council issued the *Notice on Strictly Prohibiting the Private Cultivation of Opium Poppy, the Transport and Use of Opium etc Drugs*, ordering a mass campaign be waged against drug cultivation, transport and use and that drug users be taken in for coercive drug rehabilitation.[127] The extent to which the programmes to eliminate drug use in the 1950s were successful depended largely upon the capacity of the state to mobilise large-scale popular participation as part of the Campaign to Suppress Counter-revolutionaries and, subsequently, the Three Anti and Five Anti campaigns.[128]

5 DEVELOPMENT OF RE-EDUCATION THROUGH LABOUR IN THE 1950S AND 1960S

5.1 Initial development of the power

The antecedents to the formal system of re-education through labour ('RETL') can be traced to the systems of forced labour in operation since 1951 and from cases that were investigated at the time of the Three Anti campaign but not pursued.[129] RETL itself was formally established in 1955 during the campaign for the suppression of internal counter-revolutionaries.[130]

125 Zhang, Qiuhan, 1993: 11.

126 Zhao and Yu, 2000: 17; and Ke, 1990: 25, reporting that in the early 1960s the problem of drugs had revived in some areas to the extent that the CCPCC felt it necessary to issue the *Notice on Strict Prohibition of Opium, Morphine and Harmful Drugs*, 26 May 1963.

127 Zhao and Yu, 2000: 17–18. This document reissued the February 1950 Central People's Government, *Circular on Strict Prohibition of Opium and Drug Taking*. Ke, 1990: 25, indicates that in some local areas the use of coercive drug rehabilitation continued to be used and that local regulations authorising use of this detention power were based on the 1952 CCPCC *Directive on Eradication of the Circulation of Drugs*.

128 Guo and Li, 2000: 73, reporting that in the second half of 1952, 74,590,000 people participated in propaganda and other activities related to the anti-drugs campaign. Shao, 2004: 322, reports 74,595,181. Even if the statistics quoted are overstated, the size of the mobilisation at this time remains massive.

129 Chen, 2003: 82–3, in relation to forced labour; Ma, 2001: 33 (*qing er bu li* 清而不理).

130 CCPCC, *Directive on the Thorough Elimination of Hidden Counter-Revolutionaries*, 25 August 1955; Jiang and Zhan, 1994: 96; Xia, 2001: 10, 558–9; Xie, 2000: 121–2. This campaign was launched at the end of the Campaign to Suppress Counter-revolutionaries and targeted counter-revolutionaries and 'bad elements' within the Party and state organisations. Wang, Zhongfan, 1992: 269, states RETL commenced in 1956.

The targets of the 1955 campaign were officials in the Party, government departments and the People's Liberation Army ('PLA') at central and provincial level; and people in enterprises, factories schools and residents' committees at county and local level who were politically unreliable or opposed the Party.[131] Of the targets of this campaign, some were allowed to continue in their post because their transgressions were considered minor, or they had confessed or performed meritorious acts. Others were convicted of criminal offences and then sent to reform through labour. The conduct of others was considered not sufficiently serious to warrant criminal punishment, but rendered them too unreliable to retain their position.[132] Instead of allowing these people to become unemployed, after being dismissed they were gathered up and sent to RETL. Detainees were to be paid a proportion of their pre-detention salary for their work.[133] The targets for RETL were urban residents, as, in theory, it was considered unnecessary to arrange for settlement and employment of the rural population.[134]

On 25 August 1955 the CCPCC issued the *Directive on the Thorough Elimination of Hidden Counter-revolutionaries* which provided that:

> In this campaign those counter-revolutionaries and other bad elements who have been ferreted out, except for those given the death sentence and those whose criminal circumstances are minor, who have made a thorough confession, or who may continue to be employed because of merit, should be handled in one of two ways. One method is to send them to reform through labour after being convicted of a criminal offence. The other method is to send to RETL those who cannot be convicted of a criminal offence, but politically it is no longer appropriate for them to continue to be employed, and who, if left in society will increase unemployment. That is, although they are not convicted of a criminal offence and are not completely deprived of their freedom, they should be gathered up to work for the nation and be paid a certain salary by the state.[135]

[131] Xia, 2001: 11–13.
[132] Jiang and Zhan, 1994: 96; Li and Du, 1990: 50.
[133] Xia, 2001: 11–13, and at 59–60, citing a November 1955 Internal Affairs Ministry, MPS, Ministry of Finance, *Notice on Several Questions in Drawing up the Plan for RETL*, specifying that 70 per cent of the original salary should be paid, including the amount provided for the livelihood of that person's family, and a January 1956 document, CCPCC *Instruction to Each Province City and District Immediately to Make Arrangements for RETL Organs*, which permits an adjustment to be made to the salary paid after the first two years in detention.
[134] Ren, 1992: 13.
[135] See also discussion in Xie, 2000: 121–2; Xia, 2001: 11–12, 59.

On 10 January 1956 the CCPCC issued the *Directive to Each Province and City Immediately and Without Exception to Set about Making Plans to Establish RETL Organs*, directing that RETL camps be set up at provincial and city level.[136] It required that a five-person small group be established at provincial and city level to decide who should receive a criminal punishment, those to be sent to RETL and those who should only receive an administrative penalty. RETL was established under a leadership small group comprising representatives of the civil affairs department, public security and justice departments under the leadership of provincial and municipal-level Party Committees. The public security organs were primarily responsible for management of RETL.[137] This *Directive* indicated that those people who had committed minor criminal offences and had been sentenced to control should be sent to RETL and the court should not issue a judgment in the matter.[138]

The CCPCC *Ten Person Small Group Temporary Regulations on Policy Limits on Identification and Handling of Counter-revolutionary Elements and Other Bad Elements*, issued on 10 March 1956, expanded the scope of targets to include those convicted of minor criminal offences, people of bad moral fibre and those continuing to oppose the Party and government.[139] The inclusion of minor criminal offenders within the scope of RETL was reaffirmed in a *Response by the CCPCC Ten-Person Small Group to a Request for Instructions from the Liaoning Provincial Party Committee Five-Person Small Group on Measures on RETL* on 6 September 1956. These documents formed the early basis upon which RETL organs were established.[140]

At this stage, the targets of RETL remained primarily politically defined.[141] One account states that 59 per cent of the total of 16,695

[136] Gong'an Bu Fazhisi, 1992: 235–6.

[137] Chief of the 11th Section of the MPS, Meng Zhaoliang, speech at the Third National Reform through Labour Work Conference, September 1955.

[138] A person sentenced to control was permitted to serve their sentence outside prison under the supervision of their work unit and resident committee. Zuigao Renmin Jianchayuan Jiansuo Jiancha Ting, 1992: 36.

[139] They 'include those convicted of a criminal offence and sentenced to control', 'people of extremely bad moral character, hooligans by nature, people who do bad things who will not reform after repeated education and those who are not fit to be government employees and after dismissal are unemployed' and 'relatives of people killed or arrested in the Campaign to Suppress Counter-revolutionaries and people who have not committed any counter-revolutionary offence but continue to abuse and defile the Party and government'. Cui, 1992: 17.

[140] Xie, 2000: 122; Cui, 1992: 17; Xia, 2001: 12–13.

[141] Dutton and Xu, 1998: 312–13, to transform those ideologically opposed to the regime.

detainees in the first RETL camp in Shandong province between 1957 and 1960 were taken in as a result of a political campaign.[142]

It has been argued that in 1955 RETL was not, in theory, a punishment.[143] However, even in these initial stages it was used to punish minor offenders. The CCPCC Ten-Person Small Group responsible for RETL itself acknowledged in January 1957[144] that only a portion of people sent to RETL were sent for 'settlement', to prevent them being unemployed, and that its more important function was to detain hooligans and others who were subjected to re-education as 'an administrative coercive measure'.[145]

RETL at that time had no fixed time limit.[146] In an explanation to the Standing Committee of the National People's Congress ('NPCSC') on 2 September 1957, the Minister of Public Security, Luo Ruiqing, defended the lack of a time limit for detention and rebutted suggestions that a time period of between two and three years be specified. Luo argued that, as RETL was a measure for coercive education and employment, to teach people the habit of labour and to support themselves, it was necessary to ensure that the detainee had properly reformed and had acquired the habit of work before release. He also suggested that release should be delayed until the then current unemployment situation had improved.[147]

Before 1957, RETL had no legislative basis. Luo Ruiqing raised it as an issue requiring further consideration in November 1956 with the question 'RETL, do we need legislation or not?'[148] Legislation was not passed immediately because of inconsistent views about whether legislation was required. In January 1957, the CCPCC approved a recommendation that legislation be drafted, reviewed by the CCPCC and then sent to the NPCSC for passage into law.[149]

142 Li and Du, 1990: 51, comprising 4,878 counter-revolutionaries, 2,517 rightists and 392 reactionaries.

143 Xia, 2001: 59.

144 CCPCC, approving the CCPCC Ten-Person Small Group, *Report to the CCPCC on the Current Situation regarding the Suppression of Counter-revolutionaries Campaign and 1957 Work*, 11 January 1957.

145 (*Xingzhen qiangzhi cuoshi* 行政强制措施).

146 Zhu, 1990: 6; Xia, 2001: 17.

147 Minister of Public Security, Comrade Luo Ruiqing, *Explanation on Questions about RETL at the Meeting of the NPCSC*, 2 September 1957: at 32, 152.

148 Minister of Public Security, Comrade Luo Ruiqing, *Concluding Speech at the November 1956 Conference of Provincial, City and Autonomous Self-Governing Region Party Committee Five Person Small Groups Heads*, 27 November 1956: at 34.

149 CCPCC, approving the CCPCC Ten-Person Small Group, *Report to the CCPCC on the Current Situation Regarding the Suppression of Counter-revolutionaries Campaign and 1957 Work*, 11 January 1957: at 33.

5.2 The legislative basis for RETL and expansion from 1957

The launch of the Anti-Rightist Campaign in 1957 led to an expansion of RETL. RETL became the primary method of dealing with people labelled 'rightists'.[150] In 1957, to facilitate the implementation of the Anti-Rightist Campaign, the scope of targets for RETL was increased, the numbers of people detained increased dramatically and geographical limitations on establishment of RETL camps relaxed.[151]

In 1957, after what has been described by one author as a trial period,[152] the NPCSC approved the *Decision of the State Council on the Question of RETL*.[153] This confirmed RETL as a measure for 'settlement and employment' of people without regular employment, transients and those without means of support.[154] The *Decision* provided that detainees work and receive remuneration appropriate to their work.[155] Whilst not explicitly directed at rightists, this *Decision* formed the basis upon which rightists were targeted for RETL.[156] The *Decision* did not specify any time limits for detention. The determination that it was not appropriate to fix a time limit for detention was reaffirmed by the MPS in 1958, when it noted that the situation of people in RETL was 'complex' and detainees should be released only when they had reformed.[157] As a practical result, people 'only went in and did not come out'.[158]

The *Decision* expanded the scope of RETL to include a wide range of people who harmed public order, thus making RETL more explicitly punitive in nature.[159] It listed four categories of person as targets for re-education:

1. those without proper work, hooligans or those who had committed thefts or fraud but who are not pursued for criminal responsibility, who breach public order management and who do not reform after repeated education;
2. counter-revolutionaries, anti-socialist elements whose offences are not sufficiently serious to warrant a criminal sanction, those who

150 Chen, 2003: 85–6, stating that a large proportion of rightists were sent either to RETL or to carry out supervised labour, though not providing statistics; at 89, asserting that over 99 per cent of these had been incorrectly labelled.
151 Gao, Xianduan, 1992: 40; Xia, 2001: 17; Ma, 2003: 130.
152 Yu, 1992: 403.
153 Approved by the NPCSC on 1 August 1957 and promulgated on 3 August 1957. Xia, 2001: 17, stating the *Decision* was passed to expand the scope of RETL.
154 (*Anzhi jiuye de cuoshi* 安置就业的措施). Ren, 1992: 12; Cui, 1992: 17.
155 *Decision of the State Council on the Question of RETL*, art. 2.
156 Chen, 2003: 86–8.
157 Ministry of Internal Affairs, MPS, *Response to the Work Report on Hubei Province RETL*, 17 March 1958.
158 Xia, 2001: 17 (*zhi jin bu chu* 只进不出).
159 Li and Du, 1990: 50; Ren, 1992: 13.

have been expelled from their work unit, organ, enterprise or school who have no means of support;
3. those who have work and the capacity to work but for a long time refuse to do so, or who disturb labour discipline, who harm public order, who have been expelled from a work unit, organ, enterprise or school and have no means of support; and
4. those who refuse to accept work allocation or settlement as a result of a work specialty, who refuse to accept advice, who ceaselessly and without reason cause a disturbance, obstruct official business and who do not reform after repeated education.[160]

The *Security Administrative Punishments Regulations* ('*SAPR*') passed in 1957 also provided that after receiving a punishment under the *SAPR*, those without employment and vagrants who repeatedly disturbed public order would be sent to RETL.[161] Other people who harmed public order were also identified in a range of documents issued around that time by the CCPCC and the MPS as targets for RETL. They included:

- prostitutes who make their living from prostitution;
- juveniles who had committed theft or hooliganism, who would not reform after repeated education and who had no home to return to or no head of the family to exercise control over them;
- people released from a term of reform through labour who committed further acts disrupting public order but whose acts were insufficient for a further criminal sanction;[162] and
- people released from prison who did not have a job and family to return to.[163]

The expansion of RETL to the local level coincided with the programme of rural collectivisation and establishment of people's communes, as well as with the Anti-Rightist Campaign.[164] Increasingly, RETL camps were set up at the local level, in localities, rural villages and people's communes. In August 1958 the MPS approved of

[160] Xie, 2000: 122.
[161] Xia, 2001: 16–17; Ministry of Internal Affairs, *Letter in Response to Two Questions about RETL Work*, 7 January 1958.
[162] MPS Party Group, *Regulation on the Policy Limits for Handling Criminal Elements Committing Theft, Hooliganism, Fraud, Homicide, Robbery etc.*, 23 July 1957.
[163] CCPCC, approving and issuing the Shanghai Party Committee, *Opinion on Questions about the Settlement of Personnel after Criminal Conviction where Cases were Cleared up or after Serving their Sentence*, 6 October 1957.
[164] Gao, Xianduan, 1992: 40.

establishment of RETL in communes and rural villages and acknowledged the 'effectiveness' of RETL established at these levels, especially in targeting landlords, counter-revolutionaries, wealthy peasants, bad elements and rightists.[165] One commentator asserts that at that time, nationwide, there were several hundred thousand people in RETL.[166]

By early 1959, the central authorities sought to restrict the establishment of RETL camps at the local level and required the county Party committee to approve establishment of RETL camps.[167] The CCPCC later acknowledged that RETL in a number of areas was out of control, prohibited further establishment of RETL camps at county level and below and ordered rectification of those already established.[168] In 1959 the CCPCC and the State Council jointly issued a decision providing that those people who had been 'rightists' in the campaign and who had demonstrated that they had truly reformed should have their 'rightist caps' removed, thus establishing the basis for their release from RETL.[169]

In a speech in 1962, Liu Shaoqi criticised the use of RETL as a means to expand the scope of antagonistic contradictions. He said: 'originally RETL was a measure for handling contradictions amongst the people, but [it has] ended up the same as measures for handling problems between the people and the enemy'.[170]

5.3 Controlling the scope of RETL from 1961

The 11th National Public Security Work Conference on 17 March 1961 determined that several measures needed to be taken to correct the 'leftist mistakes' of the Anti-Rightist movement.[171] On 20 April 1961, the CCPCC resolved to adopt measures to rectify RETL work, limit the scope of targets and impose a time limit of between one and three years on the period of detention, with the time period generally

[165] Ninth National Public Security Conference, *On Step by Step Strengthening the Work of Reforming the Five Categories of Elements; Landlords, the Wealthy, Counter-revolutionaries, Bad Elements and Rightists* and *Several Questions on Public Security Work (Draft)*, 16 August 1958.

[166] Xia, 2001: 17.

[167] CCPCC, approving and issuing the *Decision of the National Political-Legal Work Conference on Several Questions of Policy in the Struggle to Date against Enemies*, 20 March 1959.

[168] CCPCC, approving and issuing the MPS Party Group, *Outline of an Opinion on the Current Circumstances of the Struggle against the Enemy and Carrying out the Campaign of Social Suppression and Internal Suppression of Counter-revolutionaries (Rectification)*, 21 October 1960.

[169] Decision of the CCPCC and the State Council of the PRC, *Relating to the Problem of Dealing with Rightists who Really Demonstrate that they have Reformed*, 16 September 1959.

[170] Liu Shaoqi, *Political-legal Work and Correctly Handling Contradictions amongst the People*, 23 May 1962: at 451; Lin, 2001: 16.

[171] Xia, 2001: 17–19.

being between two and three years.[172] There was a recognition that detainees were unwilling to accept a punishment that was disproportionate to criminal punishments given for similar conduct.[173] The 1961 resolution identified a broad range of problems in the conduct of RETL such as taking in people who were not targets, ignoring education, combining the management of RETL with that of the criminal punishment of reform through labour and establishment of RETL at county level and below in breach of regulations. The 1961 resolution emphasised the importance of education over labour:

> The main task of RETL is to reform people. All RETL organs must adhere to the programme (*fangzhen*) of 'combination of labour and production and political education' and adhere to the principle of 'reform first, production second'.[174]

Although a time limit for RETL was approved, it was decided that it would not be announced publicly, but that the person to be taken in for re-education would be informed of the time limit only at the time of the decision to impose re-education. The CCPCC approval document made more detailed provision about the calculation of the time limits for detention:

> During the period of RETL, if the person is well behaved, they can be released early; if they are not well behaved, you can extend the time limit [you must also formally inform the person and their family]. Those who have carried out wrecking activities should be given criminal punishment according to the law. After release, the public security organs will be responsible for reintroducing them back to their original work unit, or get the labour department to arrange for them to be employed in a farm or factory, but they must absolutely not be returned to strategic government or sensitive military areas. If the person has no family to return to, or no employment to go to, if the person is willing, they can be retained for employment in the RETL camp.[175]

172 Approving the decision of the MPS after its 11th National Public Security Work Conference; Gao, Xianduan, 1992: 39–40; MPS, *Supplementary Provisions on Ten Specific Policy Issues Concerning Public Security Work to Date*, 17 March 1961, approved by the CCPCC on 20 April 1961.

173 Ren, 1992: 13; Zhu, Jiang, 1999: 32; Xia, 2001: 19, asserting that the lack of a time limit caused detainees to feel that they had no hope and no future, especially as RETL detainees were locked up with those convicted of criminal offences, whose imprisonment was for a fixed period.

174 From Gao, Xianduan, 1992: 39. See also the discussion in Xia, 2001: 17–18.

175 Zuigao Renmin Jianchayuan Jiansuo Jiancha Ting, 1992: 138–9, at 151.

Release at the expiration date was not automatic for those who were not well behaved during their period of re-education. The period of re-education for these people could be extended.[176] The MPS indicated that extensions should not exceed three years.[177] Some authors argue that the imposition of a time limit in 1961 indicated a change in the objectives of RETL, that it was no longer focussed purely on reform of the individual, but was also intended as a punishment.[178] If that is the case, imposition of a time limit merely made explicit the already punitive nature of the power and imposed some limits on the period of punishment.

In 1961 medium- to large-sized cities were authorised to establish centres for forced labour as an alternative to RETL, for those who had committed unlawful acts, but whose acts were not sufficiently serious to warrant RETL or a criminal sanction. In theory these camps were to be kept separate from RETL camps. In some areas specialist detention centres were established; in others, those undergoing forced labour were permitted to work in their local area and receive payment.[179]

From 1961, successive documents restricted the scope of targets for RETL. The target group shifted from political targets to those committing minor offences such as hooliganism, theft and fraud.[180] Throughout 1962, the MPS continued to restrict the scope of targets for re-education to urban residents, though with some exceptions.[181] On several occasions the CCPCC and the MPS instructed that certain groups be taken in for re-education, including counter-revolutionary and 'tertiary-level student wreckers';[182] peasants coming to Beijing to petition against grievances; insane people; and drifters who entered Beijing and caused disturbances and disrupted public order.[183] Instructions

[176] MPS, *Response to Request for Instructions from the Guangdong Provincial Reform Through Labour Office 'Several Questions on RETL Work'*, 22 January 1962.

[177] MPS, *Response to Request for Instructions from Heilongjiang Provincial Public Security Office 'Report Requesting Instructions on Questions about Fixing the Time for Continuing to Keep RETL Elements in RETL Teams and Settling RETL Personnel after their Release'*. 20 April 1962.

[178] Zhu, 1990: 6.

[179] Yu, 1992: 404; MPS, approving and issuing the *Opinion of the General Office on Seven Questions on Public Security Work to Date*, 13 November 1962.

[180] Li and Du, 1990: 52–3, reporting that between 1961 and 1965 the same RETL camp in Shandong took in a total of 7,349 people, of whom 11 per cent (821) were for political reasons, and 77.4 per cent (5,763) were for minor offences such as hooliganism, theft and fraud.

[181] Gao, Xianduan, 1992: 40, approving and issuing *the Opinion of the General Office on Seven Questions on Public Security Work to Date*, 13 November 1962.

[182] MPS, Ministry of Higher Education, *Opinion on Handling Counter-revolutionary and Bad Elements amongst Higher Education Students*, 25 August 1964.

[183] MPS, *Response to Questions Concerning the Scope of RETL*, 27 September 1965.

prohibiting RETL in rural villages and to limit the numbers of people taken in for RETL continued to be issued up to 1965.[184]

At the beginning of the Cultural Revolution, the MPS issued a notice instructing that prisoners in reform through labour and detainees in RETL, including those retained for in-camp employment, not be released when their time was complete.[185] However, other accounts assert that RETL almost ceased between May 1966 and December 1978, with some being sent to reform through labour and others released.[186] One commentator cites 1971 as the year when RETL was re-established in some cities following approval by the CCPCC of the *Summary of Minutes of the Fifteenth National Public Security Conference* convened by Zhou Enlai.[187] The MPS meeting called for the revival and re-establishment of RETL and forced labour in large- and medium-sized cities, but demanded at the same time that the power be strictly controlled.[188]

6 REGISTRATION AND DETENTION: MANAGING THE FLOATING POPULATION

The household registration system has served a number of purposes since establishment of the PRC. One, discussed above, has been to identify offenders and politically suspect people who should be subjected to special regimes of surveillance and control. Another related purpose has been to manage social order more broadly. Until recently, the household registration formed the linchpin of urban social order strategies. The household registration system enabled establishment of localised systems of 'mutual surveillance'[189] by creating urban communities modelled on rural communities[190] with relatively static populations. The police liaised with urban resident committees, which were established from December 1949, to strengthen their capacity to

184 CCPCC, approving MPS Party Group, *Post-conference Report on the Fourteenth National Public Security Conference*, 15 July 1965.
185 MPS, *Notice on Temporarily Halting the Release of Criminal Elements from Reform through Labour Units During the Period of the Cultural Revolution*, 14 October 1966.
186 Zhang and Xu, 1994: 704; Xia, 2001: 61, at 19–20, asserting that by 1969 there were only around 5,000 inmates in RETL. Xing, 2002: 5, asserts that there were only around 1,000 people detained under RETL in 1969.
187 Xia, 2001: 20; Zhang and Xu, 1994: 704; Gao, Xianduan, 1992: 40.
188 MPS, *Summary of Minutes of the Fifteenth National Public Security Conference*, 26 February 1971, point 8.
189 Dutton, 1992c: 216.
190 Lu, 1998: 91; Pan, 2004: 29–30.

manage urban localities.[191] The system of household registration was administered by the local police and designed to give them a detailed knowledge of local residents.[192] It sought to ensure that the individual was tied to the community and was not anonymous. It was at this level that residents were mobilised to participate in current campaigns, where welfare was granted by the socialist state and at which sanctioning could take place.[193] Street and resident committees played an important role in mobilising residents to participate in campaigns and neighbourhood affairs,[194] identifying those who deviated, educating, persuading and helping them to reform.[195] As discussed above, they were central to programmes in the 1950s to eradicate prostitution and drug use.

Yet another related function of the household registration system was to facilitate control over population mobility and to limit rural migration to urban areas.[196] As Kirkby points out, with limited exceptions in the period after 1949, there has been a strong popular pressure in favour of rural to urban migration. The state has vigorously resisted this pressure, using household registration, forcible repatriation to the countryside and periodic waves of sending urban residents to the countryside (*xiaxiang shangshan* 下乡上山) to limit the size of the urban population. From 1952, state agencies became increasingly concerned both to prevent peasants 'blindly floating' to urban areas and to repatriate them.[197] Itinerants, beggars and vagrants in urban areas were gathered up and placed in Labour Production Education Centres, or New Person Learn a Trade Camps.[198]

In 1957, the rural influx into cities fostered by the first Five Year plan, particularly from the Shandong, Jiangsu, Anhui, Henan and Hebei, had reached such levels that the CCPCC and the State Council jointly issued the *Directive on Preventing the Blind Outflow of the Rural Population* on 18 December 1957. This *Directive* mandated a number of measures, including establishment of the detention power that later was split into detention for repatriation (*shourong qiansong* 收容遣送) and detention for investigation (*shourong shencha* 收容审查).

191 Pan, 2004: 30–2. Hangzhou first established a resident committee in December 1949. In March 1950 Tianjin linked resident committees to the local police station.
192 Dutton, 1992c: 214–39; Ma, 1997: 130–1.
193 Dutton, 1992c: 216–18, 330.
194 Fu, 1993: 51.
195 Fu, 1993: 85–7; Lubman, 1967: 1339–49.
196 Chan and Li, 1999: 819–21; Cheng and Selden, 1994; Dutton, 1992c: 203; Yu, 1992: 248; Wang, 2005; Solinger, 1999: 35–44; Kirkby, 1985: 25.
197 Kirkby, 1985: 22–5, 34–43.
198 Yu, 1992: 8–9.

In this *Directive* the CCPCC and State Council instructed that those who refused to work, who enjoyed wandering around and encouraged others to do so, should be severely criticised. If they refused to reform after repeated education they should be forced to work under the supervision of the masses. They directed that along main transport routes such as train stations, wharves and ports, the civil administration, public security and railways should establish organs to dissuade people from leaving the countryside and to repatriate them.

The urban household register was to be used as an adjunct to identifying rural migrants and beggars who were to be taken into detention centres for repatriation to their original place of registration. Whilst in detention these people were to be organised to work to meet the cost of their return ticket. Those who were disruptive were to be punished according to the degree of severity of their offence, with the imposition of a criminal penalty or RETL for serious offences.

7 CONCLUSION

A wide range of detention powers were used at different periods and with different intensity throughout the 1950s and beyond. The different forms of detention arose in response to particular social order problems, such as the detention of prostitutes and drug users, and to assist social management, such as detention for investigation and repatriation. They were also inextricably linked with the political campaigns that were waged in the 1950s, with RETL being a prominent example. Law, to the extent that it was used to define these powers, came later and was not always made public.

From the 1950s we can see the complementary use of administrative and criminal measures. Administrative measures, including detention, were to be employed where the misconduct was not sufficiently serious to warrant a criminal sanction. The criminal law was to be used to punish enemies. Even though in theory the distinction between non-antagonistic contradictions and antagonistic contradictions and the measures to be used to resolve them was clear, in practice this was not the case, especially during campaigns. The use of RETL during the Anti-Rightist movement illustrates how elusive the line was between the two types of contradiction.

Today, discussions of strategies to resolve complex social problems such as prostitution, drug trafficking and addiction refer nostalgically to the tools of the 1950s that were reputed to be so effective.[199] However, police commentators such as Ma Weigang suggest that past experience must be used with caution in formulating strategies to attack both prostitution and drug-related offences as the social conditions that assisted eradication of prostitution and drug use in the 1950s no longer exist. He notes that society is now quite different from that of the 1950s and 1960s and that these problems have become more complex and difficult to resolve. He warns that it is no longer possible to imagine that concerted actions will be effective to eradicate these social problems and public security organs must gear themselves to wage these battles for a very long period.[200]

199 Bakken, 2000: 377, cites references asserting that the 1950s were seen as the golden age of social stability and order. Dutton, 1995a: 427; Liu, 1989: 3, portraying the 1950s as a whole as a period where honesty and law and order prevailed where 'people do not take articles left by the wayside and the doors are not bolted at night' (*lu bu shiyi, ye bu bihu* 路不拾遗, 夜不闭户).

200 Ma, Weigang, 1993b: 13.

CHAPTER FOUR

SOCIAL ORDER, THE 'HARD STRIKE' AND ADMINISTRATIVE DETENTION POWERS

1 INTRODUCTION

In the 1950s different forms of detention evolved in response to practical problems of establishing social control and to the impetus of political campaigns such as the Campaign to Suppress Counter-revolutionaries. Whilst law was not entirely absent, it tended to follow behind policies and practices. Since economic reforms were initiated in the late 1970s, the redevelopment of administrative detention powers has again been deeply influenced by their political and social order contexts, though these contexts are quite different from those of the 1950s. The possibilities for different forms of legal treatment of administrative detention are also directly influenced by the political and social order context in which those powers are developed and used. In this chapter, I set out the policy context within which police administrative detention powers have been developed and employed since the 1970s.

The social changes brought about by the economic reform programme disrupted established localised strategies for social control and crime prevention. The Party and police have responded by rejuvenating powers and reworking strategies they remember as successful in the pre-reform era. The remaking of contemporary social order policy in the shadow of its pre-reform analogue illustrates Bourdieu's observation that contemporary debates in social fields are historically and politically structured. Pre-reform strategies for social and political control have provided a vocabulary within which contemporary social order strategies have been developed, though in the process of reusing these powers in a changed social and political environment, they have been significantly altered.

I examine the transformation of community policing from voluntarist and ideologically motivated strategies into formalised, professional and remunerated mechanisms of community dispute resolution and crime prevention. However, these strategies have ultimately been inadequate to achieve social order and stability and to prevent prostitution, drug use and other forms of proscribed behaviour. Re-use of the mass campaign in the form of law and order campaigns or 'Hard Strikes' against crime, depends upon mobilisation, as it did in the 1950s and 1960s. However, increasingly the community at large has become less involved, leaving the mobilisation to state organs, particularly to the police. Whilst decisions to launch 'Hard Strikes' are politically motivated, they are waged against a backdrop of rising crime and target legally defined conduct, however vaguely defined, rather than politically defined groups or classes.

I examine the place of administrative detention powers within the social order strategy devised at the beginning of the reform era, the Comprehensive Management of Public Order ('CMPO'). Administrative detention powers are wedged between mass-line social order strategies, such as local policing and interventions by localised community organisations, at one end, and campaign-style law enforcement against crime, at the other. I argue that the failure of mass-line policing and the continuing reliance on the hard strike have both provided the impetus to increase reliance on administrative detention. In particular, the demand for flexibility in enforcement in a 'Hard Strike' has contributed to increasing reliance on flexibly defined administrative detention powers. What room does this leave for increasing legalisation and formalisation of these powers? My analysis of social order policy reveals that even though the Party continues to dominate the formulation and implementation of social order policy, as reforms progress, increasingly there is debate about the best means to maintain social order and prevent crime. These debates also attempt to depict strategies for maintaining social order as being consistent with the programme of governance according to law. The emergence of a space within which social order policy debates can take place, coupled with an acceptance that social order strategies and powers must be legally justified, arguably creates a space where legal reform of administrative detention powers becomes a possibility.

2 THE CONTEMPORARY PROBLEM OF SOCIAL ORDER AND CRIME

2.1 Characterisation of crime

In theory, in a socialist system, crime is expected to die out as the causes of crime, the exploitation and poverty inherent in capitalism, are eliminated. However, in the early 1990s police commentators noted that the crime rate had risen rapidly between 1973 and 1976, and again after 1978.[1] At the beginning of the reform era, the police came to accept that crime would not disappear.[2] In a period of rapid social change, many accepted that social cohesion had been eroded and the efficacy of traditional and popular norms of social control weakened without any new social norms yet to replace them.[3] For both ideological and practical reasons in the reform era, class background could no longer be seen as a central cause of crime, nor could theories of class struggle[4] remain at the heart of strategies to deal with crime and social disorder.

At the ideological level, the decision to downgrade the policy status of class struggle was reflected in the CCPCC resolution that the 'exploiters had been eliminated as a class'.[5] This policy was then reflected in the law. In his discussion of revisions to the 1982 *Constitution*, Peng Zhen explained that as the class of enemies had been eliminated, there was no longer an *a priori* distinction to be drawn between the 'people' and the 'enemy' as a class. As a result, he continued, all citizens had the capacity to enjoy the same rights and duties.[6] The 1982 *Constitution* thus included the provision of 'equality of all before the law'.[7]

At the practical level, at the end of the 1970s, it was recognised that social disorder and crime were no longer caused by the 'exploiting

[1] Yu, 1993: 42–3. In 1991 and 1992 Yu Lei was Deputy Minister of Public Security.

[2] Yu, 1993: 17, 191; Liu, 1989: 4. Cohen, 1968: 74–9 at 74, extracts a passage from a set of lectures on the criminal law published in 1957, asserting that crime is a product of class-based society.

[3] Chen, 1996: 400.

[4] 'Class struggle' is based on the Marxist idea that there will be political struggle between the different social classes as a result of the conflict of interest that arises between them because of their different relationship to ownership of the means of production. Collins, 1984: 8–9; Schurmann, 1968: 27. Schurmann asserts that the Chinese Communists expanded this concept to cover all conflicts, including those 'internal or external to China'. Lieberthal, 1995: at 74–5, pointing out that Mao's definition of class extended to include political attitude. As a result, being labelled 'rightists' during the Anti-Rightist campaign in 1957 could be attributed a bad class status. Schurmann, 1968: 32, arguing that it was possible for an individual to change class status by correcting their thought and 'transform[ing their] identity'.

[5] CCP Central Committee, 1981: 78.

[6] Peng, 1992a: 311.

[7] *PRC Constitution*, art. 33.

classes and the dregs of the old society',[8] but that crime 'now mainly occurs amongst the people, with the overwhelming majority [of criminal offenders] being juveniles, young workers and students, they are the children of the masses (workers, peasants, intellectuals and cadres) who grew up in new China'.[9] Fu Hualing argues that identifying juveniles from working and peasant backgrounds as the main causes of crime required a change in the orientation of crime control in the reform era. It now had to target the conduct of an individual rather than targeting a category of person based on class background.[10]

2.2 Social disorder

The increasingly complex relationship between problems of social disorder and crime has made the distinction between the people and the enemy an increasingly difficult one for enforcement agencies to draw upon when determining enforcement responses. Problems of social unrest have become increasingly serious as economic reform deepens. There is now official recognition that official corruption, inequality and unfairness in economic development are factors that tend to promote social instability.

Large and small-scale protests, labelled 'mass incidents' (*quntixing shijian* 群体性事件), against a range of injustices further complicate the policing of public order. O'Brien has labelled the range of conduct from non-co-operation, to petitioning, to protest as 'rightful resistance', as it does not seek to oppose the state but to elicit its assistance to correct local wrongdoings.[11] One academic in the public security system asserts that over 90 per cent of mass incidents arise out of public dissatisfaction with the conduct of government officials. The number of incidents involving labour disputes is also increasing, with reports of an average

8 Peng, 1992c: 249.

9 Peng, 1992c: 249; Wang, Zhongfan, 1992: 6–8. The problem of youth crime was identified in June 1979 in a joint *Report on Requesting the Whole Party to Attach Importance to Resolving the Problem of Juvenile Crime* prepared by the CCPCC Propaganda Department, Education Ministry, Ministry of Culture, MPS, State Labour Central Department, All-China Council of Trade Unions, Communist Youth League and the All-China Women's Federation, issued by the CCPCC in August 1979; Tanner, Harold, 1999: 128. See also statistics given in Bakken, 1993: 38–42. Yu, 1993: 45, asserting that from 1979–81, 70–80 per cent of those caught for criminal offences were between fourteen and twenty-five years old. Ma, 1990: 171, asserting that in 1980 juvenile crime comprised 70–80 per cent of urban crime and 60–70 per cent of rural crime. Fu, 1993: 107–8, notes that, in China, the term 'juveniles' refers to people up to the age of twenty-five.

10 Fu, 1993: 112.

11 O'Brien, 1996: 36–9.

annual increase of 30 per cent in the number of labour disputes between 1997 and 2003.[12]

Many are provoked to protest after suffering from abuse of power and corrupt practices such as the unlawful imposition of taxes, improper failure to pay wages and corrupt expropriation of farming land.[13] Unauthorised demonstrations, repeated petitioning to higher authorities, encircling and barricading government and Party offices and violent conflicts are characterised as problems of social disorder or of crime that require police intervention, even though the genesis of these protests lies in more deep-seated problems of governance.

These types of protest have been characterised as 'non-antagonistic' in nature, relating to material interests. Though non-antagonistic in nature, they are 'confrontational' in form, which affects policing responses.[14] The police have some sympathy with these protesters. However, there is a fine line between legitimate public protest which might be officially seen as 'rightful', and conduct which becomes characterised as undermining social order, or even criminal, and so 'wrongful'.

There has been a significant rise in the number of mass protests since the early 1990s. More importantly, these protests have recently become larger, better organised and more violent. They are seen as difficult to police or 'complex' because of the large numbers of people often involved, with the crowds interspersed with old, young, disabled and women, so that in the eyes of the police the 'fish and the dragons are all jumbled up together'.[15]

2.3 Contemporary problems of crime

Is crime a serious problem in China? This question is significant because social order strategies and especially the periodic harsh crackdowns on crime are justified on the basis that crime has become rampant and social order is in a parlous state. Officials agreed that crime should be determined on the basis of a person's actions rather than politically determined, thus providing a basis for a more objective analysis of the

[12] Ren, 2005: 59.

[13] Ren, 2005: 272–3, discussing the seriousness of abuses relating to farming land and forced urban housing relocations.

[14] Ren, 2005: 259–63.

[15] Ren, 2005: 263–4 (*yulong hunza* 鱼龙混杂), meaning that 'the good and bad people all jumbled up'; and Tanner, 2004: 140–2.

nature and extent of crime. However, the extent of the problem of crime in China remains highly contested.

The first 'Hard Strike' against crime was launched in 1983 in response to this so-called crime wave. Many of the juveniles identified as one of the major sources of increased crime rates also formed part of the 'floating population'.[16] This group has been identified as predominantly young, unmarried males with low education levels, in their late teens and early twenties.[17]

The problem of the floating population presents the government and Party organs, including the police, with a conundrum. Whilst they recognise the fact that both economic reform policies and the dismantling of rural communes have stimulated a movement of surplus agricultural labour to non-agricultural industries and bigger cities, and the need for this movement,[18] they attribute a disproportionate responsibility for the upsurge in urban crime to the floating population.[19] The police identify those who are 'blindly floating' as 'complicating' the public order situation of the cities.[20] Being mostly poor and very visible, it is easy for the police to identify transients who have floated from the countryside to urban areas and economically developed coastal areas as being involved in committing an ever-increasing number of criminal offences.[21] The police and the urban community alike see them as susceptible to criminal influences and as a 'reserve for criminals'.[22]

In 1982 Deng Xiaoping urged ongoing struggle against economic crime and corruption, fearing that 'without such a struggle the overall policy [of economic reform and modernisation] will fail'.[23] In the 1980s

[16] At the 1990 census in Siping (Sichuan), 90 per cent of the transients were young, 80 per cent were male and 70 per cent were from undeveloped rural areas. For many it was their first time they had left home: Zhang, Shusen 1993: 58.

[17] Li, Cheng, 1998: 46. [18] Solinger, 1999: 45–54; Wang and Lu, 1994: 137.

[19] CCPCC, *Notice approving and issuing the 'Summary of the Minutes of the National Political-Legal Work Conference' and 'Important Points in the Speech of Comrade Peng Zhen at the National Political-Legal Work Conference'*, 28 August 1982, estimating that nationwide there were over 100 000 transient criminals.

[20] Wang and Lu, 1994: 135.

[21] Yu, 1993: 70–1, 322–3. The police report that, in busy areas of Beijing and areas where a high proportion of transients live, 70 per cent of all crime is committed by transients: Gao, Han, 1992: 37. The police have also identified migrants as being involved in organised crime: Wang and Lu, 1994: 132; Gao, Han, 1992: 38.

[22] Hao, 1991: 84; Bakken, 1993: 46, discussing the popular view of the migrant population as a 'dangerous, criminal force'. Lu, 1998: 147–8, documenting local Shanghai residents' suspicion of migrant and temporary residents living in their area.

[23] Deng, 1984a: 382.

and early 1990s, the police identified the major problems of crime as violent crime,[24] property-related offences,[25] murder,[26] organised crime[27] and a group of offences labelled 'social evils', including the manufacture, transportation and sale of drugs, kidnapping and selling people, prostitution, pornography, gambling[28] and drug addiction.[29]

Since that time, with some plateaus, official statistics point to a dramatic increase in the crime rate, especially in serious and violent crime, organised crime and economic crime including corruption.

The figures in table 4.1 show a dramatic increase in the number of cases put on file by the police, especially since 1997. However, Borge Bakken and others argue that this increased crime rate correlates with a larger proportion of the population being juveniles. They predict that, as the proportion of juveniles in the overall population decreases with population ageing from its peak in the early 1990s, the high rates of crime will also decrease.[30] The dramatic increase in criminal cases put on file in 2001 may also be explained by the increased enforcement during the 2001 'Hard Strike'.

Moreover, commentators point out that, although the crime rate has increased, it began from a very low base.[31] Some criminologists, particularly Bakken, point to international survey data of both victims and perpetrators in China to support their conclusion that by international standards, China's crime rate remains low.[32] It is also well known that

[24] Yu, 1993: 9; Feng and Wang, 1991: 99.

[25] Yu, 1993: 9, asserting that between 1985 and 1993, property-related crimes, theft, armed robbery and fraud comprised 80 per cent of major cases. According to one account, in 1990, 90.1 per cent of criminal cases were property-related offences: Feng and Wang, 1991: 98–9.

[26] Yu, 1993: 9.

[27] This problem has been linked to people released from prison or from RETL: Yu, 1993: 9, as well as the re-emergence of secret societies ('black societies') and organised professional criminal groups: Cui, 1991: 65–70. The Annual Report of the Criminal Investigation Division of the MPS, 'Strike Heavily Against Group Crime', reported that, in 1991, the criminal investigation police seized 134,000 criminal gangs comprising 507,000 people. In 1992, they reported seizing more than 120,000 gangs comprising 462,000 people: reproduced in Law Yearbook Editorial Committee, 1993: 120.

[28] Yu, 1993: 9, 322.

[29] Guo and Li, 2000: 92–3, citing figures that 82.3 per cent of first-time drug users are under twenty-five years old. Liu and Yuan, 1997: 31, asserting that over 70 per cent of drug users commit crime to support their habit. Yu, 1993: 387–9, linking the use of drugs to theft and murder and the growing, sale and transport of drugs involving organised crime.

[30] Chen, Jiafang, 1998: 164–7; Bakken, 2004: 68–9.

[31] Dutton, 1992b; Dutton and Lee, 1993: 317–9; Situ and Liu, 1996: 97–101, arguing that the crime rate has increased; Chen, Jiafang, 1998: 157–8.

[32] Most agree that the crime rate in China is not as high as it is in most developed countries: Bakken, 1993: 32–5, arguing that rates of serious crime have not increased dramatically. Bakken, 2004: 73–4.

TABLE 4.1 Criminal cases

Year	Number of criminal cases put on file by the public security organs[1]
1956	190,000
1965	210,000
1976	488,000
1977	548,000
1978	535,000
1979	636,000
1980	757,000
1981	890,000
1982	740,000
1983	610,000
1984	514,000
1985	542,000
1986	547,000
1987	570,000
1988	827,000
1989	1,971,901
1990	2,216,997
1991	2,365,709
1992	1,582,659
1993	1,616,879
1994	1,660,734
1995	1,690,407
1996	1,600,716
1997	1,613,629
1998	1,986,068
1999	2,249,319
2000	3,637,307
2001	4,457,579
2002	4,336,712
2003	4,393,893
2004	4,718,122

[1] Statistics drawn from the following sources: Chen, 1998: 158; State Statistics Bureau, 'Social Statistics of China' for 1956, 1965; Zhang, 2002: 56–7, figures for 1976–83, excluding 1982, at the same time noting that these statistics understate the crime rate because of the failure of police to put many cases on file; Wang, 2004: 35, for 1982; Qin, 2004: 78, for 1983–87, rounding the statistics to the nearest 1,000. Qin provides corresponding figures for 1983–2003. Zhang, 2002: 57, for 1988; Zhang, 2002: 57; Gongan Yanjiu, 1996 (2): 47, for 1995; Gongan Yanjiu, 1997 (2): 64, for 1996; Assorted Law Year Book of China figures for 1989–2003.

official statistics in China are unreliable. A range of extrinsic factors may lead to both under-reporting and over-reporting of cases at any particular time. Bakken makes a strong argument that crime statistics are strongly influenced by enforcement policies and the skewing effect of systems that reward police officers for their success in meeting their targeted clear-up rates during anti-crime campaigns.[33] The Chinese police themselves acknowledge problems with under-reporting and failure to record complaints.[34] They support their claims of the seriousness of the crime rate by pointing to police internal surveys[35] showing a serious and ongoing under-reporting by local police of complaints to local police stations, where they are not put on file and so never enter the national crime statistics.[36]

As we will see, especially with the periodic anti-crime campaigns, there is a strongly political dimension to the question of crime and the strategies for dealing with it that leads directly to perceptions of state capacity and legitimacy. The state and the police repeatedly link ensuring social stability with the success of economic reform and social development.[37]

There has been public support for strongly punitive measures to be taken against crime and socially disruptive conduct. There also is a broad community fear of chaos and a demand for the state to give priority to the maintenance of social stability and order.[38] Surveys and other police

[33] Bakken, 2004: 75–6.

[34] MPS, *Notice on Adopting Thoroughly Effective Measures to Resolve the Problem of Incorrect Statistics*, 3 March 2000, cites ongoing failure to report correct statistics and failure to put cases on file as so serious that it was affecting national policy formation by the Party, government and MPS.

[35] Yu, 1993: 110–11. The first survey was conducted by the MPS in 1985, 1987 and 1988 into the cases received by more than 300 police stations including investigation into 25,368 individual cases. The second survey was conducted between 1988 and 1990 by the General Office of the MPS. It is described as being more extensive but details of the investigation are not specified.

[36] Yu, 1993: 6–7, 112–14, reported that the rate at which cases were put on file varied depending on the nature of the criminal offence, with serious crimes such as murder, rape and manufacture and sale of narcotics being put on file in over 80 per cent of reported cases. Offences such as kidnapping and selling women and children, theft and pick-pocketing were put on file in less than 30 per cent of cases reported to the police. The crimes of robbery, assault and hooliganism (as the offence was called prior to the 1997 reforms to the *Criminal Law*) were put on file in between 50 and 80 per cent of reported cases. Yu, 1993: 115–18, citing a survey indicating that the rate of clearing up cases put on file varied dramatically in respect of different areas and different types of offence, finding that in urban districts the clear-up rate was 20–30 per cent, suburbs 40–50 per cent, market towns 30–40 per cent and villages 40–50 per cent. Wang, 1990: 577–80, reporting similar patterns in Zhejiang province.

[37] Gong'an Bu Gonggong Anquan Yanjiusuo, 1991: 39–40; Jie and Yang, 2000.

[38] Jie and Yang, 2000, discussing survey material which shows a strong preference for stability over liberty and a strong fear of chaos, in the form of social instability and rising crime rate.

research reveal that the public support the use of punitive measures to crack down on crime.[39] Sixty per cent of respondents to a 1988 survey considered that the measures used to address crime were overly lenient, with only 2 per cent considering that the measures used to date were overly harsh.[40] A 1996 international survey on attitudes to the punishment found that the Chinese attitudes to punishment favoured very strongly punitive measures to be taken against offenders.[41] Another survey, conducted in 1995, found that 99.2 per cent of respondents supported the use of the death penalty, though more recent information points to a decline in support for it.[42] Nevertheless, such an audience remains very receptive to policies that require the severe punishment of serious criminal offences.

3 THE CONTEMPORARY SOCIAL ORDER POLICY CONTEXT OF ADMINISTRATIVE DETENTION: THE COMPREHENSIVE MANAGEMENT OF PUBLIC ORDER ('CMPO')

3.1 Introduction

In an era when class struggle was no longer at the heart of crime and with crime and social disorder on the rise, it became necessary to reconceptualise social order and crime control strategies.[43] The Comprehensive Management of Public Order ('CMPO') was devised as the state's social order and crime control umbrella. The CMPO was proposed at

Jie and Yang explain this result as indicative of the traditional view that social harmony and order is one of the most important purposes of democracy. Tang, 2001: 899, reporting that in surveys of urban residents carried out in 1997 and 1999, 58 per cent responded that political stability was more important than democratisation; Jie *et al.*, 1997; Ge, 1998: 65–9, discussing public concern about the rising crime rate and the deteriorating social order situation. Dutton, 1998: 93–115, translating a wide range of Chinese material that explores aspects of daily life, including fears in relation to deteriorating social order, uncontrolled migration to the cities, policing techniques for social control and responses to them; see also Dutton and Lee, 1993: 316–7; Petracca and Mong, 1990: 1102; Nathan, 1985: 101.

39 A survey, entitled 'Do You Feel Safe?', conducted by the Public Security Research Institute in December 1988, of 15,000 people in fifteen provinces revealed a general public dissatisfaction with the level of social disorder and crime. Gong'an Bu Gonggong Anquan Yanjiusuo, 1991: 39–42; Wang, 1991: 108, referring to an unspecified survey indicating that 59 per cent of people surveyed considered political-legal organs to be too lenient on criminals and campaign-style law enforcement was not overly harsh.

40 Gong'an Bu Gonggong Anquan Yanjiusuo, 1991: 46.

41 Cited in Bakken, 2004: 81.

42 Bakken, 2004: 82–3, citing a survey conducted by the Law Institute of the Chinese Academy of Social Sciences. Bakken, unpublished presentation, 5 July 2007.

43 Liu, 1989: 3–4.

a national meeting on public order in cities held in November 1979,[44] formally adopted by the CCPCC on 14 June 1981, and endorsed and implemented by CCPCC directives in January and August 1982.[45] It was an attempt to 'totalise and unify social forces in the fight against crime'.[46] It remains in place today.

The CMPO, however, was not an entirely new approach to problems of crime and social order. Even though crime in the reform era could no longer be construed in terms of class, strategies for prevention and punishment of crime have continued to refer to Mao Zedong's views on comprehensive management and the distinction between antagonistic and non-antagonistic contradictions.[47]

A 1993 text on Mao Zedong's legal thought describes the tools of comprehensive management as follows:

> There are many measures for [implementing] comprehensive management, dictatorship measures, administrative measures, and there are also measures of education and reform by persuasion. But the use of dictatorship measures, severe punishment of serious criminal elements according to law is the one of most importance in comprehensive management . . .[48]

As I describe in more detail below, the CMPO seeks to incorporate all these elements. The conceptual framework provided by Mao's Theory of Contradictions has also played a role in interpreting and responding to problems of crime and disorder. Though it is possible to see echoes of the distinction between antagonistic and non-antagonistic contradictions in the CMPO, this distinction no longer has class struggle as its illuminating idea. Strategies for dealing with both minor transgressions and crime have taken on a more institutionalised and punitive form. Police responses to public order offences are determined by the extent to which they are 'confrontational', even when the problem itself is characterised as non-antagonistic.[49] Even though the form of the hard

[44] The CMPO was first set out in the CCPCC approving and issuing the Central Political-Legal Committee, *Summary of the Public Order Meeting of the Five Major Cities of Beijing, Tianjin, Shanghai, Guangzhou and Wuhan*, 14 June 1981 ('Five Major Cities Meeting'); Wang, Zhongfan, 1992; Xu, 1996: 75.

[45] CCPCC, *Directive on Strengthening Political-Legal Work*, 13 January 1982; Politics and Law Teaching and Research office, 1983: 10; Central Political-legal Committee, *Summary of the National Political-Legal Work Conference*, 12 August 1982.

[46] Dutton, 2000: 75.

[47] Xiao, 1996: 90.

[48] Wang, Yuming, 1993: 347.

[49] Ren, 2005: 259–63 (*duikangxing* 对抗性).

strike retains similarities to the political-ideological campaign, it has been stripped of its political-ideological significance.

4 SOCIAL ORDER AND THE CONSTRUCTION OF A SOCIALIST SPIRITUAL CIVILISATION

The CMPO sets out strategies for establishing social order by both preventing and punishing crime. At a broader level it seeks to establish a moral basis for both government and order. Reform and political liberalisation are limited, Harry Harding argues, by Leninist and 'deeply rooted Chinese values that give the state the right – even the obligation – to promote moral conduct by educating citizens in an official doctrine believed to be morally valid'.[50] The moral basis for social order and control reflected in the CMPO is 'to promote construction of a socialist spiritual civilisation'.[51]

Mao Zedong argued that the combination of material wellbeing (material civilisation) and spiritual civilisation, correct ideological thought, were central to crime prevention.[52] Construction of a 'socialist spiritual civilisation' (*shehui zhuyi jingshen wenming* 社会主义精神文明)[53] is a core element of the Party's current vision of modernisation: 'modernisation with Chinese characteristics'[54] which places construction of a socialist spiritual civilisation alongside the establishment of an advanced material civilisation. The dual purposes of socialist modernisation were formally adopted at the 12th National Congress of the CCP held in September 1982, at which the Party resolved to 'establish

[50] Harding, 1987: 173. [51] Shu, 1996a, from the Editor's Introduction.

[52] Wang, Yuming, 1993: 342–3.

[53] Baum, 1994: 86–8. The first public call in the reform era to emphasise the creation of a high-level socialist spiritual civilisation was made by Ye Jiangying in a speech to mark the thirtieth anniversary of the establishment of the PRC on 1 October 1979. Ye said that modernisation was not limited to reform and perfection of the socialist economic system, but that at the same time emphasis should be placed on creation and perfection of the socialist political system, socialist democracy, the socialist legal system and creation of a high level of socialist spiritual civilisation. Ye called for improvement of the educational, technological and cultural levels and standards of health of the people, establishment of a lofty revolutionary idealist and revolutionary moral practice and development of a rich and varied cultural life. This portion of the speech is reproduced in Fan, 1995: 679, and discussed in Baum, 1994: 87–8. Anagnost, 1997b: 80–4, discusses the various historical and foreign roots of the concept of spiritual civilisation. Harding, 1987: 176–7, describes the term as socialist public morality.

[54] (*Zhongguoshi de xiandaihua* 中国式的现代化), distinguishing it from that of 'western industrial capitalism': Wen, 2000: 8.

socialism with Chinese characteristics'.[55] This resolution placed material civilisation, comprising economic and technological development, at the core. Creation of a high-level socialist spiritual civilisation was the guarantee, or even the precondition for achieving economic reform.[56] Socialist spiritual civilisation involves creation of a moral or ethical socialist society,[57] with Communist ideology as its core.[58]

Chinese scholars assert that Party elites understood the collapse of the Soviet Union and Eastern bloc as 'largely due to a lack of a moral and ideological education in these societies'.[59] Party elites repeatedly assert that creating a moral order is necessary to avoid the chaos that may result from the process of economic modernisation.[60]

The prevention and punishment strategies in the CMPO are based on a view that disorder results from disintegration of the moral order and dislocation in the social environment[61] and the established patterns of social control.[62] Active state intervention and strengthened social control mechanisms are required to restore normality.[63] As an indication

[55] In his report to the 12th CCP National Congress, Hu Yaobang affirmed that building of the socialist legal system was a way of codifying and institutionalising socialist democracy. Socialist democracy in turn 'provides the guarantee and support for the building of socialist material and spiritual civilisation'. Two official histories of the CCP prepared for its eightieth anniversary cite this resolution as linking socialist democracy and construction of the legal system with the construction of material and spiritual civilisation: Gai, 2001: 261–2; Benshu Bianxie Zu, 2001: 165.

[56] Hu Yaobang, in his Report to the 12th CCP National Congress, asserted that material civilisation was the foundation for socialist spiritual civilisation. Hu described spiritual civilisation as being 'manifested in a higher educational, scientific and cultural level and in higher ideological, political and moral standards'. See also Bakken, 2000: 53–4. Baum, 1994: 143–4, argues that Deng reversed the original view of the temporal relationship between material and spiritual civilisation by placing spiritual civilisation before the creation of material civilisation. For a description of material civilisation in these terms see Li, Qiyan, 1993: 278.

[57] Liu, 1994: 4.

[58] Report of Hu Yaobang made at the 12th CCP National Congress, reproduced in BBC Summary of World Broadcasts, FE/7125/C/1, accessed 19 February 2003.

[59] Discussed by Hintzen, 1999: 181.

[60] Wang, Yuming, 1993: 343–4, citing speeches of Deng Xiaoping, Chen Yun and Peng Zhen. Bakken, 2000: 58, discussing the fear that economic reform may lead to chaos.

[61] One senior policeman has asserted that the social environment must be improved and the conditions necessary for crime removed by improving the basic living standards and ethical standards of the population. The latter, spiritual civilisation, includes improving the people's cultural level, knowledge of democracy and law and socialist morality: Yu, 1993: 29. The social and political factors considered to influence crime include economic, political, cultural, psychological and environmental factors, including unemployment, poverty, the rapid increase in the population, as well as ideological factors: Yu, 1993: 12, 220–4, 189–205.

[62] Bakken argues that traditional patterns of socialisation including the 'cultural preference for moderation, balance and harmony as a cult of self-restraint' have helped to keep the crime rate low in Chinese society and have led to a fear of 'floating' and chaos in both a physical and ethical sense. He argues that changes in society since economic reform have unsettled these established patterns of thought and social control: Bakken, 1993: 43.

[63] Yu, 1993: 10–11, 232–9.

of the force of this thinking, problems of crime have been characterised as abnormal periods or 'high tides' against which there must be concerted action if the situation is to be brought back to normal. The police have identified five 'high tides' of crime since establishment of the PRC: 1950,[64] 1962,[65] 1973,[66] 1978[67] and the fifth high tide which commenced in 1986.[68] Viewed as abnormal, it is thus warranted to deal with serious crime by taking 'stern legal steps against those who are beyond education or who prove incorrigible'.[69]

5 THE CMPO

The CMPO prescribes a combination of 'moral, material and coercive' measures[70] and the combination of formal and informal techniques of social control.[71] The policy seeks to strengthen strategies for crime prevention, as well as mandating the serious punishment of crime. The CMPO seeks to replicate historical preferences for identification and control of social deviance at the local level, with formal intervention occurring only when the matter becomes sufficiently serious.[72]

In a form reminiscent of the political-ideological campaigns of the Maoist era, the CMPO calls for the mobilisation of all forces of society; state, Party and the citizenry in a co-ordinated fashion under the leadership of the Party.[73] The stated purpose of the CMPO is:

[64] Yu, 1993: 10. This was a period of transition to communist rule where the targets were counter-revolutionaries, 'bandits' left over from the old system and opponents of establishment of the new order.

[65] Yu, 1993: 11, 40–1, referring to the three 'difficult' years, after famine had displaced large numbers of people and when 421,000 cases were put on file. Yu describes the crimes committed during this period in class terms. He said 'these were mainly problems amongst the people caused as a result of natural disaster and mistakenly left policies, but because of the policy of consolidation, many serious criminal activities were not correctly identified as antagonistic contradictions'.

[66] Yu, 1993: 11–12. This high tide arose as a result of the Cultural Revolution. At this time, 535,000 cases were put on file. Yu asserts that this figure dramatically understates the amount of crime because of the widespread chaos.

[67] Yu, 1993: 12. This period began in 1978, reaching its peak in 1981 and ending in 1984. At its peak in 1981, 890,000 cases were put on file. At the end of the high tide in 1984, 510,000 cases were put on file.

[68] Yu, 1993: 12. This period began in 1986 with 540,000 cases put on file, continuing to increase until 1991, when 2,360,000 cases were put on file. Yu, 1993: 45, points out that the crime rate before 1978 was generally between 200,000 and 400,000 cases.

[69] Deng Xiaoping, *The Present Situation and the Tasks Before Us*, January 1980: 233.

[70] Wong, 1997: 304. [71] Situ and Liu, 1996: 101–2.

[72] Turk, 1989. discusses these traditional preferences at 39–40.

[73] Point seven in the *Five Major Cities Meeting* requires strengthening of the political-legal organs and Party leadership. The police, procuratorate and courts form the core of state organs falling within the category of 'political-legal organs'. See also Dutton, 2000: 75.

> to use all types of measures; political, economic, administrative, educational, cultural and legal, to prevent and punish criminal activity, educate and reform criminals, restrict the conditions which give rise to crime, create stability and a good public order situation and protect the successful implementation of the economic reform policies.[74]

In 1986 the Central Political-Legal Committee meeting determined that in essence the CMPO was a 'systematic construction' for 'education, rescue and reform'. The success of the policy, it resolved, depended upon the concerted efforts of the whole Party and people over an extended period and not merely upon the actions of several state agencies.[75]

The CMPO determines to strengthen crime prevention work by a combination of measures that form the first and second lines of defence against crime. The first line of defence against crime[76] includes strengthening basic-level local community organisations and local police work such as maintaining the household register and registers of the focal population[77] and education, especially of juveniles.[78] The second line of defence[79] includes the use of coercive administrative measures, particularly administrative detention, targeting for reform, investigation and, where necessary, repatriation of juvenile delinquents, prostitutes, transients suspected of committing crime, vagrants and beggars.[80] The CMPO calls for the severe punishment of crime by increasing co-operation between the public security organs, the procuratorate and the courts to strike hard against crime.[81]

Harold Tanner argues that the CMPO is so broad as to be 'a compulsion to total control' of the whole population.[82] However, despite its pretensions to the contrary, evidence of the comparative ineffectiveness of local-level crime prevention strategies and of 'Hard Strikes' to prevent further increases in the crime rate suggest that the CMPO was introduced as a policy precisely at the time the state's capacity and mechanisms for comprehensive surveillance had weakened;[83] and that

74 Wang, Zhongfan, 1992: 4. 75 Wang, Yuming, 1993: 347.

76 Situ and Liu, 1996: 103, use the term 'first line of defence'.

77 *Five Major Cities Meeting*, point 5.

78 Involving a range of organisations including the family and community, schools and work units in areas including political and legal education: *Five Major Cities Meeting*, points 2 and 6.

79 Xu and Fang, 1997: 97. In respect of RETL, Fu, 1993: 67.

80 *Five Major Cities Meeting*, points 4 and 5.

81 *Five Major Cities Meeting*, point 3. Michael Dutton argues that the hard strike should be viewed as an adjunct to and not a component of the CMPO: Dutton, 2000: 63–4. Others include the hard strike within the scope of CMPO: Xu, 1996: 75–88.

82 Tanner, 1995: 298. 83 Dutton, 1995b: 314.

far from being comprehensive in the way it claims, policing policy is reactive rather than proactive,[84] with many of its strategies a reworking of earlier social order strategies in an attempt to deal with new problems.[85] Evidence suggests that after the mid-1980s efforts at mass mobilisation both for the purposes of prevention and the punishment of crime have been less than successful.

6 STRENGTHENING LEADERSHIP OVER THE CMPO

From the 1980s, there have been a number of problems with implementation of the CMPO. These include uneven enforcement and the continuing deterioration of public order in some areas.[86]

In an effort to strengthen leadership and co-ordination of all programmes and policies of the CMPO, on 19 February 1991 the CCPCC and the State Council jointly issued the *Decision on Strengthening the Comprehensive Management of Public Order*. This Decision established the CMPO Committee under the joint leadership of the State Council and the CCPCC[87] and called for the strengthening of the role of the political-legal organs of state, in particular that of the police in the implementation of the CMPO.[88]

The newly established Committee was given legal status and powers by the NPCSC, *Decision on Strengthening the Comprehensive Management of Public Order*. In the area of social order management and crime control, these decisions reflect continuing direct involvement of the Party in policy formation and implementation. The Party, and the Political-Legal Committee in particular, retain control over formulation and implementation of the CMPO. However, in practice, this structure has not resulted in strengthening of the leadership and work of CMPO at the local level.[89] As I discuss in more detail below, problems of uneven enforcement and poor public order remain.

7 POLICE SOCIAL ORDER POWERS

7.1 The first line of defence: regulation and education

The first line of defence encompasses a range of strategies encompassing community policing, education and registration of groups of people considered by the police to be at risk of committing offences.

[84] Wong, 2002: 309.
[85] Dutton, 1992c: 1–6; Dutton, 1995a: 427–8. [86] Chen, 1992: 24.
[87] Chen, 1992: 25. [88] Point 6 in Chen, 1992: 31. [89] Yin, 1996: 2.

(i) *The mass-line of policing and community organisations*

At the local level, the police were responsible not only for the management of a static population through the system of household registration, but also, in the pre-reform era, for mobilisation of the masses for purposes of waging political campaigns.[90] The ideological basis of local policing in particular,[91] as with all police work, is the mass-line.[92] The mass-line of policing requires the police to rely on the masses, and to wholeheartedly serve and work in close liaison with them.[93] It is a means by which the Party mobilises the people to participate in and support its programmes.[94]

An important part of local policing in urban areas involves police liaison and co-operation with the residents' committees, their people's mediation committees and public order defence committees which are also set up in work units and judicial assistants, whose responsibilities extend to dispute resolution and the maintenance of social order in the locality.

The operation of resident committees, household registration and police liaison with local organisations was disrupted during the Cultural Revolution. Since the late 1970s, a range of strategies have been implemented to revitalise this interlocking web of local institutions of social control. For a range of reasons, including the combined effects of the Cultural Revolution; decreasing reliance on state welfare;[95] increasing population mobility;[96] increasing economic hardship in some rural

90 Zhengci Falu Jiaoyanshi, 1983: 13. The use of such a range of measures is not unique to China, see Etzioni, 2000, discussing internalisation of social norms as a basis for social order.

91 Wang, Mingxin, 1993: 250–1; Kang, 1993: 86, describes co-ordination between local police and local community organisations in respect of public order, local security and community affairs as the backbone of mass-line work and the main connection between the masses and public security organs.

92 Mao Zedong's formulation of the mass-line 'from the masses, to the masses' is set out in the 1943 essay, *Some Questions Concerning Methods of Leadership*, at 119, where he argues that practical work of the Party should involve an ongoing process of gathering scattered and unsystematic ideas from the masses, turning them into concentrated and systematic ideas and propagating them to the masses.

93 Song *et al.*, 2000b: 24–30. 94 Lubman, 1999: 42. 95 Dutton, 1992c: 333.

96 Estimates of the transient population differ. Li, Cheng, 1998: 38; Wang, Gongfan, 1997: 276; Xie, 2000: 89, estimate the floating population in 1994 to be in excess of 80 million people. Wang and Lu, 1994: 135, estimate the floating population for 1994 was 60 million. Xie, 2000: 89, citing projections at a national conference on the floating population held in August 2000 estimated that the floating population will reach 130 million by 2005 and 160 million by 2010. Mallee, 1998: 126, defines the 'floating (or transient) population' as those who have moved without changing their household registration, in contrast with 'migration', which involves changing household registration.

areas;[97] and weakening of communities,[98] this objective has been difficult to achieve.[99]

Street and resident committees and village committees

Work on reinvigorating street committees and the resident committees under them began in the late 1970s. The 1982 *Constitution* affirmed the position of urban resident committees and rural village committees as 'mass organs of self management at the grassroots level'.[100] An important part of the work of residents' committees and village committees is to undertake responsibility for the maintenance of social order. In 1987, the State Council approved the main areas of responsibility of resident committees to be: strengthening the construction of socialist spiritual civilization; actively participating in the comprehensive management of public order; initiating service enterprises for the benefit of people's lives and livelihoods; and educating residents to perform their legal duties in collaboration with the local people's government.[101] The village compact is a mechanism through which rural village committees have committed to achieving these social order objectives.[102]

The status and financial independence of urban street and resident committees was strengthened with passage on 26 December 1989 of the NPCSC *Law on Organisation of Urban Resident Committees of the PRC*.[103] The status and financial position of the committees established under the resident committee, such as the mediation committee and the public order defence committees, have also been regularised and strengthened.[104]

[97] Hao, 1991: 82–3, points to a range of destabilising changes in rural areas including the gap between actual levels of consumption and new desires and expectations, deterioration of public order committees to the point where they exist only in name in some regions and the increasing disparity between the wealthy and the poor.

[98] Yu, 1993: 233–40, 342. [99] Fu, 1993: 118; Bakken, 1993: 31.

[100] Article 111. [101] Pan, 2004: 40.

[102] Anagnost, 1997a: 349–52, discussing efforts of the state to co-opt villagers voluntarily to undertake responsibility for socialist spiritual civilisation and maintenance of social order through the use of village compacts.

[103] This law applies to resident committees of villages, nationality villages and towns at art. 21. The local government is responsible for supervision of the work of the resident committee and for its budget appropriations: *Law on Organisation of Urban Resident Committees of the PRC*, arts. 17 and 18.

[104] State Council, *Organisational Regulations of People's Mediation Committees*, 17 June 1989; Kang, 1993: 86.

As economic reform progresses, pervasive changes in China's demographic, economic and employment arrangements have fundamentally challenged the efficacy of resident committees. For example, accelerating rates of urbanisation have seen more than 100 million rural residents become city and town residents in the ten-year period to the end of 2001. In 1996 there were on average 115 temporary residents under the jurisdiction of residents' committees throughout the country, with over 1,000 in some.[105]

In 1986 the Ministry of Civil Affairs introduced the term 'community' (*shequ* 社区) into its conception of urban management.[106] This concept was later taken up under the rubric of 'community construction' (*shequ jianshe* 社区建设) as municipal governments and, from 1996, the central authorities, stressed the need to improve the work of resident committees.[107] A survey conducted in Beijing in 2001 indicates that there is work remaining to be done. Only 7.7 per cent of respondents had a clear idea of the work of the resident committee, 72.7 per cent knew a little and 19.6 per cent knew nothing at all about them; 2.7 per cent indicated that they had often been consulted by the resident committee about its work, 19.6 per cent had been consulted and 77.7 per cent had never been consulted; 91.5 per cent had never been a representative on the resident committee.[108] These results indicate that there is a low level of engagement between the resident committee and its residents, despite engagement being necessary if the resident committee is to function as a community organisation.

Judicial assistants and local mediation

In the Maoist era from 1949 to 1967, local mediation was used as a means of education, ideological indoctrination and strengthening Party control.[109] Mediation today is called in aid of grassroots strategies to promote social stability. Successful mediation of disputes is seen as a way of preventing an escalation of violence that might result from a minor dispute remaining unresolved. The mediation and legal advice work of judicial assistants and legal service offices established under the Ministry of Justice comprises an important component of these strategies.

[105] Pan, 2004: 47–8. [106] Pan, 2004: 3.

[107] Pan, 2004: 52–3, citing a national meeting in 1992, but attributing the real impetus to rebuild resident committees to a call made by Jiang Zemin at the 4th meeting of the 8th NPC in March 1996.

[108] Wei, 2003: 159–62. [109] Lubman, 1967: 1339–49; Lubman, 1999: 43–4, 59–63.

In rural areas, the CCPCC approved establishment of the system of judicial assistants and judicial offices under the county-level justice department at village and township level from 1978.[110] In 1982 urban street committees were also directed to create the post of judicial assistant.[111] By 1996 there were 16,000 such offices established.[112] Their functions are to assist the local-level government in lawful administration, to manage people's mediation work, to manage local-level legal assistance work, to represent the local people's government or street committee in handling mediation work, to organise legal education programmes, and settlement programmes and 'help and education' (*bangjiao* 帮教) for people released from prison or RETL and to participate in the work of comprehensive management of public order.[113]

The establishment of local legal service offices began at the end of 1980 in some areas such as Guangdong, Fujian and Liaoning. The Ministry of Justice encouraged their establishment nationwide after 1984. They were intended to provide free basic-level legal advice and to investigate and help resolve simple civil and economic disputes. By 2000 there were 35,000 nationwide. However, at the end of the 1990s it became clear that there were a number of serious problems with the ways in which these offices operated, including operating jointly with the local justice organ, providing poor service and advice and having unauthorised people operating legal service offices and charging fees for service.[114]

Fu Hualing's research on dispute resolution in Anxiang County, Hunan Province, concludes that it is difficult for rural people to obtain resolution of a dispute, often with the local government over the collection of taxes and fees, that is satisfactory to them. He points out that local mediation is aimed to achieve the government's objective of stability and ensuring the dispute is 'quarantined' at the local level and is not allowed to escalate to a higher level of government.[115] The police in rural areas are not necessarily interested in becoming involved in mediating disputes because such disputes are not a source of revenue for them.[116] As local police work becomes increasingly focussed on technical and professional aspects of policing, some view traditional

[110] In 1978 the CCPCC issued and approved the Summary of Minutes of the Eighth National People's Judicial Work Meeting in 1978, in Cheng, 2004: 150.

[111] CCPCC, *Directive on Strengthening Political-legal Work*, January 1980.

[112] Cheng, 2004: 151–2.

[113] Ministry of Justice, *Opinion on Strengthening the Construction of Judicial Offices*, June 1996, in Cheng, 2004: 152–2.

[114] Cheng, 2004: 157–63. [115] Fu, 2003: 122. [116] Fu, 2003: 120–1.

mass-line community work, including mediation of minor civil disputes, as increasingly irrelevant.[117] At the same time, the police complain that local mediation has been ineffective in resolving disputes and preventing their escalation, thus failing to prevent a substantial amount of violent crime.[118]

The mass-line of policing

Measures have been adopted to revitalise and strengthen police leadership over community organisations[119] and to strengthen the mass-line of policing,[120] particularly since 1984.[121] These measures include increasing the number of local police and rural police stations[122] and introducing new forms of registration based on the individual rather than the household.[123] The police have introduced more technical and professional crime prevention measures, including establishing a system of urban patrol police;[124] establishing a 110 emergency telephone number;[125] commercialising local security work with the introduction of a system of security contracts;[126] focussing on installation of security devices and surveillance equipment onto premises;[127] and improving police training and equipment.[128] In addition to public

[117] Yin and Li, 1997: 16; but see Xiao, 2000: 350–1, criticising this attitude.

[118] The police assert that in some areas 80 per cent of intentional homicide results from failure to resolve these types of disputes: Yu, 1993: 439; Wang, Zhongfan, 1992: 325.

[119] Dutton, 1992b; Dutton, 1992c; Dutton and Lee, 1993; Dutton, 1995a: 327–30; Ma, 1997: 132–3; Situ and Liu, 1996: 102–3.

[120] Xiao, 2000: 118–19.

[121] This timing has been associated with the beginning of the second campaign (January 1984) in the '1983 Hard Strike' discussed below, when the MPS directed lower-level police to make special efforts to strengthen local-level crime prevention work: Xi and Yu, 1996: 384.

[122] Dutton, 2000: 75; Chao and Dong, 1997: 51, asserting that in Dalian in the ten years to 1997, police numbers in police stations increased from 1,134 to 3,758.

[123] NPCSC, *PRC Resident Identity Card Regulations*, 6 September 1985, introduced a nationwide resident identity card system for all citizens over sixteen years old, which were superseded on 1 January 2004 by the *PRC Resident Identity Card Law*. The MPS, *Temporary Regulations on the Management of Temporary Residents in Cities and Towns*, 13 July 1985, provided for temporary registration measures.

[124] Wang and Li, 1996: 59–61. Initially, different models of patrol police were tried in Tianjin and Shanghai. In June 1993, the MPS adopted the Tianjin model to standardise and introduce a nationwide patrol system with a dedicated patrol police force. See also Fu, 1990; Ma, 1997: 132.

[125] Wang and Li, 1996: 62–3.

[126] Wang, Zhongfan, 1992: 399–400; Dutton, 2000: 76–7; Xiao, 2000: 79. An increasing number of security companies are being established under the MPS: Gong'an Bu, 1995, indicates that in 1995 there were 1,400 security companies nationwide, with 240,000 employees: at 12–13.

[127] Luo, Jueqiang, 1997: 75–6, in Shen Zhen; Chao and Dong, 1997: 51, in Shanghai.

[128] MPS, Ministry of Personnel, *Notice issuing the 'Temporary Measures on Testing the Basic Quality of the Public Security Organ Police'*, 8 May 1997, requires all police officers of specified rank and

forms of policing, public order work also includes the use of police informants, 'public order ears and eyes' (*zhi'an ermu* 治安耳目). Local police are instructed to maintain a stable of informants, preferably prior offenders who might be expected to have contacts with those currently engaged in unlawful conduct and who are willing to co-operate with the police.[129]

The police have claimed some successes, though there is much evidence that the community-based aspects of policing work continues to be both under-resourced[130] and neglected at the expense of 'Hard Strikes' against crime.[131] Police complain that despite reforms, street and residents' committees remain weak, are focussed on revenue-raising work, and that they no longer focus on, nor do they assist police in, their crime control work.[132] Fu concludes that the increased financial independence of street and residents' committees has led them to operate more in competition with the police than under their direction.[133] Public order defence teams established in work units have lost status and effectiveness as, since the introduction of economic reform policies, work units have increasingly assigned old, weak or ill-disciplined workers to work in them.[134]

These reforms illustrate that despite the stated aim of CMPO to mobilise the forces of society, the integrated localised mechanisms in place for monitoring and control of the local population have decayed and the efforts for sustained popular mobilisation on ideological grounds have lost efficacy.[135] Local committees are now legally defined and

below to undertake training and pass a test before being permitted to carry out public security work.

129 Zhi'an Guanli Bianxie Zu, 1992: 387–93.

130 Yu, 1993: 239, discussing the continuing, unresolved problem of serious understaffing at the local level of the police station, where the work load is greatest; Luo, Jueqiang, 1997: 75–6, in relation to improving funding of this work.

131 Yu, 1993: 239; Wu, 1994: 543; Su, 1994: 23; Luo, Jueqiang, 1997: 73–4, asserting the need for the hard strike (*yanda* 严打) against crime to be matched by an equivalent emphasis on crime prevention (*yanfang* 严防). Xiao, 2000: 348–9, asserting that many citizens now believe that the 'Hard Strike' is the primary method of crime control and that local-level prevention work is no longer required.

132 Wang, Gongfan, 1997: 277–9; Lu, 1998: 186–8, in a 1997 survey of local residents in Shanghai: 23.1 per cent saw themselves as activists, and only 41 per cent were willing to participate in local crime prevention programmes. At 189, finding that people living in apartment blocks were less willing to participate in crime prevention programmes than those living in low-rise areas.

133 Fu, 1993: 139–40. 134 Xiao, 2000: 350.

135 Dutton, 2000: 61; Xiao, 2000: 350–1, citing lack of interest in participating in local crime prevention work. Xinhua News Agency, 8 November 1998, reporting Cao Zhi, Vice Chairman

financially rewarded. For example, the powers and status of mediation committees are now defined by law and have as a stated objective the protection of citizens' rights.[136] Instead of ideological motivation, financial reward is an important factor in gaining support for local social control and crime prevention strategies.[137]

(ii) Registration of designated groups and locations

As discussed in chapter 3, since the founding of the PRC, the police have had systems for the identification, registration and targeting of certain groups considered politically suspect or likely to harm social order. Since the introduction of the economic reform policies, reliance on targeting certain industries, locations and groups of individuals for attention has increased.[138] Monitoring this focal population has been identified as one of the important functions of the local police and a key element in the comprehensive management of public order, an adjunct to periodic hard strikes against serious crime and other crime prevention and punishment strategies.[139] Dutton and Lee have argued with good cause that the increasing emphasis on the targeting of specially designated groups, rather than being indicative of a strengthening of effective monitoring of the general population, instead reflects the growing inability of the police and local organisations to carry out more comprehensive policing.[140]

The MPS re-issued provisional regulations defining the 'focal population' (*zhongdian renkou* 重点人口) at the end of 1980.[141] In 1985 the MPS issued regulations codifying this long-standing practice of keeping special files on certain categories of people.[142] These regulations provided that designated categories of people be subject to extensive surveillance, both overt and covert, to investigation, or to social help and education.[143] The police are required to update the material held in

of the NPCSC, reporting that after a national inspection into law enforcement and public order carried out in July 1998 by the NPCSC, there is continuing weakness or non-existence of neighbourhood committees in some areas.

136 See discussion in Liu and Li, 1999: 257–9, 287.

137 Dutton, 2000: 64, 80–7; Fu, Hualing, 2002: 187, on local mediation.

138 Dutton and Lee, 1993: 326–30; Yu, 1992: 257–60; Mou, 1992: 86–7.

139 Tian, 1999: 27; Wang, Mingxin, 1993: 251; Zhi'an Guanli Bianxie Zu, 1992: 56–7; also discussed in Dutton, 1995a: 435; Dutton and Xu, 1998: 306.

140 Dutton and Lee, 1993.

141 Wang, 2005: 105.

142 *Regulations on Management Work of the Focal Population*, March 1985, in Zhi'an Guanli Bianxie Zu, 1992: 56–7 and Dutton, 1995a: 435; including released prisoners, people released from RETL and people released from detention: Dutton and Xu, 1998: 306.

143 Zhi'an Guanli Bianxie Zu, 1992: 58–9.

respect of such people each month.[144] These regulations were amended and reissued in 1991 and again in 1998.[145] Whilst there is some information available on the existence and functioning of these registers, that information is restricted because the regulations themselves provide that the registration system is internal to the police and so not to be made public.[146]

The targeted groups are very broadly defined and include those suspected of activities harming state security and common criminal activities; those released from correctional institutions, including prisons and RETL camps; those whose activities may endanger public order, including gambling and causing a disturbance, people engaged in civil disputes that may escalate and transients without work or a fixed home.[147] Other groups who are specially identified by the police for monitoring include habitual drug users[148] and prostitutes.[149] Wang sets out a list which divides these people into five groups, with the degree to which they are monitored and controlled set out in descending order: those who threaten national security; those suspected of criminal offences including manufacture, transportation and sale of narcotics, pimps and those organising prostitution; those inclined to violent conduct or making trouble; criminals convicted of intentional crimes who have been released for less than five years; and drug users.[150] To be included on the register requires examination and approval by the chief of the local police, with the file then to be sent for report up to the county-level public security bureau.[151]

A number of police internal investigations have revealed serious shortcomings in the maintenance and efficacy of the register. These include: problems with higher-level police departments having set a quota requiring a certain proportion of the local population be included on the register and local police responding by placing people on the register and leaving them there when they should be removed; placing people on the register without the requisite approvals; not entering people on the register because of poor co-ordination between the police

144 Tian, 1999: 27. 145 Wang, 2005: 105–6.

146 Zhi'an Guanli Bianxie Zu, 1992: 60. 147 Zhi'an Guanli Bianxie Zu, 1992: 56–7.

148 CCPCC, State Council, *Urgent Directive on the Problems of Complete Prohibition of Opium*, 16 July 1982, required registration of drug users with the local government. Liu and Yuan, 1997: 40.

149 MPS, *Notice on Resolutely Prohibiting Prostitution Activities*, 10 June 1981, art. 1, requiring the focal population registers and registers on the control of targeted areas be used to identify prostitutes.

150 Wang, 2005: 108. 151 Tian, 1999: 27.

stations maintaining the register and the departments investigating and prosecuting crime, courts and penal institutions; failing to manage and control people on the register and lack of co-operation with police in other areas when inquiries about certain people are made. According to one account, of the 596,000 drug addicts registered with the police in 1998, police estimate there were between seven and eight times that number of drug users who remained unregistered.[152]

Problems arising from an increasingly mobile population and a weakening of the relationship between police and their local communities and community organisations have also been identified as prejudicial to the completeness and usefulness of the register as a social order and crime-fighting tool.[153]

(iii) Education, rescue and reform

Another strategy employed for crime prevention and preservation of social order focusses on political, moral and legal education of citizens;[154] co-opting compliance with positive norms; and improving civility (*wenming* 文明).[155] These strategies include campaigns to emulate and reward exemplary models of civility in areas such as family, school and work.[156]

The CCPCC reaffirmed continuing reliance on education and emulation as measures to create a socialist spiritual civilisation[157] after the resolution adopted at the 6th Plenum of the 14th CCPCC in October 1996.[158] This document officially recognised that social order policies to date had been unable to achieve the objectives of an orderly, civilised

152 Xiao, 2000: 174.

153 Luo and Gao, 1997, discussing Shiyan City, Hubei Province; Tian, 1999, discussing Shunyi County, Beijing.

154 Wang, Zhongfan, 1992: 363–4; *Five Major Cities Meeting*, points 2 and 6; Kang, 1993: 86, reporting that the five-year legal popularisation campaign conducted between 1986 and 1990 reached over 650 million people.

155 Anagnost examines the state's creation of a model of civility (*wenming*) whose aim is the production of a disciplined labour force suitable to the needs of foreign capital and economic reform: Anagnost, 1997b: 77–80.

156 Bakken, 2000: 175–9; Ma, 1990: 229–31, adding contractors to the list of agencies carrying out *bangjiao*.

157 Lynch, 1999: 198–9, including the identification, reward and emulation of model citizens, families and townships and encouraging 'spiritually uplifting cultural events'.

158 CCPCC, *Decision on Important Questions on Promoting Socialist Ethical and Cultural Progress* (in English), reported by the Xinhua news agency on 10 October 1996 and reproduced in BBC Summary of World Broadcasts, FE/D2740/G. Reproduced in Law Yearbook Editorial Committee, 1997: 1–9, where the title is rendered in English as *Resolution of the CPC Central Committee on Important Issues Relating to Strengthening Construction of Socialist Culture and Ethics*. See also Peerenboom, 2002a: 171; Li, 2001: 42–3.

society and documented failure to effect significant improvements in problems of public order, crime, vice and official corruption.[159]

The emphasis upon education reflects a belief that juveniles can be educated to change antisocial attitudes.[160] Early prevention is viewed as the way in which bad influences can be prevented from 'leading to the path of crime'.[161] Bakken describes as 'chain narratives' the perception that the first act that deviates from acceptable attitudes and conduct, such as small infractions of discipline or a failure to learn self-control,[162] if uncorrected, will lead to more seriously deviant acts.[163] Problems of juvenile crime have been attributed to inadequate or improper socialisation, be it in families, schools, peer groups or the community.[164]

This thinking underpins the mechanism of social help and education which is carried out by the family, school, work unit or street committee.[165] Social help and education is primarily a strategy for rehabilitation of juvenile offenders, reforming criminals and for preventing recidivism.[166] Police commentators assert that its purpose is also preventative, to identify and change unacceptable behaviour and attitudes and to prevent their deterioration into criminal behaviours.[167] It appears that the primary use of *bangjiao* is rehabilitation rather than prevention, as its targets are identified as people who have already been sanctioned, including people currently in or recently released from prison, RETL, work-study schools for juveniles[168] or coercive drug rehabilitation.[169]

159 *Decision on Important Questions on Promoting Socialist Ethical and Cultural Progress* recites the continuing seriousness of these problems.

160 Liu, Zhaoqi, 1991: 103, describing persuasion, coercion, encouragement and setting examples as the methods to deal with and rehabilitate juvenile offenders.

161 Yu, 1993: 438.

162 Bakken, 2000: 320–3, giving examples of bad habits such as laziness and selfish behaviour, liking to eat too much, hating work, running away, staying out late, failing to sit in the appropriate way in class, fidgeting and being rude.

163 Bakken, 2000: 317–25.

164 Curran and Cook, 1993: 303–9; Bakken, 1993: 47–8. Other explanations of juvenile crime are economic modernisation and the resultant worshipping of money, consumerism, decadent culture from abroad (i.e. spiritual pollution), the 'conflict in the young man's physiology and psychology' and the mistakes in school education which have allowed many students to drop out: Zhao, 1991: 72. Similar explanations are given by Liu, Zhaoqi, 1991: 102–3. A major cause of juvenile crime is attributed to the poor treatment of students who did not do well in school and large numbers of students who dropped out of school in the 1980s: Zhang, 1991: 95; Bakken, 1993: 44–5.

165 Lu, 1998: 149–57, discussing its operation in a Shanghainese community.

166 Wang, Zhongfan, 1992: 247–87, 308–22; Dutton, 1992c: 249–330; Tanner, Harold, 1999: 141–8 and at 148–53, discussing resistance to such reform.

167 Yu, 1993: 438; Bakken, 2000: 318–25.

168 Lu, 1998: 150.

169 Jiang, 2002: 31–2.

Although the programmes of prevention and education appear to be comprehensive, minor offenders, prostitutes and drug addicts are no longer being identified and dealt with at the local level in a way they previously may have been.[170] Police commentators suggest in some areas social help and rescue 'exists in name only and is becoming a mere formality'.[171]

Where prevention strategies, including education and emulation, fail, as Lynch suggests is happening,[172] social control is exercised through the use of more coercive powers.[173] Youths who 'go about in gangs, who beat and abuse people, whose families are scattered or do not have the capacity to educate or control them, who frequent public entertainment places', are seen as a 'reserve force for crime'.[174] Forms of group social protest, including people who repeatedly petition and protest against local government actions, engage in sit-ins or demonstrate and clash with the police, are seen as seriously harming social order. Against these groups, especially those who have been 'educated repeatedly and won't reform', the view is that more severe measures are appropriate.[175]

7.2 Police administrative powers: the second line of defence

With the weakening of prevention strategies encompassed by the first line of defence, the police are resorting to more formal administrative measures to prevent bad conduct further deteriorating into crime.[176] These measures are the 'second line of defence' in the strategy of crime prevention.[177] Police administrative powers that constitute the second line of defence against crime are, in theory, measures for resolving non-antagonistic contradictions amongst the people, emphasising 'education, rescue and reform'.[178] They are distinguished conceptually from the criminal law, which has been characterised as the punitive power of the state used to handle antagonistic contradictions.[179] In practice, administrative detention has been used extensively during 'Hard Strikes' against crime. As a consequence, these measures

[170] Liu *et al.*, 1997: 33, in respect of prostitution; Zhang, Shencai, 2002: 26, complaining that local government treats detention of drug offenders as more important than *bangjiao*.
[171] Mou, 1996: 129; Xiao, 2000: 351, citing the weakness of this work; Li and Cui, 1990: 437.
[172] Lynch, 1999: 201. [173] Bakken, 2000: 53–9. [174] Yu, 1993: 438.
[175] Zhu, 1991: 3. [176] Yu, 1993: 438. [177] Xu and Fang, 1997: 97; Fu, 1993: 67.
[178] Jiang and Yuan, 1990: 46; Yu, 1993: 439; Zhu, 1991: 2–4.
[179] Deng, 1984b: 238.

have become more closely associated with the punitive power of the state.[180]

(i) Strengthening of measures against socially dangerous conduct

Minor offences committed by juvenile delinquents, prostitutes, drug addicts, transients, vagrants and beggars are not seen as criminal, though their behaviour is considered morally and socially dangerous as it undermines social order and prejudices the creation of a Socialist Spiritual Civilisation.[181]

In his Report to the 12th National Congress of the NPC in 1982, Hu Yaobang called for 'resolutely eliminating all the vile social evils which had been stamped out long ago by new China but have now cropped up again'.[182] The extent to which they are viewed as socially dangerous has resulted in their inclusion in the list of problems that constituted the fourth high tide of crime.[183] This problem:

> is the re-emergence of the social evils that were eradicated in the early years of the establishment of the PRC, the manufacture, sale and use of drugs, kidnapping and selling people, prostitution etc. these evil social phenomena, not only have they rekindled but have already developed to a particularly serious stage. These evil phenomena are a hotbed to propagate crime and induce a large volume of crime like a bacteria that will infect society, poison the people and if they are not eliminated early will necessarily become a great disaster.[184]

(ii) Police powers in the second line of defence

There are several administrative powers exercised by the police as part of the second line of defence. The main powers include sanctions imposed under the *Security Administrative Punishments Law* ('SAPL'); detention for education of prostitutes; coercive drug rehabilitation; detention for training of juvenile delinquents in work study schools; and RETL. Prior to abolition of detention for investigation in 1996 and detention for repatriation in 2003, these powers were used against vagrants and the floating population.

180 Dutton and Lee, 1993: 324. 181 Yu, 1993: 438.
182 Report of Hu Yaobang made at the 12th CCP National Congress, reproduced in BBC Summary of World Broadcasts, FE/7125/C/1, accessed 19 February 2003.
183 Discussed at note 67 above. 184 Yu, 1993: 9.

The primary power to punish minor social order infringements is exercised under the 2006 *SAPL*.[185] The law provides for administrative punishments for people who disturb public order, infringe upon the personal rights of citizens or damage public or private property, but whose offences are not sufficiently serious to warrant criminal prosecution.[186] Punishments which may be given for breach of the *SAPL* are: warnings; fines; administrative detention; and revocation of a permit issued by the public security organs.[187] The *SAPL* provides for more serious punishment of those involved in prostitution and prostitution-related activities which, at the most severe, involve giving a mixture of fines and detention.[188]

RETL also falls into this intermediate category of administrative sanctions. RETL has been characterised as a sanction to be used when imposition of an ordinary administrative sanction under the *SAPL* is 'too lenient' and when imposition of a criminal sanction is 'too harsh'.[189]

Lying between punishment under the *SAPL* and RETL in degree of severity are a group of powers including detention for education of prostitutes, coercive rehabilitation of drug addicts and detention for education of juveniles.[190] These powers are discussed in more detail in the following chapters.

The legal border between unlawful conduct that is to be dealt with administratively and a criminal offence is whether the socially harmful act is 'sufficiently serious' to constitute a crime.[191] The borderline between criminal and non-criminal breaches is regulated to a great extent through specification of standards for putting a criminal case on file (*li'an biaozhun* 立案标准). For example, a dividing line was drawn in

[185] Legislation was first passed in 1957, replaced by a new *SAPR* on 5 September 1986, which was amended on 12 May 1994. That amendment increased the scope of the legislation but not the severity of the punishments. These regulations were replaced by the *SAPL* on 1 March 2006.

[186] *SAPL*, art. 2. Generally, He, 1991: 87–96.

[187] *SAPL*, art. 10.

[188] *SAPL*, art. 66 enables police to impose between ten and fifteen days' detention and impose a fine of less than RMB 5,000 on prostitutes and clients of prostitutes. Where the situation is minor the police may impose less than five days' detention and a fine of up to RMB 500. People who seek to solicit clients in public places may be subject to less than five days' administrative detention and a fine of up to RMB 500. Periods of administrative detention may be imposed on people who work as prostitutes, run brothels, introduce prostitutes or act as pimps: art. 67–9.

[189] Xu and Fang, 1997: 96.

[190] The time limit for detention under these powers is less than RETL and greater than under the *SAPL*.

[191] The amended *Criminal Law*, art. 13 provides that acts, whilst otherwise subject to criminal punishment according to the law, will not be deemed a crime 'if they are clearly minor and the harm is not great'. (English version from www.qis.net.) This provision is replicated in the *Temporary Measures*, art. 10 and the *SAPL*, art. 2.

1992 by the MPS between acts of theft that constitute a criminal offence and those which warrant RETL in the *Notice on Revision of the Statistical Methods for Filing a Case Relating to Theft.*[192] RETL is imposed where a person does not commit a criminal offence, but constantly commits misdemeanours.[193]

8 PUNISHMENT OF CRIME: THE HARD STRIKE

Administrative detention has become an important and flexible adjunct to the enforcement of the criminal law, both to increase the capacity of state agencies to detain those targeted during times of concerted action and to deal with those whose conduct falls within the expansive scope of targets, though which is not itself criminal behaviour.

The concerted and severe punishment of crime has dominated the social order strategy in the reform era. From the early 1980s senior political leaders including Deng Xiaoping and Peng Zhen drew on pre-reform models of political campaigns in devising strategies for punishment of crime.[194] They identified law as a weapon that enabled severe punishment and linked the use of law with the exercise of dictatorship over the new class of enemy, conflating law and policy. In his speech, *The Present Situation and the Tasks Before Us*, on 16 January 1980, Deng Xiaoping asserted that:

> [we] must continue to strike resolutely at various kinds of criminals, so as to ensure and consolidate a sound, secure public order. We must learn to wield the weapon of law effectively. Being soft on criminals only endangers the interests of the vast majority of the people and the overall interests of our modernisation drive.[195]

However, since the first campaign of the '1983 Hard Strike', a distinction between law and policy has emerged and doubts are being expressed about the continuing reliance on the 'Hard Strike'. The 'Hard Strike' is being remade.

192 Passed on 17 March 2000. 193 Xu and Fang, 1997: 95, in respect of RETL.

194 Xiao, 1996: 177, distinguishes the 'Hard Strike' from political campaigns by pointing to a significant difference in the terminology used to describe the campaign '*yundong*' which was not used in respect of the 'Hard Strike' in the reform era, which uses an abbreviation of the title given to the 1983 first 'Hard Strike' and refers to the mode of enforcement: '*yanda*'.

195 Deng, 'The Present Situation and the Tasks Before Us', at 238.

8.1 The Hard Strike as a method for dealing with antagonistic contradictions

In February 1980 Peng Zhen instructed police, procuratorate and court officials to 'strike fiercely' against serious crime; to punish severely, rather than lightly within the scope of the law; and to punish swiftly rather than slowly. He said: 'Of course, severely and quickly must be accurate and must be according to the law.'[196] Peng elaborated that punishing severely in accordance with the law required a consideration of both the circumstances of the offence and the current social environment. Where the social order environment was bad, severe punishment should be given.[197] He continued: 'The police, procuratorate and courts are dictatorship organs and must make the people happy and evil people afraid.'[198]

The formula to punish severely and swiftly in accordance with the law (*yifa congzhong congkuai* 依法从重从快) was adopted and reiterated in the *Summary of the Public Order Meeting of the Five Major Cities of Beijing, Tianjin, Shanghai, Guangzhou and Wuhan* ('Five Major Cities Meeting') and provided that several strikes against serious crime would be carried out in a planned and ordered fashion. It required the public security organs to improve the number of successful investigations (*po'an lü* 破案率). It also provided that 'the procuratorate must actively commence prosecutions according to the law and the courts must punish active criminal elements severely and quickly according to the law'.[199]

The description of the police, procuratorate and courts as 'dictatorship organs' harks back to the pre-reform period when their task was violently to suppress class enemies. However, in the reform era the enemy as a class had been eliminated, so the targets of suppression required redefinition. Deng Xiaoping formulated a limited sphere within which dictatorship would be exercised by analogy to class struggles of an earlier period. He said:

> But we must recognise that in our socialist society there are still counter-revolutionaries, enemy agents, criminals and other bad elements of all kinds who undermine socialist public order, as well as the new exploiters who engage in corruption, embezzlement, speculation and profiteering... The struggle against these individuals is different from the struggle of one class against the other, which occurred in the past (these individuals

[196] Peng Zhen, *Key Points of the Speech at the Report Back Meeting of the Police, Procuratorate and Court of Guangdong Province and Guangzhou City*, 1 February 1980: at 212.
[197] Peng, 1992b: 212–13. [198] Peng, 1992b: 214. [199] *Five Major Cities Meeting*, point 3.

> cannot form a cohesive and overt class). However, it is still a special form of the leftover, under socialist conditions, of the class struggles of past history. It is still necessary to exercise dictatorship over these anti-socialist elements and socialist democracy is impossible without it.[200]

The groups subjected to the state's dictatorship powers were no longer identified on the basis of political background,[201] but as those whose acts, whilst not directly seeking to undermine the political system, were fundamentally at odds with the interests of the people:

> However, there are a number of people whose acts seriously harm social order and who commit serious crime . . . Whilst their intention is not to overturn the peoples' democratic dictatorship and the socialist system, subjectively the intent of these serious criminal offenders in committing crime is extremely pernicious and objectively the ruthless and despicable methods they use cause extremely serious social harm. Their interests are at odds with the basic interests of the people. They are as incompatible with socialist construction as fire and water and so should become a target of dictatorship . . .[202]

8.2 Background to the 1983 Hard Strike

After acceptance that the bulk of crime in the period of economic reform was primarily non-antagonistic, the emphasis in law enforcement initially was upon leniency and application of the law to the circumstances of the each case.[203] In 1982 the CCPCC indicated that there should be a balance between 'punishment and leniency' and that there was only an 'extremely small number' of serious criminal elements against whom the state should exercise dictatorship and punish 'severely and quickly'.[204]

Whilst a decision had been made at the 3rd Plenary Session of the 11th CCPCC in 1978 to conduct a 'Hard Strike' against economic crime and complementary amendments were made to the law,[205]

[200] Deng, 1993: 176–7.

[201] Xiao, 1996: 100, pointing out that the principle of equality before the law does not permit enforcement agencies to take background or political status into account when handling a matter.

[202] Xiao, 1996: 111. [203] Tanner, Harold, 1999: 84.

[204] CCPCC, *Directive on Strengthening Political-Legal Work*, 13 January 1982; Wang, Zhongfan, 1992: 8–9.

[205] The NPCSC in 1981 and 1982 amended the *Criminal Law* and *CPL* by increasing the severity of punishments in respect of certain offences in the *Decision Regarding the Severe Punishment of Criminals who Seriously Undermine the Economy*, 8 March 1982 (in English) by truncating time limits for handling cases and for appeals in the *Decision Regarding the Question of the Time Limits*

differences in opinion about the proper balance of enforcement policy resulted in limited implementation of the 'Hard Strike'.[206]

This balance changed. In August 1982, the Central Political-Legal Committee emphasised the centrality of the 'Hard Strike' to the CMPO, saying that that severely cracking down on serious crime was the 'key link' of the policy.[207] It is possible to identify a range of political and narrower enforcement imperatives as motivating the decision to launch the 1983 Campaign to Severely Crack Down on Serious Criminal Activity (the '1983 Hard Strike').[208] Commentators point out that although the campaign was initiated to stop the crime wave of the 1980s, it was implemented at a time of falling crime.[209] At the broader political level, the end of 1982 saw growing conflict between reformist and conservative factions in the CCPCC. At the same time, some academics had been exploring the applicability of Western concepts of humanism and alienation in the socialist context, which was ultimately construed by conservatives as an attack on the fundamental tenets of Marxism. The backlash resulted in linking the growing crime rate with bourgeois pollution from the West and, at the end of 1983, the launch of the anti-spiritual pollution campaign.[210] White points out that all politicians saw 'Hard Strikes' against crime 'as a valid means of reaffirming political solidarity' and asserts that the campaigns against crime and spiritual pollution launched in 1983 targeted both crime and dissent.[211]

Tanner and Bakken assert that the campaign was instituted to restore the prestige and morale of the police force, which had suffered some recent embarrassing defeats after several serious criminal escapades. As a result, senior political leaders, including Deng Xiaoping, were prompted to determine that more draconian measures were required.[212] Tanner argues that the 'Hard Strike' was initiated in order to restore the 'balance of awe' over criminals and to garner support from ordinary citizens in crime prevention work.[213] A similar explanation is that the extremely

for Handling Criminal Cases, 10 September 1981 (in English), and permitting the Intermediate Peoples' Court to approve death sentences in certain cases: *Decision Regarding the Question of Approval of Cases involving Death Sentences*, 10 June 1981.

206 Sun, Shengfu, 1994: 249.
207 Wang, Zhongfan, 1992: 9.
208 *Yanli Daji Yanzhong Xingshi Fanzui Huodong.*
209 Tanner, Harold, 1999: 85; Bakken, 1993: 50; Xiao, 1996: 154, citing figures of 750,000 cases in 1980, 890,000 cases in 1981 and 840,000 cases in 1982, with increases in early 1983.
210 Baum, 1994: 150–9. 211 White, 1998: 322.
212 Xiao, 1996: 154–5; Tanner, 2000: 102–5; Tanner, Harold, 1999: 85–6.
213 Tanner, 2000: 94–5.

punitive nature of the Hard Strike was designed to frighten offenders and reassure citizens that criminals would be punished.[214]

The police believed that there was 'chaos' in many public places, people 'did not feel safe' and women were afraid to go out in the evenings to go to work.[215] Chinese police officers writing on this question also point to growing public dissatisfaction with the social order environment and demands that decisive action be taken to address these problems.[216]

Although the targets of the 'Hard Strike' were defined very broadly to cover serious crime,[217] inclusion of other offences such as hooliganism; involvement in reactionary secret societies; morally based offences such as prostitution, drug related offences and 'other acts harmful to social order' indicates that the broader political conflict and the anti-spiritual pollution campaign was instrumental in the decision to launch the '1983 Hard Strike'.[218]

8.3 The 1983 Hard Strike

In July 1983, the decision was made to launch a campaign to 'mobilise all forces of society to conducting a war against crime'.[219] In a speech shortly before the '1983 Hard Strike' was launched Deng Xiaoping said:

> Why not organise a relentless campaign against crime – or two or three campaigns? Every large or medium sized city should organise several such campaigns over the next three years . . . Just as comrade Peng Zhen said not long ago, we should conduct some investigations with the advice of veteran policemen, then we shall be able to organise campaigns. In every campaign we should crack down on a large number of criminals.

214 Dutton, 1992a: 290. 215 Wang, 2004: 35.

216 Xi and Yu, 1996: 375; Dowdle, 1997: 96, argues that the 1996 'Hard Strike' was motivated, at least in part, by demands from NPC congress members that concerted action be taken to crack down on serious crime.

217 *Decision Regarding the Severe Punishment of Criminal Elements who Seriously Endanger Public Security*, arts. 1(1)–1(6); Zhang, Qiong, 2002: 21; Xiao, 1996: 167, listing seventeen types of conduct targeted under the first campaign including murder, rape robbery, causing explosions, being leaders and members of hooligan gangs, serious injury resulting in death, kidnapping and selling people, illegal manufacture, sale and transport or theft of firearms, ammunition or explosives. *Decision Regarding the Handling of Offenders Undergoing Reform through Labour and Persons Undergoing RETL who Escape or Commit New Crimes*, 10 June 1981, arts. 1 and 3, targeting recidivists. CCPCC, approving and distributing the *Report of the Central Political-Legal Committee Summing up the Activities in the First Campaign of the Hard Strike Against Serious Crime and the Deployments for the Second Campaign*, 20 August 1984 at 115, specifically requires that those in RETL and prison not be released upon completion of their sentence but retained for in-camp employment.

218 CCPCC, State Council, *Urgent Directive on the Problems of the Complete Prohibition of Opium*, 16 July 1982.

219 Yu, 1993: 31–2.

> We have decided not to launch any more political movements, but if we are going to combat serious crime on a large scale, we must mobilise the masses . . .[220]

The targets of this 'Hard Strike' were characterised as 'wreckers' and criminal elements. The nature of the contradiction was now considered to be antagonistic and so the force of the people's democratic dictatorship should be wielded against these targets.[221] The need for conducting a 'Hard Strike' was justified by Deng Xiaoping as not only strengthening the force of dictatorship but on the basis that the Hard Strike itself constituted the dictatorship.[222] The 'Hard Strike' was the 'iron fist' of the people's democratic dictatorship.[223] The form of the 'Hard Strike', to wage three campaigns (*zhanyi* 战役) over three years,[224] was modelled on the Maoist form of campaign developed in the 1950 Campaign to Suppress Counter-revolutionaries.[225] The slogan adopted by the CCPCC was to 'punish severely and quickly, round up the whole lot in one fell swoop' (*congzhong congkuai, yi wang dajin* 从重从快, 一网打尽).[226] Enforcement quotas were set for the strike.[227] As a result, the net was cast too wide as the police feared missing one more than wrongfully seizing many (*pa luo bu pa cuo* 怕落不怕错).[228]

Tanner argues that both Deng Xiaoping and Liu Fuzhi were influential in the initial formulation of the 'Hard Strike' which led to legal constraints being abandoned in the final formulation of the Hard Strike, thus emphasising its political nature.[229] On 21 July 1983 Peng Zhen demanded that the police, procuratorates, courts and judicial departments both think and act in concert to strike hard against criminal offences that seriously harmed social order, without mentioning any

220 Deng, 1994a: 44.

221 Xiao, 1996: 155, citing Liu Fuzhi (the Minister of Public Security at the time) quoting Deng Xiaoping in 'The Hard Strike is Precisely the Dictatorship' (*yanda jiushi zhuanzheng* 严打就是专政); Xi and Yu, 1996: 372.

222 Xiao, 1996: 155; Sun, Shengfu, 1994: 249.

223 Zhu, Daren, 1996: 1.

224 Xiao, 1996: 154, 156, 174–8; Sun, Shengfu, 1994: 249; and excerpts from the collected essays of Deng Xiaoping concerning striking heavily against criminal activity and comprehensive management of public order, reproduced in Chen, 1992: 37–9.

225 Xu, 1996: 77; Dutton, 2000: 63; Xia, 2001: 9. The 1950 Campaign to Suppress Counter-revolutionaries was conducted in three stages up until 1953, including the Three Anti and Five Anti campaigns.

226 CCPCC, *Decision on Severe Punishment of Criminal Activity*, August 1983, discussed in Shu, 1996a: 28.

227 Tanner, Harold, 1999: 86–93; Leng and Chiu, 1985: 137; Epstein and Wong, 1996: 482.

228 This problem is raised in MPS, *Notice on Problems of Strictly Enforcing the CPL and the Criminal Law*, 23 January 1998: at 215.

229 Tanner, 2000: 105–8.

legal constraints on the exercise of this power.[230] Local-level Party, government and army organs were called upon to take action to support the strike.[231] The *Criminal Law* and *CPL* were amended in September 1983 to remove legal impediments to the harsh and swift punishment of the targets of the campaign by delegating authority to the Intermediate People's Courts to approve death sentences; increasing the range of offences for which the death sentence could be given; truncating procedural time limits; and investing security organs of state with the powers of the police in respect of criminal investigation and detention.[232] These amendments were the NPC's contribution to the conduct of the 'Hard Strike'. They placed a legal imprimatur on the 'Hard Strike' and concurrently removed legal procedural constraints.

The extent of abuses in the first campaign[233] led senior leaders to back away from the uncontrolled manner in which it was carried out and to re-emphasise the need for actions to be bounded by law and to be responsive to the factual situation. By November 1983, Peng Zhen instructed provincial-level public security heads that the second campaign of the 'Hard Strike' should be more focussed and that the quality of law enforcement should be improved, returning to his original formulation that the 'Hard Strike' should be carried out against the designated targets within the scope of the law, '*yifa yanda*' (依法严打), however broad it might be. The extent of abuses in the first campaign of the Hard Strike can be gleaned from comments made in his speech. Peng indicated that the capacity of prisons and detention centres had already been exceeded.[234] He instructed that the police should take account of the individual conduct and circumstances of the case when prosecuting and convicting offenders and guard against the incorrect

230 Peng Zhen, The *Whole Party Must Resolutely Carry out the Hard Strike against Serious Crime*, 21 July 1983, discussed in Xiao, 1996: 155.

231 Wang, 2004: 41.

232 Decision of the NPCSC, *Regarding the Severe Punishment of Criminal Elements who Seriously Endanger Public Security*, 2 September 1983; Decision of the NPCSC, *Regarding the Procedure for Rapid Adjudication of Cases Involving Criminal Elements who Seriously Endanger Public Security*, 2 September 1983; and Decision of the NPCSC, *Regarding the Exercise by the State Security Organs of the Public Security Organs' Powers of Investigation, Detention, Preliminary Interrogation and Carrying Out Arrest*, 2 September 1983 (in English and Chinese), in Cohen, 1984: 241–5, 246–9, 250–1.

233 Tanner, Harold, 1999: 140–1, documents a dramatic increase in the use of the death penalty during the campaign years.

234 Peng Zhen, *The Hard Strike Against Crime Must Abide by the Law, Pay Attention to Policy and Strengthen Comprehensive Management*, speech given at the National Conference of Public Security Office and Division Heads convened by the MPS between 15 and 22 November 1983.

handling of cases. Finally, he demanded that 'the few evil people within the police, procuratorate and courts' be prevented from 'intentionally handling cases incorrectly; punishing serious cases lightly, minor cases heavily and harming good people'.[235]

The problems of overcrowding in all forms of detention centres as a result of the 'Hard Strike' is documented by the MPS in its *Notice on Rectifying the Living Conditions of Detainees in Lock-ups, Administrative Detention Centres and Detention for Investigation Centres* issued on 18 December 1983:

> Since the movement to seriously crack down on crime, there has been a great increase in the numbers of those detained or arrested or taken in for detention for investigation. The facilities and equipment in the detention centres, detention for investigation camps and lock-ups are very limited. There are some people who even now are sleeping on the cement floor and have no warm clothes or quilts to ward off the cold. There is scabies, hepatitis, diphtheria and other communicable diseases and contaminated food. There are some who aren't provided with food according to the set standards and detainees are seriously hungry. Now is the coldest part of the year. In order properly to administer the lives and sanitation of detainees, to prevent them starving, freezing or dying of sickness and in order to ensure the successful implementation of the campaign against serious crime we notify as follows . . .[236]

The jurisdictional boundaries between the police, procuratorate and courts set out in the *CPL* were ignored as these agencies were organised to implement the campaign by the 'joint handling of cases' (*lianhe bangong* 联合办公).[237] The boundaries between political power and state power were abandoned as the Political-Legal Committee directly handled cases.[238]

In the second campaign of the 'Hard Strike' from early 1984 to July 1985,[239] the CCPCC sought to strengthen central controls over the conduct of the campaign, to prohibit local construction of reform through labour and RETL camps and to re-emphasise the need for co-ordination between local crime-prevention measures and the hard strike

[235] Peng Zhen, *The Hard Strike Against Crime Must Abide by the Law, Pay Attention to Policy and Strengthen Comprehensive Management*: at 351.
[236] MPS, *Notice on Rectifying the Living Conditions of Detainees in Lock-ups, Administrative Detention Centres and Detention for Investigation Centres*, 18 December 1983.
[237] Wang, 2004: 36, including that this joint office received the assistance of the People's Liberation Army ('PLA').
[238] Zhao, 2001. [239] Xi and Yu, 1996: 378.

against crime.[240] This campaign focussed on transient criminals; criminals on the run; escapees from reform through labour and RETL;[241] and morally constructed offences under the rubric of hooliganism.[242] The scope of hooligan activity was interpreted not only to extend to gang fighting and street crime, but also to include offences such as prostitution.[243] The establishment of specialist administrative detention centres for prostitutes, initially trialled in Shanghai, can be traced to this period.[244]

The third campaign of the 'Hard Strike', carried out between March and October 1986, was directed at acts which harmed society, such as prostitution-related offences, drug-related offences and gambling, as well as major theft. From August 1986, it targeted 'transient criminals'. By the time of the third campaign, Liu Fuzhi had been replaced as Minister of Public Security by Ruan Chongwu. The new Minister is credited with changing the organisation of this campaign to permit local levels to respond to their local situation when planning the focus of this campaign. It reflected an attempt to take a more balanced approach to crime-fighting by adding the strengthening of the comprehensive management of public order to its focus.[245] In this campaign, senior leaders emphasised the need for accuracy in enforcement. At a meeting convened by the MPS in August 1985 to plan for this campaign of the 'Hard Strike', it was decided that doubt about whether to arrest or send a person to RETL should be resolved in favour of not taking action against the person.[246] It was acknowledged that there had been cases wrongly handled that should be corrected, but it was decided not to reinvestigate all cases.[247] The numbers of people arrested, detained under administrative detention powers or given administrative

[240] CCPCC, approving and distributing the *Report of the Central Political-Legal Committee Summing up the Activities in the First Campaign of the Hard Strike Against Serious Crime and the Deployments for the Second Campaign*, 20 August 1984.

[241] Xi and Yu, 1996: 376, 378, noting the second campaign drew to a close in July 1985.

[242] Xi and Yu, 1996: 374, 377, including sale and distribution of pornographic materials.

[243] SPC, SPP, *Explanation and Response to Several Questions Concerning the Specific Use of Law in the Current Handling of Hooliganism Cases*, 2 November 1984, provides that hooliganism includes those who permit or arrange for women to prostitute where profit is not a motive. See also Tanner, Harold, 1999: 126–7.

[244] Discussed in *Report on Resolutely Striking against and Eliminating Prostitution Activities and Preventing the Spread of Sexually Transmitted Diseases*, point 1 and chapter 5 at 2.4.

[245] Xi and Yu, 1996: 378–380, using the slogan: 'Two hands seize; one to seize the hard strike and one to seize comprehensive management of public order'.

[246] Xi and Yu, 1996: 376, citing Peng Zhen and Liu Fuzhi: 378.

[247] Xi and Yu, 1996: 378 (*shi youcuo bijiu, dan bugao quanmian fucha* 是有错必纠, 但不搞全面复查).

sanctions during the second and third campaigns decreased substantially from those of the first campaign.[248]

In the '1983 Hard Strike', and in its first campaign in particular, legal bounds had been so loosened as to provide no impediment to local enforcement activities. Unlike the pre-reform political campaigns the purpose of the campaign was severe punishment rather than transformation.[249] Over the course of the three campaigns in the '1983 Hard Strike', the method of its implementation changed. It was only in the first campaign that local party committees and agencies were given free rein. In successive campaigns, the need for observance of the law was increasingly emphasised. By the third campaign, the need for crime prevention in concert with punishment was being reasserted.

8.4 Subsequent Hard Strikes

There have only been three 'Hard Strikes' since 1978; the first between 1983 and 1987; the second between April and July 1996;[250] and the third commencing in April 2001 and continuing for two years.[251]

The second 'Hard Strike' was announced by the General Office of the CCPCC issuing and distributing the *Central Political-Legal Committee Opinion on Strengthening Work on Several Acute Problems of Social Order and Social Stability To Date*. Against a rising crime rate, a number of serious crimes in Beijing and other major cities in early 1996 acted as a trigger for this 'Hard Strike'. The murder in his home in Beijing of a deputy committee head of the NPC, Li Peiyao, and the murder of a guard and teller during a daylight armed robbery of a branch of the Industrial and Commercial Bank of China shocked the leadership and the residents of Beijing.[252] This 'Hard Strike' targeted serious violent crimes, including murder, rape and robbery, as well as

[248] Dutton, 2000: 91, citing the numbers arrested over the first, second and third campaigns as 696,144, 200,710 and 127,911, respectively; the numbers given public order administrative punishments as 77,903, 9,850 and 7,682, respectively; and the numbers released from detention for investigation as 143,507, 18,444 and 19,012, respectively.

[249] Dutton, 1995a: 437, arguing that the first of the new-style campaign was launched by Deng Xiaoping in the campaign against crime on the railways in 1975. This type of campaign was a pragmatic anti-crime strategy stripped of its former political content. Unlike the campaign in the Maoist era, the modern-day campaign no longer has at its heart the transformation of targets.

[250] Wang, 2004: 38; Dowdle, 1997: 96, argues that NPC delegates exercised significant pressure on the authorities to launch this campaign.

[251] Zhang, Qiong, 2002: 22 (Zhang is the deputy chief of the SPP); Zhao, 2001.

[252] Wang, 2004: 37.

hooliganism, drug offences and organised crime (also referred to as 'black societies') and the 'Six Evils'.[253] In Shanghai and Henan the focus was on floating crime, in Guangdong it was on 'black societies' and violent crime, in Guangxi and Qinghai it was on the manufacture and sale of firearms and drug crimes and in Xinjiang it was on violent crime gangs.[254]

This 'Hard Strike' was also organised in three campaigns, though configured differently from those of the first Hard Strike. The first was the leadership of central Party, Congress and government organs receiving reports and resolving that this 'Hard Strike' should be given great importance and pursued to the end. The second was the mobilisation of the courts, procuratorate and police and organising for close co-operation between them in the handling of cases. The third was the extensive propaganda efforts under the joint leadership of the central Party Propaganda and Political-legal Committees to mobilise popular opinion and public support. The increase in the enforcement rate is illustrated by the following statistics. In 1996 the courts heard 570,000 criminal cases, an increase of 14.9 per cent over the previous year. Of those, 320,000 were convicted of offences of seriously harming social order and 260,000 of them were sentenced to terms of more than five years' imprisonment.[255]

The second 'Hard Strike' has been distinguished from the first on a number of grounds. It permitted local factors to be taken into account in planning both the length and focus of the strike, it placed a greater emphasis on the lawfulness of enforcement conduct and it better defined the scope of targets.[256] Co-ordination of the work of the police, procuratorate and courts took place, but did not ignore the jurisdictional boundaries between the agencies to the same extent as the first 'Hard Strike'.

253 Zhang, Qiong, 2002: 21–2, suggesting that there is not unanimity about whether the 'Six Evils' should properly be considered part of this Hard Strike as the strike was primarily implemented using administrative measures. The Six Evils included: prostitution, gambling, manufacture and sale of pornography, growing, transport and sale of drugs, kidnapping and selling women and using feudal superstition to deceive and harm the people. Zhang also expresses doubt about whether the 'Winter Punishment' (*Dongji Zhengzhi*) should be included as part of the second Hard Strike. It was carried out between December 1996 and February 1997 by the public security organs and other state judicial organs targeting activities including pornography, prostitution and drug use. Targets were primarily subject to administrative rather than criminal punishments.

254 Wang, 2004: 37. 255 Wang, 2004: 37–9. 256 Yang, 1996: 21.

The third 'Hard Strike' was initiated at a meeting of the National CMPO Committee held in Beijing on 2 and 3 April 2001.[257] Its targets were: organised crime gangs; serious violent crime including causing explosions, murder, robbery and kidnapping; and corruption.[258] In addition to the exhortation to strike 'hard and fast', the implementation of this campaign emphasised striking 'surely, accurately and relentlessly' and 'in accordance with the law'. It also emphasised combining strategies of both punishment and prevention.[259]

The degree of lawlessness in enforcement of the initial stages of the '1983 Hard Strike' has not been repeated in subsequent Hard Strikes. However, some features of enforcement have been retained. One of these is the requirement that the police, procuratorates and courts co-ordinate their work in carrying out the strike and the truncation of ordinary trial procedures. Efforts to mobilise the masses in support of the strike and to educate them can be seen in the public sentencing rallies organised by the courts. In the '2001 Hard Strike', for example, the mass sentencing rallies were an integral component of both the launch and conduct of the 'Hard Strike'.[260]

In her analysis of the '2001 Hard Strike', Trevaskes traces continuities with the ways in which earlier campaigns were initiated and conducted: gathering a group to evaluate the current crime situation and determine it is too high; labelling the intended targets as 'enemies'; making efforts to mobilise the masses including holding public mass sentencing rallies; and encouraging the police, procuratorate and courts to work together in a flexible way to achieve the objectives of the Hard Strike.[261]

It is also possible to see changes. The overwhelming political flavour of the '1983 Hard Strike' has dulled. Whilst the '1983 Hard Strike' was intended to effect a fundamental improvement in the social order situation, the '1996 Hard Strike' was intended to address pronounced problems of serious and violent crime. The '2001 Hard Strike' was designed over a two-year period to bring about a 'marked improvement' in the social order situation. The definition of targets became more carefully defined in 1996 and 2001. After the '1983 Hard Strike', law enforcement was carried out only by the police, procuratorates

[257] The political importance of the meeting was indicated by attendance of China's senior political leaders, including Jiang Zemin, Zhu Rongji, Li Peng and Hu Jintao. Luo Gan is currently the head of the CMPO. Report in the People's Court Daily (*Renmin Fayuan Bao*), 13 April 2001.

[258] Zhang, Qiong, 2002: 22. [259] Wang, 2004: 39–40 (wen zhun hen 稳准狠).

[260] Trevaskes, 2004; Trevaskes, 2003a. [261] Trevaskes, 2003b.

and courts, with local-level party organs, government and army not having a direct role in law enforcement. By the time of the '2001 Hard Strike', enforcement strategies had expanded from simply 'striking hard and fast'. They included programmes of crime prevention and efforts to improve the quality of regulatory performance and enforcement practice by focussing on corruption and preventing abuse of power.[262]

8.5 Specialist struggles and concerted actions

Since the '1983 Hard Strike', a broad array of strategies have been employed for the severe punishment of crime. In a speech given to a National Political-Legal Work Meeting in December 1996, Li Peng described the three different forms for carrying out the hard strike against crime: co-ordinated action (*jizong tongyi xingdong* 集中统一行动);[263] specialist struggles (*zhuanxiang douzheng* 专项斗争); and the regular 'Hard Strike'.[264]

A possible point of confusion is that for each of these enforcement activities, the mode of enforcement remains the severe and rapid punishment of targetted activities. The same term, hard strike, is used to describe this mode of enforcement. These types of specialist struggles have been distinguished from ordinary law enforcement activities on several grounds: they retain the characteristic of taking co-ordinated action under the leadership of the local party committee and government with close co-ordination between the political-legal organs, the police, procuratorate and courts,[265] they have defined targets and results in the forms of quotas.[266]

Specialist struggles and concerted actions differ from the 'Hard Strike' in a number of ways. They include the geographical scope of the struggle, some having a specific geographical focus and others being conducted more broadly;[267] the scope of targets and the breadth with which the targets are defined; and the purposes for which they are conducted.

Yang argues that the 'Hard Strike' should be distinguished from other forms of concerted enforcement actions on the grounds that the former is launched at the national level by central Party or state organs;

[262] Wang, 2004: 41. [263] Also referred to as the concerted action (*tongyi xingdong*).
[264] Wang, Shengjun, 1998, speech excerpted at 9–11.
[265] Tong and Wang, 1997: 259–260; Zhu, Daren, 1996: 2.
[266] Tong and Wang, 1997: 260. These are examined and set by the Party and government before the specialist struggle is launched. Su, 1994: 23; Wang, Mingxin, 1993: 9, discussing the setting of quotas in a different context.
[267] Tong and Wang, 1997: 259.

is conducted under the unified leadership of the Party;[268] and is broadly focussed. Zhang argues that the concerted action launched by the Central Political-Legal Committee in May 1990 against murder, armed robbery, manufacture and sale of drugs, hooliganism and fraud should not be considered a 'Hard Strike' as it was not national but was focussed on large and medium-sized cities, open coastal cities and transportation hubs.[269] Some specialist struggles are conducted repeatedly against intransigent problems, such as prostitution-related activities and drug-related activities.[270] Some are conducted for the purpose of ensuring the success of important activities, for example, the Winter Asian Games in Heilongjiang at the end of 1995, or are conducted seasonally.[271]

8.6 The 'Six Evils'[272]

Whilst not characterised by officials as a 'Hard Strike', the strike against the 'Six Evils' shared some of its features; it was initiated and directed by the Central Political-Legal Committee and its timing was a response to the social and political instability following the Tian'anmen Square crackdown in June 1989.[273] In the wake of Tian'anmen, the central authorities launched an attack on Western pollution and attempts to undermine socialism and promote bourgeois democracy under the banner of combating 'peaceful evolution' and 'bourgeois liberalisation'.[274]

In July 1989 and July 1990, nationwide meetings of Public Security Bureaux Heads were held in an effort to reach agreement on how to restore social and political stability.[275] The police expressed concern that because of increasing foreign contact and weaknesses of local management, the public security organs had been unable to contain socially disruptive acts including pornography, prostitution, drug use

268 Yang, 1996: 20.
269 Zhang, Qiong, 2002: 20–1. The three-year hard strike was conducted under the leadership of the CMPO Committee from 1991 against robbery, concentrating on breaking-and-entering in 1992 and crime gangs and criminals on the run in 1993: Wang, Mingxin, 1993: 182.
270 Tong and Wang, 1997: 256. An example is the hard strike conducted in Guangdong Province in May 2000 against offences including prostitution, gambling, drug abuse and kidnapping and selling women and children: China News Agency, 11 May 2000.
271 Tong and Wang, 1997: 259. 272 (*Liu Hai Tongyi Xingdong* 六害统一行动).
273 Xi and Yu, 1996: 394–5.
274 Baum, 1994: 306, 328, first conducted amongst military units then broadened by conservatives at the end of 1990.
275 Xi and Yu, 1996: 394.

and gambling, which they concluded were seriously harming socialist spiritual civilisation and disrupting the success of the economic reforms.

The manner in which the 'Six Evils' strike was formulated and implemented is illustrative of the continuing close collaboration between the Party and the police in devising and implementing law enforcement strategies. When the CCPCC and the State Council determined in 1989 to conduct a nationwide strike against pornography, the 'Yellow Evils' (*Saohuang* 扫黄), the MPS sought to include prostitution and prostitution-related offences, drug offences, gambling and deceit using feudal superstition in its scope. Later, kidnapping and selling women and children were added to the list of targets, which was then labelled the 'Six Evils' (*Liuhai* 六害).[276] The head of the Political-Legal Committee, Luo Gan, held a telephone conference on 13 November 1989 with heads of government and Party organisations at central and provincial levels to organise the nationwide strike to eradicate these evils under the titles of *Saohuang* and *Liuhai*.[277] A leadership small group comprising State Council and CCPCC Political-Legal leaders approved[278] issue by the MPS of the *Proposal for Carrying out a Nationwide Campaign for the Eradication of Prostitution and Using Prostitutes etc. 'Six Evils'*, which was issued by the MPS to lower-level departments for action on 21 November 1989.[279] The strike was conducted over a period of two months, concluding on 15 January 1990.[280]

The 'Six Evils' campaign was directed against socially harmful activities such as prostitution, gambling, manufacture and sale of pornography, growing, transport and sale of drugs, kidnapping and selling women and using feudal superstition to deceive and harm the people.[281]

[276] Xi and Yu, 1996: 394–5.

[277] Xi and Yu, 1996: 395. In Guangdong and Shen Zhen the campaign commenced earlier and was against Seven Evils (*qihai*) and included organised crime and 'black societies': Mou, 1996: 304; Law Yearbook Editorial Committee, 1991: 33.

[278] The approval is referred to in the MPS, *Notice Issuing the Proposal for Carrying out a Nationwide Campaign for the Eradication of Prostitution and Using Prostitutes etc. 'Six Evils'*, 21 November 1989, instructing agencies to take action on the Proposal.

[279] MPS, *Notice Issuing the Proposal for Carrying out a Nationwide Campaign for the Eradication of Prostitution and Using Prostitutes etc. 'Six Evils'*, 21 November 1989, and the *Proposal for Carrying out a Nationwide Campaign for the Eradication of Prostitution and Using Prostitutes etc. 'Six Evils'*; Ke, 1990: 25.

[280] Xi and Yu, 1996: 395; Chu, 1996: 1, asserting that the hard strike was to run from the second half of October 1989 until after Chinese New Year in 1990.

[281] MPS, *Proposal for Carrying out a Nationwide Campaign for the Eradication of Prostitution and Using Prostitutes etc. 'Six Evils'*, approved by the State Council and the Central Political-Legal Committee leadership small group, SPC, *Notice on Coordinating with the Public Security Organs to Carry out work to Eliminate the 'Six Evils'*, 13 November 1989; Zhang, Qiuhan, 1993.

Much of the conduct targeted during the strike against the 'Six Evils' was not criminal conduct, though the conduct was perceived to pose a real danger to society, as it was seen to poison the social atmosphere, undermine the construction of socialist spiritual civilisation and foster the development of crime.[282] Unlike the '1983 Hard Strike', there was no clear statement of whether the activities targeted as part of the 'Six Evils' strike were to be characterised as antagonistic or non-antagonistic contradictions. Here we can detect a weakening in the link between the use of coercive force and the characterisation of the conduct as antagonistic. Coercion is also available to deal with non-antagonistic contradictions.

Legislation was introduced or modified around that time to implement the concerted action against these 'evils'.[283] In the campaign against prostitution, for example, legislation was passed to create a formal legal basis for the power of detention for education which had been used for education and reform of prostitutes and their clients.[284] After the official end of the concerted action, the MPS extended the attack by public security organs, particularly in Beijing, Tianjin and Shanghai, in preparation for the Asian Games.[285]

Periodic strikes against these 'evils' have been conducted since this time. In 2000, for example, public entertainment places were targeted for increased police supervision as part of the crackdown on prostitution conducted between July and September of that year.[286] The nature of these strikes, against targeted venues and well-defined groups, coupled with complementary regulatory controls, indicate that these types of

[282] Wang *et al.*, 1997: 20, also discussed in chapters 5 and 6.

[283] They are the NPCSC, *Decision on the Punishment of Criminals who Smuggle, Produce, Traffic in and Disseminate Pornographic Articles*, 28 December 1990; *Drugs Decision*, 28 December 1990; *Decision on Punishment of Criminals who Abduct, Sell and Kidnap Women and Children*, 4 August 1991; *Prostitution Decision*, 4 August 1991. The campaign against gambling was implemented on the basis of pre-existing rules passed by the MPS and supplemented by local regulations. The campaign against feudal superstition was implemented by lower-level regulations including Ministry of Civil Affairs, MPS *et al.*, *Notice on Preventing Harm Caused by Feudal Superstitious Activities*, 29 May 1989.

[284] NPCSC, *Prostitution Decision*, 4 August 1991, gave a legal basis to the power of detention for education under which prostitutes may be detained for between six months and two years.

[285] MPS, *Notice on Deepening the Struggle to Eliminate the 'Six Evils' Strictly According to Law and Implementing Policy*, 7 May 1990.

[286] MPS, Ministry of Supervision, Ministry of Culture, Administration of Industry and Commerce, *Opinion on Launching and Strengthening Management of Public Entertainment Places and Specialist Action to Conduct a Severe Strike against Evil Social Influences including Prostitution Using Prostitutes, Gambling, Drug Use and Trafficking*, 23 June 2000.

concerted action are more directly responsive to problems of social order and crime than they are to political imperatives.

9 EXPANSION OF ADMINISTRATIVE DETENTION DURING HARD STRIKES AND OTHER SPECIALIST STRUGGLES

Although the '1983 Hard Strike' targeted crime, it acted as an impetus to expand the scope and use of a range of administrative forms of detention. Used as an adjunct to the severe punishment of crime, administrative detention became more closely associated with the punitive aspects of social order policy.

The most notable form of administrative detention was detention for investigation, the use of which was increased dramatically to hold vast numbers of people rounded up in the first campaign of the 'Hard Strike'.[287] In every area, many new detention centres were constructed at local and city level. One senior scholar has asserted that 'detention for investigation centres became large storehouses for detaining all types of offenders'.[288] The plan to integrate detention for investigation with RETL ended with the commencement of the first campaign of the 'Hard Strike' and with transfer of management of RETL from the police to the Ministry of Justice ('MoJ') in 1983.[289] Autonomy of detention for investigation as a separate power from RETL was reinforced by passage by the MPS on 15 February 1984 of the *Temporary Regulations for the Management Work of Detention for Investigation Centres* to 'strengthen and improve the work of detention for investigation centres'.[290] In January 1984, the MPS gave permission for the delegation of power to approve detention for investigation to the county level in Xinjiang.[291]

287 Actual numbers of detainees are not available. Fan and Xiao, 1991: 143, discussing the increase in numbers of detainees, asserting this was the beginning of the fourth stage of development of the power. Cui, 1993b: 92, citing the vast expansion of the use of detention for investigation during this period as the third phase of the power's development.

288 Cui, 1993b: 92.

289 MPS, *Notice on Transferring Leadership of Detention for Investigation Centres to the Preliminary Interrogation Division*, 20 December 1983.

290 These regulations were based on the 1975 *Report Concerning the Situation of the National Railways Public Order Work Meeting* by the MPS and the Ministry of Railways, approved and issued by the State Council, art. 1.

291 MPS, *Response to a Request for Instructions on the Scope of Power for Detention for Investigation*, 20 January 1984.

A notice issued by the MPS on 31 July 1986 illustrates both the use to which detention for investigation was put during the 'Hard Strike' and the extent of its abuse.

> Detention for investigation measures were of important use during the 'Hard Strike' struggle. But in some areas the management of detention for investigation was loosened and control lost. Although the issue has often been raised, abuse of detention for investigation measures remains serious. According to central statistics, this year in the 2 months of April and May there were nationally more than (x) 10,000 [actual number not given] people taken in for detention for investigation. Amongst those, only 36.2 per cent of the total detained were people suspected of being floating criminals, or who have committed minor criminal offences, and have failed to tell their true name and address and whose background is not clear.[292] The public security organs of only four provinces, autonomous regions and directly governed cities have basically implemented the relevant MPS regulations; where over 80 per cent of the people taken in for detention for investigation are these two types of people. In eight provinces, autonomous regions and directly governed cities, the proportion of these two types of people is less than 25 per cent of the people taken in for detention for investigation. There are some where the proportion is only about 10 per cent.[293]

The scope of other administrative powers, such as RETL, was also increased to accommodate more conveniently the targets of the '1983 Hard Strike'.[294] The police state that the number of people taken in for RETL during the course of this 'Hard Strike' and subsequent concerted actions increased dramatically. For example, between August 1983 and January 1987, 321,825 people were reportedly taken into RETL. During the actions against pornography, the 'Six Evils' and robbery conducted between 1989 and 1991, 301,361 people were taken into RETL.[295]

'Hard Strikes' have been central to the establishment and expansion of other forms of administrative detention.[296] In 1984, a specialist

[292] These two categories describe the official definition of targets for detention for investigation.

[293] MPS, *Notice on Immediately and Conscientiously Rectifying Detention for Investigation Work*, 31 July 1986. The annotation '(x) 10,000' means a multiple of 10,000. The text did not provide any more accurate indication of the precise number.

[294] Xu and Fang, 1997: 97, also discussed in chapter 6.

[295] Luo, 1992: 34. Luo Feng was the deputy head of the MPS Legal Affairs Office and so the statistics arguably are a correct representation of the statistics held by the MPS. He is currently Vice Minister of Public Security. However, in light of earlier discussions about problems in gathering statistics, even these figures may not be entirely reliable.

[296] Li, Yonghong, 1997: 34, noting the increase of forms of administrative coercive measures and their use as the result of hard strike enforcement policy.

centre for detention of prostitutes was set up in Shanghai and, on the basis of that experience, instructions were given for other cities to establish such centres.[297] The operation of detention for repatriation stations was also influenced by the 'Hard Strike', with a determination to increase police presence in these detention centres.[298]

10 CONTESTS OVER DEFINING THE IDEOLOGICAL NATURE OF AND PRACTICAL STRATEGIES FOR PUNISHMENT OF CRIME

10.1 Debates about the continuing emphasis on the 'Hard Strike'

Whilst it is settled policy that 'striking quickly and severely in accordance with the law' is a long-term strategy,[299] there is an ongoing debate about the proper balance of measures to be adopted in the overall social order strategy.[300]

Officially, the '1983 Hard Strike' was judged a great success.[301] Later judgments continue in the same vein. In 1993, the Minister of Public Security judged the Hard Strike policy effective in ensuring political and social stability by 'striking against serious criminal activity' and cleaning up all sorts of 'pernicious social activities'.[302] Police applauded the extent of participation by the masses in the '1983 Hard Strike'. Over the three years of the first 'Hard Strike', police asserted that citizens had given police information to the authorities in respect of over 3,170,000 cases; seized and handed over to the authorities 330,000 people;[303] and that over 290,000 people gave themselves up.[304] An

297 SPC, etc., Seven Departments, *Report on Resolutely Striking Against and Eliminating Prostitution Activities and Preventing the Spread of Sexually Transmitted Diseases*, 16 August 1985; Chen, 1992: 117, discussed in chapter 5 at 2.4.

298 MPS, Ministry of Civil Affairs, *Notice on Strengthening the Work of Detention for Repatriation*, 10 May 1984.

299 Peng Zhen, *Speech at the National Political-Legal Work Conference*, 28 January 1985: at 510; Wang, Yuming, 1993: 364–5.

300 Xu, 1996: 75–6.

301 Xi and Yu, 1996: 380–1, summarising the conclusions of the National Political-Legal Work Meeting convened in March 1987 to evaluate the results of the three-year Hard Strike. Sun, Shengfu, 1994: 249, asserting it turned around the weak, scattered and passive approach to combating crime, changed the public order situation and that it gave the 'masses a greater feeling of security'.

302 Tao Siju, *Reform and Strengthen Public Security Work Law in Order to Reform and Create an Even Better Public Order Environment*, in Law Yearbook Editorial Committee, 1993: 116.

303 Shu, 1996a: 29, also reporting that during the period of the Hard Strike, 1,647,000 criminal cases were cracked.

304 Xi and Yu, 1996: 381, citing tip-offs in 3 million cases and handing over 280,000 people.

outcome claimed for the '1983 Hard Strike' was the improvement of the people's sense of security.[305]

However, the police and police statistics call into question the effectiveness of the 'Hard Strike' to reduce crime levels after 1984, or at all.[306] The police have also noted that the problem of violent crime was exacerbated by the '1983 Hard Strike' because of the harsh treatment of detainees and the brutalising effects of locking up minor offenders with serious offenders.[307]

Some officials argue that the use of hard strike techniques is no longer appropriate in the current social order environment as it fails adequately to distinguish between the causes of minor offences and serious crime.[308] They challenge the characterisation of crime as a type of aberration, a 'high tide', that can be dealt with by a short, sharp strike and argue that some problems of crime are long term.[309] One official suggests that the hard strike has not delivered the anticipated results and that enforcement agencies should place greater emphasis on the use of administrative coercive measures to combat crime.[310] Others point out that the decision to launch a 'Hard Strike' remains a political decision made by senior leaders who are insufficiently informed of the nature and extent of crime and related social policies and that such decisions involve inadequate consultation with research and enforcement agencies.[311]

Amongst the police themselves, an increasing number argue that it is counterproductive to over-emphasise the use of the hard strike techniques at the expense of local management, education, other local crime prevention measures and regular policing work.[312] The police complain

305 Xiao, 2000: 95.

306 Zhang, 1991: 92; Zhao, 1991: 71, reporting that the rate of all violent crime began to rise again in 1985. Wang, 1990: 580, 584–6, the information reaching the MPS and senior political levels was seriously distorted in 1985 because of a more serious than usual failure to put on file cases reported to the police station. Wang attributes this to a desire of lower levels to demonstrate that the 'Hard Strike' was a success: at 588. Meng, 1994: 19, arguing that despite the proliferation of different forms of concerted action at both central and local level, they have fundamentally failed to deal effectively with the rising crime rate.

307 Wang, Mingxin, 1993: 183.

308 Zhang, Qiong, 2002: 398–9; Gao and Zhao, 1999: 566, reporting that some scholars argued it was inappropriate to include 'striking quickly and severely' as the guiding thought in the amended *Criminal Law* as it over-emphasises severe punishment of crime at the expense of education and prevention strategies.

309 Zhang, Qiong, 2002: 392–4.

310 Fang, 2002: 15, subsuming administrative coercive measures within the category of security defence punishment, see chapter 8 at section 5.

311 Wang, 2004: 42–5.

312 Tong and Wang, 1997: 263–5; Yu, 1993: 239; Wu, 1994: 543; Luo, Jueqiang, 1997: 73–4, discussing the need for the hard strike (*yanda* 严打) against crime to be matched by an equivalent

that the strikes require them to divert a disproportionate amount of resources to carrying out wave after wave of hard strikes[313] and that the strikes are planned and carried out in a formulaic way.[314] In Harbin in 1988, for example, the municipal public security organs reported being engaged in waging specialist struggles and hard strikes for 340 days out of 365.[315] One commentator has stated that local-level police are exhausted from carrying out what they see as a never-ending stream of campaigns.[316]

Police also complain that the primary burden of prosecuting hard strikes falls on them.[317] In 1994, one police officer commented that citizens are no longer particularly enthusiastic about ongoing concerted actions and hard strikes and many are unwilling to participate.[318]

Local police resistance to carrying out this type of hard strike has resulted in uneven and weak enforcement as well as in over-enforcement, which has been criticised as a form of 'elastic criminal justice'.[319] It has been reflected in manipulation of statistics by attributing to the period of the strike the number of cases that were put on file over a much longer period; the inclusion of people detained under administrative forms of detention; and repeated detention of the same people as a way of filling quotas set for that Hard Strike.[320] The problem of failing to put on file cases reported to the local police has been exacerbated by continuing use of the strike.[321]

10.2 Class struggle, the theory of contradictions and the coercive power of the state

Having rejected the centrality of notions of class struggle at the beginning of the reform era, it seems incongruous that the distinction between

emphasis on crime prevention (*yanfang* 严防). Xiao, 2000: 348–9, asserting that many citizens now believe that the 'Hard Strike' is the primary method of crime control and that local-level prevention work is no longer required.

313 Fu, 1996, citing lack of resources in carrying out strikes and mindless reliance on strikes as disrupting basic-level police work and police training as well as leading to misreporting of the actual public order situation.

314 Su, 1994: 23, asserting that they are so predictable that when one is declared criminal targets just run away.

315 Wang, Mingxin, 1993: 182–3. 316 Tong and Wang, 1997: 265.

317 Meng, 1994: 19, arguing that whilst everyone takes the credit, the real work of carrying out hard strikes is carried out by the police.

318 Su, 1994: 23. 319 Zhang, 1991: 97. 320 Wang, Mingxin, 1993: 184.

321 Wang, 1990: 580, 584–8; Cui, 1993a: 353, arguing that almost exclusive reliance on the clear-up rate to evaluate the performance of police is responsible for failure to report accurately the local public order and crime situation. He argues that there is a disparity in reporting incident occurrence rates, case filing and clear-up rates, which has led in turn to central-level policy and law-makers being unaware of the true public order situation.

antagonistic and non-antagonistic contradictions has remained so influential in policing social order. However, Deng Xiaoping drew heavily on the concepts of the enemy and upon Mao's theory of contradictions when he formulated the first campaign of the '1983 Hard Strike'. He instructed that the contradiction should be seen as 'antagonistic' and the targets the 'enemy'. Such a characterisation justified the use of punitive measures against the new enemy whose acts undermined the economic reform programme. There is an ongoing debate about the extent to which the Theory of Contradictions should be used to understand and deal with crime in the reform era, which has direct ramifications for the policing of social order and crime.[322]

One view is that the range of antagonistic contradictions is very small and the range of non-antagonistic contradictions very broad.[323] The important focus of the police is thus to protect the success of the reform and opening policy and to protect the productive forces. The police have responsibility to deal with 'destabilising forces' and to 'maintain stability and unity' (*anding tuanjie* 安定团结). As these are considered to be non-antagonistic contradictions, the techniques for resolution of these disputes are education and persuasion.[324]

Yet another view is that all criminal activity is antagonistic by nature and should be dealt with by using techniques of dictatorship.[325] This view appears not to be widely held and was strongly criticised by a senior academic, Professor Cui Ming, who warns against over-emphasis by the police on the view that 'all crime is a manifestation of class struggle'. He points out that:

> Even though some crime has a class character, by no means all does, for example sex crimes, traffic and inadvertent crime, as are the vast majority of other crimes.[326] If the police stick to the view all crime is a manifestation of class struggle then it will be impossible to understand clearly the causes of crime in the new era, there is a need to place struggle against crime on a more scientific footing.[327]

[322] This has been a longstanding issue. Cohen, 1968: 89–96, documenting a debate conducted after Mao Zedong's speech on the theory of contradictions on 27 February 1957 about the circumstances and types of offences that should be characterised as antagonistic contradictions. At 94, suggesting that both the nature of the crime and the circumstances and history of the criminal were relevant.

[323] Xiao, 1996: 96.

[324] Xiao, 1996: 109; Cui, 1993a: 354–5, describing the main tasks of the police in the early stages of socialism as striking against enemies; punishing crime; protecting the people and protecting stability; promoting economic reform; and serving the Four Modernisations.

[325] This view is discussed in Xiao, 1996: 97. [326] Cui, 1993a: 355–6.

[327] Cui, 1993a: 356.

Another point of view contained in the text of criminal justice policy edited by the then Minister of Justice, Xiao Yang, is that the Theory of Contradictions no longer has any direct impact upon the administration of justice and can no longer be a substitute for the law.[328] This text asserts that the Theory of Contradictions has continuing relevance only as a theory of criminal justice[329] and does not impinge upon the legal principle of equality before the law, which requires determination of criminal guilt and the amount of punishment be dealt with by law and based on the act, not on thought, or status.[330] Such a discussion indicates that the Theory of Contradictions has been refigured in the reform era, not only to remove its class basis, but also to make it compatible, in theory at least, with the operation of the legal system.

Whilst characterising a contradiction as antagonistic remains linked to the punitive power of the state, characterising a contradiction as non-antagonistic does not exclude the use of force. The use of administrative coercive powers as an adjunct to Hard Strikes, ostensibly to deal with non-antagonistic contradictions, illustrates the punitive nature of these powers. As we have seen in the context of 'mass incidents', characterisation of a contradiction as non-antagonistic is not determinative of the amount of force that may be used by the police where there is also a confrontational element to the dispute. This suggests that, if the characterisation of a contradiction and the use of coercive force were ever linked by more than theory, there has now been an uncoupling. Force may now equally be used to resolve non-antagonistic contradictions which are deemed to be 'confrontational' in nature as it is to deal with antagonistic contradictions.

10.3 Is the Hard Strike antithetical to legal norms?

Although there continues to be affirmation of the 'Hard Strike' strategy at the highest political levels,[331] there is growing debate about its practical usefulness and appropriateness in the current social order environment and doubt about whether it can be made compatible with the principles of governance according to law. Officially, the hard strike, broadly defined, should be carried out in accordance with the law (*yifa*

[328] Xiao, 1996: 100. [329] Xiao, 1996: 96–7, 102. [330] Xiao, 1996: 100.

[331] Law Yearbook Editorial Committee, 1999: for example, the 1998 reports on CMPO at 107; the adjudication work report of the courts at 113; the procuratorial work report at 139; and the public security work report at 157, all discussing the deepening and continuing use of hard strikes and specialist strikes.

yanda 依法严打). What does this mean? There is a range of differing views,[332] including whether the term can be given meaning at all.

Recently, officials assert that the 'Hard Strike' should be seen as a criminal enforcement policy and distinct from the substantive or procedural aspects of the law.[333] In justifying the continuing use of the 'Hard Strike', officials argue that there is a need to adjust enforcement strategies to take account of current problems of social order.[334] One purpose of the 'Hard Strike' is thus to direct the allocation of resources and personnel.[335] Factually, such an assertion is unsustainable. The 'Hard Strike' requires striking 'hard', which affects substantive interpretation of the law, and 'fast', which addresses the procedural requirements of the strike. In implementing 'hard', the unlawful conduct is to be characterised as subject to a more serious charge than might otherwise be brought. In implementing 'fast', enforcement agencies co-operate to ensure that they consolidate their efforts and expedite criminal procedures.[336] Only in this way is the mass sentencing rally possible.

To justify the continuing use of the 'Hard Strike', it has become necessary to explain its consistency with legal principle and how to prevent the conduct of a 'Hard Strike' being in breach or in disregard of the law.[337] One criticism of the use of the 'Hard Strike' is that it undermines the authority of the *Criminal Law* and *CPL*; however, officials prefer a characterisation of law and the 'Hard Strike' as complementary.[338] Some suggest that the requirement for severe and quick punishment of targeted offences must be carried out within the formal scope of the law.[339] They include the requirement that the 'Hard Strike' be conducted within the scope and spirit of the amended *Criminal Law* and the *CPL*. In particular, it must conform to the principles in the amended *Criminal Law* of equality before the law[340] and proportionality, which requires that a punishment be proportional to the degree of social harm caused by the offence.[341]

Some officials seek to interpret these basic principles in a way that supports their arguments that the hard strike is premised on law.[342] Their

332 Xiao, 1996: 158–82, canvassing a range of views.
333 Zhang, Qiong, 2002: 22; Xiong, 2001; Zhao, 2001.
334 Xiao, 1996: 170–1. 335 Zhao, 2001.
336 See, for example, discussion in Wang, 2004: 33. 337 Zhang, Qiong, 2002: 23.
338 Xiao, 1996: 169, citing this argument with disapproval.
339 Xiao, 1996: 162–6; Zhang, Qiong, 2002: 78–84. 340 *Criminal Law*, art. 4.
341 *Criminal Law*, arts. 5, 61; Xiao, 1996: 162–3; Zhang, Qiong, 2002: 70–1, arguing that the purposes of the Hard Strike are reflected in arts. 2–5 of the 1997 *Criminal Law*.
342 Xiong, 2001, an official of the SPC, uses this term in relation to the '2001 Hard Strike'.

interpretation of the principle of proportionality is that it requires the calculation of the degree of social harm to be determined not only by the specific act in question, but also by taking into account the overall social order environment. The hard strike represents a political judgment that the targeted offences cause serious harm to social order.[343] This interpretation of proportionality combines criminal policy and law in handling specific cases.[344] These commentators do not reject the need to consider and apply the *Criminal Law* provisions on mitigating factors in determining the severity of punishment, despite the requirement for severe punishment of targeted offences.[345] The effect of the hard strike, they say, is on the exercise of discretion in sentencing, where discretion is exercised against the reduction of the severity of punishment; mitigating circumstances being given less weight than usual; and exacerbating circumstances given more weight.[346] These views are reminiscent of the 1980 speech of Peng Zhen where he asserted that severe punishment required both the act itself and the social order environment to be taken into account.[347]

A senior Chinese academic asserts the task of the *Criminal Law* is to promote substantive over formal justice.[348] He argues that, apart from the principles of equality before the law and fairness of the criminal law, fundamental to justice is that the scope of criminal punishments be rational and reasonable.[349] Provisions of the amended *CPL* were designed to strengthen judicial independence;[350] procedural protections for accused persons;[351] and to clarify the jurisdictional boundaries between the police, procuratorate and courts.[352]

Those who argue that the hard strike should be replaced with newer criminal policies support their arguments by demonstrating how the hard strike is inconsistent with the programme of 'ruling the country according to law'. The rule of law, they argue, means that law is supreme; that it be for a proper purpose; that it be public, systematic and not have retrospective effect; that the administration of justice should be just and independent; and that it should embody the presumption of innocence and procedural fairness.[353] Judged against these standards,

343 Xiao, 1996: 170; Zhao, 2001. 344 Xiong, 2001. 345 Xiong, 2001. 346 Zhao, 2001.
347 Peng Zhen, *Key Points of the Speech at the Report Back Meeting of the Police, Procuratorate and Court of Guangdong Province and Guangzhou City*, 1 February 1980: at 212.
348 Chen, 1996: 392–3. 349 Chen, 1996: 396. 350 Chen and Yan, 1996: 4–5.
351 Chen and Yan, 1996: 7–8, in particular by permitting the accused access to a lawyer within twenty-four hours after being subject to a coercive measure by the police (art. 96), even though this protection is flawed in practice.
352 *CPL*, arts. 7, 8, 12, 18, 87, 169. 353 Zhang, Qiong, 2002: 360–5.

the hard strike is inconsistent with the spirit of the rule of law. Regular abuses of power lead to doubt about its justness, excessive reliance on the exercise of judicial discretion creates the conditions for abuse of power and harms the rights and freedoms of individuals and the concept of procedural fairness is undermined.[354] Thus, they conclude that the concept of carrying out a hard strike 'according to law' is unclear and ill-defined.[355]

These debates indicate that legal justification of the 'Hard Strike' has become important. Whilst interpretations of what is required for governance according to law are manipulated to suit particular agendas, the question of lawfulness can no longer be ignored. Efforts to 'legalise' the hard strike have affected the content of legislation. Officials acknowledge that the hard strike influences the drafting of and is reflected in the content of the criminal codes in the provisions that facilitate severe and rapid punishment of certain offences.[356] The revised *Criminal Law* expanded the number of criminal offences whilst at the same time providing a better definition of offences.[357] The amended *Criminal Law* also retains the power of the state to punish severely. In drafting amendments to the *Criminal Law*, it was decided that the number of crimes for which the death sentence could be given 'in principle would be neither increased nor reduced'.[358] A more direct impact of the hard strike upon legislative drafting is the continuing use of the practice of changing or interpreting law to accommodate a particular hard strike.[359] As I will discuss further, in the area of administrative detention, the legal definition of powers continues to reflect the demand for flexibility and imposes few procedural or substantive legal limits on the exercise of these powers in the way the *Criminal Law* and *CPL* increasingly do.

[354] Zhang, Qiong, 2002: 365–6, 400.

[355] Zhang, Qiong, 2002: 366. [356] Zhang, Qiong, 2002: 24–5.

[357] Wang Hanbin's explanatory speech to the NPC on the draft *Criminal Law*, 6 March 1997, stating the purpose of the amendments was to facilitate implementation of the law, see Zhou, 1997: 1.

[358] This decision was attributed to a view that the state of public order in China was very poor. As a result, the new *Criminal Law* contains fifty offences for which the death penalty may be given. Zhou, 1997: 14–15. Zhou asserts that the 1979 *Criminal Law* contained twenty-eight provisions under which the death penalty could be given, fifteen relating to counter-revolution. He asserts that under the *Criminal Law*, and subsequent amendments, sixty-six crimes were punishable by death.

[359] For example, in suppressing *Falungong*: NPCSC, *Decision on Banning Heretical Cult Organisations, and Preventing and Punishing Cult Activities*, 30 October 1999 (in English): *Explanation of the SPC and SPP Concerning Laws Applicable to Handling Cases of Organising and Employing Heretical Cult Organisations to Commit Crime*, 8 October 1999 (in English).

11 CONCLUSION

The problems in realising a comprehensive programme for social order and crime control in China's rapidly changing social, economic and political environment have forced ongoing changes to be made to each of the components of this programme. One outcome has been increasing reliance on the administrative management and detention powers of the police. As agencies struggle to respond to the challenges presented by the social order problems resulting from this social transformation, the formulation and implementation of social order policy and its relationship to law have become contested sites.

The state continues to emphasise local social order management and crime prevention strategies as a major focus of its social order policy, but the evidence suggests that efforts to strengthen grass roots organisations for these purposes have not been entirely successful. Whilst still using the rhetoric of the mass-line, there have been changes in the basis upon which local community-based control mechanisms are organised and operate, as well as in techniques of local policing. The capacity of the state to use ideology, or even its local organisational structures, to mobilise local residents is a thing of the past. Over the period of reform, the structure and powers of community organisations are being regularised and defined by law and, increasingly, members of local organisations are remunerated.

The increasing reliance on more formal administrative sanctioning powers of the police over the period of economic reform can be attributed to a combination of factors. The first is the failure of local mechanisms adequately to prevent problems such as drug use, prostitution, bad behaviour and repeated minor offences by juveniles and transients before they come to be dealt with more formally by the police. More importantly, the demand for complete enforcement during 'Hard Strikes' and other forms of concerted action has led both to net widening and increasing reliance by police on their administrative powers.

The pre-reform distinction between antagonistic and non-antagonistic contradictions continues to be used, though stripped from its traditional class basis and more recently reinterpreted in an attempt to make it compatible in theory with the policy of rule according to law. With the launch of the '1983 Hard Strike', the new enemy became those whose criminal conduct damaged economic modernisation and social order, justifying very severe punishment. However, the hard strike mode of enforcement itself has taken on many different forms since the

'1983 Hard Strike'. These changes have facilitated increasing focus on actual problems of crime and, whilst not eliminating the use of the 'Hard Strike' for central political objectives, have diminished the extent of that use compared with the '1983 Hard Strike'.[360]

In this chapter I have considered the emergence of diverging views about strategies for enforcement of social order. There is not unanimous support for continuing use of the 'Hard Strike' and other forms of concerted action. Growing doubts are being expressed about the usefulness of the hard strike as a crime control strategy. There are concerns that it not only fails to address the current crime situation but that it prevents a more rational allocation of resources to local crime prevention and social management work. Demands that the implementation of the 'Hard Strike' be conducted according to law have strengthened. Supporters of continuing use of hard strikes seek to justify them by adopting a view of law enabling them to argue that hard strikes are consistent with legal norms. Opponents of the continuing use of hard strikes adopt interpretations of the law that reveal the hard strike to be antithetical to legal norms.

I have traced a growing impetus to regularise and legalise the CMPO and its programmes in line with the policy of ruling the country according to law.[361] Recently, a commentator has suggested that there is a need to determine whether the CMPO should be implemented on the basis of policy or law. If the latter, then they argue that the remaining informal measures employed under the policy should be put on a legal footing.[362]

Recognition of the need to justify policy and specific powers in legal and not purely political terms opens for debate the legality and possibilities for reform of administrative detention powers. However, an exploration of this development in the next two chapters will reveal that the legalisation of these powers has been a slow process.

The policy of comprehensive management of public order and the continuing use of Hard Strikes were conceived to deal with crime and social order problems. What these strategies address only incompletely are the broader structural causes of social instability and unrest brought about by economic reform: economic inequality and official corruption.

[360] Wang, Mingxin, 1993: 182–3; Fu, 1993: 167, pointing out that campaigns are political as they do not address the problem of crimes committed by the powerful and target working-class youth, who are easier targets and blamed for deteriorating public order.

[361] Zhang and Wang, 2000: 26; Feng, 2000.

[362] Zhang, Wei, 2002: 56.

There is an increasing awareness that social stability rests on a broader basis of institutional capacity and improved social equality and justice. The programme of administration according to law should thus also be seen as a key element of the state's broader efforts to achieve social stability.

CHAPTER FIVE

REVIVAL OF ADMINISTRATIVE DETENTION IN THE REFORM ERA: PROSTITUTES AND DRUG ADDICTS

1 INTRODUCTION

In this chapter I trace the parallel development in the reform era of two administrative detention powers: detention for education of prostitutes and clients of prostitutes and coercive drug rehabilitation of drug addicts. These powers were both used by the CCP from around 1949. At that time, these powers, in combination with other measures, were deemed to be so successful that, according to official accounts, the problems of prostitution and drug addiction were eliminated and the powers rendered obsolete. They were both revived at the beginning of the reform era as part of the strategy for dealing with the deterioration of social order and the 'social vices' that were identified as part of the fourth 'high tide' of crime discussed in chapter 4.

Like RETL, these powers officially form part of the 'second line of defence', the ostensible purpose of which is to prevent bad and morally blameworthy conduct from deteriorating further into crime; and which have been used as an adjunct to anti-crime campaigns. Unlike RETL, both powers are directed at very specific targets, were officially abolished and only revived later during the 1970s and 1980s. The reinstatement of these powers took place after the decision was made to rebuild China's legal system. The ways in which these powers have developed from the late 1970s thus provides a very good example of the ways in which the Chinese state has managed legal reform in the context of social order. In this chapter, I focus on the ways these two powers have developed.

The impact of legal reforms on these powers is discussed further in subsequent chapters.

An examination of the development of these powers enables closer scrutiny of the enduring patterns of Party-state relations in the development and implementation of the social order strategies and the powers employed to implement those strategies discussed in chapter 4. Analysis of these powers also provides a specific context within which to examine the influence of social order policy, the hard strike in particular, on the development and use of administrative detention powers and on their legal form. I consider whether these administrative detention powers are a remnant of the pre-reform era and conclude that they differ in a number of significant ways from their pre-reform antecedents.

2 PROSTITUTION

2.1 Re-emergence of prostitution in the 1970s: characterisation of the problem

In the late 1970s and early 1980s, the re-emergence of prostitution was identified as a serious social problem requiring redress.[1] Like the 1950s, prostitution and using prostitutes is not characterised as a criminal offence. However, unlike the 1950s, it was no longer possible, after more than thirty years of Communist Party rule, to characterise prostitution as a legacy of the exploitative feudal system.[2] In the 1950s, prostitution was considered to be a form of 'social illness'[3] and a 'malignant tumour of the semi-colonial semi-feudal society'.[4] Prostitutes were characterised as victims of oppression. However, even in the 1950s, in the face of failure to eradicate prostitution after several years and recidivism of prostitutes who had already been 'liberated', prostitutes were also described as delinquents who refused to reform themselves.[5]

As prostitution spread in the late 1970s and 1980s from south-eastern and coastal parts of China inland to the centre and west of the country and from urban to rural areas, it quickly became characterised as one of the main 'public hazards' to social order.[6] From the 1970s prostitution

[1] Mou, 1996: 1, citing Deng Xiaoping as saying: 'Our cities have prostitutes, why are we not dealing with it?'

[2] Xi and Yu, 1996: 253–4; Yu, 1992: 6–10.

[3] Herschatter, 1997: 305. [4] Zhan, 2005: 416.

[5] Henriot, 1995: 469, 476; Herschatter, 1997: 309–11, indicating that the women responsible for overseeing the detention centres in Shanghai were encouraged to see prostitutes both as victims of the old exploitative system, and as being 'parasites' who lived lives of debauchery.

[6] Zhan, 2005: 417 (*gonghai* 公害).

was characterised in a way that emphasised the delinquency of prostitutes. In a report to the CCPCC and the State Council, prostitution was characterised in the following terms:

> Recently the re-emergence of prostitution activities is completely different from that of old China where prostitution arose because of being compelled to find some means of livelihood. The vast majority of prostitutes today desire material enjoyment, avoid disliked work and pursue a degenerate parasitic lifestyle.[7]

The account of prostitution given by the police also emphasises the connection between prostitution and the weakening economic and social position of women in the reform era.[8] As in the 1950s, the decision was made to eradicate prostitution.

As the amount of prostitution has expanded since the 1980s, the range of people engaging in prostitution and the circumstances in which prostitution takes place has also expanded.[9] The picture painted by the police is of an extensive and multi-layered social order problem. Although the law now adopts a more gender-neutral definition of prostitution,[10] police accounts of prostitution remain highly gendered. At one end of the scale, the police point to an increase in prostitution in rural areas and in the number of rural women and girls who have come to cities in search of employment and become prostitutes.[11] They assert that the range of venues where prostitution occurs has expanded from hotels, saunas, dance halls, hairdressers and karaoke bars to include streets, taxis, parks, factories, building sites, bus and train stations, wharves and privately owned houses. The mode of soliciting has expanded to the internet.[12] They also cite a trend towards better

[7] *Report on Striking Hard Against and Resolutely Suppressing Prostitution and Preventing the Spread of Sexually Transmitted Diseases*, submitted to the CCPCC and the State Council by the MPS, MoJ, Ministry of Health, Civil Administration and Women's Federation on 21 September 1987. Quan, 12 February 2004, reporting to Luo Feng, Vice Minister of Public Security that 80 per cent of registered female drug users engage in prostitution.

[8] Xin, 1999: 1412, 1424–9.

[9] Zhan, 2005: 425–30, setting out changes in age ranges, socio-economic background, family and employment circumstances and migration status.

[10] See, for example, the PRC *SAPL*, which uses a neutral third person pronoun (他), and the 2001 MPS *Response to a Request for Instructions on the Question of How to Determine the Nature of and Deal with Sexual Acts between People of the Same Sex with Money and Property as the Intermediary*, discussed below.

[11] Zhan, 2005: 433–4, noting that the price of sex amongst this group has decreased.

[12] Zhan, 2005: 420–31.

organisation of prostitution and a growing involvement of organised crime.[13]

Less visible forms of prostitution, including taking a 'second wife', keeping a mistress or 'secretary', whilst common, appear less frequently in police accounts of prostitution and strategies for its elimination.[14] Jeffreys notes that the practices of taking a 'second wife' or keeping a mistress are very controversial as they are often linked to official corruption, but are far less public and difficult to police.[15] These cases often come to public attention as 'sex and corruption' scandals. Examples include the dismissal in June 2006 of Beijing Government Vice Mayor Liu Zhihua and Vice Admiral Wang Shouye, both of whom, in addition to allegations about financial corruption, were found to lead 'morally degenerate' lifestyles, keeping several mistresses.[16]

The police conceptualisation of the nature of the 'problem' of prostitution has influenced the strategies that have been adopted to eradicate different forms of prostitution. Whilst maintaining the rhetoric of elimination of prostitution, the police also recognise the reality that their efforts have been unsuccessful so far and have introduced measures to strengthen regulation of prostitution, especially in public venues where prostitution occurs. As Jeffreys points out, the police not only build a picture of the problem as part of their own strategy-making processes but also, through the extensive use of media during anti-prostitution campaigns, create for the public an image of prostitution and of the harm it causes.[17]

Mainstays of police strategies to eradicate prostitution have included a series of hard strikes against prostitution and measures to regulate and manage public venues such as dance halls and bars. These strategies target the types of prostitution and sexual services that relate to public venues and so are less likely to catch more private forms of prostitution. However, in the face of continuing failure to eradicate prostitution, coupled with the recognition of the spread of sexually transmissible diseases ('STDs') and HIV/AIDS, there is increased debate about whether eradication remains the correct strategy.

13 Zhan, 2005: 427.

14 Zhang, Dunli, 2000: 20, includes this type of activity within the eight categories of prostitution, two of which include sex with a designated person or group of people.

15 Jeffreys, 2004: 169–71.

16 O'Neill, 2006, in relation to Liu Zhihua; Xinhua News Agency, 29 June 2006, in relation to Wang Shouye.

17 Jeffreys, 2004: 167–9.

2.2 Measures used to eradicate prostitution

Prostitution and using prostitutes is generally not characterised as a criminal offence, but as a public order offence primarily to be dealt with under the security administrative punishments laws.[18]

A range of measures has been adopted in the state's efforts to eradicate prostitution. These include registration at the police station as a member of the focal population, administrative sanctions under the *Security Administrative Punishments Law* ('*SAPL*') (which replaced the *SAPR* on 1 March 2006), such as a warning, fine or administrative detention and detention in specialist detention centres, or under RETL.

In June 1981, in the *Notice on Resolutely Prohibiting Prostitution Activities*, the MPS directed that prostitutes be identified from the registers of the focal population and that a consolidated strike be made against all prostitution-related activities. In this document, the MPS specified a range of measures to be taken against prostitution and related activities. Criminal sanctions were to be imposed on those who ran brothels, who forced or lured women into prostitution or who prostituted knowing they had an STD[19] in accordance with the provisions of the *Criminal Law*.[20]

Differential treatment was prescribed for prostitutes depending on the seriousness of their transgressions. Those who prostituted occasionally, or who 'hankered after petty gains' (*tantu xiaoli* 贪图小利), were to be educated and placed under the control of their head of family.[21] Those with regular employment were to be given a warning, fine or administrative detention under the *SAPR* (as it then was);[22] or a disciplinary sanction by their work unit which was also to organise for the person to be subject to help and education in their local community.[23] Those who had floated into the city from the countryside were to be gathered up for education[24] and then repatriated to their home town where they were to be subject to control and education by the local security

[18] Zhan, 2005: 418.
[19] *Notice on Resolutely Prohibiting Prostitution Activities*, art. 2.
[20] *Criminal Law*, arts. 358, 359, 361, organising, luring, forcing into prostitution and housing prostitutes; *Criminal Law*, art. 360, prostituting knowingly with a sexually transmitted disease.
[21] *Notice on Resolutely Prohibiting Prostitution Activities*, art. 3(1).
[22] Later amended by the *Decision on Strict Prohibition of Prostitution*, point 4, para. 1. *SAPR*, art. 30.
[23] *Notice on Resolutely Prohibiting Prostitution Activities*, art. 3(2).
[24] The term used in the text is *shourong jiaoyu*, which I have translated elsewhere as detention for education. However, in this context it appears that the term is being used to describe detention for the purposes of education generally, rather than to refer to a particular form of detention.

organisation.[25] Those who had no regular employment, or continued to prostitute after being educated, were to be sent to RETL.[26] Both the CMPO[27] and the *Temporary Measures on Re-education through Labour* ('Temporary Measures') passed in 1982[28] required that repeat offenders be sent to RETL.

Prostitution was targeted as part of each of the campaign of the '1983 Hard Strike'. The General Office of the CCPCC approved a report on 8 April 1983 reaffirming the use both of administrative punishments under the *SAPR* for prostitutes and clients of prostitutes and RETL for those prostitutes repeatedly caught prostituting.[29] In respect of repeat offenders, it required that all those caught be sent to RETL.[30] Local reports indicate that campaigns for the elimination of prostitution began around 1982[31] and were conducted throughout the first two campaigns of the '1983 Hard Strike'.[32] Since the '1983 Hard Strike', the police have waged an ongoing series of hard strikes against prostitution.

The current legal regime relating to prostitution replicates this range of punishments. Minor infringements are dealt with under the *SAPL*, which provides for administrative detention of prostitutes or clients of prostitutes for between ten and fifteen days, together with a fine of up to RMB 5,000. Where the situation is not serious or where a person is soliciting in a public place, administrative detention of up to five days and a fine of up to RMB 500 may be imposed.[33] The same penalties apply to people who incite, encourage or introduce a person to prostitution,[34] who organise pornographic audio visuals or performances, or who engage in licentious behaviour.[35] Where the police discover drug taking, gambling or prostitution associated with venues such as hotels, dining facilities, cultural and entertainment venues, taxis and the like, the person tipping off those engaged in prostitution will be subject to

[25] Article 3(3). [26] Article 3(1)–(3).
[27] *Five Major Cities Meeting*, point 5. [28] Article 10.
[29] General Office of the CCPCC, issuing the MPS, All-China Women's Federation, Two Party Organisations, *Report on Resolutely Suppressing Prostitution Activities*. The enforcement decisions of this Report were then issued by the SPC, SPP and the MPS in the *Opinion on How to Handle Cases Involving Prostitutes, Clients of Prostitutes and Secret Prostitutes*, 7 August 1984.
[30] General Office of the CCPCC, issuing the MPS, All-China Women's Federation, Two Party Organisations, *Report on Resolutely Suppressing Prostitution Activities*, point 4 provides '*faxian yige, shourong yige, songchu laodong jiaoyang*' (发现一个, 收容一个, 送出劳动教养).
[31] Mou, 1996: 278, in respect of Fujian province, at 310, in respect of Guangdong province, and at 344, in respect of Hubei province.
[32] Mou, 1996: 247–8, indicating that, in Liaoning province, the first campaign to eliminate prostitution was conducted between 1983 and 1985 and that several specialist struggles were carried out after that.
[33] Article 66. [34] Article 67. [35] Article 68.

administrative detention of between ten and fifteen days.[36] The *SAPL* provides that those repeatedly offending Articles 67 and 68 will be subjected to 'coercive education measures on the basis of state regulation', which at present means RETL.[37] Those who prostitute or use prostitutes and have been caught many times and fail to reform may be placed in detention for education and recidivists sent to RETL.

Where the conduct is to be subject to criminal sanction, the categories of criminal offence largely correspond with the categories of infringement set out in *SAPL*,[38] except engaging in prostitution or using prostitutes, which is not punishable as a criminal offence except where the person knows they have an STD or visits prostitutes under fourteen years old.[39] Organising or forcing others into prostitution is not punishable under the *SAPL* but is subject to criminal sanction.[40]

Regulation and control of venues associated with prostitution was strengthened in 1999 when the State Council passed the *Regulations for Management of Recreation Venues*. The regulations expressly prohibit prostitution, and permitting, inducing or encouraging prostitution in these venues. They also prohibit the provision of sexual services and any acts that 'run counter to social public morality'.[41]

2.3 Revival of specialist prostitute detention centres: detention for education (*shourong jiaoyu* 收容教育)[42]

One police source asserts that specialist detention for the education and reform of women who 'prostituted and engaged in other promiscuous hooligan activities' (*liumang yinluan* 流氓淫乱)[43] was initially set up in Shanghai and Wuhan in 1984.[44] The establishment of a prostitute detention centre in Shanghai arose out of a 1982 investigative report submitted to the Shanghai Party Committee by the Women's Federation and Party organs, recommending establishment of a specialist

36 Article 74.

37 Article 76 (按照国家规定采取强制性教育措施). See MPS, *Explanation of Several Questions on Implementation by the Public Security Organs of the 'PRC Security Administrative Punishments Law'* 23 January 2006.

38 *Criminal Law*, art. 359 (with the equivalent provision in the *SAPL*, art. 67), art. 362 (with the equivalent in the *SAPL*, art. 74) and art. 301 (with an equivalent in the *SAPL*, art. 68).

39 *Criminal Law*, art. 360.

40 *Criminal Law*, arts. 358 and 361.

41 Article 25.

42 An earlier, abbreviated and in parts outdated account of the revival of detention for education and coercive drug rehabilitation is contained in Biddulph, 2003.

43 The term is used in *Report on Resolutely Striking against and Eliminating Prostitution Activities and Preventing the Spread of Sexually Transmitted Diseases*, 16 August 1985.

44 Mou, 1996: 193.

prostitute detention centre. Funding and approval for establishment of the centre was given to the Shanghai public security organs, the Women's Federation and the civil affairs bureau, and it was to be run by the public security organs.[45] Formal establishment of the centre was approved in September 1984 by the Shanghai Party Committee and Municipal Government by issue of a local regulation.[46]

The success in Shanghai of specialist detention was noted in a report of 16 September 1985,[47] which endorsed the use of specialist prostitute detention centres and recommended that other cities follow the Shanghai example. Specifically, the report recommended that the local police, civil affairs bureau, judicial administration, health department and Women's Federation carry out investigations and prepare a report for the local government to act upon.[48] The report also required designation of certain hospitals to carry out compulsory testing for and treatment of STDs for prostitutes and their clients. Registration and reporting was required for those found to be positive.[49]

The Fujian Provincial Government issued the *Announcement on Striking Against and Eliminating Prostitution and Using Prostitutes* on 20 January 1986, approving the detention of prostitutes in Women's Education Centres (*Funü Jiaoyang Suo*) where their offences were not sufficiently serious to warrant being sent to RETL.[50] This announcement permitted detention for between six months and two years and permitted the police to approve an extension of a further year.[51] At this time the establishment of detention centres and detention of prostitutes had not yet been authorised by central government legislation.

[45] Zhan, 2005: 449; Mou, 1996: 265. The Shanghai report indicates that from the time of establishment until the end of 1993, the female detention centre had taken in 4,099 people and the clients of prostitutes centre had taken in 1,631 people.

[46] Mou, 1996: 265, *Several Regulations on the Work of Detention for Education of Female Prostitutes* and the *Opinion on Handling People who Prostitute and Clients of Prostitutes*, no dates given.

[47] Seven agencies, *Report on Resolutely Striking against and Eliminating Prostitution Activities and Preventing the Spread of Sexually Transmitted Diseases*, 16 September 1985.

[48] *Report on Resolutely Striking against and Eliminating Prostitution Activities and Preventing the Spread of Sexually Transmitted Diseases*, point 1 at 117.

[49] *Report on Resolutely Striking against and Eliminating Prostitution Activities and Preventing the Spread of Sexually Transmitted Diseases*, point 2 at 117–18.

[50] Mou, 1996: 279, approving the *Report on Resolutely Striking Against and Suppressing Prostitution and Using Prostitutes* prepared by the Fujian Bureau of Public Security requiring construction of detention for education centres. According to its report, Fujian in 1993 had nine detention centres with one in Xiamen for clients of prostitutes and a capacity for 2,000 people.

[51] Mou, 1996: 285. In 1990 the provincial government approved and issued the Bureau of Public Security, *Fujian Province Temporary Regulations on Detention for Education of Female Prostitutes*, describing the targets and approval procedures.

2.4 Specialist struggles against prostitution and the expansion of detention for education from 1986

Prostitution, and prostitution-related offences, drug-related offences and gambling were targeted as part of the third campaign of the '1983 Hard Strike' between March and October 1986.[52] The strike against prostitution was directed by the State Council *Notice on Resolutely Suppressing Prostitution Activities and Preventing the Spread of Sexually Transmitted Diseases*, issued on 1 September 1986, and complementary notices passed at that time.[53] This *Notice* pointed to the failure of efforts to eradicate prostitution and urged concerted action to eliminate it, but required that the *Notice* itself and the action taken pursuant to it not be publicly disclosed.[54]

This *Notice* required that prostitutes be punished either under the terms of the *SAPR* or be sent to RETL, but did not mention the establishment of specialist detention for education centres. This strike, however, provided impetus for more widespread construction of specialist detention centres throughout the country.[55] In Liaoning province, for example, construction of detention for education facilities for prostitutes commenced in 1986.[56]

In Guangdong in June 1987 the Standing Committee of the Guangdong People's Congress passed the *Guangdong Province Regulations on Suppressing Prostitution, Using Prostitutes and Secret Prostitution*, which provided for a range of penalties including detention of prostitutes and RETL.[57] Article 5 provides:

> Deal with prostitutes by imposing up to fifteen days' administrative detention, directing a statement of repentance be given and returning her to her family or work unit for control and education (*guanjiao* 管教).

[52] Xi and Yu, 1996: 379.

[53] MPS, *Notice on Strengthening the Public Order Management of the Hotel Industry*, 7 July 1986; regulations for management of hotel industry are set out in the MPS, *Measures on Managing Public Order in the Hotel Industry*, approved and issued by the State Council on 23 September 1987.

[54] *Notice on Resolutely Suppressing Prostitution Activities and Preventing the Spread of Sexually Transmitted Diseases*, point 9 at 229.

[55] Mou, 1996: 345, reports that in 1987 the Hubei Provincial Party Committee and the Provincial government jointly issued notices requiring detention for education of prostitutes.

[56] Mou, 1996: 252. Liaoning province reported conducting a campaign in 1986 and 1988 based on the State Council's September 1986 notice.

[57] These regulations were an amended version of 1981 public security regulations and there is an indication that detention for education centres were established in Guangdong before the 1987 regulations were passed: Mou, 1996: 311.

> Where the situation is serious, take her in for education (*shourong jiaoyang* 收容教养) for between six months and one year or impose RETL. In general fines of up to RMB 5,000 are permissible.[58]

In 1989 the Guangdong People's Government passed regulations authorising detention for education in terms not completely identical to those of other localities.[59]

The central authorities began supporting more widespread construction of detention for education centres from 1987. On 26 October 1987 the General Offices of the CCPCC and the State Council jointly issued instructions to intensify efforts to eliminate prostitution.[60] The State Council and CCPCC expressed concern that efforts to eliminate prostitution had not been particularly successful and instructed all Party and state agencies to strike hard to eliminate prostitution and related activities. Amongst the recommendations was a proposal to build specialist prostitute detention centres in areas where no detention centres had yet been established and to increase the number of areas with such detention centres from the eighteen already established on the basis of local regulations.[61] The approval document indicated that some central funding for the construction of these detention facilities would be made available after negotiation between central and local levels.[62] This document also emphasised strengthening of ongoing social order management,[63] in particular the management of entertainment venues and hotels.[64] The continuing lack of success of strikes against prostitution

[58] In 2003, approximately AUD 1,000.

[59] Ke, 1994: 48, refers to the *Temporary Regulations of Guangdong Province on Carrying out Detention for Education of Prostitutes and Users of Prostitutes etc, Seven Types of Offenders* 1989.

[60] Issuing a report prepared by the MPS, MoJ, Ministry of Health, Ministry of Civil Affairs and the National Women's Federation, entitled *Striking Hard Against and Resolutely Suppressing Prostitution Activities and Preventing the Spread of Sexually Transmitted Diseases*, 21 September 1987.

[61] *Report on Striking Hard Against and Resolutely Suppressing Prostitution Activities and Preventing the Spread of Sexually Transmitted Diseases*, submitted to the CCPCC and the State Council by the MPS, MoJ, Ministry of Health, Ministry of Civil Affairs and Women's Federation on 21 September 1987.

[62] *Report on Striking Hard Against and Resolutely Suppressing Prostitution Activities and Preventing the Spread of Sexually Transmitted Diseases*, para. 5 at 222. It proposed that they are all to be compulsorily tested for STDs and compulsorily treated at their own expense and required expansion of the STD-testing facilities set up by the Ministry of Health. Foreigners are to be expelled.

[63] General Office of the CCPCC and General Office of the State Council, issuing the *Report on Striking Hard Against and Resolutely Suppressing Prostitution Activities and Preventing the Spread of Sexually Transmitted Diseases*, 26 October 1987.

[64] At 224–6.

provided an impetus to local enforcement agencies to expand the scope of detention to include clients of prostitutes from 1987.[65]

At a public security work meeting in May 1988, the establishment by municipalities and local areas of detention for education centres was affirmed. The decision made at that meeting to expand the scope of detention nationwide was subsequently approved by the MPS in the *Summary of Minutes of Meeting on Further Attacking and Suppressing Prostitution and Using Prostitutes and Doing a Good Job of Detention for Education Work*.[66]

2.5 The concerted action against the 'Yellow Evils' and the 'Six Evils' 1989–1990

In light of the limited success of the actions taken since 1987 to eliminate prostitution and prevent the spread of STDs, on 9 January 1989 the Minister of Public Security, Wang Fang, convened a meeting attended by state, Party and other mass organisations determined to strengthen actions to eradicate prostitution.[67] The meeting approved the ongoing expansion of detention for education. The meeting decided that only a small proportion of prostitutes met the criteria for criminal prosecution or RETL, but noted that, for the vast majority, punishments given under the *SAPR* by way of a fine, detention or warning had not deterred them.[68] The meeting also determined that comprehensive management should be strengthened, in addition to strengthening the force of the hard strike and increasing use of administrative detention.[69]

Prostitution and related offences were included in the nationwide strike against the Yellow Evils and the 'Six Evils' that was approved by the CCPCC and the State Council in November 1989 and conducted

[65] Ke, 1994: 48, in cities including Shanghai, Beijing, Wuhan, Dalian and Xi'an. Mou, 1996: 265, in the Shanghai report indicates that from the time of establishment until the end of 1993, the female detention centre held 4,099 people and the prostitute client centre held 1,631 people.

[66] Referred to in Ke, 1994: 48 and Zhan, 2005: 450.

[67] *Summary of the Minutes of Meeting on Research on Striking against and Eliminating Prostitution and Using Prostitutes*: at 142. Representatives attended from the State Planning Commission, State Education Commission, Ministry of Supervision, MPS, Ministry of Civil Affairs, MoJ, Ministry of Finance, Ministry of Commerce, Ministry of Culture, Ministry of Telecommunications, Ministry of Health, State Administration of Industry and Commerce, State Tourism Bureau, Legal Bureau of the State Council, New China News Agency, Central Discipline Inspection Committee, Central Propaganda Bureau, NPCSC Legislative Affairs Committee, SPC, SPP, National Women's Federation and the Communist Youth League.

[68] *Summary of the Minutes of Meeting on Research on Striking against and Eliminating Prostitution and Using Prostitutes*: at 143.

[69] *Summary of the Minutes of Meeting on Research on Striking against and Eliminating Prostitution and Using Prostitutes*: point 3 at 144.

between November 1989 and January 1990.[70] The focus of the concerted action against the 'Yellow Evils' and the 'Six Evils' varied from locality to locality. In large cities and provinces such as Shanghai, Guangdong, Fujian, Zhejiang and Hainan, the focus was on prostitution.[71] The rate of enforcement against prostitution and prostitution-related activities under this strike increased dramatically.[72]

Although nationwide statistics are not available, statistics from several regions are illustrative of the increase in enforcement over the period of the concerted action. In Liaoning, for example, the police reported that during the period of this action, in the six-month period to March 1990, 3,333 people were seized for prostitution and related offences, compared with an average of 200 per year between 1983 and 1985 and 400 per year between 1986 and 1988.[73]

In Shanghai the rate of enforcement against prostitutes and clients of prostitutes during the 'Six Evils' action also increased dramatically. Actions taken against prostitutes in the period 1983–8 hovered in the hundreds, ranging from 244 in 1984 to 678 in 1988. In 1989, 10,869 prostitutes were given some form of sanction. This fell back to forty-two in 1990 and then increased to 1,042 in 1991.[74]

In a notice dated 7 May 1990, the MPS noted that although the official activities associated with the 'Six Evils' action were mostly finished, the public security organs would continue to concentrate on attacking the 'Six Evils' in preparation for the Asian Games,[75] focussing on Beijing, Tianjin and Shanghai.[76]

2.6 Hard strikes and concerted actions after 1990

Since 1990, further specialist struggles have been waged at regular intervals both locally[77] and nationally. Strikes conducted between 1991 and

[70] The formulation of targets and implementation of the strike are discussed in chapter 4 at 8.6.

[71] Law Yearbook Editorial Committee, 1991: 32, reporting that the focus of the strike in Jilin was gambling, in Changsha it was an attack on the 'fortune telling street'. In Sichuan, Guangxi, Shandong, Guizhou and Henan, the focus was on kidnapping and selling women and children and in Yunnan the focus was on drug offences.

[72] Law Yearbook Editorial Committee, 1991: 32, reporting that a total of 576,000 cases were handled during the two months of the 'Six Evils' strike, of which 62 per cent were gambling-related offences.

[73] Mou, 1996: 248.

[74] Mou, 1996: 277. These figures give no indication of how the cases were handled.

[75] Held between 8 September and 7 October 1990.

[76] MPS, *Notice on Deepening the Struggle to Eliminate the 'Six Evils' Strictly According to Law and Implementing Policy*, 7 May 1990.

[77] Mou, 1996: 248–9. In Liaoning between May 1991 and February 1992 the CCPCC directed that a specialist struggle under the title of the Liu Bu Ju (六部局) (6 Ministries and Commissions;

1993 against prostitution were linked with campaigns against kidnapping and selling women and forcing women into prostitution.[78]

In 1996, elimination of prostitution was identified as a key task of the public security agencies,[79] and action against prostitution and gambling was included as part of the 'Hard Strike' conducted between April and July 1996.[80] The prostitution-related cases handled during that period accounted for 43 per cent of that year's total.[81]

In 2000, another nationwide action against prostitution, gambling and drug offences was launched after the General Office State Council on 30 June issued the *Notice Issuing the MPS etc. Departments' Opinion on Commencing a Specialist Action to Strengthen Management of Public Entertainment and Service Venues and to Conduct a Severe Strike against Evil Social Influences Including Prostitution and Using Prostitutes, Gambling and Drug Use and Trafficking*. This notice mandated that concerted action be taken against activities including prostitution between July and September 2000, which resulted in sanctions being imposed on 82,000 prostitutes.[82] This was followed in 2001 by a specialist action targeting entertainment and service venues, which coincided with the '2001 Hard Strike' against serious crime.[83] It continued the strike against prostitution and prostitution-related activities, requiring the police to prefer punishment by imposing administrative detention, or detention for education over imposition of a fine. It directed that the police:

comprising the ministries and commissions of public security, administration of industry and commerce, culture, tourism and industry and the procuratorate) be conducted under the leadership of the provincial government against targeted sites, such as hotels, dance halls and taxi stands. As a result of this specialist struggle, it was reported that 4,788 prostitutes and clients of prostitutes were seized.

78 SPP, *Notice on Fully Developing Procuratorial Capacity Resolutely to Strike against Kidnapping and Selling Women and Children and the Crime of Coercing, Luring and Keeping Female Prostitutes, Actively to Co-ordinate Investigation, Prohibition and Elimination of Prostitution and Using Prostitutes*, 11 January 1991 and see excerpts of speeches made at meetings throughout the country in 1993 on the work of striking against kidnapping and prostitution extracted in Shu, 1996b: 42–7 (Shu Huaide at that time was the Secretary-General of the Central Political-Legal Committee and Director of the General Office of the Central CMPO Committee); Law Yearbook Editorial Committee, 1994: 87.

79 Zhan, 2005: 446

80 Law Yearbook Editorial Committee, 1997: 200.

81 Law Yearbook Editorial Committee, 1997: 202.

82 Law Yearbook Editorial Committee, 2001: 213.

83 MPS, Ministry of Supervision, Ministry of Culture, Administration of Industry and Commerce, *Plan for a Specialist Action to Rectify and Regularise the Order of Singing and Dancing Entertainment and Service Venues*, 11 September 2001.

> in conducting this work, resolutely stop activities such as substituting fines for detention and substituting fines for imposing criminal sanctions and increase the imposition of administrative detention and detention for education on prostitutes and clients of prostitutes.[84]

Based on available statistics, the number of prostitutes given an administrative sanction has gradually increased from 201,000 in 1991,[85] to 240,000 in 1992,[86] to 362,057 in 1995,[87] to 418,000 in 1996,[88] reducing slightly to 399,000 in 1998.[89]

The number of detention for education centres has increased over time. In June 1992 there were 111 detention for education centres established nationwide, with a capacity of over 20,000 people.[90] By the end of 1995 the police reported establishment of 150 detention for education centres nationwide, with a population of 38,000 people.[91] At the end of 1996, the number of detention centres was 160, with a total capacity of over 40,000 and 31,000 new entries for that year.[92] In 1999 there were 183 detention for education centres.[93]

2.7 Regulation of detention for education

(i) Decision on Strictly Prohibiting Prostitution and Using Prostitutes *1991*

Prior to 1991, expansion of detention for education had been based on local regulations and encouraged by policy and administrative documents issued by the CCPCC and the State Council. There was growing doubt about the capacity of provincial-level governments and congresses legally to authorise detention powers such as this and an acknowledgement that there was a need to 'legalise' and 'systematise' the detention power as quickly as possible.[94] The process for drafting the legislation to legalise this detention power illustrates continuing concentration of control by enforcement organs over the legal definition of the powers they are responsible for enforcing.

[84] Gong'an Bu Fazhi Ju, 2001: point 3.5 at 632.
[85] Law Yearbook Editorial Committee, 1992: 44.
[86] Law Yearbook Editorial Committee, 1993: 119.
[87] Law Yearbook Editorial Committee, 1996: 167.
[88] Law Yearbook Editorial Committee, 1997: 202.
[89] Law Yearbook Editorial Committee, 1999: 157; these statistics do not specify precisely what punishment has been given.
[90] Zhan, 2005: 450–1.
[91] Law Yearbook Editorial Committee, 1996: 167.
[92] Law Yearbook Editorial Committee, 1997: 202.
[93] Zhan, 2005: 451. [94] Mou, 1996: 127; Ke, 1994: 48.

The January 1989 *Summary of the Minutes of the Conference on Research on Striking against and Eliminating Prostitution and Using Prostitutes* reveals that concern was expressed that with rising levels of legal consciousness, agencies would be 'asked for an explanation' about the basis upon which people were detained for education. The meeting recognised the urgent need to provide a legal basis to justify use of the power. The meeting designated the Legal Bureau of the State Council (as it then was) with the responsibility for liaising between the NPC Legislative Affairs Committee and the MPS in preparing draft legislation for submission to the NPCSC.[95]

After what the police described as 'extensive investigations', the MPS drafted the *Decision on Strictly Prohibiting Prostitution and Using Prostitutes* ('Prostitution Decision') which was sent to the State Council with a request that the draft be sent to the NPCSC for passage into law.[96] On 4 September 1991, the NPCSC issued the *Prostitution Decision* which has since been relied upon as the 'legal basis' for detention for education.

According to the police, the *Prostitution Decision* 'provided us with an important legal basis and weapon of struggle in our work to eliminate prostitution both now and in the future',[97] This view reflects the instrumental view of law as a tool or 'weapon' to underpin enforcement policy. Unlike the drafting of legislation that affects the structure of state powers more generally,[98] the process of drafting and passing this legislation did not involve broad consultation and debate. It represents the formalist use of legislation to put a cloak of legality on a power that continues in substance to be poorly defined by policy and administrative documents.

The *Prostitution Decision* consolidated and superseded the rules and regulations passed in the 1980s for suppression and control of prostitution, setting out actions that could be taken in respect of prostitution-related activity including under the *SAPR*, Article 30.[99] It also made

95 Chen, 1992: 143.

96 Luo, 1992: 35. This report can be considered authoritative as the author was the deputy head of the Legal Affairs Division of the MPS at the time of publication of the article.

97 Mou, 1996: 120.

98 Such as the *Legislation Law*, discussed in chapter 7 at 7.4, and the *ARL*, discussed in chapter 8 at 6.5.

99 *Prostitution Decision*, para. 4. *SAPR*, art. 30 permitted imposition of a warning, a fine of up to RMB 5,000 or up to fifteen days' administrative detention; detention for education of prostitutes for between six months and two years; and RETL and a fine of up to RMB 5,000 for those who re-offend.

amendments to the criminal sanctions that could be imposed in respect of prostitution-related offences, which were later incorporated into the amended *Criminal Law*.[100] It required that all prostitutes be tested for STDs and coercively treated.[101]

Paragraph 4.2 sets out the formal legal basis for the power of detention for education in the following terms:

> Those who prostitute or use prostitutes may be coercively gathered up by the public security organs in conjunction with other relevant departments to carry out legal and moral education and to engage in productive labour to give up this evil habit. The time limit [for detention] is between six months and two years. The State Council will pass specific measures [for implementation].

The MPS issued the *Notice on Conscientiously Implementing the NCPSC Decision on Strictly Prohibiting Prostitution and Using Prostitutes* on 23 November 1991 in order to 'fill the legislative gap' until further, more detailed implementing measures could be passed by the State Council.[102] The State Council passed the *Measures for Detention for Education of Prostitutes and Clients of Prostitutes* in 1993.[103] These three documents serve as the primary regulatory basis of detention for education.

The State Council *Measures for Detention for Education of Prostitutes and Clients of Prostitutes* largely adopted the contents of the 1991 MPS *Notice*[104] and authorised the MPS to interpret and implement the *Measures*.[105] The *Measures for Detention for Education of Prostitutes and Clients of Prostitutes* made the public security organs solely responsible for the determination to send a person to detention for education, as well as for management of the detention centres.[106]

(ii) Targets

The targets for detention are 'prostitutes' and 'clients of prostitutes', apart from those to be punished under the *SAPL* and those whose conduct does not warrant RETL. Some categories of people are excluded from detention by the State Council *Measures*, including a child under the age of fourteen, a person with a serious contagious disease apart

100 The SPP issued the *Notice on Strictly Implementing the NPCSC 'Decision on Strictly Prohibiting Prostitution and Using Prostitutes'* and '*Decision on Strictly Punishing those Criminal Elements who Kidnap and Sell Women and Children*', 17 September 1991, affirming that provisions in the *Prostitution Decision* superseded any prior inconsistent law or interpretation.

101 *Prostitution Decision*, para. 4.

102 Article 4.

103 Passed to take effect on 4 September 1993.

104 Mou, 1996: 132.

105 Article 22.

106 Articles 3, 7 and 8.

from an STD, a person who is pregnant or nursing an infant under one year old and a person who has been coerced or tricked into prostitution.[107] Although the traditional premise was that prostitution was a female occupation,[108] the wording of the NPCSC *Prostitution Decision* does not use gender-specific language.[109] The indeterminacy of targets for detention relates both to the definition of prostitution and using prostitutes and to the circumstances in which this conduct will warrant imposition of detention for education rather than another sanction.

The conduct that constitutes prostitution or using a prostitute is not defined in either the NPCSC *Prostitution Decision* or the 1993 *Measures for Detention for Education of Prostitutes and Clients of Prostitutes*. In light of this lack of definition, some areas passed local regulations which set out a definition of prostitution. Such regulations include the *Decision of Guizhou Province on Prohibition of Prostitution and Using Prostitutes*, the *Regulations of Dalian Municipality for the Punishment of Prostitution and Related Activities* and the *Provisions of Hunan Province on Prohibition of Prostitution and using Prostitutes*, which defined prostitution as a woman having sex unlawfully with a man with the object of obtaining property (money and or goods).[110]

In a response to a request for instructions, in 1995 the MPS defined prostitution as referring to 'an inappropriate sexual relationship between non specified women and men with money or property as the intermediary'.[111] In 2001 this document was rescinded by the MPS *Response to a Request for Instructions on the Question of How to Determine the Nature of and Deal with Sexual Acts between People of the Same Sex with Money and Property as the Intermediary*. This document expanded the definition of prostitution to include 'inappropriate sexual acts between non specified people of different or the same sex with money or property as the intermediary, including oral sex or masturbation'. Such a document does not constitute a ministerial rule and so at best has indeterminate legal effectiveness.

An explanation of the NPCSC *Prostitution Decision* also suggests that prostitution was intended to be understood as sex acts with 'non specified person/s'.[112] When read together with the 2001 MPS document,

[107] State Council, *Measures on Detention for Education of Prostitutes and Clients of Prostitutes*, 1993, art. 7.

[108] Mou, 1996: 139.

[109] *Prostitution Decision*, para. 1 changed the wording of the criminal offence of organising, permitting encouraging 'women' to prostitute to 'other people' (*taren* 他人).

[110] Wang, 2003b, accessed 17 July 2006.

[111] In Zhu, 2001: 92.

[112] Ke and Wei, 1992: 36.

these explanations suggest that sex acts with specified persons, such as those that take place in the case of a second wife or mistress, do not fall within the definition of prostitution. Such a reading runs counter to popularly held views that this type of conduct constitutes one category of prostitution.[113] Interpretations of the conduct that will constitute prostitution vary, with some police taking a very broad view, discussed above, that morally undesirable acts involving sex and the exchange of money or gifts in circumstances such as one-night stands or extra-marital affairs may be interpreted as prostitution.[114]

However, a study guide for police officers published in 2002 explains and gives a relatively restrictive interpretation of the definition of prostitution. It asserts that for a sexual act to constitute prostitution a number of criteria must be satisfied. First, the act must be voluntary, that is the prostitute must have the capacity to make decisions, understand that the conduct can be for profit and act in pursuit of that profit. For example, where a person is coerced, the matter should be dealt with as an offence of coercing a person to prostitute.[115] Next, the act must involve the sex organs of one of the parties, so would include vaginal sex, anal sex, oral sex, masturbation. Finally, the sexual act must also involve and be motivated by an expectation of profit in the form of money or goods that represent money's worth. Xie asserts that sex acts motivated by affection or a desire to obtain benefits such as employment, a promotion or a transfer should not be considered to be 'for profit' in the relevant sense and so do not constitute prostitution.[116]

As there is a range of possible punishments that may be given to prostitutes, there is a recognition that interpretations of what acts warrant detention for education, as opposed to the imposition of other sanctions, may also vary.[117] Although the law does not require it, some police consider that targets for detention are prostitutes and clients with STDs, or those who have prostituted or used prostitutes repeatedly, but

[113] See discussions which assume that such conduct constitutes prostitution in Jeffreys, 2004: 168–71 and Zhang, Dunli, 2000.

[114] Mou, 1996: 138, 140–1, citing cases of some police who consider that if the sexual relationship is outside marriage and goods are transferred, then that will be sufficient to constitute prostitution. An example was given where a couple were having an extra-marital affair. On a particular evening, the man had bought clothing as a present for the woman and had taken the woman out for dinner and dancing. Later, they were caught having sex. The woman was sent to detention for investigation as a prostitute as she was adjudged to have had extra-marital sex for material profit. Ji, 1995: 27, criticising this confusion between unlawful acts which should be dealt with and immoral acts, such as living together or sex outside marriage, which are not unlawful, only immoral.

[115] Xie, 2002: 50–1. [116] Xie, 2002: 50–1. [117] Xie, 2000: 108.

it is difficult to prove, or where the circumstances are severe, but not sufficiently severe to warrant imposition of RETL.[118]

(iii) Time limits

The 1991 NCPSC *Prostitution Decision* provides that the time limit for detention is between six months and two years.[119] However, within these outer limits, there are few guidelines about the appropriate period of detention to be imposed in particular cases. Neither the 1991 NPCSC *Prostitution Decision* nor the 1993 State Council *Measures* set out principles to determine the length of detention to be imposed in particular cases. One commentator asserts that the amount of time actually given often depends upon the attitude of the officer handling the case, and is not based on any legal standard.[120] Another commentator proposes that the time should be determined according to what is appropriate and necessary for education and reform,[121] suggesting that the length of detention may not necessarily be determined by the degree of severity of the offending conduct but by the attitude of the detainee. The State Council *Measures* provide for a reduction in the period of detention for good behaviour and either a fine or an extension where the person refuses to submit to education or camp discipline, though the maximum period of detention may not exceed two years.[122]

The MPS allows a deduction from the time to be spent in detention for education where the person has been detained for the same conduct in other forms of detention such as administrative detention and detention for investigation when it was still extant,[123] or in criminal detention.[124] This accommodation indicates the degree of interchangeability of this form of detention with other detention powers controlled by the police.

[118] Mou, 1996: 197.
[119] *Prostitution Decision*, para. 4; *Measures on Detention for Education of Prostitutes and Clients of Prostitutes*, art. 9.
[120] Zhan, 2005: 462. [121] Mou, 1996: 197. [122] Articles 17 and 18.
[123] MPS, *Notice on Diligently Implementing the NPCSC 'Decision on Prohibiting Prostitution and Using Prostitutes'*, para. 5(3).
[124] If the administrative detention was determined to be a separate punishment, then the time spent in detention for education could not be deducted. This interpretation is based on an interpretation of State Council, *Measures for Detention for Education of Prostitutes and Clients of Prostitutes*, 1993, art. 7; MPS, *Response to a Request for Instructions on whether it is appropriate to deduct the amount of time spent in criminal detention or public order detention from the time spent in detention for education*, 11 December 1997.

(iv) Procedures

Detention for education is to be approved by the police at county level and above.[125] The 1991 MPS *Notice*[126] specifies that procedures for detention are to be carried out by analogy to *SAPR*, Article 34(2). The *SAPR* required that the police first interview the person and make a written transcript of the interview, which the person must sign as correct before a ruling is given. The person being interviewed is required to co-operate in gathering evidence upon which the determination is based. The MPS in its 1991 *Notice* at Article 5 permits administrative detention (*xingzheng juliu* 行政拘留) of a person pending a determination about sending them to detention for education. However, in some situations people are held at the lock-up for longer than fifteen days and transferred to the detention for education centre when they have only a short period of their term in detention for education remaining.[127]

These rather scanty procedural requirements were superseded by passage by the MPS of the *Regulations on the Procedures for Handling Administrative Cases by Public Security Organs* which became effective from 1 January 2004.[128] These regulations adopt the mandatory procedural requirements set out in the *Administrative Punishments Law* (*APL*) 1996,[129] though the hearing procedure remains unavailable in respect of detention.[130]

The regulations require that the unlawful act be investigated by no less than two officers who have shown their official identification.[131] A suspect may be served with a written summons to appear at the police station, or be given a verbal or coercive summons if caught on the spot.[132] A permanent written record of the interview must be made and signed as correct by the person being interviewed, who may supplement or amend it[133] or write their own statement of evidence.[134] The interview ordinarily may not exceed twelve hours but may be extended to up to twenty-four hours.[135] The police may also examine the scene for

125 State Council, *Measures on Detention for Education of Prostitutes and Clients of Prostitutes*, art. 8.
126 Article 5. 127 Zhan, 2005: 462.
128 Article 2 provides that the regulations apply to detention for education.
129 Discussed in chapter 7 at section 8.
130 Article 89 permits a person to request a hearing prior to imposition of an administrative punishment of an order to stop production or operation, to revoke a licence or for imposition of a comparatively large fine. *SAPL*, art. 98 provides that a hearing is available for punishments imposed under that law of revocation of licence or imposition of a fine of over RMB 2,000.
131 Article 37.
132 Articles 45, 46. Police also have power to take a person to the police station for questioning for up to twenty-four hours under the *People's Police Law*, 1995, art. 9 (*liuzhi panwen* 留置盘问).
133 Articles 47, 54. 134 Article 55. 135 Article 48.

evidence[136] and seize evidence if necessary to preserve it.[137] Physical searches of persons are to be carried out by two officers of the same sex as the suspect, with examination for STDs to be conducted by a doctor.[138] Prostitutes and clients of prostitutes are subjected to mandatory testing for STDs and HIV/AIDS.[139]

Written decisions to impose a sanction must set out the evidence, reasons for the decision and legal basis for the decision, inform the person of their right to appeal against the decision[140] and give them an opportunity to respond without incurring a more serious penalty.[141]

The *SAPL* now largely adopts the procedural requirements set out in the *APL* and reflected in the *Regulations on the Procedures for Handling Administrative Cases by Public Security Organs*. These legal changes reflect the growing official acceptance that the exercise of police powers to impose administrative punishments and detention must be subject to uniform procedural requirements.[142]

Whilst the law now provides certain procedural safeguards to people who might be subject to detention, practice remains some distance from that. Obtaining evidence is one example. In order to determine that prostitution has occurred, the police are required to obtain material evidence. A suspicion not supported by evidence is insufficient.[143] However, there have been a number of well-documented cases which illustrate the preference of the police to take a person into custody first and then obtain evidence by way of confession, and the severe miscarriages of justice that can result. In one, a nineteen-year-old girl, Ma Dandan, from Ma Family Village, Jingyang County, Shanxi Province was learning hairdressing in her older sister's hairdressing shop. On the evening of 8 January 2001, she was watching television in the hairdressing shop when local police burst in and took her in a police car to the police station. They interrogated her for the whole evening, demanding that she confess to being a prostitute, but she continually refused to do so. They then abused and beat her and handcuffed her underneath the police station's basketball stands. The next day they presented her with a written decision that she was to be subject to fifteen days' administrative detention for being a prostitute. She applied for review of the decision and upon undergoing a medical examination it was determined

[136] Articles 63–4. [137] Article 85. [138] Article 66.
[139] Ministry of Health, MPS, *Notice on Several Questions on Carrying out Coercive Testing and Treatment for STDs of Prostitutes and Clients of Prostitutes*, 16 December 1991.
[140] Article 133. [141] Article 134. [142] Feng, 2005: 283–4. [143] Xie, 2002: 51.

that she was a virgin. The decision to impose fifteen days' administrative detention was rescinded.[144]

2.8 Legal elasticity: the effect of concerted actions on definition and uses of *detention for education*

The recent history of detention for education illustrates the use of law to attempt to legitimate a power that during the 1980s had no proper legal basis and would now be seen as illegal. Legislation was passed by the NPCSC responding to the concern that the power had developed outside the legal framework, originally in local areas with the approval of local authorities and, later, nationwide with the joint approval of the CCPCC and the State Council. However, this legislation is expressed in the broadest possible terms. It does not truly regularise the exercise of the power but allows the police to retain a broad discretion when dealing with prostitution.

The development of the power has been intertwined with 'Hard Strikes' and other concerted actions to suppress prostitution and related activities since the 1980s. The increasing numbers of prostitutes sanctioned each year and the expansion of detention centres attest to the lack of success of these actions in dealing with the problem.

Police have been particularly ambivalent toward actions against prostitution and there are complaints that many pretend to crack down on prostitution, but in fact do very little.[145] The legal enforcement of strikes against prostitution is often severely compromised due to local corruption and police involvement in prostitution.[146]

One police officer has attributed the lack of force in striking against prostitution as one of the reasons for the continual increase in prostitution and related activities.[147] A notice issued by the MPS on 7 March 1992 urged that greater efforts be made:

> We must, moreover we certainly have the capacity to, eradicate these socially repugnant phenomena at the same time as reform and opening up. All negative thoughts and attitudes, poor resolve and lack of

[144] Wang, 2003a: 78. [145] Mou, 1996: 135.

[146] Official involvement in and profiting from prostitution was acknowledged and prohibited in Central Discipline Inspection Committee, *Temporary Regulations on Party Disciplinary Sanctions in Respect of those Party Officials and Other Responsible People who Participate in Prostitution and Prostitution Related Activities*, 28 May 1988. Liu, 16 May 2000, citing findings of an NPC investigation that found some public security personnel provide a 'protective umbrella' for prostitution in entertainment businesses.

[147] Ji, 1995: 25.

> confidence about cleaning up these repugnant social phenomena must be rapidly transformed and replaced by a resolute, positive attitude and measures taken to strengthen, persist and not to slacken off [efforts] . . .[148]

The environment in which this power has been revived differs significantly from its 1950s antecedent. First, the extensive system of local community monitoring and the capacity of the state to resettle a prostitute to another part of the country after release has been substantially eroded.

More importantly, the range of measures used to deal with prostitution in the reform era includes imposition of a fine. The broad discretion exercised by the police to punish prostitutes and their clients has enabled police to impose their preferred penalty, the fine. The MPS repeatedly warns local police against substituting fines for either administrative forms of detention or for pursuing a criminal sanction.[149] During periods of concerted action, the police are required to impose detention in preference to a fine. However, despite repeated exhortations to detain instead of fine, the police continue to issue fines rather than detain prostitutes and their clients.[150]

For example, of the 12,764 people seized during a 1993 campaign against prostitution in Liaoning province, the police reported that 260 or 2 per cent were sent to RETL; 1,095 or 8.5 per cent were sent to detention for education; and 11,117 or 87 per cent were given an administrative punishment which included 9,117 fines (71.4 per cent).[151] Figures from Shanghai indicate a similar pattern. In the eleven-year period 1983–93, the police reported seizing 42,966 prostitutes and clients of prostitutes. Of those, 650 or 1.5 per cent were given criminal sentences (five death sentences); 1,210 or 2.8 per cent were sent to RETL; 5,730 or 13.3 per cent were sent to detention for education; 1,230 or 2.8 per cent placed in detention for investigation; and 11,600

148 MPS, *Notice on Further Eradicating Repulsive Social Phenomenon such as Drug Trafficking and Prostitution*, 7 March 1992: at 78.

149 MPS, *Notice on Deepening the Struggle to Eliminate the 'Six Evils' strictly according to law and implementing policy*, 7 May 1990; MPS, *Notice on Conscientiously Implementing the NPCSC Decision on Strictly Prohibiting Prostitution and Using Prostitutes*, art. 3; MPS, Ministry of Supervision, Ministry of Culture, Administration of Industry and Commerce, *Plan for a Specialist Action to Rectify and Regularise the Order of Singing and Dancing Entertainment and Service Venues*, 11 September 2001.

150 MPS, *Notice on Strengthening the Investigation and Handling of Public Security Cases*, 14 February 1997.

151 Mou, 1996: 258, which is 82 per cent of the punishments imposed. Twenty-eight were referred for criminal investigation.

or 27 per cent given an administrative punishment.[152] In an unspecified city in Hunan in the one-year period between January 2001 and January 2002, of the 1,247 people dealt with for prostituting or using prostitutes, 1094 or 87.7 per cent were given a fine; 138 or 11 per cent were given administrative detention; 14 or 1.1 per cent were sent to detention for education, with only one person sent to RETL.[153] Police report that ten times more prostitutes are caught and punished than their clients who, in general, are fined.[154]

In addition to a preference for imposing fines, the discretion to fine has led to corrupt and abusive practices, including imposing fines in excess of the legally specified limit of RMB 5,000; imposing fines that are unfair and out of proportion to the degree of seriousness of the conduct; and unlawfully imposing on-the-spot fines, confiscating property and demanding payment of a fine for its release.[155] A person paying a fine is often able to avoid having their work unit notified.[156] In the latest attempts to curb the imposition of fines, the *Regulations on the Procedures for Handling Administrative Cases by Public Security Organs* expressly prohibit imposing an on-the-spot fine on prostitutes, clients of prostitutes and those introducing or inducing a person to prostitute.[157] Under these regulations, a person who is to be subject to a fine of greater than RMB 2,000 is able to request a hearing prior to imposition of the fine, even though a hearing is not available in respect of detention.[158]

The central role played by the fine in law enforcement is guaranteed by continuing institutional dependence upon fines to fund the local police. The revenue raised from fining prostitutes became institutionalised to the point where police were allocated quotas[159] and revenue from fines used to supplement what was otherwise an inadequate budget allocation to cover the operational costs of the local police.[160] The MPS regularly prohibits this type of activity. Its recent decision to impose

152 Mou, 1996: 264; Ji, 1995: 25, asserts that more clients are fined than prostitutes, but gives no figures in support of this assertion.

153 Zheng, 2003: 95.

154 Mou, 1996: 258 and at 196–7, reporting that in 1993, in the population of the 145 detention centres nationwide, 93 per cent comprised female prostitutes. Of the 56,351 prostitutes detained in 1993, 13,657 or 24 per cent were placed in detention for education. Of the 131,345 clients seized in 1993, 13,454 or 10 per cent were placed in detention for education.

155 Ji, 1995: 25–6. 156 Ji, 1995: 27. 157 Article 32(2).

158 Article 89; and *SAPL*, art. 98.

159 Mou, 1996: 128; Tanner, Harold, 1999: 116–17.

160 MPS, *Notice on Conscientiously Strengthening the Management of Income of Public Security Organs from Collection of Fees and Fines*, 3 January 1999, required removal from the budget of any item specifying that a proportion of fines collected be paid to the police.

individual responsibility on those in leadership positions in the areas of worst abuse is indicative of its ongoing failure to resolve the problem.[161]

Another factor limiting the number of prostitutes detained for education is the limited capacity of detention facilities. The MPS has repeatedly called for the county-level public security organs to recommend plans for construction of detention for education centres to the local government[162] and to increase the number of detention centres. In 1992 the MPS issued an instruction in which it required further construction of detention for education centres so that the capacity would be able to hold at least 25 per cent of prostitutes caught annually.[163]

Reports from Shanghai indicate that capacity is much lower than this level[164] and from Liaoning indicate that the capacity of detention facilities was about 10 per cent of the people who were eligible to be sent.[165] Although more recent figures are not available, the issue of undercapacity of detention facilities did not appear to be resolved at least by 1996.[166]

Whilst the rhetoric of 'educate, rescue and reform' remains the ostensible purpose for detaining prostitutes,[167] in the reform era this has been overlaid with the punitive aspects of strikes against prostitution being carried on in association with 'Hard Strikes' against serious crime. Although the overall rate of enforcement increases during a period of concerted action, the factors that place limits upon the number of prostitutes detained for education are not ideological, but financial, such as revenue raising by the police and the limited capacity of detention centres. The ideal of the second line of defence as a strategy to turn the wayward from a path leading to crime is undermined by practice, including the preference for imposing fines on prostitutes and their clients, a form of punishment which is not primarily focussed on rehabilitation.

161 Mou, 1996: 258. MPS, *Notice on Strengthening the Investigation and Handling of Public Security Cases*, 14 February 1997, art. 2 provides: 'Earnestly correct the incorrect practice of substituting fines for administrative detention and substituting fines for detention for education. No level public security organ is permitted to allocate a quota for collecting fines to the local level police in any form or in any name. Implementation of those quotas already issued must be stopped immediately.'

162 Article 4.

163 MPS, *Notice on Further Eradicating Repulsive Social Phenomenon such as Drug Trafficking and Prostitution*, 7 March 1992: at 79.

164 Mou, 1996: 273–4.

165 Mou, 1996: 259.

166 The MPS, *Notice on Several Questions of Implementing 'Measures on Coercive Drug Rehabilitation'*, issued on 30 May 1996, also called for speeding up of the construction of coercive drug rehabilitation facilities.

167 Hao and Li, 1998: 22.

3 DRUG ADDICTION

3.1 Re-emergence of drug addiction and measures used to address the problem

In the late 1970s the problem of drug trafficking and addiction re-emerged as a major problem in China. Officials assert that international drug trafficking problems arose first in the south-western part of China near the 'Golden Triangle', with drugs being transported through China. In the 1980s and 1990s, in addition to international trafficking the domestic market for drugs revived to the point that by the end of the 1990s commentators assert that the domestic Chinese market became the primary target of traffickers.[168]

Drug use and addiction themselves continued to be viewed as unlawful behaviour, but not as criminal offences. Official perceptions are that the levels of harm caused by drug use are extremely high, not merely because of harm to the individual, but also because of its enormous social impact. They link drug use with the spread of HIV/AIDS, STDs and infectious diseases such as hepatitis, with civil unrest in China's border regions, with drug-related crime and the spread of organised and violent crime. Official accounts of contemporary problems of drug use show a continuing sensitivity to China's historical experience of widespread drug addiction and its link to perceived national weakness.[169]

Since the beginning of the 1980s, preventing drug use and drug-related crimes has been a focus of the CMPO.[170] Concern at the worsening of drug addiction led to reinvigoration of the strategies of registration of drug users and of detention in specialist centres for treatment for drug addiction.[171] The extent of drug addiction and drug-related offences nationwide had become so great that in November 1990 the State Council established a National Drug Prohibition Committee to co-ordinate the work of drug prohibition.[172] The MPS received permission from the State Council in 1998 to establish a specialist

[168] Chen and Li, 2005: 378. [169] Song *et al.*, 2000a: 161. [170] Zhao and Yu, 2000: 128.

[171] Guo and Li, 2000: 3–6, listing targeted drugs in the following categories: narcotic drugs including opium, morphine and heroin; cocaine including snow, coke, crack and cannabis; psychoactive drugs including benzodiazepines, barbiturates; and others including ecstasy, LSD, MDMA and PCP. Chu, 1996: 13, listing targeted drugs under the following headings: opium, morphine, codein, pholcodein, cocaine, cannabis. Su, 1998: 26, asserting that heroin is the predominantly used drug, accounting for over 87 per cent of drug addicts in RETL.

[172] Zhao and Yu, 2000: 129. Chen and Li, 2005: 370–1, report that from 2004, the Drug Prohibition Committee comprises representatives of thirty-two agencies.

anti-drugs department which operates as the administrative body of the National Drug Prohibition Committee.[173] The national drugs strategy is to 'Carry out the Three Prohibits at the Same Time' (*sanjin bingju* 三禁并举), of production, trafficking and use. A proposal was made to shift the emphasis to the prohibition of drug use as the priority strategy at the second national drugs prevention work meeting in March 1997. Despite recognition that prohibition of drug use is central to China's anti-drugs strategy, many remain of the view that attacking trafficking remains the core of state drugs prevention work.[174]

State enforcement agencies have focussed their attacks on the supply side, launching a series of strikes against the criminal offences of manufacture, trafficking and sale of drugs, and have undertaken targeted actions in designated problem areas. Their aim is to invoke the 'spirit of the hard strike into everyday work'.

The other focus has been on attacking the demand for drugs, by reducing the number of drug users, curing addicts and containing the number who become addicted again. Important components of the latter strategy have been anti-drugs education and propaganda, registration of drug users, coercive drug rehabilitation and social help and rescue (*bangjiao* 帮教).[175] Drug use has also been targeted together with strikes against drug-related crime under a mixture of hard strike measures, including national-level campaigns, such as the '1983 Hard Strike', the 'Yellow Evils' and the 'Six Evils' actions in 1989[176] and a range of local[177] and national-level specialised struggles (*zhuanxiang douzheng* 专项斗争).[178] However, despite these efforts, the rate of drug use in China continues to climb.

The law provides for a range of sanctions for drug-related activities, from administrative punishments under the *SAPL* to criminal penalties imposed under the *Criminal Law*. In 1986 the *SAPR* was amended to provide for the imposition of fines and administrative detention for up to fifteen days on users of drugs, including opium and morphine.[179] The *SAPL* also provides for fines and detention for a range of drug-related activities, including cultivating, manufacturing or trafficking small quantities of drugs, being in possession of a small amount of specified drugs, providing drugs to others, tricking hospital staff to obtain

[173] Chen and Li, 2005: 371. [174] Cui, 1999: 469.
[175] Song *et al.*, 2000a: 161–2. [176] Liu and Yuan, 1997: 36.
[177] Liu and Yuan, 1997: 36. In Yunnan targeted strikes have been carried out frequently.
[178] Liu and Yuan, 1997: 36–7. [179] Article 24(3).

narcotic or stimulant drugs and encouraging or tricking others into using drugs.[180]

The work of coercive drug rehabilitation takes four forms. The first is coercive drug rehabilitation in a detention centre operated by the public security organs. The second is coercive drug rehabilitation in an RETL camp.[181] The third is voluntary drug rehabilitation carried out by the health department in clinics under the supervision of public security organs. The fourth is being directed to give up drugs within a limited period at home under the supervision of the public security agencies.[182] This latter type of rehabilitation is imposed on people who are not able to be taken into coercive drug rehabilitation because they have an acute infectious disease or serious illness, are pregnant or nursing a child under one year old or are too young for admission to coercive drug rehabilitation, or who live in an area where there is no coercive drug rehabilitation centre.[183] Coercive drug rehabilitation has been linked closely with registration of drug users and with social help and rescue of those after release from drug detention, both of which were discussed in chapter 4.

(i) Registration as part of the focal population

In a measure reminiscent of the 1950s, from the early 1980s, an important means for identifying habitual drug users has been to require them to register with the local government and give up drug use within a 'limited time'.[184] The MPS has continued to emphasise the importance of the work of registration at the local police station of drug users as part of the focal population. In the context of registration of drug users, the MPS has defined 'drug use' (or smoking drugs, *xi du* 吸毒) to include:

> smoking, eating or injecting opium, heroin, phenolpropylamine type stimulants, morphine, cocaine, marijuana and abuse for non-medicinal purposes of other addictive narcotic or stimulant drugs which are controlled by state regulation.[185]

180 *SAPL* arts. 71–4.

181 In those areas where coercive drug rehabilitation centres have not been established, a person may be sent to RETL if they have either been registered with the local government or the police and been required to give up drug use within a specified time limit, or there had been concentrated management to give up (*jizhong banban*) drug use: MPS, *Response to a Request for Instructions on Sending Drug Users to RETL*, 27 March 1992.

182 Chen and Li, 2005: 373–4.

183 Cui, 1999: 473.

184 CCPCC and State Council, *Urgent Directive on the Problems of Complete Prohibition of Opium*, 16 July 1982; Guo and Li, 2000: 317; Ke, 1990: 25.

185 MPS, *Notice on Strengthening the Work of Registration of Drug Users*, 23 May 2000.

TABLE 5.1 Number of registered drug users

Year	Number of registered drug users
1991	148,000
1994	370,000
1995	540,000
1998	681,000[1]
2000	860,000[2]
2001	901,000[3]

[1]Xiao, 2000: 174.
[2]Law Yearbook Editorial Committee, 2001: 217. In 1999, 85,000 and in 2000, 106,000 were newly registered.
[3]Law Yearbook Editorial Committee, 2002: 219.

The work of registration involves both voluntary registration and active investigation by the local police to discover the 'real situation' about drug use in the community. To achieve this purpose, the police have been directed to use a combination of measures including specially organised and ongoing routine investigations, the latter requiring close liaison with the local resident or village committee. The register of 'current drug users' includes those who have given up drugs for less than three years, those who have been released from coercive drug rehabilitation or have undertaken to give up themselves and people sentenced for drug addiction to less than three years' RETL, or prison.[186]

As discussed in chapter 4, the MPS itself has identified a number of serious shortcomings in the accuracy of the register, and with accuracy of the information reported by the local police to higher-level authorities, with problems of omission, inaccuracy, irregularities and duplication.[187] Despite these shortcomings, the register demonstrates the continuing increase in the numbers of drug users in the 1990s.

(ii) Social help and rescue and the creation of drug-free communities

The system of social help and rescue has an emphasis on the monitoring and assistance of people who have been released from a form of drug rehabilitation. Social help and rescue requires close liaison between the local police, drug rehabilitation centres, the street or village committee, work units and the family of the person in an effort to consolidate drug

[186] MPS, *Notice on Strengthening the Work of Registration of Drug Users*, 23 May 2000.
[187] MPS, *Notice on Strengthening the Work of Registration of Drug Users*, 23 May 2000.

rehabilitation after release from coercive drug rehabilitation and to reduce the rate of repeated addiction. An extension of social help and rescue has been in the creation of 'drug-free communities' (*wudu shequ* 无毒社区). It is a way of seeking to ensure that the structure of social help and rescue extends to cover all registered drug users.

The first drug-free community was established in Baotou, Inner Mongolia, in 1994, with the establishment of social help and rescue 'small groups' whose focus was the mobilisation of local members of the community, the organisation of the work of drug prevention and the ongoing rehabilitation in the community of people released from coercive drug rehabilitation. It was originally organised in a small district, such as a street committee, and expanded eventually to involve 2,169 such organisations in the city. In 1999 the National Drugs Prohibition Committee decided to expand the drug-free communities programme nationwide.[188] The primary focus of these small groups is to supervise and assist people who have been released from coercive drug rehabilitation by paying visits to their home at both fixed and random times, to have periodic chats and to assist in resolving difficulties.[189]

It has been extremely difficult to succeed in preventing addiction again after release from coercive drug rehabilitation. Even if help and rescue was a very effective strategy to prevent re-addiction, the current weakness of local communities discussed in chapter 4 acts as a limiting factor on the implementation of the strategy. In one example, of the 5,300 people recently detained at the Wuhua drug detention centre in Kunming Municipality, 68.2 per cent had been through coercive drug rehabilitation twice, and 18.2 per cent had been coercively rehabilitated more than three times, with some being rehabilitated more than five times.[190] The law requires that those who reoffend be sent to RETL, but many will become addicted again after release from RETL. Repeated drug addiction and coercive drug rehabilitation can thus become a vicious cycle, where the goal of long-term cure from drug addiction is not achieved.[191]

3.2 Reinvigoration of coercive drug rehabilitation

The revival of coercive drug rehabilitation centres was mandated in the *Notice Restating the Strict Prohibition of Opium and Drug Taking* issued by the State Council in August 1981. This notice directed co-ordinated

188 Chen and Li, 2005: 374–5. 189 Cui, 1999: 475.
190 The precise dates are not set out: Zhang, 2004: 436. 191 Zhang, 2004: 437.

efforts to be made by the public security organs, civil affairs departments and health departments to strike against drug use, including the establishment of centres for coercive drug rehabilitation. In relation to coercive drug rehabilitation, it provided: 'For users of opium and other drugs, the public security, civil administration and health, etc. departments should organise coercive drug rehabilitation.'[192] As a result, temporary drug rehabilitation organs were established in some localities. However, problems with management of local responses to this notice led to the CCPCC and the State Council jointly issuing the *Urgent Directive on the Problems of Complete Prohibition of Opium*[193] on 16 July 1982. This *Directive* required strengthening of education of drug users, and an instruction that drug users register with the local government and give up drug use within a 'limited time'. Those who refused to register or who registered and did not give up drug use were to be 'coercively taken in to give up [drug abuse] and given necessary punishment'.[194] In 1984, the scope of targets for coercive drug rehabilitation was expanded from those addicted to opium and related drugs to include those who had acquired a serious dependence on stimulant drugs.[195]

Local provisions were also passed in the early 1980s. The Guangdong Provincial Government, for example, passed temporary regulations in 1981 under which drug users could be given administrative detention, or in more serious cases be sent to RETL.[196] In the 1980s, drug rehabilitation centres were constructed and run by public security organs and a range of other organisations, including the civil affairs departments; health departments; enterprises;[197] and some street committees.[198]

In Yunnan, where the problem was considered particularly acute, a special programme to combat drugs was established in 1982 under the leadership of a local Drug Prohibition Committee, comprising representatives of agencies including the government and the public security.[199] These committees introduced a range of local measures to target drug users, with inclusion of habitual drug users as part of the focal population register at the local police station.[200] They could then be targeted

[192] Article 2; Guo and Li, 2000: 316. [193] Guo and Li, 2000: 317; Ke, 1990: 25.
[194] Article 3. [195] Chen and Li, 2005: 388.
[196] *Temporary Regulations on Prohibition of Traffic in and Use of Drugs*, 7 August 1981.
[197] Ke, 1990: 24. [198] Xie, 2000: 116.
[199] After the document issued jointly by the CCPCC and the State Council in 1982, a specialist anti-drugs force was established in Yunnan comprising 1,300 people. Chu, 1996: 63; Liu and Yuan, 1997: 35.
[200] Liu and Yuan, 1997: 40; also MPS, *Notice on Several Questions on Implementing the 'Measures on Coercive Drug Rehabilitation'*, 30 May 1996.

for a range of measures to cure addiction, including giving up drugs under the supervision of the masses; in local community organisations; in state-run detention centres (coercive drug rehabilitation); and in RETL.[201]

During the strike against the 'Six Evils' in 1989 the MPS focussed on ensuring comprehensive enforcement against all drug offenders. In particular, the MPS sought to change the balance from the imposition of fines to the use of more coercive forms of detention. It demanded that the police properly impose punishments such as administrative detention, RETL or arrest for criminal prosecution and not impose fines as a substitute. The MPS directed that drug users who had become addicted be taken in for coercive drug rehabilitation and tested for STDs.[202]

Coercive drug rehabilitation was locally regulated at this time. For example, in 1989 the Standing Committee of the Yunnan People's Congress passed the *Yunnan Provincial Administrative Punishment Provisions for Prohibiting Drugs*. These provisions specified a range of punishments for drug-related offences ranging from detention under the *SAPR*, RETL where the situation was 'serious', and criminal responsibility where the act was 'sufficient to constitute a crime'.[203] These provisions permitted drug users to be detained 'for a short time' in the police station to give up drugs and, if they failed to do so within that time, they would be confined in a coercive drug rehabilitation centre for between three months and one year. According to these provisions, those who continued to use drugs after coercive rehabilitation could be sent to RETL.[204] Provisions to similar effect were passed in other areas.[205]

During the strike against the 'Six Evils', Yunnan province focussed its enforcement efforts on drug offences, strengthening investigation into drug trafficking and admonishing addicts to give up. A mass meeting was held in Kunming on 26 June 1989 with 10,000 people in attendance. As part of the strike, fourteen serious offenders were sentenced to death. Similar mass meetings were held on 8 December in Guangzhou with 5,000 people in attendance.[206]

201 Liu and Yuan, 1997: 40.

202 MPS, *Notice on Deepening the Struggle to Eliminate the 'Six Evils' Strictly According to Law and Implementing Policy*, 7 May 1990: at 236.

203 Article 6. 204 Article 11.

205 Renmin Fayuan Chubanshe, 1992: 480–98, including the Shaan Xi Provincial People's Congress Standing Committee in 1989, the Lanzhou Municipal People's Government in 1989 and the Gansu Provincial People's Congress Standing Committee in 1990.

206 Law Yearbook Editorial Committee, 1991: 33.

TABLE 5.2 Detention of drug addicts in coercive drug rehabilitation and RETL

Year[1]		1993[2]	1994[3]	1996	1997[4]	1998[5]	1999[6]	2000[7]	2003[8]	2004[9]
Public Security	Camps	200+	251	500+	695	632	746		554	
	People	50,000	50,000	60,000	180,000	140,000	220,000 (224,000)	243,000		270,000
RETL	Camps	64	75	65	86		168			
	People	15,000	30,000	18,000	90,000	25,000	120,000 (112,000)	120,000 (new admissions 60,000)		68,000 admissions

[1]Guo, 2000: table at 318.
[2]Law Yearbook Editorial Committee, 1994: 137.
[3]Law Yearbook Editorial Committee, 1995: 129, citing the existence of 251 long-term coercive drug rehabilitation centres and 153 temporary centres.
[4]Law Yearbook Editorial Committee, 1998: 167, stating that the 695 drug rehabilitation centres have a bed capacity of 77,000 and that the RETL drug rehabilitation centres have a bed capacity of 90,000.
[5]Law Yearbook Editorial Committee, 1999: 159.
[6]Law Yearbook Editorial Committee, 2000: 184. The *White Paper on Narcotics Control*, 26 June 2000, gives numbers of detention centres and in brackets, slightly different numbers of inmates.
[7]Law Yearbook Editorial Committee, 2001: 216.
[8]Chen, 2005: 389.
[9]Chen, 2005: 374.

In 1991, a concerted action under the rubric of the 'Three Prohibits' (prohibiting production, trafficking and use) was carried out under the leadership of the national Drug Prohibition Committee. The police report that, according to incomplete statistics, 41,227 people were detained for coercive drug rehabilitation under this action.[207]

Between 1991 and 1997 public security organs reported constructing 695 coercive drug rehabilitation centres and treating 550,000 people.[208] Although there are no comprehensive figures available prior to 1993, the figures available from 1993 onwards indicate a strong increase in the numbers of people detained for rehabilitation under both coercive drug rehabilitation and RETL.

3.3 Regulation of coercive drug rehabilitation

The first national legislative instrument in the reform era to authorise detention for coercive drug rehabilitation was the NPCSC *Decision on the Prohibition of Drugs* issued on 28 December 1990 ('*Drugs Decision*'). In a manner similar to the *Prostitution Decision*, the MPS prepared the *Drugs Decision* and sent it to the State Council requesting it be sent to the NPCSC for passage as legislation.[209]

The *Drugs Decision* provided for a range of sanctions for drug-related activities and crimes. It supplemented and amended the existing criminal sanctions, later incorporated into the amended *Criminal Law*.[210] It characterises drug use as an unlawful act (*weifa xingwei* 违法行为) rather than a criminal act (*fanzui xingwei* 犯罪行为)[211] and so subject to a range of administrative measures. The *Drugs Decision* provides that administrative punishments may be given to drug users under the *SAPR* of administrative detention of up to fifteen days; increasing the amount of fine that may be given to drug users to up to RMB 2,000;[212] and permitting confiscation of drugs and equipment.[213] The *Drugs Decision* specifies that drug addicts may be taken in for coercive drug rehabilitation and that recidivists be sent to RETL.[214]

The *Drugs Decision* authorises the use of coercive drug rehabilitation in the following terms:

[207] Law Yearbook Editorial Committee, 1992: 44.
[208] Guo and Li, 2000: 318. [209] Luo, 1992: 35.
[210] See discussion in Zhao and Yu, 2000: 134. The amended *Criminal Law* then superseded the criminal law-related provisions in the *Drugs Decision*.
[211] Zhao and Yu, 2000: 134. [212] Approximately AUD 400. [213] Paragraph 8.
[214] Paragraph 8. These measures have been incorporated as part of the amended *Criminal Law* which are set out at art. 347–57.

> Where smoking or injecting drugs has become an addiction, apart from the punishment set out in the paragraph above,[215] impose coercive drug rehabilitation, carry out treatment and education. After [having been rehabilitated in] coercive drug rehabilitation, [a person who] smokes or injects drugs can be sent to RETL and made coercively to give up [drug use] during RETL.[216]

Five years after the *Drugs Decision*, on 12 January 1995 the State Council passed the *Measures on Coercive Drug Rehabilitation* which specified the length of detention under coercive drug rehabilitation and made provision for the establishment and management of coercive drug rehabilitation centres. The MPS designated these documents as the legal basis of coercive drug rehabilitation.[217]

The *Measures on Coercive Drug Rehabilitation* authorise county-level police to plan the construction of drug rehabilitation centres,[218] to determine to send a person to coercive drug rehabilitation and to be responsible for the 'management of drug rehabilitation work'. The police are also empowered to pass detailed rules to interpret the *Measures on Coercive Drug Rehabilitation* and to enforce it, as well as to manage coercive drug rehabilitation centres.[219]

(i) Targets

Originally the targets for coercive drug rehabilitation were those caught using drugs, regardless of whether they were addicted.[220] Certain categories are excluded from its scope, such as people with serious or infectious illnesses and women who are pregnant or nursing their own child less than a year old.[221] Under the *Drugs Decision*, only a person who has become addicted to drugs should be sent to coercive drug rehabilitation. A non-addicted drug user should not be a target for coercive drug rehabilitation, but subject to some other sanction.[222]

In 1998, the MPS set out the standard to be applied in determining whether a person is addicted to drugs or not for the purposes of imposing

215 Paragraph 8(1) provides for punishment under the *SAPR* of up to fifteen days' administrative detention, a fine of not more than RMB 2,000 and confiscation of drugs and equipment for drug use.

216 *Drugs Decision*, para. 8(2). The relationship between coercive drug rehabilitation and RETL was reiterated in the MPS, *Notice on Several Questions of Implementing 'Measures on Coercive Drug Rehabilitation'*, 30 May 1996. In that notice, the MPS provided that 'people released from coercive drug rehabilitation who smoke or inject drugs will by law be sent to RETL'.

217 Hao and Shan, 1999: 310–13. 218 Article 4.

219 Articles 3, 5. 220 Ke, 1990: 25.

221 *Measures on Coercive Drug Rehabilitation*, 1995, art. 20.

222 *Drugs Decision*, para. 8(2); Zhao and Yu, 2000: 134; Ke, 1990: 25.

coercive drug rehabilitation. It recognised that local conditions were inadequate to meet the standard of a medical test of addiction and that a urine test was in practice the most common method for determining drug use. Where there was evidence of drug use and the urine sample tested positive for drugs, the person should be considered addicted to drugs. It also provided that if there is evidence that a person has used drugs but that they have not continued to use them and their urine test is negative for drugs they should be considered not to be addicted. Where there is a positive blood test but insufficient evidence of drug use, the police should conduct a further urine test and carry out further investigations for evidence, or obtain a medical test of addiction where the conditions permit.[223]

Some argue that the legal definition of addiction remains inadequate.[224] One commentator asserts that, in practice, further investigations or tests are rarely undertaken and the police make a decision upon the basis of the result of the first urine test. A single test without further evidence is evidence of use but arguably is inadequate to prove addiction.[225]

(ii) Time limits

The State Council *Measures on Coercive Drug Rehabilitation* set out the framework for detention including the length of time for detention, which is between three and six months with a maximum extension of up to one year.[226] As with detention of prostitutes, the law provides no indication of the principles to be applied in determining the duration of detention or grounds for extension of the initial period.

(iii) Procedures

The public security organs at county level and above are responsible for determining whether a person should be sent to coercive drug rehabilitation. They are required to fill in a form, the *Decision on Coercive Drug Rehabilitation*, which is to be given to the detainee before they enter the drug rehabilitation centre. The family should be notified within three days of the decision to send a person to detention.[227] One commentator

223 MPS, *Response to a Request for Instructions on Determining the Standard to Determine when People who Smoke, Eat or Inject Drugs are Addicted*, 22 April 1993.

224 This issue is raised as a problem requiring more concrete legislative regulation by Zhao and Yu, 2000: 134.

225 Chen and Li, 2005: 397.

226 Article 6.

227 *Measures on Coercive Drug Rehabilitation*, 1995, art. 5.

asserts that both detention for education and coercive drug rehabilitation fall within the 'security administrative punishments system' and so principles in the *SAPR*, where applicable, are relevant to implementation of both those powers.[228] From January 2004, the procedures specified in the MPS *Regulations on the Procedures for Handling Administrative Cases by Public Security Organs*, discussed above in relation to detention for education of prostitutes and clients of prostitutes, also apply to coercive drug rehabilitation.[229]

The MPS has designated a number of circumstances where a person is not to be sent to a coercive drug rehabilitation centre and may undertake alternative treatment for drug addiction. 'Where it is not convenient to send a person to coercive drug rehabilitation' the person may be kept under the supervision of the local police station to give up drugs.[230] If they have been arrested or convicted of a crime, drug addicts may be cured of their addiction in the prisons and lock-ups where they are detained.[231]

Despite requirements that a drug addict first be sent to coercive drug rehabilitation, in one police survey[232] it was found that 11.26 per cent of the inmates in RETL had not previously been sent to coercive drug rehabilitation,[233] though there was no further explanation of the reason for sending the person directly to RETL.

3.4 Management of detention centres and revenue raising

Part of the task of drug rehabilitation centres is not merely to cure addiction and illness, and to give 'necessary punishment', but also to carry out legal and moral education, in order to 'transform' addicts.[234] The task of drug detention centres is to educate, rescue and reform.

Whilst in detention both under coercive drug rehabilitation and detention for education, living expenses and the cost of treatment are to be borne by the individual detainee or their family. For coercive drug rehabilitation, the MPS has specified that pricing guidelines be established at provincial or equivalent level by the Bureau of Public

[228] Chen, 2001.
[229] Article 2; see discussion of the procedures in relation to detention of prostitutes at section 2.7(iv) above.
[230] MPS, *Notice on Several Questions on Implementing the 'Measures on Coercive Drug Rehabilitation'*, 30 May 1996.
[231] Zhao and Yu, 2000: 137–8, set out coercive drug rehabilitation, RETL and prisons and lock-ups as the places where coercive drug rehabilitation currently takes place.
[232] Guo and Li, 2000: 130–1. The surveys were conducted in 1996 of 833 and in 1998 of 1,191 inmates in RETL who had been sent there as a result of drug addiction.
[233] Guo and Li, 2000: 144. [234] Guo and Li, 2000: 318.

Security and Pricing Authority.[235] However, if the detainee or their family have no means to pay and the detainee does not have work, the local government in principle is required to make arrangements to meet the costs.[236] Many detainees either cannot or will not pay these fees. For example, in the late 1990s, only 50 per cent of people entering the Kunming Municipal coercive drug rehabilitation centre were willing or able to pay the requisite fee.[237]

Whilst in detention, the State Council *Measures on Coercive Drug Rehabilitation* permit the detainees to be 'organised to carry out an appropriate level of labour', in addition to receiving treatment for drug addiction, psychological training, legal education and moral education.[238] In 1996, the MPS clarified the entitlement of detainees to be paid for their labour, requiring that they be paid directly and not have those amounts deducted from the fees payable to the detention centre for their living expenses.[239]

Prior to 2000, the public security organs did not have a monopoly on the operation of coercive drug rehabilitation centres. In 1995, the *Measures on Coercive Drug Rehabilitation* prohibited the operation of private drug rehabilitation centres, though continued to permit medical units to operate drug rehabilitation centres with the approval of the provincial-level health department. Drug rehabilitation centres not operated by the public security organs were to be subject to supervision by the public security organ at the same level.[240]

In 2000, the MPS criticised the poor management and security in some coercive drug rehabilitation centres and ordered a major rectification of their management. The MPS identified wide-ranging and severe problems with the administration of coercive drug rehabilitation, involving the frequent occurrence of serious 'accidents'.[241] As a result of staff shortages, some detention centres did not have personnel on duty at all times.[242] More seriously, the MPS identified an extensive problem of people who should have been sent to coercive drug rehabilitation centres instead being placed in more punitive and less

[235] MPS, *Notice on Several Questions on Implementing the 'Measures on Coercive Drug Rehabilitation'*, 30 May 1996: at 647.

[236] MPS, *Notice on Several Questions on Implementing the 'Measures on Coercive Drug Rehabilitation'*: at 647.

[237] Cui, 1999: 468. [238] Article 13.

[239] MPS, *Notice on Several Questions on Implementing the 'Measures on Coercive Drug Rehabilitation'*.

[240] *Measures on Coercive Drug Rehabilitation*, 1995, art. 21; Xie, 2000: 116.

[241] Chen and Li, 2005: 389.

[242] *Notice on Putting in Order and Rectifying Coercive Drug Rehabilitation Centres* 21 June 2000.

safe forms of detention such as the local lock-up, administrative detention centres[243] or detention for education centres. Similar problems were identified of detaining prostitutes for education in the lock-up or together with administrative detention.[244]

The MPS also identified serious problems of corruption in the operation of coercive drug rehabilitation, with coercive drug rehabilitation itself being used for revenue-raising purposes, or its proper operation being seriously affected by lack of revenue. Results were that people were detained for longer than the permitted period; people were released early; detainees were provided with drugs of addiction; people were released after having paid a fine; and additional fees such as 'head fees' and 'transport fees' were charged.[245]

Continuing problems with commercial ventures operating coercive drug rehabilitation and charging excessive fees for living expenses and medicines, and using unauthorised medicines,[246] became so serious that the MPS issued a *Notice on Putting in Order and Rectifying Coercive Drug Rehabilitation Centres*[247] demanding that all joint-venture coercive drug rehabilitation centres be closed. In March 2000, the MPS passed the *Measures for Management of Coercive Drug Rehabilitation Centres*, in which it purported to remove the capacity of all organs except public security organs to set up and operate coercive drug rehabilitation.[248]

As if to give some indication of the degree of seriousness and the widespread nature of mismanagement of detention centres both for coercive drug rehabilitation and detention for education of prostitutes, the MPS concurrently passed measures to implement a nationwide system of biennial evaluations to grade both detention for education and

243 Documenting the ongoing lack of safety of inmates in these forms of detention, MPS, *Notice on Strengthening the Work of Management of the Three Detention (Centres) and putting an end to situations where Detainees get Beaten to Death*, 22 April 1993; MPS, *Temporary Regulations on a Major Safety Inspection of Public Security Lock-ups and Rostered Inspection Tours*, 20 July 1993; and SPP, MPS, *Notice on Strengthening the Legal Supervision Work of Lock-ups*, 12 November 1999: at 190.

244 MPS, *Measures for the Management of Detention for Education Camps*, 24 April 2000.

245 MPS, *Notice on Putting in Order and Rectifying Coercive Drug Rehabilitation Centres*.

246 Many of which the MPS notice revealed were not approved by the Health Bureau for use.

247 MPS, *Notice on Putting in Order and Rectifying Coercive Drug Rehabilitation Centres*, 21 June 2000.

248 Article 4. Similar measures were passed in relation to detention for education: MPS, *Measures for the Management of Detention for Education Camps*, passed on 30 March 2000. Both sets of regulations have been identified in MPS, *Notice on Retention, Amendment and Rescission of Departmental Rules and Normative Documents*, 19 August 2004, as requiring revision in order to comply with the provisions of the *Legislation Law*.

coercive drug rehabilitation centres.[249] As a result of this rectification, 103 coercive drug rehabilitation centres were closed. Another rectification campaign was conducted in 2003, resulting in the closure of a further forty-five detention centres and the merging of seven.[250]

4 CONCLUSION

Confronted with the resurgence of prostitution and drug addiction in the reform era, the Party and the political-legal organs, particularly the police, reached back for powers that in the 1950s had been so successful. However, dislocated from some of the comprehensive mechanisms of social control that were more effective in the 1950s, these forms of detention have not delivered the desired results.

Although powers to detain prostitutes and their clients, as well as drug addicts, remain part of the second line of defence, whose aim is to educate, rescue and reform, they no longer retain the ideological significance they held in the 1950s. Police enforcement decisions are now dominated by the interplay between practical requirements for concerted action during periodic hard strikes and financial incentives that favour imposition of a fine. Police handling of prostitution and drug use has not escaped this commodification of police work. The severity and persistence of the problem of improper and corrupt revenue raising by the police has been the subject of ongoing attention by the MPS and central Party Committees such as the Central Political-Legal Committee.[251]

[249] MPS, *Measures for Evaluating the Grade of Detention for Education Camps*, 27 November 2000; MPS, *Notice on Putting in Order and Rectifying Coercive Drug Rehabilitation*, 21 June 2000. Depending on the nature of the facilities, numbers and quality of staff, the number of incidents and programmes in place, the centres would be designated first-, second- or third-grade centre. Under both sets of regulations, a detention centre organised jointly with the lock-up could not obtain a grading.

[250] Chen and Li, 2005: 389.

[251] Central Political-Legal Committee, *Notice that Political-Legal Organs Must Strictly Enforce Party Discipline and Rigorously Enforce the Law*, 18 October 1993, prohibiting imposition of fines or other exactions in breach of the law, selling official duties, substituting fines for criminal sanctions, engaging in local protectionism, accepting gifts or favours, participating in and permitting any of the 'Six Evils' and asking for payment for performance of official duties. MPS, *Regulation of the Ten Prohibitions for Public Security Organs and Public Security Officers*, 24 September 1993; MPS, *Notice on Resolutely Prohibiting Public Security Organs from Unprincipled Imposition of Fees, Fines and Exactions*, 7 June 1993; MPS, *Notice on Prohibiting the Collection of Case Handling Fees*, 2 May 1995. The MPS, *Notice on Conscientiously Strengthening the Management of Income of Public Security Organs from Collection of Fees and Fines*, 3 January 1999, gives an indication of the extent of illegal revenue-raising by the police. An audit carried out

Especially in the case of drug use, the imposition of a fine under the *SAPL* has little value as a deterrent and might only exacerbate the financial problems otherwise arising from drug use itself. The efficacy of imposing administrative detention under the *SAPL* on drug users may also be questioned on the basis that administrative detention centres are not equipped to address any special needs of addicts and that the safety of drug users may be compromised when they are placed together with a range of people who have been detained for other reasons.[252]

An analysis of the development of these two administrative detention powers in the 1980s and early 1990s illustrates the persisting dominance of the Party, State Council and the MPS in formulating social order policy and the strategies and powers for its enforcement. It demonstrates the continuing use of political and administrative directives rather than law as the primary mode for regulation of these powers, even though the politics underpinning these powers itself has changed since the 1950s. It also reveals the perseverance of the view of law held by state agencies as punitive, a weapon to be wielded by state enforcement agencies, and as providing formal legitimation for their powers. The impetus to provide a legislative basis for both detention powers appeared only when the existence and extensive use of these powers started to cause embarrassment, in particular when the policies and powers were in clear conflict with legal reform generally. Whilst there has been a willingness to comply with formalistic requirements to legalise these powers, there has been little progress in regularising the powers by tighter substantive and procedural regulation of their definition and use.

in 1996–97 of public security organs in fifteen provinces revealed that 17.8 per cent or RMB 3.166 billion (approximately AUD 633.2 million) of the total fees and fines collected were obtained illegally and in breach of discipline.

[252] See comments to this effect in Chen and Li, 2005: 396.

CHAPTER SIX

RE-EDUCATION THROUGH LABOUR

1 INTRODUCTION

In this chapter, I trace the changing uses of RETL since the late 1970s and the policy context in which these changes have taken place. Controversy has dogged the power almost since its inception in 1955. Since then, one report asserts that over 3 million people have been sent to RETL.[1]

I examine the ways in which the political and administrative modes of governance that predominated in the pre-reform era have continued to influence the development of RETL since 1978. In particular, I identify the use of RETL as a flexible tool to address changing social order problems in a way that is analogous to its use as an adjunct to political campaigns in the pre-reform era. I explore the proposition that, to date, there has been a high degree of continuity from the pre-reform era in the modes of governance and uses of the power, but that the objectives of RETL and the policy contexts in which it is used have changed. Originally RETL was implemented to consolidate state power by targeting opponents of the Party and government and other 'bad' people in order to educate and reform them.[2] In the reform era, the focus of RETL has shifted toward targeting socially disruptive behaviour and minor criminal offences for the purpose of preserving social order and maintaining political control. Many acts that were previously characterised as political errors, such as opposition to the Party or state power, are now being

[1] Chen, 2003: 102; Liu, 2001b: 18. [2] Ma, 2003: 130.

re-characterised as legal errors, such as harming social order and committing minor criminal offences.

I examine the most recent reforms to RETL which consolidate, but do not limit, the scope of targets and which regularise the procedures for the imposition of a term of RETL. The MPS has responded to the increasingly strident criticisms of abuses of RETL which indicates some recognition that steps need to be taken to establish more formalised procedures for its imposition. The pressure to legalise RETL and to make it appear consistent with the developing legal system is growing. Viewed in terms of an emerging legal field, this may be seen as an indication of the growing force of law as a means of legitimating powers previously endorsed politically.

2 REINVIGORATION OF RETL AFTER 1979

At the beginning of the reform period there was no unanimity about whether RETL should be reinvigorated. After discussion, in 1979, the CCPCC decided to retain RETL.[3] On 29 November 1979, the NPCSC gave legal approval to reinvigorate RETL by approving the *Supplementary Regulations of the State Council on RETL*, which were issued by the State Council on 5 December 1979, and by repromulgating the 1957 *Decision of the State Council on the Question of RETL*.

Expansion of RETL was incorporated as one of the components of the CMPO. In the *Five Major Cities Meeting* in 1981 the targets for RETL were described as follows:

> The small number of juveniles who have committed minor criminal offences, who have been educated repeatedly but will not reform, who cannot be managed by their family or by society and whose offences are not sufficiently serious to warrant arrest and criminal conviction, shall be sent to work study schools if they are young and if they are older shall be sent to RETL.[4]

At that meeting, Peng Zhen drew an analogy between the methods for dealing with juvenile crime and the way a parent would treat a child with an infectious disease, or a doctor would treat a sick patient. He advocated their 'education, rescue (or transformation) and reform'.[5]

[3] Li and Du, 1990: 53–4; Guo and Li, 2000: 327; Xia, 2001: 61. [4] Point 4 at 2.

[5] *Jiaoyu, ganhua, gaizao* 教育, 感化, 改造. The term *ganhua* can also be translated as to assist or to transform through persuasion. This 'Six Characters' policy was officially adopted by the CCPCC in the *Directive on Strengthening Political-Legal Work*, 13 January 1982.

The meeting adopted this programme, also reaffirming the 1961 determination discussed in chapter 3 that education and transformation should be the first priority and engaging in productive labour the second.[6]

The targets for RETL are commonly referred to as 'those who do not commit criminal offences but frequently commit misdemeanours; who drive the police to distraction; and whose offences are difficult to prosecute as criminal cases'.[7]

In 1980, the CCPCC and the State Council approved and issued an MPS report which defined the official character of RETL[8] as a method for resolving non-antagonistic contradictions, that is, as part of the second line of defence.[9] The purpose of re-education was thus to 'transform the vast majority into useful timber for socialist construction'.[10] Since the early 1980s, RETL has retained its political uses, though its political flavour has weakened as it no longer serves primarily as a tool for class struggle.[11] Its primary focus has been to address the changing problems of policing public order in the reform era.[12] The purposes of RETL are more explicitly punitive than they were in the pre-reform period; RETL is classified as an administrative measure whose targets are defined with reference to the criminal law. There is no longer any suggestion that its purpose is for resettlement and employment.[13] From near its lowest point in 1971, there were reported to be 6,623 people held in RETL. By 1978, there were 70,233.[14] By 1999, the size of RETL had increased to 310 RETL camps, containing 310,000 inmates.[15]

2.1 Targets

The scope of targets in the reform era has constantly expanded. The list of targets continues to include people adjudged politically unreliable or opposed to Party leadership. This group now includes adherents to

[6] Guo, 2005: 295; Fu, 2005a: 220–2. In his study in the economy of an RETL camp, Fu Hualing demonstrates the central importance of productive labour to the operation of an RETL camp and, so, how it is impossible in practice to give priority to education and reform.

[7] Xu and Fang, 1997: 95–6; Liu, 2001a: *dafa bufan, xiaofa changfan, qisi gong'an, nandao fayuan* 大法不犯, 小法常犯, 气死公安, 难道法院; Kang, 1992: 677.

[8] Gao, Xianduan, 1992: 39.

[9] MPS, *Temporary Measures*, art. 2 provides that RETL is a measure for resolving contradictions amongst the people.

[10] MPS, *Report on Doing Well: The Work of RETL*, 9 August 1980; Kang, 1992: 678, discussing the requirement that the priorities of RETL are education first and production second.

[11] Chen, 2003: 91–2.

[12] Jiang and Zhan, 1994: 97; Gao, Xianduan, 1992: 39.

[13] Xia, 2001: 61–2; Chen, 2003: 91–2.

[14] Guo, 2005: 294. [15] Chen *et al.*, 2002: 332.

Falun Gong and minority groups such as Uigurs and Tibetans seeking increased autonomy from the state. The emphasis, though, has shifted toward targeting those who commit minor offences, disrupt social order, disrupt economic reform, commit the 'Six Evils' and whose acts are seen as endangering the creation of a socialist morality.[16] An increasingly important use of RETL is to detain drug addicts who have become re-addicted after coercive drug rehabilitation.

(i) Expanding the scope of targets from 1980

Two documents were passed in 1980 and 1982 which expanded the targets of RETL. The first is the State Council, *Notice on Consolidation of the Two Measures of Forced Labour and Detention for Investigation into RETL*,[17] in which the targets of forced labour and detention for investigation were incorporated into the scope of RETL.[18] The reason given in the notice for combining these powers with RETL was that:

> Judging from current enforcement practice, the targets for forced labour and detention for investigation are basically the same as the targets for RETL, there is no substantive difference.[19]

The conduct previously targeted for forced labour was politically defined and included minor unlawful acts that were not sufficient to warrant criminal sanction.[20] The targets of detention for investigation were those who had committed minor offences and gave a false name and address; or had committed minor offences and were suspected of going from place to place committing crime or committing gang crimes.[21] The group of 'transient criminals' now targeted for RETL includes those who have been away from the place of their household

[16] MPS, *Temporary Measures*, art. 3 includes in its statement of objectives: transforming the person into someone who obeys the law, respects public morality, loves the motherland and loves labour.

[17] State Council, *Notice on Consolidation of the Two Measures of Forced Labour and Detention for Investigation into RETL*, 29 February 1980.

[18] This consolidation did not occur in relation to detention for investigation for the reasons discussed in chapter 4 at section 9.

[19] State Council, *Notice on Consolidation of the Two Measures of Forced Labour and Detention for Investigation into RETL*, 29 February 1980.

[20] State Council, *Notice on Consolidation of the Two Measures of Forced Labour and Detention for Investigation into RETL*, para. 1; see also Chen, 2003: 93.

[21] Targets for detention for investigation were set out in State Council, *Notice on Consolidation of the Two Measures of Forced Labour and Detention for Investigation into RETL*, 29 February 1980 and MPS, *Notice on Strictly Controlling the Use of Detention for Investigation Measures*, 31 July 1985.

registration for a long time and either commit crime for a living; or are suspected of committing crime for a living; or do not breach the criminal law but commit numerous minor offences.[22]

The second document is the *Temporary Measures on Re-education through Labour* ('*Temporary Measures*') which was approved and issued by the State Council in January 1982.[23] In redefining the targets of RETL in the *Temporary Measures*, the MPS, after investigation, determined that the previous definitions of targets were too vague, did not suit the current public order situation and were not easy to implement.[24] Since its passage, the scope of targets has been amended by numerous documents, though the *Temporary Measures* officially remain the basic definition of targets for re-education.

Under the 1982 *Temporary Measures*, targets include:

1. counter-revolutionary and anti-Party, anti-socialist elements whose crimes are not sufficiently serious to warrant criminal sanction;
2. those who form groups to commit murder, armed robbery, rape, arson and other gang crimes, whose crimes are not sufficiently serious to warrant criminal sanction;
3. those who commit unlawful or criminal acts of hooliganism, prostitution, theft, fraud, etc., who do not reform after repeated education, whose crimes are not sufficiently serious to warrant criminal sanction;
4. those who disrupt social order by inciting the masses to create disturbances and fights, pick quarrels and cause a disturbance, stir up trouble, whose crimes are not sufficiently serious to warrant criminal sanction;
5. those who have a work unit, but who, for a long time, refuse to labour or who disrupt labour discipline, ceaselessly cause trouble without cause, disrupt the order of production, work, study and teaching or living or obstruct official business, whose crimes are not sufficiently serious to warrant criminal sanction; and
6. those who instigate others to commit unlawful and criminal acts, but whose offences are not sufficiently serious to warrant a criminal sanction.

[22] MPS, *Notice Issuing the Third Bureau 'Report of the Meeting on Strengthening the Struggle Against Transient Crime'*, 1 July 1980.

[23] MPS, *Temporary Measures*, issued by the State Council on 21 January 1982. Guo, 1990: 28, asserts that this document when passed was designated for 'internal' circulation (*neibu*).

[24] Luo, 1992: 34–5.

The description of targets has since become very fragmented. One official has identified thirty-eight different categories of targets located in twenty different legislative and other instruments.[25] There is considerable overlap between the categories of targets in these documents and some targets have now been rendered redundant as a result of economic and political changes. For example, the MPS in 1988 approved RETL for people who were repeatedly caught scalping tickets allocated under the plan and would not reform.[26] Other examples are those set out in the *Temporary Measures* of 'having a job and refusing to go to work' and 'breaching labour discipline'.[27] These offences were relevant to administrative forms of labour discipline imposed in a planned economy, but not one organised along market principles. Under the *Labour Law*, these actions are treated as civil breaches of contract to be handled between the employer and employee, not as administrative offences.[28] By the early 1990s the MPS had acknowledged that the scope of targets required consolidation.[29] Some, however, applauded the fragmentation as one of the strengths of RETL, asserting that it created the flexibility needed to carry out political campaigns first and, later, hard strikes.[30]

(ii) Minor offences not sufficiently serious for criminal sanction

The punitive nature of RETL is highlighted by the extent to which targets for RETL are defined with reference to criminal offences. One commentator concludes that the targets of RETL are now entirely determined with reference to the *Criminal Law*.[31] In the 1980s the scope of RETL was expanded to cover: repeatedly scalping boat, train and bus tickets;[32] or airline tickets;[33] speculating in small amounts

[25] Gao, Xianduan, 1992: 41–2.

[26] MPS, *Response to a Request for Instructions on taking in for RETL those unlawful persons who illegally scalp tickets allocated under the plan who have been repeatedly educated and will not reform*, 29 December 1988.

[27] *Temporary Measures*, art. 10(4).

[28] *PRC Labour Law*, which took effect on 1 January 1995, at art. 16 provides that the labour relationship is established upon execution of a contract between employer and employee; art. 19 sets out the matters that must be decided in the labour contract. Chapter 10 sets out procedures for resolving labour disputes.

[29] Luo, 1992: 33. [30] Gao, Xianduan, 1992: 42. [31] Zhou, Yan, 1999: 22.

[32] MPS, Ministry of Railways and Ministry of Transportation, *Notice on Resolutely Preventing and Striking Against Scalping Vehicle and Boat Ticket Activities*, 30 November 1985, art. 2.

[33] Civil Aviation Bureau, MPS, *Notice on Resolutely Prohibiting and Striking Against Scalping Airline Ticket Activity to Ensure the Safety of Air Transportation*, 12 January 1988, art. 3.

of gold;[34] illegally felling and stealing timber;[35] committing bigamy;[36] theft carried out in cities and towns by people with rural household registrations;[37] those who are 'backbone elements of reactionary secret societies';[38] and communicating or liaising with the enemy or spies,[39] where those offences are not sufficiently serious to warrant a criminal sanction.

Eligibility for RETL requires both that the offence is not sufficiently serious to warrant a criminal sanction and that the person has been educated repeatedly and will not reform.[40] The definition of RETL with reference to the *Criminal Law* is problematic at a number of levels. The first is that it blurs the boundary between crime and non-crime,[41] as the boundary between acts that constitute a criminal offence and those that do not is adjusted from time to time by the changing standards for accepting a case.[42] An example of the slippery borderline between RETL and criminal sanctions is illustrated by an instruction issued to the courts in Wuhan in 1981. This instruction stated that if the criminal actions being tried would not warrant a criminal sanction, then the person should not be acquitted but the prosecution withdrawn and the matter referred to the police for them to impose RETL.[43] In short, instead of acquittal, the person should be sent to RETL.

The second is that criminal punishments such as control or criminal detention[44] are considerably lighter than that imposed under RETL.

[34] SPC, SPP, MPS, MoJ, *Notice on Striking Hard Against the Criminal Activity of Speculating in and Smuggling Gold*, 28 June 1987, art. 5 (rescinded 13 October 2000).

[35] Ministry of Forestry, MPS, *Notice on Several Questions on Cases of Illegal Logging and Deforestation that have been transferred to the jurisdiction of Public Security Organs*, 20 June 1985.

[36] SPC, SPP, MPS, *Notice on Questions as to Jurisdiction in Handling Bigamy Cases*, 26 July 1983, art. 3.

[37] SPC, SPP, *Supplementary Notice on Questions of the Applicable Law to Use in the Handling of Current Theft Cases*, 17 September 1986.

[38] MPS, *Circular on the Circumstances of the Hard Strike against Backbone Elements of Reactionary Secret Societies Active in Carrying out Wrecking Activities*, 1 August 1983.

[39] State Council approving and issuing the MPS, *Notice on Resolutely Striking Against Criminal Elements who Write Letters to Guomindang Espionage Agencies*, 15 August 1981; Jiang and Zhan, 1994: 98.

[40] NPCSC, *Decision of the State Council on the Question of RETL*, 3 August 1957, art. 1.

[41] Jiang and Yuan, 1990: 46–7.

[42] Such as, for example, the SPC, SPP, *Supplementary Notice on Questions of the Applicable Law to Use in the Handling of Current Theft Cases*, 17 September 1986, specifying the borderline between theft to be dealt with by RETL and that to be handled by criminal prosecution.

[43] Wuhan Municipal Public Security Bureau, Procuratorate and Court, *Notice on Several Questions on the Work of Handling Cases*, 18 August 1981: at 19.

[44] *Criminal Law*, arts. 38–41 provide that the time period of control is between three months and two years, which is served outside prison and under which the person may continue to work. *Criminal Law*, arts. 42–4 provide that criminal detention may be imposed for a period of between one month and six months and is served in the local police station.

Under RETL a person may be detained for between one and three years with a possible extension of a further year.[45] Furthermore, the requirement that a person has to have been 'educated repeatedly and won't reform' has been criticised as being an ill-defined criteria,[46] ignored in practice.[47]

In the *Regulations on Public Security Organs Handling RETL Cases* 2002 (the '*RETL Regulations*'), the MPS amended previous descriptions of targets to follow more closely the new definitions of crime set out in the amended *Criminal Law*.[48] For example, the crime of hooliganism was removed from the amended *Criminal Law* because it was considered to be so ill-defined and broad as to be arbitrary and conducive to abuse.[49] It was replaced by the crimes of molesting and humiliating women;[50] assembling a crowd to engage in promiscuous activities or repeatedly participating in those activities;[51] gathering a crowd to have brawls;[52] and wilfully attacking or chasing people and causing a disturbance in a public place that results in serious disorder.[53] The *RETL Regulations* no longer refer to hooliganism, but include within the targets the four categories of conduct listed above.[54]

The *RETL Regulations* now specify that in some cases the first offence is punishable by RETL, such as those who use secret societies, heretical cults or feudal superstition to breach the law and those who create an 'atmosphere of terror' or make the 'people feel panic stricken' or harm the public's security.[55] In other cases, the person is eligible for RETL if previously sanctioned for the offence, such as assembling a crowd to engage in promiscuous activities; scalping or forging tickets; or unlawful detention.[56]

In the early reform period the MPS recognised the need to distinguish RETL from the punishment of criminal convicts in reform through labour and to ensure that the camps no longer continued to

[45] Jiang and Yuan, 1990: 47; *Temporary Measures*, art. 13, setting out time limits for RETL.
[46] Ren, 1992: 14, pointing out who should be educating is not specified, nor is the number of times.
[47] Zhu, 1990: 259.
[48] Even though art. 9 expresses the targets to be based on the NPCSC, *Decision of the State Council on the Question of RETL*, 1957, the *Supplementary Regulations of the State Council on Re-education through Labour*, 1979, and the *Temporary Measures* set out a non-exhaustive and non-identical list of targets. These regulations may be better seen as a reinterpretation of the previous list of targets.
[49] Zhao, 1997: 15. [50] *Criminal Law*, art. 237. [51] *Criminal Law*, art. 301.
[52] *Criminal Law*, art. 292. [53] *Criminal Law*, art. 293. [54] Article 9(3).
[55] Article 9(4). [56] Article 9(5).

operate together.[57] In 1981, the Central Political-Legal Committee approved the establishment of RETL schools, and conversion of RETL camps into schools. By 2001, 86 per cent of RETL institutions were called schools.[58] However, in many respects the conceptual distinction between RETL and reform through labour continue to be blurred in terms of the stigma associated with detention.[59] An illustration is that detainees in RETL and prisoners continue to be referred to by the shorthand expression 'Two Labours' (*lianglao* 两劳).[60]

(iii) RETL as targeting social evils

RETL also targets 'social evils', including prostitution,[61] drug addiction, gambling,[62] pornography[63] and deceiving the people using feudal superstition. They were identified at the beginning of the reform era as offences comprised in the fourth high tide of crime.[64]

At the launch of the strike against the 'Six Evils' in 1989, the MPS drafted the *Proposal for Carrying out a Nationwide Campaign for the Eradication of Prostitution and Using Prostitutes etc. 'Six Evils'*. At paragraph 4, the MPS reasserted that prostitutes who re-offended after being detained by the police under detention for education should be sent to RETL. It also removed the requirement that the prostitute 'be educated many times and not reform'[65] as a pre-condition for being sent to RETL in respect of those who prostitute with foreigners; those who prostitute or use prostitutes many times; and pimps who 'make unfair profit out of prostitutes and their clients'.[66]

The 1991 *Prostitution Decision*, paragraph 4(3), provides that a person who prostitutes or uses prostitutes after being 'dealt with' by the police can be sent to RETL and fined up to RMB 5,000 by the police. This provision has been interpreted by the Legal Division of the MPS to

57 Gao, Xianduan, 1992: 39; MPS, *Report on Doing Well the Work of RETL*, 9 August 1980.
58 Guo, 2005: 300–1. 59 Dong, 2002: 3. 60 Dong, 2002: 3.
61 MPS, *Notice on Resolutely Prohibiting Prostitution Activities*, 10 June 1981.
62 SPC, SPP, MPS, *Notice on Strictly Investigating and Prohibiting Gambling Activities*, 6 August 1985, art. 3 expanded the scope of RETL as part of the '1983 Hard Strike', to include those heading up gambling rings; those who live in large- and medium-sized cities who are without regular employment and gamble; and those gamblers who have been educated repeatedly and will not reform (rescinded 13 October 2000).
63 *SAPR*, art. 32(1) and (2): production, sale, copying, lending, renting or broadcasting of pornographic material.
64 See discussion in chapter 4 at section 4. 65 *Lüjiao bugai* (屡教不改).
66 Reproduced at Chen, 1992: 148; see also Luo, 1992: 35.

mean that a person who prostitutes many times is not eligible to be sent to RETL if they have not yet been dealt with by the police.[67] To the extent that the 1989 document suggested that a person could be sent to RETL without having received any prior punishment by the police, such an interpretation has been rejected in the *Prostitution Decision*, the subsequent interpretation by the MPS Legal Division and more recently by the *RETL Regulations*.

In respect of prostitution-related offences, the *RETL Regulations* provide that RETL can be given to those who introduce, encourage or coerce people into prostitution where the circumstances are not sufficiently serious to warrant criminal prosecution[68] and prostitutes who prostitute again after having received a warning, fine or administrative detention.[69]

In relation to other 'evils', in 1990 the MPS issued a notice requiring that those who repeatedly used 'feudal superstitious' methods to disrupt social order and cheat people out of property, if not sufficiently serious to warrant a criminal sanction, were to be sent to RETL.[70] Similarly, persons using gambling to cheat people of money and who did not reform after repeated education, or if they provided the venue or equipment for gambling purposes, may be sent to RETL unless the situation warrants imposition of a criminal sanction.[71]

Possibly the largest constituent of this group are drug addicts who have become re-addicted after coercive drug rehabilitation.[72] Apart from detention in special drug rehabilitation divisions within ordinary RETL camps, some specialist RETL camps for drug addicts have been established.[73] The proportion of people in RETL as a result of drug addiction reportedly has increased dramatically. As at September 1997, one set of figures indicated that the proportion of drug addicts in RETL ranged from a minimum of 1.6 per cent of the camp population in Tianjin, to 74.1 per cent in Yunnan and 83.58 per cent in Gansu.[74]

67 Legal Division of the MPS, *Response to a Request for Instructions on Whether a Person who Repeatedly Prostitutes or Uses Prostitutes but has not been dealt with by the Public Security Organs can be sent to RETL*, 4 September 1997.
68 Article 9(7). 69 Article 9(8).
70 MPS, *Notice on Deepening the Struggle to Eliminate the 'Six Evils' Strictly According to Law and Implementing Policy*, 7 May 1990: at 237.
71 MPS, *Notice on Deepening the Struggle to Eliminate the 'Six Evils' Strictly According to Law and Implementing Policy*, 7 May 1990: at 236–7; see Gao, Xianduan, 1992: 42.
72 MPS, *Regulations on Public Security Organs Handling RETL Cases*, 1 June 2002, art. 9(9).
73 Guo and Li, 2000: 319–20; Chu, 1996: 64–5; Zhao and Yu, 2000: 141.
74 Guo and Li, 2000: 330.

Another survey reports that drug addicts in 1998 comprised 20 per cent of the total RETL population.[75]

(iv) Expanding the geographical limits on targets

At first, the scope of targets was confined to people with urban household registrations.[76] In 1980 this was increased to include people from counties, towns and rural villages who committed unlawful acts in cities, in market towns, on transportation routes or on railways.[77] In some areas, villages were allocated a quota of people who could be sent to RETL. For example, in the 1980s each year rural villages were allocated a quota of up to five people who could be sent to RETL.[78] Some argue that the geographical restriction on targets for RETL should be removed.[79] Later, specific legislation increased the circumstances in which people with a rural household registration, particularly prostitutes and drug addicts, could be sent to RETL.[80] For some time, the MPS resisted requests from local-level agencies to permit expansion of targets to include rural residents who repeatedly commit minor offences.[81] In 1998, it was decided that as social order in rural areas had deteriorated, it was necessary to impose RETL in respect of unlawful activities in rural areas, particularly those carried out by 'local riff raff, hooligans and village bullies so bitterly despised by the broad masses'.[82]

75 Su, 1998: 25; Human Rights in China, 2001b, cites an official estimate that 40 per cent of people are in RETL for drug-related offences. The size of the population is evidenced by regulations passed by the MoJ in 2003 for the separate management of drug-addicted RETL detainees: *Regulations on RETL Drug Rehabilitation Work* issued on 20 May 2003, to take effect from 1 August 2003.

76 *Supplementary Regulations on RETL*, 1979, art. 2 defines this as large- and medium-sized cities.

77 MPS, *Response to a Request for Instructions on Questions about Taking in for RETL from Counties and Towns and Operating RETL Camps in Districts and Regions*, 31 July 1980 (rescinded 5 April 2001); Ren, 1992: 13.

78 Ren, 1992: 13. 79 Luo, 1992: 37.

80 1990 *Drugs Decision*; MPS and MoJ jointly issued the *Notice on Questions of Gathering up for RETL of Prostitutes and Clients of Prostitutes*, art. 1 providing for RETL to be given to 'prostitutes with rural household registrations who have floated to county towns, or market towns or carry out prostitution in villages or their clients, whose acts are not sufficiently serious to warrant criminal punishment but who have failed to reform after repeated warnings' (rescinded in 2000); Legal Division of the MPS, *Letter of Response to the Jiangxi Provincial RETL Management Committee 'Request for Instructions on Two Questions about RETL Examination and Approval Work'*, 28 March 1990. See also chapter 5.

81 Legal Division of the MPS, *Response to a Request for Instructions to the Hainan Provincial Public Security Office 'Request for Instructions on whether Rural Unemployed who commit many offences but which are still not sufficient to pursue criminal liability can be taken in for RETL'*, 7 June 1990.

82 MPS, *Notice on Several Questions on the Scope of RETL*, 30 November 1998.

The *RETL Regulations* draw no distinction between rural and urban residents in their description of RETL targets. However, as they are expressed to be based on previous regulations that do draw such a distinction, their failure to mention this distinction is not clear evidence that the *RETL Regulations* should be interpreted to extend eligibility for imposition of RETL generally to rural residents. The *RETL Regulations* expressly exclude from their scope foreigners, stateless people, Taiwanese and Hong Kong and Macao residents.[83]

(v) The use of RETL for investigation

After the process of reincorporating detention for investigation into RETL was halted, detention for investigation was increasingly used by the police as a substitute for criminal detention to detain and interrogate criminal suspects. After detention for investigation was absorbed into the criminal coercive powers exercised by the police under the amended *CPL*,[84] police commentators complained that the remaining criminal coercive measures were inadequate.[85] RETL was used to extend the period of detention where the public security organs had been unable to complete their investigations within specified time limits,[86] or where there was insufficient evidence to support an application for arrest.[87] Police were able to continue their investigations by sending a person to RETL on the basis of the evidence of wrongdoing they already had if they considered it inappropriate to release the suspect.[88] In some areas this category of person was reported to comprise up to 20 per cent of the total RETL population.[89]

In 1999, the Central Political-Legal Committee demanded rectification of the unlawful imposition of RETL for investigation purposes.[90] The *RETL Regulations* explicitly prohibit the use of RETL to extend time limits for detention of people where the police have been unable to complete criminal investigations within the time periods specified in the *CPL*.[91]

83 Article 12.
84 Xu and Fang, 1997: 99, describe the abolition of detention for investigation as having been 'replaced by other measures'.
85 Xu and Fang, 1997: 99–100.
86 Zhou, Yan, 1999: 22; Wei, 1998: 41, referring to a 1995 document authorising this practice, issued jointly by the MPS, SPC and SPP, *Opinion on Resolving Several Problems of Enforcement Currently Faced by the Political-Legal Organs*.
87 Liu, Wenren, 1998. 88 Xu and Fang, 1997: 99–100. 89 Zhou, Yan, 1999: 22.
90 MPS, *Notice on Implementing the Central Political-Legal Committee's 'Research Opinion on the Problems of RETL'*, 14 October 1999.
91 Article 4.

(vi) The use of RETL against political targets and protestors

In the 1980s RETL continued to be used against targets defined in explicitly political terms. In this area especially, the flexibility of the broadly worded provisions in the *Temporary Measures* permitting detention of 'counter-revolutionary and anti-socialist reactionaries' was interpreted to cover a range of groups who oppose government control for one reason or another.

For example, in December 1981, in the wake of the crackdown on the Democracy Wall movement,[92] the Central Political-Legal Committee authorised RETL for those people who 'publish counterrevolutionary articles' and who 'viciously attack, spread rumours and slander Party and state leaders' whose offences were not sufficiently serious to constitute a criminal offence.[93]

A range of other groups are targets for RETL. Whilst not explicitly defined in political terms, these groups can be identified as being organised outside the bounds of state permission and control. Since the inclusion of Falun Gong within the definition of a 'heretical sect',[94] large numbers of its followers are reported to have been sent to RETL.[95] The Central Political-Legal Committee issued a notice in November 1999 instructing the coercive organs of the state to make 'full use of legal weapons' to punish unlawful activities of the Falun Gong and other heretical sects. It instructed that RETL should be imposed on those 'backbone' and 'diehard' elements who refused to give up the practice of Falun Gong and repeatedly petitioned and disrupted social order, where the conduct did not constitute a criminal offence.[96]

Potter indicates that the state has used a range of methods to suppress some religious groups, whose adherents owe their primary allegiance to their religion rather than to the state.[97] Evidence that unauthorised Christian groups, including Protestant and Catholic groups, are being

92 See Nathan, 1985: 31–40; Baum, 1994: 79–82.

93 Central Political-Legal Committee, *Opinion on Questions of whether Vilifying and Slandering Central Leadership Comrades Constitutes a Crime*, December 1981.

94 NPCSC, *Decision on Banning Heretical Cult Organisations, and Preventing and Punishing Cult Activities*, 30 October 1999; SPC, SPP, *Explanation Concerning Laws Applicable to Handling Cases of Organising and Employing Heretical Cult Organisations to Commit Crime*, 8 October 1999; *Beijing Review*, which interprets the *Criminal Law*, art. 300, to cover organisations such as Falun Gong.

95 Human Rights Watch, 2002, citing estimates of up to 10,000 detainees; Keith and Lin, 2003: 629, citing US Department of State figures of 5,000 detainees; Hung, 2003b: 35, citing figures of up to 20,000.

96 Central Political-Legal Committee, *Notice on Fully Utilising Legal Weapons to Punish the Unlawful and Criminal Actions of Falun Gong etc. Heretical Cult Organisations*, 5 November 1999.

97 Potter, 2003a: 328–36.

classified as heretical sects,[98] arguably renders their adherents vulnerable to RETL. The *RETL Regulations* now explicitly target those who use secret societies, heretical cults or feudal superstition to breach the law.[99]

The crime of counter-revolution, which was considered to be a legislative embodiment of class struggle,[100] was removed from the amended *Criminal Law* in 1997.[101] The *RETL Regulations* now follow the formula adopted in the revised *Criminal Law* and have replaced the offence of being a counter-revolutionary or anti-socialist reactionary with harming national security.[102] RETL has been used extensively in Tibet and Xinjiang, where the state has been unable to suppress opposition to Han Chinese control over those areas, or to quash local separatist movements.[103] The war on terror waged after 11 September 2001 has been used in China to strengthen suppression of religious and ethnically based separatist movements, especially in Xinjiang, where the state has associated the teaching of Islam with terrorist movements.[104] Human Rights Watch reported that the '2001 Hard Strike' campaign included those supporting independence in regions such as Xinjiang as targets.[105] Another group of people who are liable to be sent to RETL is those who repeatedly petition higher authorities and participate in mass public protests.[106]

(vii) Age limits

A person less than sixteen years old should not be sent to RETL.[107] This age limit accords with the provisions in other related areas concerning the incarceration of youths. Although it is possible for children between fourteen and eighteen to be convicted of a crime, in general a person aged under eighteen committing offences should not be liable to a criminal sanction.[108] The primary strategy to be taken with youths

98 Potter, 2003a: 330. 99 Article 9(4). 100 Xiao, 1996: 98–9.
101 *Temporary Measures*, art. 10(1).
102 Article 9(1). *Criminal Law*, arts. 102–113, setting out the offence of harming national security.
103 Potter, 2003a: 333–4. 104 Fu, 2005b: 827–8. 105 Human Rights Watch, 2001.
106 Human Rights Watch, December 2005: 56–60.
107 Cui, 1992: 18; Xia, 2001: 26; MPS, *Notice on Questions about the Age of RETL Personnel*, 30 November 1981, provides that 'in general a person sent to RETL should be over 16 years old' and offenders younger than sixteen should be sent to work study schools; MPS, MoJ, *Notice on Questions Concerning RETL and the Revocation of the Urban Household Registration of RETL Personnel*, 26 March 1984, provides that no one under sixteen years old is to be sent to RETL. The *Regulations on Public Security Organs Handling RETL Cases*, art. 9 provides that no persons under sixteen should be sent to RETL.
108 *Criminal Law*, art. 17.

under sixteen is to order the head of the family or guardian to subject the juvenile to discipline. When necessary, the juvenile may be sent to a work-study school for detention and training by the government.[109] The MPS *RETL Regulations* now set out the principle of strictly limiting the circumstances in which a minor is sent to RETL. It provides that if the parents, guardian or school have the capacity to control the offending minor, they should not be sent to RETL.[110]

2.2 Recent consolidation of targets

The view that fragmentation of the bases for defining targets was to be commended because of the flexibility it provided did not prevail. In October 1998, a national meeting was convened by the Central Political-Legal Committee to resolve issues about the scope of RETL. At that meeting it was determined that relevant agencies should work together to reach a fundamental resolution of the legal problems of RETL.[111] In October 2000 and April 2001, the MPS rescinded a number of normative documents,[112] including some setting out targets for RETL,[113] thus going some way to rationalising the targets of RETL. In the *RETL Regulations* the MPS set out a consolidated list of targets, though it did not narrow the scope of targets as it also included targets specified in 'any other regulation'.[114] Although the MPS asserts that the list of targets is based on earlier legislative instruments, and does not purport to codify the list of targets, the list has been modified to take account of changing economic and social circumstances. For example, the offence of repeatedly scalping tickets now includes scalping and forging receipts, train tickets, plane tickets and tickets that have value, but no longer requires that the tickets be allocated under the plan.[115]

109 Xia, 2001: 211–2 at 221, like the procedures for imposing RETL, the public security organs are responsible for a determination to send a juvenile to a work-study school; at 222–3, that the MoJ transferred juvenile detention to RETL, but that juveniles are detained and managed separately from adults.

110 That is, a person under eighteen: art. 10.

111 MPS, *Notice on Several Questions on the Scope of RETL*, 30 November 1998, reciting that representatives at this meeting were from the Legislative Affairs Commission of the NPC, Supreme People's Court, Supreme People's Procuratorate, Legal Office of the State Council, MPS and MoJ.

112 Keller, 1994: 722, describes normative documents as 'all administrative directives purporting to establish or modify norms of public or official behaviour'.

113 MPS, *Notice on Rescinding Some Jointly Signed Documents*, 13 October 2000; MPS, *79 Normative Documents recently rescinded by the PRC MPS*, 5 April 2001.

114 Article 9 generally and 9(10) in particular. Guo, 2005: 304, characterises this consolidation as limiting RETL to ten types of person and over forty-five types of conduct.

115 Article 9(3).

The previous offences of refusing to work and breaching labour discipline have now been removed and the new definition of targets now covers people who disrupt the order of production, work, study or life.[116]

2.3 'Hard Strike' and specialist struggles

RETL has been identified as a particularly useful and important tool in carrying out the '1983 Hard Strike' and subsequent specialist struggles,[117] as it is a component of a multi-layered system of punishments that complements the criminal justice system.[118] The use of RETL has been influenced by hard strikes in a number of ways: first, by expanding the scope of targets to include those targeted under the Hard Strike;[119] secondly, by increasing the rate of enforcement; and, thirdly, by lengthening the period of detention.[120]

The number of people sent to RETL during the initial stages of the '1983 Hard Strike' increased dramatically.[121] One commentator indicates that the number of people taken in for RETL during 1983 rose to 230,000.[122] One set of statistics indicates a total of 825,414 people were taken into RETL between 1983 and 1991; with 321,825 (or 39 per cent) taken in during the years of the '1983 Hard Strike' between August 1983 and January 1987; and 301,361 (or 36.5 per cent) taken in during the 'Six Evils' action between 1989 and 1991.[123] Prior to the launch of the campaign against the 'Six Evils' in 1989, localities were instructed to make 'necessary preparations' of detention centres in anticipation of the strike.[124]

Lengthening the period of detention was achieved by the system of retention for in-camp employment which was instituted in respect of both RETL and reform through labour.[125] Although in theory after release from RETL a person should be returned to their original work unit, in the pre-reform era some people were adjudged unable to be resettled and so remained at the RETL camp for employment.[126] The scope

[116] Article 9(5). [117] Cui, 1992: 19; Luo, 1992: 34; Xu and Fang, 1997: 96–7.
[118] Cui, 1992: 19; Zhu, Jiang, 1999: 32.
[119] Noted above, for example, in relation to the strike against the 'Six Evils'.
[120] Xu and Fang, 1997: 97; Cui, 1992: 18, asserts that retention for in-camp employment was introduced in the early 1980s as part of the Hard Strike campaign.
[121] SPP, *Notice on Implementing the Spirit of the National Political-Legal Work Conference by Strengthening the Work of Supervision over Detention Centres*, 31 August 1983, emphasising the need to improve supervision over detention centres.
[122] Xia, 2001: 21, and that the number of RETL camps expanded and their scope was increased.
[123] Luo, 1992: 34. [124] Reproduced at Chen, 1992: 148.
[125] Seymour and Anderson, 1998: 190, note that the system in respect of prisoners in reform through labour began in 1954.
[126] Jiang and Zhan, 1994: 99, citing a CCPCC regulation to this effect in 1965.

of retention for in-camp employment expanded with the passage on 19 June 1981 of the NPCSC *Decision on Handling Reform through Labour Criminals and RETL personnel who escape or commit new offences* which provided that certain types of people should have their urban household registration revoked, thus depriving them of the right lawfully to return to and live in their original place of residence.[127] Only those people whose household registration was from a large or medium-sized city (population over 300,000) could have their household registration revoked.[128]

Whilst targeted groups had their urban household registration revoked and were retained for in-camp employment, from the early 1980s others who had previously been retained for in-camp employment were progressively permitted to return to their homes, or had their status converted from detainee to ordinary worker.[129] During the first campaign of the '1983 Hard Strike', it was decided that until after the end of the first campaign, criminal inmates and RETL personnel whose sentence was complete and those who were eligible for release from in-camp employment would not be released.[130]

At the end of the first campaign of the '1983 Hard Strike', the CCPCC continued to approve the principle that those people whose criminal sentences or RETL time was complete should be retained for in-camp employment until they had truly reformed.[131] In 1985, the Party's Political-Legal Committee determined that the vast majority of those sent to reform through labour or RETL in Xinjiang should, in principle, be retained for in-camp employment after their sentence was complete.[132]

127 Article 1: 'RETL personnel who escape, or commit a crime within three years after release, or within five years after escaping, or if they are give a new term of RETL or their term is extended because of offences committed in RETL.' The *Temporary Measures*, art. 65, adds reform through labour personnel who commit an offence punished by RETL after release from reform through labour to this list.

128 Zhu, 1992: 304.

129 MPS, Ministry of Labour and Personnel, *Notice on Questions on the Remuneration of Personnel Retained for in Camp Employment after Completion of their Sentence*, 4 May 1983. For a discussion of the conditions for in-camp employment for ex-convicts in Xinjiang, Gansu and Qinghai and the gradual loosening up of the retention system during the 1980s, see Seymour and Anderson, 1998: 189–99.

130 MoJ, MPS, SPP, SPC, *Urgent Notice on Temporarily Halting the Return to Society of Criminals whose Sentence is Complete and RETL Personnel whose Time is Complete*, 19 August 1983.

131 CCPCC, approving and distributing the *Report of the Central Political-Legal Committee Summing up the Activities in the First Campaign of the Hard Strike against Serious Crime and the Deployments for the Second Campaign*, 20 August 1984.

132 Central Political-Legal Committee, *Situation Report and Opinions Concerning Work for the Coming Winter*, 21 September 1985: at 218.

However, Article 65 of the *Temporary Measures* and more recent police commentaries suggest that the period for in-camp employment is limited to three years. There is evidence to suggest that after the mid 1980s the numbers retained after their terms were completed decreased significantly.[133] Seymour and Anderson note that the parallel system of employment in reform through labour has decreased since the mid 1980s as a consequence of economic reform.[134] These trends, coupled with subsequent reforms to calculations of time limits for RETL and provisions for reduction of sentences, indicate that retention for in-camp employment has fallen into disuse.

2.4 Procedures for sending a person to RETL

(i) The changing examination and approval procedures: community participation and the RETL Management Committee

The procedures for imposing RETL have been amongst the most problematic of all police powers and have undergone a number of changes, especially since 2002. When it was first established, a range of community organisations participated in decisions to send a person to RETL. The 1957 *Decision of the State Council on the Question of RETL* provided that an application for RETL could be made to the People's Committee at the level of province; self-governing district; or directly governed city by the civil affairs bureau, public security department, local organisations, community groups, school, head of the household or guardian.[135]

As the regulation of RETL increasingly fell within the jurisdiction of government agencies in the late 1970s, community participation in the determination to send a person to RETL has diminished.[136] The *Temporary Measures* require that the decision-maker seeks the views of the local street committee or the work unit.[137] In 1999, the MPS issued a document removing the requirement to take account of the views of the local street committee and work unit. This document illustrates both the changing population demographic and the decreasing role of both the street committee and the work unit in maintaining order at the local level. It provides:

133 Epstein and Wong, 1996: 479–80, noting that since the 1980s the policy has been to release most inmates.
134 Seymour and Anderson, 1998: 197–8.
135 Article 3.
136 Zhang, Chong, 1990: 265–6.
137 Article 12.

However, now many of the people who need to be sent to RETL do not have employment or regular employment, nor do they have a fixed residence, so there is no way to obtain the views of the street committee or the work unit. Moreover, after publication of the *ARL* and the *ALL* there is a gradual strengthening of legal supervision over RETL. So when you are examining for approval RETL, according to the situation you can ask the opinion of the work unit where the person is located, or the local street committee, but you cannot base your decision solely on their opinion and gaining that opinion is not a mandatory procedural requirement.[138]

(ii) *Procedures for examination and approval by the public security organs*

In the 1979 *Supplementary Measures on RETL*, the Re-education through Labour Management Committee ('RETL Management Committee'), comprising representatives of the Civil Affairs Departments, Public Security and Labour Bureaux,[139] was given responsibility for examination and approval of applications to send a person to RETL.[140] The system of examination and approval by an RETL Management Committee has not been implemented in practice[141] and the substantive task of examination and approval of RETL is carried out by the public security organs.[142]

Prior to May 1983, all work relating to RETL, including examination and approval, was performed by the administration office of the RETL camp, which was concentrated in the hands of the RETL division of the public security organs.[143] After this time the responsibility for management of RETL camps was transferred to the MoJ.[144] The public security organs have subsequently been responsible only for examination and approval.[145]

[138] MPS, *Response to a Request for Instructions on Several Questions to do with the Procedure for Examination and Approval of RETL*, 9 June 1999.

[139] Later documents include as members of the committee the justice department and other (unspecified) departments: MPS, MoJ, *Notice on Questions Concerning RETL and the Revocation of the Urban Household Registration of RETL Personnel*, 26 March 1984.

[140] Articles 1 and 2. *Temporary Measures*, arts. 11 and 12, require the RETL Management Committee to approve a decision to impose RETL. The decision must be made at county level or above. *Temporary Measures*, art. 14 requires the RETL Management Committee to complete an 'RETL Decision Form' and an 'RETL Notification Form' before the person may be taken in for re-education.

[141] Hu, 2003: 144; Liu, 2001b: 16.

[142] Jiang and Zhan, 1994: 98; Ren, 1992: 12; Zhang, Chong, 1990: 266–7.

[143] Luo, 1992: 34; Xia, 2001: 22. [144] Xia, 2001: 347. [145] Luo, 1992: 34.

Commentators note that the RETL Management Committee exists in name only; it is at best a rubber stamp.[146] Structurally, there are several problems with the RETL Management Committee. The RETL Management Committee has no regular organisational structure to locate it within the state hierarchy; there is no hierarchical or supervisory relationship between different RETL Management Committees, the State Council and other government departments. In carrying out their duties, members' decision-making reflects the interests of government as their membership of the Committee is in their capacity as representatives of other government departments. The RETL Management Committee has no enforcement powers, and so depends upon the public security and justice departments to enforce its decisions.[147] The police consider examination and approval of RETL a natural extension of their powers to police social order.[148] Finally, the *APL*, passed in 1996, did not legally authorise the RETL Management Committee to impose an administrative punishment to deprive a person of their liberty; the public security organs are now the only state agency authorised to do this.[149]

Well before the legal incapacity of the RETL Management Committee to make decisions depriving a person of their liberty was made apparent, the MPS had been authorised to examine and approve RETL as the delegate of the RETL Management Committee. The *Notice on Questions concerning RETL and Revoking the Urban Household Registration of RETL Personnel* issued jointly by the MPS and the MoJ in 1984 provides that:

> [T]he organ for examination and approval of RETL is established within the public security organs and has been delegated by the RETL Management Committee to carry out examination and approval of people requiring RETL.[150]

As the *Temporary Measures* did not specify in any detail the procedures to be followed in the examination and approval of RETL, prior to the

[146] Ren, 1992: 12; Cheng, 1990: 253–4; Xia, 2001: 352–3.
[147] Xia, 2001: 188–9, 353.
[148] Ren, 1992: 12; Zhu, Jiang, 1999: 32; Zhang, Chong, 1990: 267–7; Hu, 2003: 144.
[149] *APL*, art. 16 limits the power to impose an administrative punishment to deprive a person of their liberty to the public security organs. See Zhu, Jiang, 1999: 32; Xia, 2001: 352.
[150] Article 2, at 104–5, discussed in Ren, 1992: 1; Zhang, Chong, 1990: 268.

passage of the *RETL Regulations* different localities established their own systems.[151]

In theory, the process for examination and approval of RETL involves several stages. The first is the preparation of a case report by the local police station or county-level public security organ.[152] Views of the street committee, family or work unit, if any, are sought at this stage.[153] These documents are then checked by the legal division of the county-level public security organ. The time limits vary between five and ten days in different areas.[154] The Application for Examination and Approval of RETL Form is completed in the name of the county-level public security organ.[155]

The application is then sent for examination and approval to the legal division of the provincial or autonomous region-level public security organ on behalf of the RETL Management Committee.[156] After approval,[157] the legal division obtains assent of the responsible officer and the seal of the RETL Management Committee is affixed[158] to the forms RETL Decision (*Laodong Jiaoyang Jueding Shu* 劳动教养决定书) and RETL Notification (*Laodong Jiaoyang Tongzhi Shu* 劳动教养通知书).[159] These documents are then sent to the original public security organ to execute the decision.[160]

The MPS continues to insist that the seal of the RETL Management Committee be affixed to the formal RETL decision and that

151 Xia, 2001: 178–9.
152 The case report (*jie'an baogao*) attaches relevant evidence and information. A form of application for examination and approval of RETL is also prepared.
153 Xia, 2001: 178–9. 154 Xia, 2001: 179.
155 *Chengqing Laodong Jiaoyang Shenpi Biao*. This standard form is reproduced in Chen *et al.*, 1996: 310–11.
156 In 1992, the responsibility for examination and approval of RETL within the public security organs was transferred from the Criminal Investigation Division and other divisions to the Legal Division: *MPS Notice on Changing the Responsibility and Leadership for Examination and Approval of RETL to the Legal Department*, 9 March 1992. Ren, 1992: 13, asserts that the responsibility for investigation and approval of RETL was not clear and so carried out by a range of divisions within the public security.
157 Xia, 2001: 180–2, examination and approval is usually a documentary examination, although it is possible for a direct investigation of the facts to take place.
158 Xia, 2001: 181–2.
159 The standard form documents are reproduced in Chen *et al.*, 1996: at 314–15 and 316–17, respectively.
160 Xia, 2001: 182, after these documents have had the seal attached, they are sent to the public security organ from which the matter originated, for delivery to the person and their family, the relevant RETL camp and the local people's procuratorate. The *Temporary Measures*, 1982, art. 14, provide that a person may not be detained unless these two documents have been properly prepared and signed.

decision-making power not be delegated to the county-level public security organs.[161]

(iii) *Problems with the approval process*

This approval process has been the subject of strong criticism. First, the legal division cannot be an impartial adjudicator of applications because its primary obligation is to act consistently with the institutional interests of the public security organs.[162] Secondly, the object of the decision has no opportunity to be heard in the decision-making process, which is carried out in secret, on the basis of documents.[163] Thirdly, the time for examination and approval is not shorter than two or three months and may be as long as eight or nine months, or longer.[164] In some cases the time may be even longer where an approval is sought to impose RETL only after an application for arrest has been refused by the procuratorate.[165] In 1987, the MPS demanded that the practice of holding people sentenced to RETL for less than one year in the local police lock-up or detention centre cease; and that all people be sent to a RETL camp within one month of their sentence being imposed.[166]

Police commentators recently acknowledged that the absence of procedural requirements for decision-making is an important deficiency in the legal definition of RETL.[167] The Legal Division of the MPS has itself identified the lack of procedural constraints in the determination to send a person to RETL as creating a subjective and unconstrained discretion which is the 'most easy to abuse'. Examination and approval of RETL has been identified by the public security organs themselves as one of the worst problems in current policing work.[168]

This abuse is both systematic and widespread. One commentator reported that a survey in 1990 of the police responsible for examination and approval of RETL considered rules about the scope of targets and procedures for approving RETL irrelevant. Their attitude was: 'We

[161] MPS, *Response to a Request for Instructions as to Whether it is Appropriate to Delegate the Examination and Approval Authority for RETL to the District or County-level Public Security Bureau*, 6 July 1989; MPS, *Notice on Several Questions about the Implementation of the ALL*, 30 October 1990.

[162] Chen, 2003: 106. [163] Chen, 2003: 106.

[164] Ren, 1992: 13. [165] Ren, 1992: 13.

[166] SPP, MPS, MoJ, *Notice that RETL Personnel Must be Sent to RETL Camps According to the Law*, 17 February 1987.

[167] Zhu, Jiang, 1999: 31–2. [168] Gong'an Bu, 1999: 20; see also Hu, 2003: 144.

fundamentally have no idea whether there are any rules about RETL' and 'We rely entirely on our experience in handling it.'[169]

The author noted that it was common to ignore the requirement that the offender 'not reform after repeated education', or 'refuse to listen to warnings and stop' and to approve RETL for the first transgression. RETL was also imposed on people who could not be sent to detention for investigation, but who also should not be sent to RETL.[170] One academic cited two examples of the abusive imposition of RETL in support of his argument that RETL be abolished. The first case involved a farmer caught stealing a purse on a public bus. The purse contained 15 Chinese cents (approximately AUD 3 cents) and the peasant was sent for two years' RETL.[171] The second involved a case in Sichuan province where an employer tried to coerce a female employee into prostituting. The girl refused and was paralysed after jumping from the building. Prior to the criminal trial, the employer was instead given one year of RETL by the local police.[172]

Chronic abuse of the examination and approval procedures has become a focus of a broader debate about the legality of RETL. Debates about whether to reform or abolish it are examined in chapter 9.

(iv) Recent reforms to regularise procedures for examination and approval of RETL

Police commentators acknowledge that the concentration of the power to investigate; to examine and approve a decision to send a person to RETL; to determine the period of detention; and to reconsider its own decisions when they are challenged is conducive to mistakes and abuse of power.[173] They acknowledge the urgent need for reform.

In 2002 the MPS passed the *RETL Regulations*, stating that one of the purposes was to regularise and address some of the major problems with the examination and approval procedures.[174] These regulations were supplemented in 2004 by the MPS, *Regulations on the Procedures for Handling Administrative Cases by Public Security Organs*, which regulate

169 Su, 1990: 261.
170 Because they were pregnant, blind, deaf, mentally disordered or had a serious disease: Su, 1990: 259–60. These categories of person are also ineligible to be sent to RETL according to art. 14(2) of the *Temporary Measures*, 1982.
171 Hu, 2003: 144–5. 172 Hu, 2003: 145.
173 Xia, 2001: 43, 87, 352–7; Su, 1990: 258–64; Xie, 2000: 123; Li, 1999: 20–1, where abuse of the examination and approval procedures for RETL was identified as one of the most serious problems in public security enforcement practice.
174 Effective on 1 June 2002.

police-imposed administrative punishments and coercive measures generally.[175]

The *RETL Regulations* require the establishment of an RETL Examination and Approval Committee within public security organs at prefectural and provincial and equivalent levels to issue RETL decisions in the name of the RETL Management Committee.[176] The Committee comprises a Chair and Vice Chair from the legal division and three to five committee members from other divisions of the public security organs, including the public order and criminal investigation divisions.[177] The regulations require that those involved in investigation of the case may not participate in its examination and approval.[178]

The *RETL Regulations* amend the existing procedures for examination and approval in a number of ways. The first specifies the form and contents required in the initial application prepared by the county-level public security organs.[179] The *Regulations on the Procedures for Handling Administrative Cases by Public Security Organs* set out procedural requirements for conducting interviews and gathering evidence.[180] The *RETL Regulations* require that the RETL application is then sent to the county-level public security legal division for verification,[181] which must be completed within three days.[182] The process of verification must be performed by at least two people and address a comprehensive list of designated matters.[183] An important difference from previous practice is that a prospective detainee must be interviewed as part of the verification procedure and a written record of interview prepared.[184]

Examination and approval of these documents is carried out at the prefectural level, or at a higher level by the RETL Examination and Approval Committee established at that level.[185] In some cases, the committee is required to re-interview the subject of the application and canvass the views of the applicant. Those situations are: where the case is serious, difficult or complex; where the subject does not make an acknowledgement or gives contradictory evidence; or where there are doubts that the evidence about the unlawful act is objective or lawful.[186] This process must be completed within three days of receipt of

[175] Article 2. See discussion in chapter 5 at section 2.7. [176] Article 2.
[177] Article 3. [178] Articles 3 and 6. [179] Articles 13, 14 and 15.
[180] Article 37, that interviews and investigations must be carried out by at least two officers; art. 48, that a person may be interviewed only for twelve hours with possible extensions of up to forty-eight hours.
[181] Article 16. [182] Article 18.
[183] Article 16; art. 18 sets out the matters to be addressed in the report.
[184] Article 17. [185] Article 20. [186] Article 20.

the application documents, but may be extended to fifteen days where further investigation or re-interviewing of the potential detainee is required.[187]

A significant departure from previous practice is to allow certain categories of person to request a hearing prior to the RETL decision being made.[188] The *RETL Regulations* provide that minors and persons who may be sent to RETL for more than two years may request a hearing. People sentenced to less than two years, drug addicts and 'people using heretical cults to wreck the implementation of national law' are excluded from exercising this right.[189]

Within two days of the RETL Examination and Approval Committee reaching its decision, it must notify those eligible to request a hearing of this right. An application for a hearing must be made within two days of receipt of notification.[190] If a hearing is not requested, the decision to impose RETL will be issued. The hearing is conducted by the RETL Examination and Approval Committee that made the RETL decision. Although the applicant may invite up to three persons who are close relatives or representatives of the work unit to attend, the *RETL Regulations* are silent on whether the applicant may have a legal representative.[191]

2.5 Limitation and time limits

The *RETL Regulations* set a limitation period of three years. If the police have not discovered the offence within three years after it was committed, the person cannot be sent to RETL for that offence, unless they have been discovered and absconded, or the victim files a complaint. In those cases there is no limitation period.[192]

Currently the term for RETL is between one and three years.[193] The RETL Examination and Approval Committee determines the initial period of detention. For the first time in 2002, the MPS specified the principles for determining the length of RETL, providing that it should

[187] Articles 18, 21.

[188] The term used here is *lingxun* 聆询. In the *APL* the term for hearing is *tingzheng* 听证. Although the process is similar, the MPS has chosen to use a different term in order to distinguish an RETL hearing from that carried out under the *APL*.

[189] Article 25. A hearing is only available under the terms of the *RETL Regulations* as the *Regulations on the Procedures for Handling Administrative Cases by Public Security Organs* do not permit a hearing in respect of RETL. The proviso in art. 89(4) that a hearing will be available where 'laws and regulations provide otherwise' suggests that these regulations are also permissive of the *sui generis* hearing procedures in the *RETL Regulations*.

[190] Article 26. [191] Article 32. [192] Article 43. [193] *Temporary Measures*, art. 13.

take account of the nature and circumstances of the offence, the motivation of the person and the degree of social harm caused. Nine discrete time periods are now prescribed, starting with one year and increasing in three-month increments up to the maximum of three years. A minor should not be given a term exceeding one-and-a-half years.[194]

Depending on the behaviour of the RETL camp detainee, the camp management may adjust the amount of time actually spent in the camp.[195] If the person at the end of their term has not reformed well, the period of detention may be extended for periods that cumulatively do not exceed one year.[196] The MoJ and the RETL organs are responsible for management, education and reform of inmates and are entrusted by the RETL Management Committee to carry out the examination and approval of giving early release, extending or shortening the time for RETL by up to three months.[197]

3 CONCLUSION

The analysis in this chapter reveals both continuity and change in the development of RETL in the reform era. There remains a high degree of continuity in the policy and administrative processes by which the scope and procedures for imposing RETL are defined. The documents that provide the ongoing definition and redefinition of targets of RETL are primarily administrative directives issued by administrative agencies, supplemented by policy documents issued by the CCPCC and other Party committees. The vague definition of targets, lack of strict procedural requirements for its imposition and concentration of examination and approval power in the hands of the public security organs ensures that RETL remains a flexible tool and facilitates its use during 'Hard Strikes' and periods of concerted enforcement action.

In the reform era, the instrumental objectives served by RETL have changed. From the outset, when RETL primarily targeted politically unreliable state employees and Party members, it has become increasingly focussed on acts that disrupt social order and harm the social fabric, such as repeated prostitution, gambling and drug addiction.

[194] *Regulations on Public Security Organs Handling RETL Cases*, art. 44.

[195] Xia, 2001: 202.

[196] Jiang and Zhan, 1994: 98; MoJ, *Response to a Request for Instructions on Extending the Time for RETL*, 27 July 1991.

[197] MPS, MoJ, *Notice on Questions Concerning RETL and the Revocation of the Urban Household Registration of RETL Personnel*, 26 March 1984.

Especially since the MPS issued the *RETL Regulations*, the targets of RETL have increasingly been defined with reference to criminal offences as set out in *Criminal Law*. Even groups such as the Falun Gong, which would generally be considered to be politically defined targets, are subjected to RETL, using the language of heretical sects which is analogous to the language used in the *Criminal Law*. Pragmatic uses of RETL are illustrated by its use as a partial substitute for detention for investigation after that power was absorbed into the amended *CPL* to fill in perceived gaps left in police criminal investigation powers.

However, it is becoming increasingly difficult for enforcement agencies to justify the flexibility of the power in light of the chorus of criticism about arbitrary and abusive uses of RETL. Recently the MPS responded to some of these criticisms when it issued the *RETL Regulations*, which have taken initial steps to consolidate and reinterpret the targets of RETL to take account of the current social and economic environment in which RETL is now used. They also impose some constraints upon the procedural flexibility previously enjoyed by the police in imposing RETL. Whilst these regulations may be interpreted as seeking to regularise the procedures for imposing RETL to some extent, they do not limit the scope of targets, or the power of the MPS to impose RETL. In the following chapters, I discuss the developing body of law that forms the basis for challenging specific decisions to impose RETL, the continuing flexibility of the power and even its continued existence in its current form.

PART THREE

LEGAL REFORM AND ITS IMPACT ON ADMINISTRATIVE DETENTION

CHAPTER SEVEN

BUILDING A LEGAL ENVIRONMENT FOR POLICE DETENTION

1 INTRODUCTION

In chapters 4, 5 and 6, my examination of the development of administrative detention powers in the context of social order policy since the late 1970s has shown the perseverance of political and administrative definitions of both the scope and procedures for imposing administrative detention. Although the purposes for the imposition of administrative detention are now more pragmatic than ideological, administrative detention remains a flexible tool for use by the public security organs.

The focus of the inquiry changes in chapters 7, 8 and 9 to consider administrative detention from the point of view of the legal system. I examine developments in the legal regulation of administrative powers of state organs and how they impact on administrative detention.

In this chapter, I first discuss Party leadership of the public security organs, both organisational and ideological, and of enforcement policy. I contend that legalisation of police power occurs within the parameters of Party leadership and that the authority of the Party in advocating 'governance according to law' has given impetus to efforts to legalise and regularise police power.

I then focus on two interrelated issues. First, the process of legalisation and rationalisation of state power since 1978 and how this has impacted on police administrative detention powers. I consider the extent to which the developments in the legal system under the policy of 'administration according to law' (*yifa xingzheng* 依法行政) have created pressure for administrative detention powers to be structured legally rather than politically and administratively. In particular, I point to recent reforms suggesting that the flexibility of these powers is increasingly in conflict with evolving principles of administrative law and that administrative detention, too, should be made to conform more closely to the legal principles of procedural regularity currently being articulated.

Secondly, I ask what evidence there is of an emerging space in which different actors, including the MPS, compete to define the law regulating administrative detention. Framed as a question as to whether these changes suggest the emergence of a legal field in Bourdieu's sense,[1] I trace the pluralisation of the uses of law; its role as a tool for institution-building; defining and constraining administrative rule-making powers; and defining the balance between empowerment and constraint in respect of specific powers. I note the contests relating to the legal principles for formulation and exercise of administrative powers generally and the applicability of these principles to administrative detention.

Pluralisation of positions and competition over determination of the law occurs within the constraints of continuing Party leadership over both the public security organs and law enforcement policy, as well as within accepted parameters of the policy of 'administration according to law'. The picture of the development of law in this area is complicated by the tensions that arise between the law reform and public order agendas of the Party and the police. These tensions are particularly pronounced at times of Hard Strikes and concerted actions against targeted groups such as the Falun Gong. I conclude that the programme of 'ruling the country according to law' has given impetus to the process of legalisation and rationalisation of police powers. The balance between law functioning to empower and to constrain police power is contested. Rather than showing this change as part of a continuum of legal change culminating in the rule of law,[2] this chapter concludes that whilst it is possible to trace both legalisation and rationalisation of police powers, these processes still remain closely tied to Party leadership. The MPS is one player amongst others, including academics and legislators. It is actively seeking to ensure that these powers have an adequate legal basis to justify their existence and to implement procedural rules in a manner that preserves flexibility in enforcement.

[1] Discussed in chapter 2 at section 2.
[2] See chapter 1, notes 53 and 54.

2 THE POLITICAL BOUNDARIES OF POLICE REFORM: PARTY LEADERSHIP OVER THE POLICE AND ENFORCEMENT POLICY

In his speech to the preparatory meeting of Third Plenum of the 11th CCPCC Meeting in December 1978, Deng Xiaoping emphasised that the reinvigoration of people's democracy[3] and the programmes of economic reform and modernisation must be institutionalised by law.[4]

For the police, adoption of these programmes required them to engage in a programme of far-reaching reform. As one of the political-legal organs of state,[5] the public security organs had been primarily responsible for suppressing class enemies and exercising the dictatorship function of the state.[6] In their own words, the public security forces were a 'sharpened weapon for suppression of class enemies'.[7] The primary function of the public security organs since their establishment in 1927 had been to protect the power of the CCP, with their organisation being transferred to the government from the Party in 1948.[8] However, the public security organs remained primarily under the leadership of the Party and drew on the army as their model.[9] Prior to 1979, the police were a revolutionary force, required primarily to resolve contradictions between the classes and to oppress and eliminate counter-revolutionaries.[10]

The revolutionary nature of police work did not change until 1979.[11] At the National Conference of Public Security Office and Bureau Chiefs in January 1979 it was resolved to change the focus of police work to protecting the success of the economic modernisation programme. The tasks of the police were to: '[C]onscientiously transform [themselves] from taking class struggle as the key link and serving political

[3] That is, democratic centralism. [4] Deng, 1978: 158.

[5] Potter, 2003b: 64–5, citing Peng Zhen, describes the CCP's Political-Legal Committees as 'responsible for directing and linking up the work of organs concerning civil affairs, public security, judicial affairs, bureaux of investigations, law courts, and supervision as well as for the disposal of mutual relations between organisations and work'.

[6] Shih, 1999: 9; Wang, Fang, 1993: 25–33, at 29, stating that the primary tasks of the police are to attack class enemies and protect the people.

[7] von Senger, 1985: 172; Wang, Fang, 1993: 26; Zhengci Falu Jiaoyanshi, 1983: 4, cites Lenin in support of the proposition that as an instrument of class rule, the police are an instrument of violence to carry out the dictatorship of the proletariat.

[8] Xi and Yu, 1996: 174–5. See also Dutton, 2005: 38–40. [9] Dutton, 2005: 139.

[10] Wang, Fang, 1993: 25; Cui, 1993a: 354; Zhengci Falu Jiaoyanshi, 1983: 3–4.

[11] Cui, 1993a: 354.

movements, to taking the path of protecting the four modernisations and serving economic construction. . . .'[12]

The National Conference determined that the focus of policing was to shift from violent large-scale mass campaigns for attacking class enemies to protecting social stability, strengthening public order management and attacking crime.[13] The primary task of the public security organs was now to protect the successful implementation of the programme of economic reform and socialist modernisation.[14] Addressing that conference, Peng Zhen emphasised the need for the public security organs, procuratorates and courts all to exercise their powers according to law.[15]

Senior Party leaders have conceived the programme of legal system reconstruction in instrumental terms; law reflects and is designed to implement Party policy. In a speech to heads of provincial-level people's congresses, Peng Zhen[16] made this view explicit. He explained that the use of law as the basis of governance was 'a step by step progression from handling affairs according to Party policy, to establishing and perfecting the legal system and handling affairs according to law'.[17] Peng argued that law is necessary for governance in the reform era. However, he saw no conflict between Party leadership and handling matters according to law, as in his view, 'law codifies Party policies and the Party leads the people in both observing and enforcing the law'.[18]

Reflecting his instrumentalist view of law, Peng saw the obligation of the public security organs to implement the Party line and law as one. According to him, the Party line and national law was the 'heaven' above the public security organs and the people, and the mass-line was the 'earth' below them.[19]

One police officer has explained that the introduction of the economic reform policy has not changed the character of the police force as a tool of the people's democratic dictatorship. Leadership of the Party and adherence to the mass-line remained unchanged as the fundamental tenets of policing.[20] The change, he asserted, only affected

[12] The *Key Points of Public Security Work* were adopted in January 1979 at a national conference of public security department and bureau heads: Xi and Yu, 1996: 367; Gao, 1994: 326–7.
[13] Xi and Yu, 1996: 367–8.
[14] Xi and Yu, 1996: 367; Peng, 1982: 282–3, emphasising this point in 1982.
[15] Peng, 1979: 186–7. At that time Peng was the Chair of the Central Political-Legal Committee.
[16] At the time of the speech in 1984, Peng was Chair of the NPCSC.
[17] Peng, 1984: 362. [18] Peng, 1984: 363; Potter, 2003b: 110–11.
[19] Peng, 1979: 185–6.
[20] Zhengci Falu Jiaoyanshi, 1983: 7; in relation to party leadership at 10–12; and the mass-line at 12–14. Wang, Fang, 1993: 25, 52.

the scope of responsibilities and specific nature of the tasks to be performed.[21]

Within these parameters, police reform has been marked by the strengthening of both legal regulation of police organisation and professional standards, despite some initial ambivalence about professionalism for fear of being accused of elitism and deviation from the mass-line.[22]

3 REBUILDING THE PUBLIC SECURITY ORGANS

3.1 Reform of the police since 1979

The task of reconstructing the public security organs began with decisions to revive the criminal investigation division; to strengthen local-level public order work;[23] and to revive the local-level organisations involved in that work, including residents' committees, mediation committees and security defence committees.[24] In April 1983, the CCPCC approved a decision of the Central Political-Legal Committee to undertake a systematic and comprehensive reform of the public security organs, including strengthening the legal basis of police organisation and powers.[25]

Since then, police reforms have gradually created a more professional force.[26] Increasingly, emphasis has been placed on education and specialist technical training of police officers, with the establishment of 101 police educational institutions between 1980 and the end of 1995.[27] In 2002, for example, 50,000 police officers studied for college diplomas; 35,000 studied for tertiary qualifications; 520,000 participated in new recruit training, professional or promotions training; 16,000 economic criminal investigation police sat proficiency tests; and 280,000 police attended skills training programmes.[28] Reform of the police force has received a strong impetus from the current Minister of Public Security, Zhou Yongkang.[29]

[21] Gao, 1994: 326. [22] Ward and Bracey, 1985: 36.
[23] Xi and Yu, 1996: 357–8. [24] Peng, 1982: 287.
[25] Xi and Yu, 1996: 395–6, referring to *Several Questions Concerning Strengthening and Reform of the Public Security Work*, adopted at that meeting. Decisions at this meeting included transfer of responsibility for management of RETL camps to the MoJ and creation of a separate, armed police force, the People's Armed Police.
[26] Dutton, 2000: 69–70. [27] Shen and Xu, 1997: 138. [28] Gong'an Bu, 2002: 65.
[29] Hu and Sun, 14 August 2003, where he is described by Wang Dawei, professor at the China Public Security University, as a 'strong minister who dares to face problems squarely, is good at grasping crucial issues and is keen on reform'. See also Fu, 2005c: 249–51.

3.2 *People's Police Law* 1995 ('PPL')

Central to the rebuilding and professionalisation of the police force was the drafting of a comprehensive *PPL*. Drafting commenced in 1982 and the final version was enacted in 1995.[30] The *PPL* is designed to be the basic organisational law of the police and to 'provide norms for modern police work'.[31]

The final version of the law did not include any reference to the nature of the police force as a 'tool of the people's democratic dictatorship'. What does this signal, if anything, about the relationship between legal reform and the political nature of policing? During the review by the NPCSC of the draft, some members of the NPCSC expressed the view that specification of police tasks adequately described the nature of the police force without need for more overtly political references in the law.[32] Although on its face the legislation may appear to be a technical and rational description of police organisation and powers, the police themselves resist any inference that the law weakens their dictatorship function.[33] In support of their position, they point to CCPCC documents issued in 1990 and 1991 that refer to the police as the 'important tool of the people's democratic dictatorship' and argue that the responsibilities enumerated in the *PPL* lead to the same conclusion.[34] However, removal of political descriptions of the nature of the police force in favour of technical definitions could also support a conclusion that the privileged political status enjoyed by the police in the pre-reform era as the senior partner in the state's coercive apparatus of *gongjianfa* is eroding.[35]

30 Effective on 28 February 1995. *Explanation of the 'PRC People's Police Law'* reproduced in Lang, 1995: 169–73. The *PPL* replaced the NPCSC *People's Police Regulations*, 25 June 1957, as the primary legislative document setting out the powers, functions and responsibilities of the police.

31 MPS, *Notice Issuing a Propaganda Outline on the PRC People's Police Law*, 28 February 1995. Ma, 1997: 113, arguing that passage of the *PPL* in 1995 represented 'the most significant event in China's efforts to create a more professional and modern police force'. See also Ward and Bracey, 1985: 36.

32 Law Committee of the NPC, *Report on the Results of the Review of the (draft) 'PRC PPL'*, 15 February 1995, in Gao, 1995: 180; Luo, 1995: 25–6, discussing the differences of opinion expressed within the NPCSC on this question.

33 Luo, 1995: 25–8.

34 Luo, 1995: 26–7, referring to the December 1990 CCPCC *Recommendation on the Ten Year Plan and 'Eighth Five year' Plan for establishment of the national economy and social development* and the October 1991, CCPCC decision on strengthening public security work (formal title not given).

35 *Gongjianfa* 公检法 refers to the police, procuratorate and courts. Fu, 1994: 280–1, discussing the loss of political prestige by the police in the reform era.

The *PPL* sets out the basic organisational structure of the police forces, specific powers of the police[36] and basic principles for the exercise of police powers. The *PPL* restates in the reform era the basic principle of 'legality in administrative action' for police work, requiring police to act in accordance with the *Constitution* and the laws and to enforce the law strictly.[37] The *PPL* specifies other basic norms upon which police must base their conduct,[38] including exercising their powers in accordance with public morality and with respect for the customs of the masses of the people.[39] The *PPL*, for the first time, explicitly prohibits extracting confessions through torture; using physical punishments;[40] unlawfully depriving a person of her or his freedom; committing illegal searches of the person, or the property or home of a person;[41] and beating, abusing or causing someone else to beat or abuse another person.[42]

The *PPL* introduces minimum criteria that must be met for recruitment into the police force and sets out requirements for education and training and criteria for promotion through the ranks and for demotion and punishment.[43]

The MPS has introduced a range of measures based on these provisions of the *PPL* to improve the professional quality of the police as well as to strengthen its oversight of the professional standards of local police.[44] Amongst other measures, it has introduced criteria to evaluate performance based on achieving set objectives;[45] changed recruitment criteria; standardised officer rankings;[46] introduced training requirements;[47] made permission to carry out police work dependent

36 *PPL*, chapter 2.

37 *PPL*, art. 4. According to the legislative hierarchy, as a basic-level law, the *PPL* must be consistent with the *Constitution*. Rules setting out specific police powers must conform to the *Constitution* and the *PPL*. The wording of the obligation of the police to obey the law differs from that set out in the *People's Police Regulations*, 1957, art. 3, which stated that the police must observe the *Constitution* and the law. *PPL*, 1995, art. 4, emphasises the role of law in regulating as well as empowering law by providing that the police 'must take the Constitution and laws as their code of conduct'.

38 Set out in *PPL*, chapter 3, Duties and Discipline.

39 *PPL*, art. 20.

40 *PPL*, art. 22(4).

41 *PPL*, art. 22(5).

42 *PPL*, art. 22(7). These provisions are not in the 1957 *People's Police Regulations*.

43 *PPL*, chapter 4; and discussion in Zhongguo Jingcha Xuehui, 2002: 181–3.

44 Meng, 1993: 1–4, citing recruitment standards, supervision of performance, strengthening internal discipline and improving pay. The need to strengthen education and professional ethical standards; to improve training; and to strengthen systems for management and control of police conduct is discussed in Gao, 1994: 331–4; and Sun, Juan, 1994: 341–4.

45 *Mubiao guanli* (目标管理): Wong, 2002: 303–4.

46 Wong, 2002: 305.

47 MPS, *Temporary Regulations on Training of the Public Security Organs' People's Police*, 16 August 1995.

upon passing a test;[48] strengthened ideological work; set more open criteria for promotion and rewards and punishments;[49] introduced systems for individual responsibility for failure to perform and for faults in performance of functions;[50] improved standards of remuneration;[51] and sought to improve the service ethic of local police.[52]

The MPS has been creating an increasingly comprehensive legislative net to regulate all aspects of police work and conduct. Law has been an important tool by which the MPS has sought to strengthen professional standards in policing and so strengthen central control over the conduct of the police at the local level.[53]

4 LIMITATIONS ON INSTITUTIONAL AUTONOMY: PARTY LEADERSHIP AND LOCAL CONTROL OVER POLICE FINANCES

In theory, creation of a comprehensive legislative infrastructure not only empowers the police but also institutionalises a complex organisational structure, making it less subject to *ad hoc* manipulation or particularised controls by the Party or local governments. This is in contrast to the pre-reform era when police were seen as an instrument of the Party.[54] For many nations, including China, increasing technical specialisation of the police and the creation of internal systems of accountability have been ways through which the police forces have asserted some degree of institutional autonomy.[55] However, the relationship between the police and the Party is more complex than simply one of subordination. Many police officers occupy senior positions in the Party and party committees at each level, and so exercise significant influence over the Party decisions that, in turn, the police are required to implement.

48 MPS, *Temporary Measures on Testing the Basic Quality of the Public Security Organ Police* (attaching the *Temporary Measures*), 8 May 1997.

49 Wong, 2002: 302–3.

50 Gong, 1994; MPS, *Regulations on the Internal Enforcement Supervision Work of Public Security Organs*, 11 June 1999; MPS *Regulations on Holding Public Security Organs People's Police Accountable for Faults in Enforcement*, 11 June 1999.

51 Meng, 1993: 3–4.

52 Zheng, 2000, discussing the programme to 'make the people satisfied' with the police (*rang renmin qunzhong manyi* 让人民群众满意).

53 Discussed in chapter 8 at section 3.

54 Fu, 1994: 278.

55 Arguments about the professional and technical nature of policing have been used to bolster the powers and independence of the police forces in many Western countries. Dixon, 1997: 6–7; in relation to China, see Fu, 1994: 277.

There are a number of structural and financial impediments to further strengthening of institutional independence of the public security organs. Party ideological and organisational leadership over the police operates as the first constraint. Control exercised by local governments is the second.

4.1 Party leadership over public security organs and enforcement policy

Party leadership over public security organs remains a basic tenet of policing.[56] The increasing professionalisation of the police and any resulting increase in institutional autonomy is limited by the nature of continuing Party ideological and organisational leadership over the police.[57] Party leadership in theory involves policy and ideological leadership and guidance but not direct involvement by the Party Committee in administrative management or examination and approval of specific cases.[58]

In 1981 Peng Zhen restated the principle that the public security organs implement law under Party leadership. He said:

> The Party leads the people in formulating law, the Party also leads the people in implementing the law. The political-legal organs are dictatorship organs, they hold the great power of life and death, so they must especially place themselves under the leadership of the Party Committee at each level. If they refuse Party leadership, have a system of their own, implement vertical leadership, become divorced from the leadership of the Party Committee at each level and don't closely rely on Party leadership, then they will not be able to do their work well and will not be able successfully to complete their duties. This is especially so for the public security organs. When the time comes that they keep secrets from the Party, close off from it, only partially report the situation to the Party, or become divorced from Party leadership, then there will certainly be chaos . . .[59]

[56] Xi and Yu, 1996: 358; Wang, Fang, 1993: 38; Fu, 1994: 278–9.

[57] Zhengci Falu Jiaoyanshi, 1983: 11–12.

[58] *CCP Constitution*, Preamble provides: 'Leadership of the Party means mainly political, ideological and organisational leadership.' Peng, 1979: 187; Potter, 2003b: 130; Zhengci Falu Jiaoyanshi, 1983: 12, citing unnamed CCPCC documents issued in 1980 (Document 5) and 1982 (Document 5), as setting out the manner in which leadership is exercised by the local Party committee over the work of political-legal organs; by managing Party programmes and policies, thought and political work and supervising the political-legal organs under it to ensure they handle matters in accordance with the state *Constitution*, laws and decrees.

[59] Peng, 1992c: 90–1, reiterating a speech he made at the 6th National Public Security Conference, *Public Security Work Must Rely on the Masses*, 9 June 1954, in Peng, 1991b: 253–4.

Potter argues that the Party sought to retain sufficient control over local-level enforcement practices to ensure implementation of its policies. By controlling the 'mechanisms and processes of state power' through law, the Party could thus ensure that the Party and the state maintained its monopoly on the use of coercion.[60]

4.2 Party organisational leadership over law enforcement: the Political-Legal Committee and the Comprehensive Management of Public Order Committee

'Police affairs' falls within the purview of the political-legal functional system,[61] the apex of which is the Political-Legal Committee of the CCP.[62] The committee is headed by a Politburo or Politburo Standing Committee member and comprises the Ministers of State Security and Public Security, the Chief of the People's Armed Police, the Chief Judge of the SPC, the Chief Procurator, the NPC Vice Chairman and the Ministers of Justice and Supervision.[63]

The Political-Legal Committee is in charge of the state's 'civilian coercive apparatus' and plays a central role in directing the social order policies and co-ordinating the work of the political-legal organs of state (primarily the public security organs, the people's procuratorates and the people's courts) in implementing those policies.[64] In a speech made at the first meeting of the Committee in 1980, Peng Zhen emphasised the co-ordinating and consensus-broking role played by the Political-Legal Committee. He asserted that its task was to ensure that all organs work in a complementary fashion to achieve the identified objectives; that a consensus about the 'right' result be reached and that all agencies implement that result.[65]

The role of the Political-Legal Committee at local levels has been described as follows:

> The Political-Legal Committee of the Party at each level is a work department of the Party Committee. It is responsible for liaising between and directing the work of the political-legal organs (the police, procuratorate

[60] Potter, 2003b: 112–16. [61] Yan, 1995: 4 (*xitong* 系统).

[62] Li, Qiyan, 1993: 353. The Committee was re-established on 24 January 1980 with Peng Zhen as its Secretary.

[63] Yan, 1995: 4; Potter, 1998: 18, describing the composition of political-legal organs.

[64] Li, Qiyan, 1993: 353, defines its tasks as: making recommendations to the CCPCC about political-legal work; co-ordinating the work of political-legal organs at each level; and directing 'unified deployments' to implement Party social order policies and to supervise implementation of Party policies. See also Lieberthal, 1995: 199.

[65] Peng, 1992b: 216–18.

> and courts), assisting the Party Committee in investigating and managing cadres and in the appropriate handling of major and important matters and organising and promoting all aspects of implementation of the Comprehensive Management of Public Order.[66]

The Political-Legal Committee was central in determinations to launch the 'Hard Strikes' of the 1980s to the 2000s and in directing the operation of those strikes.[67] Potter describes Peng Zhen's view as being one that 'the campaign was a political matter in which Party leadership was needed to ensure consistency in enforcement and in avoiding errors in the treatment and punishment of criminals; issues that were primarily of organisation and policy rather than law'.[68] Such a view could be interpreted as separating law from policy decisions about enforcement, or as describing the limits he perceived to the role of law in addressing problems of crime and social order. In either case, hard strikes insert the Party and its committees directly into law-making and enforcement activities. 'Hard Strikes' have been implemented by amending the legal definitions of targets and punishment of those targets to accommodate the needs of the hard strike. They have resulted directly in abuse of power by increasing the scope of targets and the rate of enforcement.[69]

Within China, much criticism had been levelled against the Political-Legal Committee as epitomising the lack of separation between the courts, procuratorates and police.[70] It has been criticised as undermining proper judicial process by interfering with the work of the people's procuratorates and the people's courts and interfering in the specific handling of some individual cases.[71]

Since 1979, the Political-Legal Committee's direct involvement in legislative drafting appears to have diminished. Tanner argues that it now plays an 'almost negligible role' in legislative drafting and policy, outside the sphere of criminal law.[72]

As part of the political system reform adopted by the CCPCC 13th Congress in 1987, a decision was made to abolish the Political-Legal

66 Zhengci Falu Jiaoyanshi, 1983: 12. 67 See chapters 4, 5 and 6.

68 Potter, 2003b: 131. 69 Discussed in chapters 4, 5 and 6.

70 Baum, 1994: 193–6, discussing the arguments supporting greater separation of the Party from daily administration.

71 Wang, Huanxin, 1989: 152. Trevaskes, 2003a, discussing how, during periods of hard strikes, ordinary trial processes are supplanted by more expressive forms of punishment, including mass sentencing rallies which implement more punitive and populist modes of sentencing.

72 Tanner, Murray Scot, 1999: 62–3.

Committee.[73] Tanner reports that this decision was opposed by several senior Party officials, including Peng Zhen and that, in the end the Committee was downgraded from the status of Committee to Leading Group.[74] This decision was not implemented as a result of the political backlash after the Tian'anmen Square crackdown in June 1989.[75] After that time Political-Legal Committees have become increasingly involved in directing law enforcement.[76]

As discussed in chapter 4, in order to enhance the work of the Political-Legal Committee and to strengthen control over social order policy and law enforcement, the Party established the Comprehensive Management of Public Order Committee ('CMPO Committee') in 1991 under the State Council and the CCPCC.[77] Its primary task is oversight of the implementation of the CMPO. In an effort to improve local enforcement of the CMPO, the central CMPO Committee instituted a system of leadership responsibility in 1998.[78] Under this system, the Party or government head is responsible for social order outcomes, signing a letter of responsibility. Performance is inspected and appraised and then rewards or administrative sanctions are imposed on the basis of performance against targets.[79]

There is evidence to suggest, however, that the Party's control over local-level enforcement is not as comprehensive as it may wish. The CMPO Committee was established to stem the deterioration of social order in the late 1980s and to ensure consistent enforcement of social order policy at the local level.[80] There are indications that the new structure has not resulted in increasing control over local-level social order work.[81] There is also evidence of growing local dissatisfaction

[73] Li, Qiyan, 1993: 353; Tanner, Murray Scot, 1999: 63–4.

[74] Tanner, Murray Scot, 1999: 64.

[75] Li, Qiyan, 1993: 353, in 1993 lists the Political-Legal Committee as a Committee of the CCPCC; Peng, Zhen, 1990: 447. In 1990 Peng Zhen addressed a meeting on political-legal work, calling for strengthened Party leadership over political-legal organs. Epstein, 1994: 42, citing unconfirmed reports that soon after Tian'anmen Square the Political-Legal Committees were rebuilt and strengthened.

[76] Meng, 1994: 19, referring to the ongoing role of the political-legal committees and CMPO committees in organising and directing concerted actions and 'Hard Strikes' against crime. Wang and Zhou, 1993: 9, but at 10 pointing out limitations on its capacity to exercise its leadership role.

[77] Chen, 1992: 25; Wang and Zhou, 1993: 9, noting a problem of the relationship between the CMPO Committee and the Political-Legal Committee being poorly defined.

[78] CCPCC of the CMPO Committee, *Main Points of Nationwide Comprehensive Management of Public Order Work for 1998*, in Wang, Shengjun, 2000: 23–5.

[79] Xinhua News Agency, 11 March 2000, reporting on the resolutions adopted at the March 2000 meeting of the Central CMPO Committee.

[80] CCPCC, State Council, *Decision on Strengthening the CMPO*, 1991.

[81] Yin, 1996: 2.

with continuing reliance on hard strikes and increasing resistance to carrying them out.[82]

4.3 Party organisational leadership over public security organs

Police organs at each level are under the leadership of the public security organs at the next higher administrative level, the local Party Committee[83] and the local government.[84] A political department is established in the public security organ at each level with responsibility to 'ensure implementation of the Party line and policies, ensure the successful performance of policing tasks, and be responsible for the organisational and ideological construction of police personnel and police management'.[85] The police chief exercises responsibility under the collective leadership of the Party Committee or Party Group established within that organ. The Party Committee is responsible for making decisions about matters concerning the Party line and policies, disposition of important work, appointment and dismissal, transfer and handling of important personnel, important questions impacting on the interests of the masses and matters designated by higher-level organs.[86]

The Party also scrutinises the work of the police through its Discipline Inspection Committee, which has an office in each level of public security bureau.[87] The Party's Discipline Inspection Committee is responsible for ensuring Party members adhere to Party discipline and follow the Party line in carrying out enforcement activities. It has power to investigate acts in breach of Party discipline and to impose an internal Party disciplinary sanction.[88]

82 Zhang, 1991: 97 and chapter 4, at section 10.

83 Lieberthal, 1995: 200, describing this as a system of 'dual leadership'. However, he does not explicitly take into account the control exercised by the local government over the police.

84 *PPL*, art. 116; Hui, 2000: 82–4. Vertical leadership (*tiaotiao* 条条) by the higher-level public security organs and horizontal leadership by the local people's government (*kuaikuai* 块块) is called the system of dual supervision. The relationship between vertical and horizontal leadership is described as being unified leadership, management according to level, combining vertical and horizontal leadership with horizontal leadership predominant (*tongyi lingdao, fenji guanli, tiaokuai jiehe, yikuai weizhu* 统一领导, 分级管理, 条块结合, 以块为主).

85 Hui, 2000: 79–80, comprising the Party Committee and specialist political instruction personnel.

86 Hui, 2000: 82.

87 The office is jointly operated with the Ministry of Supervision, discussed in chapter 8 at section 4.

88 Li, Qiyan, 1993: 352; the Third Plenum of the 11th CCPCC determined to re-establish this Committee in December 1978.

4.4 Party ideological leadership and professional ethos

In the early 1980s, Johnson commented that despite growing professionalism within the police force, the ethical obligations of the police continued to be conceived in terms of political ideology rather than through creation of a professional ethos separate from that of the Party/state.[89]

Since that time, although Party organisational leadership over the public security organs has remained intact, problems have arisen as a result of the diminishing ideological power of the Party over the police force. Building a professional ethos is ongoing though incomplete. Conservatives claim that the effect of creating a socialist market economy, with emphasis on 'paid employment and the principle of commodity exchange based on an equivalence of value' has undermined the significance of Party leadership and adherence to the mass-line for many police officers. Many police feel left behind in the race for wealth and disillusioned with the differential results of the policy of economic reform,[90] sentiments which have had a serious effect on police morale and the quality of law enforcement activities.[91] Overvaluing money has been characterised as an ideological problem leading to bad work habits and corruption requiring rectification.[92]

The mass-line remains a basic tenet of policing, though the strained and increasingly alienated relationship between the police and the people is viewed with deepening concern.[93] One reason given for the decline in adherence to the mass-line has been the dramatic increase in police numbers since the 1980s,[94] up from 600,000 in 1987 to 1.4 million at the end of 1997[95] and to 1.7 million by 2003.[96] As a result, over 70 per cent of police are under forty years old, with the vast majority less than thirty years old.[97] Their experience of policing has been dominated by campaign-style policing and so, as one policeman

[89] Johnson, 1983: 10. [90] Wong, 2002: 291–2.

[91] Zhang, Changgong, 1993: 15; Gao, 1994: 329, surveys in 1990 and 1994 amongst local-level police and police patrols identified salary (96 per cent) and housing conditions (85 per cent) as prime motivating factors. Sun, Juan, 1994: 336–8; Meng, 1993: 1.

[92] Xu, 1994: 299–302. [93] Yin and Li, 1997: 13–14.

[94] In 1987 there were 600,000 professional police, of which 320,000 were public order police and 150,000 were criminal investigation police: Wang, Zhongfan, 1992: 481. In 1990, those numbers had increased to 769,000 professional police of which 150,000 were public order police, 159,000 household registration police and 79,000 criminal investigation police: Law Yearbook Editorial Committee, 1991: 947; Brady, 1981: 18, reports that in 1950 there were less than 80,000 police.

[95] Li, Zhongxin, 1998: 44. Li at that time was the chief of the Number 4 Research Unit of the MPS.

[96] New China News Agency, 7 January 2004. [97] Yin and Li, 1997: 28.

commented, 'they care little for anything except striking hard and cracking cases'.[98]

Commentators point to bad police attitudes and corrupt behaviour as evidence of poor professional standards that undermine community relations. Examples include: refusing to handle a matter unless a fee is paid; not handling a matter unless income may be derived from it in some way; and involvement of police in corrupt, violent and illegal behaviour, including organising prostitution and the distribution of drugs.[99] The extensive use of temporary contract police to overcome police shortages at local levels has also been identified as a major source of breaches of discipline and unlawful behaviour.[100]

Repeated efforts have been made to improve the ethical and ideological basis of the police. Recently this has taken the form of strengthening the 'socialist spiritual civilisation' of the public security agencies during the ninth five-year plan between 1996 and 2000:

> Since the open door policy, the public security organs have supported the Party's basic line and its basic programmes, wholeheartedly serving the people and getting rid of corruption. At the same time as protecting socialist economic construction, they have also promoted the construction of socialist spiritual civilisation . . . But, because of a range of negative social influences, problems remain of worshipping money, hedonism, individualism and amongst some police this problem is growing; torture and other uncivilised acts still exist and corruption occurs . . .[101]

The specific programme to address problems of low ethical standards amongst public security personnel does not rely entirely on ideological training, but also involves setting clearer standards for the performance of specific policing tasks; strengthening systems for internal supervision over police work; and carrying out more public relations work.[102] The weakening of political ideology as a guide to police conduct is now being

[98] Yin and Li, 1997: 14–28; Meng, 1993: 1. [99] Yin and Li, 1997: 14–15.

[100] Zhang, Chengfeng, 1994: 279–80, citing figures that in some areas contract police are responsible for 65 per cent of breach of discipline cases. In relation to the use of contract police to overcome shortage in numbers, see Fu, 1990: 114.

[101] MPS, '9.5' *Opinion on Implementing the Construction of Socialist Spiritual Civilisation in the Public Security Organs*, 15 January 1997, point 2 at 245–6. This Opinion was passed to implement the CCPCC *Decision on Several Important Questions on Strengthening the Construction of Socialist Spiritual Civilisation*, 10 October 1996. See also discussion of spiritual civilisation in chapter 4 at section 4.

[102] The '9.5' *Opinion on Implementing the Construction of Socialist Spiritual Civilisation in the Public Security Organs* includes, amongst the tasks necessary to strengthen socialist spiritual civilisation, protecting political stability by cracking down on enemies and cracking down on the 'Six Evils'.

counterbalanced by efforts to build professional standards and controls. However, the problems of corruption and abuse of power within the police force remain acute.

4.5 The contest for control between the MPS and local Party committees and governments

For the MPS, some aspects of local government control over policing remain problematic, especially in light of MPS efforts to regularise police conduct and establish a professional ethos. Higher-level public security organs exercise vertical supervision over lower-level organs,[103] primarily in respect of professional policing work. This covers issuing regulations and instructions concerning police work and police standards;[104] and co-ordinating and planning police work including undertaking targeted concerted actions.[105]

Horizontal supervision, exercised by the local people's government and local Party committees, relates to the administration of the police and designating policing priorities in the local area.[106] In practice, the local government wields a great deal of power over local policing as it provides virtually their whole budget, including equipment, salaries, police station buildings and offices. It also exercises power over the appointment of police personnel after consultation with higher-level police departments.[107] Local police see themselves as beholden to the local government and obliged to perform tasks as directed, even though many of these are not police duties.[108] As they say 'one is under the control of the person from whose bowl one eats'.[109]

The power of local government and the Party committee over the local police weakens the capacity of the MPS to supervise and control the conduct of local-level public security organs and limits the capacity of central authorities to discipline lower-level police officers.[110] Fu argues that local Party committees exercise control over local policing to the point that reform policies cannot be implemented without their support.[111] Fu also argues that efforts of Zhou Yongkang since 2003 to institute uniform recruitment criteria for the police reflects a desire

[103] Hao and Shan, 1999: 3–4; Hui, 2000: 78–9; Wang and Zhang, 1983: 202.

[104] Including enforcement procedures, training and professional conduct requirements and recruitment standards.

[105] Discussed in Ma, 1997: 126–8 and set out in the *PPL*, art. 116.

[106] Hui, 2000: 82–4. [107] Hui, 2000: 83–4; Ma, 1997; *PPL*, art. 116.

[108] Yu and Zhang, 1999: 259, document a survey in 1992 at one police station in Shandong province in which 40 per cent of police time was spent performing non-policing tasks.

[109] Ding, 1999: 11. [110] Zhang, Chengfeng, 1994: 278, 281. [111] Fu, 2005c: 243–4.

to strengthen central control over the police at the expense of local control.[112]

For example, a survey published in 2000 of police in twenty counties in Gansu indicated that at the local level, police continue to be required to perform non-police duties, including collection of a range of local taxes; enforcing the family planning policy; enforcing planning and building regulations; enforcing policies concerning use of agricultural land; and interfering in economic disputes by detaining one party to the dispute to obtain payment of the disputed amount.[113] Despite efforts by central authorities to regularise the criteria for calculation of the local police budget,[114] funding in some areas remains problematic as the calculated budget is not made available.[115] Despite repeated prohibitions by the CCPCC, the practice of using fines to supplement local police budgets continues.[116]

4.6 Individual interference in police work

Whilst the CCPCC has prohibited it, some leaders continue to view the police and procuratorate as personal agents. In 1986, the CCPCC issued the *Notice that the Whole Party Must Resolutely Protect the Socialist Legal System*:

> In general, the legal consciousness of each level of Party group and the vast majority of Party members and cadres has continually strengthened and there has been a continual improvement in consciously handling matters according to law. But, it must be pointed out that there are some Party organisations and officials and cadres, especially those in Party and Military leadership organs and leadership positions, who still consider themselves to be a special case, who substitute their word for law, use

[112] Fu, 2005c: 250. [113] Wang *et al.*, 2000: 21–2; see also Fu, 1994: 277–91.

[114] MPS, Ministry of Finance, *Decision on the Scope of Expenditure and Measures for Management of Expenses of Public Security Work*, 20 September 1991. The *Decision*, art. 2, specifies items of public security work which are to be included in the annual budget, including paying police informants. Finance departments at each level are to include these amounts in the annual budget 'according to the actual needs of the public security organ according to the current financial system and on the basis of what is possible, to do the best possible to make arrangements for the annual expenditure budget'. Article 31 indicates that the annual budget is to be negotiated and determined at provincial, autonomous region and directly governed city level.

[115] Wang, 1999: 58; Hu and Sun, 14 August 2003, reporting that this problem remains unresolved.

[116] In 1993, the Standing Committee of the CCPCC Political Bureau in the *Important Directive on the Work of CMPO* prohibited what it identified as the widespread practice of the finance department returning to the agency 30 per cent of the monies paid in by that agency. The MPS *Notice on Conscientiously Strengthening the Management of Income of Public Security Organs from Collection of Fees and Fines*, 3 January 1999, also required that any budget item specifying that a proportion of fines collected be paid to the police be removed from the budget.

> their power to suppress the law and who bend the law to help their friends, placing themselves above the law and outside the scope of the law. Some of them disrupt the regular work of the judicial organs and force them to handle matters according to their own demands, who in disrespect for the *Constitution* and *CPL* wantonly detain people, or demand that the public security organs perform acts which breach the personal and democratic rights of citizens and treat the police and procuratorate as tools to carry out their own personal affairs. Even though these problems are not widespread, they have a particularly bad influence and are viewed with great seriousness by the whole Party.[117]

These concerns remain apposite. Law provides one channel, however weak at present, for police to resist demands by individuals, Party organs and local governments to perform work outside the scope of their legally defined authority and responsibilities. The *PPL* permits police to refuse to accede to demands to act in excess of the law or outside their legally specified powers and requires the matter be reported to a higher-level organ.[118] Scholars have noted that the police have already resorted to legal arguments to resist demands both by the Party to conduct hard strikes,[119] and to protect themselves against demands at the local level to do the local government's 'dirty work'.[120]

5 AFFIRMING LAW AS THE BASIS FOR GOVERNANCE

5.1 Administration according to law

For the police, leadership of the Party is felt not only in terms of strategies for maintaining social order and law enforcement but also in the requirement that administration be carried out according to law. Establishing law as a basis for governance and regime legitimation has become a central Party policy. In theory, all are equally subject to the law, including the Party and the police.[121] As we have seen, the basic requirement that the state's coercive powers be exercised by the application of law was first articulated by Peng Zhen in 1984.[122] The requirement that government officials carry out administration according to law was later set out in the resolution of the Third Plenum of the 14th Party

117 Gong'an Bu, 1990: 271. 118 *PPL*, art. 33.
119 Fu, 1994: 281–3; Zhang, Chengfeng, 1994: 279. 120 Fu, 1994: 277–91.
121 *Constitution*, art. 5. The *CCP Constitution*, art. 3(4) and preamble provide that: 'The Party must conduct its activities within the framework of the *Constitution* and other laws.'
122 Peng, 1984: 362.

CCPCC in November 1993, which emphasised the role of law in underpinning establishment of a socialist market economy. The Resolution directed that 'government at all levels must carry out administration according to law and handle affairs according to law'.[123] What was not clear was what types of documents constituted 'law'. Was it sufficient that the law was in the form of local rules or ministerial rules, or was something more authoritative such as legislation passed by the NPC or its Standing Committee required? What types of substantive and procedural matters must the law address? What values should the law reflect? The initial definition of administration according to law did not answer these questions. It adopted the formalist position that administrative actions are valid if they conform to the substantive and procedural requirements of the laws and rules upon which those acts are based and that those laws and rules themselves are legally valid.[124] The first task was to give police administrative powers some form of legal basis.

The policy status of rule according to law was further elevated in 1996 when Jiang Zemin directed that the Party and state 'rule the country according to law, protect the long-term peace and order of the country'.[125] In November 1999, the State Council passed the *Decision on Comprehensively Carrying Forward Administration According to Law*, in which it stressed the importance of 'administration according to law' as a way of consolidating the leadership of the Party and state power. It emphasised the importance of the lawful exercise of power by local officials to the welfare of the people and to their relationship with government.[126] At a national meeting convened by the State Council in 1999 to discuss implementation of this policy, the then Premier, Zhu Rongji, affirmed both its centrality and the continuing instrumentalist characterisation of law as the implementation of Party policy. He explained:

[123] CCPCC, *Decision on Several Questions on Establishing a Socialist Market Economy System*, 14 November 1993: at 8; Fu, Siming, 2002: 1.

[124] For a formalist conception of the rule of law, see chapter 1, notes 67–8. Ying, 1992a: 415, defines *yifa xingzheng* as:
1. the administrative department must be established and its powers conferred by law. If the organ or any official acts outside the scope of organisational laws, acts where there is no delegated power, or acts in excess of delegated powers, the act will be void;
2. administrative acts must not be in conflict with the law and discretionary powers and must be exercised within the scope permitted by law; and
3. any act not carried out within the legally specified procedure will be in excess of power and so void.

[125] See discussion in chapter 2.

[126] Law Yearbook Editorial Committee, 2000: 503.

> Administration according to the law is the implementation of the Party line, programme and policies, it is the basic guarantee for protection of the interests of the people. Our government is a people's government and wholeheartedly serving the people is the basic purpose of the Party and government. Our Party leads the people in seizing political power and, through legislation, which is the integration of the Party's correct position and the collective will of the people, it becomes national law. The *Constitution* and laws are the high level, unified and focussed expression of the Party line and programme and of the basic interests of the people.[127]

In 1999 the MPS issued the *Notice on Implementing the 'State Council Decision on Comprehensively Carrying Forward Administration According to Law'*. In this notice, the MPS mapped out a broad ranging programme to consolidate and rectify defects and inconsistencies in the legal basis of police powers; to improve standards of local law enforcement; and to strengthen mechanisms for supervision of law enforcement activity and the punishment of those abusing their power or acting unlawfully.[128] On 10 June of the same year, the MPS issued the *Notice on General Implementation in Public Security Organs Nationwide of the System of Openness in Police Work*, which implemented the programme of rule according to law and was a means of institution-building.[129] This policy was reiterated in the Preamble to the CCP *Constitution*, which provided '[s]tate legislation and law enforcement should be strengthened so as gradually to put all work of the state on a legal footing'.

In 2000, the MPS set out its plan to establish a comprehensive and regularised set of laws, regulations and rules dealing with police organisation, regulating police powers and establishing a comprehensive and effective system for the supervision of police enforcement work by 2005.[130] These priorities were reiterated in 2004 in the MPS, *Opinion on Public Security Organs Implementing the 'Outline on Comprehensively Carrying Forward the Implementation of Administration According to Law'*. This time, however, the call to complete the task of legal reform of police powers and effective legal regulation of police work was more urgent. The Opinion was issued in response to increasing central pressure to deal with the serious police misconduct that had been exposed

[127] Zhu, Rongji, 1999: 2; Luo, 1989: 39, refers to this as the principle of lawfulness; Yang, 2001: 38–40, criticises what he calls a campaign style of legal construction which he argues threatens to deny the autonomy of law as well as its claims to internal coherence, rationality and stability.

[128] At 368. See chapter 8 at section 3. [129] Hao and Shan, 1999: 329.

[130] MPS, *Decision on Strengthening Public Security Legal System Construction*, 3 June 2000.

during 2002 and 2003. These policing scandals had led to a public outcry and demands from the highest levels of Party and state that these problems be redressed.[131]

5.2 Competing interpretations of administration according to law

(i) *Formalist approaches: law as empowering and regularising police power*

For the public security organs, administration according to law is simply one policy governing police administrative management which is to be implemented alongside leadership of the Party, adherence to the mass-line and implementation of the CMPO.[132] Law has been viewed as a way of granting powers and protecting the public security organs in the exercise of their duties.[133] The police argue that they require adequate legal empowerment and clear legal protection for the exercise of powers enabling them to carry out their law enforcement functions.[134] For example, one purpose of the amended *Criminal Law* was to criminalise activities that were previously not offences and to facilitate implementation of the law by the better definition of offences.[135] The instrumental uses of law as empowering police enforcement activities is illustrated most clearly by the legislation introduced authorising and later providing legal justification for hard strikes, such as that against the 'Six Evils', discussed in chapters 4 and 5.[136]

Law is seen as a way to regularise, and to impose a clear standard on, the enforcement activities of local agencies. In its 2000 *Notice on Implementing the 'State Council Decision on Comprehensively Carrying Forward*

131 In response to these concerns, the CCPCC issued the *Work Plan for Resolving Acute Problems of Law Enforcement and Promoting the Construction of the Law Enforcement System of the Public Security Organs* on 7 June 2004.

132 Jiang and Zhan, 1994: 9–10, discuss the concept of *yifa xingzheng* 依法行政 as one of the four basic principles governing police administrative management activities; at 4–11 setting out the other basic principles of leadership of the party, adherence to the mass-line and implementation of CMPO.

133 *PPL*, art. 5; MPS, *Notice Issuing a Propaganda Outline on the PRC PPL*, 28 February 1995: 451.

134 Huang *et al.*, 1988: 46, gives examples where the police have called for legislative empowerment to deal with prostitution, demonstrations and strikes.

135 Zhou, 1997: 1, referring to Wang Hanbin's explanatory speech to the NPC on the draft *Criminal Law*, 6 March 1997.

136 NPCSC, *Decision on the Punishment of Criminals who Smuggle, Produce, Traffic in and Disseminate Pornographic Articles*, 28 December 1990; *Drugs Decision*, 28 December 1990; *Prostitution Decision*, 4 August 1991; *Decision on Punishment of Criminals who Abduct, Sell and Kidnap Women and Children*, 4 August 1991; Ministry of Civil Affairs, MPS, State Administration of Industry and Commerce, State Council Religious Affairs Bureau, *Notice on Preventing Harm Caused by Feudal Superstitious Activities*, 29 May 1989; SPC, *Notice on Coordinating with the Public Security Organs in Carrying out the Work of Eliminating the 'Six Evils'*, 13 November 1989.

Administration According to Law', the MPS required public security personnel to:

> fundamentally transform traditional concepts of administrative enforcement, work habits and work methods that have become inappropriate. Acquire a firm grasp of legal system concepts in both thought and action, use law as the accurate measure, study how to be good at using legal methods to manage state administration work and to carry out management functions . . .[137]

The use of law to regularise state administration, prevent arbitrary decisions and to ensure that 'government officials faithfully implemented the ruler's decrees' is a consistent theme of governance throughout China's history.[138] Turner notes that 'this theme, that the state's legitimacy rested in part on its ability to curb bureaucratic misbehaviour, is one that is repeated in studies from Qin and Han through to the Qing'.[139] Some developments in administrative law, such as the *Administrative Litigation Law* ('ALL') and the *State Compensation Law*, go beyond law as a means by which to implement specific policies, to law as a method to impose constraints on the exercise of power by making officials accountable for their conduct.[140]

(ii) Debates over the purpose of administrative law: balance theory

Administrative law scholars argue that it is no longer sufficient for administration according to law to be interpreted simply as empowerment and regularisation of administrative power, but that it should also limit the power of state agencies[141] and promote values that are not simply defined by Party policy.[142] Whilst administrative law scholars agree that administrative law has at its heart prevention of abuse of power by officials,[143] they have disagreed over the correct balance between empowerment and constraint.

Scholars have proposed a range of divergent theories.[144] Debate has focussed on two main theories:[145] first, that the primary aim of administrative law is to control state power and to protect individual

137 At 368. 138 Peerenboom, 2002a: 41.
139 Turner *et al.*, 1994: 31; see also Nathan, 1985: 67–71.
140 Jiang, Mingan, 1998: 3–5. 141 Ma, 2000: 242–4.
142 Jiang, Mingan, 1998: 13–16; Yang, 2001: 207–8. 143 Yang, 2001: 204.
144 Pi and Ma, 1997: 75, lists them as management theory (*guanli lun* 管理论), control of power theory (*kongquan lun* 控权论), serve the people theory (*wei renmin fuwu lun* 为人民服务论), public power theory (*gonggong quanli lun* 公共权力论); see also a list of different definitions in Lin, 1996: 3–6.
145 Luo, 2003: 13–14.

rights;[146] and the second emphasises the role of law as a basis for efficient management and in providing a normative basis for organisation of agencies and official action and supervising the exercise of state power.[147]

The current dominant view represents an accommodation of both these theories. Balance theory (*pingheng lun* 平衡论) seeks to find a balance between the role of law in empowering and facilitating efficient management and in protecting the rights of citizens.[148] Proponents of this theory argue that this type of balance is a necessary basis for stable development of the socialist market economy.[149] There is disagreement, however, over how balance should be achieved. Proponents of the balance theory admit that at present the balance remains heavily in favour of the state, with insufficient restrictions on and overly weak supervision of the exercise of administrative power.[150] One scholar concludes that the way to achieve balance is through emphasis on controlling state power.[151] How to strengthen supervision over administrative action remains disputed. One scholar criticises Western-inspired demands to strengthen judicial supervision of administrative action as unrealistic, instead favouring emphasising administrative supervision over administrative action.[152] Other administrative law scholars conclude that balance cannot be achieved between state power and individual rights, asserting that the primary object of administrative law must be to supervise and control officials (*zhi guan* 治官) and that law should not be seen as a tool of administration.[153]

(iii) Rule of law administration

Some scholars criticise the formalist conception of administration according to law as not imposing sufficiently onerous constraints on

[146] Luo, Haocai, 1997a: 1–6, based on the Anglo-American tradition; Zhu, 2000: 2, equates the theory of controlling state power with the 'red light theory' she attributes to Richard Rawlings.
[147] Zhu, 2000: 20–1. This view has been attributed to the German, French, Japanese and especially the former Soviet and pre-reform Chinese views which, despite differences between them, privilege state power and emphasise the role of law in empowering state action. The ultimate purpose for ensuring efficient management in this scheme is to ensure that state power is used to serve the people. Zhan, 1997: 106, calls this reasoning 'serve the people-ism', asserting that it is distinct from management theory.
[148] Luo, Haocai, 1997b: 1–7; Jiang, Mingan, 1997: 242.
[149] Luo, 2003: 15–16; Zhan, 1997: 108–9, arguing that balance theory is distinct from Western theories, in particular control theory, which reflect the historical particularities that gave rise to them.
[150] Luo and Gan, 1997: 33–4. [151] Fan, 2003: 420–3.
[152] Zhu, 2000: 20–2. [153] Yang, 2001: 204–5.

state action. They argue that administrative rules (*guizhang* 规章) passed by ministries and commissions should be excluded from the scope of 'law'. That is, ministries should not be able to pass and administer rules that protect their institutional interests and empower themselves without regard as to whether these rules accord with the interest of the people, or whether they are just and proper.[154] Proponents of this view also assert that not only must everyone be subject to law, but that the laws themselves must reflect more general values. Law must also be 'good'.[155] It must protect human rights and be in the public interest.[156] Law must also impose limits on administrative discretion,[157] require that all decision-making be reasonable[158] and strengthen external supervision over both administrative rule-making and enforcement.[159]

(iv) Flexibility as a problem of discretion

Debates about the meaning and scope of administration according to law have re-characterised the continuing flexibility of police powers as a legal question about the proper scope of police discretionary power. Whilst accepting that a certain amount of discretion is necessary to improve administrative efficiency, it is also generally acknowledged that uncontrolled power will inevitably lead to abuse.[160] In a 1992 survey, 95.4 per cent of judges and 92.5 per cent of lawyers considered it necessary to limit the scope of administrative discretionary powers.[161]

Even the police recognise that, although discretion greatly enhances enforcement efficiency, excessive discretion enables unreasonable and unjust outcomes in enforcement.[162] In particular, the use of administrative coercive measures to implement law and order strikes, coupled with the lack of detailed substantive and procedural definition of the

154 Yang, 2001: 201–3, 207–9. 155 Jiang, Mingan, 1998: 13–16. 156 Yang, 2001: 198, 208.

157 Zhang and Zhang, 1991: 69–73; Yang, 2001: 198, discussing the need to limit discretion and to ensure that administrative actions conform to the principle of reasonableness.

158 Jiang, Lishan, 1998: 17, describing reasonableness in terms similar to English principles of natural justice, that there be due process, restrictions on abuse of power and including substantive requirements that the act be fair (*gongping* 公平), just (*zhengyi* 正义), in the broad social interest and protect individual rights and procedural requirements.

159 Jiang, Mingan, 1998: 17; Zhou, Guangyang, 1999: 34–6; Zhou and Zhang, 1990: 45.

160 Fu, Siming, 2002: 179, 184–6; Tang, 1993: 42.

161 Tang, 1993: 42, citing results of a 1992 survey in which 86.6 per cent of judges, 98.3 per cent of lawyers and 85.6 per cent of administrators responded that if the exercise of power was uncontrolled it would inevitably be abused.

162 Hu, 1998: 50, blaming low ethical professional standards.

powers, has facilitated abuse and made these coercive powers almost uncontrollable.[163]

Limiting the scope of discretion is seen as a way of rationalising the exercise of local enforcement powers and limiting abuse of power. In the leading Chinese police research journal, one commentator asserts that:

> [t]he large volume of discretionary actions have not been made the subject of effective norms, [as a result] in the process of the administration of public security, a vast number of problems of unfairness and unreasonableness have not been effectively resolved, which has seriously influenced the image of public security enforcement activities.[164]

Scholars and some police agree that the exercise of discretion should be constrained by basic principles in order to prevent the use of discretion for improper purposes, such as protecting local or institutional interests.[165] These basic principles include that the exercise of discretion should be just and reasonable, objectively fair, in conformity with the requirements of the legislation and proportional.[166] In addition, scholars argue that the exercise of discretion should take into consideration individual rights and the public interest.[167]

These arguments have been influential in shaping the extensive programme of legal reform that has taken place, especially since 1996. One recent example is the *SAPL*, which took effect on 1 March 2006. In a book written to explain the amendments to the law to the police, the authors assert that the principles for restricting discretion and strengthening procedural requirements that were included in the *SAPL* were designed to enact the 'old English principle of natural justice, that all powers must be exercised in a just manner'. They go on to assert that the principle of natural justice is fundamental to contemporary notions of the rule of law in China.[168]

[163] Zhou, Guangyang, 1999: 33, acknowledging that at present administrative power remains paramount over and unconstrained by law. Li, Zhongxin, 1998: 44; Zhang, Changgong, 1993: 15, acknowledging that uncontrolled power will lead to its abuse, asserting that the range of supervision mechanisms used to date have been ineffective to curb the use and abuse of administrative power. Hu, 1998: 50, asserting that interchangeability of one form of punishment with another has facilitated corruption and abuse, with it common for fines to be substituted for other punishments and people sent to RETL who should be dealt with in the criminal justice system.

[164] Hu, 1998: 49. [165] Zhang and Guan, 1992: 193.

[166] Hu, 1998: 50; Jiang, Mingan, 1998: 17; Fu, Siming, 2002: 184–6.

[167] Jiang, Mingan, 1998: 17; Zhang and Guan, 1992: 192; Sun, 1999: 285–9.

[168] Feng, 2005: 286.

6 LEGISLATING POWERS

6.1 Building a basis of laws and rules

Administration according to law requires at least that powers exercised by government agencies are based on law, and that those laws are validly passed.[169] These formal requirements raise a number of questions. What documents will be sufficient to provide a legal basis for a power? Which agencies should be authorised to pass those laws?

Since the beginning of the reform era, state agencies at all levels have been busy creating a legal infrastructure. The 1982 *Constitution* concentrates the power to make law (*falü* 法律) in the NPC and the NPCSC, which exercise the highest legislative power of state.[170] The *Constitution* empowers the State Council to pass administrative regulations (*xingzheng fagui* 行政法规);[171] ministries and commissions under the State Council to pass administrative rules (*xingzheng guizhang* 行政规章);[172] local people's congresses to pass local regulations (*difangxing fagui* 地方性法规);[173] and local people's governments to pass local rules (*guizhang* 规章).[174] This was the first time since establishment of the PRC that ministries and commissions under the State Council were constitutionally authorised to issue rules.[175] The results have been stunning. In 1999, the Premier, Zhu Rongji, reported that apart from the *Constitution*, from 1979 to June 1999 there had been 250 laws and 106 decisions (*jueding* 决定) passed by the NPC and the NPCSC; 830 administrative regulations passed by the State Council; more than 7,000 local regulations passed by local people's congresses and their standing committees; and more than 30,000 administrative rules passed by central-level ministries and commissions and by local people's governments.[176]

Officially, Zhu commended the rate at which this legal infrastructure is being established.[177] However, some scholars express consternation at the volumes of legislation passed since 1979.[178] They fear, with justification, that the passage of vast quantities of legislation in an uncontrolled and unco-ordinated fashion may result in a form of

169 Ying, 1992a: 415. 170 *Constitution*, art. 58.
171 *Constitution*, art. 89(1). 172 *Constitution*, art. 90.
173 *Constitution*, art. 100; Ying, 1993: 127–8. These local rules must be lodged with the NPCSC and the State Council in accordance with the State Council, *Regulations and Rules Reporting Regulations*, effective 1 January 2002.
174 *PRC Organic Law of Local People's Congresses at Each Level and Local People's Governments at Each Level*, arts. 7, 51; Ying, 1993: 127–8; Keller, 1994: 726.
175 Sun, 2000: 174–5. 176 Zhu, Rongji, 1999: 5–6. 177 Zhu, Rongji, 1999: 5–6.
178 Korzec, 1991, describes this flood of rule-making as 'administrative lawlessness'.

'dictatorship by law' (*falü tongzhi* 法律统治), with laws covering a range of areas that do not require regulation; administrative rules and other documents overwhelming legislation as the basis for the imposition of legal rights and obligations; and a mass of unco-ordinated and contradictory rules undermining the authority of law.[179] An official report found that duplication, conflict and inconsistency between different rules have resulted in a reduction in efficiency and a waste of resources.[180] The systems for supervision of subordinate rule-making have been unable effectively to address this problem.[181]

Rule-making has commonly been used by central administrative agencies, local governments and congresses to protect their own interests and to expand their power.[182] Administrative agencies have not only empowered themselves through passing rules, they have also commonly drafted legislation for passage by higher-level institutions for which they will later have the responsibility both to interpret and enforce.[183] In contrast with the trend of increasing openness in legislative drafting, the process of rule-making has not been open to public comment and many rules passed by the MPS have not been publicly available after passage.

As I discussed in chapters 5 and 6, ministerial and local rule-making has been the primary basis for establishment and definition of administrative detention powers. For example, the power to detain prostitutes and their clients, prior to passage by the NPCSC of the *Prostitution Decision* on 4 August 1991, was based entirely on local regulations and MPS documents. As noted in chapter 5, these rules continued to give the

179 Yang, 2001: 44–6, 52–3.

180 Zhang, Chunsheng, 2000: 312–15, reproducing a report prepared during drafting of the *Legislation Law* entitled *Analysis and Research of Laws, Administrative Regulations and Local Regulations that Regulate in Respect of the Same Matter*.

181 Sun, 2000: 202–3; Li, Peng, 2000: 305, in 1999, describing the rule reporting system as passive and ineffective. Supervision over subordinate rule-making is exercised by the NPC in respect of laws and decisions passed by the NPCSC; *Constitution*, art. 62(11), by the NPCSC in respect of State Council administrative regulations; *Constitution*, art. 67(7), and local regulations passed by provincial-level people's congresses; *Constitution*, art. 67(8), by the State Council in respect of administrative rules passed by ministries and commissions; *Constitution*, art. 89(13); and in respect of rules passed by provincial level governments, *Constitution*, art. 89(14). Sun, 2000: 200–2, describing the system of reporting rules to the State Council under the *Regulation and Rule Reporting Regulations*, 18 February 1990.

182 Sun, 2000: 198–9. Perry Keller has labelled 'bureaucratic dominance' the self-empowerment of administrative agencies through exercise of their rule-making power: Keller, 1994: 738–42. Li, Lin, 1998: 785–8, pointing out that strengthening administrative power in relation to legislative power is not confined to China.

183 Keller, 1994: 738–42.

police an almost unfettered discretion in the exercise of these powers. The legislation passed subsequently did not constrain the scope of their discretion.

6.2 Redefining law and its values

(i) Efforts by the NPC to increase control over legislation

Since 1978, control over law-making has been an area of intense competition between the NPCSC and the State Council.[184] The NPC and, especially, the NPCSC have sought to exercise greater control over law-making activities.[185] Through its control of the legislative agenda, the NPCSC determines whether legislation will be drafted in a certain area and who has responsibility for drafting that legislation.[186] This has enabled it to strengthen controls over the rule-making activities of administrative agencies. The NPCSC has asserted more control over legislative drafting at the expense of the State Council, especially where the legislation affects a range of state agencies. For example, specialist drafting groups, comprising academic specialists and permanent employees of the NPCSC, were appointed to research and prepare the first draft of legislation including the *ALL*,[187] *Criminal Law*,[188] *CPL*,[189] *APL*[190] and *Legislation Law*.[191] Although the organs responsible for enforcement of the law were consulted throughout the drafting process, they were not involved in the preparation of the first draft, thus weakening their control over the drafting process. In contrast, the legislation passed by the NPCSC which authorised detention for education and coercive drug rehabilitation was drafted by the MPS.[192]

184 Tanner, Murray Scot, 1999: 44–9.

185 Tanner, Murray Scot, 1999: 101–3, noting the extensive legal professional expertise of the permanent staff in the committees of the NPCSC, particularly the Legislative Affairs Committee.

186 Dowdle, 1997; Tanner, Murray Scot, 1999: 115–16, noting that this has occurred especially after the Tian'anmen Square crackdown in 1989.

187 Chai, 1990: 46–7; Potter, 1994a: 274–5.

188 Chen, Jianfu, 1999a: 170; Gao and Zhao, 1999: 565–6.

189 Described in Hecht, 1996: 13–18.

190 Editorial Committee, 1996: 2. In 1990 the State Council Legal Department (as it then was) commenced drafting *Administrative Punishment Regulations*. The work of drafting an *Administrative Punishments Law* was taken over in 1991 by a drafting group established by the Legislative Affairs Commission of the NPCSC.

191 Zhang, Chunsheng, 2000: 287, a specialist drafting group within the Legislative Affairs Commission commenced drafting the *Legislation Law* in the second half of 1993. At 302–4, excerpting speeches by Li Peng (then Chair of the NPCSC) discussing the work of specialist committees in drafting important legislation.

192 See discussion in chapter 5.

The *PRC Legislation Law* 2000 sought to regularise the system of rule-making by codifying the hierarchy of legislative power; and then set out procedures for passing legislation and mechanisms for the supervision of rule-making, including the resolution of conflicts and inconsistencies between different types of rules. It specified certain subjects upon which law-making power was confined to the NPC or the NPCSC, including the establishment of administrative measures for the deprivation of personal liberty.[193] Scholarly criticism of the continuing uncertainty surrounding which official documents constitute law and the values reflected in law were central issues in drafting the *Legislation Law*. In addition, the *Legislation Law* and subsequent implementing documents increasingly require that rules take into account and protect the rights and interests of citizens. They seek to shift the balance away from the use of law as a means of empowerment, to law as a vehicle for protecting rights and interests and creating a more open system for rule-making.

(ii) Constraining the scope of MPS rule-making power

There are competing interpretations of the scope of rule-making power given to administrative organs under the *Constitution*. The first and most commonly accepted view is that administrative agencies are authorised by the *Constitution* to pass rules in respect of all matters falling within the scope of their functional competence, unless expressly prohibited or otherwise regulated by a higher-level legislative instrument.[194] Under this interpretation the MPS has power to pass rules with respect to matters including preventing, stopping and investigating unlawful and criminal activity, protecting social order and stopping acts that harm social order.[195]

The contrary view is that the *Constitution* enables administrative agencies to carry out administration within the scope of their functional power, but that they are not empowered to pass rules or to create legal norms in respect of those functions. This more restrictive view allows administrative agencies only to exercise rule-making power if there is a specific delegation or authorisation to pass implementing regulations or interpretations.[196]

The *Legislation Law* enacted the restrictive view of agency rule-making power.[197] Article 71 provides, *inter alia*, that the 'matters

193 Article 8; see discussion below.
194 Ying, 1993: 105–13, 127; Xu and Pi, 1991: 207–10; Sun, 2000: 183.
195 *PPL*, art. 6(1) and (2). 196 Xu, 1997: 88–90.
197 Zhang, Chunsheng, 2000: 215–17.

about which ministries and commissions may enact administrative rules should be matters within the scope of the implementation of laws or administrative regulations, decisions and orders of the State Council'. A similar limitation in respect of local government rules is set out in Article 73. The MPS is now authorised to pass administrative rules within the scope of its functional power to specify in more detail or to implement provisions in a law or administrative regulation. This provision is not uncontroversial, as one commentator argues it is in conflict with the terms in which ministries and commissions are empowered in Article 90 of the *Constitution*.[198] Another interpretation is that the *Legislation Law* has failed to prescribe clear limits to the legislation-making power of ministries and commissions.[199]

Article 71 has arguably removed the power of the MPS and local governments to pass rules establishing administrative detention powers. In contrast to the way detention for education was rebuilt on the back of administrative rules in the 1980s, agency power is now confined to interpreting and implementing higher-level legislation. However, in practice this limitation places few restrictions on the rule-making power of the MPS as the *Legislation Law* has not limited the capacity of the MPS to issue broad-ranging interpretations of laws and administrative rules such as the *RETL Regulations*.[200] In the case of powers such as detention for education and coercive drug rehabilitation, the generality of the NPCSC decisions authorising these detention powers imposes few constraints on the ways in which its interpretation powers are exercised.

The competition for superiority in rule-making status between central government ministries and local governments also remained unresolved.[201] This was one of the most controversial issues in drafting

[198] Article 90, *inter alia*, empowers ministries and commissions to 'issue orders, directives and regulations within the jurisdiction of their respective departments and in accordance with the law and administrative rules and regulations, decisions and orders issued by the State Council' (English from the translation prepared by the Legislative Affairs Commission of the NPCSC); Yang, 2001: 105.

[199] Sun, 2000: 199.

[200] Zhang, Chunsheng, 2000: 139–40, asserting that the *Legislation Law*, art. 42, authorises the NPCSC to issue interpretations of law and does not affect power to issue interpretations in respect of the application of the law. Article 42 thus does not affect the pre-existing power of the SPC and the SPP to issue judicial interpretations, nor the power of the State Council and ministries and commissions to issue administrative interpretations.

[201] The *Legislation Law*, art. 82, provides that local rules and ministerial rules have the same level of authority. Neither local rules (arts. 63, 64, 78, 79, 80) nor ministerial rules (arts. 71, 78, 79, 80) may be inconsistent with national-level law or administrative regulations.

the *Legislation Law*.[202] The MPS argued strongly that ministerial rules should have priority over local government rules.[203] Some localities argued that in relation to certain matters, including coercive measures for the deprivation of liberty such as coercive drug rehabilitation and detention for repatriation, local governments should be given enhanced powers.[204] Neither view prevailed. Both types of rules have equal status, a result which leaves unresolved the basic problem of conflict between these categories of rules. This conflict means that disputes about which rules should be applied to determine the lawfulness of decision-making, for example, for the purpose of administrative review, may need to be determined by the State Council on a case-by-case basis.[205] This debate is another reflection of the ongoing tension between the MPS and local governments over control of the definition of administrative coercive powers and local policing.

(iii) Regularising rule-making

The *Legislation Law* and interpretations subsequently issued seek to regularise the processes of law and rule-making and to impose obligations of publicity on all laws, regulations and rules.[206]

The *Legislation Law* authorised the State Council to pass administrative regulations to specify mandatory procedures for rule-making.[207] The State Council then promulgated the *Procedural Regulations for Formulating Administrative Regulations*, which specify the procedures for initiation, drafting, examination, promulgation and interpretation of administrative regulations of the State Council. It also passed the *Procedural Regulations for Formulating Rules* to specify the same matters in respect of administrative rules of central government departments and

202 Sun, 2000: 177.

203 Reported by the NPCSC Legislative Affairs Committee, *Opinions of Each Province and Relevant Central Ministries on the Scope of Law Making Power in the (Draft) Legislation Law*, in Zhang, Chunsheng, 2000: 331.

204 *Opinions of Each Province and Relevant Central Ministries on the Scope of Law Making Power in the (draft) Legislation Law*.

205 Such as, for example: State Council, Legal Affairs Office, *Letter in Response to 'Request for Instructions about Whether to Apply Local Regulations or Ministerial Rules in Examining the Case of Zhang Xiaoli Applying for Administrative Review'*, 4 September 2001.

206 The *Legislation Law* sets out this obligation in respect of laws passed by the NPC and the NPCSC at arts. 23, 41, 52, amendments to those laws at art. 53, administrative regulations at art. 62, local-level and autonomous self-governing regions' regulations at art. 70, ministerial rules at art. 77 and local rules at art. 77, providing that those rules must be published in the locality.

207 Article 74. These regulations are to be drafted with reference to the procedures set out in *Legislation Law*, chapter 3 for passage of State Council administrative regulations.

people's governments at the level of province. These regulations took effect on 1 January 2002. Rules passed in breach of these regulations are void.[208] The regulations fail, however, to specify the procedures by which a rule is to be declared void or what might happen where decisions are made on the basis of a rule which is subsequently declared to be void.

In an effort to standardise the use of official documents by central ministries and local people's governments and to distinguish these documents from rules, the State Council issued the *Measures on the Handling of Official Documents by State Administrative Agencies*, effective from 1 January 2001.[209]

Addressing some of the criticisms of self-empowerment by administrative agencies, the *Procedural Regulations for Formulating Rules* require the rule be formulated to protect the rights of citizens and legal entities and that rules balance empowerment with the responsibilities of the administrative organ to the public welfare. Rules are now required to reflect governmental values of economic regulation, management of society and public service.[210]

The *Procedural Regulations for Formulating Rules* seek to regularise and formalise the process of drafting and to encourage transparency in the drafting process.[211] They provide that if the rule is of immediate concern to the interests of the people (*qieshen liyi* 切身利益) or the subject of a major divergence of opinion (*zhongda yiyi fenqi* 重大利益分歧), the agency drafting the rule may arrange for public hearings to enable different views to be heard, questions to be addressed and the issues to be debated. Records are required to be made of the comments and questions raised at these public meetings.[212] The drafting organ must also consult with other interested departments of the State Council.[213] The draft must be examined by

[208] *Procedural Regulations for Formulating Rules*, art. 2.

[209] The measures specify procedures for drafting, issuing and handling official documents and the circumstances in which different types of documents should be issued. Official documents are divided into categories whose purpose is designated. They are the order (*mingling* 命令); decision (*jueding* 决定); announcement (*gonggao* 公告); public announcement (*tonggao* 通告); notice (*tongzhi* 通知); circular (*tongbao* 通报); proposal (*yi'an* 议案); report (*baogao* 报告); request for instructions (*qingshi* 请示); response to a request for instructions (*pifu* 批复); opinion (*yijian* 意见); official letter (*han* 函); and summary of minutes of meeting (*huiyi jiyao* 会议纪要): art. 9. Article 16 specifies circumstances where an official document may be issued jointly by an administrative agency and a Party organ.

[210] *Procedural Regulations for Formulating Rules*, arts. 4 and 5.

[211] The *Procedural Regulations for Formulating Administrative Regulations*, chapters 2, 3 and 4 contain similar provisions for administrative regulations passed by the State Council.

[212] *Procedural Regulations for Formulating Rules*, art. 15.

[213] *Procedural Regulations for Formulating Rules*, art. 16.

the legal department of the relevant ministry, which may arrange for a public hearing with leadership approval.[214] The document will then be promulgated[215] and must then be published in the designated *Gazette* and newspaper.[216]

These regulations represent a clear intention to transform administrative rule-making to make it more open, regularised and rights-oriented. Whilst these regulations are comparatively new, there are some indications that local governments and administrative agencies have taken steps to introduce public consultation into their rule-making processes.[217] As part of its specific instructions on how to implement the State Council's 2004 *Outline on Comprehensively Carrying Forward Implementation of Administration According to Law*, the MPS instructed that where possible the agency responsible for drafting the rule should conduct public consultation, either by organising 'hearing meetings' (*tingzheng hui* 听证会), discussion forums or a meeting of experts, or, where the proposed rule was of immediate concern to the interests of the people, conducting a consultation through online forums or publication of the draft in newspapers.[218]

(iv) Strengthening supervision over rule-making

Systems for supervision of rule-making follow the administrative hierarchy of the state, requiring lower-level agencies such as the MPS and local governments to report rules to the State Council for the record.[219] The higher-level agency has power to avoid or amend regulations and rules, and to resolve conflicts between subordinate rules.[220]

214 *Procedural Regulations for Formulating Rules*, art. 23.

215 *Procedural Regulations for Formulating Rules*, art. 30, signed by the relevant head of department including the minister or mayor specifying the name of the rule, its document series number, its date of passage, effectiveness and promulgation.

216 *Procedural Regulations for Formulating Rules*, art. 31.

217 In relation to local government legislative hearing, see Yang and Chen, 2004.

218 MPS, *Opinion on Public Security Organs Implementing 'Outline on Comprehensively Carrying Forward Implementation of Administration According to Law'*, 2 July 2004: point 3.

219 State Council, *Regulations and Rules Reporting Regulations*, 1 January 2002, arts. 2 and 3, replacing the State Council, *Regulation and Rule Reporting Regulations*, 18 February 1990, provide that the Legal Office of the State Council is responsible for scrutiny of rules if it determines that the rule was not passed in accordance with procedure or conflicts with a higher-level regulation or law: Articles 14, 15. The Legal Office should refer issues to the state agency with functional power to deal with them.

220 Exercised by the NPC in respect of laws and decisions of the NPCSC: *Constitution*, art. 62(11); by the NPCSC in respect of State Council administrative regulations: *Constitution*, art. 67(7); and local regulations passed by provincial-level people's congresses: *Constitution*, art. 67(8); by the State Council in respect of administrative rules passed by ministries and commissions: *Constitution*, art. 89(13); and in respect of rules passed by provincial-level governments: *Constitution*, art. 89(14).

Whilst not expanding the channels for carrying out supervision of subordinate rule-making, the *Procedural Regulations for Formulating Rules* enable actors outside government to submit to the Legal Office of the State Council written requests for review of rules they consider to be in contravention of administrative regulations or laws.[221] The Legal Affairs Office of the State Council reported that for the period 1 January 2003 to 31 March 2004, it had received and examined forty-eight complaints from administrative agencies, social groups, enterprises and individuals that a local rule was inconsistent with a higher-level regulation or law.[222] Even though the primary mode of supervision of rule-making remains the system of reporting the rule for the record, there now appears to be some scope for other actors to seek reconsideration of agency rule-making.

7 GIVING ADMINISTRATIVE DETENTION POWERS A LEGAL BASIS

7.1 The beginning: the *Security Administrative Punishment Regulations* ('SAPR'), Re-education through Labour ('RETL') and the *Criminal Procedure Law* ('CPL')

After the decision to re-establish the legal system and to give a legal basis to the coercive power of the state, the NPC and the NPCSC passed and repromulgated laws in respect of both criminal and administrative powers.

The *Criminal Law* and the *CPL* were amongst the first laws passed.[223] The *CPL* authorised the public security organs to take a range of coercive measures in exercising their criminal investigation powers.[224] On 29 November 1979, the NPCSC reinvigorated RETL by approving the *Supplementary Regulations of the State Council on RETL* and repromulgating the 1957 *Decision of the State Council on the Question of RETL*.[225] On 23 February 1980, the NPCSC repromulgated the 1957 *SAPR*[226] to

[221] Article 35, permitting state organs, social organisations, industrial and enterprise organisations and citizens to make such applications. *Regulations and Rules Reporting Regulations*, art. 9, also authorises citizens and organisations to make submissions requesting the Legal Affairs Office to examine contested rules.

[222] Law Yearbook Editorial Committee, 2004: 98–9.

[223] These laws were passed on 1 July 1979 and came into effect on 1 January 1980.

[224] *CPL*, General Part, chapter 6: obtaining a guarantor and awaiting trial out of custody, criminal detention, summons for detention, residential surveillance and arrest.

[225] In the *Supplementary Regulations of the State Council on RETL*.

[226] Zhu, 1991: 4–5.

provide a legal basis for the imposition of punishments for public order infringements.

To take account of the changed social order and economic environment, the MPS drafted amendments to the rules on RETL, passed in 1982,[227] and drafted amendments to the *SAPR* which were handed to the NPCSC for examination and passage in 1986.[228]

7.2 The *Administrative Litigation Law*

Prior to the *ALL* coming into effect on 1 October 1990 there was no legal challenge that could be made to the imposition of administrative detention on the grounds that the power was not established, or justified, by law.[229] The *ALL* empowered courts to examine the lawfulness of specific administrative actions[230] including administrative acts 'depriving a person of their liberty'.[231] Where a person claims that their lawful rights have been infringed as the result of an administrative action, the decision-maker has the onus of proving the lawfulness of the decision,[232] thus bringing into question the legal basis upon which the decision was made.

The basis upon which the court determines lawfulness was one of the most controversial areas of debate during the drafting of the *ALL*. Some scholars argued that administrative rules, not just administrative actions, should be subjected to scrutiny by the courts to determine their lawfulness. Administrative agencies asserted that administrative regulations should be a basis for determining the legality of the administrative act in question.[233] The current provisions in Articles 52 and 53 were seen by some scholars as a poor compromise.[234]

Article 52 provides that the court determines the lawfulness of a particular action according to 'laws and administrative regulations'.[235] These are laws of the NPC and the NPCSC; administrative regulations of the State Council; and regional legislation. Article 53 requires the people's courts to 'refer to' administrative rules 'formulated and promulgated' by ministries and commissions under the State Council, and rules

227 *Temporary Measures*, 21 January 1982.

228 Zhu, 1991: 5, asserting that the MPS commenced drafting in 1983, handed the amended *SAPR* to the NPCSC in March 1986 and that this draft was passed in September 1986.

229 The concern amongst public security organs that after passage of the *ALL* their powers needed to have adequate legal basis is discussed in Guo, 1990: 28–9.

230 *ALL*, art. 5. 231 *ALL*, art. 11(2). 232 *ALL*, art. 32. 233 Zhang, 1992: 50–2.

234 Zhang, 1992: 51–2; Zhang, Shuyi, 2000: 37–8, stating that one reason is that the structure of state allocates power to higher-level administrative organs to amend and rescind administrative rules and that the courts do not have power to review the lawfulness of rules.

235 *ALL*, art. 52.

passed by local governments. Courts, in theory, are able to ignore a local rule they consider contradicts a higher-level rule. The matter should then be referred to the SPC, which may ask the State Council for a ruling on the validity of the law.[236] As a result, the documents constituting the legal bases of administrative detention powers needed to be specified so that the decisions by public security organs to impose detention could be justified as being 'lawful' before a court. Based on the definition in the *ALL*, at the time the *ALL* took effect in October 1990, detention for education and coercive drug rehabilitation had no legal basis.

The *ALL* raised two important issues. The first was to determine whether these powers were administrative or criminal in nature. If administrative, the second was to determine their legal basis. Categorisation of the powers as administrative was acknowledged by the MPS through the inclusion of these detention powers in the *Notice on Several Questions about the Implementation of the 'Administrative Litigation Law' by Public Security Organs*, issued on 30 October 1990. However, with powers such as detention for investigation, which were in fact used for criminal investigation, the distinction could be blurred. In practice, the police often sought to avoid the jurisdiction of the *ALL* by asserting that they were carrying out a criminal investigation.[237] In May 1991, the SPC issued an interpretation of the *ALL* confirming that its jurisdiction under *ALL*, Article 11, included examination of decisions to send a person to RETL and to detain a person for investigation.[238]

The MPS in the 1990 notice then designated the documents that constitute the 'legal basis' of RETL; detention for investigation; detention for education; and coercive drug rehabilitation for the purpose of determining whether a specific decision to detain was lawful.[239]

(i) Detention for education

In its 1990 notice, the MPS designated three documents as the legal basis of the power to detain for education.[240] Not one sets any parameters for imposing detention. The list highlights the dearth of rules regulating the scope of detention that conformed, even slightly, with the

[236] *ALL*, art. 53; Xiao, 1989: 32; Luo and Ying, 1990: 236–7.
[237] Qinghe County People's Court, 1992, reporting on a case where the police refused to provide evidence of the basis upon which the detainee, Geng Weijun, had been detained.
[238] SPC, *Opinion on Several Questions on Implementation of the 'PRC Administrative Litigation Law'*, 29 May 1991.
[239] Paragraphs 2, 3, 4 and 5, at 667–70.
[240] Paragraph 5.

requirements of *ALL*, Article 52. The first is the State Council *Notice on Resolutely Suppressing Prostitution Activities and Preventing the Spread of Sexually Transmitted Diseases* of 1 September 1986. Whilst this document falls within the scope of Article 52, it does not explicitly mention detention for education. The second is the *Report on Resolutely Striking Against and Suppressing Prostitution Activities and Preventing the Spread of Sexually Transmitted Diseases*, 16 September 1985, which approved the construction of specialist detention centres. This document was jointly issued by a number of ministries and the Women's Federation. Arguably it could be characterised as falling within the scope of Article 53, although the Women's Federation is an organisation that does not exercise formal governmental power and so has no status to make laws or rules. The third is the *Report on Striking Hard Against and Resolutely Suppressing Prostitution Activities and Preventing the Spread of Sexually Transmitted Diseases* of 26 October 1987, issued jointly by the General Office of the CCPCC and General Office of the State Council. This report directed that more specialist detention centres be built, though it does not provide any normative basis for detention for education.

In August 1991, the problem of the lack of a legislative basis for detention for education was resolved when the NPCSC passed the *Prostitution Decision*. The *Prostitution Decision* reflects a minimalist response to the requirement that such powers be put on a legal footing as it empowers police in the broadest possible terms to detain prostitutes and clients of prostitutes. Apart from setting the time limits for detention, this decision imposes no constraints, substantive or procedural, on the police in respect of their use of this power. The police themselves viewed this decision as a form of legislative empowerment and legitimation.[241]

(ii) Coercive drug rehabilitation

In its 1990 notice, the MPS specified the State Council *Notice Restating the Strict Prohibition of Opium and Drug Taking*, 27 August 1981, as the legal basis of coercive drug rehabilitation. This document merely asserts the need for coercive rehabilitation of drug users and provides no normative framework for coercive drug rehabilitation.[242] In designating this document as the legal basis for coercive drug rehabilitation, the MPS acknowledged that this was a temporary measure until legislation on coercive drug rehabilitation could be passed. The NPCSC

[241] See chapter 5 at section 2. [242] Paragraph 4.

Drugs Decision was passed on 28 December 1990 explicitly to provide the required legal basis for the power to detain drug addicts.

(iii) RETL

In the *Notice on Several Questions about the Implementation of the 'Administrative Litigation Law' by Public Security Organs*, the MPS nominated three documents as constituting the legal basis of RETL.[243] They are the 1957 *Decision of the State Council on the Question of RETL*, approved by the NPCSC and repromulgated in 1979; the *Supplementary Regulations on RETL*, approved by the NPCSC on 29 November 1979 and issued by the State Council on 5 December 1979; and the *Temporary Measures*, passed by the MPS and approved and issued by the State Council in January 1982.

The legal basis for sending prostitutes and drug addicts to RETL was subsequently provided by the NPCSC *Drugs Decision* and the *Prostitution Decision*.[244] Prior to passage of the 1990 *Drugs Decision*, there were no legal grounds for detaining rural drug addicts in RETL.[245] Prior to its replacement by the *SAPL*, the MPS confirmed that the provisions in the *SAPR* (Articles 30 and 32) providing for imposition of RETL on recidivist prostitutes and gamblers also constituted a legal basis for imposition of RETL.[246]

The MPS provided that other MPS documents dealing with RETL may also be referred to as the legal basis of RETL if they were not inconsistent with documents designated as the legal basis of RETL; if they had been approved by the State Council; or if they had been jointly issued with the SPP or the SPC. In doing this, the MPS highlights the inadequacy of the designated documents to define the scope of RETL.

7.3 The *Administrative Punishments Law* ('*APL*')

The *ALL* confronted the police with the problem of categorising all of their detention powers and designating their legal basis. Where no document could suffice, the MPS had to obtain legal authorisation for these powers, which it did in the form of the *Drugs Decision* and *Prostitution*

243 Paragraph 2.
244 Guo and Li, 2000: 328; Ren, 1992: 12, asserting that these documents together constitute the legal basis for detention in RETL.
245 Guo and Li, 2000: 319.
246 MPS, *Response to a Request for Instructions on Whether or Not the 'Security Administrative Punishments Regulations' can act as a Basis for Examination and Approval of RETL*, 31 May 2002.

Decision issued by the NPCSC. The next legal challenge to administrative detention powers came with passage of the *APL* in 1996. The challenge lay in determining whether these administrative detention powers should be characterised as administrative punishments (*xingzheng chufa* 行政处罚), and so within the scope of the *APL*, or administrative coercive measures (*xingzheng qiangzhi cuoshi* 行政强制措施), and so outside the scope of the law.

The *APL* codifies what punishments may be created; the agencies empowered to create and enforce them; and the principles and procedures that underpin their enforcement. This legislation predominately affected the public security organs which imposed the bulk of administrative punishments.[247] The *APL*, Article 9(2), specifies that an administrative punishment depriving a person of personal freedom may only be established by a law passed by the NPC or the NPCSC.[248] Administrative rules may now only be used to authorise imposition of a fine or a warning.[249] The *APL*'s transitional provisions required punishments not in conformity with the *APL* be rectified before 31 December 1997, and renders void the imposition of any administrative punishment not based on a publicly promulgated law or regulation.[250]

After passing the *SAPR* in 1986, scholarly attention focussed on administrative punishments.[251] The *ALL* introduced the concept of an administrative coercive measure.[252] After this time, scholarly attention refocussed on the distinction between administrative punishments,[253] administrative coercive measures[254] and administrative

[247] He, 2002: 56, reporting that in Hangzhou each year the public security organs impose around 800,000 or 80 per cent of all punishments imposed by government organs.

[248] *APL*, art. 9(2); Ying and Liu, 1996: 64. [249] *APL*, art. 12. [250] *APL*, arts. 3 and 4.

[251] Zhang and Zhang, 1991: 220. [252] Fu, 2001: 250–1; Hu, 2002: 34–5.

[253] Jiang and Zhan, 1994: 110–13, lists administrative punishments as including: notice of criticism, warning, ordering writing of a letter of regret, requirement that an action be performed such as replanting trees or returning goods, fines, compulsory sale of products, confiscation of illegally obtained goods or proceeds from sale of goods, revocation of licence or permit and administrative detention.

[254] Academics and commentators within the public security system include in the list of administrative coercive measures against the person the powers of detention for investigation (*shourong shencha* 收容审查); detention for repatriation (*shourong qiansong* 收容遣送); stopping for questioning (*dangchang panwen*, 当场盘问), detention for questioning (*liuzhi panwen* 留置盘问); coercive drug rehabilitation (*qiangzhi jiedu* 强制戒毒); detention for education (*shourong jiaoyu* 收容教育); RETL (*laodong jiaoyang* 劳动教养); coercive summons (*qiangzhi zhuanhuan* 强制传唤); coercive detention (*qiangzhi juliu* 强制拘留); prohibition (*yue shu* 约束); coercive removal from the scene (*qiangzhi daili xianchang* 强制带离现场); coercive repatriation (*qiangxing qiansong* 强行遣送); coercive examination for STDs (*qiangzhi jiancha xingbing* 强制检查性病); coercive treatment (*qiangzhi zhiliao* 强制治疗); expulsion from the country (*qiansong chujing* 遣送出境); refusal to permit exit from the country (*buzhun chujing* 不准出境); and refusal to permit entry into the country (*buzhun rujing* 不准入境): Jiang and Zhan, 1994 at 94–102; Fu, 1991: 153–7; and generally Xie, 2000.

dispositions (*chuzhi* 处置).[255] The institutional interest in distinguishing between these different classes of administrative action became more focussed after the passage of the *APL*, which regulated only administrative punishments. These laws, and the *APL* in particular, did not limit the capacity of administrative agencies to determine the classification of their own powers, as the *APL* does not specify what powers constitute an 'administrative punishment'. The scope of *APL*, Article 9(2) remains the subject of debate.[256]

Administrative coercive measures have been distinguished in principle from administrative punishments on the grounds that administrative punishments are imposed for breach of a legal provision, where the evidence is clear and complete.[257] Coercive measures, on the other hand, may be imposed to prevent or stop the occurrence or continuation of an unlawful action; to preserve evidence; or to clarify a situation where the facts are not sufficiently clear to impose a punishment.[258] The police state that coercive measures may be employed by the public security organs to carry out searches and examinations; coercively to educate and reform; to compel citizens to perform an obligation; and coercively to enforce a decision.[259]

Arguing that the purpose of coercive drug rehabilitation and detention of prostitutes is for education, treatment and reform, not punishment, academics and officials within the public security system have asserted that the administrative detention powers that do not fall within the *SAPR* (and now the *SAPL*) should be characterised as coercive measures, not punishments.[260] These arguments depend upon formalistic interpretations of the wording of the documents describing the powers. The MPS defined the power of detention for education as a 'coercive administrative education power administered by the public security organs'.[261] Coercive drug rehabilitation has been defined under the *Measures on Coercive Drug Rehabilitation* as 'an administrative measure coercively to carry out medical and psychological treatment

255 Jiang and Zhan, 1994: 84–91, including orders, prohibitions, licensing and inspection.
256 Yang, 2001: 128–9, criticises this as a weakness of the law.
257 Zhang and Zhang, 1991: 220–2; Fu, 1991: 149–50.
258 Fu, 1991: 149–50. 259 Jiang and Zhan, 1994: 92.
260 Jiang and Zhan, 1994 at 94–102; Fu, 1991: 153–7; Xie, 2000: 107, 115–16.
261 MPS, *Notice on Conscientiously Implementing the NPCSC 'Decision on Strictly Prohibiting Prostitution and Using Prostitutes'*, 23 November 1991, art. 4. This definition is replicated in State Council, *Measures for Detention for Education of Prostitutes and Clients of Prostitutes*, 4 September 1993, art. 2.

and education about laws and morals in order to give up drug addiction'.[262]

The characterisation of RETL has been more controversial. Views of academics and enforcement agencies remain polarised.[263] Police and justice officials assert that RETL is an administrative coercive measure.[264] They point to the CCPCC *Directive on Strengthening Political-Legal Work* issued on 13 January 1982, describing the work of RETL as to 'educate, rescue and reform'.[265] They argue that there is no clear rule stating that RETL is a punishment. They rely for legal support of this assertion on the *Temporary Measures*, which describe RETL as 'an administrative measure for coercive education and reform carried out against people being re-educated through labour, it is one method of handling internal contradictions amongst the people'.[266]

Arguments that RETL should properly be characterised as a punishment point to the purposes for which it has been used since the early 1980s.[267] Some administrative law scholars suggest that after passage of the *APL*, it is no longer appropriate to characterise RETL as a coercive power.[268] One scholar argues that the coercive reform aspects of RETL cannot be used to define the legal character of the power as they are also the objectives of administrative punishment.[269] Legislative support for this argument was found in the *SAPR*, which specified that RETL may be given for repeated prostitution and gambling, and the Human Rights White Paper published by the State Council Information Office in 1991, which identifies RETL as an administrative punishment.[270]

At stake in this debate are the questions of whether these powers are now lawful and whether the police in exercising them are subject to the requirements of the *APL* for openness and fairness in decision-making; proportionality in determining the period of detention; and compliance

262 Article 2. 263 Xia, 2001: 54.

264 For example, Xie, 2000: 121–3; Li and Liu, 1992: 175; Xue, 1996: 35, also arguing that RETL is not a punishment because it is imposed by the RETL Management Committee and only the public security organs have capacity to impose administrative punishments; Mou, 1992: 196; Jiang and Zhan, 1994: 96, but at the same time expressing reservations about whether this characterisation can remain; Li and Du, 1990: 48, 54.

265 Tong, 1990: 68.

266 Jiang and Zhan, 1994: 97, asserting that claims that RETL is an administrative punishment are without basis. Xia, 2001: 54–5, describing this position without adopting or rejecting it.

267 Xia, 2001: 60–3, reciting these arguments.

268 Ying and Ma, 1996: 67–8; Cui, 1992: 18; Gao, Xianduan, 1992: 38; Yang and Liu, 1990: 80, provide a counterintuitive argument that RETL must be an administrative punishment otherwise it would be contrary to *Constitution*, art. 37.

269 Yang and Liu, 1990: 78–80. 270 Luo, 1992: 37.

with the mandatory procedures specified in the *APL*.[271] In the case of RETL, this debate forms part of the broader debate about whether to reform or to abolish it.[272]

7.4 The *Legislation Law*

The distinction between the appropriate type of legislative instrument that could constitute the legal basis for administrative punishments and administrative coercive measures depriving a person of freedom was removed by the *Legislation Law* 2000. The *Legislation Law* contains a list of areas which may be regulated only by law passed by the NPC or the NPCSC. Article 8(5) includes in this list 'deprivation of a citizen's political rights, coercive measures and punishments for restriction of personal freedom'.[273] Since this law was passed, the State Council, local congresses and governments and the MPS no longer have power to pass regulations and rules upon which a person may be deprived of personal liberty. Article 9 prevents the NPC and the NPCSC from delegating the power to pass laws in respect of these matters.

The drafting of Articles 8 and 9 in the *Legislation Law* was strongly contested. One lobby group argued that, to suit the needs of administrative efficiency, it should be permissible for administrative coercive measures to be based on administrative regulations and local regulations. They advocated that limitations on administrative rule-making in respect of coercive measures to deprive personal freedom should apply only to judicial deprivation of personal liberty under the *CPL*, the *Civil Procedure Law* and the *ALL*.[274]

This view prevailed until the final draft of the *Legislation Law* was submitted to the NPC for examination. During the final review of the draft legislation conducted by the Law Committee of the NPC, a different view prevailed. This alternative view placed citizens' rights above the demands of administrative efficiency by asserting that freedom of the person was a fundamental right protected by the *Constitution*.[275]

[271] Procedural requirements of the *APL* are discussed below.

[272] Discussed in chapter 9 at section 4.

[273] Zhang, Chunsheng, 2000: 45–50, explaining the basis for such a provision as recognising that personal freedom and political rights are fundamental rights of citizens guaranteed by the *Constitution* and as such should not be lightly impinged upon. Zhang argues freedom of the person is the basis for other freedoms and rights.

[274] Zhang, Chunsheng, 2000: 48–9, discussing the debate without specifying the members of this lobby group (Zhang Chunsheng is the Deputy Chair of the NPCSC Legislative Affairs Committee).

[275] Article 37 provides: 'Freedom of the person of citizens of the PRC is inviolable. No citizen may be arrested except with the approval or by decision of a people's procuratorate or by decision of

On this view, any power by which a person was deprived of freedom must be based upon law and not on subordinate legislation.[276] In the report issued by the NPC Law Committee, *Results of Review of the (Draft) PRC Legislation Law*, the draft legislation was amended to add coercive measures to the list of powers that may only be based upon law.[277] It was for this reason that the power of the NPC and the NPCSC to pass laws in this respect was made non-delegable.[278]

After passage of the *Legislation Law*, the MPS, along with other government agencies, undertook a major review of the continuing lawfulness of the rules they had passed. As a result of its review, the MPS rescinded a large volume of rules. For example, in 2002, the MPS issued a notice in which it rescinded forty-seven normative documents relating to RETL which did not conform to the requirements of the *Legislation Law*.[279] In September 2003, the MPS commenced a thorough review of all its rules and normative documents. In 2004, the MPS issued the *Notice on Retention, Amendment and Recision of Departmental Rules and Normative Documents* in which it reviewed 1,871 rules and normative documents issued by the MPS and by provincial-level public security organs. It divided these documents into categories for retention, for rescission or for amendment. The MPS identified a number of rules or normative documents that required amendment by passage of legislation to cover the subject matter previously regulated by MPS documents.[280] The MPS, *Measures for Management of Coercive Drug Rehabilitation Centres* 2000, and the *Measures for the Management of Detention for Education Camps* 2000, fall within this category of document.

7.5 Are administrative detention powers lawful?

Although the *Legislation Law* requires that punishments and coercive measures resulting in deprivation of personal freedom be established by law, it leaves several issues at the heart of judging the lawfulness of administrative detention powers unresolved. First, what requirements,

a people's court, and arrests must be made by the public security organs. Unlawful detention or deprivation or restriction of citizens' freedom of the person by other means is prohibited, and unlawful search of the person of citizens is prohibited.' From the translation of the *Constitution* prepared by the NPCSC Legislative Affairs Commission.

276 Zhang, Chunsheng, 2000: 48–9.

277 At 295. 278 *Legislation Law*, art. 9; Zhang, Chunsheng, 2000: 71–2.

279 MPS, *Notice on Rescinding a Proportion of Normative Documents on Re-education through Labour*, 20 September 2002.

280 Gong'an Bu Fazhi Ju, 2004: 300–1.

if any, should be specified in the law concerning the substantive and procedural details of a power? Secondly, what constitutes a delegation within the meaning of Article 9? Thirdly, what principles determine whether implementing regulations in substance defining the scope and procedures for imposing detention is an unlawful delegation of power or a lawful exercise of the power to implement the law? These questions centre around an interpretation of what is legally required to 'establish' (*sheding* 设定) an administrative detention power. These ambiguities about the degree of specificity required of the law in setting out substantive as well as procedural matters and the extent to which those matters may be specified in administrative regulations and rules create scope for the ongoing debate about the lawfulness of administrative detention powers. These issues are considered further in chapter 9.

7.6 Are administrative detention powers constitutional?

Arguments that administrative detention powers should be reformed or abolished commonly begin with an assertion that these powers are in conflict with the *Constitution* and that they constitute an 'unlawful detention or deprivation of a citizen's freedom of the person'. This provision has proved to be a valuable rhetorical tool for arguing that administrative detention powers should be abolished.

Article 37 provides that:

> The freedom of the person of citizens in the PRC is inviolable. No citizen shall be arrested except with the approval or by decision of a people's procuratorate or by decision of a people's court and arrests must be made by public security organs. Unlawful detention or deprivation or restriction of citizens' freedoms of the person by other means is prohibited and unlawful search of the person of citizens is prohibited.[281]

In 2004 the *Constitution* was further amended to add a promise that the state respects and protects the human rights of citizens.[282]

In order to safeguard the constitutional promise to protect human rights and the rights of the citizen under Article 37, Mo Jihong argues that a person may only be detained on the basis of a constitutional provision or a law passed by the NPC or its Standing Committee. He acknowledges, though, that the question of the degree of specificity

[281] English version from http://www.qis.net/chinalaw.

[282] A paragraph was added to art. 33 which provides: 'The State respects and preserves human rights.'

required of such legislation in terms of both substantive and procedural regulation remains unresolved.[283] These are the questions that are also left unresolved by the *Legislation Law*.

8 PROCEDURAL REQUIREMENTS IN EXERCISING ADMINISTRATIVE POWERS

8.1 The growing importance of procedural regularity

Since passing the *ALL*, scholars and officials have been pressing for better regulation of administrative procedures.[284] Scholars argue that mandatory procedural requirements may be one method of achieving fairness and stability in the law, at a time when rapid social and economic transition makes achievement of stability in substantive legal norms difficult.[285] Better regulation of administrative procedures is now a 'hot topic' and the need for stronger procedural rules to protect citizens' rights, encourage procedural fairness and impose constraints on administrative decision-making is supported by academics.[286]

Unable to agree on a comprehensive law of administrative procedure, various aspects of administrative procedure have been passed as specific laws, including the 1989 *ALL*; the 1996 *APL*; the 1995 *State Compensation Law*; the 1999 *ARL*; and the 2003 *Administrative Licences Law*. These laws, and in particular the hearing provisions of the *APL*, were intended to be models for drafting a more comprehensive law of administrative procedure, the *Administrative Procedure Law*.[287] The draft *Administrative Coercion Law* also contains procedural requirements similar to those of the *APL*. Increasingly, legislation governing police powers has adopted these procedural regulations.

The 2006 *SAPL* is the most recent legislative reform which saw the enactment of the procedural requirements set out in the *APL* in respect of minor public order infringements. One of the objectives in revising this law was to ensure that the procedural regulations of the *SAPL* were consistent with those of the current legislative regime embodied in the *APL*, the *ALL* and the *ARL*. This was seen as one of the significant deficiencies in the existing law.[288]

Concerted efforts have been made to overcome political and institutional opposition to the idea of a comprehensive code of administrative

[283] Mo, 2005: 53. [284] Ma, 2000: 42. [285] Wang, Xixin, 1998: 256–8.
[286] Fu, Siming, 2002: 239; Ma, 2000: 42; Wu, 1999: 75; Ji, 1993: 18.
[287] Zhang, 1998: 6; Ma, 2000: 56–7. [288] Feng, 2005: 267.

procedure.[289] Recently, in principle, approval for an *Administrative Procedure Law* has been obtained and the law has been included in the 2004 legislation plan of the NPCSC.[290]

Advocates claim that this law will go a long way towards applying the principles of procedural fairness, participation, openness, efficiency and accountability to all administrative behaviour.[291] A discussion draft has been prepared by senior administrative law academics, specifying procedural rules in respect of both abstract administrative acts (rules and normative documents), and specific administrative acts (particular decision-making).[292] This draft at Article 60(4) enables a person to request a hearing prior to a final determination being made in respect of any administrative act resulting in deprivation of personal freedom. If accepted, such a provision would be broader than the current law.

This draft reflects the aspirations that administrative law academics and some senior officials in the NPCSC have for law to serve as a tool to promote fairness and openness and to protect the rights of citizens in an expansive fashion. It is evidence of the influence of academics and the people's congresses in the emerging legal field in establishing a comprehensive set of basic principles for the exercise of administrative power.

8.2 The strengthening of procedural regulations for administrative detention

The procedural regulation of administrative detention has developed in a piecemeal fashion. This aspect of administrative detention is now governed by a number of overlapping and interrelated laws and rules. The rules particular to RETL are discussed in chapter 6 at section 2.

The 1991 MPS *Notice on Conscientiously Implementing the NPCSC 'Decision on Strictly Prohibiting Prostitution and Using Prostitutes'* provides that procedures for imposing detention for education be carried out with reference to those of the *SAPR*.[293] This notice also permits administrative detention of the person pending a determination about imposing detention for education. Although there is no like regulation in respect

[289] Ma, 2000: 51–5; Ying, 2001: 208–13.

[290] Ma, 2000: 42–3; drafting has been included in the 2003 legislative plan of the NPCSC.

[291] Ma, 2000: 43, and at 59, setting out the outline of proposed draft legislation; Pi, 2000: 69–105, setting out basic principles of administrative procedure as fairness (*gongping* 公平), justice (*gongzheng* 公正), participation (*canyu* 参与), openness (*gongkai* 公开) and efficiency (*xiaolü* 效率).

[292] Pi, 2000: 567–82. Chapter 4 of the draft law relates to abstract administrative acts and chapter 5 to specific administrative acts.

[293] Article 5.

of coercive drug rehabilitation, one commentator asserts that the principles of the *SAPR* apply to both detention for education and coercive drug rehabilitation as they fall within the 'security administrative punishments system'.[294]

Some procedural provisions in respect of coercive drug rehabilitation are set out in the 1995 State Council *Measures on Coercive Drug Rehabilitation*. These *Measures* prescribe that the public security organs at county level and above are responsible for determining whether a person should be sent to coercive drug rehabilitation. They are required to fill in a form of Decision on Coercive Drug Rehabilitation and hand it to the person before they enter the drug rehabilitation centre. The family should be notified within three days of the decision being made.[295]

8.3 The next step: *APL*, the *Regulations on the Procedures for Handling Administrative Cases by Public Security Organs*, 1 January 2004, and the *SAPL*

Acts characterised as administrative punishments, including those within the scope of the *SAPL*, are subject to the mandatory procedural requirements set out in the *APL*. However, as discussed in section 7.3 above, after passage of the *APL*, authorities insisted that detention for education, coercive drug rehabilitation and, less convincingly, RETL, were administrative coercive measures and so not within the scope of the *APL*. However, the MPS was unable to sustain this interpretation of the powers so as to exclude these mandatory procedures for long. In 2004 the MPS extinguished the tenuous legal boundary between punishments and coercive measures in so far as it relates to procedures when it passed the *Regulations on the Procedures for Handling Administrative Cases by Public Security Organs*. These regulations purported to be an interpretation of the *APL* and to cover administrative cases involving 'administrative punishments as well as coercive drug rehabilitation, detention for education etc coercive measures'.[296]

These regulations adopt the *APL* principles that the punishment be timely, just, open and based on facts.[297] Openness is defined in the *APL* as requiring that, before imposition of a punishment, the official must inform the accused party of the facts, evidence and law upon which

[294] Chen, 2001. [295] Article 5. [296] Article 2.

[297] *APL*, art. 4, which includes a requirement that the punishment be proportionate to the degree of social harm caused by the act. These regulations are silent on that point. *Regulations on the Procedures for Handling Administrative Cases by Public Security Organs*, arts. 3, 4.

the decision is based and give reasons for the decision.[298] That party is permitted to respond to the facts and evidence of the accusation, provide contradictory or mitigating evidence and debate the basis for the decision without exacerbating their punishment for doing so.[299]

Following the *APL*, these regulations specify three mandatory procedures for handling administrative cases: summary, ordinary and hearing procedures, thus strengthening considerably the procedural requirements for imposition of detention. Summary procedures, enabling the punishment to be given on the spot, apply in respect of warnings and fines of individuals up to RMB 50 and legal entities of up to RMB 1,000.[300] As discussed in chapter 5 at 2.8, police are now prohibited from imposing on-the-spot fines in cases involving prostitution, introducing or inducing a person to prostitute or using prostitutes.[301]

The ordinary procedure applies in respect of punishments not subject to summary procedure.[302] Ordinary procedure requires that at least two officials, who have shown their credentials,[303] to investigate and gather evidence in a manner that is 'complete, objective and just'.[304] Evidence is to be reviewed by the head of that administrative agency and a written determination made.[305] The *Regulations on the Procedures for Handling Administrative Cases by Public Security Organs* provide that evidence gathered by deceit, torture or which is otherwise unlawfully obtained cannot be used as the basis of the decision.[306] They also provide that a person may not ordinarily be held for questioning for longer than twelve hours.[307] The person is to be notified in person of the decision.[308]

The *APL* permits a person to request a hearing by the decision-making agency prior to imposition of a punishment such as a relatively large fine, revocation of a business licence or suspension of production.[309] However, neither the *APL* nor the *Regulations on the Procedures for Handling Administrative Cases by Public Security Organs*, nor the *SAPL*, make a hearing available where the proposed punishment is deprivation of personal freedom. The *APL* refers a person dissatisfied with

298 *APL*, art. 31. 299 *APL*, art. 32.
300 *APL*, art. 33; *Regulations on the Procedures for Handling Administrative Cases by Public Security Organs*, effective on 1 January 2004, art. 32.
301 *Regulations on the Procedures for Handling Administrative Cases by Public Security Organs*, art. 32.
302 *APL*, art. 36. 303 *APL*, art. 37. 304 *APL*, art. 36.
305 *APL*, art. 38. 306 Article 26.
307 Article 48, with a possible extension up to twenty-four hours where the situation is complex. A person is not to be questioned for continuous twelve-hour periods or restrained during questioning.
308 *APL*, art. 40. 309 *APL*, arts. 42–3, *tingzheng* (听证).

a decision to detain to the review provisions of the *SAPR*[310] (now replaced by the *SAPL*), which permitted a person to seek review only after the decision to detain had been made.[311] The *SAPL* allows a person to challenge a decision to impose administrative detention by commencing either review or litigation. The person may seek a stay of execution pending the outcome of review or litigation and may apply for release upon obtaining an acceptable guarantor or providing surety.[312]

An explanation for exclusion of the right to a hearing in respect of detention under the *APL* is that detention is a 'sufficiently difficult punishment to execute', it 'often requires immediate implementation' and 'the procedural provisions of the *SAPR* provide adequate protection of an individual's rights' without further enabling that person to require a hearing.[313] The *SAPL* continues these provisions and was only amended to prevent the accumulated time for detention from exceeding twenty days.[314] These statements, coupled with the continuing exclusion of the right to a hearing for administrative detention under the new regulations, illustrate how detention remains an area where considerations of efficiency and protection of state power continue to outweigh other considerations of due process.

The new regulations make the ordinary procedures available in respect of police administrative detention. To this extent, they represent a statement in principle that public security organs are required to conform to principles of lawfulness, openness and justice in the exercise of their powers.[315]

9 CONCLUSION

The status of the Party's programme of administration according to law has been elevated significantly since 1996, resulting in increasing focus by state agencies, including public security, on the legalisation and rationalisation of their organisational structure and powers. Law has

310 *APL*, art. 42. 311 *SAPR*, art. 40; Li, 2002: 81–3.

312 *SAPL*, art. 107, replacing the *SAPR*, art. 40; MPS, *Temporary Regulations on Guarantor and Surely Monies in the SAPR*, effective on 1 January 1997, art. 6. *SAPL*, arts. 108–11 require that the guarantor be a close family member and take responsibility for ensuring that the person does not abscond or, if they do, actively to locate them.

313 Editorial Committee, 1997: 279–80. These views are authoritative as the book was co-authored by members of the NPCSC Legislative Affairs Committee, Zhang Chunsheng and Zhang Shicheng, SPC Administrative Division, Jiang Bixin and the State Council Legal Office Li Jiang and others.

314 Feng, 2005: 266. This provision was enacted at *SAPL*, art. 16. 315 Article 4.

become a significant factor in competitions between different organs of state for power, status and control. The MPS has sought to shape legal developments and to use law for a range of different purposes.

The MPS has sought to use law as a way of regularising the structure of the police force and of imposing upon it increasingly detailed professional standards. Law has become one mechanism through which the MPS has sought to strengthen institutional autonomy from incursions by local governments, influential people and even from demands to carry out politically directed hard strikes. Debates surrounding the drafting of the *Legislation Law* reveal efforts by both the MPS and local governments to strengthen their rule-making power at the expense of the other, though on that occasion both were unsuccessful.

The police have viewed the process of legalisation and rationalisation of their powers primarily as a means of empowerment and of regularisation of the local exercise of police powers. To an extent, this view has been challenged. After the *ALL*, the MPS was compelled to find ways legally to justify its powers. When this proved difficult, the NPCSC provided a broad legislative approval for both detention for investigation and coercive drug rehabilitation. The form of empowerment did not impose any legislative constraints on the flexibility of the powers. The more complex legislative history of RETL enabled the MPS to nominate documents as legal basis of RETL which, at the time, could arguably satisfy the criteria set out in the *ALL* in a formalistic way.

Different groups have sought to invest the policy of 'administration according to law' with their own values and preferred content. A range of diverging positions has been adopted about a number of central questions. What types of rules will be sufficient to constitute the legal basis and legal justification for administrative detention powers? What values should be reflected in laws? What types of mandatory procedural requirements should be imposed on the exercise of police power? To what extent should police discretion be limited and how should this be achieved? Academics, in particular, have disagreed with the narrow conception of administration according to law. Some have argued strongly that administration according to law not only requires that law empowers and regularises administrative decision-making, but that it also constrains power and protects the rights of citizens. Others have advocated a 'rule of law administration', which reflects broader values of fairness, openness and protection of human rights. They have been successful to an extent in obtaining legislative acceptance of these principles.

Academics and NPC delegates and officials have successfully ensured that the legal basis for detention powers, both punishments and coercive measures, be restricted to laws passed by the NPC and the NPCSC, despite strong opposition by the MPS. The *Legislation Law* also led to specification of principles of openness and public interest as the basis for rule-making. However, this law fails to limit the interpretation power of the MPS, an increasingly important basis upon which the MPS shapes its powers and the responsibilities of the local police.

Whilst academics have succeeded in entrenching more stringent procedural requirements into the law governing administrative punishments, this success was initially limited by the exclusion of administrative detention from the hearing provisions of the *APL*. The MPS sought to exclude its detention powers from the scope of the *APL* by defining them as coercive powers, though finally making the principles of the *APL* applicable to detention of prostitutes, drug addicts and RETL. The MPS has not been entirely opposed to improving procedural regularity in its decision-making, particularly in areas where systematic abuse has made these powers controversial. Recognising that its current procedures for determining to send a person to RETL led to widespread abuse, the MPS has passed regulations that impose stricter procedural parameters for decision-making. It remains to be seen how effective these will be in practice.

There has been strong advocacy for imposing substantive and procedural restraints on the exercise of administrative discretion and for ensuring that administrative action is based on principles such as reasonableness, fairness, openness and proportionality. The enactment of principles such as these, which would undermine the ongoing informality in the exercise of powers of administrative detention, remains to be achieved.

These contests are evidence of a legal space in which diverging positions may be adopted in relation to the establishment of basic principles for the exercise of administrative power, as well as particular regulatory regimes affecting the exercise of administrative detention powers. They also suggest the growing force of law as a means to define and strengthen institutional positions and powers. This is demonstrated, for example, by the imposition by the MPS of procedural rules drawn from the *APL* in respect of its administrative detention powers when it had previously sought to exclude them from the scope of the *APL* as administrative coercive powers.

Leadership of the Party sets the parameters within which these debates and the legalisation and regularisation of police power take place. The Party continues to exercise organisational controls over the police force and over policing policy and strategy. Party leadership presents an apparent paradox. To the extent that the Party is directly involved in policing and enforcement strategy, especially during campaigns of hard strikes, they serve to frustrate the processes of legalisation and professionalisation of the police. Yet, at the same time, it is the Party's authority that gives importance to the programme of administration law reform, that ensures the participation of state agencies, and that endorses the increasingly vigorous debate about the meaning and implementation of the policy of administration according to law.

CHAPTER EIGHT

SUPERVISION OF POLICE CONDUCT: LEGALISATION AND CONTEST

1 INTRODUCTION

Ensuring that central policies are implemented at the local level in China has been understood as key to the maintenance of political power.[1] Party elites have sought to ensure that the local political-legal organs, the police, procuratorates and courts comply with Party policy and directives, especially when conducting hard strikes.[2] For leaders such as Peng Zhen, Party leadership over the police and law enforcement was essential to ensure that law and order policy was consistently enforced, as well as to prevent abuse of power.[3] Decentralisation of power as a consequence of economic reform has made these objectives difficult to achieve.

In May 1988, the Legislative Affairs Bureau of the State Council[4] discussed two major problems of poor law enforcement amongst administrative agencies. The first was inadequate legal empowerment of administrative agencies. The second was serious problems of dereliction of duty, abuse of power and unlawful actions by officials exercising their enforcement powers.[5] To address these problems, the meeting resolved to provide a more complete legal basis for administrative action; to improve procedural law; and to strengthen mechanisms for controlling

[1] Potter, 2003b: 112–13, discusses Peng Zhen's view that law was a way of ensuring that the Party state maintained its monopoly on coercion.

[2] Potter, 2003b: 115–16. [3] Potter, 2003b: 116.

[4] It has now changed its name to Legal Affairs Office.

[5] Zhou and Zhang, 1990: 45; Tang, 1993: 42. In a 1992, survey 68.5 per cent of judges responded that abuse of administrative power in China had become chronic.

administrative conduct. To strengthen supervision, the meeting proposed instituting systems for supervision, improving self-regulation and raising the standard of officials.[6]

The problem of abuse of power is most acute amongst the public security organs.[7] In a 1992 survey sampling eighteen provinces, 35.1 per cent of respondents identified the public security organs as leaving the worst impression of all government departments.[8] The police themselves acknowledge that abuse of power, corruption, torture and abuse of detainees is endemic,[9] and there is alarm at the most senior political levels about police abuses.[10]

In this chapter, I focus on supervision of police conduct, initiated both as part of the management of police work and at the suit of aggrieved individuals. I investigate the matrix of supervision mechanisms and the extent to which supervision is being framed as a standard of lawfulness rather than as one that is politically and administratively defined. I consider the extent to which recent reforms to supervisory powers such as litigation and review have sought to regularise and constrain the exercise of police power in terms of lawfulness and how the concept of lawfulness has expanded to include principles of fairness and the protection of citizen's rights.

Administrative detention is supervised under several mechanisms, though they have not, either alone or in combination, been effective

[6] Zhou and Zhang, 1990: 45, citing a speech given by Zhang Bixin to the meeting.

[7] Gong'an Bu, 1999: 20, noting that abuse of procedures in exercise of their duties is common and identified, along with torture and abuse of examination and approval of RETL, as one of the most serious problems of law enforcement at present.

[8] Gong, 1993: 256, 289–90. Respondents were drawn from citizens, judges, lawyers, government officials. The industry and commerce departments was rated second worst at 13.5 per cent.

[9] Zhang, Chengfeng, 1994: 276–7; Gao, 1994: 330; Zhang, Chunhu, 1994: 351. In respect of detention centres see, for example, MPS, *Notice on Strengthening the Work of Management of the Three Detention (Centres) and putting an end to situations where Detainees get Beaten to Death*, 22 April 1993; MPS, *Temporary Regulations on a Major Safety Inspection of Public Security Lock-ups and Rostered Inspections Tours*, 20 July 1993; SPP, MPS, *Notice on Strengthening the Legal Supervision Work of Lock-ups*, 12 November 1999, at 190, identifying the poor safety of people held in detention and the prevalence of practices such as police beating and abusing detainees, locking up different categories of detainees together, detaining people who should not be detained and releasing those who should not be released. In respect of torture: Li, 1999; Central Political-Legal Committee, *Notice that Political-Legal Organs Must Strictly Enforce Party Discipline and Rigorously Enforce the Law*, 18 October 1993; MPS, *Notice on Conducting a Major Nationwide Investigation into Public Security Enforcement and Implementing Concentrated Education and Rectification*, 6 March 1998.

[10] Xinhua News Agency, 6 November 1999, reporting concern at the top political levels; New China News Agency, 7 January 2004, reporting that the CCPCC Political Bureau gave instructions for an immediate clean-up after hearing a report in 2003 by the Minister of Public Security about enforcement problems.

to control or limit abuses of administrative detention.[11] I explore the ways in which agencies, including the MPS, have sought to strengthen their supervision powers and so strengthen their institutional positions. Further, I consider the extent to which agencies both compete and collaborate in exercising their supervision powers in a way which is indicative of actors in an emerging legal field.

2 STRENGTHENING SUPERVISION AS A KEY COMPONENT OF ADMINISTRATION ACCORDING TO LAW

Academics argue that introduction of a legal order to legitimate state power requires more than enactment of legislation: it depends upon the public having confidence that the legal system is fair and delivers justice.[12] A formalist view of law requires that administrative agencies enforce the law as the minimum necessary to achieve justice. Development of the legal system has expanded from a view that law is something that the police enforce, to include a requirement that the law enforcers themselves are subject to law in the exercise of their powers. The balance to be struck between empowerment and constraint is a delicate one. Many commentators argue that the Party's claims to political legitimacy are based upon its success in building a legal system to achieve the goals of economic reform and modernisation[13] and social stability.[14] However, social stability increasingly depends not only upon the exercise of the state's coercive powers, but also upon the state controlling arbitrary and abusive uses of power by state officials through strengthening legal controls over them.[15] The police themselves recognise this. In a paper given at a seminar on police management in Beijing in 1993, one policeman said:

[11] Hu and Sun, 14 August 2003, citing Wang Taiyuan, a professor at the China Peoples Public Security University, who asserts that poor co-ordination between different supervision mechanisms resulted in supervision being chaotic.

[12] Liang, 1995: 31.

[13] Potter, 1995b: 16–17; McCormick, 1990: 103; Lieberthal, 1995: 147, emphasising the importance of material benefits accruing to citizens as a result of economic reform.

[14] von Senger, 2000: 53, discussing official views that law is a good way of guaranteeing social stability; Brugger, 1989: 13, in relation to economic reforms; Bakken, 2000: 6, arguing that legitimacy is premised on both economic growth and social control; Peerenboom, 2002a: 169–70; Lubman, 1995: 10, citing Jiang Zemin's calls in 1992 for a strong legal system 'to maintain political stability and good social order'. Epstein, 1994: 19; McCormick, 1990: 103, describing the legal system as 'a way of restoring order in a fundamental sense'.

[15] Li, Linda Chelan, 2000: 214–15.

> Also, being an important liaison between the Communist Party, the government and the people, the public security organs play a vital role in building the prestige and image of the government. Problems of public security men will produce more harmful consequences than those in average government circles.[16]

An ongoing problem is the perception of many officials that they are law enforcers and not subject to the law themselves.[17] However, administrative officials, judges and lawyers overwhelmingly agree that the uncontrolled exercise of power will inevitably lead to abuse.[18]

Supervision of public security work is carried out by a range of state organs.[19] Party leadership includes controls over policy enforcement, party discipline and corruption through the local Party Committee and more specifically in respect of discipline, through the Discipline Inspection Committee, whose offices are established within public security organs.[20] State scrutiny over police work and strategy is carried out by people's congresses and governments at different levels: the procuratorate; and state audit agencies.[21] As part of the mass-line, the public security organs are also subject to social supervision by the masses, primarily through the letters and visits system, social organisations and the popular press.

To improve self-regulation, the public security organs have strengthened mechanisms for supervision over police management and professional training, policy and law enforcement and individual conduct. In the early 1990s, the MPS sought to improve its channels for receiving complaints about police work from the public by establishing complaints centres.[22]

[16] Zhang, Changgong, 1993: 14 (quotation from the English version).

[17] Jiang, Mingan, 1998: 2.

[18] Tang, 1993: 42, citing results of a 1992 survey in which 86.6 per cent of judges, 98.3 per cent of lawyers and 85.6 per cent of administrators responded that if the exercise of power was uncontrolled it would inevitably be abused.

[19] Hui, 2000: 262–3; Jiang and Zhan, 1994: 229–43. Enforcement strategies include strengthening the law and carrying out concerted actions such as that carried out in 1998 to deal with problems of illegal conduct and breach of duty by law enforcement personnel, including police officers and judges: Xinhua News Agency, 17 February 1999.

[20] Jiang and Zhan, 1994: 229–31, describing supervision by the Party as the primary mechanism of external supervision over the work of the police, corresponding to its leadership over the public security organs and the high proportion of police officers who are Party members. It has joint offices with the Ministry of Supervision. *PPL*, art. 42, provides for supervision over public security organs and their personnel by the supervision organs of state.

[21] Ying, 1993: 641–2, discussing the role of the state audit bureau to supervise the revenue and expenditure of government and government agencies.

[22] MPS, *Measures for Trial Implementation on the Work of the Complaints Reporting Centre*, 3 May 1990, to take complaints about police work from the public. Another is MPS, *Supervision Bureau*

In addition to these methods for supervision of police conduct, since 1986 the capacity of citizens to complain about administrative detention to review agencies and the courts has gradually been expanded. In 1986, the *SAPR* enabled citizens to complain to the courts about the imposition of an administrative punishment. Although required to seek review first from the higher-level public security organ, an aggrieved citizen could then appeal to the courts.[23] This introduced a more public form of supervision of police conduct that was not controlled by the public security organs' own internal disciplinary procedures. The *SAPL* now gives an aggrieved person a choice to commence either litigation or review, thus removing the requirement that the person seek review before being permitted to commence litigation.[24] The scope of administrative litigation was increased with passage of the *ALL*, which enabled citizens to sue the police for unlawful acts, including imposition of administrative detention.

Supervision of the decision to impose RETL provides an illustration of the range of ineffective, overlapping supervision mechanisms applicable to that decision.[25] A person dissatisfied with a decision to impose RETL is required by the *Temporary Measures* to seek re-examination of the findings of fact from the original decision-maker.[26] The system of re-examination has been judged ineffective to address any of the issues that may arise from the original decision.[27] In 1990, one commentator noted that petitioners against an RETL decision 'waited until their terms were complete without obtaining a response'.[28]

In the *RETL Regulations*, the MPS interpreted this provision to include the capacity to seek review of the decision either by the people's government at the same level as the decision-maker, or by the higher-level public security organ. If dissatisfied with the result of the review, the subject of the decision is able to commence administrative litigation.[29] A person may petition the local public security organ if they exceed the time limits to apply for review.[30]

System for Reporting Cases of Police Officers Unlawfulness and Breach of Discipline, 29 December 1990.

23 *SAPR*, art. 39.

24 *SAPL*, art. 102.

25 Li, 1999: 20–1, the MPS identifying decision-making processes to impose RETL as one of the worst abused areas of police power.

26 Article 12(2). *RETL Regulations*, art. 76, permitting an application for re-examination to be made to the RETL Management Committee that made the original decision.

27 Ren, 1992: 14.

28 Cheng, 1990: 254.

29 Articles 72, 73.

30 *RETL Regulations*, art. 77, in accordance with the MPS, *Temporary Regulations on Public Security Organs Receiving Complaints and Appeals*, effective from 1 May 1995.

The 2002 *RETL Regulations* provide that the public security organs handling RETL examination and approval are subject to supervision by the procuratorate; the supervision bureaux; the masses;[31] and the RETL Management Committee at the same level.[32] However, the regulations do not specify how these supervision powers are to be exercised. Prior to the *RETL Regulations*, the procuratorate had interpreted its supervisory role as relating only to the management of RETL camps and decisions to lengthen or shorten terms of detention, and not to the examination and approval process.[33] Arguably this interpretation has not been changed by the *RETL Regulations* as the MPS cannot bind the procuratorate by its own rules.

3 THE MPS AND DEPARTMENTS

3.1 Strengthening internal supervision as a way of controlling local abuses

As part of its efforts to address current failures in the supervision of local enforcement, the MPS and the State Council have strengthened both the institutional and regulatory frameworks for internal supervision of police conduct.[34]

Not unlike police forces in other countries, the MPS asserts that it has the technical expertise and knowledge of operational procedures and practices required effectively to supervise enforcement activities.[35] Officials argue that the primary mechanism for supervision of enforcement activities is vertical supervision within the public security organs. Other mechanisms for supervision, they argue, are at best an adjunct.[36] Public security officials argue, with some cause, that other internal mechanisms of supervision carried out by the Discipline Inspection Committee and the state supervision organs have been ineffective to restrict abuse of power.[37]

In its *Decision on Strengthening Construction of the Public Security Legal System* 2000, the MPS signalled its intention to strengthen and

[31] *RETL Regulations*, art. 68. [32] *RETL Regulations*, art. 69.
[33] *People's Procuratorate Measures on the Work of Supervision over RETL (for trial implementation)*, art. 1 at 72, art. 2 at 75; Xia, 2001: 186, 195.
[34] Hao and Shan, 1999: 13.
[35] Jiang and Zhan, 1994: 240–1; Dixon, 1997: 6–7; Reiner, 1994: 742–52, discussing the changing balance of autonomy and external oversight in the British police force in the 1980s and 1990s.
[36] Jiang and Zhan, 1994: 240–1. [37] Li, Zhongxin, 1998: 44.

systematise internal supervision and to control better abuse of power.[38] It set the target that:

> In three years or so we must achieve distinct results in dealing with pronounced enforcement problems about which there is strong public reaction including: torture, exceeding the time limits for detention, abuse of coercive measures and the chaotic imposition of fines, levying of fees and distraint of property.[39]

Public security supervision includes vertical management systems, enabling higher-level departments to supervise and review the professional work of lower-level departments; *ad hoc* investigation of particular matters; supervision of individual cases or areas of enforcement activity; standard form reporting of certain types of incidents;[40] gathering statistics; sending specialist investigation teams; and calling for reports to be prepared on certain issues.

In 1999, in the face of serious abuses of the examination and approval procedures, the Central Political-Legal Committee directed that the public security organs strengthen their internal supervision over the examination and approval of RETL.[41] The *RETL Regulations* provide that if a higher-level public security organ discovers that an RETL decision of the lower-level public security organ is incorrect, it can either rescind or change the decision in the name of the lower-level organ or order the lower-level organ to correct the decision within a specified time.[42] The system of public complaints received by public security complaints centres mentioned above, and the handling of individual protests,[43] provides information to higher-level public security departments. However, this form of supervision remains *ad hoc* as there is no system for automatic review of RETL decisions.

[38] At 376.

[39] MPS, *Decision on Strengthening Public Security Legal System Construction*, 3 June 2000, at 376.

[40] The MPS, has established a number of standardised reporting procedures in respect of unlawful behaviour including MPS, *Supervision Bureau System for Reporting Cases of Police Officers' Unlawful Conduct and Breaches of Discipline*, 29 December 1990. More recent reporting requirements carry penalties for failure to report within the specified time limit.

[41] MPS, *Notice on Implementing the Central Political-Legal Committee's 'Research Opinion on the Problems of RETL'*, 14 October 1999.

[42] *RETL Regulations*, art. 71.

[43] Received under the MPS, *Temporary Regulations on Public Security Organs Receiving Complaints and Appeals*, 1 May 1995.

3.2 The Public Security Supervision Committee

The strengthening of internal supervision and especially that conducted by higher-level public security organs over the work of lower-level public security organs was given a specialist organisational structure with the establishment of the Public Security Supervision Committee in 1995.[44] The supervision committee system was given a more detailed organisational structure in 1997[45] when the State Council mandated establishment of a Public Security Supervision Committee, headed by the Minister of Public Security.[46] The MPS issued implementing regulations in 2001.[47] This committee has responsibility for co-ordinating and implementing supervision work carried out by subordinate supervision committees.[48] Supervision committees are to be established at county level and above, with staff assigned exclusively to them.[49]

The supervision committee supervises the lawfulness of conduct of personnel in subordinate departments and lower-level organs and their conformity with police disciplinary rules.[50] In addition to regular supervision work, the committee is also able to conduct focussed or special investigations.[51] After approval from the police chief, the committee may order performance of a duty,[52] or take direct disciplinary action

[44] Based on *PPL*, art. 47, requiring establishment of an internal supervision system.

[45] By the State Council, *Regulations on Supervision of Public Security Organs*, 20 June 1997; Hui, 2000: 282.

[46] Hao and Shan, 1999: 13, discussing the establishment of supervision committees (*gong'an ducha weiyuanhui* 公安督察委员会) to supervise law enforcement activities of the police and internal management matters including rewards, punishments and promotions and discipline.

[47] MPS, *Measures on Implementing the Regulations on Supervision of Public Security Organs*, 2 January 2001.

[48] Article 2.

[49] Article 3; Hui, 2000: 283–4; MPS, *Notice Implementing the Regulations on Supervision of Public Security Organs*, 18 July 1997, although by 1999 the establishment of supervision committees was incomplete: MPS, *Notice on Establishing and Regularising the Organ for Supervision of Police Work in Public Security Organs at Each Level*, 2 August 1999, providing that the Secretary of the Discipline Inspection Committee within the public security organ could be appointed chief of the supervision department in order better to co-ordinate work. Members of the Committee were to receive at least one month's training before taking up their position.

[50] Article 4, including the management of public order, criminal investigations, determinations to put a case on file for handling, handling of public complaints against the police and functions such as the allocation of personnel. *China Daily*, 13 August 2003, reporting that on 22 January the MPS published the Five Prohibitions. Hu and Sun, 14 August 2003, citing them as prohibitions on using firearms in breach of regulations, drinking alcohol on duty, drinking bearing firearms, drunk driving and gambling.

[51] MPS, *Measures on Implementing the Regulations on Supervision of Public Security Organs*, 2 January 2001, art. 20.

[52] Article 9, in the case of nonfeasance.

in respect of unlawful conduct.[53] Supervision personnel may also recommend that an officer be suspended, or given a disciplinary sanction including demotion, transfer or removal; or may transfer the matter to the procuratorate for investigation in respect of breaches of the criminal law.[54] A police officer who fails to perform a directive issued by a higher-level agency where it could lead to serious consequences, engages in torture or beating of criminal suspects, wrongfully gives an administrative punishment or imposes fines where the situation is serious or accepts gifts or other monies, may be suspended from duty or detained.[55]

Increasingly, these mechanisms for internal supervision over local uses of administrative detention are judged against standards of lawfulness and reasonableness. They impose liability on individual police officers for their conduct. In 1999, the MPS provided that a police officer committing an intentional or negligent 'fault' in enforcement would be liable to disciplinary sanction[56] or, if the matter is serious, criminal sanction.[57] A 'fault' in enforcement includes unlawfulness and unreasonableness in imposing RETL, detention for education and coercive drug rehabilitation, administrative detention and coercive measures.[58] Faults extend to those with responsibility who fail to ensure the required conditions in all forms of police-run detention are met.[59] A 'fault' has been defined to include a successful challenge to a decision under administrative litigation or review where there was a 'mistake of the

[53] Article 10, such as directing an unlawful action be corrected, confiscating weapons, vehicles and restraints that are being improperly used or, if the matter is serious, by compelling the person to leave the scene.

[54] Article 11; MPS, *Notice Issuing the Public Security Supervision Regulations Standard Form Documents*, 19 June 1998, issuing standard forms in respect of decision-making by the supervision committee.

[55] MPS, *Regulation on Implementing the Prohibitive Measure of Stopping the Performance of Duties*, 29 August 1998, art. 3. This notice is based on *PPL*, art. 48(3), and *Public Security Supervision Regulations*, art. 11(1).

[56] MPS, *Regulations on Internal Enforcement Supervision Work in Public Security Organs*, 11 June 1999, chapter 2, including demotion, leaving the post for training, suspension from duty, revocation of qualification, a written investigation, circulating a notice of criticism, expulsion.

[57] MPS, *Regulations on Holding Public Security Organs' People's Police Accountable for Faults in Enforcement*, 1999 art. 18.

[58] MPS, *Regulations on Public Security Organs Internal Enforcement Supervision Work*, 1999, art. 6(4), the lawfulness and reasonableness of the use and enforcement of administrative detention, fines, confiscation of illegally obtained property, revocation of a licence or permit, sealing up, distraint, or freezing of assets, RETL, detention for education, coercive drug rehabilitation and other administrative punishments and coercive measures.

[59] Article 6(5), including lock-ups (*kanshousuo* 看守所), criminal detention centres (*juyi suo* 拘役所), public order detention centres (*zhi'an jiliu suo* 治安拘留所), detention for education centres, coercive drug rehabilitation centres, detention for questioning rooms (*liuzhi shi* 留置室) and other sites for the deprivation of personal freedom.

main facts, or a gross abuse of procedure'.[60] If compensation is payable under the *State Compensation Law*, the responsible individual will be required to pay part or all of the compensation awarded.[61]

Regulations have been implemented to hold heads of public security organs accountable for both their own conduct and serious breaches committed within the organ under their control.[62] Where a death results from torture, the criminal investigation division must be brought in to investigate and police chiefs of higher-level public security organs will be liable to sanction.[63] Complementary measures were passed jointly by the CCPCC and the State Council to strengthen the management and supervision of leadership cadres.[64]

These supervision powers appear very comprehensive. It is too early to judge how effective they will be on a day-to-day basis. However, an early indication is the clean-up campaign launched by the MPS between August and November 2003 in response to instructions by the CCPCC Political Bureau to deal with problems in enforcement. As a result of this campaign, 33,761 police officers were dismissed as unqualified and 10,940 'substandard workers' were 'cleared out'.[65]

3.3 The Legal Division

To strengthen legal aspects of police work, including internal supervision of police enforcement work, the MPS has focussed on building and then strengthening the Legal Division. Passage of the *ALL* in 1989 provided impetus.[66] By 1991 over 70 per cent of public security organs at county level and above had established legal divisions.[67] In its 2000 decision to complete the construction of the legal infrastructure of

[60] Article 3. [61] Article 19.

[62] MPS, *Notice issuing 'Temporary Regulations on Leadership Accountability in Public Security Organs'*, 3 April 1997, art. 6 setting out serious breaches of discipline and law for which the chief and in some cases the section head will bear responsibility: misuse of weapons leading to death, torture leading to death; not supervising detention resulting in the escape or a person being killed in detention; failure to investigate or pursue a breach of discipline.

[63] MPS, *Notice on Further Strengthening Leadership Accountability in Cases of Torture Resulting in Death and the System of Reporting and Self-criticism in these cases etc.*, 16 June 1999: if there are two deaths by torture in one year the police chief at provincial level will be liable to disciplinary sanction.

[64] General Office of the CCPCC, General Office of the State Council, *Notice Issuing 'Regulations on Leadership Officials Reporting Personal Large and Important Matters'*, 31 January 1997.

[65] New China News Agency, 7 January 2004. The report does not indicate what 'cleaning out' involved.

[66] Guo, 1990: 29.

[67] Law Yearbook Editorial Committee, 1992: 47; Law Yearbook Editorial Committee, 1991: 36, reporting that in 1990 one-third of public security organs at county level and above had established legal divisions.

public security organs within five years, the functions and staffing of the legal division were given greater importance.[68]

The Legal Division has broad responsibilities in respect of all law-related matters. It is responsible for drafting rules (and standardised forms used in enforcement activities), checking rules drafted by other departments within the Ministry, legal interpretation and examining and responding to difficult problems relating to particular enforcement issues referred by departments or from lower-level public security organisations.[69] The legal department in the MPS organises and carries out *ad hoc* investigations into targeted problems in law enforcement, involving scrutiny of local rules and documents and the random selection of cases for examination.[70] It has responsibility along with the Supervision Committee to determine liability of officers for faults in enforcement.[71] In 2001, the MPS established a system for the annual examination and appraisal of the quality of police law enforcement work. It examines, *inter alia*, the lawfulness of decisions to impose detention for education, coercive drug rehabilitation and RETL and the management of the detention centres in which these people are held. It also examines the timeliness and lawfulness in handling administrative review and litigation cases.[72] This appraisal process is organised by the Legal Division and reviewed by the public security organ at the next higher level.[73] One stated objective of these regulations is to strengthen higher-level supervisory control over lower-level public security organs.[74]

The legal division also performs a range of other related legal functions such as legal training and legal guidance and consultation, legal research and investigation.[75] Its primary responsibility for supervision of individual cases is exercised through participation in the examination and approval of decisions to send a person to RETL;[76] detention for training of juvenile delinquents in work-study schools; carrying out

[68] MPS, *Decision on Strengthening Public Security Legal System Construction*, 3 June 2000.
[69] MPS, *Decision on Strengthening Public Security Legal System Construction*, 3 June 2000; Jiang and Zhan, 1994: 243.
[70] Annual Report on Public Security Work, Law Yearbook Editorial Committee, 2002: 225, reporting, for example, that in 2001 the Legal Division of the Fujian Public Security Bureau carried out an investigation of 41,881 cases on administrative coercive measures involving 148,494 people, correcting 5,431 cases involving 7,047 people.
[71] MPS, *Decision on Strengthening Public Security Legal System Construction*, 3 June 2000.
[72] MPS, *Regulation on Examination and Appraisal of the Quality of Law Enforcement*, 10 October 2001, arts. 7, 9, 10.
[73] Articles 17, 18.
[74] Article 2.
[75] Ding, 2000: 73.
[76] *RETL Regulations*, chapter 3.

administrative review; and representing public security in administrative litigation and cases involving claims for compensation.[77]

Police officials argue that there is still a need to strengthen the legal division by improving its institutional relationships with other public security organs, such as the supervision committee, the Party's Discipline Inspection Committee and the state supervision organs, which have not been clearly defined and are worked out in an *ad hoc* way; by appointing better qualified personnel; and by giving the Division more autonomy over the appointment of its staff.[78]

4 SUPERVISION BY THE DISCIPLINE INSPECTION COMMITTEE AND THE MINISTRY OF SUPERVISION

As noted previously, all public security organs are subject to supervision by the Party's Discipline Inspection organs[79] and the state supervision departments,[80] which have a joint office in each public security organ at county level and above.[81] The responsibilities of these agencies are broadly framed: to investigate unlawful acts[82] and breaches of Party-discipline.[83] In recent years their main focus has been on targeting official corruption.[84]

Part of the responsibility of the discipline inspection organs is to ensure implementation of Party-directed hard strikes and to investigate police officers suspected of being engaged in the unlawful activities targeted by the hard strike. For example, the discipline organs carried out investigations into the activities of state officials as part of the '1996 Hard Strike' against pornography, gambling and drugs. They also scrutinised the manner and degree of vigour with which the 'Hard Strike' was carried out by the agency. Leaders who did not allocate sufficient resources to carrying out the 'Hard Strike' or whose subordinates did not

77 Jiang and Zhan, 1994: 241; Ding, 2000: 75.

78 Ding, 2000: 74–5.

79 Li, Qiyan, 1993: 352. The Discipline Inspection Commission was re-established in December 1978 by decision of the 11th CCPCC Third Plenum; CCP Central Committee, 1978: 16.

80 Jiang, Bixin, 1997: 4. The Ministry of Supervision was re-established in 1986 by decision of the NPCSC.

81 Jiang and Zhan, 1994: 233–4; Li, Zhongxin, 1998: 46. In 1993, after the 14th CCP Congress, the CCPCC determined that the work of these two agencies be conducted jointly; Jiang, Bixin, 1997: 71.

82 *PRC Administrative Supervision Law*, 1997, art. 18, to ensure that public security personnel implement laws, decisions and orders and perform their duties in a lawful and proper manner.

83 Li, Qiyan, 1993: 352, to ensure Party members adhere to Party discipline and follow the party line in carrying out enforcement activities and to investigate and give a Party disciplinary sanction for breaches.

84 Ceng, 1995: 112–41.

strike with sufficient force were criticised, and in serious circumstances Party and/or administrative disciplinary sanctions were imposed.[85]

Despite the apparent breadth of power to supervise policy implementation and individual conduct, police sources suggest that the discipline inspection organs are comparatively ineffective. They point to low numbers, old age and lack of training, and a lack of clarity in the internal organisation and control by the local Party Committee and government as eroding the capacity of these organs to carry out independent investigations.[86]

5 THE NPC AND LOCAL PEOPLE'S CONGRESSES

An area in which the NPC and local congresses have been particularly active is the supervision of law enforcement practices and in some cases the handling of individual cases by the courts, police and other agencies.[87]

At the central level, each year the NPC Internal and Judicial Work Committee has conducted investigations into different aspects of law enforcement.[88] For example, in 1998, it carried out an investigation into the administration of justice and implementation of the CMPO.[89] In 2000, it investigated the enforcement of the amended *CPL*, paying particular attention to problems of detention in excess of the legal time limits.[90] In 1993, 1994 and 1996, it investigated the enforcement of the CMPO, including actions taken to prohibit prostitution, and examined particularly serious enforcement problems existing amongst local political-legal organs.[91] In some cases the responsible minister is called to present a report and answer questions on an especially acute problem. For example, in 1990, the Minister of Public Security was required to respond to questions in respect of the continuing failure to curb the

85 A *Survey of the Work of the National Discipline Inspection and Supervision Organs Participating in the CMPO* (1995–1996): 303.

86 Li, Zhongxin, 1998: 46, pointing out that there are around 8,000 personnel to supervise the 1.4 million police officers, their average age is around fifty and that they need to obtain support and approval for investigations from the local party and government.

87 Young, 2002: 726. The *Constitution*, art. 71, empowers congresses to organise investigation groups to investigate these issues.

88 The scope and procedures for such inspections are set out in NPCSC, *Provisions of the NPCSC on Strengthening Inspection and Supervision of Law Enforcement*, 2 September 1993 (in English).

89 Law Yearbook Editorial Committee, 1999: 76–7.

90 Law Yearbook Editorial Committee, 2001: 110.

91 Law Yearbook Editorial Committee, 1998: 92.

gross abuses of detention for investigation.[92] In 1999, the Minister of Public Security reported on efforts to improve enforcement standards of public security organs.[93] At the level of the NPC, congress delegates are empowered to ask for an explanation in respect of particular enforcement issues and cases where there has been a major breach of the law. The responsible minister may provide either a written response to the NPC Chairman's Committee or an oral response.[94]

From the mid 1980s, provincial-level congresses have established systems to carry out supervision over general law enforcement issues.[95] Since adoption of the policy of ruling the country according to law, one scholar argues that their position has been strengthened, enabling more forceful supervision.[96] Their success has largely been achieved through co-operation with the local Party Committee and government to gain support for their supervision activities and with the encouragement of the NPC and its leaders.[97] Some congresses have tried to improve their status by issuing reports on their supervision to government, identifying problem areas and specifying actions required to redress those problems.[98]

The subjects of investigation may include areas of work especially targeted by the Party and state and areas of law where there have been particularly serious problems with enforcement, or problems that have given rise to strong public opinion.[99] The continuing poor conditions in police-operated detention have been a particular focus. Indeed, it became necessary in 1997 for the MPS to issue special instructions to all local-level public security bureaux to co-operate with inspections of police-run detention centres by congress delegates. Local police had resisted inspections carried out by local congress delegations by denying them access to these centres, including lock-ups, detention for education centres, and coercive drug rehabilitation centres. Further, the MPS required local police to take note of the comments of congress inspection

92 Discussed in chapter 1 at section 3. Yang, 1991: 42, reporting on an inquiry in 1990 into enforcement practices conducted by the Internal Affairs and Judicial Work Committee. MPS, *Notice on Urgently Rectifying the Abuse of Detention for Investigation Measures*, 15 February 1992, referring to an investigation in December 1991 into abuses of detention for investigation conducted by the Office of the Law Committee of the NPC and the NPCSC Legislative Affairs Committee.

93 Xinhua News Agency, 6 November 1999.

94 NPC, *Organisation Law*, arts. 16, 17; Jiang and Zhan, 1994: 231–3.

95 Liu and Cheng, 2002: 84–5, tracing this development to the mid 1980s and expanding in the early 1990s. For instance, between 1991 and the end of the first half of 1994, provincial congresses carried out 997 different investigations into a range of law enforcement issues.

96 Young, 2002: 729–31.

97 Young, 2002: 729–30, Fu *et al.*, 8 November 1999.

98 Young, 2002: 736.

99 Liu and Cheng, 2002: 25.

teams and report them to the MPS.[100] Despite efforts to strengthen supervision over police conduct, the need for the MPS to intervene and instruct local police officers to co-operate with these investigations indicates the continuing weakness of local congress powers to supervise the police.

Starting at the end of the 1980s, many provincial-level people's congresses began to require the chief judge, the chief procurator or the head of the relevant administrative agency to present a report on the handling of particular cases, as well as introducing a responsibility system under which the chief judge, procurator, administrative department official and the individual involved would be rendered personally liable for wrongful handling of matters.[101]

The exercise of these forms of supervision has now been validated by specific legislation. On 27 August 2006, the long-awaited PRC *Supervision Law of the Standing Committees of Congresses at Each Level* ('*Supervision Law*') was passed by the NPCSC to take effect on 1 January 2007. The *Supervision Law* strengthens and puts on a legal footing the power of the standing committee to carry out supervision of the conduct of the local government, courts and procuratorates.[102] The *Supervision Law* empowers the standing committee of congresses at each level to require the local government, court or procuratorate to prepare a specialist work report on questions of public concern, or issues that closely affect the interests of the people, including law enforcement problems discovered during inspections carried out by the standing committee, matters about which there have been many letters and visits, or matters of general public concern.[103] After examination of the report and suggestions for amendment made to the relevant agency, including proposals for corrective action, the report is then presented to the standing committee for consideration. Where necessary, the standing committee may pass a resolution requiring the agency to take certain actions and to report within a specified time on implementation of the resolution.[104] Both the annual plan for enforcement investigations and the investigation report, including the report prepared by the relevant agency, should be made public.[105] This element of publicity is likely to expand the influence of such investigations.

[100] MPS, *Notice on Actively Accepting the Inspection and by Congresses and Political Consultative Conferences of the Work of Lock-ups*, 15 January 1997.

[101] Liu and Cheng, 2002: 33–4, 89 (*cuo'an zerenzhi* 错案责任制.).

[102] Article 5.

[103] Articles 8 and 9.

[104] Articles 10–14.

[105] Articles 23 and 27.

The standing committee may also establish investigation committees to carry out periodic investigations into specific issues of the enforcement of laws, regulations, rules or normative documents, or can establish an *ad hoc* investigation committee to investigate a particular problem or issue in the name of the standing committee.[106] When the standing committee convenes to review a proposal or a report, the relevant government or department, court or procuratorate should send the person responsible for that area of work to attend to answer questions or to listen to advice.[107] The standing committee may receive a request from a group of standing committee members to conduct inquiries about the conduct by the local government, courts or procuratorates of particular matters.[108] The *Supervision Law* also affirms the power of the standing committee to scrutinise local government budgets and final accounts and to remove senior government, court and procuratorate officials from their posts.[109]

6 SUPERVISION INITIATED BY CITIZEN COMPLAINT

6.1 Letters and visits

One of the simplest and oldest ways for citizens to lodge a complaint against the police conduct has been the letters and visits system (xinfang 信访). This is often the first mode of complaint where a person is dissatisfied with a decision by an agency such as the police. Each state agency is required to have an office to which people can complain, either in person or by other forms of correspondence. Unlike administrative review and litigation, a complaint is not confined to failure to meet a legal standard, be it lawfulness or reasonableness, but may be a broad statement of discontent with the process or outcome of the exercise or non-exercise of agency responsibilities. The police have observed that a majority of complaints about police conduct relate to decisions relating to public order and household registration, as well as the failure of the police to act on complaints. A significant number of complaints also relate to the abuse of administrative detention powers, including administrative detention, detention for education and RETL.[110]

The letters and visits system has been criticised for its ineffectiveness in resolving complaints. One problem is that the letters and visits office does not have authority to supervise activities of other divisions of

[106] Articles 22–7, 40. [107] Article 34. [108] Article 35.
[109] *Supervision Law*, chapters 3 and 8. [110] Hua, 2005: 32–3.

public security and is not empowered to direct the relevant enforcement division to change a decision or deal with a matter in any particular way.[111] As discussed below, the increasing problem of social unrest arising from the failure to deal with complaints has prompted the Political-Legal Committee to call for greater attention to be paid to regularising enforcement work and improving the justice of law enforcement activities.[112] This call coincided with the passage by the State Council of the *Letters and Visits Regulations* in 2005, directed at strengthening the letters and visits offices of local governments. These regulations have moved to specify the procedures, responsibilities and powers of the letters and visits offices in an effort to ensure that complaints are dealt with in a timely and efficient manner. They also seek to limit the capacity of people to make simultaneous complaints through letters and visits where they have already commenced litigation or review.

6.2 Expanding and regularising systems for external scrutiny of police decision-making

Passage of the *ALL* in 1989 marked an abrupt departure from the traditional conception of the relationship between citizens and state organs, challenging established notions that citizens do not sue officials and that those who do are troublemakers. As the head of the Administrative Division of the SPC at the time, Huang Jie, pointed out:

> In addition, the feudal ideas of thousands of years in our country are deep-rooted in some people's minds. A major part of feudal thought is the concept of rigid hierarchy. From antiquity on down, the officials are high above and the people are down below. The people cannot sue officials. People suing officials was considered to be opposing superiors and creating a disturbance.

Huang Jie also pointed to the 'need to change the notion of some citizens that they would prefer to die unjustly rather than sue an official'.[113]

The enormous symbolic importance of the *ALL* lies in its ambition to remould deeply entrenched customs of power and to render the decision-making of administrative agencies subject to external scrutiny.[114] It also marks the success of academic proponents of legal reform in gaining

[111] Chen, Xiaobo, 1998: 37.
[112] *Ministry of Public Security: Step by Step Pay Close Attention to Collectively Dealing with the Problems of Letters and Visits by the Masses*, 10 June 2005, People's Net, accessed at http://politics.people.com.cn/GB/1027/3460720.html on 16 August 2006.
[113] Huang, 1992. [114] Potter, 1994a: 287–8.

political support for passage of the law over the objections of administrative agencies.[115] Proponents of administrative litigation contend that by providing a formalised and regular channel for complaints, administrative litigation promotes social stability by diverting popular dissatisfaction with poor local administration from being expressed more directly.[116] Administrative litigation impacts on the institutional relationship between the courts and administrative agencies, as courts are the agents through which the acts of administrative organs have become subject to greater external supervision.[117]

The scope of the *Administrative Review Regulations* ('*ARR*') passed by the State Council in 1990[118] followed that of administrative litigation and consolidated existing powers of administrative agencies to review administrative decisions.[119] Commentators agree that a purpose for expanding the scope of review at that time was to reduce the number of matters that were the subject of litigation, as well as to strengthen the internal procedures by which higher-level organs supervised administrative decision-making at the local level.[120] There is some statistical support for this conclusion. In 1990, one policeman asserts that there were 22 million punishments given under the *SAPR*. Of those cases, 30,000 people sought review. Only 4,500, or 15 per cent, of reviewed cases were subsequently the subject of litigation.[121]

Implementation of administrative litigation and review has met with considerable resistance from local officials, who consider a citizen challenging the decision of an official disruptive and improper.[122] Many administrative organs and officials have found it unpalatable that courts have been authorised to scrutinise the lawfulness of administrative decision-making.[123] The attitudes of individuals in senior Party and

[115] Potter, 1994a: 274–5, 287–8; Jiang, 2000: 604–5, asserting that there is strong support at highest Party levels for the system of administrative litigation. Jiang Bixin is a senior judge in the Administrative Division of the SPC and so his comments about implementation and problems with administrative litigation are very authoritative and relied upon extensively in this chapter.

[116] Jiang, 2000: 560–1. See also Epstein, 1989: 1, asserting that: 'The new law is clearly designed to ease popular discontent with maladministration.'

[117] Potter, 1994a: 290.

[118] Now superseded by the *ARL* 1999.

[119] Ying, 1992b: 5. The scope of matters that may be accepted under the *ALL* are listed at art. 11 and under the *ARL* at art. 9.

[120] Ying, 1992b: 6; Zhang and Zhang, 1991: 317; Mou, 1992: 227–8.

[121] Hu, 1992: 36.

[122] Li, Peizhuan, 1993: 27, 64 (then deputy head of the Legal Affairs Bureau (as it was then) of the State Council). Yang, 2001: 160–1; Pei, 1997: 834, cites a survey showing that of the eighty municipal, county and district agencies surveyed, 95 per cent of officials considered the proposed law to be premature.

[123] Jiang, 2000: 583–95.

government positions have been critical of the implementation of systems of review and litigation.[124] Their differing attitudes are reflected in the uneven implementation of review and litigation throughout the country. One official in the legal division of the Liaoning government complained in 1991 that 'some leaders do not respect the systems of review and litigation and have [adversely] influenced proper commencement of this type of work'.[125]

The police have also been reluctant to submit to such an external mechanism of supervision.[126] At the time the law was passed, the Vice Minister of Public Security expressed concerns that the new law would place a strain on resources because of both the anticipated number of cases brought against the police and the urgent need to rectify the inadequacies and inconsistencies in the legislative basis for coercive detention powers. Both he and the head of the legal division of the MPS argued that the law would have a deleterious impact on the efficiency of police enforcement work.[127]

In the police force as well, there is evidence that particular attitudes of senior local officials may explain uneven implementation of review and litigation in different localities. Soon after administrative litigation and review commenced, the MPS Legal Division reported that in the first quarter of 1991, the number of review cases in provinces including Sichuan, Zhejiang, Henan and Hunan were comparatively high, whereas the numbers in Tianjin, Jiangsu, Hainan, Ningxia and Qinghai were comparatively low.[128] The regional disparity in the number of public security-related administrative litigation cases for the second quarter of 1991 is illustrated by the following statistics: Zhejiang 153; Sichuan 115; Henan and Liaoning 92; Jiangsu 12; Qinghai 10; Ningxia 9; Tianjin 8; Beijing 4; and Hainan 2. This regional disparity is also reflected in the overall numbers of administrative litigation and review cases for that period.[129] These results suggest that factors including

[124] Jiang, 2000: 564.

[125] Li, Peizhuan, 1993, *Report on the Situation Concerning Work of Administrative Review in Liaoning*: 19–23 at 22–23.

[126] Chen, 1993: 42–45.

[127] Tao Siju (then Vice Minister of Public Security), *Response to Questions from a Reporter of the People's Public Security News about the (Draft) ALL*, 31 March 1989; Jiang Bo (then head of the Legal Division of the MPS), *Responding to Questions from a Reporter for the Legal Daily on Implementation of the ALL*, 28 March 1989.

[128] Li, Peizhuan, 1993: 578. The first three provinces reported 916, 874 and 755 cases, respectively. Jiangsu reported 177 and Hainan forty-five. In the second quarter of 1991 Ningxia received sixty-eight and Qinghai forty-seven review cases.

[129] Li, Peizhuan, 1993: 103.

attitude and quality of law enforcement, in addition to economic development and levels of wealth, have influenced the extent to which these review mechanisms have been implemented.[130]

6.3 Questioning the complementary nature of review and litigation

The *ALL* permits a person to choose between commencing either litigation or review, unless laws and regulations require the person to seek review first.[131]

The official explanation of the relationship between litigation and review is that they complement each other.[132] In review, administrative agencies have an opportunity to correct their own mistakes, to strengthen higher-level supervision over the decision-making of lower-level organs and to reduce the inconvenience of a court appearance. The courts are spared by having their caseload reduced. However, the relationship in many situations has not been particularly complementary and may hinder the capacity of a person to have their complaint heard.[133]

In its notice implementing the *ALL*, the MPS specified that a person dissatisfied with decisions to impose administrative forms of detention must first seek review before being able to commence litigation.[134] Although rules issued by the MPS do not bind the courts, the State Council subsequently issued regulations confirming the requirement for review in respect of detention for education[135] and coercive drug rehabilitation.[136] In the case of RETL, the requirement in the *Temporary Measures* that a person first seek re-examination of a decision from the original decision-maker[137] has been interpreted by the MPS to enable a person to seek review and, if dissatisfied with the results of the review, to commence litigation.[138] The status of the *Temporary Measures* is unclear as the State Council approved but did not pass these regulations.[139] However, it appears to be accepted that these rules are sufficient to impose a requirement for review. Critical comments by

[130] Li, Peizhuan, 1993: 578. [131] *ALL*, art. 37(2).
[132] Ma, Yuan, 1993: 15. [133] Wang, 2001: 69.
[134] MPS, *Notice on Several Questions about the Implementation of the 'Administrative Litigation Law' by Public Security Organs*, 30 October 1990, paras. 4 and 5.
[135] State Council, *Measures for Detention for Education of Prostitutes and Clients of Prostitutes*, 1993, art. 20.
[136] State Council, *Measures on Coercive Drug Rehabilitation*, 1995, art. 7.
[137] Article 12(2). [138] *RETL Regulations*, arts. 72 and 73.
[139] Approving and issuing (*pizhuan* 批转) may be used by the State Council to raise the status of a document passed by a lower-level agency such as the MPS, and make it binding on all

judges on the difficulties of dealing with RETL cases have not identified the requirement for review as one of the problems.[140]

A person in administrative detention is required to seek review before being able to commence litigation and so is vulnerable to delays in the review agency accepting and dealing with the case. A more serious problem is that administrative agencies have often been unwilling to accept applications for review and, where they do, have been unwilling to rescind unlawful or improper decisions.[141] Requiring a person to seek review first has proved to be a way of discouraging or even depriving a person of the opportunity to commence litigation.[142] Failing to give a decision in a review case has been one way of excluding the court's jurisdiction under the *ALL*. One judge complains that the police will often not inform a person sent to RETL of their rights to seek review, or will intentionally delay handling the review in order to exceed the time limits for commencing litigation, or will neglect to hand over the RETL decision documents and prevent family and lawyers having access to the person.[143] As I discuss below, the Supreme People's Court has sought to address some of these problems in its 1999 *Interpretation* of the *ALL*.

6.4 Administrative litigation

(i) Scope of litigation and accepting a case

The scope of administrative litigation is limited in a number of ways that have impinged upon its practical effectiveness in supervising administrative detention. The local people's court[144] is empowered to receive and determine complaints about the lawfulness, though not the appropriateness, of listed specific administrative acts.[145] The *ALL* distinguishes a 'specific administrative act' from an 'abstract administrative

agencies under the State Council. It is not clear that approval and issue raises the document to the same status as an administrative regulation which must be passed and promulgated by the State Council according to procedures now set out in the State Council, *Procedural Regulations for Formulating Administrative Regulations* 2002. See also Keller, 1989; and Ying, 1993: 279, arguing that it is no longer appropriate to use *pizhuan*.

140 Zhang, 1996: 39, complains that the police do not give detainees an opportunity to seek review or delay handling review cases, but does not challenge the need to obtain review first.

141 Yang Jingyu (Head of the State Council Legal Office), *Explanation of the draft 'PRC ARL'*, at 451. These problems were given as a reason for amending the law.

142 Discussed in more detail below. 143 Zhang, 1996: 39.

144 *ALL*, art. 13. If the matter is important or complex it may be heard by the Intermediate People's Court (art. 14), or if it involves a major or complicated matter then the High People's Court may exercise first instance jurisdiction (art. 15). *Interpretation on Several Questions on the Enforcement of the 'PRC ALL'*, art. 8(1), includes within this category cases where the defendant is the people's government at county level and above.

145 *ALL*, arts. 2 and 5; Xiao, 1989: 30.

act', defining the latter as 'an administrative normative document which does not have a specified target and which may be applied repeatedly'.[146] The rules and other documents upon which the police base their decision are thus excluded from the litigation. The scope of litigation is specified as a list of matters,[147] including administrative punishments and coercive measures, but excluding workplace disciplinary sanctions.[148] Judges now argue that there is an urgent need to expand the matters that may be subject to litigation.[149]

The jurisdiction of courts under the *ALL* excludes criminal coercive measures.[150] Although administrative detention powers were classified by the MPS as administrative, in some cases public security organs have tried to avoid the court's jurisdiction by claiming the detention falls under the criminal coercive powers of the police, or substituting the administrative detention with a criminal coercive measure.[151] This is an issue when the administrative power is used for the purposes of criminal investigation, as is sometimes the case with RETL and was commonly the case in detention for investigation.[152] The court, however, has asserted that if the power exercised is not one contained in the *CPL*, it is administrative in nature.[153]

For example, the case of Geng Weijun involved his detention for investigation on the grounds of suspected fraud. He was employed by his uncle who had been involved in a contractual dispute with a third

[146] *ALL*, art. 12(2) and *Interpretation on Several Questions on the Enforcement of the 'PRC ALL'*, art. 3, Ying *et al.*, 1999: 114–15, defining an abstract administrative act as a rule with binding effect; Ma, 2000: 88–9.

[147] During the drafting of the *ALL* there were two views about the scope of accepting cases: the 'listing method' and the 'summary method'. The *ALL*, art. 11 currently implements the former. Zhang, 1992: 47–9; Zhang and Zhang, 1991: 387–90, are advocates of the summary method and argued that the scope of accepting cases should be based on and protect the fundamental rights of citizens. Those in favour of the listing method argued that if the powers given to the courts were too wide, then the courts would be unwilling to accept cases or would not be able to handle the volume of cases.

[148] *ALL*, art. 11(1) (ii), provides that the courts may accept a case where a person is dissatisfied with an administrative coercive measure such as restriction of personal freedom, or the sealing up arresting or freezing of property. Article 12(3) excludes from the scope of review internal administrative acts, which are decisions by the workplace to reward, punish, appoint or dismiss personnel.

[149] Zhu, Guoxiong, 1996: 528–33. There has been some uncertainty about whether the courts have jurisdiction to accept cases that fall neither within the scope of art. 11 nor of art. 12. Recently, the SPC defined its jurisdiction expansively by deciding courts could accept cases in respect of administrative acts (*xingzheng xingwei* 行政行为), excluding only the matters set out in art. 12.

[150] This exclusion is made explicit in the 1999 *Interpretation on Several Questions on the Enforcement of the 'PRC ALL'*, art. 1.

[151] Liu, Yan, 1991: 63–4, such as obtaining a guarantor pending trial.

[152] Discussed in chapter 6 at section 2. [153] Yang, 1998: 13.

party. He commenced administrative litigation, claiming the detention was unlawful. The public security organs claimed that they were in fact holding Geng Weijun to investigate suspected criminal activities and that the administrative litigation proceedings would prejudice the criminal investigation. In this case, the applicant was in court during the hearing of the administrative litigation when the public security organs sought to re-detain him. The police were only dissuaded after the people's court sent a judge to remonstrate with them.[154]

The broad discretionary power of the public security organs to impose either an administrative or criminal coercive measure enables them to avoid administrative litigation by changing the legal basis on which a person is detained to one exercised under the *CPL*.[155] For example, the court no longer has jurisdiction over the case of a detainee where the public security organ imposes a criminal coercive measure such as criminal detention or residential surveillance.[156]

(ii) Lawfulness of a specific administrative act

Lawfulness is determined by whether the decision was made in conformity with substantive and procedural laws and administrative regulations.[157] The courts may not review the exercise of discretion if it is within formal legal boundaries, unless it is an abuse of power.[158] In chapter 7, I discussed the documents constituting the 'legal basis' of these administrative detention powers, noting that they describe the scope of these powers in very broad terms. Defined in this way, it becomes difficult for an applicant to succeed unless there is some very clear error in application of the relevant substantive rules or procedures. However, recent reforms imposing mandatory procedural regulations on the imposition of administrative detention have expanded the scope of matters that go to the lawfulness of a decision.[159]

For example, Chen Weiguo, an unemployed twenty-four-year-old man, was sent to RETL for being involved on two occasions in drunken brawls, attacking people and disrupting public order. He alleged that he was detained by the police but not informed of the power under

[154] In the case concerning the detention of Geng Weijun, the public security organs refused to provide evidence about the grounds upon which he was held on the grounds that it would prejudice the criminal investigation. The case is discussed in Qinghe County People's Court, 1992: 28–30.

[155] Zhang, 1996: 38–9, in respect of RETL.

[156] Jiang, 2000: 580.

[157] *ALL*, art. 52.

[158] See discussion below.

[159] See discussion in chapter 6 of the *APL* and MPS, *Regulations on the Procedures for Handling Administrative Cases by Public Security Organs*, effective on 1 January 2004.

which he was detained, nor did he or his family receive any written notification of the RETL decision. The decision to impose RETL was overturned for failing to comply with the procedural requirements that he sign an acknowledgement of the RETL decision and that his family be notified.[160] Taking an expansive interpretation, it is arguable that the requirement of the *APL* in respect of administrative punishments that acts conform to the principles of justice, openness and proportionality might also be viewed as pertinent to a consideration of the lawfulness of the decision.[161]

In discussing the definition of targets for RETL in chapter 6, I examined the expansion of targets through rules issued by the MPS. It is arguable since passage by the State Council of rules imposing procedural requirements for passing administrative rules, that these documents should be categorised as internally issued documents which, in principle, fall outside the scope of the *ALL*, Article 53.[162] There is some indication that the courts in determining the lawfulness of RETL have not been willing to apply rules that expand the scope of targets beyond those set out in laws and administrative regulations.[163] However, courts are explicitly permitted to refer to rules and normative documents by Article 62 of the SPC *Interpretation on Several Questions on the Enforcement of the 'PRC Administrative Litigation Law'* which permits courts to cite 'lawful and effective rules and other normative documents' in their judgments.

(iii) Parties to litigation: the applicant

To facilitate administrative litigation, an applicant need only assert the infringement of lawful rights by the act of an administrative agency.[164]

160 Decision on the case, *Chen Weiguo is dissatisfied with the RETL decision of the Shizui Shan People's Government RETL Management Committee*, 1992. The procedures in this case were set out in the *Temporary Measures*, 1982, art. 12. Provisions for service and acknowledgement of the RETL Decision are now set out in the *RETL Regulations*, arts. 49, 52

161 *APL*, art. 4.

162 Requirements to promulgate administrative rules are contained in State Council, *Procedural Regulations for Formulating Rules* 2002. Official documents are regulated by State Council, *Measures on the Handling of Official Documents by State Administrative Agencies*, 2001.

163 Lin, 2001: 13, referring to a 1997 SPC, *Response to a Request for Instructions on the question of whether it is possible to send to RETL an unlawful person who commits offences in the countryside and whose residence is in the countryside but whose acts are insufficient to pursue criminal charges*, which required the courts determine the scope of targets for RETL on the basis of NPCSC laws and State Council administrative regulations only. Analogously, the SPC, *Opinion on Several Questions on the Implementation of the Administrative Litigation Law of the PRC* (for trial implementation), 1991, art. 3, provides that the court's jurisdiction to hear a case cannot be excluded by either administrative regulation or rule.

164 *ALL*, art. 2.

However, applicants face difficulties in making a complaint about administrative detention because of strategies adopted by some local police to limit administrative litigation against them and inadequacies in the law that make these strategies possible. In 1999, the SPC issued a judicial interpretation, the *Interpretation on Several Questions on the Enforcement of the 'PRC Administrative Litigation Law'* as part of its ongoing efforts to overcome these difficulties.[165]

To commence administrative litigation, the applicant must demonstrate the existence of the administrative act complained about. In the case of detention, such as coercive drug rehabilitation, the existence of the act is evidenced by the document, Decision on Coercive Drug Rehabilitation, that the public security organ is required to hand to the person prior to them entering the detention centre.[166] However, if the necessary documentation is not provided then proving the existence of the administrative act becomes more difficult.[167] Another example is if a fine is paid and the agency refuses to issue a receipt, the person seeking to commence litigation will be unable to present the official documentation that would normally constitute proof that the fine was imposed and paid. A similar problem arises if family members commence litigation on behalf of a detainee to whom the police have refused to permit access and there is no documentary proof of detention.[168] The SPC has tried to circumvent the problems caused by refusal to issue receipts and other documentation by instructing lower-level courts to accept any evidence showing the act took place where the documentation that would normally be required to show performance of the act is absent.[169]

A more serious problem for people in detention occurs when the detainee has not been informed of her or his right to seek review or commence litigation, or is not given an opportunity to exercise those rights. Whilst unlawful, it creates a practical problem of how to seek review and then litigation prior to release from detention. If a detainee

165 Passed on 24 November 1999, to take effect on 10 March 2000, art. 98 rescinds the *Opinion of the SPC on Several Questions on the Implementation of the 'PRC Administrative Litigation Law' (for trial implementation)*, issued on 29 May 1991.

166 State Council, *Measures on Coercive Drug Rehabilitation*, 12 January 1995, art. 5, also requires the person's family be notified within three days of detention.

167 Zhang, 1996: 39, cites this as a problem with commencing litigation in respect of RETL.

168 Wang, Zhenguang, 1992: 59, describing this as a common occurrence in detention for investigation cases (Wang is a judge in the Intermediate People's Court, Fuzhou). Liu, Yan, 1991: 63, noting that judges have difficulty gaining access to a person in detention when hearing administrative litigation cases.

169 Jiang, 2000: 587–8; SPC, *Interpretation on Several Questions on the Enforcement of the 'PRC Administrative Litigation Law'*, 1999, art. 40.

is unable to commence an action her or himself, an agent *ad litem*[170] can be appointed in writing.[171] It may be very difficult for the detainee to give this authorisation if no access is granted to them or they are not informed of their rights.[172] Under the SPC *Opinion on Several Questions on Implementation of the 'PRC Administrative Litigation Law'*, issued on 29 May 1991, the agent was required to present a written authority to the court. If the agent could not gain access to the detainee, the detainee had not approved, or was unaware of the attempt to commence the action, the court was not able to accept the case.[173]

In the Chen Yingchun case, an eighteen-year-old secretary had been detained without her family being informed. Her father, upon discovering her whereabouts, unsuccessfully sought to commence litigation during her detention to have the detention decision rescinded. He had no access to her and so had not obtained the necessary written authorisation. There is some anecdotal evidence that judges would sometimes visit the detainee in these circumstances to inquire whether they gave permission and obtain authorisation that way.[174] Further, the SPC in 1999 directed courts to accept an oral entrustment if the applicant was unable to give a written authority. Where a person is in detention and the authorities refuse to allow access to that person, the SPC directed that the court is to presume that a valid entrustment has been given.[175]

Some cases have been documented where public security organs have taken retribution against a person commencing litigation by imposing a more severe punishment for the same conduct. In one case in which a person commenced litigation in respect of a RMB 20 fine imposed under the *SAPR*, the public security organ responded by increasing the punishment to fifteen days' administrative detention. The reasoning was that the public security organ had previously exercised its discretion to impose a light punishment but, given the person's attitude, it decided the act should be punished more severely.[176]

170 *ALL*, art. 29. 171 *ALL*, art. 29.

172 Administrative Division, 1993: 82. These problems apply equally to all forms of administrative detention. The commentator in the Chen Yingchun case acknowledges that detainees often cannot exercise their litigation rights: at 173.

173 Point 24 provides that the agent must show the written appointment as agent to the court for its approval. *Civil Procedure Law*, arts. 58, 59 and 60, requiring that a written signed power of attorney be submitted to the People's Court specifying the subject matter and limits of the authority granted.

174 Wang, Zhenguang, 1992: 60, suggests this as a solution in respect of detention for investigation cases.

175 *Interpretation on Several Questions on the Enforcement of the 'PRC Administrative Litigation Law'*, art. 24.

176 Jiang, 2000: 580.

TABLE 8.1 Numbers of cases and administrative litigation compared

Year	First instance cases accepted by people's courts	First instance administrative cases accepted (percentage of total cases)	Public security administrative cases first instance accepted (percentage of administrative litigation cases)
1990[1]	2,916,774	13,006 (0.44%)	4,519 (34.75%)
1991	2,901,685	25,667 (0.88%)	7,720 (30.08%)
1992	3,051,157	27,125 (0.89%)	7,863 (28.98%)
1993	3,414,845	27,911 (0.82%)	7,018 (25.14%)
1994	3,955,475	35,083 (0.88%)	8,624 (24.58%)
1995	4,545,676	52,596 (1.15%)	11,633 (22.12%)
1996	5,312,580	79,966 (1.51%)	15,090 (18.87%)
1997	5,288,379	90,557 (1.71%)	14,171 (15.65%)
1998	5,410,798	98,350 (1.82%)	14,288 (14.53%)
1999	5,692,434	97,569 (1.71%)	14,611 (14.97%)
2000	5,356,294	85,760 (1.6%)	13,173 (15.36%)
2001	5,936,368	100,921 (1.7%)	14,525 (14.39%)
2002	5,132,199	80,728 (1.56%)	11,707 (14.5%)
2003	5,130,760	87,919 (1.7%)	10,816 (12.3%)
2004	5,072,881	92,613 (1.8%)	11,199 (12.1%)
2005	5,161,170	96,178 (1.86%)	9,514 (9.9%)

[1] Statistics drawn from the Statistical Materials and from the reports on Public Security Work contained in the annual *Law Year Books* for the years 1990–2003. Statistics for the years 2004–5 are drawn from the *Gazette* of the PRC Supreme People's Court.

Although senior judges assert that the number of cases involving direct retribution is small, for many the prospect of retribution or of souring an ongoing relationship with government officials is a strong disincentive to commencing litigation.[177] The continuing low rate of administrative litigation and review compared with both the total number of first instance cases accepted by the courts and the number of administrative punishments imposed is set out in tables 8.1 and 8.2.

[177] Wang, 2001: 69; Jiang, 2000: 577–8, referring to three surveys, one conducted by the Intermediate Court in one city, another by the People's Court of Pi County, Henan and the last in 1992 investigating the implementation of the *ALL*, nationwide. Around 70 per cent of respondents indicated they would not commence litigation even if their rights were infringed for fear of retributions.

TABLE 8.2 Public Security Administrative Litigation and Review

Year	Public security administrative punishments given	Administrative review (percentage of total cases)	Administrative litigation cases accepted (percentage of total cases)
1990[1]	1,965,663	–	4,519 (0.23%)
1991	2,414,055	22,513 (0.93%)	7,720 (0.32%)
1992	2,956,737	24,442 (0.83%)[2]	7,863 (0.265%)
1993	3,351,016	23,122 (0.69%)	7,018 (0.21%)
1994	3,300,972	–	8,624 (0.26%)
1995	3,289,760	–	11,633 (0.35%)
1996	3,363,636	–	15,090 (0.45%)
1997	3,227,669	21,985 (0.68%)	14,171 (0.44%)
1998	3,232,113	29,742 (0.92%)	14,288 (0.44%)
1999	3,356,083	29,022 (0.86%)	14,611 (0.43%)
2000	4,437,417	36,275 (0.82%)	13,173 (0.29%)
2001	4,851,600	31,210 (0.64%)	14,525 (0.29%)

[1]Statistics drawn from the Statistical Materials and from the reports on Public Security Work contained in the annual *Law Year Books* for the years 1990–2003. The MPS did not provide detailed figures of the number of review and litigation cases for the years 2002–3. Law Yearbook Editorial Committee, 1992: 861–2, 47.
[2]Li, Peizhuan, 1993: 101. However, the Legal division of the MPS reports accepting 27,196 review cases in 1992.

However, in the case of detention, these disincentives may be outweighed by the degree of severity of the decision. Figures provided by the MPS Legal Division indicate that in 1991 and 1992 over 50 per cent of all review and litigation cases brought against police decision-making were against administrative detention, including RETL and detention for investigation.[178] In 1992 the MPS reported that the number of litigation cases was 5,676, with 42 per cent of cases concerning administrative detention and 15 per cent concerning fines.[179] Table 8.2 shows that whilst the rate at which people commence review is greater than that for litigation, both litigation and review constitute a very low proportion of the total number of administrative punishments given by the

178 Li, Peizhuan, 1993: 102.

179 Law Yearbook Editorial Committee, 1993: 936–7. In 1992 the MPS report (at 124) asserts that in review cases, 49 per cent of decisions were upheld, 25 per cent decisions were rescinded, 13 per cent were amended and 12 per cent withdrew the review application.

police. It also indicates that there has been no significant increase in the rate of litigation and review and after an initial increase, and since 1996, the rate has declined slightly.

(iv) Parties to litigation: the respondent

The respondent must be a state administrative agency.[180] Authority to impose administrative detention rests solely with the public security organs.[181] Detention by other agencies is unlawful. However, where other agencies, such as the procuratorate, community organisations such as local security committees or security defence teams, the Party committee or the discipline inspection committee, have unlawfully imposed detention on parties, they are not *prima facie* subject to the court's jurisdiction under the *ALL*.[182] The SPC has sought to redress this problem by providing that if the organ has been authorised to exercise administrative power, the administrative agency that entrusted that agent will be the defendant, regardless of whether the entrustment was lawful nor not.[183]

The legal division of the public security organ at the same level as the RETL Management Committee, in whose name the RETL decision is made, acts as respondent in the name of the Committee.[184] It is unclear now whether the RETL Management Committee has authority to impose RETL. If RETL is classified as an administrative punishment, it clearly does not.[185]

(v) The role of lawyers

The role of lawyers in assisting people who are the subject of administrative detention is very limited, not least because the number of decisions which are the subject of administrative litigation is very small.[186] Their role is also constrained by their obligation to promote and preserve social order in the exercise of their responsibilities.

[180] *ALL*, art. 25 provides the respondent is the administrative organ that performed the specific administrative act. If the matter has been reviewed, the review organ is the respondent.

[181] *APL*, art. 16.

[182] Jiang, 2000: 580–2.

[183] SPC, *Interpretation on Several Questions on the Enforcement of the 'PRC Administrative Litigation Law'*, arts. 20, 21.

[184] *RETL Regulations*, art. 73.

[185] *APL*, art. 16, provides that only the police have the capacity to impose an administrative punishment for deprivation of personal liberty. Approval procedures are discussed in chapter 6 at section 2.4.

[186] Alford, 2003: 186, noting that lawyers play little if any role in the informal dispute-resolution processes usually adopted in respect of administrative decision-making.

The importance of legal representation in administrative litigation is unclear. Pei points out that the rate of legal representation rose until 1992, after which time it fell.[187] He suggests the role of lawyers in administrative litigation declined because lawyers were not seen as decisive in influencing the outcomes of litigation, because of the willingness of administrative agencies to amend their decisions and because of the rapid expansion in the volume of administrative litigation.[188] Pei asserts that respondents have a lower rate of representation than applicants and concludes that this is because of the high rate of negotiated settlements. He concludes that respondents do not treat legal representation seriously.[189] However, before such a conclusion can be drawn, it would be necessary to examine data to prove that the level of representation amongst respondents is significantly lower, and to consider whether the reason for lower levels of legal representation is because of the availability of specialist legally trained personnel within the agency, such as the legal division of public security organs, whose role is to represent the agency in administrative litigation.

A 1997 survey in Anhui showed 83.33 per cent of applicants considered having a good lawyer was important in succeeding in administrative litigation, 100 per cent considered a just verdict; 88 per cent legal knowledge; and 80.95 per cent a meritorious case important to success.[190] Peerenboom interprets this material as suggesting that lawyers play an important role in administrative litigation and not only are involved in negotiating a resolution to disputes, but also act as a buffer between the applicant and defendant.[191] His conclusion that lawyers are actively involved in negotiating resolutions to disputes is supported by the results of an investigation into the role of lawyers carried out in Yunnan in 1997.[192] However, the Anhui survey also revealed that only 15.48 per cent of respondents would retain a lawyer in conducting administrative litigation, whilst 67.86 per cent preferred to conduct the case themselves under the guidance of a representative. The authors interpret these responses as indicating that applicants seek to supplement their own legal knowledge but do not trust lawyers sufficiently to entrust them to handle their case.[193] Statistics provided by

[187] Pei, 1997: 853. [188] Pei, 1997: 853. [189] Pei, 1997: 854.
[190] Jiang, Mingan, 1998: 430. [191] Peerenboom, 2002a: 405–6.
[192] Jiang, Mingan, 1998: 414–16, reporting that in 1996, 55.2 per cent of applicants had legal representation and 44.8 per cent of respondents had legal representation and that lawyers were actively involved in negotiating settlements and that they were also involved in administrative review.
[193] Jiang, Mingan, 1998: 430.

the MoJ indicate the level of legal representation in respect of administrative litigation is increasing, though these figures provide no information about the rate of representation in cases against the public security organs.[194]

The responsibility of lawyers to promote social order and the development of the 'harmonious society' in their role as representative for applicants to administrative litigation cases was articulated in the *Guiding Opinion of the All China Lawyers' Association on Lawyers Handling Mass Cases* issued on 20 March 2006.[195] In that document lawyers entrusted to represent clients in collective or representative litigation involving more than ten people are required to report their entrustment to the bureau of justice, the lawyers' association in their place of registration as well as to the lawyers association in the place of the litigation and to conduct the matter subject to their supervision. Lawyers are required to represent their clients' lawful interests but at the same time are required to liaise with relevant parties including the local government with a view to minimising social disruption and resolving the dispute. In more sensitive areas of administrative decision-making, lawyers are actively discouraged from representing applicants, such as during the state suppression of the Falun Gong in 1999.[196]

(vi) Jurisdiction

The local people's court in the location of the public security organ deciding to impose a punishment under the *SAPL* will prima facie have jurisdiction. However, if the decision is to restrict personal freedom, the applicant may choose the location in which to commence the action, either in the location of the decision-maker, or the review agency if the matter has been subject to review, or in the location of the applicant.[197] The applicant thus is able to minimise the possibility of the local public security organ influencing the acceptance and conduct of the proceedings.

194 To 43,800 in 2001, with 3,649 legal aid cases, from 19,360 in 1996 and 14,307 in 1991. Law Yearbook Editorial Committee, 2002, 1997 and 1992, respectively.

195 *Zhonghua Quanguo Lüshi Xiehui Guanyu Lüshi Banli Quntixing Anjian Zhidao Yijian*, reproduced at www.dffy.com/faguixiazai/ssf/200606/20060620110110.htm accessed 18 August 2006.

196 Alford, 2003: 188.

197 *ALL*, art. 14. The location of the applicant is either their registered residence, the place where they commonly reside or where they were detained. SPC, *Interpretation on Several Questions on the Enforcement of the 'PRC Administrative Litigation Law'*, art. 8(4) excludes this choice of jurisdiction if a sanction has been levied against property in addition to the detention.

One problem with litigation is that the courts are often unwilling to accept a case, or are pressured by the local authorities not to accept it, and so the court either delays or does not make a decision to put the case on file.[198] To address this problem, the SPC provided that if an application is lodged, the court must put that matter on file within seven days of receipt and decide whether the case can be accepted.[199] However, if the court has not put the case on file within seven days, the applicant is entitled to lodge the application at the next higher-level people's court, thus avoiding possible local pressure on the courts.[200]

(vii) Procedural issues

The respondent has the onus of proving the lawfulness of the decision.[201] The respondent is not permitted to collect evidence from the applicant or witnesses.[202] Evidence collected by the defendant from the applicant or witnesses in contravention of this prohibition is not admissible as evidence of the lawfulness of the act.[203] The MPS *Regulations on the Procedures for Handling Administrative Cases by Public Security Organs* 2004 and the *SAPL* also exclude evidence obtained by torture, trickery, deception or other unlawful means.[204] Such a provision allows much greater scope to challenge evidence obtained, especially from those in detention.

A person must commence litigation within three months from the date the person knew or ought to have known of the administrative decision, or fifteen days from the date of a review decision.[205] The SPC has made provision to take account of the special disadvantage of a person who has been detained and so unable to exercise their litigation rights, directing that the time limit will start to run from the date of their release.[206] If the applicant is unable to attend court for a reason beyond their control, the court is required to suspend the litigation until that situation has ended.[207]

198 Jiang, 2000: 560, 582–3; Gong, 1993: 264–8. 199 *ALL*, art. 42.
200 *ALL*, *Interpretation*, art. 32. 201 *ALL*, art. 32. 202 *ALL*, art. 33.
203 *ALL*, *Interpretation*, art. 30. 204 Article 12. *SAPL*, art. 79. 205 *ALL*, art. 39.
206 *Interpretation on Several Questions on the Enforcement of the 'PRC Administrative Litigation Law'*, art. 43. This provision replaces the earlier interpretation which provided that the maximum period of extension is one year: *Opinion of the SPC on Several Questions on the Implementation of the 'PRC ALL'* (for trial implementation), art. 35.
207 *Interpretation on Several Questions on the Enforcement of the 'PRC Administrative Litigation Law'*, art. 51.

Administrative agencies have often been unwilling to be a defendant and sometimes impede the conduct of administrative litigation.[208] They sometimes refuse to co-operate with litigation, either by not signing to acknowledge receipt of process; not appearing in court; not providing evidence to support the lawfulness of the act; not performing a judgment against them; or threatening or offering inducements to judges.[209] A report from the early 1990s revealed that in one court a judge tried seventy-seven public security-related cases without the defendant responding to any of the allegations.[210] In another case, the legal representative of the defendant public security agency refused to attend court, but during the hearing sat in the public gallery and interfered with the court proceedings.[211] Another judge complained of police obstruction in the handling of RETL cases, arguing that they prevented the court from gathering evidence and refused to produce relevant evidence.[212] However, a judge of the SPC, whilst acknowledging such cases of interference by public security organs, asserts that these are a small minority of cases.[213]

Both the SPC and the MPS have adopted measures seeking to address these problems. One aspect of the annual appraisal of the quality of law enforcement practice considers whether administrative litigation and review responsibilities have been carried out lawfully, with a particular focus on whether there was a refusal to appear in court, to provide evidence in a timely manner and whether there was delay or a perfunctory handling of complaints.[214]

The SPC has sought to ensure that failure by the respondent to co-operate in the proceedings will not frustrate the litigation. It has directed that, if the administrative organ fails to appear in court or fails to provide any evidence to the court without good reason within ten days of being served with the duplicate application, the court may judge the act unlawful on the basis of insufficiency of evidence.[215] This becomes an

[208] Ma, 2000: 126; and generally Jiang, 2000; but for a more optimistic view, Tang, 1993: 6, asserting that administrative litigation is becoming an important mechanism for resolving disputes; generally, Pei, 1997.

[209] Jiang, 2000: 590–4; Jiang, Mingan, 1998: 419–20, a 1997 survey of lawyers in Yunnan showed that lawyers also had difficulty obtaining evidence of the act and the legal basis for the act from respondents.

[210] Chen, 1993: 41. [211] Chen, 1993: 41. [212] Zhang, 1996: 39. [213] Jiang, 2000: 580.

[214] MPS, *Regulation on Examination and Appraisal of the Quality of Law Enforcement*, 10 October 2001, art. 10.

[215] *ALL*, art. 48, deals with failure to appear in court. *ALL*, art. 43 and the *ALL, Interpretation*, art. 26 deal with failure to provide evidence. The basis for the decision is *ALL*, art. 54(2)(a).

important issue for a detainee, as the courts will generally not suspend enforcement of the administrative decision, based on the presumption that administrative actions are effective and valid.[216]

Judges have difficulties independently exercising their adjudicative power in administrative litigation cases.[217] Jiang Bixin reports that many judges are unwilling to accept or determine cases which are unfavourable to the administrative agency and are either unwilling or unable to exercise their powers to sanction defendants interfering in the conduct of administrative litigation or refusing to perform judgments.[218] The evidence indicates that the SPC has sought to overcome many of the practical and legal difficulties faced by local courts in conduct of administrative litigation through the avenue open to it, the use of its judicial interpretation power.

(viii) Withdrawal of applications

The *ALL*, Article 50 prohibits mediation between the parties to negotiate a settlement. Despite this prohibition, the practice of 'consultation', 'co-ordination' and 'doing work out of court' is extremely common and has contributed to the high rate at which actions are withdrawn by applicants.[219] In some areas, there are reports that up to 70 per cent of cases are withdrawn after acceptance by the court.[220] An applicant may apply to the court to withdraw the litigation after the matter has been accepted, though the court should determine whether or not to accept the withdrawal application.[221] One judge indicates, though, that courts

[216] Hu and Wang, 1991: 119–20; *ALL*, art. 44, setting out the circumstances for ordering suspension of the decision, including: where continuing performance would cause irreparable loss and suspension would not harm the public interest or the respondent decides to suspend performance.

[217] Tang, 1993: 33–5, at 28, reported on a 1992 survey of judges in which 25.3 per cent reported that interference in the conduct of administrative adjudication work was a disincentive to carrying out administrative adjudication.

[218] Jiang, 2000: 595–8. Courts are empowered to impose a fine or detain for up to fifteen days any person interfering in the conduct of the case: *ALL*, art. 49.

[219] Chen, 1993: 41–2; Han, 1994: 29, who gives figures for Shandong province of the 948 first instance administrative cases in 1991, 369 were withdrawn; that is 38.9 per cent. In 1992, of the 875 first instance cases, 379 were withdrawn, which is 43.3 per cent. In 1993, of the 1,436 first instance administrative cases, 790 were withdrawn, which is 53.6 per cent.

[220] Jiang, 2000: 582.

[221] Hu and Wang, 1991; these issues are discussed in cases No. 65; 'Yuangao Ziyuan Yaoqiu Chehiu Susong shifou Zunyu' (Should the Applicant be Permitted to Voluntarily Seek Withdrawal of Litigation) at 137–8; No. 66 '"Lianxi Huiyi" Shang Jueding Chesu Bu Fuhe Falü Guiding' (Deciding to withdraw litigation at a 'Joint Conference' does not Comply with the legal regulation) at 138–9; No. 67 'Yuangao Tichu Chesu, Fayuan Caiding Zhunxu' (The Plaintiff requested withdrawal of the litigation and the Court Determined to permit it) at 139–41.

TABLE 8.3 Administrative litigation in respect of public security administrative punishments[1]

Year	Total cases accepted	Total cases decided	Uphold decision (percentage of total)	Rescind decision (percentage of total)	Withdrawn (percentage of total)
1990	4,519	4,044	1,913 (47.3%)	698 (17.3%)	1,236 (30.6%)
1991	7,720	7,644	2,905 (38%)	1,464 (19.2%)	2,532 (33.1%)
1992	7,863	7,837	2,452 (31.3%)	1,457 (18.6%)	2,894 (36.9%)
1993	7,018	6,993	1,796 (25.7%)	1,201 (17.2%)	2,980 (42.6%)
1994	8,624	8,454	1,704 (20.2%)	1,343 (15.9%)	3,992 (47.2%)
1995	11,633	11,427	1,907 (16.7%)	1,781 (15.6%)	5,731 (50.2%)
1996	15,090	15,095	2,353 (15.6%)	2,450 (16.2%)	7,696 (51%)
1997	14,171	13,932	2,340 (16.8%)	2,205 (15.8%)	(8,903)[2] (63.9%)
1998	14,288	14,278	2,574 (18.%)	2,157 (15.1%)	6,150 (43.1%)
1999	14,611	14,907	3,048 (20.5%)	2,071 (13.9%)	5,905 (39.6%)
2000	13,173	13,173	2,940 (22.3%)	1,879 (14.3%)	4,792 (36.4%)
2001	14,525	14,554	3,508 (24.1%)	1,865 (12.8%)	5,017 (34.5%)
2002	11,707	11,761	3,634 (30.9%)	1,593 (13.5%)	3,351 (28.5%)
2003	10,816	10,950	3,166 (28.9%)	1,342 (12.3%)	3,373 (30.8%)
2004	11,199	11,247	3,317 (29.5%)	1,326 (11.8%)	3,167 (28.2%)
2005	9,514	9,602	2,806 (29.2%)	969 (10.1%)	2,780 (29%)

[1]Statistics are drawn from the annual *Law Year Book* for the years 1990–2003. Statistics for the years 2004–5 are drawn from the *Gazette* of the PRC Supreme People's Court.
[2]This figure appears to represent withdrawals although it appeared under a different heading in a table that did not otherwise contain a section listing the number of cases withdrawn.

commonly accept applications to withdraw the case without considering whether it is appropriate to do so or not.[222] Table 8.3 shows the increase in the rate of withdrawals in cases involving the police from around 30 per cent in 1990; up to a high of 51 per cent in 1996; and gradual decrease back to 29 per cent in 2005.

Differing explanations have been given for the high rate at which matters are withdrawn prior to judgment. The reluctance of respondents to have an award made against them is one of the primary factors. Many officials are reluctant to be made a defendant as they fear the resulting loss of face and authority, loss of bonuses and possible personal

222 Han, 1994: 29.

liability to pay compensation if the act is adjudged unlawful and compensation awarded.[223] In one report in 1992, the Yangzhou City Public Security Sub-Bureau of Henan Province instituted a system to punish police officers whose conduct resulted in the public security bureau losing administrative litigation by imposing individual liability on the officer responsible. In addition to bearing the costs of litigation and paying compensation, the officer was to be penalised by having a salary deduction imposed, together with losing the opportunity for promotion in that year.[224] The scope of individual liability was extended in 1999 when the MPS passed regulations to impose a disciplinary sanction or require payment of compensation by the individual officer where there was a 'mistake of the main facts, or a gross abuse of procedure'.[225]

Pei argues that the high rate of withdrawal of cases occurs because of out-of-court settlements where the administrative agency either rescinds or amends its decision so that the applicant was willing to withdraw the litigation.[226] Based on a selection of cases, he states that 38 per cent of cases in 1994 and 54 per cent in 1995 were withdrawn for these reasons. As a result, he argues that if a person is able to have their case accepted, even without a court decision, their chance of obtaining a satisfactory result is substantial: 36.7 per cent in 1994 and 38.3 per cent in 1995.[227] Similar statistics emerge from the annual report of court work for 1999, indicating that of the total 28,681 cases withdrawn by the applicant, in 15,714 (55 per cent) of those cases, the respondent changed the administrative decision.[228] Similarly, in 2000, of the 21,967 cases withdrawn, in 9,855 (45 per cent) of those cases, the respondent had changed the administrative decision.[229]

However, some earlier local data suggests a more complex picture. An analysis in the journal of the Shandong People's High Court of the reasons for withdrawing cases in Shandong province for the years 1991–93 indicated that pressure by the government agency to withdraw the case constituted 50 per cent of withdrawals; 20 per cent were attributed to

223 Jiang, 2000: 583–5. See also discussion in section 3.2 above and MPS, *Regulations on Public Security Organs Internal Enforcement Supervision Work*, 1999.
224 Report (author not attributed) in (1992) No. 2, *Jingcha Wenzhai* (Police Magazine) 22.
225 MPS, *Regulations on Internal Enforcement Supervision Work in Public Security Organs*, 11 June 1999, art. 3.
226 Pei, 1997: 842–3. However, it is important to note that the selection of cases in the *Selection of Cases of the People's Courts* compiled by the SPC is not representative of the overall types and outcomes of administrative cases as lower-level courts select the cases themselves for inclusion.
227 Pei, 1997: 842–3.
228 Law Yearbook Editorial Committee, 2000: 129.
229 Law Yearbook Editorial Committee, 2001: 165.

the applicant realising that their case was weak; and 30 per cent were attributed to mediation of the outcome. Of this 30 per cent, no indication was give of how satisfactory the result was to the applicant.[230]

The high withdrawal rate illustrates the reluctance of administrative agencies to have a judgment made against them and their efforts to avoid this result. Pei's arguments suggest that the high withdrawal rate may not be at the expense of substantive justice.[231] Some case reports, such as the case involving the illegal detention and beating of Li Jinsheng, support such a conclusion. This case is an example of a situation where commencing litigation brought the attention of the leadership of the public security organ to the abuse complained of and led to internal supervision mechanisms being initiated.

In 1997, Li Jinsheng, a forty-seven-year-old farmer, was detained and beaten by an officer of the Yanshi City Public Security Bureau, Gao Kefeng, and two members of the local security defence team, following a complaint made by his wife.[232] Li was hospitalised as a result of the injuries suffered. He commenced administrative litigation against the Yanshi City Public Security Bureau, claiming he had been unlawfully detained and seeking compensation. After the chief of the Yanshi Public Security Bureau was served with the initiating process, he instructed Discipline Inspection and Supervision officers to investigate the facts of the case and obtain written statements from the perpetrators. At the same time, the police chief suspended Gao for seven days then assigned him to other duties and required the parties involved to study documents on police conduct and discipline. The police chief directed Gao to make an apology to Li and pay RMB 3,000 compensation for loss of wages and medical expenses.[233] Satisfied, Li Jinsheng applied to withdraw the case, which the court granted.[234]

Imposition of individual liability, discussed above, may not necessarily promote higher standards of law enforcement, but may encourage use of avoidance tactics. After passage of the *ALL*, figures showed that between 1990 and 1991 the rate of law enforcement decreased. In twenty government departments in an undisclosed municipal district, the number of cases dealt with involving unlawful acts decreased

230 Han, 1994: 29.

231 See also table 8.3 which, whilst ambivalent, does not contradict this conclusion showing that prior to 1999, the rate of cases where the court upheld the decision has decreased and the rate of withdrawal of cases has increased, whilst the rate at which decisions have been rescinded has remained relatively constant.

232 Zuigao Renmin Fayuan, 1998: 280–3.

233 In 2004, approximately AUD 600.

234 Zuigao Renmin Fayuan, 1998: 280–3.

by 68.6 per cent and the number of administrative punishments given decreased by 80.8 per cent.[235] In another area, in the year after the *ALL* was implemented, the number of punishments imposed dropped by between 35 per cent and 42 per cent.[236] To avoid litigation, enforcement agencies either imposed lighter fines than specified, gave a fine instead of imposing a more severe form of sanction[237] or accepted the truism that if you do nothing, you can't be wrong, and so did nothing.[238]

The MPS also noted that after passage of the *ALL* there was a 22.7 per cent drop in the number of people sent to RETL. In 1991, 87,518 people were sent to RETL, a decrease of 22.7 per cent from the previous year. In some areas the decrease was between 40 and 50 per cent between 1990 and 1991. The MPS attributed this to inadequate legal specification of examination and approval procedures, coupled with an aversion to being a defendant in an administrative litigation suit.[239] Such a dampening effect was only temporary, with the MPS reporting that RETL approvals in 1994 increased 33 per cent nationwide, with some areas reporting a 50 per cent increase over the previous year.[240]

(ix) Decisions

Courts may rescind or uphold an administrative decision, require the agency to perform the act in accordance with legal procedure and, in very limited circumstances, alter an administrative punishment.[241] Judges report that courts generally defer to the factual findings of the decision-maker. The courts are able to rescind a decision where the main evidence is insufficient; where the incorrect laws or regulations were applied; where there were breaches of procedural rules; or where the act was in excess of or abuse of power.[242] The definition of abuse of power invites an inquiry into the propriety of the purpose for which a decision was taken[243] and could, if the courts chose, facilitate expansion of their capacity to examine appropriateness of a decision and of the exercise of discretion under the rubric of an inquiry into abuse of power.

[235] Jiang, 2000: 556–7, though the total value of fines imposed decreased by only 5.6 per cent.
[236] Jiang, 2000: 586.
[237] Jiang, 2000: 557–8, cites research by the legal department in 1991 in an undisclosed district, revealing that 80 per cent of fines imposed were improperly light.
[238] Jiang, 2000: 586. [239] Luo, 1992: 35–6.
[240] Law Yearbook Editorial Committee, 1995, 134. No figures were reported for the years 1992 or 1993.
[241] *ALL*, art. 54. [242] *ALL*, art. 54(2).
[243] Xiao, 1989: 34; Luo and Ying, 1990: 250.

The definitions of acting in excess of power and abuse of power remain poor. These two grounds are capable of being interpreted either expansively or narrowly. One commentator describes the scope of excess of power as acting beyond the extent of lawful authorisation, in respect of administrative functional capacity, or substantive or procedural limitations.[244] There is some difference of scholarly opinion about the scope of abuse of power. Some argue that there must be a subjective intention to use the power for an improper purpose, while others contend that it would be sufficient for the act to be unreasonable or disproportionate.[245]

Professor Ying Songnian states that abuse of power should be understood as an act that falls within the formal limits of power, but contravenes the purpose, spirit and principle of the legislation, for example, where the motivation for the action is improper or unlawful, carried out for personal gain or to help relatives and friends. Ying provides instances of abuse of power, such as where a fine is imposed within the formal limits provided by law, but the purpose for imposing the fine is to meet the financial needs of the agency or to receive a bonus; where the fine is disproportionate to the unlawful behaviour; or where there is grossly differential handling of similar types of unlawful behaviour.[246] Ying's interpretation of the scope of abuse of power thus encompasses both subjective improper purpose and an objective determination that the act was disproportionate. A determination that an act is in abuse of power results in the act being unlawful.

A court may amend an administrative punishment only where it is manifestly unjust, a term which has been interpreted restrictively. One scholar defines 'manifestly unjust' as a subset of abuse of power, in that it is a serious abuse of power.[247] This limitation is in contrast with the much broader power of a review agency to amend administrative decisions on grounds including that the specific administrative act was 'obviously improper'.[248]

244 Ying *et al.*, 1999: 293.

245 Peerenboom, 2002a: 423, discusses the different possible views.

246 Ying *et al.*, 1999: 294. 247 Sun, 1999: 288–9.

248 *ARL*, art. 28(5). Although there is no strict definition of what conduct constitutes obviously improper behaviour, a number of examples describe the intent of the provision, including acts which are otherwise within the formal scope of the law, but which are such that a person of ordinary ethical standards would consider to be improper, such as a disproportionately heavy or light punishment in relation to the seriousness of the offending conduct, or where one punishment such as administrative detention was given when it should have been a warning: Ying *et al.*, 1999: 294–5.

Where a court finds some fault with enforcement during litigation it is able to issue a judicial recommendation to the administrative department at the level higher than the decision-maker, or to the supervisory department in charge of the decision-maker.[249]

(x) Social order policy, Party leadership and independence in adjudication

The courts are vulnerable to the influence of the local Party, government and its agencies when exercising their adjudication powers.[250] Administrative litigation over administrative detention is further complicated by the use of administrative detention in carrying out hard strikes and the involvement of the Political-Legal Committee in implementing social order policy.[251]

As one of the political-legal organs of the state, the courts are also required to implement social order and crime-fighting policies under the leadership of the Political-Legal Committee and the CMPO Committee. The chief judge of the people's court at each level is a member of the Party's Political-Legal Committee. The Political-Legal Committee remains very influential in directing enforcement policy and in dealing with 'important and difficult cases'.[252]

The co-ordinating role played by the Political-Legal Committee in the exercise of their functions by the police, procuratorate and courts is illustrated in a speech given by Peng Zhen in 1980.[253] At the first meeting of the Central Political-Legal Committee, Peng Zhen mapped out the tasks of the Political-Legal Committee. These included to organise and co-ordinate the work of the political-legal organs, to help them reach a common understanding of the tasks to be performed, to act in unison and to co-ordinate in 'doing battle'.[254] Although affirming that each could express different views, in accordance with the principles of democratic centralism, once a decision was made, Peng asserted that all agencies must implement it.[255] Although this speech was made in 1980, the sentiments remain relevant to the work of the courts today, especially when they are handling sensitive or difficult issues such as

[249] *ALL*, art. 65(3); Zhang and Zhang, 1991: 572–3.
[250] Lubman, 1999: 263–4; Clarke, 1996: 50–2.
[251] Discussed in chapter 7 at section 4.2. [252] Clarke, 1996: 50.
[253] At that time he was Secretary of the Central Political-Legal Committee.
[254] Peng Zhen, *Summary of a Speech Given at the First Meeting of the Central Political-Legal Committee*, 6 February 1980, at 217.
[255] Peng Zhen, *Summary of a Speech Given at the First Meeting of the Central Political-Legal Committee*, 6 February 1980, at 218.

those that touch on social order and the implementation of campaigns of hard strikes.

Shortly afterwards, Peng Zhen reiterated the basic proposition that the courts, procuratorate and police must co-operate in handling cases:

> In some cases, the police, procuratorate and courts have different viewpoints. If you have different viewpoints, why can't they be discussed and resolved? Facts, law and policy are all one, why should consultation be seen as unlawful? You should know how to use law, you should know the use of law.[256]

Peng emphasised that different views about how to handle cases, especially big or difficult ones should be discussed first and an agreement reached.[257]

These views on the relationship between the work of the courts, procuratorate and police persist, particularly at the time of hard strikes.[258] A recent example of an instruction issued by the Central Political-Legal Committee that directly affects the handling of administrative litigation arose from a meeting convened in 1998 by the Committee to discuss issues about the scope of RETL. That meeting decided to extend RETL to 'rural riff raff, hooligans and village bullies'. The courts were instructed that in handling administrative litigation cases involving this group they should 'fully consider the actual situation in rural villages, handle the matter carefully and don't decide lightly to make a judgment against the decision of the RETL examination and approval authority'.[259]

This close relationship between the use of police coercive powers, administrative detention and implementation of hard strikes makes administrative litigation of administrative detention a particularly sensitive issue. At the time of a hard strike, judges are required to co-operate with the police in carrying out the strike and at the same time deal with questions of lawfulness of administrative detention. A further complicating factor is where the local police chief is also head of the local Political-Legal Committee. The police chief's superior status on the

[256] Peng Zhen, *Conduct Investigation and Study, Handle Matters According to The Actual Situation*, 26 April 1980, at 227.

[257] Peng Zhen, *Conduct Investigation and Study, Handle Matters According to The Actual Situation*, 26 April 1980.

[258] Lubman, 1999: 264.

[259] This meeting was referred to in MPS, *Notice on Several Questions on the Scope of RETL*, 30 November 1998.

Political-Legal Committee can be used to pressure the chief judge of the court in respect of pending litigation.[260]

Another strong influence on administrative litigation is the local government, which is responsible for allocation of the court's budget and other benefits such as housing.[261] Chief judges and division chiefs are appointed and removed by the local congress[262] on the advice of the local Party Committee.[263] Another impediment to the vigorous implementation of the *ALL* is the realistic perception by judges of the need for a co-operative relationship with government departments. Although infrequent, there are examples of retaliation by the local government against courts when they lost an administrative litigation case. In one instance, the local government refused for three years to approve construction of a new courthouse. In another case, an allocation was not made to cover the court's budget deficit. In another, the judges' medical expenses were not covered. In a case where there was a judgment against the public security organs, they later refused to attend to protect the security of the court when demonstrators converged on the court building.[264]

The difficulty of exercising judicial independence is illustrated by responses to a survey of judges in twenty-two cities in 1992. In this survey, 63 per cent reported interference from government agencies in the conduct of administrative litigation.[265] The lack of independence and interference in adjudication was identified as the most influential factor impeding administrative litigation.[266] A significant proportion of judges, 32.6 per cent, reported that the just adjudication of administrative litigation was influenced by the view that it was not appropriate for the courts to get administrative agencies offside and 41.9 per cent pointed to other factors external to the courts.[267]

There is evidence that the attitude of senior political and government officials has influenced the volume of administrative litigation in different areas.[268] In a speech given at the second meeting of administrative division judges of Gansu province on administrative adjudication work in December 1993, the Deputy President of the Gansu High People's Court listed some of the difficulties faced in implementing the administrative litigation system, including refusing to accept cases for fear of falling foul of the local government and Party committees. To

[260] Chen, 1993: 44. [261] Lubman, 1999: 264; Jiang, 2000: 598.
[262] *PRC Judges Law*, Chapter 5. [263] Lubman, 1999: 252, 264.
[264] Chen, 1993: 44. [265] Gong, 1993: 259. [266] Tang, 1993: 31. [267] Tang, 1993: 33.
[268] Pei, 1997: 838, setting out regional variations in acceptance of administrative litigation cases.

illustrate the disparity in the rates of litigation in different areas, he reported that there had been more cases in Pingding Mountain City, Henan province in the first nine months of 1993 than in the whole of Gansu province for the previous three years. He attributed the difference to the support of local leadership for administrative litigation and extensive education and publicity to inform citizens of their rights under the law.[269]

The judge's approach to dealing with interference in administrative litigation is illustrative of consultative and co-operative approaches used by courts in dealing with these problems. Li suggested that difficult problems should be referred either to the local Party Committee, to the people's congress or to the higher-level people's court for supervision and direction and that a consultative approach be adopted in the court's efforts to handle matters 'according to the law and to adjudicate properly'.[270]

Efforts have been made to strengthen the professional standing of judges and improve the independence of the courts. The *Judges Law* passed in 1995 sought to improve the professional status of judges by setting out judges' professional standards.[271] In 1997, Jiang Zemin announced a programme for 'promoting judicial reform and providing systematic guarantees for the judicial organs to exercise independently and fairly their adjudicatory power and prosecutorial power'.[272]

In 1999, the SPC outlined a five-year reform agenda.[273] It is a broad, institution-building project to improve the professionalism of personnel, to institute procedural reforms and to crack down on corruption. A nationwide judicial examination has been implemented to ensure that all judges meet basic criteria of legal and professional competence.[274] Increasing attention has been paid to introducing reforms to strengthen the independence of courts in adjudication, represented by the interpretation issued by the SPC to strengthen administrative litigation work.

These reforms are suggestive of a shift in the balance of power between the police, procuratorate and courts. The political-legal relationship between these three agencies, represented by the term *gongjianfa*, allocated a vast preponderance of power to the police, especially in

[269] Li, Gangde, 1993: 7–8; Peerenboom, 2002a: 399, suggests this problem is widespread.
[270] Li, Gangde, 1993: 10. [271] *PRC Judges Law*, 1995, Chapter 4.
[272] Cited in Xin, 2002: 88.
[273] See discussion of the implementation of this programme in the Supreme People's Work Report to the NPC delivered at the third session of the Ninth NPC on 10 March 2000: see also Xin, 2002: 85.
[274] *PRC Judges Law*, 1995, art. 46.

the pre-reform era.[275] However, in the emerging space of the legal field, the power of the courts to scrutinise the lawfulness of police conduct, albeit still very limited, begins to disrupt this subservient position. Passing the *ALL* raised the debate about the nature of police power and the extent to which the courts should be able to scrutinise the exercise of police power.[276] In a trial, the police are theoretically, though not in practice, in an equal position to the citizen complainant and police power is subordinated to the adjudicative power of the courts. Efforts by the courts to strengthen implementation of the *ALL* are an illustration of how the process of legalisation and regularisation of police powers in the legal field creates the possibility to change the relationship between the police and the courts.

6.5 Administrative review

The purpose of administrative review is to enhance efficiency in administration[277] and to strengthen the internal supervision mechanisms of public security organs.[278] The State Council asserts that administrative review is 'an important supervisory system by which administrative agencies can correct their own errors'.[279] In 2000, the MPS reported that over 70 per cent of all cases of administrative review nationwide involved review of decision-making by public security organs.[280]

Whilst the scope of matters subject to administrative review initially replicated those subject to administrative litigation, the scope of inquiry in review is broader. A review agency is empowered to consider both the lawfulness and the appropriateness of a decision.[281] Since 1999, the review agency is empowered to scrutinise the lawfulness of the rule or document upon which the specific decision is based.[282]

When the *ARR* were passed in 1990, review was primarily to be carried out by the higher-level administrative department in charge, emphasising vertical lines of supervision.[283] Amendments in 1994 expanded the choice of forum for review, enabling an application to be made to the review organ in the government at the same level,

275 Lubman, 1999: 163, 168–9. 276 Gong, 1991. 277 Ying, 1993: 658.

278 Mou, 1992: 227–8. In relation to state agencies generally, Yang Jingyu, Head of the State Council Legal Office, *Explanation of the (Draft) 'PRC ARL'*; Ying, 1992b: 22.

279 State Council, *Notice on Implementing the 'PRC ARL'*, 6 May 1999, at 91; Yang Jingyu, *Explanation of the (Draft) 'PRC ARL'*.

280 MPS, *Notice on Implementing the 'State Council Decision on Comprehensively Carrying Forward Administration According to Law'*, 23 February 2000, at 368.

281 *ARR*, 1990, art. 7; Ying, 1992b: 5, 40.

282 *ARL*, art. 7. 283 Article 11.

strengthening the horizontal lines of supervision.[284] However, the vast majority of public security review cases are still heard by the higher-level public security organ.[285]

Eight years after introducing the system of administrative review, a number of serious problems remained, including an overly narrow scope of review; inconvenience in commencing review; unwillingness of review agencies to accept applications; and unwillingness of agencies to rescind or amend unlawful or improper decisions.[286] Statistics for the number of review and litigation cases accepted in respect of decisions by public security organs are drawn from the *China Law Year Book*.[287] They can only be taken as a guide as categories have not been clearly defined and some inconsistencies exist between these statistics and statistics provided in other sources. For example, in a book on implementation of the systems of administrative review and litigation, the MPS Legal Division gave a breakdown of the category of public order administrative decisions. It reported that in 1991, public security organs received 22,513 cases for review,[288] comprising 18,502 complaints about administrative punishments and 3,103 complaints about coercive measures. In 1992, it reported a total of 27,196 cases,[289] comprising 22,186 complaints about administrative punishments and 3,417 complaints about coercive measures.[290] Despite the disparity in these statistics from those in table 8.2, they do show that the number of litigation and review cases compared with the number of public order decisions made by the public security organs remains extremely low.[291]

In an effort to address problems of the low rate of review and problems in bringing review cases,[292] the system of administrative review was amended and expanded with passage by the NPCSC of the *ARL*.[293]

The *ARL* now requires administrative review to be carried out on the basis of 'justice, openness, timeliness, being convenient to the people, correcting mistakes where they occur and protecting the correct implementation of law and regulations'.[294] The *ARL* has been implemented by the MPS in 2004 in the *Procedural Regulations for Handling Administrative Review Cases*. These *Regulations* replicate many of the

284 State Council, *Decision on Amending the 'Administrative Review Regulations'*, 9 October 1994.
285 Hui, 2000: 301. 286 Yang Jingyu, *Explanation of the (Draft) 'PRC ARL'*, at 451.
287 In tables 8.1–8.3 above. 288 The same as that reported in the *Law Year Book*.
289 Diverging from the figures reported in the *Law Year Book*, see table 8.2.
290 Li, Peizhuan, 1993: 101. 291 Table 8.2 above. 292 Ying *et al.*, 1999: 2–3.
293 Passed on 29 April 1999, effective on 1 October 1999. The *ARR* were revoked by *ARL*, art. 43.
294 *ARL*, art. 4.

measures introduced by the SPC to address impediments to litigation, indicating a similarity between the weaknesses and forms of resistance by the decision-maker to both litigation and review. The reforms to both the systems of administrative review and litigation demonstrate the state's desire to regularise and strengthen scrutiny of administrative decision-making.

(i) Scope of review

Decisions to impose an administrative punishment[295] or coercive measure[296] may be reviewed under the *ARL*. Prior to the *ARL*, a person dissatisfied with a decision to impose RETL had a right to ask for re-examination of the decision from the original decision-maker.[297] The relationship between this right and the right to seek review was not clarified until the *ARL*. In September 1999, the MPS issued the *Opinion on Several Questions Concerning the Implementation by Public Security Organs of the 'PRC Administrative Review Law'* providing that:

> Where a person is dissatisfied with a RETL decision issued by the RETL Management Committee, that person may apply for review either to the people's government at the same level as the decision-maker or to the higher-level RETL Management Committee.[298]

Recognising that many problems of arbitrary and unfair decision-making for which people sought review were caused by the overlap and inconsistency between the increasing number of local and ministerial rules,[299] the *ARL* increased the scope of review to include local and ministerial rules. At the same time as applying for review of a specific decision, Article 7 allows an applicant to request the review agency to scrutinise regulations passed by ministries, people's governments and government agencies and township and district governments, which are the basis for the specific decision under review. Use of the term 'regulation' (*guiding* 规定) in Article 7 has been given an expansive meaning to include administrative regulations and rules passed according to formal legislative procedures; public documents of agencies and governments,

295 *ARL*, art. 6(1).
296 *ARL*, art. 6(2); for a discussion of expansion of the scope of review generally, see Ma, 2000: 101–6; Yang, 2001: 154.
297 *Temporary Measures*, art. 12(2).
298 MPS, *Opinion on Several Questions Concerning the Implementation by Public Security Organs of the 'PRC ARL'*, 27 September 1999. This provision is now also contained in the *RETL Regulations*, art. 76.
299 Ma, 2000: 91.

also called normative documents (*guifanxing wenjian* 规范性文件); and any other public document issued by an administrative agency upon which a particular decision has been based.[300] Such an expansive interpretation enables the review agency to examine any document upon which the decision was based, regardless of its formal legal categorisation.

The MPS has directed that, in the course of review, the review agency scrutinise normative documents passed at the same level as the review agency, or lower.[301] The review agency may deal with the normative document itself if it has functional power to do so. The review organ must rescind or amend unlawful documents passed at the same level within thirty days and either rescind or direct the lower-level agency to rescind or amend unlawful documents passed at the lower level.[302] If the review agency does not have functional capacity to make a binding determination about the validity of the rule, it is required to refer the matter to an agency that does have that capacity,[303] by transferring it to a higher-level agency.[304] Increasing the scope of review in this way not only makes review significantly broader than administrative litigation, it also provides a practical way of strengthening the scrutiny by higher-level public security organs over local-level rule-making, norm-setting and decision-making.

(ii) Lawfulness and appropriateness of the specific administrative act

Administrative review is also broader than litigation in that inquiry is made into the appropriateness as well as the lawfulness of the decision. The purpose of review is to correct unlawful and inappropriate acts.[305] One senior academic who participated in drafting the *ARL* argues that appropriateness is an extension of the principle of lawfulness as it inquires whether the act and any exercise of discretion was reasonable, just, carried out objectively and appropriate in degree (*shidu* 适度).

300 Ying *et al.*, 1999: 113–14.

301 MPS, *Opinion on Several Questions Concerning the Implementation by Public Security Organs of the 'PRC ARL'*, 27 September 1999, section 2 at 624–625; MPS, *Procedural Regulations for Handling Administrative Review Cases*, 2003, arts. 43 and 44. Normative document refers generally to any internal directive that sets out norms for exercise of functional powers by that agency.

302 MPS, *Procedural Regulations for Handling Administrative Review Cases*, 2003, arts. 45 and 46.

303 *ARL*, arts. 26, 27 provide that the review agency must carry out the investigation within thirty days or, if it does not have authority, refer the question to an agency with capacity within seven days.

304 MPS, *Procedural Regulations for Handling Administrative Review Cases*, 2003, art. 47.

305 *ARL*, arts. 1, 3(3); MPS, *Procedural Regulations for Handling Administrative Review Cases*, 2003, art. 1.

Considerations of appropriateness include consideration of whether discretion was exercised for the purpose of the legislation, whether it was based on a proper consideration of the relevant facts and accords with reason (*hehu lixing* 合乎理性) and does not take into account irrelevant factors.[306]

(iii) Procedures

The procedures for review have been amended in an effort to remove impediments to those seeking review. The *ARL* requires that the review process be just, open and based on the principle of correcting mistakes where they occur.[307] Incorporation of these principles was designed to extend to administrative review the applicability of principles of justice and openness which were originally set out in the *APL*.[308]

Upon passage of the *ARL* in 2000, the MPS designated the legal division of the higher-level public security department to be responsible for carrying out review.[309] In 2003, the MPS issued regulations replacing those passed in 2000, specifying that review is to be conducted by the legal division of specialist review organs established within the public security organs, not legal divisions within other functional departments.[310]

The time limit for seeking review has been extended to sixty days from the day on which the applicant knew of the decision, unless the law stipulates a longer period.[311] A person requesting that the public security organs perform an obligation may seek review if the act has not been performed within sixty days of the request.[312] The time limits for applying for review will not start to run until a person has been informed, or knew, of their right to seek review.[313] An application for

[306] Ying *et al.*, 1999: 20–1.

[307] *ARL*, art. 4 provides that the review organ shall carry out its functions adhering to the principles of lawfulness, justice, openness, timeliness, being convenient for the people and adhering to the principle that mistakes must be corrected, and protecting the proper implementation of law and regulations.

[308] Ma, 2000: 98–100.

[309] In MPS, *Procedural Regulations for Handling Administrative Review Cases*, 24 October 2000.

[310] MPS, *Procedural Regulations for Handling Administrative Review Cases*, passed on 10 October 2002 to take effect on 1 January 2003, art. 3.

[311] *ARL*, art. 9, compared with fifteen days under the *ARR*; Ying *et al.*, 1999: 138–9. The time starts to run on the date that the person receives written notice of the contents of the decision or from the date on which a public announcement of the contents of the decision is published. The time may not be shortened and the time limit may be extended in the case of *force majeure*, that is, objective circumstances which are not able to be anticipated, unavoidable and unable to overcome, or other proper reasons, such as sicknesss or difficulty with transport.

[312] MPS, *Procedural Regulations for Handling Administrative Review Cases*, 2003, art. 23.

[313] MPS, *Procedural Regulations for Handling Administrative Review Cases*, 2003, art. 21.

review may be made either orally or in writing.[314] In a provision that replicates that made in respect of litigation, the decision-maker will not be able to avoid review by failing to deliver the prescribed documentation to prove that the decision was made, as the person seeking review is permitted to use any evidence to prove the existence of the administrative act.[315]

The MPS has affirmed the rights of detainees to request review and has required co-operation from the detention centres by providing that the detention centre must register any request for review and send it to the review agency within three days of its receipt.[316] The principle method for carrying out review is based on documents provided by the applicant and the decision-maker.[317] The review agency may decide or the applicant may request that the review agency carry out investigations itself and hear oral arguments from the parties as well as from third parties.[318]

In reviewing the imposition of coercive measures, the review organ is instructed to pay particular attention to whether the decision-maker was acting within the scope of their power; whether the act was lawful, within the lawful scope and time limits of the act; whether the evidence upon which the decision was based is correct; and whether procedures have been followed.[319] The fact that these matters needed to be specified provides an indication of the problems most frequently encountered in the imposition of administrative coercive detention measures.

In an attempt to address problems of non-co-operation and delay by the original decision-maker, the *ARL* requires that the original decision-maker must provide documents and other relevant materials upon which the decision was based within ten days of receiving a copy of the application for review.[320] If the original decision-maker does not provide the relevant materials, the act may be rescinded on the grounds of insufficiency of evidence to support the decision.[321] Provisions seeking to prevent delays are of particular importance to people in

[314] Article 11. Where the application is made orally, the MPS, requires that a written record of the oral application be completed on a standard form, which is reproduced at Gong'an Bu Fazhi Ju, 1999: 619; MPS, *Procedural Regulations for Handling Administrative Review Cases*, 1 January 2003, art. 17.

[315] MPS, *Procedural Regulations for Handling Administrative Review Cases*, 2003, art. 21. Inclusion of such a provision in respect of both litigation and review indicates the prevalence of this problem.

[316] MPS, *Procedural Regulations for Handling Administrative Review Cases*, 2003, art. 24.

[317] Ying *et al.*, 1999: 244–5. [318] *ARL*, art. 22.

[319] MPS, *Procedural Regulations for Handling Administrative Review Cases*, 2003, art. 40.

[320] Article 23. [321] Article 28(4).

detention, as the enforcement of the specific administrative act under review will generally not be suspended.[322] Reluctance to suspend performance of a decision has been explained on several grounds: the presumption that the decision is *prima facie* lawful, to prevent abuse of the review process and to protect the public interest.[323]

(iv) Jurisdiction of review organs

A person given administrative detention may choose to commence review in the review organ of the higher-level public security organ or of the people's government at the same level.[324] During drafting of the *ARL*, the MPS sought, unsuccessfully, to strengthen its vertical supervision over administrative detention at the expense of horizontal supervision. The MPS argued that its decisions to impose administrative detention should only be reviewable by review agencies within the public security hierarchy. Initially, this argument was successful as the draft and two discussion drafts of the law submitted to the NPCSC for examination excluded decisions of public security organs to impose administrative detention from the scope of review by government review agencies.[325]

However, during examination by the NPCSC, congress members, academics and some officials in administrative agencies strongly objected to such a limitation.[326] In the final version of the law, this attempt to exclude review by local governments over administrative detention was rejected. The reasons for such strong opposition to this proposal included views that the decisions of public security organs should be subject to scrutiny by local government; that there had been problems of misuse of detention powers; and that in some areas, the public security organs had passed rules themselves to exclude the jurisdiction of local government review agencies to review cases concerning administrative detention. This rejection was also supported by the

[322] *ARL*, art. 21. The decision-maker or the review agency may, itself or upon application by the applicant, suspend enforcement pending the outcome of review. Ying *et al.*, 1999: 237–8, setting out grounds for suspension during review that parallel grounds for recision of the act, including the decision that is based on a document that has been revoked, facts were not taken into account that should have been, there is a mistake of fact, there is inadequate evidence to support the decision and great damage would be caused by performing the decision where the consequences would be difficult to undo.

[323] Ying *et al.*, 1999: 236–7.

[324] *ARL*, art. 12 sets out the matters where a person may only apply to the higher-level review organ, including customs, finance, taxation, foreign exchange management organs and decisions by state security organs.

[325] Yang Jingyu, *Explanation of the (Draft) 'PRC ARL'*, at 454; Ying *et al.*, 1999: 161–2.

[326] Ying *et al.*, 1999: 162.

view that fundamental rights of citizens such as their personal freedom should be protected to the greatest extent possible.[327] The protection of rights relating to personal freedom has thus been an important consideration in framing the powers to review the imposition of administrative detention as well as in determining the power of the public security organs to regulate administrative detention.[328] These reforms are indicative of a change in priorities in dealing with police administrative detention powers. They represent a retreat from the view that legal regulation of police administrative detention powers should reflect administrative convenience and efficiency, to include a consideration of the importance of protecting citizens' rights.

(v) Decisions

Unlike administrative litigation, the review agency has extensive powers to amend decisions, direct that the decision be amended, or direct that a new decision be made.[329] The review organ also exercises powers to scrutinise and deal with rules and other documents issued at lower levels. The decision-maker will be held to have acted in abuse of power where the act was lawful but carried out for an improper reason.[330] An act will be obviously improper where there is an obvious disparity between the handling of the case and other similar cases.[331]

6.6 Compensation

The *PRC State Compensation Law*[332] enables a person to claim compensation for losses suffered as the result of unlawful acts by state functionaries exercising criminal jurisdiction and administrative powers.[333] The claim may be made either together with an application for review or litigation or independently.[334] Where a person is claiming compensation for unlawful detention, the calculation of damages will be made on the basis of the average salary for the previous year.[335] The amount of compensation payable is not affected by the actual salary of the person. The intention of the law was to provide a minimum standard of compensation in respect of the breach of the fundamental right of personal

327 Ying *et al.*, 1999: 161–2.
328 See the discussion of the debates surrounding the drafting of the *Legislation Law* in chapter 7 at section 7.4.
329 MPS, *Procedural Regulations for Handling Administrative Review Cases*, 2003, arts. 66–72.
330 MPS, *Procedural Regulations for Handling Administrative Review Cases*, 2003, art. 71.
331 MPS, *Procedural Regulations for Handling Administrative Review Cases*, 2003, art. 72.
332 1 January 1995, art. 35.
333 *State Compensation Law*. 334 Article 9. 335 Article 26.

freedom, which is not dependent upon the wealth or poverty of the person whose right has been infringed.[336] Damages may also be assessed in respect of property losses, personal injury, illness, disability and death suffered as a result of the unlawful act in accordance with the formula set out in the law.[337]

6.7 Citizen empowerment, disillusionment and public order issues

Despite the low numbers of cases of litigation and review brought by citizens, the impact of the *ALL* on the conceptualisation of the relationship between citizen and state should not be underestimated. By creating rights to sue, the *ALL* has empowered a diverse group of people to use the law to assert and protect their rights.[338] O'Brien and Li have illustrated the use of administrative litigation as a strategy of rural people to obtain redress in respect of grievances. They conclude that administrative litigation empowers and enlarges the rights of villagers.[339] They also point out that one of the consequences of administrative litigation has been to educate local officials about the law, either for better, by encouraging them to improve the standard of law enforcement, or for worse, by strengthening their resolve to discourage complaints about their conduct.[340] Pei also points to the use of the *ALL* by lower socio-economic groups to protect themselves from acts of law enforcement agencies.[341]

However, the pursuit of redress for infringements of a citizen's rights can also lead to disillusionment with the legal system where their efforts are stymied at every turn.[342] More seriously, failure to address citizen complaints can exacerbate social order problems. Whilst the police are mostly required to handle 'mass incidents' that do not arise as a result of police conduct, the failure of police supervision mechanisms to deal with complaints about police conduct may also lead to public protests. One police report suggests that social order problems are exacerbated when citizens unsuccessfully seek redress in respect of police decision-making through the letters and visits system. A 1998 report from the Hongqiao district of Tianjin indicates that a small number of

336 Xiao, 1994: 241.
337 In respect of property, arts. 25, 28; in respect of harm to the person, art. 27.
338 Potter, 1994a: 288–9; Pei, 1997: 848–52, pointing to distinct groups including state-owned enterprises and private entrepreneurs who use administrative litigation to resolve disputes. He concludes that the *ALL*, has been used to advantage by a number of groups to assert their legal rights.
339 O'Brien and Li, 2004: 92.
340 O'Brien and Li, 2005: 42.
341 Pei, 1997: 848–52.
342 O'Brien and Li, 2005: 42.

people, who were dissatisfied with the handling of their case because their complaint was either treated with disdain or was not properly resolved, became serial petitioners (*shangfang laohu* 上访老虎). These people are seen as causing serious problems for the police as they petition repeatedly to the local police station, petition the local government and higher-level authorities and often gather increasingly large groups to protest.[343]

There has been serious public criticism not only of police abuse of power but also of police failure to deal with complaints. There is high-level recognition that the failure to deal adequately with citizens' complaints about police enforcement practices and abuse itself becomes a cause of social unrest, especially the failure to deal with citizens' complaints made through the letters and visits system. To deal with this problem, police chiefs were directed to receive and deal with citizens' complaints in person. During the period of this concerted action, which took place between 18 May and the end of September 2005, the police reported that they received 71,000 complaints.[344] The Minister of Public Security, Zhou Yongkang, emphasised that such a concerted action had as its objects: improving the relationship between the police and citizens; improving the lawfulness of police enforcement practice; promoting an harmonious society; and eliminating factors that contribute to social instability.[345]

7 CONCLUSION

An examination of the different mechanisms for supervision of police decision-making illustrates both continuation of Party supervision of enforcement and a strengthening of legally defined standards for supervision of police conduct. Internal supervision within the public security system now applies the standards of lawfulness and appropriateness that were originally developed in the context of administrative litigation and review. With recent legislative reforms, in particular the passage of the *APL*, the MPS *Regulations on the Procedures for Handling Administrative Cases by Public Security Organs* and the *SAPL*, the standard of

343 Chen, Xiaobo, 1998: 35.

344 *Nationwide Public Security Organs have Already Opened the Door and Received 71,000 Letters and Visits from the Masses*, People's Net at http://legal.people.com.cn/GB/42735/3461027.html, accessed on 16 August 2006.

345 Zhou Yongkang, 'Collectively Deal with the Letters and Visits Problem, Promote Social Harmony and Stability' in *People's Daily*, 12 July 2005, accessed at http://gov.people/com.cn/GB/46742/3534612.html on 16 August 2006.

lawfulness itself has been expanded to incorporate increasingly comprehensive and detailed procedural requirements and, arguably, standards of justice, openness and proportionality.

These developments, however, do not lead to a conclusion that increasing legalisation has been successful in controlling abuses of administrative detention.[346] There is evidence that administrative detention continues to be an area of enforcement that is chronically abused. The very low rates of litigation and review illustrate the continuing reluctance of citizens to use formal channels to complain against the public security organs. The high rate of withdrawals of administrative litigation cases and the drop in enforcement activities after passage of the *ALL*, whilst not inevitably leading to an adverse result for citizens, illustrate that one of the consequences of strengthening external supervision and imposing individual liability on officials in respect of their conduct has been to avoid, rather than comply with, the law.

My examination of the different forms of supervision over police administrative detention points to an increasingly complex range of institutional and individual interests in exercising supervision power. The first is the central–local relationship. This is illustrated by the efforts of the MPS to strengthen its own scrutiny of local rule and decision-making, both through strengthening its array of internal supervision mechanisms and through the strengthening of administrative review. The difficulty in carrying out administrative review reveals not just a weakness in the legal normative framework for administrative detention and lack of widespread understanding and acceptance of legal standards, but also the structural difficulties in higher-level agencies exercising effective oversight and control over local conduct. Unevenness in implementing both litigation and review illustrates the important role played by local Party and government officials in either promoting or thwarting the successful implementation of supervision. Although the MPS sought to strengthen its own supervision capacity and, at the same time, to limit the capacity of local governments to review administrative detention, its efforts to entrench this restriction in the *ARL* were rebuffed at the last minute by the NPCSC and the committees reviewing the draft *ARL*.

The second set of relationships that is affected by the exercise of supervision power is those which exist between different agencies of

[346] He, 2002: 56–7. In respect of Hangzhou, He asserts that the standard of administrative enforcement has improved since the introduction of these supervision mechanisms.

the state. Agencies such as local people's congresses have collaborated with local Party committees and government to carry out repeated inspections of the conditions in police-run detention centres. Their efforts in the past to supervise police-run detention revealed that their own authority was insufficient to ensure co-operation by the local police. The *Supervision Law* now imposes a legislative obligation on these agencies to co-operate and to act on suggestions and directives issued by the local congresses to correct problems in enforcement. The SPC has also made efforts to improve the capacity of local courts to exercise their powers to scrutinise police decision-making by using its interpretation power to militate against some of the methods employed by local police to subvert and impede the conduct of administrative litigation. These efforts are limited by the vulnerability of local courts to pressure from local government and its agencies and the need to have a collaborative relationship with them. The approach of the people's courts in handling administrative detention cases is also influenced by the requirement to implement the state's social order strategy and facilitate the implementation of hard strikes as one of the political-legal organs of state.

The third relationship that is affected by the potential to initiate supervision of police conduct is that which exists between the citizen and the state. Even though the rate of litigation and review is very low, there are some who do seek to exercise their rights through these channels. In doing so, they continue to disrupt the traditional conception that 'officials do not regret their actions'.[347] The use by citizens of different channels to complain about police abuse of power is having a number of effects. One is to provide an incentive to central public security organs to strengthen mechanisms for supervision and control of police conduct and to seek to improve responses to citizen-initiated complaints. Another is to educate and empower citizens, even if the result is to disillusion them about the effectiveness of the legal system to protect their rights. Yet another is to raise the legal consciousness of police officers.

The tensions and contestations mapped in this chapter are indicative of the emergence of a legal field. There is evidence of a diverse array of agencies and individuals, each with distinct interests, with a stake not only in participating but also in expanding their role in supervision over police decision-making. The expansion of legal standards of supervision

[347] Huang, 1992: 43–5.

from administrative litigation and review to internal supervision conducted within the public security organs suggests the application of legal concepts and vocabulary in areas previously not defined in legal terms and the growing force of law. These developments, however, remain ineffective to deal with the continuing problems of abuse of police power.

CHAPTER NINE

LEGAL REFORM CATCHES UP WITH ADMINISTRATIVE DETENTION

1 INTRODUCTION

The Party policy of ruling according to law has finally begun to have an impact on administrative detention. Despite some minor reforms, the police detention powers examined in this book have become increasingly inconsistent with the standards of the evolving administrative legal regime, both in terms of the legal basis of the powers and of the regulation of their scope and procedure. As I discussed in chapter 8, mechanisms for supervision of police detention have failed to curb abuses. With official acceptance that the law must not only protect administrative efficiency and empower the police but also protect the rights of citizens, the ongoing systemic abuse of these powers by local police is becoming socially and politically unjustifiable. There is a recognition that these powers, if they are to be retained, must be reformed to make them more compatible with the developing legal framework and that there is a need to create a rational structure for the coercive powers of state. Where a decision is made not to reform, or where a power cannot be reformed, the conditions are now conducive for their abolition.

Legal reform of administrative detention powers has begun, usually taking the form of incremental changes to regulation of the power and to the principles for exercise of that power. Occasionally, reform takes a form that is dramatic and thoroughgoing. An example of such radical reform occurred in 2003. Chronic abuse of the power of detention for repatriation and the lack of a legal basis to justify its continuing existence led to calls to abolish the power.[1] These voices were galvanised following publicity over the detention and beating to death of a college graduate, Sun Zhigang, and the presentation of a petition by scholars to the NPC to abolish the power.[2] On 18 June 2003, the Premier, Wen Jiabao, announced that the power to detain would be abolished and replaced with provisions for the shelter and welfare of vagrants.[3] The State Council passed regulations to give effect to this decision.[4]

In this chapter, I argue that law provides both a forum for and a vocabulary within which ongoing contests over reform and restructuring of police powers take place. These contests reveal characteristics of an emerging legal field where the force of law is now sufficient to require administrative detention powers to be reconstituted in legally defined terms. First, I examine the debates surrounding the incorporation in 1996 of detention for investigation into the *CPL*. Next I consider the current issues about the restructuring or abolition of RETL. At present there is a range of possible options for reform and legalisation of this power. The issue of reform of these powers involves sensitive political issues of police power and social control, but as the example of detention for investigation shows, diverging positions could be and were adopted in the legal debate about its future. In addition to reform of individual powers, I consider the broader ongoing debates about how to improve the legal rationality and regularity of administrative detention powers as a group. The main objective of the latter debates has been to find a legal justification for RETL, though the impetus for reform has not been confined to that power.

2 LEGAL REFORM OF ADMINISTRATIVE DETENTION POWERS: THE DEMISE OF DETENTION FOR INVESTIGATION

2.1 The problems with detention for investigation[5]

An example of radical reform of administrative detention powers is detention for investigation. Detention for investigation was described as

[1] Xie, 2000: 101–3, documents systemic abuse of the power; Human Rights in China, 1999; Liu, 2001c; Wang, 2002.
[2] Reported by Eric Eckholm in the *New York Times* on 2 June 2003.
[3] Reported by Daniel Kwan in the *South China Morning Post* on 19 June 2003.
[4] State Council, *Measures on the Administration of Aiding Vagrants and Beggars Having no Means of Livelihood in Cities*, 18 June 2003, effective 1 August 2003.
[5] An earlier version of this discussion about the abolition of detention for investigation can be found in Biddulph, 2005: 217–24.

the 'longstanding difficult problem' (*laodanan wenti* 老大难问题) between construction of a socialist legal system and enforcement practice.[6] In 1987 the MPS described the power as:

> a type of coercive administrative investigation measure used by public security organs in accordance with State Council regulations against those who are suspected of roaming around committing offences, or have committed a criminal act and do not tell their correct name and address and whose background is not clear. It is not a type of criminal punishment, nor is it a public order administrative punishment.[7]

By 1987, local public security organs had been repeatedly criticised by the MPS for a range of serious abuses of the power of detention for investigation.[8] The MPS sought to provide a better definition of the scope of the power and enforcement standards, exhorted local public security organs to curb abuse of the power, and even suggested that, should abuses continue unabated, the power itself might be lost.[9]

In a notice issued in 1987, the MPS not only criticised continuing abusive practices but also sought to limit the public outcry against abuse of detention for investigation by restricting public disclosure or discussion of it. The reasons given were that public and media discussions of the use of detention for investigation in handling criminal investigations had led to 'misunderstandings' and had given a 'bad impression' and because there remained no clear legislative basis for the power.[10]

The continuing problems of serious abuse of this power led to concern at senior political levels,[11] increasing public dissatisfaction with the abuse and greater scrutiny by state organs outside the public security organs themselves. Amongst the numerous notices issued by the MPS demanding lower-level organs curb abuse of the power,[12] the MPS

6 Liu, 1990: 22.

7 MPS, *Notice on the Inappropriateness of Publicly Reporting Detention for Investigation*, 27 January 1987.

8 These notices included: MPS, *Notice on Strengthening the Management Work of Detention Centres and Detention for Investigation Centres*, 23 November 1983; MPS, *Notice on Strictly Controlling the Use of Detention for Investigation Measures*, 31 July 1985; MPS, *Notice on Immediately and Conscientiously Rectifying Detention for Investigation Work*, 31 July 1986.

9 MPS, *Notice on Immediately and Conscientiously Rectifying Detention for Investigation Work*, 31 July 1986: 381–2.

10 MPS, *Notice on the Inappropriateness of Publicly Reporting Detention for Investigation*, 27 January 1987.

11 Wong, 1996: 372.

12 MPS, *Notice on Further Controlling the Use of Detention for Investigation Measures*, 11 June 1991; MPS, *Notice on Urgently Rectifying the Abuse of Detention for Investigation Measures* 15 February 1992; MPS, *Notice on Strengthening the Work of Management of the Three Detention [Centres] and*

indicated that abuses of detention for investigation had been the subject of complaint and investigation by people's congresses at both the local and national levels.[13]

2.2 Finding a legal basis for detention for investigation

At the same time that the MPS was seeking to curb abuse and deal with the growing criticism of police misconduct, it was also trying to address the criticism that there was no clear legal basis for detention for investigation. The clearest legal basis had been provided by the Notice issued by the State Council on 29 February 1980, *On Supporting the Unification of the Two Measures of Forced Labour and Detention for Investigation with RETL*. Although this *Notice* sets out the scope of targets for detention for investigation,[14] it was unsatisfactory as a legal basis in several respects,[15] not the least of which was that the main purpose of the *Notice*, to merge detention for investigation with RETL, was never carried out.[16] This *Notice* did not clarify the relationship between detention for investigation and other police powers to detain and interrogate criminal suspects set out in the *CPL*, nor its relationship to administrative sanctions for minor public order infringements that could be punished under the *SAPR*.[17] The MPS supplemented this document by

putting an end to situations where Detainees get Beaten to Death, 22 April 1993; MPS, *Notice Strictly Prohibiting Public Security Organs from Interfering in Economic Disputes and Illegally Seizing People*, 25 April 1992.

13 MPS, *Notice on Further Controlling the Use of Detention for Investigation Measures*, 1991; Yang, 1991: 42, reporting on an inquiry in 1990 into enforcement practices made by the Internal Affairs and Judicial Work Committee which noted systematic abuse of detention for investigation. MPS, *Notice on Urgently Rectifying the Abuse of Detention for Investigation Measures*, 15 February 1992, referring to an investigation in December 1991 into abuses of detention for investigation carried out by the Office of the Law Committee of the NPC and the NPCSC Legislative Affairs Committee.

14 Article 2 provides:
Those people who have committed minor criminal offences and do not tell their name and address and whose background is not clear, or they have committed a minor criminal offence and are suspected of floating from place to place committing crime, committing multiple crimes or forming a group to commit crime who need to be taken in to investigate their criminal acts, should be sent to a specially formed unit in RETL camps to carry out investigation. In general where the danger would not be great if they were placed in society, can be placed under house arrest, or released on bail etc in accordance with the provisions of the *CPL* whilst carrying out investigation.

15 One argument was that it was beyond the power of the State Council to regulate detention powers, discussed below.

16 The process was commenced but never completed because of commencement of the Hard Strike which started in August 1983 (Gao, 1990: 18–19) and transfer in May 1983 of responsibility for management of RETL camps from the MPS to the MoJ: Luo, 1992: 34; Xia, 2001:22.

17 Passed by the NPCSC on 5 September 1986 and amended 12 May 1994.

providing a more detailed directive setting out targets and procedures for exercising the power in the 1985 *MPS Notice on Strictly Controlling the Use of Detention for Investigation Measures*.

In May 1983, the CCPCC gave a clear instruction that detention for investigation required a legislative basis and that detention for interrogation be subject to strengthened legal supervision.[18] One police officer asserts that the MPS prepared numerous drafts of a *Detention for Investigation Law (Shourong Shencha Fa)*. However, it had been unable to have any proposed draft accepted for inclusion in the NPCSC's legislation plan because of its inability to obtain a consensus view on the major issues.[19] The *ALL* made it more urgent that the power be given a legislative basis in order for the police to be able to justify its use as lawful.[20]

2.3 Debates about reform or abolition of detention for investigation

Despite the Ministry's efforts to stifle public discussion of detention for investigation, debate about proposals for reform of the power began appearing in law and police journals in the late 1980s[21] and early 1990s and became incorporated into broader discussions about reform of the *CPL*.[22] A range of proposals for reform of detention for investigation included either passing *sui generis* legislation by the NPC or administrative regulations by the State Council; incorporating the substance of the power into the revised *CPL*; or merging the power with RETL.[23]

Many legal academics and some representatives of people's congresses,[24] and even one legal academic in the public security system, argued that the power was arbitrary and illegal and should be abolished.[25] The arguments were framed in both legal and practical

18 CCPCC, *Notice Approving and Issuing the Two Documents of the National Public Security Work Conference*, 28 May 1983; Gao, 1990: 20.

19 Gao, 1990: 20; Guo, 1990: 28.

20 Guo, 1990: 28, arguing that the 'only way out' to preserve the existence of the power was for the NPC to pass legislation, to use legal means to regularise its existence. The MPS, *Notice on Several Questions about the Implementation of the 'Administrative Litigation Law' by Public Security Organs*, 30 October 1990, set out the rules that were to constitute the legal basis of the power. Chapter 7 at section 7 discusses determination of the legal bases for detention for education, coercive drug rehabilitation and RETL.

21 Hsia and Zeldin, 1992, list articles published between 1987 and 1991.

22 Zhongguo Faxue Hui Susong Fa Yanjiu Hui, 1992: 142–3; Fan and Xiao, 1991: 146–7; Wang, Jiancheng, 1992: 179; Hecht, 1996: 14–15, suggests that organised academic discussions on revision of the *CPL* commenced in late 1991.

23 Gao, 1990: 20; Fan and Xiao, 1991: 148.

24 Noted in Cui, 1993b: 95.

25 Cui, 1993b: 96–7. Professor Cui is professor in the Chinese People's Public Security University. Wang, Xixin, 1993; Zhang and Li, 1994.

terms. Legal arguments rested on three assertions that the existence of the power was unconstitutional. The first aspect of this argument was that it was contrary to the spirit of Article 37 of the *Constitution*, which guarantees freedom of the person unless arrested.[26] The second was that the State Council was not competent to pass laws authorising detention.[27] The third was that the power to detain administratively undermined the integrity of the system of criminal procedure as it was in practice a substitute for criminal detention, but was outside the *CPL*.[28]

Practical arguments proffered against retention of the power were that it was ineffective in the investigation of crime[29] and that reform would not solve the problem of abuse.[30]

Police, government officials[31] and academics who argued for retention of the power agreed that reform was needed to rectify its inadequate legal and regulatory basis, but that the power was nonetheless very effective[32] and accorded with the 'national spirit'.[33] Views differed amongst academics discussing revisions to the *CPL* as to whether the incorporation of detention for investigation as a criminal coercive measure was desirable.[34]

Central to debates about reform or abolition of detention for investigation was the question of whether the power should be characterised as administrative or criminal in nature.[35] The question was settled by the SPC in its 1991 interpretation of the scope of the *ALL*. The SPC asserted the jurisdiction of the people's courts to receive complaints from citizens alleging unlawful exercise of detention for investigation.[36] The MPS accepted this characterisation and specified the documents

[26] Cui, 1993b: 95; Wang, Xixin, 1993: 111.

[27] Cui, 1993b: 95, citing arguments that the power to pass laws authorising detention was outside the powers of the State Council specified in the *Constitution*, art. 89. Cai, 1991: 56, asserting that only the NPC or the NPCSC has power to pass laws that restrict personal freedom.

[28] Cui, 1993b: 96. [29] Zhang and Li, 1994: 58–9. [30] Cui, 1993b: 96–7.

[31] Cui, 1993b: 94, cites leadership of public security organs and government at different levels as the main proponents of its retention.

[32] Li and Liu, 1992: 183; Gao, 1990: 20–1; Fan and Xiao, 1991: 146; Chen and Zhang, 1992b: 172; Wang, Jiancheng, 1992: 181; Jiang and Zhan, 1994: 95–6.

[33] Chen and Zhang, 1992b: 172.

[34] Fan and Xiao, 1991: 148, argued the power should be incorporated into the revised *CPL*. Song, 1992: 143; Chen and Zhang, 1992b: 173–4, argued it should not.

[35] Mao, 1991: 13; Zhang and Zhang, 1991: 267; Chen and Zhang, 1992a: 87; Chen and Zhang, 1993: 114, arguing that the power is administrative and should not be abolished. Wang, Xixin, 1993: 112, arguing that the power is substantively criminal in nature and should be abolished.

[36] *Opinion of the SPC on Several Questions on the Implementation of the ALL of the PRC (for trial implementation)*, 29 May 1991, art. 2, para. 2 at 659.

constituting the legal basis for judging the lawfulness of any act of detention.[37]

A discussion draft published by the committee drafting amendments to the *CPL* in 1995 provided for abolition of detention for investigation.[38] Acknowledging that abolition of detention for investigation would be inconvenient to the police,[39] the draft amendments provided for lowering the standard of evidence required to approve arrest to 'where there is evidence to support a strong suspicion that a crime has been committed where the criminal suspect could be sentenced to punishment of no less than imprisonment . . .'.[40] The drafting group considered that even though detention for investigation was to be abolished, it was inappropriate to lengthen the time limits for detention which, under the 1979 law, was a total of ten days.[41]

In the meetings attended by interested state organs held after publication of the discussion draft, the MPS negotiated inclusion of substantive elements of detention for investigation into the amended *CPL*.[42] Proposals included decreasing the standard of evidence required for arrest,[43] expanding the scope of targets for detention to include those previously within the scope of detention for investigation[44] extending the time permitted for detention of persons who would previously have fallen within the scope of targets for detention for investigation[45] and not commencing the calculation of the time for detention until their

[37] MPS, *Notice on Several Questions on the Implementation of the Administrative Litigation Law by Public Security Organs*, 30 October 1990, at point 3, discusses the documents comprising the normative legal basis for reviewing legality of imposition of detention for investigation at 668.

[38] Chen and Yan, 1995: 19, 195. [39] Chen and Yan, 1995: 205–6.

[40] Chen and Yan, 1995: art. 98 at 22. The requirement for arrest in art. 40 of the 1979 *CPL* was that 'the principal facts of the crime have been clarified and [the defendant] could be sentenced to a punishment of not less than imprisonment'.

[41] 1979 *CPL*, art. 48. The maximum time for detention was three days with a possible extension of up to four days. The procuratorate was required to approve or reject the application within three days of receipt of the application. *Draft CPL*, art. 96; Chen and Yan, 1995: 203 204.

[42] The MPS document is entitled *Plan for Specific Revision of Provisions of the CPL Relevant to the Public Security Organs (Draft Soliciting Opinions)*, private papers, not published, no date.

[43] Proposed amendment to 1979 *CPL*, art. 40, to enable arrest where 'there is evidence to show a criminal act or suspicion of a crime, where it is necessary to pursue criminal responsibility . . . ': *Plan for Specific Revision of Provisions of the CPL Relevant to the Public Security Organs (Draft Soliciting Opinions)* at 6.

[44] Suggesting amendments to 1979 *CPL*, art. 41 to include those suspected of committing crime, who do not give their true name and address and whose status is unclear, those who have committed a minor crime, who are suspected of going from place to place committing crime and those who have committed a minor crime who are strongly suspected of committing many crimes or committing crimes in a gang. *Plan for Specific Revision of Provisions of the CPL Relevant to the Public Security Organs (Draft Soliciting Opinions)* at 7.

[45] At 8, proposing that art. 48 of the 1979 *CPL* be revised to extend the time limits for applying for arrest to seven days and for a possible extension of between five and ten days, 'where there

identity, address and background was clarified, where there was a serious suspicion that the person had committed a crime, had not given their true name and address or whose background was unclear.[46]

2.4 Incorporation of detention for investigation into the amended *CPL* and ongoing interpretations

Abolition of detention for investigation was proclaimed by Gu Angran, Chairman of the Legislative Affairs Commission of the NPCSC, in his explanatory speech on the draft amended *CPL* to the Fourth National Peoples' Congress Meeting on 12 March 1996. In that speech he said:

> Detention for investigation is a type of administrative coercive measure that has been of positive use for clarifying and investigating crime, especially for investigating those who float from place to place committing crime and whose identity is not clear. But, the time of detention in detention for investigation is comparatively long, moreover because it doesn't involve any other judicial organ and the decision is made by the public security organs alone, it lacks a system for supervision and restriction and does not conform to the relevant requirements of the *CPL*.
>
> In order gradually to strengthen socialist democracy and legal system construction, better to protect the rights and interests of citizens, we have absorbed the contents of detention for investigation needed in practice for the struggle against crime into the *CPL* by supplementing and amending the relevant criminal coercive measures and have not retained the administrative coercive measure of detention for investigation.

In the final version of the *CPL* passed by the NPC, the public security organs had managed to claw back more power than allowed by the discussion draft. The standard for approval of arrest had been further reduced to where 'the principal facts of the crimes have been clarified and [the criminal suspect] could be sentenced to a term of not less than imprisonment'.[47] The scope of targets for detention was expanded to include targets of the former detention for investigation, where 'there is a strong suspicion that the person goes from place to place committing crimes, who repeatedly commits crimes or who gangs up with others to commit crime'.[48] The time limits for requesting arrest of certain

is a serious suspicion that they have gone from place to place committing crimes, committed many crimes or committed crimes in a gang, where the facts are complicated'.

46 Proposing amendment to art. 48 of the 1979 *CPL* in *Plan for Specific Revision of Provisions of the CPL Relevant to the Public Security Organs (Draft Soliciting Opinions)*.

47 *CPL*, art. 60.

48 *CPL*, art. 61(7).

categories of detainees, including some previous targets of detention for investigation,[49] were increased from a maximum of seven days to thirty-seven days.[50]

After passage of the amended *CPL*, a police commentator suggested that, in theory, the broadening of coercive powers in the *CPL* provided the public security organs with sufficient power to perform their criminal investigation functions and to compensate for their loss of detention for investigation.[51] The amendments, this author suggested, required the public security organs to 'change their traditional work style' from an emphasis on obtaining evidence through interrogation of suspects held in detention to a broader range of investigation techniques and competencies.[52] The author noted that the requirements that the police change their work style and improve their technical investigation skills may be difficult to achieve.[53]

The amended *CPL* did not put an end to the ongoing process of construction and reconstruction of related police detention powers. After passing the *CPL*, the MPS issued a notice interpreting police-related provisions of the *CPL* which further expanded the time limits for detention of criminal suspects who were targets of the former power of detention for investigation.[54] In particular, the interpretation asserted that the time limits for detention would not commence until clarification of the name, address and background of the detainee. The *CPL*, Article 128 permits the 'investigation and detention period' (*zhencha jiya qixian* 侦查羁押期限) for those 'who do not tell their true name and address or whose identity is unclear' to commence from the date their identity is clarified. Article 112 of the MPS's interpretation document explained the scope of Article 128 of the *CPL* as follows:

> Criminal suspects who do not tell their true name and address, whose identity is not clear, if within thirty days it has not been possible to clarify these matters and to apply for arrest, after receipt of approval from

[49] *CPL*, art. 69, para. 2: 'Major suspects who are on the run, who repeatedly commit crime, or who gang up with others to commit crime.'

[50] *CPL*, art. 69. This category of person can be held for thirty days before the public security organs are required to apply for arrest. The people's procuratorate is required either to approve or reject the request for arrest within seven days of receipt.

[51] Cui, 1996: 36. [52] Cui, 1996: 36–7.

[53] In relation to the difficulty in implementing reforms to the *CPL*, Hecht, 1996: 77–9; Human Rights in China, 2001a; Fu, 1998: 43–7, in respect of access of an accused person in detention to a lawyer. Tanner, Harold, 1999: 188–9, considers that in the 1980s many enforcement problems were due in part to problems of poor payment and lack of training.

[54] MPS, *Regulations on the Procedures for Handling Criminal Cases*, passed on 20 April 1998, effective 14 May 1998.

> the responsible person in the public security bureau at county level or above, the time period for detention will commence from the date on which the identity of the person is clarified, but it is not permitted to halt the investigation into their criminal actions.

One academic claims that the original intent of Article 128 was to permit the extension of the period of detention after arrest and not prior to arrest, and that in no circumstances could the period of pre-arrest criminal detention be extended past a total of thirty-seven days.[55] The commentator suggests that such an interpretation should be abolished, otherwise 'it would be easy for the previous detention for investigation to remain unchanged'.[56]

3 LAW AS THE FORUM FOR DEBATES ABOUT ADMINISTRATIVE COERCIVE POWERS

The debate surrounding reform of detention for investigation was fuelled by concerns over its serious and endemic abuse and over the inability of the MPS to justify the power in legal terms. It may have been politically expedient to permit removal of a power that had become the focus of so much adverse publicity. However, the processes by which detention for investigation was finally abolished and brought within the scope of the *CPL* illustrates that the outcomes of the reform debate were quite open-ended.

This story demonstrates the importance of legally based arguments in reforming detention powers such as detention for investigation and providing legitimation for them. Framed in legal terms, a range of different positions could be and were adopted. The MPS and some academics within the public security sector were actively engaged in all stages of negotiations, seeking to characterise the power legally to justify preserving it, then reconstituting it within the amended *CPL*. By refusing to include a *Detention for Investigation Law* in the legislative plan, congress representatives ensured that detention for investigation could no longer continue in its original form. Academics took different positions. One group was entrusted with drafting the amended *CPL* and so was able to shape the terms of debate in that respect. Although detention for investigation was abolished, the power of the public security organs to detain and interrogate criminal suspects was not dramatically reduced,

[55] Wang, Jiancheng, 2000: 93–5. [56] Wang, Jiancheng, 2000: 95.

just re-organised, indicating that legal reform may not necessarily limit police power.

This analysis demonstrates that although police administrative detention powers were developed in the politically dominated context of social order policy, their reform and restructuring is now being debated in legal terms. This is illustrated through the ongoing debates about reform of RETL, and, to a lesser extent, detention for education and coercive drug rehabilitation.

4 THE DEBATE ABOUT RETL

Arguments about whether to abolish or reform RETL are longstanding and ongoing. In 1979, the CCPCC decided, after debate, that RETL should be retained.[57] After the *ALL* took effect in 1990 there was again concern expressed amongst the public security organs that the legal basis of RETL was overly vague, facilitated the arbitrary exercise of power and that the then current draft of the RETL law did not address these problems.[58] The question of RETL was discussed again seriously during the drafting of amendments to the *Criminal Law*.[59] The ongoing debates about either reform or abolition of RETL have starting points similar to those about detention for investigation and detention for repatriation discussed above, that is, chronic abuse and an inadequate legal basis.[60]

Lack of a proper legal basis is viewed by the police and others as a serious defect in RETL and in the legal regime governing police powers.[61] Since the early 1980s in particular, there has been common agreement that the regulatory basis of RETL is inadequate, fragmented and internally contradictory.[62] These problems in turn have been identified as facilitating arbitrary uses of the power, placing it in conflict with the developing legal system and increasingly rendering decisions vulnerable to claims of illegality.[63] Critics of RETL also emphasise its irrationality in the system of punishments. A key complaint is that the length of a sentence is more than the criminal punishments of control[64] and

[57] Zhu, 1990: 4–5. [58] Guo, 1990: 28–9.
[59] Song and Song, 2003:244–5; Liu, Wenren, 1998: 23. [60] Gong'an Bu, 1999: 21.
[61] Zhu, Jiang, 1999: 30; Li, 1999: 21; Zhang, Chong, 1990: 40–4.
[62] For example, Ren, 1992: 13; Zhu, Jiang, 1999: 30.
[63] Zhu, Jiang, 1999: 30; Zhang and Xu, 1994: 707.
[64] *Criminal Law*, arts. 38 and 39, enable a person to serve a sentence of between three months and two years out of prison.

criminal detention,[65] whilst the degree of severity of the offence for imposing RETL is, by definition, less than that required for a criminal sanction.[66]

More importantly, the current legal form of the power and the manner of determining to send a person to RETL have been seen as being in substantial conflict with the policy of ruling the country according to law. It has been argued that the power is unconstitutional,[67] offends against the protection of the fundamental right to personal freedom in the *Constitution*[68] and breaches China's international obligations under the *International Covenant on Economic, Social and Cultural Rights*[69] and the *International Covenant on Civil and Political Rights*.[70]

4.1 Proposals for reform of RETL

There is a range of views on how to reform RETL. The divergence of opinions is particularly evident between academics and the political-legal organs,[71] although opinion within the political-legal organs is not unanimous.

Some take the view that RETL is fundamentally inconsistent with the legal system and should be abolished. Within the NPCSC it has been argued that RETL is illegal under the *Legislation Law* and should be abolished.[72] A number of judges assert that the severity of punishment under RETL contradicts legal principles for imposition of punishments and is inconsistent with the system of administrative and criminal punishments. They conclude that RETL is fundamentally at odds with basic requirements of the legal system and should be abolished.[73] Even one commentator from within the police, whilst emphasising the need for legislation, notes the inadequacy of the current regulatory regime to legalise RETL, asserting that the documents designating the legal basis of RETL should be characterised as administrative regulations, as the

[65] *Criminal Law*, art. 42, provides that criminal detention is for a period of between one and six months.
[66] Liu, 2001a; Zhou, Yan, 1999: 22.
[67] See, for example, the collection of views in Vol. 5 (2001) *Faxue*, including Chen, 1996: 20–2.
[68] Li, Yonghong, 1997: 34, arguing that the proper interpretation is that art. 37 prohibits imposition of any measure depriving a person of their liberty that is more severe than arrest.
[69] 993 UNTS 3 (entered into force 3 January 1967).
[70] Song and Song, 2003: 243–5. 999 UNTS 171 (entered into force 23 March 1976). China has signed but not yet ratified this convention.
[71] Gao, Xianduan, 1992: 38, Legal Division of the Guanxi Zhuang Autonomous Region Public Security Department.
[72] Dong, 2002: 3–4.
[73] Zhang, 1996: 41–2, Beijing Municipal High People's Court; Wang, Faqiang, 1997, Zhangjiajie Intermediate People's Court, Hunan.

documents approved by NPCSC were not passed and promulgated by them.[74]

There is also a broad range of proposals that involve the retention and reform of RETL. One is that Article 37 of the *Constitution* guaranteeing freedom of the person from arbitrary deprivation should be interpreted as requiring that a person may only be deprived of their personal liberty for a considerable amount of time by a court judgment.[75] A similar proposal is that the police retain power to impose RETL, but that the decision be automatically reviewed by either a court or the procuratorate. Another suggestion is that administrative coercive measures resulting in deprivation of liberty for an extended period, such as RETL, detention for education and detention of juvenile offenders if they are not abolished, should be brought within the scope of the *Criminal Law*.[76] Others propose that RETL should be treated as a public order punishment, emphasising prevention and education.[77] Another view is that reform of the system of administrative punishments such as RETL should re-emphasise education and reform of people committing minor offences. Supporters of this reform proposal advocate abolishing the criminal sanction of control, substituting it with RETL, and expanding the capacity of social and community organisations to carry out guidance and education in the community in order to restrict the scope of incarceration under RETL.[78] Other police advocate expanding the scope of RETL and the power of the RETL Management Committee.[79]

4.2 Legislation: RETL law

The debate over the RETL reforms and proposals to draft a RETL law have been ongoing since the late 1980s.[80] In an argument reminiscent of the debates around detention for investigation, the view favoured by many in the public security and justice organs is passage of *sui generis* legislation, the *Re-education through Labour Law* (*Laodong Jiaoyang Fa*) to rationalise and consolidate the legal basis of the power.[81] Such legislation would provide a legal justification for the power, even if

74 Zhu, Jiang, 1999: 31; the same view is expressed by Professor Xu Xianming, also an NPC delegate in *Nanfang Dushi Bao*, 8 March 2004.
75 Chen, 2002: 20–1; Zhai, 2002: 32; Peng, Yunfei, 1990: 85–9, rejects this view.
76 Li, Yonghong, 1997: 35. 77 Liu, 2001a.
78 Jiang and Yuan, 1990: 48. 79 Ren, 1992: 15.
80 Su, 1990: 262, in 1990, discussing the 'passage of the PRC Re-education through Labour Law which is currently being speeded up'. Discussions within the MoJ were published as a book of essays in Zhu, 1990; Wang, Zhongfan, 1992: 280.
81 Gong'an Bu, 1999: 21; Jiang and Yuan, 1990: 48; Zhu, Jiang, 1999: 30.

the scope and procedures of public security organs for imposing RETL were constrained as a result.[82] However, efforts to draft such legislation to date have been fraught with difficulty as there has been no consensus on basic issues such as the fundamental purpose and nature of the power,[83] except that RETL is a method for resolving non-antagonistic contradictions.[84]

Before drafting of an RETL law can commence, a number of basic legal issues must be resolved. In these debates, many of the issues that had been resolved for pragmatic purposes have been re-opened. Is the power a criminal or administrative power? Is it a punishment or a coercive measure? Or is it in a category of its own as a 'special administrative measure'?[85] How can RETL be formulated in such a way that it complies with constitutional guarantees of freedom of the person and China's international treaty obligations? Adding to the complexity of these issues has been the accretion of functions to RETL in the 1980s and 1990s, particularly the detention of drug addicts in specialist RETL camps. RETL now serves divergent functions, including punishment of minor offenders; detention of criminal suspects for investigation; detention of dissidents; and detention of those whose conduct is considered dangerous to the wellbeing of society and conducive to crime, such as drug addicts and prostitutes.[86]

On 6 May 1999, the Criminal Law Office of the NPCSC Legislative Affairs Committee convened a meeting to discuss the legal characterisation of RETL.[87] At that meeting four possibilities were raised. RETL could be characterised as an administrative coercive measure; a type of public order administrative punishment; a judicially imposed punishment; or a minor criminal punishment.[88]

One of the preliminary issues that remains unresolved is whether RETL should be characterised as a criminal or administrative power. Despite the present characterisation of RETL as administrative, the continuing debate about whether RETL is in substance a criminal sanction recognises that targets are largely defined with reference to the *Criminal Law*. The relationships between the criminal law and RETL include recognition that many who could be subject to criminal prosecution

[82] See discussion of the *Legislation Law* 2000 in chapter 7.
[83] Ren, 1992: 15.
[84] Ren, 1992: 15; Cui, 1992: 17; Luo, 1992: 36; Gao, Xianduan, 1992: 38. The theory of contradictions is discussed in chapters 3 and 4.
[85] Zhu, Jiang, 1999: 31; Gong'an Bu, 1999: 21, setting out the alternative interpretations.
[86] Discussed in chapter 6. [87] Xia, 2001: 58. [88] Xia, 2001: 58.

are sent instead to RETL[89] and its use in practice as an adjunct to the criminal law, especially at times of hard strikes and specialist struggles.[90]

Others describe the power as administrative in nature but as supplementary to criminal sanctions because of the close relationship between the definition of targets of RETL and criminal targets.[91] A more common characterisation is that the sanctioning system is multilayered and that RETL sits between public order administrative punishments and the *Criminal Law* as a power that fills the gap between the two.[92] The police support this interpretation, arguing that RETL should be retained as a separate power and used as a supplement to the criminal law.[93]

In March 2004, a Chinese newspaper reported that the NPCSC had responded to a proposal put by 127 delegates to the NPC meeting that RETL be reformed by placing drafting of a *Law on the Correction of Misdemeanours* (*Weifa Xingwei Jiaozhi Fa* 违法行为矫治法) on its legislation plan.[94] The report indicates that the Legislative Affairs Commission recommended drafting a law that would cover public order infringements rather than confining the scope of the law to RETL. As the proposed legislation is currently at the stage of research and investigation, Professor Xu Xianming, the NPC delegate interviewed about the law, indicated that it would still be some time before the drafting process was complete.[95] Despite the initial wave of publicity about the drafting of this new law in early 2004, momentum for reform was lost for some years. However, it is inevitable that RETL will be reformed.

5 CREATING A NEW CATEGORY OF PUBLIC ORDER PUNISHMENT: THE SECURITY DEFENCE PUNISHMENT

Some do not limit law reform proposals to RETL but argue that there is a need for more wide-ranging reforms of the system of administrative punishments and public order coercive measures as a whole.[96] One such

[89] Ren, 1992: 14; Zhu, Jiang, 1999: 32; Cui, 1992: 19; Gao, Xianduan, 1992: 39, citing a speech given by Luo Feng, at that time Deputy Head of the Legal Division of the MPS in Zhuhai, in which he said that over 90 per cent of the targets of RETL should be subjected to criminal punishment but for some reason criminal prosecutions could not be pursued. Yang and Liu, 1990: 80–2.

[90] Zhu, Jiang, 1999: 32; Yang and Liu, 1990: 80–2. [91] Cui, 1992: 19.

[92] Zhu, Jiang, 1999: 30; Xia, 2001: 57; Gong'an Bu, 1999: 21.

[93] Gao, Xianduan, 1992: 39; Jiang, Yihuai, 1997.

[94] Literally, the *Unlawful Acts Correction Law*. *Nanfang Dushi Bao*, 8 March 2004.

[95] *Nanfang Dushi Bao*, 8 March 2004. [96] For example, Song and Song, 2003; Liu, 2001a: 5.

proposal has been to reorganise public order coercive powers under the category of the security defence punishment (*bao'an chufen* 保安处分).[97]

Some Chinese scholars have sought to develop a criminological basis for the security defence punishment, drawing from several European traditions.[98] The theory of the security defence punishment has been developed with reference to theories of social defence developed in nineteenth- and early twentieth-century Europe, which emphasised the need to protect society against those types of people who are inherently dangerous and pose a threat to society.[99] Advocates of the security defence punishment argue that Western ideas can be used to serve China's needs in its current stage of development.[100] Some see the concept of security defence as a vehicle for transformation of offenders in the same way as powers such as RETL, detention for education and coercive drug rehabilitation are supposed to be. They have re-employed the slogan 'educate, rescue and reform' as the context and aim of security defence punishments.[101]

Although the category of security defence punishment remains a proposal, many scholars point out that in China there is already a range of powers similar to the security defence punishment in both the criminal and administrative law[102] that are in fact imposed on the grounds of individual dangerousness.[103] Those in the administrative law include the coercive powers of detention for education; coercive drug rehabilitation; detention of juvenile offenders; revocation of household registration; retention for in-camp employment; coercive examination and treatment for STDs; confiscation of illegal items; preventative detention of those who pose a present threat and are mentally unstable

97 Song and Song, 2003; Gao and Chen, 2003. A category labelled administrative criminal is also used, see Li, 2003.

98 Song and Song, 2003: 232–42, discussing Italy, Germany, Austria, Switzerland, Sweden and France.

99 Song and Song, 2003: 232–5, building on theories developed from works of Becaria in the eighteenth century and Lombroso in the nineteenth; Gao and Chen, 2003: 58, also drawing on these theories to propose bases for detention to protect society against the harm from 'natural-born criminals, people who pose a danger to society because of insanity or because of sexually transmitted diseases'.

100 Yu, 1996: 16.

101 Li, Weihong, 1997: 30, replicating the slogans used in respect of powers including RETL and detention for education; Gao and Chen, 2003: 57.

102 Yu, 1996: 11; Zhou, Yan, 1999: 23, pointing out similarities and dissimilarities.

103 Epstein and Wong, 1996: 473, 478; Zhou, Yan, 1999: 24, arguing that Chinese criminology does not include the concept of dangerousness, but that dangerousness is in practice a factor in calculation of the punishment to be imposed and could be included in considerations for imposing RETL.

or incompetent; protective custody; and RETL.[104] Scholars argue that the legal basis for these powers is currently fragmented and inadequate and that it is necessary to pass general legislation both to legalise and rationalise this broad range of coercive measures.[105]

It is not inevitable, though, that reform of police administrative detention powers will take the form of re-categorising these powers as security defence punishments. Some Chinese scholars and police officials assert that the security defence punishment is inappropriate as a model on which to reform police powers, including RETL, as the idea of security defence itself is constrained by its own particular historical origins.[106] Others argue that the reason the system of security defence punishments has not been adopted is that the potential for abuse of power is very high.[107] Many others support the concept of the security defence punishment though they disagree as to how it should be implemented.

Broader questions remain. One question is whether the police should be broadly empowered to act proactively to manage and preserve social order, or whether they are only able to act where dangers to public order presently exist.[108] Another is which organ – the police, procuratorate or courts – should have power to impose a security defence punishment.

One proposal that was debated, but not resolved in drafting the amended *Criminal Law*, was that the *Criminal Law* should include a chapter for security defence punishments.[109] Some continue to advocate this solution.[110] Powers such as RETL would thus be brought within the ambit of the criminal law and lose their status as administrative powers.[111] Others propose separate legislation for security defence

104 Yu, 1996: 11; Hou, 1994: 42–46; Gao and Chen, 2003: 57. 105 Yu, 1996: 16.

106 Xia, 2001: 56, 58, 116–31; Han, 2000: 106, adding to these objections that judicial approval of security defence punishments would create too broad a discretion in the courts.

107 Zhai, 2002: 28; Song and Song, 2003: 245, arguing abuse is likely if administrative coercive powers are reorganised under a unified criminal system of security defence punishments.

108 This debate as it relates to the German police from before 1933, the use of the police by the Nazi regime and reforms after 1945, in particular the powers of the administrative police to act pre-emptively, is discussed in Thomaneck, 1985; Harlan, 1997.

109 Gao and Zhao, 1999: 571, setting out the different views expressed at that time: that RETL should be incorporated into the *Criminal Law* as a form of security defence punishment; that it be added as one of the forms of criminal punishment; and others who argued it was not appropriate for RETL to be included in any way in the *Criminal Law*.

110 Xu, 2001: 134, advocating that security defence punishments be included as a separate chapter in the *Criminal Law*.

111 Song and Song, 2003: 244–5, discussing this view; Yu, 1996: 15, advocating this view; Zhou, Yan, 1999: 25, arguing that RETL should be brought within the scope of the *Criminal Law*.

punishments to act as a form of 'special deterrent' to supplement the criminal law.[112] Security defence punishments under this proposed regime would be imposed by a court in addition to, or as a substitute for, a criminal sanction.[113] Others consider that the security defence punishment should be retained as a separate category that is an adjunct to and substitute for a criminal sanction.[114]

6 ONGOING ADMINISTRATIVE LEGISLATIVE REFORM

In parallel with discussions about reform of the state's sanctioning system, ongoing reforms to the system of administrative law are having increasingly significant impacts on administrative detention. After passage of the *ALL* and *APL*, in addition to the now-successful efforts to obtain support for passing a comprehensive *APL*,[115] scholars and members of the NPC have also successfully advocated passing an *Administrative Coercion Law* that would, *inter alia*, set basic legal standards for all administrative coercive powers.[116] In support of these claims, scholars point to the proliferation of administrative coercive measures and their fragmented legal basis, reporting that since 1950 there have been 10,369 laws, administrative regulations and rules specifying 263 different types of coercive measures. Coercive measures are predominately specified by rules, with very few regulated by law.[117]

Scholars have attributed the expanding number and scope of administrative coercive measures to hard strike enforcement policies.[118] They argue that there is now a need for administrative coercive measures to be legally defined.[119] Since the *APL*, they report that administrative agencies have been using coercive measures instead of punishments to avoid the legal constraints imposed on the use of administrative

[112] Yu, 1996: 11, 14; Bao, 1997.
[113] Gao, Xianduan, 1992: 39, the so-called narrow definition. The broad definition is imposition of coercive measures to prevent crime outside the scope of the criminal law.
[114] Gao and Chen, 2003: 57; Fang, 2002: 16, advocating that the security defence system continue to be included in part in the criminal law and in part as administrative sanctions to enhance the convenience of administrative enforcement.
[115] Discussed in chapter 7.
[116] Fu, 2001: 270; Hu, 2002: 34, reporting in 2002 that a draft of the law had been submitted to the NPCSC for examination, dealing with administrative coercive measures and coercive enforcement.
[117] Hu and Jin, 2000: 32, noting that of the legal instruments specifying coercive measures, 3 per cent are laws, 15 per cent are administrative regulations and 82 per cent are ministerial rules. (They include RETL within the category of administrative coercive measures.)
[118] Li, Yonghong, 1997: 34. [119] Li, Yonghong, 1997: 34.

punishments,[120] making legal definition of the boundary between punishments and coercive measures more urgent.[121]

The proposed law defines coercive powers to include administrative coercive measures and coercive enforcement.[122] Passage of this law will complement the *APL* and will ensure that all administrative powers exercised by the public security organs are subject to the same requirements in respect of their legislative basis, procedures for imposing a coercive measure and supervision. Commentary suggests that the power to impose an administrative coercive measure will remain with the administrative agency. The most recent draft of this law requires that a coercive measure for deprivation of personal liberty be established by legislation passed by the NPC or the NPCSC. It provides a more detailed description than the *Legislation Law* or the *APL* of what matters must be specified by the legislation. Article 10(2) provides:

> Where an administrative coercive measure has already been established by law, administrative regulations and local regulations may only regulate specific implementing procedures, and must not amend or supplement the regulation of the targets, scope, conditions, methods, etc., specified in the law.

This draft provision appears to be taking a restrictive view of the proper scope of interpretation by lower-level administrative regulations and rules. Such a provision would clearly restrict the capacity of the MPS, for example, to amend the scope of targets for RETL and the procedures for determining to send a person to RETL in the ways it has done in 2002 and 2004.

Other proposals for reform are to diffuse the current concentration of power in the hands of the police, both to impose detention and administer the detention centres. One proposal for reform is to remove management of detention for education from the control of the public security organs. One procurator argues that the failure to separate the power of the public security organs, both to decide to send a prostitute to detention for education and to manage the detention centres, has led to abuse and restricted the capacity of the procuratorate to exercise its supervision powers.[123] One senior academic advocates that the courts should be the organ primarily responsible for determinations to impose detention, by introducing the principle of 'application to a court for the

[120] Fu, 2001: 270. [121] Hu and Jin, 2000: 34.
[122] Hu, 2002: 36–8. *Draft Administrative Coercion Law*, art. 2. [123] Li, Yonghong, 1997: 35.

use of a coercive measure as the norm with administrative imposition of coercive measures the exception'.[124] This model would take the form of an application and examination and approval by the court. These debates are ongoing and, as yet, unresolved.

7 CONCLUSION

The debates surrounding RETL have a sense of *déjà vu* about them as they bear a strong similarity to the debates in the 1990s about reform and abolition of detention for investigation. These debates reflect the increasingly contested nature of police administrative detention powers. They also illustrate an emerging consensus amongst all contestants that these powers must now be redefined and reorganised in ways that are consistent, or at least not overtly in conflict with, the structure and principles of the legal system.

Legalisation and regularisation of administrative detention is progressing on several fronts. The ongoing process of building a comprehensive administrative law infrastructure is increasingly resulting in the imposition of procedural constraints upon the use of administrative detention by the police. A current focus is the reorganisation of individual powers such as RETL and of administrative coercive measures as a group.

Proposals to consolidate police coercive powers under the concept of security defence punishments may both legalise and rationalise these powers to an extent. However, as the outcomes of reorganisation of detention for investigation illustrate, legalisation and rationalisation do not necessarily result in limitation of police coercive powers. If implemented, a proposal to reorganise administrative coercive powers within a category of security defence punishment may preserve the broad scope of police power and its discretionary nature. In a climate where a principal complaint about police abuse of power at the local level is that the police respond to instructions to implement hard strikes by expanding the scope of targets beyond their already vaguely defined boundaries, the dangers of basing powers to detain on the grounds of social dangerousness must be self-evident.

124 Ma, 2000: 23.

PART FOUR

ANALYSIS AND CONCLUSION

CONCLUSION: THE FIELD OF LAW, THE FORCE OF LAW AND THE POWERS THAT BE

1 INTRODUCTION

I return now to consider the questions posed in chapter 1 of this book. My hypothesis is that legal reform is having an impact on administrative detention powers, but that the outcomes of the reform process are not predetermined as the processes of legal change are themselves dynamic and contested.

This book has addressed the ways in which processes of legal reform have impacted on administrative detention powers. I posed three questions, two of which address substantive issues. First, what are the continuities and discontinuities between administrative detention in the reform and the pre-reform era? Secondly, to what extent is it possible to trace legalisation and regularisation of these powers? Thirdly, how does the use of the legal field as an analytical construct illuminate our understanding of the process of legal change as it relates to police administrative detention powers?

2 WHAT ARE THE CONTINUITIES AND DISCONTINUITIES BETWEEN ADMINISTRATIVE DETENTION IN THE REFORM AND PRE-REFORM ERA?

Chapters 2 and 3 reviewed analyses of administrative detention in the pre-reform era which characterised the powers as part of the class-based, mass-line strategies that were representative of informal or populist modes of justice. This characterisation contrasts with formal modes of justice that emphasise procedural justice[1] through reliance on codified laws and the concentration of legal authority in the 'hands of trained specialists'.[2] The continuing use of these forms of police-administered

[1] Baum, 1986: 79–84. [2] Brady, 1981: 16.

detention, coupled with analyses suggesting that the modernisation and professionalisation of the police force in the reform era has been only partial, frames the question of the extent to which administrative detention bears hallmarks of the pre-reform era.

An examination in chapter 3 of the development and use of detention for education, coercive drug rehabilitation and RETL from the early 1950s and the development of these powers during the reform era discussed in chapters 5 and 6 reveal continuities and discontinuities with the pre-reform antecedents of these powers. What appears to be a continuation of pre-reform strategies of social control, on closer examination, is revealed to be quite distinct in a number of respects.

2.1 Administrative detention viewed in the context of social order policy: repetition with a difference

Official propaganda has extolled the effectiveness of efforts in the 1950s to eliminate prostitution and drug use and to create social stability and order. In chapter 3, my examination of the strategies used to achieve these objectives indicates that these successes depended upon the use of administrative detention powers as part of a broader social order strategy that was both comprehensive and ideologically driven. Elimination of prostitution was achieved through a mixture of registration and surveillance, detention and education of prostitutes, arranged marriages or relocation of those released to other parts of the country, and through the creation of local communities where everyone was known. Elimination of drug addiction, in addition, relied on massive mobilisation of the population during the Three Anti and Five Anti campaigns. RETL began as part of a political campaign and was used initially as a means of dealing with those adjudged politically unreliable. These pre-reform strategies for social control were grounded in class-based distinctions between antagonistic and non-antagonistic contradictions, discussed in chapters 3 and 4.

As we have seen in chapter 4, confronted with problems of increasing crime and social disorder at the beginning of the reform era, the Party sought to reinstate a comprehensive social order strategy which included powers of administrative detention. However, these powers were reinstated in a changed political and social environment. My consideration of the implementation of the CMPO in the reform era illustrates that the ideal of the 1950s could not be reconstituted. Community-based prevention strategies were weakened and have been reconstructed in ways that no longer depend on ideological mobilisation. The police increasingly rely on more professional policing techniques such as patrols, emergency telephone numbers, registration of the 'focal population' to identify and monitor targeted groups and on hard strikes to target problems of social order and crime.

My examination in chapter 4 of the use of the 'Hard Strike' in the reform era traces how its form was modelled on the campaigns used in the pre-reform period, but emphasises that its purpose and ideological significance today have changed. In direct contrast to the pre-reform era, when the campaign was an anti-bureaucratic device used to attack class enemies and whose purpose was to transform society, in the reform era the 'Hard Strike' has become a feature of crime control strategies designed to strengthen state control, to protect economic reform and to attack those whose conduct threatens to disrupt order. As Dutton concludes, in the reform era, the 'Hard Strike' against crime is no longer grounded in notions of class struggle or the transformation of the offender but is a pragmatic, repressive tool to combat crime and frighten the people into behaving lawfully.[3]

The continuing use of the distinction between antagonistic and non-antagonistic contradictions in social order strategies illustrates the enduring influence of this conceptual distinction. However, even the notion of contradiction has been remade in the reform era. In 1983, Deng Xiaoping shifted the focus of the state's powers of dictatorship from class enemies to a new category of person whose criminal conduct was seen as undermining the economic reform programme and public order, but most of whom came from the working classes. In doing this, he confirmed the dissociation between pre-reform notions of class and antagonistic contradictions.

From an analysis in chapter 4 of the series of hard strikes waged against differing activities since 1983 and the proliferation of specialist struggles that rely on hard strike strategies, it could be concluded that the scope of antagonistic contradictions is now defined on an ongoing basis by the targets of the strike. Targeting under the hard strike and labelling the struggle against those targeted as an antagonistic contradiction can now be seen as a conceptual device to justify the use of extreme force.

In theory, administrative detention forms part of the second line of defence in the state's crime prevention strategy. It is a strategy for

[3] Dutton, 1995a: 436–8; Tanner, 2000: 94–5, reinforces this reasoning with his argument that the '1983 Hard Strike' was designed to restore the 'balance of awe'. See the discussion on this point in chapter 4.

dealing with non-antagonistic contradictions which should be dealt with by techniques of education, persuasion and other forms of regulation. However, we have seen in chapter 4 that where a contradiction becomes confrontational, the characterisation of the dispute as non-antagonistic is no barrier to the use of force. The interchangeable use of detention and a fine in respect of prostitution and drug use discussed in chapter 5 reveals that administrative detention is in fact viewed by the police as one of the array of punishments they may impose. This contradicts the official rhetoric that administrative detention is imposed as a coercive measure to rescue and transform transgressors, rather than to punish them.

A common thread in my analysis of each of these administrative detention powers in the reform era has been the extent to which their expanding scope and increasing use has been intertwined with the continuing heavy reliance on hard strikes as a strategy to attack crime and to deal with broader problems of social order. As the forms of hard strike expanded to cover socially harmful conduct such as prostitution, drug use and gambling, administrative detention has become used increasingly as an adjunct to criminal punishment, thus blurring the distinction between antagonistic and non-antagonistic contradictions. Another illustration of this blurring can be seen in the redefinition of the targets of RETL with reference to the *Criminal Law* by the 2002 *RETL Regulations* discussed in chapter 6, and the ongoing discussions about subsuming RETL and other administrative detention powers within a category of minor criminal offences, discussed in chapter 9 at sections 4–5.

This analysis leads to the conclusion that, whilst pre-reform social order strategies for social order inspired the social order strategy of the reform era, they differ significantly. Familiar categories and practices such as the CMPO, antagonistic and non-antagonistic contradictions and campaign-style policing in the form of 'Hard Strikes' continue to exist. However, as this discussion shows, aspects of these concepts have been disaggregated from their ideological roots and redeployed in the reform era to meet a changed political agenda and a changing social order situation.

2.2 Administrative detention and continuities in the institutional mechanisms for policy and rule formation

My examination of the institutional processes for the production of social order policy and development of the powers to implement that policy reveals the enduring nature of the political-legal organisational system in the reform era.

One of the most marked continuities is that administrative detention continues to be a flexible tool in the hands of the police to address current social order problems. These powers continue to be chronically abused. Chapter 5 considers how, in the cases of detention for education and coercive drug rehabilitation, power is concentrated in the hands of the police to impose detention, to manage the detention centres and to interpret the law defining these detention powers. In chapter 6 we see how, in respect of RETL, the police have the same powers, but since 1983 are no longer responsible for the management of RETL camps.

2.3 Significance of repetition with a difference for the possibilities for legal change

The continuities between pre-reform conceptual frameworks, strategies and institutional structures for policy formation, noted above, indicate that the possibilities for change in the reform era are structured and constrained. Within these apparent continuities I have also noted areas of significant difference between the strategies for social order and crime control in the pre-reform and reform eras. How do these continuities and differences influence the possibilities for legal reform of administrative detention powers?

In chapter 4, I conclude that the pragmatic orientation to social order policy now leaves open the possibility for diverging views about what strategies will be the most effective to achieve social order and political stability. I document a growing number of voices criticising the continuing reliance on the hard strike as a law and order strategy. Their criticisms are pragmatic: it has not been effective; it does not accurately address the causes of crime; the hard strike is not the best strategy to deal with contemporary problems of crime; and it is an irrational allocation of policing resources.

Even those who argue in support of the continuing use of the hard strike strategy are at pains to justify it on the grounds that it is an effective means of reducing crime. Recent supporters of the hard strike strategy assert that the 'hard strike is conducted according to law'. By characterising the hard strike as an enforcement policy, the hard strike is, in theory, transformed into a decision about the allocation of law enforcement resources, rather than a device that is conceptually antithetical to the requirements of rule according to law and to legal norms such as equality before the law. The desire to legalise the CMPO, 'Hard

Strikes' and administrative detention thus makes sense when they are understood as pragmatic strategies for crime control and punishment. This desire also indicates that legalisation of what might be considered to be policy, and so an inappropriate subject of legislation, is seen as a tool for legitimation and entrenchment of these policies.

In the reform era, the policy of ruling the country according to law and the reorientation of social order policy toward the more pragmatic objectives of achieving social order and stability have created an environment more conducive to a pluralisation of views about what strategies are the most effective and appropriate. We have seen this debate in relation to social order policy and specific parts of it, including the use of administrative detention powers. This, in turn, has enabled the development of a space within which differing positions may be adopted about whether and, if so, how powers exercised in pursuit of social order are to be legally defined and justified.[4]

3 TO WHAT EXTENT DOES LAW STRUCTURE POLICE POWERS RELATING TO ADMINISTRATIVE DETENTION?

The questions of legalisation and regularisation of administrative detention powers set out in chapter 1 is a two-pronged inquiry. First, it looks at the extent to which administrative detention powers themselves have been defined in legal as opposed to political and administrative terms. Secondly, it considers the broader environment in which police law-making and interpretation powers are defined and in which legal systems for the supervision of enforcement practice are established and implemented.

3.1 Legalisation of administrative detention powers

Administrative detention powers remain poorly defined by law. In chapters 5 and 6, I examine the documentary basis of the three administrative detention powers in this book and the political and social environments in which they have been reinvigorated in the reform era. This analysis reveals that the development and definition of each of these powers has been integrally connected to the process of formulating and implementing social order policy, and to 'Hard Strikes' in particular.

[4] See chapter 4 at section 10 and the discussion in chapter 7 at section 5 about differing views of what principles should be reflected in 'administration according to law'.

My discussion of detention for education in chapter 5 provides an example of this process. This form of detention was reintroduced in Shanghai and Wuhan in 1984. The successes in Shanghai were noted by central-level agencies in 1985 and other localities were encouraged to formulate plans for the construction of like detention centres. It was only in 1987 that the General Office of the CCPCC and the General Office of the State Council issued instructions to expand the construction of these detention centres nationwide as part of overall instructions to take concerted action to eliminate prostitution.

Legislation which provided a legal basis for detention for education was passed by the NPCSC in 1991 after a meeting attended by a wide range of state and Party agencies expressed concern that the power was not underpinned by legislation. The meeting resolved that the MPS, in consultation with the Legal Bureau of the State Council, should draft legislation. This example illustrates how the development of these powers has been an integral part of the established administrative and political processes through which social order policy and strategies are developed and implemented. Legislation in this case was a way of preventing embarrassment and providing legal grounds to justify the existence of the power.

This is an example of the continuing instrumental uses of law: to empower the police and to preserve their discretion to use administrative detention as a flexible and ultimately abusive tool.[5] This example also illustrates the continuing interrelationship between Party and state administrative organs within the political-legal framework in policy formation and in the development of the specific powers required to implement policy in the area of social order. My analysis of the development of these powers in the reform era also shows the process of policy formation and implementation, and the development of these powers involves ongoing interactions between local and central organs of Party and state. It does not indicate that the development of this power was initiated and directed in a top-down manner by central Party organs.

Whilst this example illustrates the instrumental uses of law as a tool of empowerment, there is also evidence discussed in chapters 6 and 7 to conclude that, in the absence of detailed legislation, administrative agencies are now issuing regulations to regularise the scope and

[5] Epstein, 1994: 22, describing instrumental uses of law as being law as an instrument of political power, where power may be exercised according to legal rules but is not legitimated by them.

enforcement of administrative detention powers. Chapter 6 demonstrates that in respect of RETL, the documents passed or approved by the NPCSC have long since ceased accurately to describe the targets for detention, or the procedures for making a determination to send a person to RETL. During the reform period, the gradual accretion of targets for detention has been achieved primarily by way of administrative rules, both by central agencies and local congresses and governments.

Recently, the MPS has sought to consolidate the categories of people who are targets for RETL and to provide better definitions of the procedures for making a determination to send a person to RETL. The conclusion that the MPS itself is seeking to regularise the powers exercised by the police is supported by the introduction by the MPS of rules governing the management and grading of detention for education and coercive drug rehabilitation centres, discussed in chapter 5; introduction of a *sui generis* hearing procedure in some cases prior to imposition of RETL, discussed in chapter 6; and the strengthening of internal supervision over local enforcement practice, discussed in chapter 8.

3.2 Legalisation of the environment in which administrative detention powers are defined, enforced and supervised

Although administrative detention powers themselves remain poorly defined by law, my examination in chapters 7 and 8 of the developments in the area of administrative law reveals that this lack of legal definition is increasingly at odds with the more general legal principles now being established. In chapter 9 I illustrate this tension in the debates now being conducted about reform and possible abolition of RETL. As I conclude in section 2 above, social order policy and the powers exercised under its rubric, such as administrative detention, are no longer insulated from the policy imperative to implement 'administration according to law'.

Reforms in constitutional and administrative law have sought to impose constraints upon the rule-making powers of the police in respect of their administrative detention powers,[6] to impose procedural requirements on administrative punishments that are now being applied to some administrative coercive measures, such as RETL,[7] and

6 See discussion of the *APL*, *Legislation Law* and documents implementing the *Legislation Law* in chapter 7 at section 6.

7 Chapter 6 in respect of RETL and chapter 7 at section 8 in respect of introduction of laws regulating procedures for exercising administrative powers.

to strengthen a range of mechanisms for supervision of the exercise of police powers.[8]

Elevation of the status of the policy of administration according to law by the Party has provided a strong impetus to encourage the MPS and other state agencies to create legal bases for police power and to regularise that power in legal terms. This process has seen an expansion of legally defined concepts, such as the concept of lawfulness, from its initial use as the criteria for supervision of administrative decision-making by the courts, to use as the criteria for imposition of internal disciplinary sanctions on police officers, discussed in chapter 8. This book reveals concern at all levels at the endemic abuse of power by the police. Emphasis on the need to strengthen supervision over police decision-making illustrates a recognition that the preservation of social order extends beyond enforcement of law and order to controlling abuse of power and corruption by local police.

Despite the substantial changes that have been made to the regulation of administrative powers generally, their impact on administrative detention has been limited by the degree of generality with which the administrative detention powers themselves are defined.

How do we evaluate these substantive changes in the law, in particular the unevenness of these developments? Viewed in a rule of law framework, it would be difficult to conclude that the regulatory regime governing administrative detention could be characterised as progressing toward the rule of law. Despite developments in administrative law generally that seek to make police powers subject to legal norms, the rules governing administrative detention could not be considered at present to impose any meaningful constraints on the exercise of these powers. This is a minimum requirement for the rule of law. The close interconnection between regulation of administrative detention powers and social order policy and the central role played by the Party in both formation and implementation of social order policy and in promoting the legalisation of police powers makes it difficult to conclude that law-making in this area is gaining autonomy from Party control. Nor has the legal regime that is being built to regulate and control the exercise of state power yet been effective to control chronic abuse by the police of their administrative detention powers.

An examination of the extent of legalisation of police administrative detention powers reveals a complex and seemingly inconsistent

[8] Discussed in chapter 8.

picture. In an overall environment where state power is increasingly legally defined, the form of administrative detention powers appears to remain heavily determined by social order policy and the political-legal environment in which that policy is formulated and implemented. Yet indications are that the demand to legalise state powers has now reached the policing of social order and the process of creating a legal basis for police administrative detention powers is under serious contemplation. Finally, there appears to be a real possibility for legally inspired change to administrative detention powers, with a radical restructuring of detention for investigation, abolition of detention for repatriation and ongoing discussions about how to reform RETL and possibly all police administrative detention powers, as discussed in chapter 9.

How do we interpret this picture? In the section below, I consider the ways in which the legal field might provide a framework within which to understand these seemingly contradictory processes of change, highlighted in the examination of the substantive legal changes relating to administrative detention above.

4 HOW DOES THE USE OF THE LEGAL FIELD AS AN ANALYTICAL CONSTRUCT ILLUMINATE OUR UNDERSTANDING OF THE PROCESSES OF LEGAL CHANGE OF POLICE ADMINISTRATIVE DETENTION POWERS?

My consideration of the substantive changes to administrative detention, both in the context of social order between the pre-reform and reform eras and in the context of legal reform in the reform era, reveals a process which is both complex and disparate. My discussion in section 2 above illustrates the extent to which social order policy and administrative detention have been modelled upon pre-reform institutions but are not the same as them. I noted how, in the reform era, these changes leave space for discussions and different positions to be adopted about the manner and extent to which these powers should be defined and justified in legal terms. In section 3, I trace the expansion of legal concepts to cover administrative detention and how these developments increasingly highlight the inadequacy of the legalisation of administrative detention powers themselves. I also note that whilst law still lacks a high degree of autonomy from the Party and political-legal institutions, the central Party elites do not exercise single control. The expansion and increasing importance of law and legal concepts to define and justify police powers and the existence of actors who, within existing policy constraints, are able to adopt differing positions in relation to the process and content of legalisation, point to the emergence of a Party-state sanctioned legal field.

4.1 The emergence of a legal field

As discussed in chapter 2, Bourdieu's conception of the legal field is of a semi-autonomous space within which competitions between actors to determine the law are historically and politically structured, but where the outcomes of these competitions are not pre-ordained. The field is conceived as operating consonant with and legitimating the state's vision of order.[9] Bourdieu's conception of the field as a semi-autonomous space reaches its limits when law is used as an instrument to serve the interests of one dominant party. The legal field, whilst functioning in a close relationship with, and reflecting the power controlled by, the state gains autonomy as it becomes organised around its own internal protocols and acquires its own institutions, actors, practices and values.

It is only as the programme of legal reform progresses that it has been possible to posit the emergence of a legal field with its own actors and distinctive vocabulary and logic. Its autonomy remains low, but has the potential to increase.

My examination in chapter 4 of the development of social order policy and the powers necessary to implement it in the reform era shows that the Party seeks to retain its leadership of political-legal organs of the state, especially the police, and policy implementation, in particular, in directing hard strikes. Chapter 7 shows that leadership of the Party is the political boundary of police reform. Within this boundary, the Party has invested its authority in the policy of 'ruling the country according to law' and 'administration according to law'. The Party's determination that governance must be legally based has provided the impetus for establishment of a more comprehensive system of state law. Party leadership over political-legal organs has provided impetus for implementation of this policy. Party leadership has facilitated the legalisation of police structure and powers, whilst at the same time the Party continues to exercise direct leadership over enforcement practice when it determines to implement a 'Hard Strike'.

[9] Chapter 2 at section 2.3.

My examination of the process of legalisation and regularisation of police powers in chapters 7 and 8, and the debates over reform of administrative detention in chapter 9, indicate that the objectives and means by which 'administration according to law' is to be given form is sufficiently open-textured to enable a range of different positions to be adopted. The idea of pluralisation from within, discussed in chapter 2, contemplates the accommodation of an increasingly complex and diverse range of interests and positions within the expanding confines of acceptable debate.

4.2 The boundaries of the field

In Bourdieu's terms, the expansion of legal norms, or legalisation of police powers, can be understood as a process of appropriation to the legal field. As I have discussed in section 3 above, legalisation of administrative detention powers has not taken place at the same rate as the development of more general administrative law norms. However, the establishment of an increasingly comprehensive set of administrative law norms has required the gradual appropriation of administrative detention powers to the legal from the political realm. This process began with passage of the *ALL*, discussed in chapter 7, which required that the police justify their powers and the exercise of those powers in terms of their lawfulness. The MPS was required to respond by designating the documents that constituted the 'legal bases' of the powers. The *ALL* required that administrative detention be located within the legal categories it had created, such as specific administrative act, administrative punishment, administrative coercive measure, discretion and abuse of power.

Passage of the *APL* continued this process by introducing into the law relating to administrative punishments the concepts of proportionality, openness and fairness in decision-making. Initially, the MPS, with the concurrence of the State Council and the NPCSC, was able to define these powers as outside the purview of the *APL*. However, in 2002 the MPS itself passed rules to regularise the procedures for imposition of RETL with reference to the *APL* and, in 2004, applied these principles to the exercise of its administrative decision-making in general, illustrating the growing symbolic and practical importance of being able to demonstrate conformity with broader norms of procedural fairness set out in the *APL*.

In chapter 8 I have documented the expansion of the concept of 'lawfulness' as the criterion for supervising police conduct, not only for external forms of review such as litigation and review, but also for internal supervision conducted within the public security system and as the basis for imposition of internal disciplinary sanctions.

The inadequacy of the existing regulatory basis of these powers to legitimate them in legal terms was finally highlighted with passage of the *Legislation Law* discussed in chapter 7. Even though it is arguable that the *Prostitute Decision* and the *Drugs Decision* conform to the formal requirements of the *Legislation Law* that detention powers be based on law, my analysis of these laws reveals that they are purely devices to empower the police. As my discussion in chapter 9 of recent debates about reform of RETL illustrates, the comparative failure to provide a comprehensive legal basis for administrative detention powers that is consistent with the growing body of administrative law calls into question whether these laws remain adequate to make these powers lawful.

4.3 Actors: the growing competition over the establishment of legal norms

Within the emerging legal field it has become possible to discern different roles and positions amongst potential legal actors. Debates over legal norms have taken place in respect of specific laws as well as at the level of jurisprudence.

At the level of jurisprudence, chapter 7 discusses how contests have been concerned with the question of what principles are encompassed within the term 'administration according to law'. These debates address issues concerning the appropriate balance between the use of law to empower state agencies, to place limits on the scope and manner of the exercise of those powers and to protect citizens against infringement of those powers, a question addressed in chapter 8. This question is fundamental to the definition of the field itself and the establishment of the principles to underpin specific legislation. Academics have played an important role in this area, especially in their advocacy of enhanced procedural rules, and introduction of principles of openness in government, transparency and fairness in decision-making.

Academics and congress officials in particular have used the opportunity presented by the policy of 'ruling according to law' to obtain support for a raft of legislation designed to create a more comprehensive legislative regime for the regulation of state power. There is evidence that the formation of alliances has proved decisive in obtaining support for some controversial legislative changes. An example was when academics obtained senior Party support to pass the *ALL* over the opposition of administrative agencies. Their success in setting out the fundamental legal norms for the definition and exercise of administrative power as a whole has required the MPS to respond within these terms.

It is indicative of the increasing significance of law that the MPS itself has been actively engaged in the legal regulatory process, both in influencing the developing administrative legal system and in strengthening its capacity to determine the law relating to police powers in a range of ways. One way the MPS has engaged in the legal process is in its interventions in the drafting of important legislation. This includes the *CPL* in respect of its powers to detain and interrogate criminal suspects, discussed in chapter 9; the *Legislation Law* in seeking to preserve its power to pass rules, to legislate for administrative coercive measures and to remove this power from local congresses and governments, discussed in chapter 7; and the *ARL* in seeking to restrict the channels for review in respect of administrative coercive powers to public security review organs, discussed in chapter 8. Although the MPS draws on the dominance it previously enjoyed under the politically structured political-legal organisation of the police, procuratorate and courts (*gongjianfa*), it has not been able consistently to dominate, especially in respect of legislative drafting, as the outcome of these contests demonstrates.

Chapter 8 demonstrates how the MPS has also sought to strengthen its supervision of local police by strengthening its internal supervision mechanisms and expanding the standard of lawfulness of their conduct as the criteria for imposition of internal disciplinary sanctions on police officers, though other agencies, such as local congresses, have actively sought to expand their own competency to supervise the management of administrative detention centres. There is evidence to suggest that the police have also used law to seek to resist demands to perform non-police work.

The debates about abolition of detention for investigation and the ongoing debates about reform of RETL discussed in chapter 9 are indicative of the different positions and interests represented: academics, judges, procurators, congresses, justice departments and public security organs. These positions in turn are reflective of the emergence of a semi-autonomous legal field.

4.4 The growing force of law

Law is becoming an increasingly important means of legitimating police powers, of assisting in institution-building and of enhancing the status of the players. This is illustrated in the general acknowledgement that detention for education required a legal basis and the consensus reached between agencies allocating responsibility to the MPS to draft the legislation. An illustration of the consequences of failure to obtain approval for passage of legislation to provide a legal basis for detention for investigation is the abolition of the power. As I suggest above, the non-conformity of administrative detention powers such as RETL with the increasingly comprehensive legal structures and vocabulary has become an important element in the debate surrounding their abolition.

4.5 Limits to the force of law: the problem of law enforcement

The force of law, however, should not be overstated. Some commentators suggest that the process of economic reform is leading inevitably to the political decline of the Party.[10] While this may be true in general, it has become clear in this study that reforms to legalise and rationalise police administrative detention powers remain constrained by Party leadership[11] and continue to be instituted within the context of the existing political-legal apparatus. The pluralisation of positions is taking place within these constraints.

Another important limit to the force of law is the extent to which law enforcers have accepted the 'rules of the game' and, consequently, the capacity of law to legitimate the specific exercise by the police of their powers. In chapter 8 I documented efforts to address ongoing problems of abuse of power and unlawful conduct by police officers. A recurring theme is the continuing weakness of legal norms in influencing police enforcement culture and practice and the efforts by state agencies to strengthen their normative force. However, to date, strengthening legal supervision over police decision-making has not inevitably improved the lawfulness of police conduct. Faced with resistance by local organs, some local courts have been reluctant to exercise their powers under the *ALL*.

Bourdieu argues that the capacity of law to legitimate the established order lies in its appearance of impartiality and universality. The perception that individual decision-making is based upon universal and impartial laws creates a 'chain of legitimation' which removes these decisions 'from the category of arbitrary violence'.[12] In an environment where the

10 Walder, 1995: Introductory chapter; Burns, 1999, describing the processes of adaptation by the Party to changed situations brought about by economic reform.
11 McCormick, 1990: 90–1, makes this point in relation to legal reform as a whole.
12 Chapter 2 at section 2; Bourdieu, 1987: 824.

legal field is emerging out of the broader field of power, the shared views and values of the field have not yet been firmly established. The establishment of shared legal habitus of actors, their shared practices, views, values and ways of acting,[13] is a slow and ongoing process.

Viewing the public security organs themselves as a semi-autonomous field, the strength of the legal habitus must be seen as mediated by the force of the legal field in relation to other fields and the direct influence of politics and other social norms on enforcement practice. In chapter 7, I document the ongoing processes of legalisation and professionalisation of the police force in the reform era. This process has involved the reinterpretation of objectives of the pre-reform values of the mass-line and Party leadership as being for the purpose of class struggle. Police power is now exercised to ensure the success of economic reform. Unsurprisingly, adherence to law is still viewed as only one priority of policing.

My discussion in chapter 7 of the transformation of the police in the reform era indicates that the processes of instilling a professional, legally based police ethic continues but remains incomplete. At the same time, the ideologically based system of police ethics has dramatically weakened. In this environment, the MPS has struggled to contain disenchantment amongst local police with their position in the reform era, with corruption and with systemic abuse of power.

The development of the legal field in the area of social order to date is at its initial stages. It is possible to trace the development of a legal field in which actors compete to determine law and in which law is accepted as necessary to legitimate police powers. However, the legitimating force of law remains limited whilst law and enforcement practice lack the appearance of justice and where law fails to control arbitrary and abusive police enforcement practices.

4.6 Structure and change: the functioning of the field

The processes of change within the legal field and the law that is produced are subject to a number of influences. First, the 'rules of the game' that frame the terms of the contests between actors in any social field are historically, socially and politically structured. My discussion of the development of administrative detention powers in the reform era reveals the direct influence of social order policy. Within the broader structure of social order policy, administrative detention continues to

[13] Chapter 2 at section 1; Terdiman, 1987: 811.

be located between localised, informal mechanisms for social control and criminal justice, a pattern that is replicated from the pre-reform era. It thus appeared natural that administrative detention was reinvigorated as a component of the CMPO in the reform era. My discussion of the development of administrative detention powers in chapters 5 and 6 shows that legal reform in this area has also been structured, or stymied, by concepts such as the distinction between the two types of contradiction, campaign-style policing in the form of the 'Hard Strike' and efforts to implement comprehensive strategies of social control, which have been redeployed and modified in the reform era. These continuities illustrate that there is still a limited range of concepts available to characterise and deal with social order problems in this changed environment.

Secondly, changes in fields are directly influenced by changes in other social fields and the field of power. Adoption of the policy of economic modernisation and its emphasis upon governance according to law have directly influenced the ways in which social order strategies and powers are conceptualised. An illustration is the fading of class struggle as the conceptual framework for structuring social order policies and the increasing importance of governance according to law which has led to discussions about legalisation of the CMPO, carrying out 'hard strikes according to law' and legalisation of administrative detention.

Thirdly, the boundaries of the field and, whilst the field is emerging, the rules of the game, are susceptible to contest and change. While structured, Bourdieu suggests that the logic and rules produced as a result of the competitions between actors in the field are not pre-ordained. The active nature of this competition also contemplates the appropriation of novel and foreign ideas to the terms of the debate and that influential actors, individuals or groups may be instrumental in shaping the rules, effecting change within certain subfields and expanding the boundaries of the field. The status of the rule of law and human rights in international discourse, together with the endorsement of protection of human rights by the state, helps improve the status and influence of advocates of the rule of law and protection of human rights within China.

In section 4.3 above, I have discussed the influence of different groups in developing bodies of law and establishing the values that law reflects. I have documented contests over the processes of change in respect of the basic principles of constitutional and administrative law, as well as in respect to specific legislation and the impact of this legislation on the legal regulation of administrative detention, illustrating the dynamic and contested process of change. In some areas, such as debates over the basic purposes of administrative law, discussed in chapter 7, and reforms of RETL and police administrative coercive powers, discussed in chapter 9, Western legal concepts have been influential. The outcomes of these most recent debates about the reform of administrative detention are difficult to predict.

An examination of the debates over detention for investigation, detention for repatriation and the current debates about reform of RETL indicate that developments in the legal system have created both the conditions and the imperative for reform of these powers. The impetus for legal reform has been strengthened by the policy of administration according to law. Reforms to constitutional and administrative law have increasingly thrown into relief the current failure to reform administrative detention powers and the extent to which they are inconsistent with the established requirements for legality of police powers.

The legal imperatives for reform are bolstered by increasing public and official dissatisfaction with the chronic and severe abuses of these powers, an important factor underlying the abolition of detention for repatriation and detention for investigation. In the case of detention for repatriation, this reform, to date at least, is radical: a complete abolition of the power. In the case of detention for investigation, the reform involved a radical restructuring of the power, though not a substantial diminution in police powers to detain criminal suspects for questioning. With RETL, the outcome is not yet determined. Several proposals exist, ranging from reorganisation, radical legal restructuring, to an overhaul of the entire system of police administrative coercive powers. At present, public debates about reform of detention for education and coercive drug rehabilitation appear to be subsumed within the broader discussions about whether to establish a category of security defence to regulate these powers.

Whilst these debates provide some hope that the balance of reform is in favour of constraint of police power and protection of individual rights against abuse, there appears to be no indication of a willingness radically to curtail police power. The *RETL Regulations* appear to remove politically defined transgressions from the scope of targets, while retaining broad powers to target dissent, which has been redefined with reference to criminal offences. Developments in administrative law that give more content to the concept of lawfulness, strengthen procedural requirements for the imposition of detention and seek to strengthen supervision over the exercise of detention powers, have sought to regularise rather than limit police power.

5 CONCLUSION

The legal field provides a useful analytical construct through which to examine legal change relating to administrative detention as it focusses attention on several factors that influence the processes of change. First is the historical, political and social structuring of the legal field and the rules of the game. Second is the impact of changes in other fields, such as the social, economic, governmental fields and the field of power, on the terms of legal debate. The third factor is the positions adopted by different actors and the influence they have on the terms and outcomes of contests about the production of legal norms and rules. Each of these factors has been influential in the process of legal change as it relates to administrative detention.

The outcomes of the contests between legal actors are significant not only for the law that is produced but also because of the potential for these contests to strengthen the force of the legal field. The boundaries of the legal field and its attractive force are strengthened by the appropriation of powers and state functions into the legal field through redefining and then judging their exercise in legal terms and by the increasing status this brings to legal players. The diversity of legal actors, which includes academics, judges, congress-people, Party elites, the MPS and local police, as well as other government departments and lawyers, each with their own positions and interests, also warns against an assumption that increasing legalisation of state power will necessarily result in the limitation of state or police power.

In China, the development of the legal field and the pluralisation of positions that it reflects remains constrained within the limits of Party policy and political orthodoxy. This book has not revealed an increasing tolerance of dissent, quite the reverse. As Bourdieu suggests, the legal field has developed in a way that is not antagonistic to state power, but in a way that reinforces it. The impetus for legal reform to define police power, to curb abuse and to better protect the rights of citizens is to regularise and so protect state and Party power. However, the emergence of a legal field with its own particular vocabulary, logic and values suggests that there is the possibility of longer-term structural change toward greater autonomy in the ways in which law is developed and enforced and its relationship to political power.

Bourdieu's conception of society as comprising a series of overlapping and interrelated fields[14] provides a conceptual framework through which to examine the interaction between different fields. This book has shown, through an examination of the specific example of administrative detention, that law is becoming increasingly important in defining the structure of the police force, police powers and standards of police conduct. Law has had limited impact to date, however, on law enforcement strategies and police culture. The relationship between the field of policing and the legal field is a dynamic one, where the police influence the functioning of the legal field and the development of legal norms. In turn, the police are influenced by developments in law and the legal field.

Similarly, the development of the legal field has been directly influenced by the changes in the field of power and the Party's determination to change its mode of exercising power, from direct involvement in day-to-day decision-making to increasingly indirect involvement by establishing a legal system to provide the basis for day-to-day decision-making. Whilst this book has been quite narrowly focussed, the larger question of the changing ways in which political power is exercised, even the changing nature of politics in China, has been ever present in the background. This question remains to be examined more explicitly.

The central question underlying this book is how to approach an analysis of rapid legal change in a modernising country such as China. This is a question of broader interest to studies of law and development, comparative law and the sociology of law. Focussing on the processes of change and the ways in which law is produced draws attention to the interrelationship between the legal field and other social fields, the changing balance between autonomy and instrumentalism and the active roles that actors play in appropriating domestic and foreign ideas, institutions and rules for use in legal reform. An analysis of the processes of change is not a substitute for evaluations of the outcomes of legal reform, whether judged against the standard of the rule of law or some other standard, but it provides an important adjunct to them. An analysis of the processes and dynamics of reform suggests that we may indulge in cautious optimism that administrative detention powers in China will gradually be legalised and regularised and that stronger powers for supervision of the exercise of these powers will be implemented. This book does not, however, support a conclusion that administrative

[14] Trubek *et al.*, 1994: 414.

detention powers used in relation to social order issues will be abolished wholesale or that a citizen-centred notion of individual human rights will be embraced any time soon. In the case of administrative detention, the pressure for legal reform is such that these detention powers cannot remain in their current form. The continuing power of the political-legal apparatus and its capacity to influence the reform process suggests that it is unlikely that reforms will result in a reduction of power to deal with problems of crime and social order. There may, however, be a redistribution of power between the different agencies of state that comprise the state's coercive apparatus.

APPENDIX ONE

INDEX OF LEGISLATION, ADMINISTRATIVE REGULATIONS, RULES, NORMATIVE DOCUMENTS, PARTY DOCUMENTS, SPEECHES AND CASES

LEGISLATION

National People's Congress ('NPC')

PRC Criminal Law, passed on 1 July 1979, effective on 1 January 1980, amended in 1997, promulgated on 14 March 1997 to come into effect on 1 October 1997, reproduced in Law Yearbook Editorial Committee, 1998: 206–41.	Zhonghua Renmin Gongheguo Xingfa 中华人民共和国刑法
PRC Criminal Procedure Law, passed on 1 July 1979, effective on 1 January 1980, amended in 1996, promulgated on 17 March 1996 to come into effect on 1 January 1997 ('CPL'), reproduced in Law Yearbook Editorial Committee, 1997: 251–67.	Zhonghua Renmin Gongheguo Xingshi Susong Fa 中华人民共和国刑事诉讼法
PRC Constitution 1982, promulgated to take effect on 4 December 1982, amended on 12 April 1988, 29 March 1993, 15 March 1999 and 14 March 2004 (English translation of the 1982 law from the translation prepared by the Legislative Affairs Commission of the NPCSC, printed in 1987 by the Foreign Languages Press, Beijing).	Zhonghua Renmin Gongheguo Xianfa 中华人民共和国宪法

PRC Administrative Litigation Law, passed on 4 April 1989, effective on 1 October 1990 ('ALL'), reproduced in Huang, 1993: 651–9.	Zhonghua Renmin Gongheguo Xingzheng Susong Fa 中华人民共和国行政诉讼法
PRC Administrative Punishments Law, 17 March 1996 ('APL'), reproduced in Law Yearbook Editorial Committee, 1997: 236–40.	Zhonghua Renmin Gongheguo Xingzheng Chufa Fa 中华人民共和国行政处罚法
PRC Legislation Law, passed on 15 March 2000 to take effect on 1 July 2000, reproduced in Law Yearbook Editorial Committee, 2001: 257–63.	Zhonghua Renmin Gongheguo Lifa Fa 中华人民共和国立法法

National People's Congress Standing Committee ('NPCSC')

NPCSC, People's Police Regulations, 25 June 1957, reproduced in Wang, Huaian, 1989: 1500–1.	Quanguo Renmin Daibiao Dahui Changwu Weiyuanhui, Zhonghua Remin Gongheguo Remin Jingcha Tiaoli 中华人民共和国人民警察条例
NPCSC, Decision of the State Council on the Question of Re-education through Labour, approved by the NPCSC on 1 August 1957 and promulgated on 3 August 1957, reproduced in Wang, Huaian, 1989: 1573 ('Decision of the State Council on the Question of RETL').	Quanguo Renmin Daibiao Dahui Changwu Weiyuanhui, Guowuyuan Guanyu Laodong Jiaoyang Wenti de Jueding 国务院关于劳动教养问题的决定
NPCSC, Supplementary Regulations of the State Council on Re-education through Labour, 29 November 1979, reproduced in Wang, Huaian, 1989: 1574.	Quanguo Renmin Daibiao Dahui Changwu Weiyuanhui, Guowu Yuan Guanyu Laodong Jiaoyang de Buchong Guiding 国务院关于劳动教养的补充规定
NPCSC, Decision Regarding the handling of offenders undergoing Reform through Labour and persons undergoing Re-education through Labour who escape or commit new crimes, 10 June 1981 (in English and Chinese), reproduced in Foreign Languages Press, 1984: 220–5, Chinese text reproduced in Wang, Huaian, 1989: 112.	Guanyu Chuli Taopao huozhe Chongxin Fanzui de Laogaifan he Laojiao Renyuan de Jueding 关于处理逃跑或者重新犯罪的劳改犯和劳教人员的决定

Decision of the NPCSC Regarding the Question of Approval of Cases involving Death Sentences, 10 June 1981, reproduced in Foreign Languages Press, 1984: 217–19 (in English and Chinese, translation by Jerome Cohen).	Quanguo Renmin Daibiao Dahui Changwu Weiyuanhui, Guanyu Sixing Anjian Hezhun Wenti de Jueding 全国人民代表大会常务委员会关于死刑案件核准问题的决定
Decision of the NPCSC Regarding the Question of the Time Limits for Handling Criminal Cases, 10 September 1981, reproduced in Foreign Languages Press, 1984: 226–8 (in English and Chinese, translation by Jerome Cohen).	Quanguo Renmin Daibiao Dahui Changwu Weiyuanhui Guanyu Xingshi Anjian Banan Qixian de Jueding 全国人民代表大会常务委员会关于刑事案件办案期限问题的决定
Decision of the NPCSC Regarding the Severe Punishment of Criminals who Seriously Undermine the Economy, 8 March 1982, reproduced in Foreign Languages Press, 1984: 229–40, in English and Chinese, translation by Jerome Cohen).	Quanguo Renmin Daibiao Dahui Changwu Weiyuanhui Guanyu Yancheng Yanzhong Pohuai Jingji de Zuifan de Jueding 全国人民代表大会常务委员会关于严惩严重破坏经济的罪犯的决定
Decision of the NPCSC Regarding the Severe Punishment of Criminal Elements who Seriously Endanger Public Security, 2 September 1983 (in English and Chinese), reproduced in Cohen, 1984: 241–5.	Quanguo Renmin Daibiao Dahui Changwu Weiyuanhui Guanyu Yancheng Yanzhong Weihai Shehui Zhi'an de Fanzui Fenzi de Jueding 全国人民代表大会常务委员会关于严惩严重危害社会治安的犯罪分子 的决定
Decision of the NPCSC Regarding the Procedure for Rapid Adjudication of Cases Involving Criminal Elements who Seriously Endanger Public Security, 2 September 1983 (in English and Chinese), reproduced in Cohen, 1984: 246–9.	Quanguo Renmin Daibiao Dahui Changwu Weiyuanhui Guanyu Xunsu Shenpan Yanzhong Weihai Shehui Zhi'an de Fanzui Fenzi de Chengxu de Jueding 全国人民代表大会常务委员会关于迅速审判严重危害社会治安的犯罪分子的程序的决定
Decision of the NPCSC Regarding the Exercise by the State Security Organs of the Public Security Organs' Powers of Investigation, Detention, Preliminary Interrogation and Carrying Out Arrest, 2 September 1983, excerpted in Wang, Huaian, 1989: 1503–4.	Quanguo Renmin Daibiao Dahui Changwu Weiyuanhui Guanyu Guojia Anquan Jiguan Xingshi Gong'an Jiguan de Zhencha, Juliu, Yushen he Zhixing Daibu de Zhiquan de Jueding 关于国家安全机关行使公安机关的 侦察，拘留，预审和执行逮捕的职权的决定

NPCSC, PRC Resident Identity Card Regulations, 6 September 1985, reproduced in Chen, 1992: 370–2.	Quanguo Renmin Daibiao Dahui Changwu Weiyuanhui, Zhonghua Renmin Gongheguo Jumin Shenfenzheng Tiaoli 中华人民共和国居民身份证条例
NPCSC, Law on Organisation of Urban Resident Committees of the PRC, 26 December 1989, reproduced in Chen, 1992: 489–92.	Quanguo Renmin Daibiao Dahui Changwu Weiyuanhui, Zhonghua Renmin Gongheguo Chengshi Jumin Weiyuanhui Zuzhi Fa 中华人民共和国城市居民委员会组织法
NPCSC, PRC Security Administrative Punishment Regulations, passed in 1957, reproduced in Zuigao Renmin Jianchayuan Jiansuo Jiancha Ting, 1992: 478–9; replaced by the SAPR passed by the NPCSC on 5 September 1986, reproduced in Wang, Huaian, 1989: 1529–34 and Gong'an Bu Fazhi Si, 1994: 11–24 ('SAPR'), replaced by the Security Administrative Punishments Law ('SAPL') effective from 1 March 2006.	Quanguo Renmin Daibiao Dahui Changwu Weiyuanhui, Zhonghua Renmin Gongheguo Zhi'an Guanli Chufa Tiaoli 中华人民共和国治安管理处罚条例
NPCSC, Decision on the Punishment of Criminals who Smuggle, Produce, Traffic in and Disseminate Pornographic Articles, 28 December 1990, reproduced in Renmin Fayuan Chubanshe, 1992: 100–4.	Quanguo Renmin Daibiao Dahui Changwu Weiyuanhui, Quanguo Renmin Daibiao Dahui Changwu Weiyuanhui Guanyu Chengzhi Zousi, Zhizuo, Fanmai, Chuanbo Yinhui Wupin de Fanzuifenzi de Jueding 全国人民代表大会常务委员会关于惩治走私，制作，贩卖，传播淫秽物品的犯罪分子的决定
NPCSC, Decision on the Prohibition of Drugs, 28 December 1990, reproduced in Renmin Fayuan Chubanshe, 1992: 357–61 ('Drugs Decision').	Quanguo Renmin Daibiao Dahui Changwu Weiyuanhui, Guanyu Jindu de Jueding 全国人民代表大会委员会关于禁毒的决定
NPCSC, Decision on Strengthening the Comprehensive Management of Public Order, 2 March 1991, reproduced in Chen, 1992: 34–6.	Quanguo Renmin Daibiao Dahui Changwu Weiyuanhui Guanyu Jiaqiang Shehui Zhi'an Zonghe Zhili de Jueding 全国人民代表大会常务委员会关于加强社会治安综合治理的决定

NPCSC, Decision on Strictly Prohibiting Prostitution and Using Prostitutes, 4 August 1991, reproduced in Renmin Fayuan Chubanshe, 1992: 18–22 and Chen, 1992: 163–5 ('Prostitution Decision').	Quanguo Renmin Daibiao Dahui Changwu Weiyuanhui, Guanyu Yanjin Maiyin Piaochang de Jueding 全国人民代表大会常务委员会关于严禁卖淫嫖娼的决定
NPCSC, Decision on Punishment of Criminals who Abduct, Sell and Kidnap Women and Children, 4 August 1991, reproduced in Renmin Fayuan Chubanshe, 1992: 310–15 and Chen, 1992: 166–8.	Quanguo Renmin Daibiao Dahui Changwu Weiyuanhui, Guanyu Yancheng Guaimai, Bangjia Funü, Ertong de Fanzui Fenzi de Jueding 全国人民代表大会常务委员会关于严惩拐卖，绑架妇女，儿童的犯罪分子的决定
NPCSC, Provisions of the NPCSC on Strengthening Inspection and Supervision of Law Enforcement, 2 September 1993 (in English from Isinolaw Reference ID 0–235–131668), Chinese version reproduced in Law Yearbook Editorial Committee, 1994: 360–1.	Quanguo Renmin Daibiao Dahui Changwu Weiyuanhui, Guanyu Jiaqiang Dui Falü Shishi Qingkuang Jiancha Jiandu de Ruogan Guiding 全国人民代表大会常务委员会关于加强对法律实施情况检查监督的若干规定
NPCSC, PRC State Compensation Law, passed and effective from 12 May 1994, reproduced in Law Yearbook Editorial Committee, 1995: 165–8; Gong'an Bu Fazhi Si, 1994: 25–36.	Quanguo Renmin Daibiao Dahui Changwu Weiyuanhui, Zhonghua Renmin Gongheguo Guojia Peichang Fa 中华人民共和国国家赔偿法
NPCSC, PRC Labour Law, passed on 5 July 1994 to take effect on 1 January 1995, reproduced in Law Yearbook Editorial Committee, 1995: 181–6.	Quanguo Renmin Daibiao Dahui Changwu Weiyuanhui, Zhonghua Renmin Gongheguo Laodong Fa 中华人民共和国劳动法
NPCSC, PRC Judges Law, passed on 28 February 1995, promulgated to take effect on 1 July 1995, reproduced in Law Yearbook Editorial Committee, 1996: 214–18.	Quanguo Renmin Daibiao Dahui Changwu Weiyuanhui, Zhonghua Renmin Gongheguo Faguan Fa 中华人民共和国法官法
NPCSC, PRC People's Procurators Law, passed on 28 February 1995 to take effect on 1 July 1995, reproduced in Law Yearbook Editorial Committee, 1996: 218–21.	Quanguo Renmin Daibiao Dahui Changwu Weiyuanhui, Zhonghua Renmin Gongheguo Jianchaguan Fa 中华人民共和国检察官法
NPCSC, PRC People's Police Law, passed and effective on 28 February	Quanguo Renmin Daibiao Dahui Changwu Weiyuanhui, Zhonghua

1995 ('PPL'), reproduced in Law Yearbook Editorial Committee, 1996: 221–4.	Renmin Gongheguo Renmin Jingcha Fa 中华人民共和国人民警察法
NPCSC, PRC Lawyers' Law, passed on 15 May 1996 to take effect on 1 January 1997, reproduced in Law Yearbook Editorial Committee, 1997: 276–9.	Quanguo Renmin Daibiao Dahui Changwu Weiyuanhui, Zhonghua Renmin Gongheguo Lüshi Fa 中华人民共和国律师法
NPCSC, PRC Administrative Supervision Law, 9 May 1997, reproduced in Law Yearbook Editorial Committee, 1998: 245–8.	Quanguo Renmin Daibiao Dahui Changwu Weiyuanhui, Zhonghua Renmin Gongheguo Xingzheng Jiancha Fa 中华人民共和国行政监察法
NPCSC, PRC Administrative Review Law, passed on 29 April 1999, promulgated to take effect on 1 October 1999 ('ARL'), reproduced in Law Yearbook Editorial Committee, 2000: 244–8.	Quanguo Renmin Daibiao Dahui Changwu Weiyuanhui, Zhonghua Renmin Gongheguo Xingzheng Fuyi Fa 中华人民共和国行政复议法
NPCSC, Decision on Banning Heretical Cult Organisations, and Preventing and Punishing Cult Activities, 30 October 1999 (in English), Chinese version reproduced in Law Yearbook Editorial Committee, 2000: 314–15.	Quanguo Renmin Daibiao Dahui Changwu Weiyuanhui, Guanyu Qudi Xiejiao Zhizhi, Fangfan he Chengzhi Xiejiao Huodong de Jueding 全国人民代表大会常务委员会关于取缔邪教组织，防范和惩治邪教活动的决定
NPCSC, PRC Resident Identity Card Law, passed on 28 June 2003 to take effect on 1 January 2004, reproduced in Law Yearbook Editorial Committee, 2004: 228–30.	Quanguo Renmin Daibiao Dahui Changwu Weiyuanhui, Zhonghua Renmin Gongheguo Jumin Shenfenzheng Fa 中华人民共和国居民身份证法
NPCSC, PRC Security Administrative Punishment Law ('SAPL'), passed on 28 August 2005 and promulgated to take effect on 1 March 2006, reproduced in Ke and Wu, 2005: 5–29.	Quanguo Renmin Daibiao Dahui Changwu Weiyuanhui, Zhonghua Renmin Gongheguo Zhi'an Guanli Chufa Fa 中华人民共和国治安管理处罚法
NPCSC, PRC Supervision Law of the Standing Committees of Congresses at Each Level ('Supervision Law'), passed on 27 August 2006, promulgated to take effect on 1 January 2007, reproduced at http://news.xinhuanet.com.legal/2006-08/27content_5013597.htm, accessed on 28 August 2006.	Zhonghua Renmin Gongheguo Geji Renmin Daibiao Dahui Changwu Weiyuanhui Jiandu Fa 中华人民共和国各级人民代表大会常务委员会监督法

Other documents issued by the NPCSC and its subcommittees

Report of the Law Committee of the NPC on the Results of the Review of the (draft) 'PRC People's Police Law', 15 February 1995, reproduced in Gao, 1995: 180–4 and Luo, 1995: 202–8.	Quanguo Renda Falü Weiyuanhui Guanyu 'Zhonghua Remin Gongheguo Renmin Jingcha Fa (Cao'an)' Shenyi Jieguo de Baogao 全国人大法律委员会关于'中华人民共和国人民警察法（草案）'审议结果的报告
NPCSC Legislative Affairs Committee, Report on Opinions of Each Province and Relevant Central Ministries on the Scope of Law Making Power in the (draft) Legislation Law, 1999, reproduced in Zhang, Chunsheng, 2000: 326–35.	Fazhi Gongzuo Weiyuanhui, Gedi he Zhongyang Youguan Bumen dui Lifa Fa (Cao'an) Guanyu Lifa Quanxian Wenti de Yijian 法制工作委员会，各地和中央有关部门对立法法（草案）关于立法权 限问题的意见
9th NPC Law Committee, Report on the Results of Review of the '(draft) PRC Legislation Law', 14 March 2000, reproduced in Zhang, Chunsheng, 2000: 294–6.	Di Jiujie Quanguo Renmin Daibiao Dahui Falü Weiyuanhui Guanyu 'Zhonghua Renmin Gongheguo Lifa Fa (Cao'an)' Shenyi Jieguo de Baogao 第九届全国人民代表大会法律委员会关于'中华人民共和国立法法（草案）'审议结果的报告

JUDICIAL INTERPRETATIONS

Supreme People's Court ('SPC')

SPC, Measures on Resolutely Abolishing Specialist and Commercial Fines in Handling Drug Criminals, November 1950, referred to in Ma, Weigang, 1993a: 56.	Zuigao Renmin Fayuan, Chuli Dufan Ying Jianjue Feizhi Zhuanke yu Yike Fajin Banfa 最高人民法院处理毒犯应坚决废止专科与易科罚金办法
SPC, Opinion on Several Questions on the Implementation of the Administrative Litigation Law of the PRC (for trial implementation), discussed and passed at the 499th meeting of the Adjudication Committee of the Supreme People's Court on 29 May 1991, reproduced in Huang, 1993: 659–66.	Zuigao Renmin Fayuan, Guanyu Guanche Zhixing 'Zhonghua Renmin Gongheguo Xingzheng Susong Fa' Ruogan Wenti de Yijian 最高人民法院关于贯彻执行'中华人民共和国行政诉讼法'若干问题的意见

SPC, Notice on Coordinating with the Public Security Organs in Carrying out the Work of Eliminating the 'Six Evils', 13 November 1989, reproduced in Renmin Fayuan Chubanshe, 1992: 2–4.

Zuigao Renmin Fayuan, Guanyu Peihe Gong'an Jiguan Kaizhan Chu 'Liuhai' Gongzuo de Tongzhi 最高人民法院关于配合公安机关开出'六害'工作的通知

SPC, Response to a Request for Instructions on the question of whether it is possible to impose RETL on a person who commits offences in the countryside and whose residence is in the countryside but whose acts are insufficient to pursue criminal charges, 1997, referred to in Lin, 2001: 13.

Zuigao Renmin Fayuan, Guanyu Dui Jiazhu Nongcun Bing Zai Nongcun Zuo'an, Shang bu Gou Zhuijiu Xingshi Zeren de Weifa Renyuan Kefou Laodong Jiaoyang Wenti de Dafu 最高人民法院关于家居农村并在农村作案，尚不够追究刑事责人的违法人员可否劳动教养问题的答复

SPC, Interpretation on Several Questions on the Enforcement of the 'PRC Administrative Litigation Law', passed on 24 November 1999 to take effect on 10 March 2000 ('ALL Interpretation'), reproduced in Law Yearbook Editorial Committee, 2001: 633–41 and Gong'an Bu Fazhi Ju, 2000: 886–907.

Zuigao Renmin Fayuan, Guanyu Zhixing 'Zhonghua Renmin Gongheguo Xingzheng Susong Fa' Ruogan Wenti de Jieshi 最高人民法院关于执行'中华人民共和国行政诉讼法'若干问题的解释

Supreme People's Procuratorate ('SPP')

SPP, Notice on Implementing the Spirit of the National Political-Legal Work Conference by Strengthening the Work of Supervision over Detention Centres, 31 August 1983, extracted in Zuigao Renmin Jianchayuan Jiansuo Jiancha Ting, 1992: 65–6.

Zuigao Renmin Jianchayuan, Guanyu Guanche Quanguo Zhengfa Gongzuo Huiyi Jingshen Jiaqiang Jiansuo Jiancha Gongzuo de Tongzhi 最高人民检察院关于贯彻全国政法工作会议精神加强监所检察工作的通知

SPP, Measures on the Work of Supervision over Re-education through Labour (for trial implementation), 23 July 1987, extracted in Zuigao Renmin Jianchayuan Jiansuo Jiancha Ting, 1992: 498–505.

Zuigao Renmin Jianchayuan, Renmin Jianchayuan Laodong Jiaoyang Jiancha Gongzuo Banfa (Shixing) 最高人民检察院劳动教养检察工作办法（试行）

SPP, Notice on Fully Developing Procuratorial Capacity Resolutely to Strike against Kidnapping and

Zuigao Renmin Jianchayuan, Guanyu Chongfen Fahui Jiancha Zhineng Jianjue Daji Guaimai Funü,

Selling Women and Children and the Crime of Coercing, Luring and Keeping Female Prostitutes, Actively to Coordinate Investigation, Prohibition and Elimination of Prostitution and Using Prostitutes, 11 January 1991, reproduced at Gong'an Bu Fazhi Si, 1991: 194–6.	Ertong he Qiangpo, Yinyou Rongliu Funü Maiyin de Fanzui Jiji Peihe Chajin Qudi Maiyin Piaochang Huodong de Tongzhi 最高人民检察院关于充分发挥检察职能坚决打击拐卖妇女，儿童和强迫,引诱容留妇女卖淫的犯罪积极配合查禁取缔卖淫嫖娼活动的通知
SPP, Notice on Strictly Implementing the NPCSC 'Decision on Strictly Prohibiting Prostitution and Using Prostitutes' and 'Decision on Strictly Punishing those Criminal Elements who Kidnap and Sell Women and Children', 17 September 1991, reproduced in Gong'an Bu Fazhi Si, 1991: 274–6.	Zuigao Renmin Jianchayuan, Guanyu Yange Zhixing Quanguo Renda Changweihui 'Guanyu Yanjin Maiyin Piaochang de Jueding' he 'Guanyu Yancheng Guaimai Bangjia Funü, Ertong de Fanzui Fenzi de Jueding' de Tongzhi 最高人民检察院关于严格执行全国 人大常委会‘关于严禁卖淫嫖娼的决定和关于严惩拐卖绑架妇女，儿童的犯罪分子的决定的通知

ADMINISTRATIVE REGULATIONS

State Council

Central People's Government, Circular on Strict Prohibition of Opium and Drug Taking, 24 February 1950, reproduced in Renmin Fayuan Chubanshe, 1992: 366–7.	Zhongyang Renmin Zhengfu Zhengwuyuan Guanyu Yanjin Yapian Yandu de Tongling 中央人民政府政务院关于严禁鸦片烟毒的通令
Central People's Government, PRC Regulations for the Punishment of Counter-revolutionaries, 21 February 1951, referred to in Xi and Yu, 1996: 261.	Zhonghua Renmin Gongheguo Chengzhi Fangeming Tiaoli 中华人民共和国惩治反革命条例
Administrative Council, Temporary Measures on Control of Counter-revolutionary Elements, 27 June 1952, reproduced in Zhonggong Zhongyang Wenxian Yanjiu Shi, 1992c: 244–6.	Zhengwuyuan Guanzhi Fangeming Fenzi Zanxing Banfa 政务院管制反革命分子暂行办法
PRC Regulations on Punishment of Drug Crimes, November 1952 referred to in Shao, 2004: 321.	Zhonghua Renmin Gongheguo Chengzhi Dufan Tiaoli 中华人民共和国惩治毒贩条例

State Council, Notice on Strictly Prohibiting the Private Cultivation of Opium Poppy, the Transport and Use of Opium etc. Drugs, 1973, referred to in Zhao and Yu, 2000: 18.	Guowuyuan Guanyu Yanjin Sizhong Yingsu he Fanmai, Xishi Yapian deng Dupin de Tongzhi 国务院关于严禁私种罂粟合叛卖，吸食鸦片等毒品的通知
State Council, approving and issuing MPS, Ministry of Railways Report of the National Conference on the work of Public Order on Railways, 15 July 1975 (excerpted in photocopy materials at 3), referred to in Cui, 1993b: 91.	Guowuyuan Pizhuan Gong'an Bu, Tiedao Bu Guanyu Quanguo Tielu Zhi'an Gongzuo Huiyi de Qingkuang Baogao 国务院批转公安部，铁道部，关于全国铁路治安工作会议的情况报告
State Council, Notice promulgating the 'Supplementary Regulations of the State Council on Re-education through Labour', 5 December 1979, reproduced in Wang, Huaian, 1989: 1574.	Guowuyuan Guanyu Gongbu 'Guowu Yuan Guanyu Laodong Jiaoyang de Buchong Guiding' de Tongzhi 国务院关于公布 '国务院关于劳动教养的补充规 定' 的通知
State Council, Notice on Consolidation of the Two Measures of Forced Labour and Detention for Investigation into Re-education through Labour, 29 February 1980, reproduced in Wang, Huaian, 1989: 1582–3 and Gong'an Bu Fagui Ju, 1980: 238–9.	Guowuyuan, Guanyu Jiang Qiangzhi Laodong he Shourong Shencha Liang Xiang Cuoshi Tongyi yu Laodong Jiaoyang de Tongzhi 国务院关于将强制劳动和收容审查两项措施统一于劳动教养的通知
State Council, Approving and Issuing the MPS Notice on Resolutely Striking Against Criminal Elements who Write Letters to Guomindang Espionage Agencies, 15 August 1981, excerpted in Gong'an Bu Fazhisi, 1992: 49.	Guowuyuan Pizhuan Gong'an Bu Guanyu Jianjue Daji Xiang Guomindang Tewu Jiguan Xiexin Guagou de Fanzui Fenzi de Tongzhi (Jielu) 国务院批转公安部关于坚决打击向国民党特务机关写信挂钩的犯罪分 子的通知（节录）
State Council, Notice Restating the Strict Prohibition of Opium and Drug Taking, 27 August 1981, reproduced in Renmin Fayuan Chubanshe, 1992: 368–9 and Wang, Huaian, 1989: 1547–8.	Guowuyuan, Guanyu Chongshen Yanjin Yapian Yandu de Tongzhi 国务院关于重申严禁鸦片烟毒的通知
State Council, Notice on Resolutely Suppressing Prostitution Activities and Preventing the Spread of Sexually Transmitted Diseases, 1 September 1986, reproduced in Gong'an Bu Fagui Ju, 1986: 227–9.	Guowuyuan, Guanyu Jianjue Qudi Maiyin Huodong he Zhizhi Xingbing Manyan de Tongzhi 国务院关于坚决取缔卖淫活动和制止性病蔓延的通知

State Council, Organisational Regulations of People's Mediation Committees, passed on 5 May 1989 to take effect on 17 June 1989, reproduced in Chen, 1992: 486–8.	Guowuyuan, Renmin Tiaojie Weiyuanhui Zuzhi Tiaoli 国务院人民调解委员会组织条例
State Council, Regulation and Rule Reporting Regulations, 18 February 1990, reproduced in Wang, Huaian *et al.*, 1993: 928–30.	Guowuyuan, Fagui Guizhang Bei'an Guiding 国务院法规规章备案规定
State Council, Administrative Review Regulations, passed on 24 December 1990 to take effect on 1 January 1991 ('ARR'), reproduced in Wang, Huaian *et al.*, 1993: 1981–6 (now replaced by the ARL).	Guowuyuan, Xingzheng Fuyi Tiaoli 国务院行政复议条例
State Council, Measures for Detention for Education of Prostitutes and Clients of Prostitutes, 4 September 1993, reproduced in Gong'an Bu Fazhi Si, 1993: 74–7.	Guowuyuan, Maiyin Piaochang Renyuan Shourong Jiaoyu Banfa 国务院卖淫嫖娼人员收容教育办法
State Council, Decision on amending the 'Administrative Review Regulations', 9 October 1994, reproduced in Gong'an Bu Fazhi Si, 1994: 276.	Guowuyuan, Guanyu Xiuzheng 'Xingzheng Fuyi Tiaoli' de Jueding 国务院关于修正‘行政复议条例’的决定
State Council, Measures on Coercive Drug Rehabilitation, 12 January 1995, reproduced in Gong'an Bu Fazhi Si, 1995: 157–60.	Guowuyuan, Qiangzhi Jiedu Banfa 国务院关于强制戒毒办法
State Council, Regulations on Supervision of Public Security Organs, 20 June 1997, reproduced in Gong'an Bu Fazhi Si, 1997: 153–5.	Guowuyuan, Gong'an Jiguan Ducha Tiaoli 国务院，公安机关督察条例
State Council, Notice on Implementing the 'PRC Administrative Review Law', 6 May 1999, reproduced in Gong'an Bu Fazhi Ju, 1999: 91–5.	Guowuyuan, Guanyu Guanche Shishi 'Zhonghua Renmin Gongheguo Xingzheng Fuyi Fa' de Tongzhi 国务院关于贯彻实施‘中华人民共和国行政复议法’的通知
State Council, Decision on Comprehensively Carrying Forward Administration According to Law, 8 November 1999, reproduced in Law Yearbook Editorial Committee, 2000: 503–4.	Guowuyuan, Guanyu Quanmian Tuijin Yifa Xingzheng de Jueding 国务院关于全面推进依法行政的决定

State Council, Measures on the Handling of Official Documents by State Administrative Agencies, effective from 1 January 2001, reproduced in Gong'an Bu Fazhi Ju, 2000: 243–53.	Guowuyuan, Guojia Xingzheng Jiguan Gongwen Chuli Banfa 国务院国家行政机关公文处理办法
State Council, Regulations and Rules Reporting Regulations, effective on 1 January 2002, reproduced in Gong'an Bu Fazhi Ju, 2001: 289–93.	Guowuyuan, Fagui Guizhang Bei'an Tiaoli 国务院法规规章备案条例
State Council, Procedural Regulations for Formulating Administrative Regulations, effective on 1 January 2002, reproduced in Gong'an Bu Fazhi Ju, 2001: 269–75.	Guowuyuan, Xingzheng Fagui Zhiding Chengxu Tiaoli 国务院行政法规制定程序条例
State Council, Procedural Regulations for Formulating Rules, effective on 1 January 2002, reproduced in Gong'an Bu Fazhi Ju, 2001: 276–83.	Guowuyuan, Guizhang Zhiding Chengxu Tiaoli 国务院规章制定程序条例
State Council, Measures on the Administration of Aiding Vagrants and Beggars Having no Means of Livelihood in Cities, 18 June 2003 to take effect on 1 August 2003, reproduced in Law Yearbook Editorial Committee, 2004: 335–6.	Guowuyuan, Chengshi Shenghuo Wuzhao de Liulang Qitao Renyuan Qiuzhu Guanli Banfa (Chinese from Xinhua Web reference number 2003–06–22 16:41:13) 国务院城市生活无照的流浪乞讨人员求助管理办法
State Council, Notice Issuing the Implementing Outline on Comprehensively Carrying Forward Implementation of Administration According to Law, 22 March 2004, reproduced in Gong'an Bu Fazhi Ju, 2004: 62–76.	Guowuyuan Guanyu Yinfa Quanmian Tuijin Yifa Xingzheng Shishi Gangyao de Tongzhi 国务院关于印发全面推进依法行政实施纲要的通知
State Council, Letters and visits Regulations, 1 May 2005, reproduced at http://news.xinhuanet.com/zhengfu/2005-01/17/content_2471020.htm.	Guowuyuan Xinfang Tiaoli 国务院信访条例

Other documents of the State Council

Information Office of the State Council of the PRC, White Paper on Narcotics Control, 26 June 2000 (in English), from www.china.org.cn/e-white/1/.	
State Council, General Office Notice issuing the MPS etc. Departments Opinion on Commencing a Specialist Action to Strengthen Management of Public Entertainment and Service Venues and to Conduct a Severe Strike against Evil Social Influences including Prostitution and Using Prostitutes, Gambling and Drug Use and Trafficking, 30 June 2000, reproduced in Gong'an Bu Fazhi Ju, 2000: 227.	Guowuyuan Bangongting Zhuanfa Gong'an Bu Deng Bumen Guanyu Kaizhan Jiaqiang Yule Fuwu Changsuo Guanli Yanli Daji Maiyin Piaochang Dubo Xidu Fandu Deng Shehui Chou'e Xianxiang Zhuanxiang Xingdong Yijian de Tongzhi 国务院办公厅转发公安部等部门关于开展加强娱乐服务场所管理严厉打击卖淫嫖娼赌博吸毒贩毒等社会丑恶现象专项行动意见的通知
State Council, Legal Affairs Office Letter in Response to 'Request for Instructions about Whether to Apply Local Regulations or Ministerial Rules in Examining the Case of Zhang Xiaoli Applying for Administrative Review', 4 September 2001, reproduced in Gong'an Bu Fazhi Ju, 2001: 168.	Guowuyuan Fazhi Bangongshi Dui 'Guanyu Shencha Zhang Xiaoli Shenqing Xingzheng Fuyi Yi'an Ying Yong Difangxing Fagui, Haishi Shiyong Bumen Guizhang de Qingshi' de Fuhan 国务院法制办公室对'关于审查张晓利申请行政复议一案应用地方性法 规，还是适用部门规章的请示'的复函

ADMINISTRATIVE RULES ISSUED BY CENTRAL MINISTRIES, COMMISSIONS AND OTHER AGENCIES

Documents jointly issued by Central Ministries and Commissions

Internal Affairs Ministry, MPS, Ministry of Finance, Notice on Several Questions in Drawing up the Plan for Re-education Through Labour, November 1955, discussed in Xia, 2001: 59–60.	Neiwu Bu, Gong'an Bu, Caizheng Bu Guanyu Bianzhi Laodong Jiaoyang Jihua Zhong de Ruogan Wenti de Tongzhi 内务部，公安部，财政部关于编制劳动教养计划中的若干问题的通知
Internal Affairs Ministry, Letter in Response to Two Questions about	Neiwu Bu, Guanyu Laodong Jiaoyang Gongzuo Shang Liangge

RETL Work, 7 January 1958, excerpted in Zuigao Renmin Jianchayuan Jiansuo Jiancha Ting, 1992: 31, 152.	Wenti de Fuhan 内务部关于劳动教养工作上两个问题的复函
Internal Affairs Ministry, MPS, Response to the Work Report on Hubei Province Re-education through Labour, 17 March 1958, excerpted in Zuigao Renmin Jianchayuan Jiansuo Jiancha Ting, 1992: 30–1.	Neiwu Bu, Gong'an Bu, Dui Hubei Sheng Laodong Jiaoyang Gongzuo Baogao de Pifu 内务部，公安部对湖北省劳动教养工作报告的批复
MPS, Ministry of Higher Education, Opinion on Handling Counter-revolutionary and Bad Elements amongst Higher Education Students, 25 August 1964, excerpted in Zuigao Renmin Jianchayuan Jiansuo Jiancha Ting, 1992: 137.	Gong'an Bu Gaodeng Jiaoyu Bu, Guanyu Dui Gaodeng Xuexiao Xuesheng Zhong Fangeming Fenzi, Huai Fenzi de Chuli Yijian 公安部，高等教育部，关于对高等学校学生中反革命分子，坏分子的处意见
MPS, Ministry of Labour and Personnel, Notice on Questions on the Remuneration of Personnel Retained for in-camp Employment after Completion of their Sentence, 4 May 1983, reproduced in Zuigao Renmin Jianchayuan Jiansuo Jiancha Ting, 1992: 223–4.	Gong'an Bu, Laodong Renshibu, Guanyu Xingman Liuchang (chang) Jiuye RenyuanYouguan Daiyu Wenti de Tongzhi 公安部，劳动人事部，关于刑满留场（厂）就业人员有关待遇问题的通知
Supreme People's Court, Supreme People's Procuratorate, MPS, Notice on Questions as to Jurisdiction in handling Bigamy Cases, 26 July 1983, excerpted in Gong'an Bu Fazhisi, 1992: 53.	Zuigao Renmin Fayuan, Zuigao Renmin Jianchayuan, Gong'an Bu Guanyu Chonghun Anjian Guanxia Wenti de Tongzhi 最高人民法院，最高人民检察院，公安部关于重婚案件管辖问题的通知（节录）
MoJ, MPS, Supreme People's Procuratorate, Supreme People's Court, Urgent Notice on Temporarily Halting the Return to Society of Criminals whose Sentence is Complete and Re-education through Labour Personnel whose Time is Complete, 19 August 1983, excerpted in Zuigao Renmin Jianchayuan Jiansuo Jiancha Ting, 1992: 200–1.	Sifa Bu, Gong'an Bu, Zuigao Renmin Jianchayuan, Zuigao Renmin Fayuan, Guanyu dui Fanren Xingman he Laojiao Qiman de Ren Yuan Zanting Fanghui Shehui de Jinji Tongzhi 司法部，公安部，最高人民检察院，最高人民法院'关于对犯人刑满和劳教期满的人员暂停放回 社会的 紧急通知'
MPS, MoJ, Notice on Questions Concerning Re-education through	Gong'an Bu, Sifa Bu, Guanyu Laodong Jiaoyang he Zhuxiao

Labour and the Revocation of the Urban Household Registration of Re-education Through Labour Personnel, 26 March 1984, reproduced in Gong'an Bu Fazhi Si, 1991: 517–8 and excerpted in Zuigao Renmin Jianchayuan Jiansuo Jiancha Ting, 1992: 104–5, 127	Laodong Jiaoyang Renyuan Chengshi Hukou Wenti de Tongzhi 公安部，司法部关于劳动教养和注销劳动教养人员城市户口问题的通知
MPS, Ministry of Civil Affairs, Notice on Strengthening the Work of Detention for Repatriation, 10 May 1984, reproduced in Gong'an Bu Fagui Ju, 1984: 328–9.	Gong'an Bu, Minzheng Bu, Guanyu Jiaqiang Shourong Qiansong Gongzuo de Tongzhi 公安部民 政部关于加强收容遣送工作的通知
Supreme People's Court, Supreme People's Procuratorate, MPS, Opinion on How to Handle Cases Involving Prostitutes, Clients of Prostitutes and Secret Prostitutes, 7 August 1984, reproduced in Renmin Fayuan Chubanshe, 1992: 38.	Zuigao Renmin Fayuan, Zuigao Renmin Jianchayuan, Gong'an Bu, Guanyu Maiyin, Piaochang, Anchang Ying Ruhe Chuli de Yijian 最高人民法院，最高人民检察院，公安部，关于卖淫，嫖 娼，暗娼案件应如何处理的意见
Supreme People's Court Supreme People's Procuratorate, Explanation and Response to Several Questions Concerning the Specific use of law in the Current Handling of Hooliganism Cases, 2 November 1984, excerpted in Renmin Fayuan Chubanshe, 1992: 39.	Zuigao Renmin Fayuan, Zuigao Renmin Jianchayuan, Guanyu Dangqian Banli Liumang Anjian Zhong Juti Yingyong Falü de Ruogan Wenti de Jieda 最高人民法院，最高人民检察院关于当前办理流氓案件中具体应用法律的若干问题解答（节录）
Ministry of Forestry, MPS, Notice on Several Questions on Cases of Illegal Logging and Deforestation that have been transferred to the jurisdiction of Public Security Organs, 20 June 1985, reproduced in Gong'an Bu Fazhisi, 1992: 112–14.	Linye Bu, Gong'an Bu, Guanyu Daofa, Lanfa Senlin Anjian hua gui Gong'an Jiguan Guanxia hou you guan Wenti de Tongzhi 森林部，公安部关于盗伐,滥伐森林案件划归公安机关管辖后有关问题的通知
Supreme People's Court, Supreme People's Procuratorate, MPS, Notice on Strictly Investigating and Prohibiting Gambling Activities, 6 August 1985 (rescinded 13 October 2000), Gong'an Bu Fazhisi, 1992: 64.	Zuigao Renmin Fayuan, Zuigao Renmin Jianchayuan, Gong'an Bu, Guanyu Yange Chajin Dubo Huodong de Tongzhi 最高人民法院，最高人民检察院，公安部关于严格查禁赌博活动的通知
Supreme People's Court, Supreme People's Procuratorate, MPS, Ministry of Civil Affairs, MoJ,	Zuigao Renmin Fayuan, Zuigao Renmin Jianchayuan, Gong'an Bu, Minzheng Bu, Sifa Bu, Weisheng Bu,

Ministry of Health, Secretariat of the Women's Federation, Report on Resolutely Striking Against and Suppressing Prostitution Activities and Preventing the Spread of Sexually Transmitted Diseases, 16 September 1985, excerpted in Chen, 1992: 117–19.	Quanguo Fulian Ji Shuji Chu Guanyu Jianjue Daji Qudi Maiyin Huodong he Fangzhi Xingbing Manyan de Baogao 最高人民法院，最高人民检察院，公安部，民政部，司法部，卫生部，全国妇联及书记处关于坚决打击取缔卖淫活动和防治性病蔓延的报告（节录）
MPS, Ministry of Railways and Ministry of Transportation, Notice on Resolutely Preventing and Striking Against Scalping Vehicle and Boat Ticket Activities, 30 November 1985 (rescinded 13 October 2000), excerpted in Gong'an Bu Fazhisi, 1992: 67.	Gong'an Bu, Tiedao Bu, Jiaotong Bu, Guanyu Jianjue Zhizhi he Daji Daomai Che Chuan Piao Huodong de Tongzhi 公安部，铁道部，交通部关于坚决制止和打击倒卖车船票活动的通知（节录）
Supreme People's Court, Supreme People's Procuratorate, MPS and MoJ Notice on Several Questions to which Attention Must be Paid in Carrying out the Hard Strike against Transient Crime, 23 August 1986, reproduced in Gong'an Bu Fagui Ju, 1986: 101–3.	Zuigao Renmin Fayuan, Zuigao Renmin Jianchayuan, Gong'an Bu, Sifa Bu, Guanyu Zai Daji Liucuan Fanzui Huodong Zhong Xuyao Zhuyi Jige Wenti de Tongzhi 最高人民法院，最高人民检察院，公安部，司法部关于在打击流窜犯罪活动需要注意几个问题的通知
Supreme People's Court, Supreme People's Procuratorate, Supplementary Notice on Questions of the Applicable Law to use in the Handling of Current Theft Cases, 17 September 1986, excerpted in Zuigao Renmin Jianchayuan Jiansuo Jiancha Ting, 1992: 122–3.	Zuigao Renmin Fayuan, Zuigao Renmin Jianchayuan Guanyu Banli Dangqian Daoqie Anjian zhong Shiyong Falü Wenti de Buchong Tongzhi 最高人民 法 院，最高人民检察院关于办理当前盗窃案件中适用法律问题 的补充通知
Supreme People's Procuratorate, MPS, MoJ Notice that Re-education through Labour Personnel Must be Sent to Re-education through Labour Camps According to the Law, 17 Februrary 1987, reproduced in Gong'an Bu Fagui Ju, 1987: 481.	Zuigao Renmin Jianchayuan, Gong'an Bu, Sifa Bu, Guanyu Laojiao Renyuan Yingdang Yilü Song Laodong Jiaoyang Changsuo Shourong de Tongzhi 最高人民检察院，公安部，司法部关于劳教人员应当一律送劳动教养场所收容的通知
Supreme People's Court, Supreme People's Procuratorate, MPS, MoJ, Notice on Striking Hard Against the Criminal Activity of Speculating in and Smuggling Gold, 28 June 1987	Zuigao Renmin Fayuan, Zuigao Renmin Jianchayuan, Gong'an Bu Sifa Bu Guanyu Yanli Daji Daomai Zousi Huangjing Fanzui Huodong de Tongzhi 最高人民法院，最高人民检察院，公安

(rescinded 13 October 2000), excerpted in Zuigao Renmin Jianchayuan Jiansuo Jiancha Ting, 1992: 122.
部，司法部，关于严厉打击倒卖走私黄金犯罪活动的通知

MPS, MoJ, Notice On Questions of Gathering up for Re-education through Labour of Prostitutes and Clients of Prostitutes, 24 August 1987 (rescinded 13 October 2000), reproduced in Gong'an Bu Fazhisi, 1992: 72–3.
Gong'an Bu, Sifa Bu, Guanyu Maiyin Piaosu Renyuan Shourong Laodong Jiaoyang Wenti de Tongzhi 公安部，司法部关于卖淫嫖宿人员收容劳动教养问题的通知

Civil Aviation Bureau, MPS, Notice on Resolutely Prohibiting and Striking Against Scalping Airline Ticket Activity to Ensure the Safety of Air Transportation, 12 January 1988, reproduced in Gong'an Bu Fazhisi, 1992: 78–9.
Minhang Ju, Gong'an Bu, Guanyu Jianjue Zhizhi he Daji Daomai Feiji Piao Huodong Quebao Hangkong Yunche Anquan de Tongzhi 民航局，公安部关于坚决制止和打击倒卖飞机票活动确保航空运车安全的通知

Ministry of Civil Affairs, MPS, State Administration of Industry and Commerce, State Council Religious Affairs Bureau, Notice on Preventing Harm Caused by Feudal Superstitious Activities, 29 May 1989, reproduced in Renmin Fayuan Chubanshe, 1992: 697–9.
Minzheng Bu, Gong'an Bu, Guojia Gongshang Xingzheng Guanli Ju, Guowuyuan Zongjiao Shiwu Ju Guanyu Zhizhi Sangzang Zhong de Fengjian Mixin Huodong de Tongzhi 民政部，公安部，国家工商行政管理局，国务院宗教事务局关于制止丧葬中的封建迷信活动的通知

MPS, Ministry of Finance, Notice issuing the 'Decision on the Scope of Expenditure and Measures for Management of Expenses of Public Security Work', 20 September 1991, reproduced in Gong'an Bu Fazhi Si, 1991: 604–14.
Gong'an Bu, Caizheng Bu, Gong'an Yewufei Kaizhi Fanwei he Guanli Banfa de Guiding 公安部，财政部关于印发'公安业务费开支范围和管理办法的 规定'的通知

Ministry of Health, MPS, Notice on Several Questions on Carrying out Coercive Testing and Treatment for STDs of Prostitutes and Clients of Prostitutes, 16 December 1991, referred to in Xie, 2000: 104–5.
Weisheng Bu, Gong'an Bu Guanyu Dui Maiyin Piaochang Renyuan Qiangzhi Jinxing Xingbing Jiancha Zhiliao Youguan Wenti de Tongzhi 卫生部，公安部关于对卖淫嫖娼人员强制进行性病检查治疗有关问题的 通知

MPS, Ministry of Personnel, Notice issuing the 'Temporary Measures on Testing the Basic Quality of the Public Security Organ Police', 8 May 1997, reproduced in Gong'an Bu Fazhi Si, 1997: 231; and Temporary
Gong'an Bu, Renshi Bu, Guanyu Yinfa 'Gong'an Jiguan Renmin Jingcha Jiben Suzhi Kaoshi Kaohe Zanxing Banfa' de Tongzhi 公安部人事部，关于印发'公安机关人民警察基本素质考试 考核暂行办法'

Measures on Testing the Basic Quality of the Public Security Organ Police, reproduced in Gong'an Bu Fazhi Si, 1997: 232–6.	的通知, 'Gong'an Jiguan Renmin Jingcha Jiben Suzhi Kaoshi Kaohe Zanxing Banfa' 公安机关关于人民警察基本素质考试考核暂行办法
Supreme People's Court, Supreme People's Procuratorate, Explanation Concerning Laws Applicable to Handling Cases of Organising and Employing Heretical Cult Organisations to Commit Crime, 30 October 1999 (in English), reproduced in Chinese in Law Yearbook Editorial Committee, 2000: 597–8.	Zuigao Renmin Fayuan, Zuigao Renmin Jianchayuan, Guanyu Banli Zuzhi he Liyong Xiejiao Zuzhi Fanzui Anjian Juti Yingyong Falü Ruogan Wenti de Jieshi 最高人民法院, 最高人民检察院关于办理组织和利用邪教组织犯罪案件具体应用法律若干问题的解释
Supreme People's Procuratorate, MPS, Notice on Strengthening the Legal Supervision Work of Lock-ups, 12 November 1999, reproduced in Gong'an Bu Fazhi Ju, 1999: 190–3.	Zuigao Renmin Jianchayuan, Gong'an Bu, Guanyu Jiaqiang Kanshousuo Falü Jiandu Gongzuo de Tongzhi 最高人民检察院, 公安部关于加强看守所法律监督工作的通知
MPS, Ministry of Supervision, Ministry of Culture, Administration of Industry and Commerce, Opinion on Launching a Specialist Action to Strengthen Management of Public Entertainment and Service Venues and to Conduct a Severe Strike against Evil Social Influences Including Prostitution and Using Prostitutes, Gambling and Drug Use and Trafficking, 23 June 2000, reproduced in Gong'an Bu Fazhi Ju, 2000: 227–31.	Gong'an Bu, Jiancha Bu, Wenhua Bu Gongshang Ju, Guanyu Kaizhan Jiaqiang Yule Fuwu Changsuo Guanli Yanli Daji Maiyin Piaochang Dubo Xidu Fandu deng Shehui Chou'e Xianxiang Zhuanxiang Xingdong de Yijian 公安部, 监察部, 文化部, 工商局关于开展加强娱乐服务场所管理严厉打击卖淫嫖娼赌博吸毒贩毒等社会丑恶现象专项行动的意见
MPS, Ministry of Supervision, Ministry of Culture, Administration of Industry and Commerce, Plan for a Specialist Action to Rectify and Regularise the Order of Singing and Dancing Entertainment and Service Venues, 11 September 2001, reproduced in Gong'an Bu Fazhi Ju, 2001: 6305.	Gong'an Bu, Jiancha Bu, Wenhua Bu Guojia Gongshang Xingzheng Guanli Zongju, Zhengdun he Guifan Gewu Yule Fuwu Changsuo Chengxu Zhuanxiang Xingdong Fang'an 公安部, 监察部, 文化部, 国家工商管理总局整顿和规范歌舞娱乐服务场所程序专项行动方案

Ministry of Public Security ('MPS')

MPS, (Draft) Temporary Measures on the Management of the Special Population, August 1950, referred to in Yu, 2002: 15.	Gong'an Bu, Guanyu Tezhong Renkou Guanli de Zanxing Banfa 公安部关于特种人口管理的暂行办 法（草案）
MPS, Temporary Regulations on Management of Urban Household Registration, July 1951, referred to in Yu, 2002: 15.	Gong'an Bu, Chengshi Hukou Guanli Zanxing Tiaoli 公安部，城市户口管理暂行条例
MPS, Supplementary Provisions on Ten Specific Policy Issues Concerning Public Security Work to Date, 17 March 1961, approved by the CCPCC on 20 April 1961, excerpted in Zuigao Renmin Jianchayuan Jiansuo Jiancha Ting, 1992: 151.	Gong'an Bu, Guanyu Dangqian Gong'an Gongzuo Shige Juti Zhengce Wenti de Buchong Guiding 公安部关于当前公安工作十个具体政策问题的补充规定
MPS, Response to a Request for Instructions from the Guangdong Provincial Reform Through Labour Office 'Several Questions on Re-education Through Labour Work', 22 January 1962, excerpted in Zuigao Renmin Jianchayuan Jiansuo Jiancha Ting, 1992: 150–1.	Gong'an Bu, Dui Guangdong Sheng Gong'an Ting Laogai Ju 'Guanyu Laojiao Gongzuo Ruogan Wenti de Qingshi' de Pifu 公安部对广东省公安厅劳改局'关于劳教工作若干问题的请示'的批复
MPS, Response to Request for Instructions from Heilongjiang Provincial Public Security Office 'Report Requesting Instructions on Questions about Fixing the Time for Continuing to Keep Re-education Through Labour Elements in Re-education through Labour Teams and Settling Re-education through Labour Personnel after their Release', 20 April 1962, extracted in Zuigao Renmin Jianchayuan Jiansuo Jiancha Ting, 1992: 150.	Gong'an Bu, Dui Heilongjiang Sheng Gong'an Ting 'Guanyu Dui Jixu Liu Budui Laodong Jiaoyang Fenzi Dingqi he Laojiao Renyuan Jiechu Hou Anzhi Wenti de Qingshi Baogao' de Pifu 公安部对黑龙江省公安厅'关于对继续留部队劳动教养分子定期和劳教人员解除后安置问 题的请示报告'的批复
MPS, Approving and Issuing the Opinion of the General Office on Seven Questions on Public Security Work to Date, 13 November 1962, extracted in Zuigao Renmin Jianchayuan Jiansuo Jiancha Ting, 1992: 25–7.	Gong'an Bu, Pizhuan Bangongting Guanyu Dangqian Gong'an Gongzuo Qige Wenti de Yijian 公安部批转办公厅关于当前公安工作七个问题的意见

MPS, Response to Questions Concerning the Scope of Re-education through Labour in the Notice of 10 September, 27 September 1965, excerpted in Zuigao Renmin Jianchayuan Jiansuo Jiancha Ting, 1992: 136–7.	Gong'an Bu, Guanyu Jiuyue Shiri Tongzhi Zhong Youguan Laojiao Fanwei Wenti de Dafu 公安部关于九月十日通知中有关劳教范围问题的答复
MPS, Notice on Temporarily Halting the Release of Criminal Elements from Reform through Labour Units during the Period of the Cultural Revolution, 14 October 1966, extracted in Zuigao Renmin Jianchayuan Jiansuo Jiancha Ting, 1992: 203.	Gong'an Bu, Guanyu Zai Wenhua Dageming Qijian Laogai Danwei Zanting Jiefang Fanzui Fenzi de Tongzhi 公安部关于在文化大革命期间劳改单位暂停解放犯罪分子的通知
MPS, Summary of Minutes of the Fifteenth National Public Security Conference, 26 February 1971, extracted in Zuigao Renmin Jianchayuan Jiansuo Jiancha Ting, 1992: 24.	Gong'an Bu, Di Shiwuci Quanguo Gong'an Huiyi Jiyao 第十五次全国公安会议纪要
MPS, Notice on Doing a Good Job of Ferreting out Floating Criminals during the New Year and Spring Festival Period, December 1975, referred to in Cui, 1993b: 91.	Gong'an Bu, Guanyu Zuohao Yuandan, Chunjie Qijian Qingcha Liucuan Fan Gongzuo de Tongzhi 公安部，关于作好元旦，春节期间清查流窜犯工作的通知
MPS, Notice issuing the Third Bureau 'Report of the Meeting on Strengthening the Struggle Against Transient Crime', 1 July 1980, excerpted in Zuigao Renmin Jianchayuan Jiansuo Jiancha Ting, 1992: 135–6.	Gong'an Bu, Zhuanfa San Ju 'Guanyu Jiaqiang dui Liucuan Fanzui Douzheng Zuotanhui de Baogao' de Tongzhi 公安部转发三局'关于加强对流窜犯罪斗争座谈会 的报告'
MPS, Response to a Request for Instructions on Questions about Taking in (people) for RETL from Counties and Towns and Operating RETL Camps in Districts and Regions, 31 July 1980 (rescinded 5 April 2001), reproduced in Gong'an Bu Fagui Ju, 1980: 240–1.	Gong'an Bu, Guanyu Xian, Zhen Shourong Laodong Jiaoyang he Di Qu Juban Laodong Jiaoyang Changsuo Wenti de Pifu 公安部关于县，镇收容劳动教养和地区举办劳动教养场所问题的批复
MPS, Report on Doing Well the Work of Re-education through Labour, 9 August 1980, excerpted in Gong'an Bu Fagui Ju, 1980: 243–7.	Gong'an Bu, Guanyu Zuohao Laodong Jiaoyang Gongzuo de Baogao 公安部关于做好劳动教养工作的报告

MPS, Notice on Resolutely Prohibiting Prostitution Activities, 10 June 1981, excerpted in Zhonghua Renmin Gong'an Bu, 1994: 1148–50.	Gong'an Bu, Guanyu Jianjue Zhizhi Maiyin Huodong de Tongzhi 公安部关于坚决制止卖淫活动的通知
MPS, Notice on Questions about the Age of Re-education Through Labour Personnel, 30 November 1981 (rescinded 5 April 2001), excerpted in Zuigao Renmin Jianchayuan Jiansuo Jiancha Ting, 1992: 131.	Gong'an Bu, Guanyu Laodong Jiaoyang Renyuan Nianling Wenti de Tongzhi 公安部关于劳动教养人员年龄问题 的通知
MPS, Temporary Measures on Re-education through Labour, 21 January 1982 ('Temporary Measures') (issued by the State Council and passed by the MPS), reproduced in Wang, Huaian, 1989: 1583–9.	Gong'an Bu, Laodong Jiaoyang Shixing Banfa 劳动教养试行办法
MPS, Circular on the Circumstances of the Hard Strike against Backbone Elements of Reactionary Secret Societies Active in Carrying out Wrecking Activities, 1 August 1983, excerpted in Gong'an Bu Fazhisi, 1992: 111.	Gong'an Bu, Guanyu Yanli Daji you Xianxing Pohuai Huodong de Fandong Huidaomen Gugan Fenzi de Qingkuang Tongbao 公安部关于严厉打击有现行破坏活动的反动会道门骨干分子的情况通报
MPS, Notice on Strengthening the Management Work of Detention Centres and Detention for Investigation Centres, 23 November 1983, reproduced in Gong'an Bu Yushen Ju, 1985.	Gong'an Bu, Guanyu Jiaqiang Juliu Suo, Shoushen Suo Guanli Gongzuo de Tongbao 公安部关于加强拘留所，收审所管理工作的通报
MPS, Notice on Earnestly Doing a Good Job of the Living Conditions of Detainees in Lock-ups, Administrative Detention Centres and Detention for Investigation Centres, issued on 18 December 1983, reproduced in Gong'an Bu Yushen Ju, 1985: 191 (and photocopy materials pp. 24–5).	Gong'an Bu, Guanyu Renzhen Gaohao Kanshousuo, Juliusuo, Shoushenzhan Guanya Renyuan Shenghuoli de Tongzhi 公安部关于认真搞好看守所，拘留所，收审站关押人员生活里的通知
MPS, Notice on Transferring Leadership of Detention for Investigation Centres to the	Gong'an Bu, Guanyu Shourong Shencha Suo Jiaoyou Yushen Bumen Lingdao de Tongzhi

Preliminary Interrogation Division, 20 December 1983 (reproduced in photocopy materials pp. 26–7).	公安部关于收容审查所交由于预审部门领导的通知
MPS, Response to a Request for Instructions on the Scope of Power for Detention for Investigation, 20 January 1984 (reproduced in photocopy materials p. 31).	Gong'an Bu, Guanyu Shoushen Quanxian de Pifu 公安部关于收审权限的批复
MPS, Regulations on Management Work of the Focal Population, March 1985, referred to in Zhi'an Guanli Bianxie Zu, 1992: 56.	Gong'an Bu, Zhongdian Renkou Guanli Gongzuo Guiding 公安部重点人口管理工作规定
MPS, Temporary Regulations on the Management of Temporary Residents in Cities and Towns, 13 July 1985, reproduced in Chen, 1992: 368–9.	Gong'an Bu, Guanyu Chengzhen Zanzhu Renkou Guanli Zanxing Guiding 公安部关于城镇暂住人口管理的暂行规定
MPS, Notice on Strictly Controlling the Use of Detention for Investigation Measures, 31 July 1985, reproduced in Gong'an Bu Yushen Ju, 1985: 229–31 and Gong'an Bu Fagui Ju, 1985: 263–5.	Gong'an Bu, Guanyu Yange Kongzhi Shiyong Shourong Shencha Shouduan de Tongzhi 公安部关于严格控制使用收容审查手段的通知
MPS, Notice on Strengthening the Public Order Management of the Hotel Industry, 7 July 1986, reproduced in Renmin Fayuan Chubanshe, 1992: 49–50.	Gong'an Bu, Guanyu Jiaqiang Lüguan Hangye Zhi'an Guanli Gongzuo de Tongzhi 公安部关于加强旅馆行业治安管理工作的通知
Notice on Immediately and Conscientiously Rectifying Detention for Investigation Work, 31 July 1986, reproduced in Gong'an Bu Fagui Ju, 1986: 381–2 and Wang, Huaian, 1989: 1572.	Gong'an Bu, Guanyu Liji Renzheng Zhengdun Shourong Shencha Gongzuo de Tongzhi 公安部关于立即认真整顿收容审查工作的通知
MPS, Temporary Regulations on Guarantors and Surety Monies in Public Order Administrative Punishments, passed on 20 December 1986 to take effect on 1 January 1987, reproduced in Gong'an Bu Fagui Ju, 1986: 175–7.	Gong'an Bu, Guanyu Zhi'an Guanli Chufa Zhong Danbao Ren he Baozheng Jin de Zanxing Guiding 公安部关于治安管理处罚中担保人和保证金的暂行规定
Notice on the Inappropriateness of Publicly Reporting Detention for Investigation, 27 January 1987, reproduced in Gong'an Bu Fagui Ju, 1987: 511–12.	Gong'an Bu, Guanyu Buyi Gongkai Baodao Shourong Shencha de Tongzhi 公安部关于不宜公开报道收容审查的通知

MPS, Measures on Managing Public Order in the Hotel Industry, issued by the MPS on 10 November 1987 and approved by the State Council on 23 September 1987, reproduced in Gong'an Bu Fagui Ju, 1987: 187–90 and Wang, Huaian, 1989: 1559–60.

Gong'an Bu, Lüguan Ye Zhi'an Guanli Banfa 公安部旅馆业治安管理办法

MPS, Summary of Minutes of Meeting on Further Attacking and Suppressing Prostitution and Using Prostitutes and Doing a Good Job of Detention for Education Work, May 1988, referred to in Ke, 1994: 48.

Gong'an Bu, Jinyibu Daji Qudi Maiyin Piaochang Huodong de Zuohao Shourong Jiaoyu Gongzuo Zuotanhui Jiyao 公安部进一步打击取缔卖淫嫖娼活动的做好收容教育工作座谈会 纪要

MPS, Response to a Request for Instructions on Taking in for RETL those Unlawful Elements who Illegally Scalp Tickets Allocated under the Plan who have been Repeatedly Educated and Will Not Reform, 29 December 1988 (rescinded 5 April 2001), reproduced in Gong'an Bu Fagui Ju, 1988: 166 and excerpted in Zuigao Renmin Jianchayuan Jiansuo Jiancha Ting, 1992: 119–20.

Gong'an Bu, Guanyu dui Feifa Daomai Gezhong Piaozheng er you Lüjiao Bugai de Weifa Fenzi Geiyu Shourong Laodong Jiaoyang 公安部关于对非法倒卖各种票证而又屡教不改的违法分子给与收容劳动教养

MPS, Response to a Request for Instructions as to Whether it is Appropriate to Delegate the Examination and Approval Authority for Re-education through Labour to the District or County-level Public Security Bureaux, 6 July 1989, reproduced in Gong'an Bu Fagui Ju, 1989: 387.

Gong'an Bu, Guanyu Kefou Jiang Laodong Jiaoyang Shenpi Quan Weituo Quxian Gong'an Ju Xingshi Wenti de Pifu 公安部关于可否将劳动教养审批权委托区县公安局行使问题的批复

MPS, Notice Issuing the 'Proposal for Carrying out a Nationwide Campaign for the Eradication of Prostitution and Using Prostitutes etc. 'Six Evils', 21 November 1989, reproduced in Chen, 1992: 145. Proposal for Carrying out a Nationwide Campaign for the Eradication of Prostitution and Using Prostitutes etc. 'Six Evils', reproduced in Chen, 1992: 146–9.

Gong'an Bu, Yinfa 'Guanyu Zai Quanguo Kaizhan Saochu Maiyin Piaochang deng 'Liu Hai' Tongyi Xingdong de Fang'an' 公安部印发'关于在全国开展扫除卖淫嫖娼等'六害'统一行动的方案'的通知, 关于在全国开展扫除卖淫嫖娼等'六害'统一行动的方案

Measures for Trial Implementation on the Work of the Complaints Reporting Centre, 3 May 1990, reproduced in Gong'an Bu Fazhi Si, 1990: 455–7.	Gong'an Bu, Jubao Zhongxin Gongzuo Shixing Banfa 公安部举报中心工作实行办法
MPS, Notice on Deepening the Struggle to Eliminate the 'Six Evils' strictly on the basis of law and implementing policy, 7 May 1990, reproduced in Gong'an Bu Fazhi Si, 1990: 231–8.	Gong'an Bu, Guanyu Yange Yifa Banshi, Zhixing Zhengce, Shenru Kaizhan Chu 'Liu Hai' Douzheng de Tongzhi 公安部关于严格依法办事，执行政策，深入开展除'六害'斗争的通知
MPS, Notice on Several Questions about the Implementation of the 'Administrative Litigation Law' by Public Security Organs, 30 October 1990, reproduced in Huang, 1993: 667–70.	Gong'an Bu, Guanyu Gong'an Jiguan Guanche Shishe 'Xingzheng Susong Fa' Ruogan Wenti de Tongzhi 公安部关于公安机关贯彻实施'行政诉讼法'若干问题的通知
MPS, Supervision Bureau System for Reporting Cases of Police Officers' Unlawful Conduct and Breaches of Discipline, 29 December 1990, reproduced in Gong'an Bu Fazhi Si, 1990: 458–60.	Gong'an Bu, Gong'an Ganjing Weifa Weiji Anjian Baogao Zhidu 公安干警违法违纪案件报告制度
MPS, Notice on Further Controlling the Use of Detention for Investigation Measures, 11 June 1991, reproduced in Gong'an Bu Fazhi Si, 1991: 520–2.	Gong'an Bu, Guanyu Jinyibu Kongzhi Shiyong Shourong Shencha Shouduan de Tongzhi 公安部进一步控制使用收容审查手段的通知
MPS, Notice on Conscientiously Implementing the NPCSC 'Decision on Strictly Prohibiting Prostitution and Using Prostitutes', 23 November 1991, reproduced in Gong'an Bu Fazhi Si, 1991: 318–22 and Zhonghua Renmin Gong'an Bu, 1994: 1152–6.	Gong'an Bu, Guanyu Renzhen Guanche Zhixing Quanguo Renmin Daibiao Dahui Changwu Weiyuanhui 'Guanyu Yanjin Maiyin Pioachang de Jueding' de Tongzhi 公安部关于认真贯彻执行全国人民代表大会常务委员会'关于严禁卖淫嫖娼的决定'的通知
MPS, Notice on Urgently Rectifying the Abuse of Detention for Investigation Measures, 15 February 1992, reproduced in Gong'an Bu Fazhi Si, 1992: 469–72.	Gong'an Bu, Guanyu Jianjue Jiuzheng Lanyong Shoushen Shouduan de Tongzhi 公安部关于坚决纠正滥用收审手段的通知
MPS, Notice on Further Eradicating Repulsive Social Phenomena such as Drug Trafficking and Prostitution,	Gong'an Bu, Guanyu Jinyibu Saochu Fandu Maiyin Deng Shehui Chou'e Xianxiang de Tongzhi

7 March 1992, reproduced in Gong'an Bu Fazhi Si, 1992: 77–81.	公安部关于进一步扫除贩毒，卖淫等社会丑恶现象的通知
MPS, Notice on Changing the Responsibility and Leadership for Examination and Approval of Re-education through Labour to the Legal Department, 9 March 1992, reproduced in Gong'an Bu Fazhi Si, 1992: 474.	Gong'an Bu, Guanyu Laodong Jiaoyang Shenpi Gongzuo Gai Yu Fazhi Si Zeren Zhidao de Tongzhi 公安部关于劳动教养审批工作改与法制司责任指导的通知
MPS, Response to a Request for Instructions on Sending Drug Users to Re-education through Labour, 27 March 1992, reproduced in Gong'an Bu Fazhi Si, 1992: 475.	Gong'an Bu, Guanyu dui Xiduzhe Song Laodong Jiaoyang Wenti de Pifu 公安部关于对吸毒者送劳动教养问题的批复
MPS, Notice on Strictly Prohibiting Public Security Organs from Interfering in Economic Disputes and Illegally Seizing People, 25 April 1992, reproduced in Gong'an Bu Fazhi Si, 1992: 148–50.	Gong'an Bu, Guanyu Yanjin Gong'an Jiguan Chashou Jingji Jiufen Weifa Zhuaren de Tongzhi 公安部关于严禁公安机关插手经济纠纷违法抓人的通知
MPS, Notice on Amending the Procedural Regulations for Appeal for Prostitutes and Clients of Prostitutes who are dissatisfied with a Decision on Detention for Education, 14 August 1992, reproduced in Zhonghua Renmin Gong'an Bu, 1994: 1157.	Gong'an Bu, Guanyu Xiugai Maiyin Piaochang Renyuan bu Fu Shourong Jiaoyu de Shensu Chengxu Guiding de Tongzhi 公安部关于修改卖淫嫖娼人员不服收容教育的申诉程序规定的通知
MPS, Notice on Strengthening the Work of Management of the 'Three Detention (Centres)' and putting an end to situations where Detainees get Beaten to Death, 22 April 1993, reproduced in Gong'an Bu Fazhi Si, 1993: 215–17.	Gong'an Bu, Guanyu Jiaqiang 'Sansuo' Guanli Gongzuo Dujue Zai Ya Renyuan Bei Ouda Zhisi Shijian de Tongzhi 公安部关于加强'三所'管理工作杜绝在押人员被殴打致死 事件的通知
MPS, Notice Reiterating the Resolute Prohibition on Public Security Organs from the Unprincipled Imposition of Fees, Fines and Exactions, 7 June 1993, reproduced in Gong'an Bu Fazhi Si, 1993: 512–14.	Gong'an Bu, Guanyu Chongshen Jianjue Jinzhi Gong'an Jiguan Guanyu Luan Shoufei, Luan Fakuan, Luan Tanpai de Tongzhi 公安部关于重申坚决禁止公安机关 关于乱收费，乱罚款，乱摊派的通知
MPS, Temporary Regulations on a Major Safety Inspection of Public Security Lock-ups and Rostered	Gong'an Bu, Gong'an Jiguan Kanshousuo Anquan Da Jiancha yu Zhiban Xunshi Zanxing Guiding

Inspection Tours, 20 July 1993, reproduced in Gong'an Bu Fazhi Si, 1993: 225–7.	公安部，公安机关看守所安全大检查与值班巡视暂行规定
MPS, Regulation of the Ten Prohibitions for Public Security Organs and Public Security Officers, 24 September 1993, reproduced in Gong'an Bu Fazhi Si, 1993: 525–6.	Gong'an Bu, Gong'an Jiguan he Gong'an Ganjing Shi Buzhun de Guiding 公安部，公安机关和公安干警十不准的规定
MPS, Notice Issuing a Propaganda Outline on the 'PRC People's Police Law', 28 February 1995, reproduced in Gong'an Bu Fazhi Si, 1995: 450; Outline of Information on the PRC People's Police Law reproduced in Gong'an Bu Fazhi Si, 1995: 451–9.	Gong'an Bu, Guanyu Yinfa 'Zhonghua Renmin Gongheguo Renmin Jingcha Fa' Xuanquan Tigang de Tongzhi 公安部关于印发'中华人民共和国人民警察法'宣传提纲的通知 '中华人民共和国人民警察法'宣传提纲
MPS, Temporary Regulations on Public Security Organs Receiving Complaints and Appeals, passed on 11 January 1995 to take effect on 1 May 1995, reproduced in Gong'an Bu Fazhi Si, 1995: 478–82.	Gong'an Bu, Guanyu Shouli Konggao Shensu Zanxing Guiding 公安部关于受理控告申诉暂行规定
MPS, Notice on Prohibiting the Collection of 'Case Handling Fees' by Public Security Organs, 2 May 1995, reproduced in Gong'an Bu Fazhi Si, 1995 440–1.	Gong'an Bu, Guanyu Gong'an Jiguan Yanjin Shouqu 'Ban'an Fei' de Tongzhi 公安部关于公安机关严禁收取'办案费'的通知
MPS, Response to a Request for Instructions on the Question of How to Determine the Nature of and Deal with Oral Sex, Masturbation etc. with Profit as the Motive, 10 August 1995, referred to in Zhu, 2001: 92.	Gong'an Bu 'Guanyu Dui Yi Yingli Wei Mudi de Shouyin, Kouyin Deng Xingwei Dingxing Chuli Wenti de Pifu' 公安部关于对以营利为目的的手淫，口淫等行为定性处理问题的批复
MPS, Temporary Regulations on Training of the Public Security Organs' People's Police, distributed on 16 August 1995, reproduced in Gong'an Bu Fazhi Si, 1995: 393–7.	Gong'an Bu, Gong'an Jiguan Renmin Jingcha Peixun Zanxing Guiding 公安机关人民警察培训暂行规定
MPS, Notice on Several Questions on Implementing 'Measures on Coercive Drug Rehabilitation', 30 May 1996, reproduced in Gong'an Bu Fazhi Si, 1996: 645–9.	Gong'an Bu, Guanyu Guanche Zhixing 'Qiangzhi Jiedu Banfa' You Guan Wenti de Tongzhi 公安部关于贯彻执行'强制戒毒办法'有关问题的通知
MPS, Issuing the '9.5' Opinion on Implementing the Construction of Socialist Spiritual Civilization in the	Gong'an Bu, Guanyu Yinfa 'Jiu wu' Gong'an Jiguan Shehui Zhuyi Jingshen Wenming Jianshe Shishi

Public Security Organs, 15 January 1997, reproduced in Gong'an Bu Fazhi Si, 1997: 244; and '9.5' Opinion on Implementing the Construction of Socialist Spiritual Civilization in the Public Security Organs, reproduced in Gong'an Bu Fazhi Si, 1997: 245–52.	Yijian 公安部关于印发 '九五' 公安机关社会主义精神文明建设实 施意见
MPS, Notice on Actively Accepting the Inspection and Supervision by Congresses and Political Consultative Conferences of the work of Lock-ups, 15 January 1997, reproduced in Gong'an Bu Fazhi Si, 1997: 255–6.	Gong'an Bu, Guanyu Zhudong Jieshou Renda, Zhengxie dui Kanshousuo Gongzuo Jiancha Jiandu Wenti de Tongzhi 公安部关于主动接受人大，政协对看守所工作检查监督问题的通知
MPS, Notice on Strengthening the Investigation and Handling of Public Security Cases, 14 February 1997, reproduced in Gong'an Bu Fazhi Si, 1997: 422–4.	Gong'an Bu, Guanyu Jiaqiang Zhi'an Anjian Chachu Gongzuo de Tongzhi 公安部关于加强治安案件查处工作 的通知
MPS, Notice issuing 'Temporary Regulations on Leadership Accountability in Public Security Organs', 3 April 1997, reproduced in Gong'an Bu Fazhi Si, 1997: 261–4.	Gong'an Bu, Guanyu Yinfa Gong'an Bu, Gong'an Jiguan Zhuijiu Lingdao Zeren Zanxing Guiding' de Tongzhi 公安部公安机关追究领导责任暂行规定的通知
MPS, Notice Implementing the Regulations on Supervision of Public Security Organs, 18 July 1997, reproduced in Gong'an Bu Fazhi Si, 1997: 265–8.	Gong'an Bu, Guanyu Guanche Shishi 'Gong'an Jiguan Ducha Tiaoli' de Tongzhi 公安部关于贯彻实施 '公安机关督察条例' 的通知
MPS, Response to a Request for Instructions on whether it is appropriate to deduct the amount of time spent in criminal detention or public order detention from the time spent in detention for education, 11 December 1997, reproduced in Gong'an Bu Fazhi Si, 1997: 391.	Gong'an Bu, Guanyu Dui Xingshi Juliu, Zhi'an Juliu Qixian Shifou Zhedi Shourong Jiaoyu Qixian Wenti de Pifu 公安部关于对刑事拘留，治安拘留期 限是否折抵收容教育期限问题的批复
MPS, Notice on Problems of Strictly Enforcing the Criminal Procedure Law and the Criminal Law, 23 January 1998, reproduced in Gong'an Bu Fazhi Ju, 1998: 214–17.	Gong'an Bu, Guanyu Yange Zhixing Xingshi Susong Fa, Xingfa Youguan Wenti de Tongzhi 公安部关于严格执行刑事诉讼法，刑法有关问题的通知
MPS, Notice on Conducting a Major Nationwide Investigation into	Gong'an Bu, Guanyu Zai Quanguo Gong'an Jiguan Kaizhan Zhifa Da

Public Security Enforcement and Implementing Concentrated Education and Rectification, 6 March 1998, reproduced in Gong'an Bu Fazhi Ju, 1998: 127–31.	Jiancha he Jingxing Jizhong Zhengdun de Tongzhi 公安部关于在全国公安机关开展执法大检查和进行集中教育整顿的通知
MPS, Response to a Request for Instructions on Determining the Standard to Determine When People who Smoke, Eat or Inject Drugs are Addicted, 22 April 1998, reproduced in Zhonghua Renmin Gongheguo Gong'an Bu, 2005: 2284.	Gong'an Bu Guanyu Xishi Zhushe Dupin Renyuan Chengyin Biaozhun Jieding Wenti de Pifu 公安部关于吸食注射毒品人员成瘾标准界定问题的批复
MPS, Regulations on the Procedures for Handling Criminal Cases, passed on 20 April 1998 to come into effect on 14 May 1998, reproduced in Gong'an Bu Fazhi Ju, 1998: 255–319.	Gong'an Bu, Gong'an Jiguan Banli Xingshi Anjian Chengxu Guiding 公安部公安机关办理刑事案件程序规定
MPS, Notice Issuing the Public Security Supervision Regulations' Standard Form Documents, 19 June 1998, reproduced in Gong'an Bu Fazhi Ju, 1998: 136–9.	Gong'an Bu, Guanyu Yinfa Gong'an Jiancha Falü Wenshu Shiyang de Tongzhi 公安部关于印发公安检查法律文书式样的通知
MPS, Notice Issuing 'Regulations on Public Security Organs Implementing the Prohibitive Measure of Stopping the Performance of Duties', 29 August 1998, reproduced in Gong'an Bu Fazhi Ju, 1998: 163; 'Regulations on Public Security Organs Implementing the Prohibitive Measure of Stopping the Performance of Duties', reproduced in Gong'an Bu Fazhi Ju, 1998: 164–75.	Gong'an Bu, Guanyu Yinfa 'Gong'an Jiguan Shishi Tingzhi Zhixing Zhiwu de Jinbi Cuoshi de Guiding' de Tongzhi 公安部关于印发 '公安机关实施停止执行职务和禁闭措施的规定' 的通知' Gong'an Jiguan Shishi Tingzhi Zhixing Zhiwu de Jinbi Cuoshi de Guiding' de Tongzhi 公安机关实施停止执行职务和禁闭措施的规定
MPS, Notice on Several Questions on the Scope of RETL, 30 November 1998, reproduced in Liu, 2002: 421–2.	Gong'an Bu Guanyu Laodong Jiaoyang Fanwei Youguan Wenti de Tongzhi 公安部关于劳动教养范围有关问题的通知
MPS, Notice on Conscientiously Strengthening the Management of Income of Public Security Organs from Collection of Fees and Fines, 3 January 1999, reproduced in Gong'an Bu Fazhi Ju, 1999: 131–2.	Gong'an Bu, Guanyu Qieshi Jiaqiang Gong'an Jiguan Shoufei he Fa Mei Shouru Guanli de Tongzhi 公安部关于切实加强公安机关收费和罚没收入管理的通知

MPS, Response to a Request for Instructions on Several Questions to do with the Procedure for Examination and Approval of Re-education through Labour, 9 June 1999, reproduced in Gong'an Bu Fazhi Ju, 1999: 602.	Gong'an Bu, Guanyu Shenpi Laodong Jiaoyang Youguan Chengxu Wenti de Pifu 公安部关于审批劳动教养案件有关程序问题的批复
MPS, Notice on General Implementation in Public Security Organs Nationwide of the System of Openness in Police Work, 10 June 1999, reproduced in Hao and Shan, 1999: 329–32.	Gong'an Bu, Guanyu Zai Quanguo Gong'an Jiguan Pubian Shixing Jingwu Gongkai Zhidu de Tongzhi 公安部关于在全国公安机关普遍实行警务公开制度的通知
MPS, Regulations on Holding Public Security Organs' People's Police Accountable for Faults in Enforcement, 11 June 1999, reproduced in Gong'an Bu Fazhi Ju, 1999: 177–82.	Gong'an Bu, Gong'an Jiguan Renmin Jingcha Zhifa Guocuo Zeren Zhuijiu Guiding 公安部公安机关人民警察执法过错责任追究规定
MPS, Regulations on the Work of Internal Supervision of Enforcement in Public Security Organs, 11 June 1999, reproduced in Gong'an Bu Fazhi Ju, 1999: 171–6.	Gong'an Bu, Gong'an Jiguan Neibu Zhifa Jiandu Gongzuo Guiding 公安部公安机关内部执法监督工作规定
MPS, Notice on Further Strengthening Leadership Accountability in Cases of Torture Resulting in Death and the System of Reporting and Self-criticism in these Cases etc., 16 June 1999, reproduced in Gong'an Bu Fazhi Ju, 1999: 183–5.	Gong'an Bu, Guanyu Jinyibu Jiaqiang dui Xingxun Bigong Zhi Ren Siwang Anjian Zhuijiu Lingdao Zeren he Zhuji Huibao Jiantao Deng Xiang Gongzuo de Tongzhi 公安部关于进一步加强对刑讯逼供致人死亡案件追究领导责任和逐级汇报检讨等项工作的通知
MPS, Notice on Establishing and Regularising the Organ for Supervision of Police Work in Public Security Organs at Each Level, 2 August 1999, reproduced in Gong'an Bu Fazhi Ju, 1999: 129–30.	Gong'an Bu, Guanyu Jianli he Guifan Difang Geji Gong'an Jiguan Jingwu Ducha Jigou de Tongzhi 公安部关于建立和规范地方各级公安机关警务督察机构的通知
MPS, Opinion on Several Questions concerning the Implementation by Public Security Organs of the 'PRC Administrative Review Law', 27 September 1999, reproduced in Gong'an Bu Fazhi Ju, 1999: 622–6.	Gong'an Bu, Guanyu Gong'an Jiguan Guanche Shishi 'Zhonghua Renmin Gongheguo Xingzheng Fuyi Fa' Ruogan Wenti de Yijian 公安部关于公安机关贯彻实施'中华人民共和国行政复议法'若干问题的意见

MPS, Notice on Implementing the Central Political-Legal Committee's 'Research Opinion on the Problems of RETL', 14 October 1999, reproduced in Liu, 2002: 444–5.	Gong'an Bu Guanyu Guanche Zhongyang Zhengfa Weiyuanhui 'Guanyu Dui Laodong Jiaoyang Wenti de Yanjiu Yijian' de Tongzhi 公安部关于贯彻中央政法委员会'关于对劳动教养问题的研究意见'的通知
MPS, Notice on Implementing the 'State Council Decision on Comprehensively Carrying Forward Administration According to Law', 23 February 2000, reproduced in Gong'an Bu Fazhi Ju, 2000: 367–73.	Gong'an Bu, Guanyu Guanche Luoshi 'Guowuyuan Guanyu Quanguo Tuijin Yifa Xingzheng de Jueding' de Tongzhi 公安部关于贯彻落实'国务院关于全面推进依法行政 的决定'的通知
MPS, Notice on Adopting Thoroughly Effective Measures to Resolve the Problem of Incorrect Statistics, 3 March 2000, reproduced in Gong'an Bu Fazhi Ju, 2000: 304–7.	Gong'an Bu, Guanyu Caiqu Youli Cuoshi Cong Genben Shang Jiuzheng Tongji Bushi Wenti de Tongzhi 公安部关于采取有力措施从根本上纠正统计不实问题的通知
MPS, Measures for Management of Coercive Drug Rehabilitation Centres, passed on 30 March 2000 to take effect on 17 April 2000, reproduced in Gong'an Bu Fazhi Ju, 2000: 804–13.	Gong'an Bu, Qiangzhi Jiedu Suo Guanli Banfa 公安部强制戒毒所管理办法
MPS, Measures for the Management of Detention for Education Camps, passed on 30 March 2000 to take effect on 24 April 2000 reproduced in Gong'an Bu Fazhi Ju, 2000: 814–24.	Gong'an Bu, Shourong Jiaoyu Suo Guanli Banfa 公安部收容教育所管理办法
MPS, Notice on Strengthening the Work of Registration of Drug Users, 23 May 2000, reproduced in Zhonghua Renmin Gongheguo Gong'an Bu, 2005: 2286.	Gong'an Bu Guanyu Jiaqiang Xidu Renyuan Dengji Gongzuo de Tongzhi 公安部关于加强吸毒人员登记工作的通知
MPS, Decision on Strengthening Construction of the Public Security Legal System, 3 June 2000, reproduced in Gong'an Bu Fazhi Ju, 2000: 374–80.	Gong'an Bu, Guanyu Jiaqiang Gong'an Fazhi Jianshe de Jueding 公安部关于加强公安法制建设的决定
MPS, Notice on Putting in Order and Rectifying Coercive Drug Rehabilitation Centres, 21 June 2000, reproduced in Gong'an Bu Fazhi Ju, 2000: 412–19.	Gong'an Bu, Guanyu Qingli Zhengdun Qiangzhi Jiedu Suo de Tongzhi 公安部关于清理整顿强制戒毒所的通知

MPS, Procedural Regulations for Handling Administrative Review Cases, 24 October 2000, reproduced in Gong'an Bu Fazhi Ju, 2000: 912–14. (Note: replaced by regulations of the same name on 1 January 2003.) — Gong'an Bu, Banli Xingzheng Fuyi Anjian Chengxu Guiding 公安部办理行政复议案件程序规定

MPS, Measures Evaluating the Grade of Detention for Education Camps, 27 November 2000, reproduced in Gong'an Bu Fazhi Ju, 2000: 348–62. — Gong'an Bu, Shourong Jiaoyu Dengji Pingding Banfa 公安部收容教育等级评定办法

MPS, Measures on Implementing the Regulations on Supervision of Public Security Organs, 2 January 2001, reproduced in Zhou, 2005: 231–41. — Gong'an Bu Guanyu Jiancha Tiaoli Shishi Banfa 公安部关于检查条例实施办法

MPS, Regulation on Examination and Appraisal of the Quality of Law Enforcement, 10 October 2001, reproduced in Zhou, 2005: 258–62. — Gong'an Bu Guanyu Zhifa Zhiliang Kaoshi Pingyi Guiding 公安部关于执法质量考核评议规定

MPS, Response to a Request for Instructions on the Question of How to Determine the Nature of and Deal with Sexual Acts between People of the Same Sex with Money and Property as the Intermediary, 28 December 2001, reproduced at http://gaj.fuyang.gov.cn/news/ZCWJ_5867/20048234842.aspx, accessed on 17 July 2006. — Gong'an Bu Guanyu Dui Tongxing Zhijian Yi Qiancai Wei Meijie de Xing Xingwei Dingxing Chuli Wenti de Pifu 公安部关于对同性之间以钱财为媒介的性行为定性处理问题的批复

MPS, Response to a Request for Instructions on Whether or Not the 'Security Administrative Punishments Regulations' can act as a Basis for Examination and Approval of RETL, 31 May 2002, reproduced in Gong'an Bu Fazhi Ju, 2002: 533. — Gong'an Bu Guanyu 'Zhi'an Guanli Chufa Tiaoli' Nengfou Zuowei Laodong Jiaoyang Shenpi Yiju Wenti de Pifu 公安部关于'治安管理处罚条例'能否作为劳动教养审批依据问题的 批复

MPS, Regulations on Public Security Organs Handling Re-education through Labour Cases, 1 June 2002 (the 'RETL Regulations'), reproduced in Gong'an Bu Fazhi Ju, 2002: 509–31 and Xing, 2002: 216–36. — Gong'an Bu, Gong'an Jiguan Banli Laodong Jiaoyang Anjian Guiding 公安部公安机关办理劳动教养案件规定

MPS, Notice on Rescinding a Proportion of Normative Documents on Re-education through Labour, 20 September 2002, reproduced in Gong'an Bu Fazhi Ju, 2002: 534–47.	Gong'an Bu Guanyu Feizhi Bufen Youguan Laodong Jiaoyang de Guifanxing Wenjian de Tongzhi 公安部关于废止部分关于劳动教养的规范性文件的通知
MPS, Procedural Regulations for Handling Administrative Review Cases, passed on 10 October 2002 to take effect on 1 January 2003, reproduced in Gong'an Bu Fazhi Ju, 2002: 549–67.	Gong'an Bu, Banli Xingzheng Fuyi Anjian Chengxu Guiding 公安部办理行政复议案件程序规定
MPS, Regulations on the Procedures for Handling Administrative Cases by Public Security Organs, passed on 26 August 2003 to take effect on 1 January 2004, reproduced in Zhou, 2005: 310–39.	Gong'an Bu, Gong'an Jiguan Banli Xingzheng Anjian Chengxu Guiding 公安部公安机关办理行政案件程序规定
MPS, Notice Issuing 'Work Plan for Resolving Acute Problems of Law Enforcement and Promoting the Construction of the Law Enforcement System of the Public Security Organs', 15 June 2004, reproduced in Gong'an Bu Fazhi Ju, 2004: 281–3.	Gong'an Bu Guanyu Yinfa 'Guanyu Jiejue Zhifa Tuchu Wenti Tuijin Gong'an Zhifa Zhidu Jianshe de Gongzuo Jihua' de Tongzhi 公安部关于印发'关于解决执法突出问题推进公安执法制度建设的工作计划'的通知
MPS, Opinion on Public Security Organs Implementing 'Outline on Comprehensively Carrying Forward Implementation of Administration According to Law', 2 July 2004, reproduced in Gong'an Bu Fazhi Ju, 2004: 294–9.	Gong'an Bu Gong'an Jiguan Guanche Shishi 'Quanmian Tuijin Yifa Xingzheng Shishi Gangyao' de Yijian 公安部公安机关贯彻实施'全面推进依法行政是实纲要'的意见
MPS, Notice on Retention, Amendment and Recission of Departmental Rules and Normative Documents, 19 August 2004, reproduced in Gong'an Bu Fazhi Ju, 2004: 300–477.	Gong'an Bu Guanyu Baoliu Xiugai Feizhi Bumen Guizhang Ji Guifanxing Wenjian de Tongzhi 公安部关于保留修改废止部门规章及规范性文件

Documents issued by other organs within the MPS, other documents

Northeast Public Security Central Office, Measures on Temporary Management of Household Registration, June 1948, cited in Xi and Yu, 1996: 171.	Dongbei Gong'an Zongchu Guanyu Hukou Zanxing Guanli Banfa 东北公安总处'关于户口暂行管理办法'

MPS Party Group, Regulations on the Policy Limits for Handling Criminal Elements Committing Theft, Hooliganism, Fraud, Homicide, Robbery etc., 23 July 1957, excerpted in Zuigao Renmin Jianchayuan Jiansuo Jiancha Ting, 1992: 144–5.	Gong'an Bu Dangzu Guanyu Chuli Daoqie, Liumang, Zhapian, Xiongsha, Qiangjie Deng Xingshi Fanzui Fenzi Zhengce Jiexian de Guiding 公安部党组关于处理盗窃，流氓，诈骗，凶杀，抢劫等刑事犯罪分子政策界限的规定
Ninth National Public Security Conference on Step by Step Strengthening the Work of Reforming the Five Categories of Elements; Landlords, the Wealthy, Counter-Revolutionaries, Bad Elements and Rightists, 16 August 1958, excerpted in Zuigao Renmin Jianchayuan Jiansuo Jiancha Ting, 1992: 29.	Di Jiuci Quanguo Gong'an Huiyi Guanyu Jinyibu Jiaqiang dui Di, Fu, Fan, Huai, You Wu Lei Fenzi Gaizao de Jueyi 第九次全国公安会议'关于进一步加强对地，富，反，坏，右五类分子改造工作的决议'
Ninth National Public Security Conference approving 'Several Questions on Public Security Work (Draft)', 16 August 1958, excerpted in Zuigao Renmin Jianchayuan Jiansuo Jiancha Ting, 1992: 29–30.	Di Jiuci Quanguo Gong'an Huiyi Pizhun 'Gong'an Gongzuo de Yixie Wenti (Cao'an)' 第九次全国公安会议批准'公安工作的一些问题（草案）'
Legal Division of the MPS, Letter of Response to the Jiangxi Provincial Re-education through Labour Management Committee 'Request for Instructions on Two Questions about RETL Examination and Approval Work', 28 March 1990, reproduced in Gong'an Bu Fazhisi, 1992: 121.	Gong'an Bu Fazhi Si, Dui Jiangxi Sheng Laodong Jiaoyang Guanli Weiyuanhui 'Guanyu Laodong Jiaoyang Shenpi Gongzuo Liang ge Wenti de Qingshi' de Fuhan 公安部法制司对江西省劳动教养管理委员会'关于劳动教养审批工作两个问题 的请示'的复函
Legal Division of the MPS, Response to a Request for Instructions to the Hainan Provincial Public Security Office 'Request for Instructions on whether Rural Unemployed who commit many offences but which are still not sufficient to pursue criminal liability can be taken in for Re-education through Labour', 7 June 1990, reproduced in Gong'an Bu Fazhisi, 1992: 124–5.	Gong'an Bu Fazhi Si, Dui Hainan Sheng Gong'an Ting 'Guanyu Jiaju Nongcun, Duoci Zuo'an, Shangbugou Zhuiqiu Xingshi Zeren de Weifa Renyuan Keshou Laodong Jiaoyang de Qingshi' de Pifu 公安部法制司对海南省公安厅'关于家居农村，多次作案，尚不够追求刑事责任的违法人员可收容劳动教养的请示'的批复

Legal Division of the MPS, Response to a Request for Instructions on Whether a Person who Repeatedly Prostitutes or Uses Prostitutes but has not been dealt with by the Public Security Organs can be sent to RETL, 4 September 1997, reproduced in Liu, 2002: 419.
Gong'an Bu Fazhi Si, Guanyu Duoci Maiyin, Piaochang Wei Bei Gong'an Jiguan Chuli de Nengfou Shixing Laodong Jiaoyang de Dafu
公安部法制司关于多次卖淫嫖娼未被公安机关处理的能否实行劳动教养的答复

MPS, Plan for Specific Revision of Provisions of the Criminal Procedure Law Relevant to the Public Security Organs (Draft Soliciting Opinions), no date (photocopy materials).
Gong'an Bu, Xingshi Susong Fa Zhong yu Gong'an Jiguan Xiangguan Tiaokuan de Juti Xiugai Fang'an) (Zhengqiu Yijian Gao)
公安部刑事诉讼法中与公安机关相关条款的具体修改方案（征求意见稿）

Administrative rules issued by other government departments

Ministry of Internal Affairs, Directive on Implementing the Work of Strict Prohibition of Drug Taking, 12 September 1950, cited in Ma, Weigang, 1993a: 55–6.
Neiwu Bu Guanyu Guanche Yanjin Yandu Gongzuo de Zhishi
内务部关于贯彻严禁烟毒工作的 指示

Ministry of the Interior, Instructions Relating to the Work of Placement and Reform of City Vagrants, 11 July 1956 (in English), translated and reproduced in Cohen, 1966: 244–8.

Ministry of Internal Affairs, Letter in Response to Two Questions about RETL Work, 7 January 1958, extracted in Zuigao Renmin Jianchayuan Jiansuo Jiancha Ting, 1992: 31.
Neiwu Bu, Guanyu Laodong Jiaoyang Gongzuo Shang Liangge Wenti de Fuhan
内务部关于劳动教养工作上两个问 题的复函

MoJ, Response to a Request for Instructions on Extending the time for Re-education through Labour, 27 July 1991, reproduced in Gong'an Bu Fazhi Si, 1991: 523.
Sifa Bu, Guanyu Yanchang Laodong Jiaoyang Qi Wenti de Pifu 司法部，关于延长劳动教养期问题的批复

MoJ, Opinion on Strengthening the Construction of Judicial Offices, June 1996, referred to in Cheng, 2004: 152–3.
Sifa Bu, Guanyu Jiaqiang Sifa Suo Jianshe de Yijian 司法部，关于加强司法所建设的意见

MoJ, Regulations on Re-education through Labour Drug Rehabilitation Work, issued on 20 May 2003 to take
Sifa Bu, Laodong Jiaoyang Jiedu Gongzuo Guiding
司法部劳动教养戒毒工作规定

effect from 1 August 2003, accessed at www.legalinfo.gov.cn/moj/ldjyglj/2003-06/10/content_31260.htm.

PROVINCIAL REGULATIONS AND RULES

Provincial people's congresses

Beijing People's Congress, Resolution on Closing Brothels, 21 November 1949, referred to in Ma, 1994: 57.	Beijing Shi Renmin Daibiao Dahui, Guanyu Fengbi Jiyuan de Jueyi 北京市人民代表大会关于封闭妓院 的决议
Guangdong Province Regulations on Suppressing Prostitution, Using Prostitutes and Secret Prostitution, 19 June 1987, reproduced in Renmin Fayuan Chubanshe, 1992: 65–7.	Guangdong Sheng Guanyu Qudi Maiyin, Piaochang Anchang de Guiding 广东省关于取缔卖淫，嫖娼暗娼的规定

Provincial governments

Guangdong Province People's Government Temporary Regulations on Prohibition of Traffic in and Use of Drugs, 7 August 1981, reproduced in Renmin Fayuan Chubanshe, 1992: 480–1.	Guangdong Sheng Renmin Zhengfu, Guanyu Jinzhi Fandu Xidu de Zanxing Guiding 广东省人民政府关于禁止贩毒吸毒 的暂行规定
Fujian People's Government Announcement on Striking Against and Suppressing Prostitution and Using Prostitutes, 20 January 1986, excerpted in Chen, 1992: 120.	Fujian Sheng Renmin Zhengfu, Guanyu Daji, Qudi Maiyin Piaochang Huodong de Tonggao 福建省人民政府关于打击取缔卖淫嫖娼活动的通知
Temporary Regulations of Guangdong Province on Carrying out Detention for Education of Prostitutes and Users of Prostitutes etc., Seven Types of Offenders, 1989, discussed in Ke, 1994: 48.	Guangdong Sheng, Dui Maiyin Piaochang Deng Qi zhong Weifa Renyuan Shixing Shourong Jiaoyu de Zanxing Guiding 广东省对卖淫嫖娼等七种违法人员实行收容教育的暂行规定
Fujian People's Government, Fujian Province Temporary Regulations on Detention for Education of Female Prostitutes, 13 October, 1990, reproduced in Chen, 1992: 285–8.	Fujian Sheng, Shourong Jiaoyu Maiyin Funü Zanxing Guiding 福建省收容教育卖淫妇女暂行规定

(Shanghai Municipal Government – not clearly specified in text), Several Regulations on the Work of Detention for Education of Female Prostitutes (no date given), referred to in Mou, 1996: 265.	Guanyu Dui Shourong Jiaoyu Maiyin Funü Gongzuo de Ruogan Guiding 关于对收容教育卖淫妇女工作若 干规定
(Shanghai Municipal Government), Opinion on Handling People who Prostitute and Clients of Prostitutes (no date given), referred to in Mou, 1996: 265.	Guanyu Dui Maiyin Piaochang Renyuan de Chuli Yijian 关于对卖淫嫖娼人员的处理意见

Provincial government departments, jointly issued provincial level documents

Fujian Public Security Bureau, Report on Resolutely Striking Against and Suppressing Prostitution Activities, October 1985, referred to in Mou, 1996: 279.	Fujian Sheng, Gong'an Ting Guanyu Jianjue Daji Qudi Maiyin Huodong de Baogao 福建省公安厅关于坚决打击取缔卖淫活动的报告
Wuhan Municipal Public Security Bureau, Procuratorate and Court Notice on Several Questions on the Work of Handling Cases, 18 August 1981, referred to in Cui, 1992: 19.	Wuhan Shi Gong'an Ju, Jianchayuan, Fayuan Guanyu Ban'an Gongzuo Zhong Jige Youguan Wenti de Tongzhi 武汉市公安局，检察院，法院关于办 案工作中几个有关问题的通知

DOCUMENTS ISSUED BY THE CHINESE COMMUNIST PARTY ('CCP') AND ORGANS OF THE CCP

CCP National Congress

Constitution of the CCP amended at the 16th National Congress on 14 November 2002 (English version from english.peopledaily.com.cn), last accessed on 30 March 2004.

CCP Central Committee ('CCPCC')

CCPCC, Directive on Suppression of Counter-revolutionary Activities, 18 March 1950, referred to in Xia, 2001: 9.	Zhonggong Zhongyang, Guanyu Zhenya Fangeming Huodong de Zhishi 中共中央关于镇压反革命活动的指示

CCPCC, Directive on Suppression of Counter-revolutionary Activities, 10 October 1950, reproduced in Zhonggong Zhongyang Wenxian Yanjiu Shi, 1992a: 420–3.	Zhonggong Zhongyang Guanyu Zhenya Fangeming Huodong de Zhishi 中共中央关于镇压反革命活动的 指示
CCPCC, Approving and Issuing Central Ministry of Public Security 'Report on the Meeting of National Public Security Conference', 28 November 1950, reproduced in Zhonggong Zhongyang Wenxian Yanjiu Shi, 1992a: 441–6.	Zhonggong Zhongyang Pizhuan Zhongyang Gong'an Bu 'Guanyu Quanguo Gong'an Bu Huiyi de Baogao' 中共中央批转公安部 '关于全国公安会议的报告'
CCPCC, Directive on the Question of Labour, Production and Employment of Landlords in Areas where Land Reform is Already Complete, 10 May 1951, reproduced in Zhonggong Zhongyang Wenxian Yanjiu Shi, 1992b: 259–60.	Zhonggong Zhongyang Dui Tudi Gaigeye Yi Wancheng Diqu de Dizhu Canjia Laodong Shengchan Ji Jiuye Wenti de Zhishi 中共中央对土地改革业已完成地区 的地主参加劳动生产及就业问题的 指示
CCPCC, Directive on the Problem of Cleaning up the 'Mid-levels' and 'Internal Levels', 21 May 1951, reproduced in Zhonggong Zhongyang Wenxian Yanjiu Shi, 1992b: 274–8.	Zhonggong Zhongyang Guanyu Qingli 'Zhongceng' "Neiceng' Wenti de Zhishi 中共中央关于清理 '中层' '内层' 问题的指示
CCPCC, Directive on Eradication of the Circulation of Drugs, April 1952, referred to in Ke, 1990: 25.	Zhonggong Zhongyang, Guanyu Suqing Dupin Liuxing de Zhishi 中共中央关于肃清毒品流行的指示
CCPCC, Directive on the Thorough Elimination of Hidden Counter-revolutionaries, 25 August 1955, extracted in Zuigao Renmin Jianchayuan Jiansuo Jiancha Ting, 1992: 38–9.	Zhonggong Zhongyang, Guanyu Chedi Suqing Ancang Fangeming Fenzi de Zhishi 中共中央 '关于彻底肃清暗藏反革命分子 的指示
CCPCC, Directive to Each Province and City Immediately and without Exception to Make Arrangements to Establish Re-education through Labour Organs, 10 January 1956, excerpted in Zuigao Renmin Jianchayuan Jiansuo Jiancha Ting, 1992: 36–7 and Gong'an Bu Fazhisi, 1992: 235–6.	Zhonggong Zhongyang, Guanyu Ge Sheng, Shi Ying Liji Chouban Laodong Jiaoyang Jigou de Zhishi (Jielu) 中共中央关于各省，市应立即筹办 劳动教养机构的指示（节录）
CCPCC Ten-Person Small Group, Temporary Regulations on Policy	Zhonggong Zhongyang Shiren Xiaozu, Guanyu Fangeming Fenzi he

Limits on Identification and Handling of Counter-revolutionary Elements and Other Bad Elements, 10 March 1956, excerpted in Zuigao Renmin Jianchayuan Jiansuo Jiancha Ting, 1992: 146–7.	Qita Huai Fenzi de Jieshi Ji Chuli Zhengce Jiexian de Zanxing Guiding 中共中央批准中央十人小组 '关于反革命分子和其他坏分子的解释及处理的政策界限的暂行 规定'
Response by the CCPCC Ten-Person Small Group to a request for instructions from the Liaoning Provincial Party Committee Five-Person Small Group on Measures on RETL, 6 September 1956, excerpted in Zuigao Renmin Jianchayuan Jiansuo Jiancha Ting, 1992: 34–5.	Zhongyang Shi Ren Xiaozu, Fu Liaoning Shengwei Wuren Xiaozu Guanyu Laodong Jiaoyang Banfa de Qingshi 中央十人小组复辽宁省委五人小组关于劳动教养办法的请示
CCPCC, approving the CCPCC Ten-Person Small Group 'Report to the CCPCC on the Current Situation Regarding the Suppression of Counter-revolutionaries Campaign and 1957 Work', 11 January 1957, excerpted in Zuigao Renmin Jianchayuan Jiansuo Jiancha Ting, 1992: 33–4.	Zhonggong Zhongyang Pizhun Zhongyang Shiren Xiaozu, 'Guanyu Sufan Yundong de Dangqian Qingkuang he 1957 nian de Gongzuo Xiang Zhongyang de Baogao' 中共中央批准中央十人小组 '关于肃反运动的当前情况和一九五七年工作向中央的报告'
CCPCC, approving and issuing the Shanghai Party Committee 'Opinion on Questions about the Settlement of Personnel after Criminal Conviction where Cases were Cleared up or after Serving their Sentence', 6 October 1957, excerpted in Zuigao Renmin Jianchayuan Jiansuo Jiancha Ting, 1992: 142.	Zhongyang Pizhuan Shanghai Shiwei 'Guanyu Qingan Shifang he Xingman Shifang Renyuan Anzhi Wenti' de Yijian 中央批转上海市委 '关于清案释放和刑满释放人员安置问题' 的意见
CCPCC, approving and issuing 'Decision of the National Political-Legal Work Conference on Several Questions of Policy in the Struggle to Date Against Enemies', 20 March 1959, excerpted in Zuigao Renmin Jianchayuan Jiansuo Jiancha Ting, 1992: 28.	Zhonggong Zhongyang, Pizhuan 'Quanguo Zhengfa Gongzuo Huiyi Guanyu Dangqian Duidi Douzheng zhong Jige Zhengce Wenti de Jueding 中共中央批转 '全国政法工作会议与当前对敌斗争中几个政策问题' 的规定
CCPCC, approving and issuing MPS Party Group 'Outline of an Opinion on the Current Circumstances of the Struggle Against the Enemy	Zhonggong Zhongyang, Pizhuan Gong'an Bu Dangzu 'Guanyu Dangqian Diwo Douzheng Xingshi he Kaizhan Shehui Zhengfan, Neibu

and Carrying out the Campaign of Social Suppression and Internal Suppression of Counter-revolutionaries (Rectification)', 21 October 1960, excerpted in Zuigao Renmin Jianchayuan Jiansuo Jiancha Ting, 1992: 28.

Sufan (Qingli) Yundong de Yijian Tigang' 中共中央批准公安部党组 '关于当前敌我斗争形势和开展社会镇压，内部肃反（清理）运动的意见 提纲'

CCPCC, approving the 11th MPS National Public Security Conference 'Supplementary Provisions on Ten Specific Policy Issues Concerning Public Security Work to Date', 17 March 1961, on 20 April 1961, extracted in Zuigao Renmin Jianchayuan Jiansuo Jiancha Ting, 1992: 138–9, 151 and Gong'an Bu Fazhisi, 1992: 5.

Zhonggong Zhongyang, Pizhun Di Shiyici Quanguo Gong'an Huiyi 'Guanyu Dangqian Gong'an Gongzuo Shige Juti Zhengce Wenti de Buchong Guiding 中共中央批准第十一次全国公安 会议 '关于当前公安工作十个具体政策问题的补充规定'

CCPCC, approving and issuing the MPS, Ministry of Internal Affairs Party Committee Report on Urgently Preventing the Free Movement of the Population, 7 November 1961, referred to in Fan and Xiao, 1991: 142.

Zhonggong Zhongyang, Pizhuan Gong'an Bu Neiwu Bu Dangzu 'Guanyu Jianjue Zhizhi Renkou Ziyou Liudong de Baogao' 中共中央批转公安部，内务部 党组 '关于坚决制止人口自由流动的 报告'

CCPCC, approving and issuing the two documents 'On Ten Public Order Measures' and 'On the Problems of Preventing the Free Movement of the Population', 7 November 1961, excerpted in (photocopy materials p. 2).

Zhongyang, Pizhuan 'Guanyu Shixiang Zhi'an Cuoshi' he 'Guanyu Zhizhi Renkou Ziyou Liudong Wenti' de Liangge Wenjian (Jielu) 中央批转 '关于十项治安措施' 和 '关于制止人口自由流动问题' 的两个文件（节录）

CCPCC, Notice on Strict Prohibition of Opium, Morphine and Harmful Drugs, 26 May 1963, referred to in Ke, 1990: 25.

Zhonggong Zhongyang, Guanyu Yanjin Yapian, Mafei Duhai de Tongzhi 中共中央关于严禁鸦片，吗啡毒害的通知

CCPCC, Approving MPS Party Group 'Post-Conference Report on the Fourteenth National Public Security Conference', 15 July 1965, excerpted in Zuigao Renmin Jianchayuan Jiansuo Jiancha Ting, 1992: 24.

Zhonggong Zhongyang, Pizhun Gong'an Bu Dangzu 'Guanyu Di Shisi Ci Quanguo Gong'an Huiyi de Huihou Baogao' 中共中央批准公安部党组 '关于第十四次全国公安会议的会后报告'

CCPCC, approving and issuing the Summary of Minutes of the Eighth

Zhonggong Zhongyang Zhuanpi 'Di Ba Ci Quanguo Renmin Sifa

National People's Judicial Work Meeting in 1978, referred to in Cheng, 2004: 150.	Gongzuo Huiyi Jiyao 中共中央转批第八次全国人民司法工作会议纪要
CCPCC, Notice issuing CCPCC Propaganda Department etc. Eight Units 'Report on Requesting the Whole Party to Attach Importance to Resolving the Problem of Juvenile Crime', 17 August 1979, reproduced in Chen, 1992: 174–7.	Zhonggong Zhongyang Zhuanfa Zhongyang Xuanchuan Bu, Deng Bage Danwei, 'Guanyu Tiqing Quandang Zhongshi Juejue Qingshaonian Weifa Fanzui Wenti de Baogao' de Tongzhi 中共中央转发中央宣传部等八个单位'关于提请全党重视解决青少年犯罪问题的报告'的通知
CCPCC, approving and issuing the Central Political-Legal Committee Summary of the Public Order Meeting of the Five Major Cities of Beijing, Tianjin, Shanghai, Guangzhou and Wuhan, 14 June 1981 ('Five Major Cities Meeting'), reproduced in Chen, 1992: 1–4.	Zhonggong Zhongyang Pizhuan Zhonggong Zhengfa Weiyuanhui Zhaokai de Jing, Jin, Hu, Sui, Han Wu Da Chengshi Zhi'an Zuotanhui de Jiyao 中共中央批转中央政法委员会召开的京，津，沪，穗，汉五大城市治安座谈会的纪要（节录）
CCPCC, Directive on Strengthening Political-Legal Work, 13 January 1982, reproduced in Chen, 1992: 5–8.	Zhonggong Zhongyang Guanyu Jiaqiang Zhengfa Gongzuo de Zhishi 中共中央关于加强政法工作的指示
CCPCC, Notice approving and issuing the 'Summary of the Minutes of the National Political-Legal Work Conference' and 'Important Points in the Speech of Comrade Peng Zhen at the National Political-Legal Work Conference', 28 August 1982, excerpted in (photocopy materials p. 9).	Zhonggong Zhongyang Pizhuan 'Quangou Zhengfa Gongzuo Huiyi Jiyao' he 'Peng Zhen Tongzhi zai Quanguo Zhengfa Gongzuo Huiyi shang de Jianghua Yaodian' de Tongzhi (Jielu) 中共中央批转'全国政法工作会议纪要'和'彭真同志在全国政法工作会议上的讲话要点'的通知（节录）
CCPCC, Notice approving and issuing the Two Documents of the National Public Security Work Conference, 28 May 1983 (Zhong fa 1983 #23 Document) (excerpted in photocopy materials p. 10).	Zhonggong Zhongyang Pizhuan Quanguo Gong'an Gongzuo Huiyi de Liangge Wenjian de Tongzhi 中共中央批转全国公安工作的两个文件的通知（节录）
CCPCC, Decision on Severe Punishment of Criminal Activity, 25 August 1983, http://news.xinhuanet.com/ziliao/2005-02/07/content_2558498.htm.	Zhonggong Zhongyang, Guanyu Yanli Daji Xingshi Fanzui Huodong de Jueding 中共中央关于严厉打击刑事犯罪活动的决定

CCPCC, approving and issuing the Report of the Central Political-Legal Committee Summing up the Activities in the First Campaign of the Hard Strike Against Serious Crime and the Deployments for the Second Campaign, 20 August 1984, excerpted in Chen, 1992 112–16, extracted in Zuigao Renmin Jianchayuan Jiansuo Jiancha Ting, 1992: 200.	Zhonggong Zhongyang Pizhuan Zhongyang Zhengfa Weiyuanhui 'Guanyu Yanli Daji Yanzhong Fanzui Huodong Di yi Zhanyi Zongjie he Di Er Zhanyi Bushu de Baogao 中共中央批转中央政法委员会 '关于严厉打击严重刑事犯罪活动 第一战役总结和第二战役部署的报告' 的通知 (节录)
CCPCC, Notice that the Whole Party Must Resolutely Protect the Socialist Legal System, 10 July 1986, reproduced Gong'an Bu, 1990: 271–5.	Zhonggong Zhongyang Guanyu Quandang Bixu Jianjue Weihu Shehui Zhuyi Fazhi de Tongzhi 中共中央关于全党必须坚决维护 社会主义法制的通知
CCPCC, Resolution on Guiding Principles for Construction of Socialist Spiritual Civilisation, 29 September 1986, reproduced in Chen, 1992: 11–12.	Zhonggong Zhongyang Guanyu Shehui Zhuyi Jingshen Wenming Jianshe Zhidao Fangzhen de Jueyi 中共中央关于社会主义精神文明 建设指导方针的决议
CCPCC, Decision on Several Questions on Establishing a Socialist Market Economy System, 14 November 1993, reproduced in Law Yearbook Editorial Committee, 1994: 1–9.	Zhonggong Zhongyang, Guanyu Jianli Shehui Zhuyi Shichang Jingji Tizhi Ruogan Wenti de Jueding 中共中央关于建立社会主义市场 经济体制若干问题的决定
CCPCC, Decision on Several Important Questions on Strengthening the Construction of Socialist Spiritual Civilisation, 10 October 1996 (translated in English as CCPCC Decision on Important Questions on Promoting Socialist Ethical and Cultural Progress, reproduced in BBC Summary of World Broadcasts FE/D2740/G).	Zhonggong Zhongyang, Guanyu Jiaqiang Shehui Zhuyi Jingshen Wenming Jianshe Ruogan Zhongyao Wenti de Jueyi 中共中央关于加强社会主义精神 文明建设若干重要问题的决议
CCPCC, Work Plan for Resolving Acute Problems of Law Enforcement and Promoting the Construction of the Law Enforcement System of the Public Security Organs, 7 June 2004, reproduced in Gong'an Bu Fazhi Ju, 2004: 284–93.	Zhonggong Zhongyang, Guanyu Jiejue Zhifa Tuchu Wenti Tuijin Gong'an Zhifa Zhidu Jianshe de Gongzuo Jihua 中共中央关于解决执法突出问题 推进公安执法制度建设的工作计划

Committees of the CCPCC

Central Committee East China Division Directive on implementing '(Draft) Regulation on Control and Reform of Landlords after Land Reform', reproduced in Zhonggong Zhongyang Wenxian Yanjiu Shi, 1992b: 346–55.	Zhonggong Zhongyang Huadong Ju Dui Zhixing 'Guanyu Tudi Gaige Hou Guanzhi he Gaizhao Dizhu de Guiding (Cao'an)' de Zhishi 中共中央华东局 对执行 '关于土地改革后管制和改造地主 的规定（草案）' 的指示
Central Political-Legal Committee, Opinion on Questions of whether Vilifying and Slandering Central Leadership Comrades Constitutes a Crime, December 1981, reproduced in Zuigao Renmin Jianchayuan Jiansuo Jiancha Ting, 1992: 130–1.	Zhongyang Zhengfa Weiyuanhui, Guanyu Dui E'du Gongji, Feibang Zhongyang Lingdao Tongzhi Shifou Goucheng Fanzui Wenti de Yijian 中央政法委员会关于对恶毒攻击，诽谤中央领导同志是否构成犯罪 的意见
Central Political-Legal Committee, Summary of the National Political-Legal Work Conference, 12 August 1982, reproduced in Chen, 1992: 9–10.	Zhongyang Zhengfa Weiyuanhui, Quanguo Zhengfa Gongzuo Huiyi de Jiyao (Jielu) 中央政法委员会全国政法工作会议的纪要（节录）
General Office of the CCPCC, Issuing the MPS, All-China Women's Federation, Two Party Organisations 'Report on Resolutely Suppressing Prostitution Activities', 8 April 1983, reproduced in Renmin Fayuan Chubanshe, 1992: 28–32 and Gong'an Bu Fazhisi, 1992: 51–2.	Zhonggong Zhongyang Bangongting Zhuanfa Gong'an Bu, Quanguo Fulian Liang Dangzu 'Guanyu Jianjue Qudi Maiyin Huodong de Baogao 中共中央办公厅转发公安部，全国妇联两党组 '关于坚决取缔卖淫活动的报告'
Central Political-Legal Committee, Situation Report and Opinions Concerning Work for the Coming Winter, 21 September 1985, extracted in Zuigao Renmin Jianchayuan Jiansuo Jiancha Ting, 1992: 218.	Zhonggong Zhengfa Weiyuanhui Qingkuang Tongbao he Jindong Gongzuo Yijian 中共政法委员会情况通报和今冬工作意见
Central Discipline Inspection Committee, Temporary Regulations on Party Disciplinary Sanctions in Respect of those Party Officials and Other Responsible People who Participate in Prostitution and Prostitution Related Activities, 28 May 1988, reproduced in Renmin Fayuan Chubanshe, 1992: 36–7.	Zhonggong Zhongyang Jilü Jiancha Weiyuanhui, Dui Canyu Piaochang, Maiyin Huodong de Gongchan Dangyuan ji Youguan Zerenzhe Dang Ji Chufen de Zanxing Guiding 中共中央纪律检查委员会对参与 嫖娼，卖淫活动的共产党员及有关责任者党籍处分的暂行规定

Central Political-Legal Committee, Notice that Political-Legal Organs Must Strictly Enforce Party Discipline and Rigorously Enforce the Law, 18 October 1993, reproduced in Gong'an Bu Fazhi Si, 1993: 527–30. — Zhonggong Zhongyang Zhengfa Weiyuanhui, Guanyu Zhengfa Bumen Yansu Jilü Yange Zhifa de Tongzhi 中共中央政法委员会关于政法部门严肃纪律严格执法的通知

Standing Committee of the CCPCC Political Bureau, Important Directive on the Work of Comprehensive Management of Public Order, 1993, reproduced in Shu, 1996b: 4–6. — Zhonggong Zhongyang Zhengzhi Ju Changweihui Dui Shehui Zhi'an Zonghe Zhili Gongzuo de Zhongyao Zhishi 中共中央政治局常委会对社会治安综合治理工作的重要指示

Central Political-Legal Committee, Notice on Fully Utilising Legal Weapons to Punish the Unlawful and Criminal Actions of Falungong etc. Heretical Cult Organisations, 5 November 1999, reproduced in Liu, 2002: 423–5. — Zhonggong Zhongyang Zhengfa Weiyuanhui Guanyu Chongfen Yunyong Falü Wuqi Chengzhi Falungong Deng Xiejiao Zuzhi Weifa Fanzui Huodong de Tongzhi 中共中央政法委员会关于充分运用法律武器惩治法轮功等邪教违法犯罪活动的通知

Other documents, reports

(Draft) Measures on Dealing with Prostitution in Beiping City, 26 September 1949, referred to in Ma, 1994: 57. — Beiping Shi Chuli Jinü Banfa (Cao'an) 北平市处理妓女办法（草案）

South-west Military Committee, Implementing Measures on Strictly Prohibiting Opium Smoking, 31 July 1950, referred to in Zhao and Yu, 2000: 17. — Xinan Junweiyuanhui, Guanyu Jinjue Yapian Yandu de Shishi Banfa 西南军政委员会关于禁绝鸦片烟 毒的实施办法

Inner Mongolia Autonomous Region People's Government, Inner Mongolia Autonomous Region Implementing Measures on Strictly Prohibiting Opium Smoking, April 1951, referred to in Zhao and Yu, 2000: 17. — Nei Menggu Zizhiqu Renmin Zhengfu, Nei Menggu Zizhiqu Jinjue Yapian Yandu Shishi Banfa 内蒙古自治区人民政府，内蒙古自治区禁绝鸦片烟毒实施 办法

North-east People's Government Order on Strictly Prohibiting Opium Smoking and other Drugs, February 1952, referred to in Zhao and Yu, 2000: 17. — Dongbei Renmin Zhengfu, Guanyu Yanjin Yapian Yandu ji Qita Dupin de Mingling 东北人民政府关于严禁鸦片烟毒及其他毒品的命令

Summary of the Minutes of the Conference on Research on Striking Against and Suppressing Prostitution and Using Prostitutes (meeting held on 9 January 1989), reproduced in Chen, 1992: 142–4.	Guanyu Yanjiu Daji Qudi Maiyin Piaochang Huodong de Huiyi Jiyao 关于研究打击取缔卖淫嫖娼活动的会议纪要
MPS, MoJ, Ministry of Health, Civil Administration and Women's Federation Report on Striking Hard Against and Resolutely Suppressing Prostitution and Preventing the Spread of Sexually Transmitted Diseases, submitted to the CCPCC and the State Council on 21 September 1987, reproduced in Gong'an Bu Fagui Ju, 1988: 222 and excerpted in Chen, 1992 133–4.	Gong'an Bu, Sifa Bu, Weisheng Bu, Minzheng Bu Quanguo Fulian, Guanyu Yanli Daji Jianjue Qudi Maiyin Huodong he Zhizhi Xingbing Manyan de Baogao (Jielu) 公安部，司法部，卫生部，民政部，全国妇联，关于严厉打击坚决取缔卖淫活动和制止性病蔓延的报告（节录）
General Office of the Central Discipline Inspection Committee, General Office of the Ministry of Supervision, 1995–96, A Survey of the Work of the National Discipline Inspection and Supervision Organs Participating in the Comprehensive Management of Public Order, 23 August 1996, reproduced in Wang, Shengjun, 1998: 302–5.	Zhongyang Jiwei Bangongting, Jiancha Bu Bangongting, 1995–1996 Nian Quanguo Jijian Jiancha Jiguan Canyu Shehui Zhi'an Zonghe Zhili Gongzuo Gaikuang 中央纪委办公厅，监察部办公厅，1995–6 年全国纪检监察机关参与社会治安综合治理工作概况

DOCUMENTS ISSUED JOINTLY BY STATE AND PARTY ORGANS

Documents issued jointly by CCP organs and state organs

CCPCC, State Council, Directive on Preventing the Blind Outflow of the Rural Population, 18 December 1957, reproduced in Guowuyuan Fazhi Ju, 1958 (translated and reproduced in Cohen, 1968: 251, as 'Instruction on Preventing the Blind Outflowing of People from Rural Areas').	Zhonggong Zhongyang, Guowuyuan Fabu 'Guanyu Zhizhi Nongcun Renkou Mangmu Wailiu de Zhishi 中共中央，国务院发布关于制止农村人口盲目外流的指示

Decision of the CCPCC and the State Council of the PRC Relating to the Problem of Dealing with Rightists who Really Demonstrate that they have Reformed, 16 September 1959 (translated into English and reproduced in Cohen, 1968: 268).	
CCPCC Propaganda Department, Ministry of Education, Ministry of Culture, MPS, State Labour Central Department, All-China Council of Trade Unions, Communist Youth League and the All-China Women's Federation, Report on Requesting the Whole Party to Attach Importance to Resolving the Problem of Juvenile Crime, 19 June 1979, reproduced in Chen, 1992: 178–83.	Zhongyang Xuanchuan Bu, Jiaoyu Bu, Wenhua Bu, Gong'an Bu, Guojia Laodong Zongju, Quanguo Zong Gonghui, Gongqing Tuan Zhongyang, Quanguo Fulian, Guanyu Tiqing Quandang Zhongshi Juejue Qingshaonian Weifa Fanzui Wenti de Baogao 中央宣传部，教育部，文化部，公安部，国家劳动总局，全国总工会，共青团中央，全国妇联关于提请全党重视解决青少年犯罪问题的报告
CCPCC, State Council, approving and issuing MPS Report on Doing a Good Job of Re-education through Labour Work, 14 September 1980, reproduced in Gong'an Bu Fagui Ju, 1980: 242, attaching the report at 243–7.	Zhonggong Zhongyang, Guowuyuan, Pizhuan Gong'an Bu Guanyu Zuohao Laodong Jiaoyang Gongzuo de Baogao 中共中央国务院批转公安部关于做好劳动教养工作的报告
CCPCC, State Council, Urgent Directive on the Problem of Complete Prohibition of Opium, 16 July 1982, reproduced in Chen, 1992: 102–4.	Zhonggong Zhongyang, Guowuyuan, Guanyu Jinjue Yapian Yandu Wenti de Jinji Zhishi 中共中央，国务院关于禁绝鸦片烟毒 问题的紧急指示
CCPCC, Notice that the Whole Party Must Resolutely Protect the Socialist Legal System, 10 July 1986, (reproduced in photocopy materials pp. 271–5).	Zhonggong Zhongyang, Guanyu Quandang Bixu Jianjue Weihu Shehui Zhuyi Fazhi de Tongzhi 中共中央关于全党必须坚决维护社会主义法制的通知
General Office of the CCPCC and General Office of the State Council issuing the 'Report on Striking Hard Against and Resolutely Suppressing Prostitution Activities and Preventing the Spread of Sexually Transmitted Diseases', 26 October 1987, reproduced in Gong'an Bu Fagui Ju, 1988: 218–19.	Zhonggong Zhongyang Bangongting, Guowuyuan Bangongting Zhuanfa 'Guanyu Yanli Daji Jianjue Qudi Maiyin Huodong he Zhizhi Xingbing Manyan de Baogao' 中共中央办公厅，国务院办公厅转发 '关于严厉打击坚决取缔卖淫活动和制止性病蔓延' 的报告

CCPCC, State Council, Decision on Strengthening the Comprehensive Management of Public Order, 19 February 1991, reproduced in Chen, 1992: 24–33.	Zhonggong Zhongyang, Guowuyuan, Guanyu Jiaqiang Shehui Zhi'an Zonghe Zhili De Jueding 中共中央，国务院关于加强社会治安综合治理的决定
General Office of the CCPCC, General Office of the State Council, Notice Issuing the 'Regulations on Leadership Officials Reporting Personal Large and Important Matters', 31 January 1997, reproduced in Gong'an Bu Fazhi Si, 1997: 257; Regulations on Leadership Officials Reporting Personal Large and Important Matters, reproduced in Gong'an Bu Fazhi Si, 1997: 258–60.	Zhonggong Zhongyang Bangongting Guowuyuan Bangongting Guanyu Yinfa 'Guanyu Lingdao Ganbu Baogao Geren Zhongda Shixiang de Guiding' de Tongzhi 中共中央办公厅，国务院办公厅关于印发'关于领导干部报告个人重大事项的决定'的通知 Guanyu Lingdao Ganbu Baogao Geren Zhongda Shixiang de Guiding 关于领导干部报告个人重大事项的决定

SPEECHES, REPORTS AND CASES

Speeches and reports

Mao Zedong, Some Questions Concerning Methods of Leadership, 1 June 1943, reproduced in Mao, 1967: 117–22 (in English).	
Peng Zhen, Public Security Work must Rely on the Masses, 9 June 1954, reproduced in Peng, 1991b: 253–4.	Peng Zhen, Gong'an Gongzuo Yao Yikao Qunzhong 公安工作要依靠群众
Chief of the 11th Section of the MPS, Meng Zhaoliang, speech at the Third National Reform through Labour Work Conference, September 1955, excerpted in Zuigao Renmin Jianchayuan Jiansuo Jiancha Ting, 1992: 37.	Gong'an Bu Shiyi Ju Juzhang Meng Zhaoliang Tongzhi zai Disan Ci Quanguo Laogai Gongzuo Huiyi shang de Baogao 公安部十一局局长孟昭亮同志在第三次全国劳改工作会议上的报告
Minister of Public Security, Comrade Luo Ruiqing, Concluding Speech at the November 1956 Conference of Provincial, City and Autonomous Self-Governing Region Party Committee Five Person Small	Gong'an Bu Buzhang Luo Ruiqing Tongzhi zai Yijiu Wuliu Nian Shiyi Yue Ge Sheng, Shi Zizhiqu Dangwei Wuren Xiaozu Zhang Huiyi shang de Zongjie Fayan 公安部部长罗瑞卿同志在一九五六

Groups Heads, 27 November 1956, excerpted in Zuigao Renmin Jianchayuan Jiansuo Jiancha Ting, 1992: 34.	年十一月个省，市，自治区党委五人 小组长会议上的总结发言
Mao Zedong, On the Correct Handling of Contradictions Among the People, 27 February 1957, reproduced in Mao, 1972 (in English) and Cohen, 1968: 83–8 (in English).	
Minister of Public Security, Comrade Luo Ruiqing, Explanation on Questions about RETL at the Meeting of the NPCSC, 2 September 1957, extracted in Zuigao Renmin Jianchayuan Jiansuo Jiancha Ting, 1992: 32, 152.	Gong'an Bu Buzhang Luo Ruiqing Tongzhi zai Renda Changweihuiyi Shang Guanyu Laodong Jiaoyang Wenti de Shuoming 公安部部长罗瑞卿同志在人大常委会议上关于劳动教养问题的说明
Liu Shaoqi, Political-legal work and correctly handling contradictions amongst the people, 23 May 1962, reproduced in Liu, 1985: 450–2.	Liu Shaoqi, Zhengfa Gongzuo he Zhengque Chuli Renmin Neibu Maodun 刘少奇，政法工作和正确处理人民内部矛盾
Deng Xiaoping, Emancipate the Mind, Seek Truth from Facts and Unite as One in looking to the Future, 13 December 1978 (in English), reproduced in Deng, 1978: 151–65.	
Peng Zhen, Explanation of the Drafts of Seven Laws, 26 June 1979, reproduced in Peng, 1992b: 156–70.	Peng Zhen, Guanyu Qige Falü Cao'an de Shuoming 彭真关于七个法律草案的说明
Peng Zhen, Speech given at the National Conference of Provincial-level Public Security Chiefs, 16 September 1979, reproduced in Peng, 1992b: 182–9.	Peng Zhen, Zai Quanguo Gong'an Juzhang Huiyi de Jianghua 彭真在全国公安局长会议的讲话
Deng Xiaoping, The Present Situation and the Tasks Before Us, 16 January 1980, reproduced in Deng, 1984b: 224–58 (in English).	
Peng Zhen, Key Points of the Speech at the Report Back Meeting of the Police, Procuratorate and Court of Guangdong Province and Guangzhou City, 1 February 1980, reproduced in Peng, 1992b: 212–15.	Peng Zhen, Zai Guangdong Sheng he Guangzhou Shi Gongjianfa Huibaohui de Jianghua Yaodian 彭真在广东省广州市公检法汇报 上的讲话要点

Peng Zhen, Summary of a Speech given at the First Conference of the Central Political-Legal Committee, 6 February 1980, reproduced in Peng, 1992b: 216–18.	Peng Zhen, Zai Zhongyang Zhengfa Weiyuanhui Di Yi Ci Huiyi de Jianghua Jiyao 彭真在中央政法委员会第一次会 议上的讲话纪要
Peng Zhen, Conduct Investigation and Study, Handle Matters According to the Actual Situation, 26 April 1980, reproduced in Peng, 1992b: 226–8.	Peng Zhen, Kaizhan Diaocha Yanjiu, An Shiji Qingkuang Banshi 彭真开展调查研究，按实际情况办事
Peng Zhen, Speech given to the Five Major Cities' Public Order Meeting, 21–22 May 1981, reproduced in Peng, 1992b: 248–63.	Peng Zhen, Zai Wu Da Chengshi Zhi'an Zuotanhui Shang de Jianghua 彭真在五大城市治安座谈会上的 讲话
Vice Minister of Public Security, Comrade Ling Yun, Speech at the Meeting on Improving Reform Work, 7 August 1981, excerpted in Zuigao Renmin Jianchayuan Jiansuo Jiancha Ting, 1992: 40.	Gong'an Bu Fubuzhang Ling Yun Tongzhi Zai Gaijin Gaizao Gongzuo Zuotanhui shang de Jianghua 公安部副部长凌云同志在改进改造工作座谈会上的讲话
Peng Zhen, Political-Legal Work in the New Era, 22 July 1982, reproduced in Peng, 1992b: 282–91.	Peng Zhen Xin Shiqi de Zhengfa Gongzuo 彭真新时期的政法工作
Deng Xiaoping, Crackdown on Crime, 19 July 1983 (in English), reproduced in Deng, 1994a 44–5.	
Peng Zhen, The Whole Party Must Resolutely Carry out the Hard Strike against Serious Crime, 21 July 1983, reproduced in Peng, 1992b: 345–7.	Peng Zhen, Yanli Daji Yanzong Xingshi Fanzui Huodong Yao Quandang Xia Juexin 彭真，严厉打击严重犯罪活动要全 党下决心
Peng Zhen, The Hard Strike Against Crime Must Abide by the Law, Pay Attention to Policy and Strengthen Comprehensive Management, 15–22 November 1983, Speech given at the National Meeting of Public Security Office and Division Heads convened by the MPS between 15 and 22 November 1983, reproduced in Peng, 1992b: 348–51.	Peng Zhen, Yanli Daji Xingshi Fanzui Yao Zunshou Falü, Zhuyi Zhengce Jiaqiang Zonghe Zhili 彭真，严厉打刑事犯罪要遵守法律，注意政策，加强综合治理
Peng Zhen, Not Only is it Necessary to Rely on Party Policy, it is also Necessary to Handle Matters	Peng, Zhen Bujin Yao Kao Dang de Zhengce Erqie Yao Yifa Banshe 彭真不仅要靠党的政策，而且要依 法办事

According to Law, 13 March 1984, reproduced in Peng, 1992b: 361–6.	
Peng Zhen, Speech at the National Political-Legal Work Conference, 28 January 1985, reproduced in Peng, 1991b: 509–19.	Peng Zhen, Zai Quangguo Zhengfa Gongzuo Huiyi Shang de Jianghua 彭真在全国政法工作会议上的 讲话
Deng Xiaoping, The Two Basic Elements in China's Policies, 4 July 1987, reproduced in Deng, 1994b 244–6 (in English).	
Tao Siju, Vice Minister of Public Security, Response to Questions from a Reporter of the People's Public Security News about the (Draft) Administrative Litigation Law, 31 March 1989, reproduced in Liu and Bao, 1989: 188–90.	Gong'an Bu Fu Buzhang Tao Siju, Jiu Xingzheng Susong Fa (Cao'an) Da Renmin Gong'an Bao Jizhe Wen 公安部副部长陶驷驹就'行政诉讼法（草案）'答人民公安报'记者问
Jiang Bo (then head of the Legal Division of the MPS), Responding to Questions from a reporter for the Legal Daily on Implementation of the Administrative Litigation Law, 28 March 1989, reproduced in Liu and Bao, 1989: 191–3.	Gong'an Bu Fazhi Si Sizhang Jiang Bo Jiu Ruhe Zhexing Xingzheng Susong Fa Da 'Fazhi Ribao' Jizhe Wen 公安部法制司司长江波就如何执行行政诉讼法答法制日报' 记者问
Peng Zhen, Key Points of a Speech at the National Political-Legal Work Conference, 5 March 1990, reproduced in Peng, 1992b: 444–8.	Peng, Zhen Zai Quanguo Zhengfa Gongzuo Huiyi Shang de Jianghua Yaodian 彭真在全国政法工作会议上的讲话要点
Minister of Public Security, Tao Siju, Reform and Strengthen Public Security Work in Order to Reform and Create an even better Public Order Environment, 1993, reproduced in Law Yearbook Editorial Committee, 1993: 115–18.	Gong'an Bu Buzhang Tao Siju, Gaige he Jiaqiang Gong'an Gongzuo, Wei Gaige he Jianshe Chuangzao Genghao de Zhi'an Huanjing 公安部部长陶驷驹，改革和加强公安 工作，为改革和建设创造更好的治安 环境
Wang Jiafu, Issues in Constructing a Legal System for a Socialist Market Economy, 21 January 1995, reproduced in Sifa Bu Fazhi Xuanquan Si, 1995: 78–106.	Wang Jiafu, Shehui Zhuyi Shichang Jingji Falü Zhidu Jianshe Wenti 王家福社会主义市场经济法律制度 建设问题
Jiang Zemin, Hold High the Great Banner of Deng Xiaoping Theory for an All-round Advancement of the Cause of Building Socialism with	

Chinese Characteristics into the 21st Century, 12 September 1997, Report delivered at the 15th National Congress of the CCP (in English), reproduced in (1997), Vol. 40, No. 40, *Beijing Review*, 10–33.	
Yang Jingyu, Head of the State Council Legal Office, Explanation of the (Draft) 'PRC Administrative Review Law', reproduced in Ying *et al.*, 1999: 451–7 (undated).	Yang Jingyu, Guanyu 'Zhonghua Renmin Gongheguo Xingzheng Fuyi Fa (Cao'an)' de Shuoming 杨景宇，国务院法制办公室主任 关于 '中华人民共和国行政复议法（草案）' 的说明

Cases

Case where Chen Yingchun sues Lishi County Public Security Bureau for Detaining her for Investigation, 1991 ('Chen Yingchun case'), reproduced in Lin, 1992: 170–5.	Chen Yingchun Su Lishi Xian Gong'an Ju dui Qi Shourong Shencha An 陈迎春诉离石县公安局对其收容审查案
Qinghe County People's Court, How We Heard our First Detention for Investigation Administrative Litigiaton Case (case involving Geng Weijun), discussed in Qinghe County People's Court, 1992.	Qinghe Xian Renmin Fayuan Women shi ruhe Shenli Shouci Shoushen Xingzheng Anjian de 青河县人民法院我们是如何审理首次收审案件的
Case where Chen Weiguo is dissatisfied with the RETL decision of the Shizui Shan People's Government RETL Management Committee, 1992, reproduced in Zhu, 1994: 1301–3.	Chen Weiguo Bufu Shizui Shan Shi Renmin Zhengfu Laodong Jiaoyang Guanli Weiyuanhui Laodong Jiaoyang Jueding An 陈卫国不服石嘴山市人民政府劳动教养管理委员会劳动教养决定案
Case where Li Jinsheng Sues the Yanshi City Public Security Bureau for Unlawful Deprivation of Personal Freedom, reproduced in Zhu, 1998: 280–3.	Li Jinsheng Su Yanshi Shi Gong'an Ju Feifa Xianzhi Qi Renshen Ziuyou An 李金胜诉偃师市公安局非法限制其人身自由案

BIBLIOGRAPHY

Administrative Division of the Chongqing Municipal Intermediate People's Court, (1993) 'Shenli Shourong Shencha Xingzheng Anjian Muqian Ying Zhuyi de Jige Wenti (Several Problems in Trying Detention for Investigation Administrative Litigation Cases to Date)', 4, *Xingzheng Faxue Yanjiu (Administrative Law Studies)*, 81–84.

Alford, William, (1986) 'On the Limits of "Grand Theory" in Comparative Law', 61, *Washington Law Review*, 945–56.

Alford, William, (1995) 'Tasselled Loafers for Barefoot Lawyers: Transformation and Tension in the World of Legal Workers', 141, *The China Quarterly*, 22–40.

Alford, William, (2000) 'Law, Law, What Law? Why Western Scholars of China Have Not Had More to Say About Its Law', in *The Limits of the Rule of Law in China*, Turner, K.G, Feinerman, J.V. and Guy, R.K. (eds.), Seattle, University of Washington Press, 45–64.

Alford, William, (2003) 'Of Lawyers Lost and Found: Searching for Legal Professionalism in the People's Republic of China', in *East Asian Law-Universal Norms and Local Cultures*, Rosett, Arthur, Cheng, Lucie and Woo, Margaret (eds.), London, RoutledgeCurzon, 182–204.

Allars, Margaret, (1997) *Administrative Law: Cases and Commentary*, Sydney, Butterworths.

Amnesty International, (1991) *China: Punishment Without Crime*, London and New York, Amnesty International Publications.

Amnesty International, (1992) *Detention Without Trial, A System for Extra-Judicial Punishment*, London and New York, Amnesty International Publications, 10–13.

Amnesty International, (1996) *China: No-one is Safe: Political Repression and Abuse of Power in the 1990s*, London and New York, Amnesty International Publications.

Amnesty International, (1997) *People's Republic of China: Law Reform and Human Rights*, London and New York, Amnesty International Publications.

Anagnost, Ann, (1997a) 'Constructing the Civilized Community', in *Culture and State in Chinese History: Conventions Accommodations and Critiques*,

Huters, Theodore, Wong, R. Bin and Yu, Pauline (eds.), Stanford, Stanford University Press, 346–65.

Anagnost, Ann, (1997b) *National Past Times: Narrative, Representation and Power in Modern China*, Durham, Duke University Press.

Bakken, Borge, (1993) 'Crime, Juvenile Delinquency and Deterrence Policy in China', 30, *The Australian Journal of Chinese Affairs*, 29–58.

Bakken, Borge, (2000) *The Exemplary Society, Human Improvement, Social Control and the Dangers of Modernity in China*, New York, Oxford University Press.

Bakken, Borge, (2004) 'Moral Panics, Crime Rates and Harsh Punishment in China', 37, *The Australian and New Zealand Journal of Criminology*, 67–89.

Balbus, Isaac, (1977) 'Commodity Form and and Legal Form: An Essay on the "Relative Autonomy of Law"', 11, *Law and Society Review*, 571–89.

Bao, Suixian, (1997) 'Woguo Bao'an Chufen Ying Dandu Lifa (China's Security Defence Punishments Should Have *sui generis* Legislation)', *Renmin Gong'an* (*People's Police*), 34–5.

Baum, Richard, (1986) 'Modernization and Legal Reform in Post-Mao China: The Rebirth of Socialist Legality', 19, *Studies in Comparative Communism*, 69–103.

Baum, Richard, (1994) *Burying Mao: Chinese Politics in the Age of Deng Xiaoping*, Princeton, Princeton University Press.

Benshu Bianxie Zu (Book Editorial Committee) (ed.), (2001) *Zhongguo Gongchandang Bashi Nian Xuexi Duben* (*Reader on 80 Years of the Chinese Communist Party*), Beijing, Zhonggong Zhongyang Dangxiao Chubanshe (Central Party School Press).

Berman, Harold J., (1963) *Justice in the USSR. An Interpretation of Soviet Law*, Cambridge, Harvard University Press.

Biddulph, Sarah, (2003) 'The Production of Legal Norms: A Case Study of Administrative Detention in China', 20, *UCLA Pacific Basin Law Journal*, 217–77.

Biddulph, Sarah, (2005) 'Mapping Legal Change in the Context of Reforms to Chinese Police Powers', in *Asian Socialism & Legal Change*, Gillespie, John and Nicholson, Pip (eds.), Canberra, Asia Pacific Press, 212–38.

Bonnin, Michel and Chevrier, Yves, (1996) 'The Intellectual and the State: Social Dynamics of Intellectual Autonomy During the Post-Mao Era', in *The Individual and the State*, Hook, Brian (ed.), Oxford, Clarendon, 149–74.

Bourdieu, Pierre, (1987) 'The Force of Law: Toward a Sociology of the Juridical Field (Terdiman, R. translator)', 38, *Hastings Law Journal*, 814–54.

Bourdieu, Pierre, (1990) *In Other Words: Essays Towards a Reflexive Sociology*, Cambridge, Polity Press.

Bourdieu, Pierre and Wacquant, Loic, (1992) *An Invitation to Refexive Sociology*, Chicago, Univeristy of Chicago Press.

Boxer, John T., (1999) 'China's Death Penalty: Undermining Legal Reform and Threatening the National Economic Interest', *Suffolk Transnational Law Review*, 593–618.

Bracey, D.H., (1989) 'Policing in the People's Republic', in *Social Control in the People's Republic of China*, Troyer, R., Clark, J. and Rojek, D. (eds.), New York, Praeger, 130–40.

Brady, James, (1981) 'The Transformation of Justice under Socialism: The Contrasting Experiences of Cuba and China', 10, *The Insurgent Socialist*, 5–24.

Brady, James, (1982) *Justice and Politics in People's China: Legal Order or Continuing Revolution?* London, Academic Press.

Brady, James, (1983) 'The People's Republic of China', in *International Handbook of Contemporary Developments in Criminology: Europe, Africa, the Middle East and Asia*, Johnson, E.H. (ed.), Westport, Greenwood Press, 107–41.

Brewer, John, (1988) *The Police, Public Order and the State*, London, Macmillan Press.

Brook, Timothy and Frolic, Michael, (1997) *Civil Society in China*, New York, M.E. Sharpe.

Brugger, Bill, (1989) 'Ideology, Legitimacy and Marxist Theory in Contemporary China', in *China: Modernisation in the 1980s*, Cheng, Joseph Y.S. (ed.), Sydney, Allen & Unwin, 1–33.

Brugger, Bill and Reglar, Stephen, (1994) *Politics, Economy and Society in Contemporary China*, Hong Kong, Macmillan Press.

Buckley, Chris, (19 August 2006) 'Activist Trial Ends in Disarray: Lawyers Defend Blind Rights Advocate', *The Age*, 21.

Burns, John, (1999) 'The People's Republic of China at 50: National Political Reform', 159, *The China Quarterly*, 580–94.

Cai, Dingjian, (1991) 'Guojia Quanli Jiexian Lun (Discussion of the Limits of State Power)', *Zhongguo Faxue* (*Chinese Legal Science*), 54–61.

Cao, Lan, (1997) 'Law and Economic Development: A New Beginning?' 32, *Texas International Law Journal*, 545–59.

CCP Central Committee, (1978) *Communique of the Third Plenary Session of the 11th Central Committee of the Communist Party of China, Adopted 22 December 1978*, 6–16.

CCP Central Committee, (1981) *Resolution on Certain Questions in the History of Our Party Since the Founding of the People's Republic of China.*

Ceng, Fanqi (ed.), (1995) *Zhongguo Gongchangdang Jilu Jiancha Gailun* (*Introduction to China's Communist Party Discipline Inspection*), Beijing, Zhongguo Fangzhen Chubanshe.

Chai, Fabang (ed.), (1990) *Xingzheng Susongfa Jiaocheng* (*Administrative Litigation Law Teaching Materials*), Beijing, Zhongguo Renmin Gong'an Daxue Chubanshe (Chinese People's Public Security University Press).

Chan, Janet, (1996) 'Changing Police Culture', 36, *British Journal of Criminology*, 109–34.

Chan, Kam Wing and Li, Zhang, (1999) 'The Hukou System and Rural–Urban Migration in China: Processes and Changes', 160, *The China Quarterly*, 818–55.

Chao, Lianshan and Dong, Fuyi, (1997) 'Zhongguo Shi de Zhi'an Gongzuo Shehuihua de Lilun yu Shijian (Theory and Practice of a Chinese Model of Socialisation of Public Order)', in *Lun Zhongguo Tese de Gong'an* (*Discussion of Public Security with Chinese Characteristics*), Kang, Damin (ed.), Beijing, Qunzhong Chubanshe (Masses Press), 47–57.

Chen, Albert, (1999) 'Toward a Legal Enlightenment: Discussions in Contemporary China on the Rule of Law', 17, *UCLA Pacific Basin Law Journal*, 125–65.

Chen, Duanhua (2003) 'Laodong Jiaoyang de Lishi Kaocha yu Fansi (Study and Rethinking of the History of Re-education through Labour)', in *Zhi'an Guanli Zhidu Sicun (Reflection on the Regulation of Public Order*), Zhu, Weiguo (ed.), Beijing, Falu Chubanshe (Law Press), 79–126.

Chen, Guangzhong and Yan, Duan (eds.), (1995) *Zhonghua Renmin Gongheguo Xingshi Susong Fa Xiugai Jianyi yu Lunzheng* (*Preliminary Version for Revision of the 'Criminal Procedure Law of the People's Republic of China' and its Annotations*), Beijing, Zhongguo Fangzheng Chubanshe (China Fangzheng Press).

Chen, Guangzhong and Yan, Duan (eds.), (1996) *Zhonghua Renmin Gongheguo Xingshi Susong Fa Shiyi yu Yingyong* (*Annotations and Application of 'The Criminal Procedure Law of the People's Republic of China'*), Chanchung, Jilin People's Press.

Chen, Jiafang, (1998) 'Crime in China's Modernization', in *Social Transition in China*, Zhang, Jie and Li, Xiaobing (eds.), Lanham, University Press of America, 155–70.

Chen, Jianfu, (1999a) *Chinese Law: Towards an Understanding of Chinese Law, Its Nature and Development*, The Hague, Kluwer Law International.

Chen, Jianfu, (1999b) 'Market Economy and the Internationalisation of Civil and Commercial Law in the People's Republic of China', in *Law, Capitalism and Power in Asia*, Jayasuriya, Kanishka (ed.), London, Routledge, 69–94.

Chen, Jianfu (2000) 'Coming Full Circle: Law-Making in the PRC from a Historical Perspective', in *Law-Making in the People's Republic of China*, Otto, Jan Michiel, Polak, Maurice V., Chen, Jianfu and Li, Yuwen (eds.), The Hague, Kluver Law International, 19–39.

Chen, Puxian, Zhang, Kangnian and Zhang, Jie (eds.), (1996) *Gong'an Yingyong Xiezuo Liwen Xuanping (Selection and Appraisal of Precedent Documents for use by the Public Security)*, Beijing, Zhongguo Renmin Gong'an Daxue Chubanshe (China People's Public Security University Press).

Chen, Shouyi, (1988) 'A Review of Thirty Years of Legal Studies in New China', *Journal of Chinese Law*, 181.

Chen, Weidong and Zhang, Tao, (1992a) 'Shourong Shencha de Ruogan Wenti Yanjiu (An Examination of Several Questions about Detention for Investigation)', 13, *Zhongguo Faxue* (*Chinese Legal Science*), 82–7.

Chen, Weidong and Zhang, Tao, (1992b) 'Shourong Shencha Ruogan Wenti Yanjiu (Research on Several Questions about Detention for Investigation)', in *Xingshi Susong Fa de Xuigai yu Wanshan* (*Revision and Perfection of the Criminal Procedure Law*), Zhongguo Faxue Hui Susong Fa Yanjiu Hui (Procedure Law Association of the China Law Society) (ed.), Beijing, Zhongguo Zhengfa Daxue Chubanshe (China University of Politics and Law Press), 170–8.

Chen, Weidong and Zhang, Tao, (1993) 'Zai Tan Shourong Shencha Buyi Feichu (Another Discussion of why Detention for Investigation Should not be Abolished)', *Zhongguo Faxue* (*Chinese Legal Science*), 113–14.

Chen, Xiaobo, (1998) 'Gong'an Xinfang Gongzuo Zhong Shangfang Laohu de Chengyin, Tedian Ji Duice (Causes, Characteristics and Countermeasures for Serial Petitioners in Public Security Letters and Visits Work)', *Hubei Gong'an Gaodeng Zhuanke Xuexiao Xuebao* (*Journal of the Hubei Public Security Specialist College*), 35–7.

Chen, Xingyou and Li, Shuyin, (2005) 'Zhongguo dui Xidu Chengyin zhe Qiangzhi Jiedu Zhidu Yanjiu Baogao (Research Report on China's System of Coercive Rehabilitation of Drug Addicts)', in *Xianzhi dui Renshen Ziyou de Xianzhi* (*To Refrain from the Restrictions of Personal Freedom*), Guo, Jian'an and Zheng, Xiaze (eds.), Beijing, Falu Chubanshe (Law Press), 367–415.

Chen, Xinliang, (1996) 'Xingshi Lifa Gongzhenglun (Discussion of Fairness in Criminal Legislation)', in *Fazhi Xiandaihua Yanjiu* (*Studies on Modernization of the Legal System*), Vol. 2, Nanjing Normal University Legal System Modernization Research Centre (ed.), Nanjing, Nanjing Normal University Press, 388–405.

Chen, Xinliang, (2002) 'Laodong Jiaoyang zhi Quanli Guishu Fenxi (An Analysis of Classification of Power of Re-education Through Labour', 5, *Faxue* (*Law Science*), 20–2.

Chen, Youfeng, (2001) 'Zhi'an Guanli Chufa Tiaoli Xiuding Silu (Thoughts on Revisions to the Security Administrative Punishments Regulations)', in *Falu Lunwen Ziliao Ku* (*Collection of Law Theses Materials*), Vol. 2002, www.cpd.com.cn/20010605/GB/2834^3B08.htm.

Chen, Yourong (ed.), (1992) *Shehui Zhi'an Zonghe Zhili Zhengci Fagui: Huibian (Collection of Laws and Regulations of the Policy of Comprehensive Management of Public Order)*, Beijing, Qunzhong Chubanshe (Masses Press).

Chen, Youxi, (1993) 'Dui Xingzheng Susong Kunjing de Hongguan Sikao (Macroscopic Reflections on the Predicament of Administrative Litigation'), 4, *Xingzheng Faxue Yanjiu (Administrative Law Studies)*, 41–2.

Chen, Zexian, Liu, Wenren, Qu, Xuewu and Feng, Rui, (2002) 'Guanyu Laodong Jiaoyang Zhidu de Yanjiu Baogao (Research Report on the System of Re-education Through Labour)' in *Lixing yu Chengxu: Zhongguo Laodong Jioyang Zhidu Yanjiu (Rationality and Order: Research on China's System of Re-education Through Labour)*, Chu, Huaizhi, Chen, Xinliang and Zhang, Shaoyan (eds.), Beijing, Falu Chubanshe (Law Press), 331–43.

Cheng, Shanzong, (1990) 'Laodong Jiaoyang Jiandu Chengxu Chutan (Preliminary Discussion of the Procedure for Supervision of Re-education Through Labour)', in *Laodong Jiaoyang Yanjiu Lunwen Xuanji (Selected Collection of Theses on Re-education Through Labour Research)*, Zhu, Hongde (ed.), Beijing, Qunzhong Chubanshe (Masses Press), 253–7.

Cheng, Tiejun and Selden, Mark, (1994) 'The Origins and Social Consequences of China's Hukou System', 139, *The China Quarterly*, 644–68.

Cheng, Weirong, (2004) *Dangdai Zhongguo Sifa Xingzheng Zhidu (The Contemporary Chinese Judicial Administrative System)*, Shanghai, Xuelin Chubanshe (Xuelin Press).

Chibundu, Maxwell, (1999) 'Globalizing the Rule of Law: Some Thoughts at and on the Periphery', *Indiana Journal of Global Legal Studies*, 79–116.

China Daily, (13 August 2003) 'Public Security No Excuse for Police Excesses', *Financial Times*, Information.

China News Agency, (11 May 2000) '"Strike-hard" Crime Crackdown Successes Noted', BBC Summary of World Broadcasts, Asia Pacific Stories.

Chiu, Hongdah, (1992) 'China's Criminal Justice System and the Trial of Pro-Democracy Dissidents', 24, *New York University Journal of International Law and Politics*, 1181–201.

Chu, Huaizhi, (1996) *'Liuhai' Zhili Lun (Discussion of Management of the 'Six Evils')*, Beijing, Zhongguo Jiancha Chubanshe (China Procuratorate Press).

Chu, Mike, (2000) 'Criminal Procedure Reform in the People's Republic of China: The Dilemma of Crime Control and Regime Legitimacy', 18, *UCLA Pacific Basin Law Journal*, 157–208.

Clark, David, (1999) 'The Many Meanings of the Rule of Law', in *Law, Capitalism and Power in Asia*, Jayasuriya, Kanishka (ed.), London, Routledge.

Clarke, Donald, (1985) 'Concepts of Law in the Chinese Anti-crime Campaign', 98, *Harvard Law Review*, 1890–908.

Clarke, Donald, (1991) 'What's Law Got To Do With It? Legal Institutions and Economic Reform in China', 10, *UCLA Pacific Basin Law Journal*, 31.

Clarke, Donald, (1995) 'Justice and the Legal System in China', in *China in the 1990s*, Benewick, Robert and Wingrove, Paul (eds.), London, Macmillan, 83–93.

Clarke, Donald, (1996) 'Power and Politics in the Chinese Court System: The Enforcement of Civil Judgments', 10, *Columbia Journal of Asian Law*, 1.

Clarke, Donald, (2003) 'Puzzling Observations in Chinese Law: When is a Riddle Just a Mistake?' in *Understanding China's Legal System*, Hsu, C. Stephen (ed.), New York, New York University Press, 93–121.

Clarke, Donald and Feinerman, James, (1995) 'Antagonistic Contradictions: Criminal Law and Human Rights in China', 141, *The China Quarterly*, 135–54.

Cohen, Jean and Arato, Andrew, (1992) *Civil Society and Political Theory*, Cambridge, MIT Press.

Cohen, Jerome, (1966) 'The Criminal Process in the People's Republic of China: An Introduction', 79, *Harvard Law Review*, 469–533.

Cohen, Jerome, (1968) *The Criminal Process in the People's Republic of China 1949–1963*, Cambridge, Mass., Harvard University Press.

Cohen, Jerome (translator), (1984) *The Criminal Law and the Criminal Procedure Law of China*, Beijing, Foreign Languages Press.

Cohen, Jonathon, (1993) 'One Nation's "Gulag" is Another Nation's "Factory Within a Fence": Prison-labor in the People's Republic of China and the United States of America', 12, *UCLA Pacific Basin Law Journal*, 190–236.

Collins, Hugh, (1984) *Marxism and Law*, Oxford, Oxford University Press.

Conner, Alison (2000) 'True Confessions? Chinese Confessions Then and Now', in *The Limits of the Rule of Law in China*, Turner, K.G., Feinerman, J.V. and Guy, R.K. (eds.), Seattle, University of Washington Press, 132–62.

Cooney, Sean, Lindsey, Tim, Mitchell, Richard and Zhu, Ying, (2002a) 'Labour Law and Labour Market Regulation in East Asian, States', in *Law and Labour Market Regulation in East Asia*, Cooney, Sean, Lindsey, Tim, Mitchell, Richard and Zhu, Ying (eds.), London, Routledge, 1–26.

Cooney, Sean, Lindsey, Tim, Mitchell, Richard and Zhu, Ying (eds.), (2002b) *Law and Labour Market Regulation in East Asia*, London, Routledge.

Cooney, Sean and Mitchell, Richard, (2002) 'What is Labour Law Doing in East Asia?', in *Law and Labour Market Regulation in East Asia*, Cooney, Sean, Lindsey, Tim, Mitchell, Richard and Zhu, Ying (eds.), London, Routledge, 246–74.

Cotterrell, Roger, (1983) 'Legality and Political Legitimacy in the Sociology of Max Weber', in *Legality, Ideology and the State* Sugarman, David (ed.), London and New York, Academic Press.

Cotterrell, Roger, (1992) *The Sociology of Law: An Introduction*, London, Butterworths.

Cotterrell, Roger, (1995) *Law's Community: Legal Theory in Sociological Perspective*, Oxford, Clarendon Press.

Craig, Paul, (1997) 'Formal and Substantive Conceptions of the Rule of Law: An Analytical Framework', *Public Law*, 467–87.

Cui, Hongxin, (1992) 'Laodong Jiaoyang shi Texu de Xingzheng Chufa (Reeducation Through Labour is a Special Administrative Punishment)' 2, *Gong'an Yanjiu* (*Public Security Studies*), 17–19.

Cui, Ming, (1991) 'Firmly Guard Against the Development and Spread of Secret Society Forces', in *Crime Trend in the 1990s and its Countermeasures of Prevention and Control*, Beijing, Chinese People's Public Security University Press (ed.), 9–12.

Cui, Ming, (1993a) 'Shehui Zhuyi Chuji Jieduan yu Gong'an Jianshe (Preliminary Stages of Socialism and Public Security Construction)', in *Zhongguo Dangdai Xing yu Fa* (*China's Contemporary Crime and Law*), Cui, Ming (ed.), Beijing, Qunzhong Chubanshe (Masses Press), 353–7.

Cui, Ming, (1993b) 'Shourong Shencha de Lishi, Xianzhuang Yu Chulu (The History, Present Situation and Prospects of Detention for Investigation)', in *Zhongguo Dangdai Xing Yu Fa* (*China's Contemporary Crime and Law*), Cui, Ming (ed.) Beijing, Qunzhong Chubanshe (Masses Press), 90–8.

Cui, Ming (ed.), (1999) *Dupin Fanzui* (*Drug Crimes*), Beijing, Jingguan Jiaoyu Chubanshe (Police Officers Education Press).

Cui, Xin, (1996) 'Xingshi Susong Fa Xiugai Hou Gong'an Gongzuo Mianling de Xingshi Ji Renwu (The Situation and Tasks of Public Security Work after Revision of the Criminal Procedure Law)', 3, *Gong'an Yanjiu* (*Public Security Studies*), 36–8, at 31.

Curran, Daniel and Cook, Sandra, (1993) 'Growing Fears, Rising Crime: Juveniles and China's Justice System', 39, *Crime and Delinquency, Special Issue: Crime and Justice in China and Japan*, 296–315.

Deng, Xiaoping, (1978) 'Emancipate the Mind, Seek Truth from Facts and Unite as One in Looking to the Future', in *Selected Works of Deng Xiaoping (1975–1982)*, Vol. 2, Bureau for the Compilation and Translation of Works of Marx, Lenin, Engels and Stalin under the Central Committee of the Communist Party of China (ed.), Beijing, Foreign Languages Press, 151–65.

Deng, Xiaoping, (1984a) 'Combat Economic Crime', in *Selected Works of Deng Xiaoping 1975–1982*, Vol. 2, Beijing, Foreign Languages Press, 380–2.

Deng, Xiaoping (ed.), (1984b) *Selected Works of Deng Xiaoping (1975–1982)*, Beijing, Foreign Languages Press.

Deng, Xiaoping, (1993) 'Uphold the Four Cardinal Principles, 30 March 1979', in *Selected Works of Deng Xiaoping (1975–1982)*, Vol. 2, Bureau for the Compilation and Translation of Works of Marx, Lenin, Engels and Stalin under the Central Committee of the Communist Party of China (ed.), Beijing, Foreign Languages Press, 166–91.

Deng, Xiaoping, (1994a) 'Crack Down on Crime, 19 July 1983', in *Selected Works of Deng Xiaoping*, Vol. 3, Bureau for the Compilation and Translation of Works of Marx, Lenin, Engels and Stalin under the Central Committee of the Communist Party of China (ed.), Beijing, Foreign Languages Press, 44–5.

Deng, Xiaoping, (1994b) *Selected Works of Deng Xiaoping (1982–1992)*, Vol. 3, Bureau for the Compilation and Translation of Works of Marx, Lenin, Engels and Stalin under the Central Committee of the Communist Party of China (ed.), Beijing, Foreign Languages Press.

Dezalay, Yves and Garth, Bryant, (2001) 'The Import and Export of Law and Legal Institutions: International Strategies in National Palace Wars', in *Adapting Legal Cultures*, Nelken, David and Feest, Johannes (eds.), Oxford, Hart Publishing, 241–55.

Dicks, Anthony, (1995) 'Compartmentalized Law and Judicial Restraint: An Inductive View of Some Jurisdictional Barriers to Reform', 141, *The China Quarterly*, 84–109.

Dikotter, Frank, (2002) *Crime, Punishment and the Prison in Modern China*, New York, Columbia University Press.

Dikotter, Frank, Laamann, Lars and Zhou, Xun, (2002) 'Narcotic Culture: A Social History of Drug Consumption in China', 42, *British Journal of Criminology*, 317–36.

Ding, Xiang, (2000) 'Xin Shiqi Gong'an Fazhi Gongzuo Gaige yu Fazhan (Reform and Develoment of Public Security Legal System Work in the New Age)', 1, *Gong'an Yanjiu (Public Security Studies)*, 73–5, 46.

Ding, Xinfa, (1999) 'Zhengque Chulihao Liuge Guanxi, Cujin Gong'an Gongzuo Xietiao Fazhan (Correctly Handle Six Relationships, Advance the Coordinated Development of the Public Security Organs)', 1, *Gong'an Yanjiu (Public Security Studies)*, 11–13, 10.

Dixon, David, (1997) *Law in Policing: Legal Regulation and Police Practices*, Oxford, Clarendon Press.

Dobinson, Ian, (2002) 'The Criminal Law of the People's Republic of China (1997): Real Change or Rhetoric?' 11, *Pacific Rim Law and Policy Journal*, 1–62.

Dong, Gaoqun, (2002) 'Laodong Jiaoyang Zhidu Yinggai Feizhi (The Reeducation Through Labour System Should be Abolished)', *Renmin Daibiao Bao (People's Representatives Newspaper)*, 3.

Dowdle, Michael, (1997) 'The Constitutional Development and Operations of the National People's Congress', Spring, *Columbia Journal of Asian Law*, 1–125.

Dowdle, Michael, (1999) 'Heretical Laments: China and the Fallacies of "Rule of Law"', 11, *Cultural Dynamics*, 287–314.

Dreyer, June, (1996) *China's Political System: Modernization and Tradition*, Boston, Allyn and Bacon.

Dutton, Michael, (1992a) 'Disciplinary Projects and Carceral Spread: Foucauldian Theory and Chinese Practice', 21, *Economy and Society*, 276–94.

Dutton, Michael, (1992b) 'A Mass Line Without Politics, Community Policing and Economic Reform', in *Economic Reform and Social Change in China*, Watson, Andrew (ed.), London, Routledge, 200–27.

Dutton, Michael, (1992c) *Policing and Punishment in China, From Patriarchy to 'the People'*, Cambridge, Cambridge University Press.

Dutton, Michael, (1995a) 'Dreaming of Better Times: "Repetition with a Difference" and Community Policing in China', 3, *positions east asia cultures critique*, 415–47.

Dutton, Michael, (1995b) 'One Story, Two Readings: A Response to Harold Tanner', 20, *Law and Social Inquiry*, 305–16.

Dutton, Michael, (1998) *Streetlife China*, Cambridge, Cambridge University Press.

Dutton, Michael, (2000) 'The End of the (Mass) Line? Chinese Policing in the Era of Contract', 27, *Social Justice*, 61–105.

Dutton, Michael, (2005) *Policing Chinese Politics: A History*, Durham, Duke University Press.

Dutton, Michael and Lee, Tianfu, (1993) 'Missing the Target? Policing Strategies in the Period of Economic Reform', 39, *Crime and Delinquency, Special Issue: Crime and Justice in China and Japan*, 316–36.

Dutton, Michael and Xu, Zhangrun, (1998) 'Facing Difference: Relations, Change and the Prison Sector in Contemporary China', in *Comparing Prison Systems: Toward a Comparative and International Penology*, Weiss, Robert and South, Nigel (eds.), Amsterdam, Gordon and Breach Publishers, 289–336.

Editorial Committee, (1997) *Xingzheng Chufa Fa Yinan Wenti Jieda (Answers to Difficult Questions on the Administrative Punishments Law)*, Beijing, Zhongguo Renmin Gong'an Daxue Chubanshe (China People's Public Security Press).

Editorial Committee, PRC Administrative Punishments Law Explanation and Cases (1996) *Zhonghua Renmin Gongheguo Xingzheng Chufa Fa Shiyi yu Anli (PRC Administrative Punishments Law Explanation and Cases)*, Beijing, Renmin Fayuan Chubanshe (People's Court Press).

Epstein, Edward, (1989) 'Administrative Litigation Law: Citizens can Sue the State but not the Party', *China News Analysis*, 3.

Epstein, Edward, (1992) 'A Matter of Justice', in *China Review*, Hong Kong, The Chinese University Press, 1–30.

Epstein, Edward, (1994) 'Law and Legitimation in Post-Mao China,' in *Domestic Law Reforms in Post-Mao China*, Potter, Pitman (ed.), Armonk, M.E. Sharpe.

Epstein, Edward and Wong, Simon Hing-Yan, (1996) 'The Concept of "Dangerousness" in the People's Republic of China and its Impact on the Treatment of Prisoners', 36, *British Journal of Criminology*, 472–97.

Etzioni, Amitai, (2000) 'Social Norms: Internalization, Persuasion and History', 34, *Law and Society Review*, 157–78.

Fan, Chongyi and Xiao, Shengxi (eds.), (1991) *Xingshi Susong Fa Yanjiu Zongshu Yu Pingjia* (*Summary and Appraisal of Criminal Procedure Law Study*), Beijing, Zhongguo Zhengfa Daxue Chubanshe (China University of Politics and Law Press).

Fan, Gang and Xin, Chunying, (1998) *The Role of Law and Legal Institutions in Asian Economic Development: The Case of China*, Boston, Harvard University, Harvard Institute for International Development, 1–41.

Fan, Gu (ed.), (1995) *Ye Jianying Zhuan* (*Biography of Ye Jianying*), Beijing, Dangdai Zhongguo Chubanshe (Contemporary China Press).

Fan, Ping and Yao, Huan, (1998) *Zhongguo Gongchandang Danzhang Jiaocheng* (*Teaching Materials on the Chinese Communist Party Constitution*), Beijing, Zhongguo Fangzhen Chubanshe (China Fangzhen Press).

Fan, Yunhua, (2003) 'Kongquan de Pingheng Lun de Hexin (Controlling Power is the Core of Balance Theory)', in *Xiandai Xingzheng Fa de Pingheng Lilun* (*Balance Theory in Contemporary Administrative Law*), Vol. 2, Luo, Haocai (ed.), Beijing, Beijing Daxue Chubanshe (Beijing University Press), 415–23.

Fang, Qingxia, (2002) 'Goujian Woguo Wanzheng de Bao'an Chufen Zhidu de Shexiang (Envisaging Constructing China's Integrated Security Defence Punishment System)', 20, *Hebei Faxue* (*Hebei Law Science*), 13–17.

Feinerman, James, (1994) 'Legal Institution, Administrative Device, or Foreign Import: The Roles of Contract in the People's Republic of China', in *Domestic Law Reforms in Post-Mao China*, Pitman, Potter (ed.), New York, M.E. Sharpe, 225–44.

Feng, Shuangxing and Wang, Zhilin, (1991) 'Trend Prediction: China's Criminal Offences in the 1990s', in *Crime Trends in the 1990s and its Countermeasures of Prevention and Control*, Chinese People's Public Security University (ed.), Beijing, 98–101.

Feng, Suozhu (ed.), (2005) *Zhonghua Renmin Gongheguo Zhi'an Guanli Chufa Fa Shiyi yu Shiyong Zhinan* (*Guide to the Interpretation and Practice of the PRC Security Administrative Punishments Law*), Beijing, Zhongguo Renmin Gongan Daxue Chubanshe (China People's Public Security Press).

Feng, Xinhua, (2000) 'Shehui Zhi'an Zonghe Zhili Lifa Tanyao (A Probe into Comprehensive Management of Public Order Legislation)', 2, *Hubei Gong'an Gaodeng Xuexiao Xuebao* (*Journal of the Hubei Public Security Institute*), 22–4, 64.

Fenwick, Colin, (2001) *Private Benefit from Forced Prison Labour: Case Studies on the Application of ILO Convention 29*, for the International

Confederation of Free Trade Unions, available at www.ictfu.org/ displaydowmentoasp? Index=991212919&Language=EN>, Chapter 4, The People's Republic of China.

Finder, Susan, (1989) 'Like Throwing an Egg Against a Stone? Administrative Litigation in the PRC', 3, *Journal of Chinese Law*, 1–28.

Finder, Susan, (1993) 'The Supreme People's Court of the People's Republic of China', 7, *Journal of Chinese Law*, 145–224.

Fitzpatrick, Peter, (1983) 'Law, Plurality and Underdevelopment', in *Legality, Ideology and the State*, Sugarman, David (ed.), London and New York, Academic Press, 159–81.

Foreign Languages Press (ed.), (1984) *The Criminal Law and the Criminal Procedure Law of China*, Beijing, Foreign Languages Press.

Forster, Keith, (1985) 'The 1982 Campaign Against Economic Crime in China', 14, *The Australian Journal of Chinese Affairs*, 1–19.

Freckmann, Anna and Wegerich, Thomas, (1999) *The German Legal System*, London, Sweet & Maxwell.

Friedman, Lawrence, (1969a) 'Legal Culture and Social Development', 4, *Law and Society Review*, 29–44.

Friedman, Lawrence, (1969b) 'On Legal Development', 24, *Rutgers Law Review*, 11–64.

Friedman, Lawrence, (2001) 'Erewhon: The Coming Global Legal Order', 37, *Stanford Journal of International Law*, 347.

Fu, Hongjie, (1996) 'Qianxi Dangqian Gong'an Gongzuo de Wuqu (Simple Analysis of Errors in Current Public Security Work)', 1, *Gong'an Yanjiu (Public Security Studies)*, 31–3.

Fu, Hualing, (1990) 'Patrol Police: A Recent Development in the People's Republic of China', 13, *Police Studies*, 111–17.

Fu, Hualing, (1993) *Formalizing Popular Justice: Police and Community in Post-Mao China*, Toronto, Osgoode Hall Law School, York University.

Fu, Hualing, (1994) 'A Bird in the Cage: Police and Political Leadership in Post-Mao China', 4, *Policing and Society*, 277–91.

Fu, Hualing, (1998) 'Criminal Defence in China: The Possible Impact of the 1996 Criminal Procedure Law Reform', 153, *The China Quarterly*, 31–48.

Fu, Hualing, (2002) 'Shifting Landscape of Dispute Resolution in Rural China', in *Implementation of Law in the People's Republic of China*. Chen, Jianfu, Li, Yuwen and Otto, Jan Michiel (eds.), The Hague, Kluwer Law International, 179–95.

Fu, Hualing, (2003) 'The Politics of Mediation in a Chinese County: The Case of Luo Lianxi', 5, *The Australian Journal of Asian Law*, 107–27.

Fu, Hualing, (2005a) 'Punishing for Profit: Profitability and Rehabilitation in a *Laojiao* Institution', in *Engaging the Law in China: State, Society, and Possibilities for Justice*, Diamant, Neil, Lubman, Stanley and O'Brien, Kevin (eds.), Stanford, Stanford University Press, 213–29.

Fu, Hualing, (2005b) 'Re-education Through Labour in Historical Perspective', 184, *The China Quarterly*, 811–30.

Fu, Hualing, (2005c) 'Zhou Yongkang and the Recent Police Reform in China', 38, *Australian and New Zealand Journal of Criminology*, 241–53.

Fu, Huazong *et al.* (eds.), (1991) *Shiyong Xingzheng Chengxu Fa* (*Practical Administrative Procedure Law*), Beijing, Zhongguo Renmin Gong'an Daxue Chubanshe (Chinese People's Public Security University Press).

Fu, Shicheng, (2001) *Xingzheng Qiangzhi Yanjiu* (*Study of Administrative Coercion*), Beijing, Falu Chubanshe (Law Press).

Fu, Siming, (2002) *Zhongguo Yifa Xingzheng de Lilun yu Shijian* (*Theory and Practice of Administration According to Law in China*), Beijing, Zhongguo Jiancha Chubanshe (China Procuratorate Press).

Fu, Xu, Zhu, Dongju and Wang, Leiming, (8 November 1999) 'Parliament Leader Urges More Supervision by Local Legislatures', BBC Summary World Broadcasts, Asia Pacific Stories.

Funk, Albrecht, (1995) 'The German Police System in a European Context', in *Comparisons in Policing: An International Perspective*, Brodeur, Jean-Paul (ed.), Aldershot, Avebury, 69–86.

Gai, Jun (ed.), (2001) *Zhongguo Gongchandang 80 Nian Lishi Jianbian* (*A Short History of the 80 Years of the Chinese Communist Party*) Beijing, Zhonggong Zhongyang Dangxiao Chubanshe (Central Party School Press).

Galligan, Dennis, (1990) *Discretionary Powers. A Legal Study of Official Discretion*, Oxford, Clarendon Press.

Gao, Chuanli, (1998) 'Xuexi Yifa Zhiguo Jianshe Shihui Zhuyi Fazhi Guojia Jiben Fanglue: Tuidong Shiwu Da Jingshen de Guanche Luoshi (Study Ruling the Country by Law to Construct the Basic Plan for Ruling the Country by Law: Promote Implementation of the Spirit of the Fifteenth Central Committee)', in *Yifa Zhiguo Jiben Fanlue Lunwenji* (*Collection of Essays on the Basic Plan for Ruling the Country by Law*), Sifabu Sifa Yanjiu Suo (Judicial Research Office of the Bureau of Justice) (ed.), Beijing, Falu Chubanshe (Law Press), 1–16.

Gao, Han, (1992) 'Dangqian Liuchong Fanzui de Tedian yu Duice (The Current Characteristics and Tactics to Deal with Floating Criminals)', *Fanzui yu Duice* (*Crime and Countermeasures*), 37–9.

Gao, Huanyue (ed.), (1995) *Zhonghua Renmin Gongheguo Renmin Jingcha Fa Jianghua* (*Discussion of the People's Police Law of the PRC*), Beijing, Zhongguo Jiancha Chubanshe (China Procuratorate Press).

Gao, Mingxuan and Zhao, Bingzhi (eds.), (1999) *Xin Zhongguo Xingfa Xue Yanjiu Licheng* (*The Course of Criminal Law Studies in New China*), Beijing, Fangzheng Chubanshe (Fangzheng Press).

Gao, Weixin and Chen, Xin, (2003) 'Bao'an Chufen Zhidu de Fali Jichu Ji Qi Zai Woguo de Goujian (The Jurisprudential Basis of the System of

Security Defence Punishments and their Establishment in China)', 3, *Shihezi Daxue Xuebao (Journal of Shihezi University)*, 57–60.

Gao, Xianduan, (1990) 'Shourong Shencha de Wenti yu Chulu (The Problem and Prospects for Detention for Investigation)', 3, *Gong'an Yanjiu (Public Security Studies)*, 18–21.

Gao, Xianduan, (1992) 'Shilun Woguo Laodong Jiaoyang Zhidu de Tedian (A Tentative Discussion of my Country's System of Re-education Through Labour)', 5, *Gong'an Yanjiu (Public Security Studies)*, 38–42.

Gao, Yiyu, (1994) 'Qiantan Xin Shiqi Jingcha Xingxiang (Brief Discussion of Police Image in the New Era)', in *Zhongguo Renmin Gong'an Daxue Xiaoqing Shi Zhou Nian Lunwen Xuanji (Selection of Essays for the Tenth Anniversary of the China People's Public Security University)*, Xiaoqing Chouban Bangongshi Xueshu Xiaozu (Anniversary Preparation Office Academic Small Group) (ed.), Beijing, Zhongguo Renmin Gong'an Daxue Chubanshe (China People's Public Security Press), 325–34.

Ge, Fei, (1998) 'Second Class Citizen: A Record of China's First "Severe Strike" Campaign', in *Streetlife China*, Dutton, Michael (ed.), Cambridge, Cambridge University Press, 65–9.

Gillespie, John, (2002) 'Transplanted Company Law: An Ideological and Cultural Analysis of Market Entry in Vietnam', 51, *International and Comparative Law Quarterly*, 641–72.

Goldsmith, Andrew, (1990) 'Taking Police Culture Seriously: Police Discretion and the Limits of Law', 1, *Policing and Society*, 91–114.

Goldstein, Joseph, (1960) 'Police Discretion not to Invoke the Criminal Process: Low Visibility Decisions in the Administration of Justice', in *Policing*, Vol. 2, Reiner, Robert (ed.), Aldershot, Dartmouth, 3–54.

Gong, Taihua, (1991) 'Jingcha Quan yu Xingzheng Susong (Police Power and Administrative Litigation)', 4, *Gong'an Daxue Xuebao (Journal of the Public Security University)*, 46–7, 50.

Gong, Taihua, (1994) 'Jianli Cuiqiu Gong'an Ganjing Zhefa Guocuo Zeren Zhidu Chutan (Preliminary Exploration of Establishment of a System for Accountability of Public Security Officers for Faults in Enforcement)', in *Zhongguo Renmin Gong'an Daxue Xiaoqing Shi Zhou Nian Lunwen Xuanji (Selection of Essays for the Tenth Anniversary of the China People's Public Security University)*, Xiaoqing Chouban Bangongshi Xueshu Xiaozu (Anniversary Preparation Office Academic Small Group) (ed.), Beijing, Zhongguo Renmin Gong'an Daxue Chubanshe (China People's Public Security Press), 367–75.

Gong, Xiangrui, (1993) *Fazhi de Lixiang yu Xianshi (The Ideal and Reality of Rule of Law)*, Beijing, Zhongguo Zhengfa Daxue Chubanshe (China University of Politics and Law Press).

Gong'an Bu (Ministry of Public Security), (1995) *Zhongguo Gong'an Gongzuo* (*Policing in China*), Beijing, Gong'an Bu (Ministry of Public Security).

Gong'an Bu (Ministry of Public Security), (2002) *Zhongguo Gong'an Gongzuo* (*Policing in China*), Beijing, Gong'an Bu (Ministry of Public Security) 1–90.

Gong'an Bu Fagui Ju (ed.), (1980) *Zhifa Shouce*, Beijing, Qunzhong Chubanshe (Masses Press).

Gong'an Bu Fagui Ju (ed.), (1984) *Zhifa Shouce*, Beijing, Qunzhong Chubanshe (Masses Press).

Gong'an Bu Fagui Ju (ed.), (1985) *Zhifa Shouce*, Beijing, Qunzhong Chubanshe (Masses Press).

Gong'an Bu Fagui Ju (ed.), (1986) *Zhifa Shouce*, Beijing, Qunzhong Chubanshe (Masses Press).

Gong'an Bu Fagui Ju (ed.), (1987) *Zhifa Shouce*, Beijing, Qunzhong Chubanshe (Masses Press).

Gong'an Bu Fagui Ju (ed.), (1988) *Zhifa Shouce*, Beijing, Qunzhong Chubanshe (Masses Press).

Gong'an Bu Fagui Ju (ed.), (1989) *Zhifa Shouce*, Beijing, Qunzhong Chubanshe (Masses Press).

Gong'an Bu Fazhi Ju (ed.), (1998) *Gong'an Jiguan Zhifa Xuzhi*, Beijing, Jingguan Jiaoyu Chubanshe (Police Officer's Education Press).

Gong'an Bu Fazhi Ju (ed.), (1999) *Gong'an Jiguan Zhifa Xuzhi*, Beijing, Jingguan Jiaoyu Chubanshe (Police Officer's Education Press).

Gong'an Bu Fazhi Ju (ed.), (2000) *Gong'an Jiguan Zhifa Xuzhi*, Beijing, Zhongguo Renmin Gong'an Daxue Chubanshe (China People's Police University Press).

Gong'an Bu Fazhi Ju (ed.), (2001) *Gong'an Jiguan Zhifa Xuzhi*, Beijing, Zhongguo Renmin Gong'an Daxue Chubanshe (China People's Police University Press).

Gong'an Bu Fazhi Ju (ed.), (2002) *Gong'an Jiguan Zhifa Xuzhi*, Beijing, Zhongguo Renmin Gong'an Daxue Chubanshe (China People's Police University Press).

Gong'an Bu Fazhi Ju (ed.), (2004) *Gong'an Jiguan Zhifa Xuzhi*, Beijing, Zhongguo Renmin Gong'an Daxue Chubanshe (China People's Police University Press).

Gong'an Bu, Fazhi Ju Disi Yanjiusuo, (1999) 'Dangqian Gong'an Zhifazhong Cunzai de Zhuyao Wenti Ji Duice Zhengwen Zongshu (Summary of Solicited Contributions on the Main Problems Existing in Contemporary Public Security Enforcement and Counter-measures)', 2, *Gong'an Yanjiu* (*Public Security Studies*), 19–21.

Gong'an Bu Fazhi Si, (1992) *Gong'an Jiguan Banli Laodong Jiaoyang Anjian Fagui Huibian* (*Collections of Laws and Regulations on Public Security Officals*

Handling Re-education Through Labour Cases), Beijing, Jingguan Jiaoyu Chubanshe (Police Officer's Education Press).

Gong'an Bu Fazhi Si (ed.), (1990) *Zhifa Shouce*, Beijing, Qunzhong Chubanshe (Masses Press).

Gong'an Bu Fazhi Si (ed.), (1991) *Zhifa Shouce*, Beijing, Qunzhong Chubanshe (Masses Press).

Gong'an Bu Fazhi Si (ed.), (1992) *Zhifa Shouce*, Beijing, Qunzhong Chubanshe (Masses Press).

Gong'an Bu Fazhi Si (ed.), (1993) *Zhifa Shouce*, Beijing, Qunzhong Chubanshe (Masses Press).

Gong'an Bu Fazhi Si (ed.), (1994) *Zhifa Shouce*, Beijing, Qunzhong Chubanshe (Masses Press).

Gong'an Bu Fazhi Si (ed.), (1995) *Zhifa Shouce*, Beijing, Qunzhong Chubanshe (Masses Press).

Gong'an Bu Fazhi Si (ed.), (1996) *Zhifa Shouce*, Beijing, Qunzhong Chubanshe (Masses Press).

Gong'an Bu Fazhi Si (ed.), (1997) *Gong'an Jiguan Zhifa Xuzhi*, Beijing, Jingguan Jiaoyu Chubanshe (Police Officer's Education Press).

Gong'an Bu Gonggong Anquan Yanjiusuo (Ministry of Public Security, Public Security Research Institute) (ed.), (1991) *Ni Gandao Anquan Ma? (Do you Feel Safe*), Beijing, Qunzhong Chubanshe (Masses Press).

Gong'an Bu Yushen Ju (ed.), (1985) *Yushen Kanshoushuo Gongzuo Shouce* (*Handbook of Investigative Dentention and Lock-up Work*), Beijing, Qunzhong Chubanshe (Masses Press).

Gong'an Bu, Zhengzhi Bu (ed.), (1990) *Gong'an Zhengzhi Shouce* (*Handbook of Public Security Political Work*), Beijing, Qunzhong Chubanshe (Masses Press).

Gramckow, Heike, (1995) 'The Influence of History and the Rule of Law on the Development of Community Policing in Germany', 18, *Police Studies*, 17.

Gu, Xin, (1998) 'Plural Institutionalism and the Emergence of Intellectual Public Spaces in Contemporary China: Four Relational Patterns and Four Organizational Forms', 7, *Journal of Contemporary China*, 271–301.

Guo, Daohui, (4 February 2000) 'Legal Paper on Developing the Rule of Law, Media Freedom', BBC Summary of World Broadcasts, Asian Pacific Stories.

Guo, Dawei, (1990) 'Zuohao Shishi Xingzheng Susong Fa de Zhunbei Baozheng Gong'an Jiguan Yifa Xingzheng (Do a Good Job of Preparation for Implementation of the Administrative Litigation Law to Ensure Public Security Organs Carry out Administration According to Law)', 1, *Gong'an Yanjiu* (*Public Security Studies*), 27–9.

Guo, Jian'an, (2005) 'Zhongguo Laodong Jiaoyang Zhidu Yanjiu Baogao (Research Report on China's System of Re-educationThrough Labour)', in *Xianzhi dui Renshen Ziyou de Xianzhi* (*To Refrain from the Restictions on Personal Freedom*), Guo, Jian'an and Zheng, Xiaze (eds.), Beijing, Falu Chubanshe (Law Press), 278–366.

Guo, Jian'an and Li, Rongwen, (2000) *Xidu Weifa Xingwei de Yufang yu Jiaozhi* (*Prevention and Treatment of Drug Abuse*), Beijing, Falu Chubanshe (Law Press).

Guowuyuan Fazhi Ju (ed.), (1958) *Zhonghua Renmin Gongheguo Fagui Huibian* (*Collection of the Laws and Regulations of the PRC*), Beijing, Falu Chubanshe (Law Press).

Hamrin, Carol Lee and Zhao, Suisheng (eds.), (1995) *Decision-Making in Deng's China: Perspectives from Insiders*, Armonk, New York, M.E. Sharpe.

Han, Wei, (2000) 'Bao'an Chufen Shi fou Shiyong yu Xianjieduan de Zhongguo (Is the Security Defence Punishment Suitable in Contemporary China)', 14, *Jiangsu Gong'an Zhuanke Xuexiao Xuebao* (*Journal of Jiangsu Public Security College*), 105–7.

Han, Yong, (1994) 'Xingzheng Susong Chesu Duo de Xianxiang Burong Hushi (It Cannot be Ignored that there is an Increase in the Number of Administrative Cases that are Withdrawn)', 6, *Shandong Shenpan* (*Shandong Adjudication*), 29–31.

Hao, Chiyong and Shan, Zhou, (1999) *Jingwu Gongkai yu Gongmin Quanli* (*Openness in Police Work and Citizens' Rights*), Beijing, Xiandai Chubanshe (Modern Press).

Hao, Hongkui, (1991) 'Impact of Chinese Rural Community Changes on Crimes-Sociological Thinking on Rural Crimes', in *Crime Trend in the 1990s and its Countermeasures of Prevention and Control*, Beijing, Chinese People's Public Security University Press (ed.), 77–85.

Hao, Zhangsheng and Li, Zhenguo, (1998) 'Shourong Jiaoyu Gongzuo Chutan (Preliminary Exploration of Detention for Education Work)', 5, *Henan Gong'an Xuekan* (*Henan Public Security Studies Journal*), 22–5.

Harding, Harry, (1987) *China's Second Revolution: Reform After Mao*, Sydney, Allen & Unwin.

Harlan, John, (1997) 'The German Police: Issues in the Unification Process', 20, *Policing*, 532–54.

Hawes, Colin, (2003) 'Seeds of Dissent: The Evolution of Published Commercial Law Court Judgments in Conetmporary China', 5, *Australian Journal of Asian Law*, 1–41.

Hawkins, Keith, (1986) 'On Legal Decision-Making', 43, *Washington and Lee Law Review*, 1116–242.

Hazard, John, (1969) *Communists and their Law*, Chicago, University of Chicago Press.

He, Fuqiang, (2002) 'Gong'an Xingzheng Chufa Helixing Yuance de Liangdian Sikao (Reflecting on Two Points about the Principle of Reasonableness in Public Security Administrative Punishments)', 71, *Zhejiang Gong'an*

Gaodeng Zhuanke Xuexiao Bao 'Gong'an Xuekan' (*Journal of Zhejiang Police College 'Public Security Science Journal'*), 56–8.

He, Jiangui (ed.), (1991) *Xingzheng Chufa Tonglun* (*General Survey of Administrative Punishment*), Beijing, Falu Chubanshe (Law Press).

Hecht, Jonathon, (1996) *Opening to Reform? An Analysis of China's Revised Criminal Procedure Law*, New York, Lawyers Committee for Human Rights.

Heng, Russell Hiang Khng, (2001) 'Media Negotiating the State: In the Name of the Law in Anticipation', 16, *Sojourn*, 213–37.

Henriot, Christian, (1995) "La Fermature": The Abolition of Prostitution in Shanghai, 1949–58', 142, *The China Quarterly*, 467–86.

Herschatter, Gail, (1997) *Dangerous Pleasures: Prostitution and Modernity in Twentieth-Century Shanghai*, Berkeley, University of California Press.

Hintzen, Geor, (1999) 'The Place of Law in the PRC's Culture', 11, *Cultural Dynamics*, 167–92.

Hou, Baotian, (1994) 'Woguo Xianxing Fa zhong de Bao'an Chufen (The Security Defence Punishment in China's Contemporary Law)', 56, *Falu Kexue* (*Legal Science*), 41–6, 58.

Hsia, Tao Tai and Zeldin, Wendy, (1992) 'Sheltering for Examination (Shourong Shencha) in the Legal System of the People's Republic of China', 7, *China Law Reporter*, 97–128.

Hu, Jiansen, (2002) 'Lun Zhongguo "Xingzheng Qiangzhi Cuoshi" Gainian de Yanbian ji Dingwei (Discussing the Evolution and Position of China's "Administrative Coercive Measures")', 6, *Zhongguo Faxue* (*Chinese Legal Science*), 34–42.

Hu, Jiansen and Jin, Weifeng, (2000) 'Zhongguo Xianxing Falu Fagui Guizhang suo she Xingzheng Qiangzhi Cuoshi zhi Xianzhuang Ji Shizheng Fenxi (An Analysis of the Current Situtaion and Substantial Evidence on China's Current Laws, Regulations and Rules Relating to Administrative Coercive Measures)', 6, *Faxue Luntan*, 31–4.

Hu, Jiansen and Wang, Lianxing (eds.), (1991) *Xingzheng Susong Shilun yu Anli* (*Administrative Litigation Law: Explanation and Cases*), Beijing, Falu Chubanshe (Law Press).

Hu, Jintao, (20 February 2005) 'Shenke Renshi Goujian Shehui Zhuyi Hexie Shehui de Zhongda Yiyi Zhazha Shishi Zuohao Gongzuo Dali Cujin Shehui Hexie Tuanjie (Profoundly Understand the Major Significance of Constructing a Socialist Harmonious Society, Solidly do a Good Job of Strongly Promoting Social Harmony and Unity)', in *Renmin Ribao* (*People's Daily*), Beijing.

Hu, Kangsheng and Li, Fucheng, (1997) *Zhonghua Renmin Gongheguo Xingfa Shiyi* (*Explanation of the Criminal Law of the People's Republic of China*), Beijing, Falu Chubanshe (Law Press).

Hu, Kui and Sun, Zhan, (14 August 2003) A *Powerful Drive to Exercise Management over the Police*, London, BBC Monitoring International Reports.

Hu, Rengu, (1992) 'Tan Gong'an Xingzheng Susong Anjian (Discussion of Public Security Administrative Litigation Cases)', *Jingcha Wenzhai (Police Digest)*, citing *Renmin Gong'an (People's Police)*, 36–7.

Hu, Weilie, (2003) 'Laodong Jiaoyang Zhidu Ying yu Feichu (The System of Re-education Through Labour Should be Abolished)', in *Zhi'an Guanli Zhidu Sicun* (*Reflection on the Public Order Regulation*), Zhu, Weiguo (ed.), Beijing, Falu Chubanshe (Law Press), 136–47.

Hu, Yanfei, (1998) 'Lun Gong'an Xingzheng Ziyou Cailiangquan (On Public Security Administrative Discretion)', 3, *Gong'an Yanjiu* (*Public Security Studies*), 49–51.

Hua, Jingfeng, (2005) 'Banli Zhi'an Anjian Yinfa Xinfang Wenti de Yuanyin Ji Xiangguan Duice (Causes and Related Counter-Measures for Letters and Visits Problems Triggered by the Handling of Public Order Cases)', 131, *Gongan Yanjiu* (*Police Research*), 32–5.

Huang, Daphne, (1998) 'The Right to a Fair Trial in China', 7, *Pacific Rim Law and Policy Journal*, 171–96.

Huang, Jie, (1992) 'On the Administrative Litigation Law', 24, *Chinese Law and Government*, 43–46.

Huang, Jie (ed.), (1993) *Xingzheng Susong Shiyong Daquan* (*Encyclopedia of Administrative Litigation*), Hebei, Hebei Renmin Chubanshe (Hebei People's Press).

Huang, Jingping, Li, Tianfu and Wang, Zhiming, (1988) 'Gong'an Guanli Xianzhuang (The Situation with Regard to Public Security Management)', 4, *Gong'an Yanjiu* (*Public Security Studies*), 42–6.

Huang, Yao, (1994) *Sanci Danan Busi de Luo Ruiqing Dajiang* (*Senior General Luo Ruiqing who Survived Three Great Disasters*), Beijing, Zhonggong Dangshi Chubanshe (Central Party History Press).

Huang, Yao and Zhang, Mingzhe (eds.), (1996) *Luo Ruiqing Zhuan* (*Biography of Luo Ruiqing*), Beijing, Dangdai Zhongguo Chubanshe (Contemporary China Press).

Hui, Shengwu (ed.), (1991) *Jingcha Xingzhengfa Gailun* (*An Introduction to Police Administrative Law*), Shanxi, Shanxi Renmin Jiaoyi Chubanshe (Shanxi People's Education Press).

Hui, Shengwu (ed.), (2000) *Jingcha fa Lungang* (*Outline Discussion of the Police Law*), Beijing, Zhongguo Zhengfa Daxue Chubanshe (China Politics and Law University Press).

Human Rights Delegation to China, (1991) *Report of the Human Rights Delegation to China.*

Human Rights in China, (1999) *Not Welcome at the Party: Behind the 'Clean-up' of China's Cities – A Report on Administrative Detention under Custody and Repatriation*, New York, Human Rights in China, 1–52.

Human Rights in China, (2001a) *Empty Promises: Human Rights Protection and China's Criminal Procedure Law in Practice*, New York, Human Rights in China, 1–94.

Human Rights in China, (2001b) *Re-education Through Labour (RTL): A Summary of Regulatory Issues and Concerns*, Hong Kong, Human Rights in China, 1–9.

Human Rights Watch, (2001) 'Opportunism in the Face of Tragedy: Repression in the Name of Anti-terrorism', www.hrw.org/campaigns/september11/opportunismwatch.htm.

Human Rights Watch, (2002) *Dangerous Meditation: China's Campaign Against Falungong*, New York and Washington, Human Rights Watch

Human Rights Watch, (December 2005) 'We Could Disappear At Any Time: Retaliation and Abuses Against Chinese Petitioners', 17, *Human Rights Watch*, 1–87.

Hung, Veron Meiying, (2003a) 'Improving Human Rights in China: Should Re-education Through Labour be Abolished?' *Columbia Journal of Transnational Law*, 303–26.

Hung, Veron Meiying, (2003b) 'Reassessing Re-education Through Labour', 2, *China Rights Forum*, 35–41.

Hunt, Alan, (1993) *Explorations in Law and Society: Toward a Constitutive Theory of Law*, New York and London, Routledge.

Hunt, Alan and Wickham, Gary, (1994) *Foucault and Law: Towards a Sociology of Law as Governance*, London, Pluto Press.

Jayasuriya, Kanishka, (1999) 'Introduction: A Framework for Analysis of Legal Institutions in East Asia', in *Law, Capitalism and Power in Asia*, Jayasuriya, Kanishka (ed.), London, Routledge, 1–27.

Jeffreys, Elaine, (2004) *China, Sex and Prostitution*, London, RoutledgeCurzon.

Ji, Haibing, (1995) 'Dui Maiyin Piaochang Weifa Fanzui Huodong Daji Bu Li de Biaoxian Ji Duice (The Manifestations and Countermeasures against Striking Without Force against Prostitution and Related Unlawful and Criminal Activities)', 3, *Gong'an Yanjiu* (*Public Security Studies*), 25–8.

Ji, Weidong, (1993) 'Chengxu Bijiao Lun (A Discussion of Comparative Procedure)', 7, *Bijiao Fa Yanjiu* (*Journal of Comparative Law*), 1–46.

Jiang, Bixin, (2000) 'Xingzheng Guanli Xiangdui Ren de Quanli Qiuqi (Enforcement Mechanisms for the Citizens' Rights Against Unlawful Administrative Actions)', in *Zouxiang Quanli de Shidai* (*Toward an Age of Rights*), Xia, Yong (ed.), Beijing, Zhongguo Zhengfa Daxue Chubanshe (China University of Politics and Law Press), 552–611.

Jiang, Bixin (ed.), (1997) *Xingzheng Jiancha Fa Shiyong Quanshu* (*Practical Encyclopedia on the Administrative Supervision Law*), Beijing, Renmin Fayuan Chubanshe.

Jiang, Bo and Zhan, Zhongle, (1994) *Gong'an Xingzheng Fa* (*Public Security Administrative Law*), Beijing, Zhongguo Renshi Chubanshe (China Personnel Press).

Jiang, Lishan, (1998) 'Fazhi Xiandaihua Fangan Tantao (An Inquiry into the Programme of Legal System Modernisation)', in *Fazhi Xiandaihua Yanjiu* (*Studies on Modernization of the Legal System*), Vol. 4, Nanjing Normal University Modernization of the Legal System Research Centre (ed.), Nanjing, Nanjing Normal University Press, 94–120.

Jiang, Mingan, (1997) 'Lun 'Pingheng Lun' Ji Xingzheng fa Lilun Jichu Yanjiu de Yidian Qianjian-yu Ji Wei Tonghang Pengyou de Yici Duihua (Discussing a Few of My Humble Opinions about "Balance Theory" and the Theoretical Basis of Administrative Law Study – A Conversation with Several Colleagues and Friends)', in *Xiandai Xingzhengfa de Pingheng Lilun* (*Balance Theory in Contemporary Administrative Law*), Luo, Haocai (ed.), Beijing, Beijing Daxue Chubanshe (Peking University Press), 242–5.

Jiang, Mingan, (1998) *Zhongguo Xingzheng Fazhi Fazhan Jincheng Diaocha Baogao* (*Report on an Investigation on the Course of Development of Chinese Administration by Law*), Beijing, Falu Chubanshe (Law Press).

Jiang, Qihan and Yuan, Kaiying, (1990) 'Laodong Jiaoyang Wenti Shulue (Discussion of Problems of Re-education Through Labour)', 4, *Gong'an Yanjiu* (*Public Security Studies*), 46–8.

Jiang, Qingming, (2002) 'Dui Xidu Renyuan Kaizhan Shehui Bangjiao de Diaocha yu Sikao (Investigation into and Reflections on Social Help and Education of Drug Users)', 5, *Gong'an Xuekan* (*Public Security Science Journal*), 31–4.

Jiang, Yihuai, (1997) 'Lun Jianli Zhongguo Tese de Bao'an Chufen Zhidu (Discussing Establishment of a System of Security Defence Punishments with Chinese Characteristics)', 3, *Gong'an Yanjiu* (*Public Security Studies*), 41–3, 62.

Jie, Chen and Yang, Zhong, (2000) 'Valuation of Individual Liberty vs. Social Order among Democratic Supporters: A Cross Validation', 53, *Political Research Quarterly*, 427–39.

Jie, Chen, Yang, Zhong, Hillard, Jan and Scheb, John, (1997) 'Assesing Political Support in China: Citizens' Evaluation of Government Effectiveness and Legitimacy', 6, *Journal of Contemporary China*, 551–66.

Johnson, E.H., (1983) 'Neighbourhood Police in the People's Republic of China', *Police Studies, the International Review of Police Developments*, 8–12.

Johnston, Gordon and Percy-Smith, Janie, (2003) 'In Search of Social Capital', 31, *Policy and Politics*, 321–34.

Jones, Carol, (1994) 'Capitalism, Globalization and the Rule of Law: An Alternative Trajectory of Legal Change in China', 3, *Social and Legal Studies*, 195–221.

Jones, Carol, (1999) 'Politics Postponed: Law as a Substitute for Politics in Hong Kong and China', in *Law, Capitalism and Power in Asia: The Rule of Law and Legal Institutions*, Jayasuriya, Kanishka (ed.), London, Routledge, 45–68.

Kahn-Freund, Otto, (1974) 'On the Uses and Misuses of Comparative Law', 37, *Modern Law Review*, 1–27.

Kang, Damin, (1993) 'Mass Line of Public Security in China', in *Seminar on Police Management; A Paper Collection*, Chinese People's Public Security University, Foreign Affairs Office (ed.), Beijing, 84–89.

Kang, Shuhua (ed.), (1992) *Fanzuixue Tonglun* (*General Discussion of Criminology*), Beijing, Beijing Daxue Chubanshe (Peking University Press).

Ke, Liangdong, (1990) 'Qiangzhi Jiedu Lifa Lun (Discussion about Legislation for Coercive Drug Rehabilitation)', 6, *Gong'an Yanjiu* (*Public Security Studies*), 23–7.

Ke, Liangdong and Wei, Monan (eds.), (1992) *Guanyu Yanjin Maiyin Piaochang de Jueding, Guanyu Yancheng Guaimai Bangjia Funu Ertong de Fanzui Fenzi de Jueding Shiyi* (*Explanation of the Decision on Strictly Prohibiting Prostitution and Using Prostitutes and the Decision on the Severe Punishment of Criminal Elements who Kidnap and Sell Women and Children*), Beijing, Qunzhong Chubanshe (Masses Press).

Ke, Liangdong and Wu, Mingshan (eds.), (2005) *Zhi'an Guanli Chufa Fa Shiyi yu Shiwu Zhinan* (*Guide to the Explanation and Implementation of the Security Administrative Punishments Law*), Beijing, Zhongguo Renmin Gong'an Daxue Chubanshe (China People's Public Security Press).

Ke, Meisen, (1994) 'Tantan Shourong Jiaoyu de Jige Wenti (Discussing Several Questions about Detention for Education)', 1, *Zhengfa Xuekan* (*Journal of Political Science and Law*), 48–52.

Keith, Ronald, (1994) *China's Struggle for the Rule of Law*, New York, St Martin's Press.

Keith, Ronald and Lin, Zhiqiu, (2001) *Law and Justice in China's Marketplace*, New York, Palgrave.

Keith, Ronald and Lin, Zhiqiu, (2003) 'The 'Falungong Problem': Politics and the Struggle for the Rule of Law in China', 175, *The China Quarterly*, 623–42.

Keller, Perry, (1989) 'Legislation in the People's Republic of China', 23, *University of British Columbia Law Review*, 653–88.

Keller, Perry, (1994) 'Sources of Order in Chinese Law', 42, *The American Journal of Comparative Law*, 711–59.

Kirkby, R, (1985) *Urbanization in China: Town and Country in a Developing Economy 1949–2000 AD*, New York, Columbia University Press.

Korzec, Michal, (1991) 'Administrative Lawlessness in China', *Review of Socialist Law*, 145–59.

Lang, Sheng (ed.), (1995) '*Zhonghua Renmin Gongheguo Renmin Jingcha Fa' Shiyong Wenti Jiexi* (*Explanation and Analysis of Practical Questions of the 'PRC Peoples' Police Law*), Beijing, Zhongguo Minzhu Fazhi Chubanshe (China Democracy and Legal System Press).

Law Yearbook Editorial Committee (ed.), (1991) *Law Yearbook of China*, Beijing, Press of Law Yearbook of China.

Law Yearbook Editorial Committee (ed.), (1992) *Law Yearbook of China*, Beijing, Press of Law Yearbook of China.

Law Yearbook Editorial Committee (ed.), (1993) *Law Yearbook of China*, Beijing, Press of Law Yearbook of China.

Law Yearbook Editorial Committee (ed.), (1994) *Law Yearbook of China*, Beijing, Press of Law Yearbook of China.

Law Yearbook Editorial Committee (ed.), (1995) *Law Yearbook of China*, Beijing, Press of Law Yearbook of China.

Law Yearbook Editorial Committee (ed.), (1996) *Law Yearbook of China*, Beijing, Press of Law Yearbook of China.

Law Yearbook Editorial Committee (ed.), (1997) *Law Yearbook of China*, Beijing, Press of Law Yearbook of China.

Law Yearbook Editorial Committee (ed.), (1998) *Law Yearbook of China*, Beijing, Press of Law Yearbook of China.

Law Yearbook Editorial Committee (ed.), (1999) *Law Yearbook of China*, Beijing, Press of Law Yearbook of China.

Law Yearbook Editorial Committee (ed.), (2000) *Law Yearbook of China*, Beijing, Press of Law Yearbook of China.

Law Yearbook Editorial Committee (ed.), (2001) *Law Yearbook of China*, Beijing, Press of Law Yearbook of China.

Law Yearbook Editorial Committee (ed.), (2002) *Law Yearbook of China*, Beijing, Press of Law Yearbook of China.

Law Yearbook Editorial Committee (ed.), (2004) *Law Yearbook of China*, Beijing, Press of Law Yearbook of China.

Lee, David, (2000) 'Legal Reform in China: A Role for Nongovernmental Organizations', 25, *Yale Journal of International Law*, 363–433.

Legrand, Pierre, (2001) 'What "Legal Transplants"?', in *Adapting Legal Cultures*, Nelken, David and Feest, Johannes (eds.), Oxford, Hart Publishing, 55–70.

Leng, Shaochuan and Chiu, Hongdah, (1985) *Criminal Justice in Post-Mao China: Analysis and Documents*, Albany State, University of New York Press.

Li, Baozhen (scribe for Legal Division of the Ministry of Public Security and Number Four Research Unit), (1999) 'Dangqian Gong'an Zhefa zhong Cunzai de Zhuyao Wenti Ji Duice Zhengwen Zongshu (Summary of Solicited Articles on the Main Problems and Counter-measures Existing in Current Public Security Enforcement)', 2, *Gong'an Yanjiu* (*Public Security Studies*), 19–21.

Li, Cheng, (1998) 'Surplus Rural Labourers and Internal Migration in China', in *Migration in China*, Bakken, Borge (ed.), Copenhagen, Nordic Institute of Asian Studies, 17–65.

Li, Chunhua, (2002) *Zhi'an Guanli Chufa Shilun yu Xin Anli Pingxi* (*Explanation and Discussion of Security Administrative Punishments and Commentary on New Cases*), Beijing, Zhongguo Renmin Gong'an Daxue Chubanshe (China People's Public Security Press).

Li, Gangde, (1993) 'Zai Quanshen Di er zi Xingzheng Shenpan Gongzuo Huiyi Shang de Jianghua (Talk Given at the Second Provincial Administrative Adjudication Work Conference)', 6, *Gansu Shenpan* (*Gansu Adjudication*), 6–8.

Li, Huayin and Liu, Baiyang (eds.), (1992) *Gong'an Xingzheng Chengxu Yu Zingzheng Susong* (*Public Security Administrative Procedure and Administrative Litigation*), Beijing, Qunzhong Chubanshe (Masses Press).

Li, Jieli, (1996) 'The Structural Strains of China's Socio-legal System: A Transition to Formal Legalism?' 24, *International Journal of the Sociology of Law*, 41–59.

Li, Junren and Du, Fuzhi, (1990) 'Lun Laodong Jiaoyang de Xingzhi Wenti (Discussion of the Nature of Re-education Through Labour)', in *Laodong Jiaoyang Yanjiu* (*Studies in Re-education Through Labour*), Beijing, Qunzhong Chubanshe (Masses Press), 48–58.

Li, Lin, (1998) 'Lifa Jiguan (Legislative Organs)', in *Xianfa Bijiao Yanjiu* (*Comparative Study of Constitutional Law*), Li, Buyun (ed.), Beijing, Falu Chubanshe (Law Press), 755–836.

Li, Linda Chelan, (2000) 'The "Rule of Law" Policy in Guangdong: Continuity or Departure? Meaning, Significance and Processes', 161, *The China Quarterly*, 199–220.

Li, Peizhuan (ed.), (1993) *Xingzheng Fuyi Gailan* (*General Overview of Administrative Review*), Beijing, Zhongguo Fazhi Chubanshe (China Legal System Press).

Li, Peng, (2000) 'Li Peng Weiyuanzhang Guanyu Quanguo Renda Changweihui Lifa Gongzuo de Zhongyao Lunshu (Important Expositions by Li Peng Commission Head on the Legislation Work of the Standing Committee of the NPC)', in *Zhonghua Renmin Gongheguo Lifa Fa Shiyi* (*Explanation of the PRC Legislation Law*), Zhang, Chunsheng (ed.), Beijing, Falu Chubanshe (Law Press), 300–5.

Li, Qian and Cui, Xiaofang, (1990) 'Laogai Jiefang, Laojiao Jiechu Renyuan Zhongxin Fanzui Wenti Yuanyin Tanxi (Exploration and Analysis of the Causes for Recidivism amongst People Released from Reform Through Labour and Re-education Through Labour)', in *Zhongguo Xian Jieduan Fanzui Wenti Yanjiu (Lunwen Ji)* (*Study of the Problem of Crime in China's*

New Era (Essay Collection)), Vol. 2, Yu, Lei (ed.), Beijing, Zhongguo Renmin Gong'an Daxue Chubanshe (Chinese People's Public Security Press), 434–41.

Li, Qiyan, (1993) *Zhongguo Gongchangdang Dangwu Gongzuo Da Cidian (Dictionary of CCP Party Work)*, Beijing, Xinhua Chubanshe (New China Press).

Li, Victor, (1970) 'The Role of Law in Communist China', *China Quarterly*, 66–111.

Li, Weihong, (1997) 'Bao'an Chufen yu Zuixing Junheng (The Balance Between Security Defence Punishments and Criminal Punishments)', *Yantai Daxue Xuebao (Journal of Yantai University)*, 27–31.

Li, Xiaoming, (2003) *Xingzheng Xingfa Xue Daolun (The Guidelines of Administrative Criminal Law)*, Beijing, Falu Chubanshe (Law Press).

Li, Yanhua, (2001) 'Yide Zhiguo – Shehui Zhuyi Daode Jianshe de Xin Jingjie (Rule by Virtue – The New Realm of Socialist Moral Construction)', 2, *Zhengzhou Qinggongye Xueyuan Xuebao (Shehui Kexue Bao) (Journal of the Zhengzhou Institute of Light Industry) (Social Sciences)*, 41–4.

Li, Yonghong, (1997) 'Xianzhi Gongmin Renshen Ziyou de Xingzheng Qiangshi Cuoshi Ji Lifa Wanshan (Administrative Coercive Measures for the Deprivation of Personal Freedom and the Perfection of its Legislation)', 9, *Faxue (Law Science)*, 32–5.

Li, Zhongxin, (1998) 'Guanyu Renmin Jingcha de Zhefa Jiandu (On Supervision of the Law Enforcement of the People's Police)', 1, *Gong'an Yanjiu (Public Security Studies)*, 44–7.

Liang, Zhiping, (1989) 'Explicating "Law": A Comparative Perspective of Chinese and Western Legal Culture', 3, *Journal of Chinese Law*, 55–91.

Liang, Zhiping, (1995) 'Zhuanxing Shiqi de falu de shehui zhengyi', 2, *China Perspectives*, 28–31.

Lieberthal, Kenneth, (1995) *Governing China From Revolution Through Reform*, New York, W.W. Norton.

Liebman, Benjamin, (1999) 'Legal Aid and Public Interest Law in China', Spring, *Texas International Law Journal*, 211–86.

Lin, Feng, (1996) *Administrative Law Procedures and Remedies in China*, Hong Kong, Sweet and Maxwell.

Lin, Wenjun, (2001) *Laodong Jioayang Zhidu Ruogan Wenti Lifa Yanjiu (Legislative Study of Several Questions on the System of Re-education Through Labour)*, Xiamen University, Xiamen.

Lin, Zhun (ed.), (1992) *Renmin Fayuan Anlixuan (Selection of Cases of the People's Courts)*, Beijing, Renmin Fayuan Chubanshe (People's Court Press).

Lindsey, Tim and Masduki, Teten, (2002) 'Labour Law in Indonesia after Suharto: Reformasi or Replay', in *Law and Labour Market Regulation in East Asia*, Cooney, Sean, Lindsey, Tim, Mitchell, Richard and Zhu, Ying (eds.), London, Routledge, 27–54.

Liu, Baiyang and Bao, Hongxia (eds.), (1989) *Gong'an Jiguan Xingzheng Susong Zhinan* (*Guide to Public Security Organ's Administrative Litigation*), Beijing, Zhongguo Renmin Gong'an Daxue Chubanshe (Chinese People's Public Security University Press).

Liu, Enqi, (1989) 'Gaige Kaifang yu Shehui Zhi'an (Reform and Opening Up and Social Order)', 5, *Gong'an Yanjiu* (*Public Security Studies*), 3–7.

Liu, Guang'an and Li, Cunpeng, (1999) 'Mediation and the Protection of Rights', in *Zouxiang Quanli de Shidai* (*Toward an Age of Rights*), Xia, Yong (ed.), Beijing, Zhongguo Zhengfa Daxue Chubanshe (China University of Politcs and Law Press), 251–90.

Liu, Hainian, (1996) 'Qian Yan (Foreword)', in *Yifa Zhiguo Jianshe Shehui Zhuyi Fazhi Guojia* (*Ruling the Country According to Law, Establishing a Socialist Nation Ruled According to Law*), Wang, Jiafu, Liu, Hainian, Li, Buyun and Li, Lin (eds.), Beijing, China Legal System Press, 1–4.

Liu, Hainian, Li, Buyun and Li, Lin (eds.), (1996) *Yifa Zhiguo Jianshe Shehuizhuyi Fazhi Guojia* (*Ruling the Country According to Law Establishing a Socialist Nation Ruled According to Law*), Beijing, Zhongguo Fazhi Chubanshe (China Legal System Press).

Liu, Huayin and Liu, Baiyang (eds.), (1992) *Gong'an Xingzheng Chengxu yu Xingzheng Susong* (*Public Security Administrative Procedure and Administrative Litigation*), Beijing, Qunzhong Chubanshe (Masses Press).

Liu, Jianguo (ed.), (2002) *Laodong Jiaoyang Tonglan* (*An Overview of Re-educatin Through Labour*), Beijing, Zhongguo Jiancha Chubanshe (China Procuratorate Press).

Liu, Naimin, Zhang, Genli and Shen, Yongkang, (1997) 'Guanyu Jiada Chajin Maiyin Piaochang Huodong Lidu de Jidian Renshi (Several Understandings on Strengthening Activities for Banning Prostitution and Using Prostitutes)', 2, *Gong'an Yanjiu* (*Public Security Studies*), 32–6.

Liu, Shaoqi, (1985) *Liu Shaoqi Xuanji* (*Collected Works of Liu Shaoqi*), Beijing, Renmin Chubanshe (People's Press).

Liu, Shipu, (1990) 'Guanyu Shourong Shencha de Sikao (Reflections on Detention for Investigation)', 5, *Gong'an Yanjiu* (*Public Security Studies*), 22–6.

Liu, Wenren, (1998) 'Laodong Jiaoyang Ji Xu Lifa (Re-education Through Labour Urgently Needs Legislation)', 5, *Faxue Zhazhi* (*Legal Studies Journal*), 22–3.

Liu, Wenren, (2001a) 'Laodong Jiaoyang Zhidu Ji Qi Gaige (The System of Re-education Through Labour and its Reform)', in *Falu Lunwen Ziliaoku* (*Collection of Law Theses Materials*), Vol. 2002, www.jcrb.com.cn/ournews/asp/readNews.asp?id=18870.

Liu, Wenren, (2001b) 'Laodong Jiaoyang Zhidu Ji Qi Gaige (The System of Re-education Through Labour and its Reform)', 4, *Xingzheng Faxue Yanjiu* (*Administrative Law Studies*), 13–21.

Liu, Wenren, (2001c) 'Shourong Qiansong Gongzuo Buyi Jixu Baoliu (It is not Appropriate to Preserve Detention for Repatriation)', in *Falu Lunwen Ziliao Ku* (*Collection of Law Theses Materials*), Vol. 2002, www.jcrb.com.cn/ournews/asp/readNews.asp?id=18860.

Liu, Xiaochuan, (1994) *The Present Situation and Strategical Measures of Public Security in China*, Conference for the Tenth Anniversary Celebrations of the Founding of the China People's Public Security University, Beijing.

Liu, Xin, (2003) 'Xingzheng Xingfa – Xingzheng Fa yu Xingfa de Jiejie (Administrative Criminal Punishment – the Intersection of Administrative Law and Criminal Law)', in *Zhi'an Guanli Zhidu Sicun* (*Reflection on the Public Order Regulation* (English title)), Zhu, Weiguo (ed.), Beijing, Falu Chubanshe (Law Press), 173–82.

Liu, Xuanlue and Yuan, Cheng, (1997) 'Dui You Zhongguo Tese de Jingdu Gongzuo de Tansuo yu Sikao (Exploration and Reflection on the Work of Drug Prohibition with Chinese Characteristics)', in *Lun Zhongguo Tese de Gong'an* (*Discussion of Public Security with Chinese Characteristics*), Kang, Damin (ed.), Beijing, Qunzhong Chubanshe (Masses Press), 30–46.

Liu, Yan, (1991) 'Qiantan Shenli Shourong Shencha Anjian Ying Jiejue de Liangge Wenti (A Brief Discussion of Two Problems that Must be Resolved in Hearing Detention for Investigation Cases)', 6, *Faxue yu Shijian* (*Law and Practice*), 63–64.

Liu, Yongping, (1998) *Origins of Chinese Law, Penal and Administrative Law in its Early Development*, Hong Kong, Oxford University Press.

Liu, Youde, (16 May 2000) *Organized Crime Characterized by Official Collusion, London*, BBC Summary of World Broadcasts.

Liu, Zhaoqi, (1991) 'On Educating Juvenile Law Breakers', in *Crime Trends in the 1990s and its Countermeasures of Prevention and Control*, Beijing, Chinese People's Public Security University, 102–6.

Liu, Zheng and Cheng, Xiangqing, (2002) *Renda Jiandu Tansuo* (*Exploration of Supervision by People's Congresses*), Beijing, Zhongguo Minzhu Fazhi Chubanshe (China Democracy and Law Press).

Lo, Carlos Wing-Hung, (1997) 'Socialist Legal Theory in Deng Xiaoping's China', 11, *Columbia Journal of Asian Law*, 469–86.

Lu, Hong, (1998) *Community Policing – Rhetoric or Reality? The Contemporary Chinese Community-Based Policing System in Shanghai*, Ann Arbor, UMI Company.

Lubman, Stanley, (1967) 'Mao and Mediation: Politics and Dispute Resolution in Communist China', 55, *California Law Review*, 1284–359.

Lubman, Stanley, (1991) 'Studying Contemporary Chinese Law: Limits, Possibilities and Strategy', 39, *The American Journal of Comparative Law*, 293–341.

Lubman, Stanley, (1995) 'Introduction: The Future of Chinese Law', 141, *The China Quarterly*, 1–21.

Lubman, Stanley, (1999) *Bird in a Cage: Legal Reform in China after Mao*, Stanford, Stanford University Press.

Lubman, Stanley, (2000) 'Bird in a Cage: Chinese Law Reform after Twenty Years', *Northwestern Journal of International Law and Business*, 383–423.

Luo, Feng, (1992) 'Laodong Jiaoyang Shenpi Gongzuo de Huigu yu Sikao (Retrospect and Thoughts on Investigation and Approval of Re-education Through Labour)', 5, *Gong'an Yanjiu* (*Public Security Studies*), 33–7.

Luo, Feng, (1995) *Zhonghua Renmin Gongheguo Renmin Jingchafa Shiyi* (*Explanation of the PRC People's Police Law*), Beijing, Qunzhong Chubanshe (Masses Press).

Luo, Haocai, (1997a) 'Guanyu Xiandai Xingzheng fa Lilun Jichu Yanjiu (On the Study of the Theoretical Basis of Contemporary Administrative Law)', in *Xiandai Xingzhengfa de Pingheng Lilun* (*Balance Theory in Contemporary Administrative Law*), Luo, Haocai (ed.), Beijing, Beijing Daxue Chubanshe (Peking University Press), 1–7.

Luo, Haocai (ed.), (1997b) *Xiandai Xingzhengfa de Pingheng Lilun* (*Balance Theory in Contemporary Administrative Law*), Beijing, Beijing Daxue Chubanshe (Peking University Press).

Luo, Haocai (ed.), (1989) *Xingzheng Faxue* (*Administrative Law Study*), Qinghuangdao, Zhongguo Zhengfa Daxue Chubanshe (China University of Politics and Law Press).

Luo, Haocai, (2003) 'Xingzheng Faxue yu Yifa Xingzheng (The Study of Administrative Law and Administration According to Law)', in *Xiandai Xingzheng Fa de Pingheng Lilun* (*Balance Theory in Contemporary Administrative Law*), Vol. 2, Luo, Haocai (ed.), Beijing, Beijing Daxue Chubanshe (Beijing University Press), 9–22.

Luo, Haocai and Gan, Wen, (1997) 'Xingzheng Fa de "Pingheng" ji "Pingheng Lun" Fanchou (The Scope of "Balance" and "Balance Theory" in Administrative Law)', in *Xiandai Xingzheng Fa de Pingheng Lilun* (*Balance Theory of Contemporary Administrative Law*), Luo, Haocai (ed.), Beijing, Beijing Daxue Chubanshe (Peking University Press).

Luo, Haocai and Ying, Songnian (eds.), (1990) *Xingzheng Susong Faxue* (*The Study of Administrative Litigation Law*), Beijing, Zhongguo Zhengfa Daxue Chubanshe (China Univeristy of Politics and Law Press).

Luo, Jueqiang, (1997) 'Shen Zhen Shequ Zhi'an Gongzuo Xin Tedian Chutan (Preliminary Analysis of the New Characteristics of Public Order Work in Shen Zhen Residential Districts)', in *Lun Zhongguo Tese de Gong'an* (*Discussion of Public Security with Chinese Characteristics*), Kang, Damin (ed.), Beijing, Qunzhong Chubanshe (Masses Press), 71–81.

Luo, Qin and Gao, Weidong, (1997) 'Zhongdian Renkou Guanli de Wuda Wenti (Five Major Problems with the Management of the Focal Population)', *Qingshaonian Fanzui Wenti* (*Issues on Juvenile Crime and Delinquency*), 21–2.

Lustgarten, Laurence, (1986) *The Governance of Police*, London, Sweet and Maxwell.

Lynch, Daniel, (1999) 'Dilemmas of "Thought Work" in *Fin-de-Siècle* China', 157, *The China Quarterly*, 173–201.

Ma, Huaide, (1999) *Zhonghua Renmin Gongheguo Xingzheng Fuyifa Shijie* (*Explanation of the Administrative Review Law of the PRC*), Beijing, Zhongguo Fazhi Chubanshe (China Legal System Press).

Ma, Huaide, (2000) *Xingzheng Fa Zhidu Jiangou yu Panli Yanjiu* (*Study of the Administrative Legal System Construction and Case Law*), Beijing, Zhongguo Zhengfa Daxue Chubanshe (China University of Politics and Law Press).

Ma, Jie, (1990) *Zhongguo Shehui Zhi'an Zonghe Zhili Yanjiu* (*Research into China's Comprehensive Management of Public Order*), Beijing, Falu Chubanshe (Law Press).

Ma, Longhu, (2001) 'Dui Woguo Laodong Jiaoyang Zhidu de Lixing Fenxi (Analysis of the Rationality of My Country's System of Re-education Through Labour)', 6, *Zhengfa Luncong* (*Collected Essays on Politics and Law*), 33–5.

Ma, Longhu, (2003) 'Dui Woguo Laodong Jiaoyang Zhidu de Lixing Fenxi (Analysis of the Rationality of My Country's System of Re-education Through Labour)', in *Zhi'an Guanli Zhidu Sicun* (*Reflections on the System of Public Order Regulation*), Zhu, Weiguo (ed.), Beijing, Falu Chubanshe (Law Press), 129–35.

Ma, Weigang, (1993a) 'Jianguo Chuqi Jinyan Jindu Yundong Shulue (Outline of the Campaign to Prohibit Smoking and Drug Use in the Early Period of Establishing the Nation)', 6, *Gong'an Yanjiu* (*Public Security Studies*), 55–8.

Ma, Weigang (ed.), (1993b) *Jinchang Jindu: Jianguo Chuqi de Lishi Huigu* (*Prohibition of Prostitution and Drugs: An Historical Review of the Early Period in Establishing China*), Beijing, Jingguan Jiaoyu Chubanshe (Police Officer Education Press).

Ma, Weigang, (1994) 'Jianguo Chuqi Jinchang Shulue (Outline of Prohibition of Prostitution in the Early Period of Establishing the Nation)', 2, *Gong'an Yanjiu* (*Public Security Studies*), 56–8.

Ma, Yuan (ed.), (1993) *Xingzheng Shenpan Shiwu* (*Practical Tasks of Administrative Adjudication*), Beijing, Beijing Shifan Daxue Chubanshe (Beijing Normal University Press).

Ma, Yue, (1997) 'The Police Law 1995: Organization, Functions Powers and Accountability of the Chinese Police', 20, *Policing: An International Journal of Police Strategies and Management*, 113–35.

Mallee, Hein, (1998) 'Definitions and Methodology in Chinese Migration Studies', in *Migration in China*, Bakken, Borge (ed.), Copenhagen, Nordic Institute of Asian Studies, 107–44.

Mao, Zedong, (1937a) 'On Contradiction', in *Selected Works of Mao Tse-tung*, Vol. 1, Beijing, Foreign Languages Press, 311–47.

Mao, Zedong, (1937b) 'On Practice', in *Selected Works of Mao Tse-Tung*, Vol. 1, Beijing, Foreign Languages Press, 295–309.

Mao, Zedong, (1967) *Selected Works of Mao Zedong*, Beijing, Foreign Languages Press.

Mao, Zedong, (1972) 'On the Correct Handling of Contradictions Among the People', in *Quotations from Chairman Mao Tsetung*, Foreign Languages Press (ed.), Beijing, Foreign Languages Press, 45–57.

Mao, Zedong, (1977) 'On the People's Democratic Dictatorship', in *Selected Works of Mao Tse-Tung*, Vol. 4, Mao, Zhibin (ed.), Beijing, Foreign Languages Press, 411–24.

Mao, Zhibin, (1991) 'Shourong Shencha shi Xingzheng Qiangzhi Cuoshi (Shelter and Investigation is an Administrative Coercive Measure)', 5, *Gong'an Daxue Xuebao* (*Journal of the Public Security University*), 13–14.

Mattei, Ugo, (1997) 'Three Patterns of Law: Taxonomy and Change in the World's Legal Systems', 45, *American Journal of Comparative Law*, 5–44.

McBarnet, Doreen, (1984) 'Law and Capital: The Role of Legal Form and Legal Actors', 12, *International Journal of the Sociology of Law*, 231–8.

McCormick, Barrett, (1990) *Political Reform in Post-Mao China: Democracy and Bureaucracy in a Leninist State*, Berkeley, University of California Press.

McCormick, Barrett and Kelly, David, (1994) 'The Limits of Anti-Liberalism', 53, *The Journal of Asian Studies*, 804–31.

Meng, Qingfeng, (1993) 'The Police Force in the Reform Era', in *Seminar on Police Management*, Foreign Affairs Office, Chinese People's Public Security University (ed.), Beijing, Zhongguo Renmin Gong'an Daxue Chubanshe (Chinese People's Public Security Press), 1–4.

Meng, Qingfen, (1994) 'Dui Xingshi Fanzui Daji Bu Li Wenti Jidai Caiqu de Jiben Duice (The Urgent Need for Basic Countermeasures in respect of the Problem of Failing to Strike Forcefully against Crime)', 6, *Gong'an Yanjiu* (*Public Security Studies*), 18–21.

Miliband, R., (1985) 'State Power and Class Interests', in *Lloyd's Introduction to Jurisprudence*, Lloyd, Lord of Hampstead and Freeman, M.D.A. (eds.), London, Stevens & Sons, 1028–36.

Mo, Jihong, (2005) 'Studies on the Legal Sanction on the Restriction of Personal Freedom from the Perspective of the Constitution', in *Xianzhi Dui Renshen Ziyou de Xianzhi* (*To Refrain from the Restrictions of Personal Freedom*), Guo, Jian'an and Zheng, Xiaze (eds.), Beijing, Falu Chubanshe (Law Press), 47–78.

Monjardet, Dominique, (1995) 'The French Model of Policing', in *Comparisons in Policing: An International Perspective*, Brodeur, Jean-Paul (ed.), Aldershot, Avebury, 49–68.

Moore, Sally Falk, (1978) *Law as Process: An Anthropological Approach*, London, Routledge and Kegan Paul.

Mou, Shihuai (ed.), (1992) *Gong'an Xingzheng Guanli Yu Xingzheng Fuyi Susong* (*Public Security Administrative Management and Administrative Review and Litigation*), Beijing, Zhongguo Renmin Gongan Daxue Chubanshe (Chinese People's Public Security University Press).

Mou, Xinsheng (ed.), (1996) *Zhili Maiyin Piaochang Duice* (*Countermeasures for the Control of Prostitution and Use of Prostitutes*), Beijing, Chunzhong Chubanshe (Masses Press).

Munro, Robin, (2000) 'Judicial Psychiatry in China and its Political Abuses', 14, *Columbia Journal of Asian Law*, 1–128.

Nanfang Dushi Bao (The Southern Metropolis), (8 March 2004) 'Laojiao Zhidu Jiang Zuo Zhongda Bianhua (The System of Re-education Through Labour will Undergo Significant Changes)'.

Nathan, Andrew, (1985) *Chinese Democracy*, Berkeley, University of California Press.

Nelken, David, (1995) 'Disclosing/Invoking Legal Culture: An Introduction', 4, *Social and Legal Studies*, 435–52.

Nelken, David, (2001) 'Towards a Sociology of Legal Adaptation', in *Adapting Legal Cultures*, Nelken, David and Feest, Johannes (eds.), Oxford, Hart Publishing, 7–54.

New China News Agency, (7 January 2004) 'China Dismisses over 30,000 Unqualified Policemen in Clean-Up Campaign', *BBC Monitoring International Reports*.

O'Brien, Kevin, (1996) 'Rightful Resistance', 49, *World Politics*, 31–55.

O'Brien, Kevin and Li, Lianjiang, (2004) 'Suing the Local State: Administrative Litigation in Rural China', 51, *The China Journal*, 75–96.

O'Brien, Kevin and Li, Lianjiang, (2005) 'Suing the Local State: Administrative Litigation in Rural China', in *Engaging the Law in China*, Diamant, Neil, Lubman, Stanley and O'Brien, Kevin (eds.), Stanford, Stanford University Press, 31–53.

O'Neill, Mark, (2006) 'The Rise and Fall of a Career Cadre', *South China Morning Post*, 11.

Orts, Eric, (2001) 'The Rule of Law in China', *Vanderbilt Journal of Transnational Law*, 43–115.

Pan, Xiaojuan, (2004) *Zhongguo Jiceng Shehui Zhonggou* (*The Main Structures of China's Grassroots Society*), Beijing, Zhongguo Fazhi Chubanshe (China Legal System Press).

Parsons, Talcott, (1964) 'Evolutionary Universals in Society', 29, *American Sociological Review*, 339–57.

Peerenboom, Randall, (1999) 'Ruling the Country in Accordance with Law: Reflection on the Rule and Role of Law in Contemporary China', 11, *Cultural Dynamics*, 315–51.

Peerenboom, Randall, (2001) 'Globalization, Path Dependency and the Limits of Law: Administrative Law Reform and the Rule of Law in the People's Republic of China', 19, *Berkeley Journal of International Law*, 161–264.

Peerenboom, Randall, (2002a) *China's Long March Toward Rule of Law*, Cambridge, Cambridge University Press.

Peerenboom, Randall, (2002b) 'Law Enforcement and the Legal Profession in China', in *Implementation of Law in the People's Republic of China*. Chen, Jianfu, Li, Yuwen and Otto, Jan Michiel (eds.), The Hague, Kluwer Law International, 125–47.

Peerenboom, Randall, (2002c) 'Let One Hundred Flowers Bloom, One Hundred Schools Contend: Debating Rule of Law in China', 23, *Michigan Journal of International Law*, 471–544.

Peerenboom, Randall, (2005) 'Law and Develoment of Constitutional Democracy in China: Problem or Paradigm?' 19, *Columbia Journal of Asian Law*, 185–234.

Pei, Minxin, (1995) '"Creeping Democratization" in China', 6, *Journal of Democracy*, 65–79.

Pei, Minxin, (1997) 'Citizens v. Mandarins: Administrative Litigation in China', 152, *The China Quarterly*, 832–62.

Peng, Yunfei, (1990) 'Cong Laodong Jiaoyang Gongzuo Shijian Qiantan Woguo Laodong Jiaoyang de Xingzhi (A Brief Discussion from the Practice of Re-education Through Labour of the Nature of My Country's Re-education Through Labour)', in *Laodong Jiaoyang Yanjiu Lunwen Xuanji (Re-education Through Labour Research, Selected Collection of Theses)*, Zhu, Hongde (ed.), Beijing, Qunzhong Chubanshe (Masses Press), 84–92.

Peng, Zhen, (1979) 'Zai Quanguo Gong'an Juzhang Huiyi de Jianghua (Speech given at the National Conference of Provincial-level Public Security Chiefs)', in *Lun Xin Zhongguo de Zhengfa Gongzuo (Discussion of the Political Legal Work in New China)*, Beijing, Zhongyang Wenxian Chubanshe (Central Documents Press), 182–9.

Peng, Zhen, (1982) 'Xin Shiqi de Zhengfa Gongzuo (Political-Legal Work in the New Era)', in *Lun Xin Zhongguo de Zhengfa Gongzuo (Discussion of the Political Legal Work in New China)*, Beijing, Zhongyang Wenxian Chubanshe (Central Documents Press), 282–91.

Peng, Zhen, (1984) 'Bujin Yao Kao Dang de Zhengce Erqie Yao Yifa Banshe (Not Only is it Necessary to Rely on Party Policy it is Also Necessary to Handle Matters According to Law)', in *Lun Xin Zhongguo de Zhengfa Gongzuo (Discussion of the Political Legal Work in New China)*, Beijing, Zhongyang Wenxian Chubanshe, 361–6.

Peng, Zhen, (1990) 'Zai Quanguo Zhengfa Gongzuo Huiyi Shang de Jianghua Yaodian (Key Points of a Speech at the National Political-legal Work

Conference)', in *Lun Xin Zhongguo de Zhengfa Gongzuo* (*Discussion of the Political Legal Work in New China*), Beijing, Zhongyang Wenxian Chubanshe (Central Documents Press), 444–8.

Peng, Zhen, (1991a) 'Guanyu Qige Falu Cao'an de Shuoming (Explanation of the Drafts of Seven Laws)', in *Peng Zhen Wenxuan, 1949–1990* (*Selection of Documents of Peng Zhen, 1949–1990*), Zhonggong Zhongyang Wenxian Bianji Weiyuanhui (Central Documents Editorial Committee (ed.), Beijing, Renmin Chubanshe (People's Press), 368–82.

Peng, Zhen (ed.), (1991b) *Peng Zhen Wenxuan (1941–1990)* (*Collected Essays of Peng Zhen*), Beijing, Renmin Chubanshe (People's Press).

Peng, Zhen, (1992a) 'Guanyu Zhonghua Renmin Gongheguo Xianfa Xiugai Cao'an de Baogao (Report on Draft Revisions to the PRC Constitution) 26 January 1982', in *Lun Xin Zhongguo de Zhengfa Gongzuo* (*Discussion of the Politics and Law Work in New China*), Beijing, Zhongyang Wenxian Chubanshe (Central Documents Press), 304–32.

Peng, Zhen (ed.), (1992b) *Lun Xin Zhongguo de Zhengfa Gongzuo* (*Discussion of Political Legal Work in New China*), Beijing, Zhongyang Wenxian Chubanshe (Central Documents Press).

Peng, Zhen, (1992c) 'Zai Wu Da Chengshi Zhi'an Zuotanhui Shang de Jianghua (Address given to the Five Major Cities Public Order Meeting) 21, 22 May 1981', in *Lun Xin Zhongguo de Zhengfa Gongzuo* (*Discussion of the Political Legal Work in New China*), Beijing, Zhongyang Wenxian Chubanshe (Central Documents Press).

Petracca, Mark and Mong, Xiong, (1990) 'The Concept of Chinese Neo-Authoritarianism: An Exploration and Democratic Critique', 30, *Asian Survey*, 1099–117.

Pi, Chunxie (ed.), (2000) *Xingzheng Chengxu Fa Bijiao Yanjiu* (*Comparative Study of Administrative Procedure Law*), Beijing, Zhongguo Renmin Gong'an Daxue Chubanshe (Chinese People's Public Security University Press).

Pi, Chunxie and Ma, Jun, (1997) 'Guanyu Pinghenglun de Jidian Sikao (Several Reflections on Balance Theory)', in *Xiandai Xingzhengfa de Pingheng Lilun* (*Balance Theory in Contemporary Administrative Law*), Luo, Haocai (ed.), Beijing, Beijing Daxue Chubanshe (Peking University Press), 75–93.

Politics and Law Teaching and Research Office (ed.), (1983) *Gong'an Gongzuo Gailun* (*Introduction to Public Security Work*), Zhongguo Xingshi Jingcha Xueyuan (China Criminal Police Institute).

Potter, Pitman, (1994a) 'The Administrative Litigation Law of the PRC: Judicial Review and Bureaucratic Reform', in *Domestic Law Reforms in Post-Mao China*, Pitman, Potter (ed.), Armonk, M.E. Sharpe.

Potter, Pitman, (1994b) 'Riding the Tiger: Legitimacy and Legal Culture in Post-Mao China', 138, *The China Quarterly*, 325–58.

Potter, Pitman, (1995a) 'Foreign Investment Law in the People's Republic of China: Dilemmas of State Control', 141, *The China Quarterly*, 155–85.

Potter, Pitman, (1995b) *From Leninist Discipline to Socialist Legalism: Peng Zhen on Law and Political Authority in the PRC*, Hong Kong, The Chinese University of Hong Kong.

Potter, Pitman, (1998) 'Curbing the Party: Peng Zhen and Chinese Legal Culture', 45, *Problems of Post-Communism*, 17–28.

Potter, Pitman, (1999) 'The Chinese Legal System: Continuing Commitment to the Primacy of State Power', 159, *The China Quarterly*, 673–83.

Potter, Pitman, (2000) 'Law-Making in the PRC: The Case of Contracts', in *Law-Making in the People's Republic of China*, Otto, Jan Michiel, Polak, Maurice V., Chen, Jianfu and Li, Yuwen (eds.), The Hague, Kluwer Law International, 189–206.

Potter, Pitman, (2003a) 'Belief in Control: Regulation of Religion in China', 174, *The China Quarterly*, 317–37.

Potter, Pitman, (2003b) *From Leninist Discipline to Socialist Legalism: Peng Zhen on Law and Political Authority in the PRC*, Stanford, Stanford University Press.

Potter, Pitman, (2003c) 'Globalization and Economic Regulation in China: Selective Adaptation of Globalized Norms and Practices', 2, *Washington University Global Studies Law Review*, 119–50.

Qinghe County People's Court, (1992) 'Women shi Ruhe Shenli Shouci Shoushen Xingzheng Anjian de.' (How we Heard our First Shelter and Investigation Administrative Case)', *Shandong Shenpan* (*Shandong Adjudication*), 28–30.

Quan, Xiaoshu, (12 February 2004) 'More than 70 per cent of Chinese Drug Addicts Are Youths under 35', *WorldSources, Inc. from Xinhua*.

Radin, Margaret, (1989) 'Reconsidering the Rule of Law', 69, *Boston University Law Review*, 781–819.

Reimann, Mathias, (2002) 'The Progress and Failure of Comparative Law in the Second Half of the Twentieth Century', 50, *American Journal of Comparative Law*, 671–700.

Reiner, Robert, (1994) 'Policing and the Police', in *The Oxford Handbook of Criminology*, Maguire, Mike, Morgan, Rod and Reiner, Robert (eds.), Oxford, Clarendon Press, 705–72.

Ren, Enshun, (1992) 'Laodong Jiaoyang de Wenti yu Chulu (The Problems and Prospects for Re-education Through Labour)', 2, *Gong'an Yanjiu* (*Public Security Studies*), 12–16.

Ren, Hongjie, (2005) *Shehui Wending Wenti Qianyan Tansuo* (*A Preliminary Exploration of Problems of Social Stability*), Beijing, Zhongguo Renmin Gong'an Daxue Chubanshe (Chinese People's Public Security University Press).

Renmin Fayuan Chubanshe, 'Daji Liuhai Weifa Fanzui Shiyong Falu Shouce' Bianxuanzu (People's Court Press 'Strike Against the Six Evils' Unlawfulness and Crime Practical Handbook' Editorial Group) (ed.), (1992) *Daji Liuhai Weifa Fanzui Shiyong Falu Shouce* (*Practical Legal Handbook on Striking Against the Six Evils' Unlawful and Criminal Conduct*), Beijing, Renmin Fayuan Chubanshe (People's Court Press).

Roebuck, Derek, (1992) *The Past is Another Country: Legal History as Comparative Law*, International Conference on Comparative Law, Peking University, 122–44.

Rosenfeld, Michel, (2001) 'The Rule of Law and the Legitimacy of Constitutional Democracy', 74, *Southern California Law Review*, 1307–50.

Schurmann, Franz, (1968) *Ideology and Organization in Communist China*, Berkeley, University of California Press.

Seita, Alex, (1997) 'Globalization and the Convergence of Values', 30, *Cornell International Law Journal*, 429–91.

Seymour, James and Anderson, Richard, (1998) *New Ghosts Old Ghosts: Prisons and Labor Reform Camps in China*, Armonk, New York, M.E. Sharpe.

Shao, Yong, (2004) *Zhongguo Jindai Fandu Shi* (*A History of Prohibition of Drugs in Modern China*), Fuzhou, Fujian Renmin Chubanshe (Fujian People's Press).

Shen, Long, (1990) 'Xiaomian Changji Zhenhua Shehui (Eradicate Prostitution, Rectify Society)', 1, *Gong'an Yanjiu* (*Public Security Studies*), 55–7, 63.

Shen, Long, (1991) 'Zhonggguo Jinyan Jindu de Guochu yu Xianzai (The Past and Present of China's Prohibition of Smoking and Drug Use)', 3, *Gong'an Yanjiu* (*Public Security Studies*), 55–8.

Shen, Yuan, (2000) 'Conceptions and Receptions of Legality: Understanding the Complexity of Law Reform in Modern China', in *The Limits of the Rule of Law in China*, Turner, K.G, Feinerman, J.V and Guy, R.K. (eds.), Seattle, University of Washington Press, 20–44.

Shen, Zhongmin and Xu, Zhenqiang, (1997) 'Lun Zhongguo Jingcha Jiaoyu de Fazhan Zouxiang (Discussing Trends in the Development of China's Police Education)', in *Lun Zhongguo Tese de Gong'an* (*Discussion of Public Security with Chinese Characteristics*), Kang, Damin (ed.), Beijing, Qunzhong Chubanshe (Masses Press), 138–56.

Shih, Chih-yu, (1996) 'China's Socialist Law Under Reform: The Class Nature Reconsidered', 44, *American Journal of Comparative Law*, 627–46.

Shih, Chih-yu, (1999) *Collective Democracy, Political and Legal Reform in China*, Hong Kong, The Chinese University Press.

Shu, Huaide (ed.), (1996a) *Zhongguo Shehui Zhi'an Zonghe Zhili Nianjian, 1991–1992* (*Yearbook of the Comprehensive Management of Public Order 1991–1992*), Beijing, Falu Chubanshe (Law Press).

Shu, Huaide (ed.), (1996b) *Zhongguo Shehui Zhi'an Zonghe Zhili Nianjian, 1993–1994* (*Yearbook of the Comprehensive Management of Public Order 1993–1994*), Beijing, Falu Chubanshe (Law Press).

Sifa Bu Fazhi Xuanquan Si, (Ministry of Justice Legal System Propaganda Department) (ed.), (1995) *Zhonggong Zhongyang Juban Falu Zhishi Jiangzuo Jishe* (*Record of the Course of Lectures on Legal Knowledge held by the CCP Central Committee*), Beijing, Falu Chubanshe (Law Press).

Situ, Yingyi and Liu, Weizhang, (1996) 'Comprehensive Treatment to Social Order: A Chinese Approach against Crime', 20, *International Journal of Comparative and Applied Criminal Justice*, 95–115.

Skinner, Quentin (ed.), (1985) *The Return of Grand Theory in the Human Sciences*, Cambridge and New York, Cambridge University Press.

Solinger, Dorothy, (1999) *Contesting Citizenship in Urban China: Peasant Migrants, the State, and the Logic of the Market*, Berkeley, Univeristy of California Press.

Sommer, Matthew, (2000) *Sex, Law and Society in Late Imperial China*, Stanford, Stanford University Press.

Song, Haiying and Song, Yan, (2003) 'Bao'an Chufen Zhidu yu Xing Fa zhong de Renquan Baozhang Jizhi (The Mechanisms for Protection of Human Rights in the System of Social Defence Punishments and the Criminal Law)', in *Zhi'an Guanli Zhidu Sicun* (*Reflection on the Public Order Regulation*), Zhu, Weiguo (ed.), Beijing, Falu Chubanshe (Law Press), 231–45.

Song, Qiang, (1992) 'Lun Woguo Xingshi Qiangzhi Cuoshi Xin Tixi (Discussing the New System of China's Criminal Coercive Measures)', in *Xingshi Susong Fa de Xuigai yu Wanshan* (*Revision and Perfection of the Criminal Procedure Law*), Zhongguo Faxue Hui Susong Fa Yanjiu Hui (Procedure Law Association of the China Law Society) (ed.), Beijing, Zhongguo Zhengfa Daxue Chubanshe (China University of Politics and Law Press), 136–45.

Song, Zhansheng, Wang, Zhimin, Song, Wannian, Zhang, Wenqing, Song, Yongzhi and Liu, Yilin (eds.), (2000a) *Zhongguo Gong'an Dabaike Quanshu* (*Encyclopedia of China's Public Security*), Vol. 1, Changchun, Jilin Renmin Chubanshe (Jilin People's Press).

Song, Zhansheng, Wang, Zhimin, Song, Wannian, Zhang, Wenqing, Song, Yongzhi and Liu, Yilin (eds.), (2000b) *Zhongguo Gong'an Dabaike Quanshu* (*Encyclopedia of China's Public Security*), Vol. 2, Changchun, Jilin Renmin Chubanshe (Jilin People's Press).

Spence, Jonathon, (1990) *The Search for Modern China*, New York, London, W.W. Norton and Company.

Su, Li, (1998) 'Dangqian Xidu Laodong Jiaoyang Renyuan de Tedian yu Jiedu Duice (Characteristics and Strategies for Giving up Drugs amongst Current Drug Addicted Personnel in Re-education Through Labour)', 1, *Zhongguo Sifa* (*Judicature Today*), 25–7.

Su, Shuyuan, (1990) 'Laodong Jiaoyang Shenpi Gongzuo Bixu Shixing Falu Jiandu (Legal Supervision Must be Carried Out over the Work of Examination and Approval of Re-education Through Labour)', in *Laodong Jiaoyang Yanjiu Lunwen Xuanji* (*Re-education Through Labour Research, Selected Collection of Theses*), Zhu, Hongde (ed.), Beijing, Qunzhong Chubanshe (Masses Press), 258–64.

Su, Yingjie, (1994) 'Dui Dangqian "Yanda" Tongyi Xingdong Wenti de Jidian Sikao (Several Reflections on Problems with the Current "Hard Strike" Concerted Action)', 6, *Gong'an Yanjiu (Public Security Studies)*, 22–4, 35.

Sun, Juan, (1994) 'Jingcha Xingwei Dongli de Diaocha (Survey and Reflection on the Motivation for Police Action)', in *Zhongguo Renmin Gong'an Daxue Xiaoqing Shi Zhou Nian Lunwen Xuanji* (*Selection of Essays for the Tenth Anniversary of the China People's Public Security University*), Xiaoqing Chouban Bangongshi Xueshu Xiaozu, (Anniversary Preparation Office Academic Small Group) (ed.), Beijing, Zhongguo Renmin Gong'an Daxue Chubanshe (China People's Public Security Press), 335–44.

Sun, Shengfu, (1994) 'Guanyu Jianchi "Yanda" Fanzhen de Yixie Sikao (Some Reflections on Upholding the Guiding Principle of the "Hard Strike")', in *Zhongguo Renmin Gong'an Daxue Xiaoqing Shi Zhou Nian Lunwen Xuanji* (*Selection of Essays for the Tenth Anniversary of the China People's Public Security University*), Beijing, Zhongguo Renmin Gongan Daxue Chubanshe (China People's Public Security University Press), 248–54.

Sun, Xiaoxia, (1999) *Falu dui Xingzheng de Kongzhi – Xiandai Xingshengfa de Fali Jieshi* (*Control of Administration by Law – Jurisprudential Interpretation of Modern Administrative Law*), Jinan, Shandong Renmin Chubanshe (Shandong People's Press).

Sun, Yimin, (2000) 'Lun Guowuyuan Bumen Lifa (On Legislation of the Ministries under the State Council)', in *Lifa Yanjiu* (*Legislation Review of China*), Zhou, Wangsheng (ed.), Beijing, Falu Chubanshe (Law Press), 172–216.

Swartz, David, (1997) *Culture & Power: The Sociology of Pierre Bourdieu*, Chicago, The University of Chicago Press.

Taiwo, Olufemi, (1999) 'The Rule of Law: The New Leviathan?' 12, *Canadian Journal of Law and Jurisprudence*, 151–68.

Tamanaha, Brian, (2000) 'A Non-Essentialist Version of Legal Pluralism', 27, *Journal of Law and Society*, 296–321.

Tamanaha, Brian, (28 February 2003) *The Rule of Law for Everyone?* http://ssrn.com/abstract=312622.

Tang, Wenfang, (2001) 'Political and Social Trends in the Post-Deng Urban China: Crisis or Stability?', 168, *China Quarterly*, 890–909.

Tang, Yongjin, (1993) 'Yichang Jingqiaoqiao de Geming (A Quiet Revolution)', in *Fazhi de Lixiang yu Xianzhuang (The Ideal and Reality of Rule of Law)*, Gong, Xiangrui (ed.), Beijing, Zhongguo Zhengfa Daxue Chubanshe (China Politics and Law University Press), 5–77.

Tanner, Harold, (1994) *Crime and Punishment in China 1979–1989*, unpublished PhD thesis, Columbia University.

Tanner, Harold, (1995) 'Policing, Punishment and the Individual: Criminal Justice in China', 20, *Law and Social Inquiry*, 277–303.

Tanner, Harold, (1999) *Strike Hard! Anti-Crime Campaigns and Chinese Criminal Justice, 1979–1985*, Ithaca, Cornell University Press.

Tanner, Murray Scot, (1999) *The Politics of Lawmaking in China: Institutions, Processes and Democratic Prospects*, Oxford, Clarendon Press.

Tanner, Murray Scot, (2000) 'State Coercion and the Balance of Awe: The 1983–1986 "Stern Blows" Anti-Crime Campaign', 44, *The China Journal*, 93–125.

Tanner, Murray Scot, (2002) 'Changing Windows on a Changing China: The Evolving "Think Tank" System and the Case of the Public Security Sector', 171, *The China Quarterly*, 559–74.

Tanner, Murray Scot, (2004) 'China Rethinks Unrest', 27, *The Washington Quarterly*, 137–56.

Terdiman, Richard, (1987) 'Translator's Introduction: The Force of Law: Toward a Sociology of the Juridical Field', 38, *Hastings Law Journal*, 805–13.

Teubner, Gunther, (1998) 'Legal Irritants: Good Faith in British Law or How Unifying Law Ends up in New Divergences', 61, *Modern Law Review*, 11–32.

Thomaneck, Jurgen, (1985) 'Police and Public Order in the Federal Republic of Germany', in *Police and Public Order in Europe*, Roach, John and Thomaneck, Jurgen (eds.), Beckenham, Croom Helm Ltd, 143–84.

Thornton, Sarah, (1995) 'Importing Prison Labor Products from the People's Republic of China: Re-examining U.S. Enforcement of Section 307 of the Trade and Tariff Act of 1930', 3, *Pacific Rim Law & Policy Journal*, 437–63.

Tian, Jinsheng, (1999) 'Dui Woxian Zhongdian Renkou Guanli Gongzuo de Diaocha yu Sikao (An Investigation and Reflections on My County's Focal Population Management Work)', 3, *Beijing Renmin Jingcha Xueyuan Xuebao (Journal of the Beijing People's Police Academy)*, 27–30.

Tong, Baocai and Wang, Qingbin, (1997) 'Lun Zhuanxiang Douzheng Zai Jiejue Tuchu de Zhi'an Wenti Zhong de Zhanlue Zuoyong (Discussing the Strategy of Specialist Struggles in Resolving Acute Public Order Problems)', in *Lun Zhongguo Tese de Gong'an (Discussion of Public Security with Chinese Characteristics)*, Kang, Damin (ed.), Beijing, Qunzhong Chubanshe (Masses Press), 256–65.

Tong, Yan, (1990) 'Guanyu Laodong Jiaoyang Xingzhi de Chubu Tantao (Preliminary Inquiry into the Nature of Re-education Through Labour)', in *Laodong Jiaoyang Yanjiu (Studies in Re-education Through Labour)*, Qunzhong Chubanshe (Masses Press), 59–68.

Trevaskes, Susan, (2003a) 'Public Sentencing Rallies in China: The Symbolizing of Punishmnet and Justice in a Socialist State', 39, *Crime, Law & Social Change*, 359–82.

Trevaskes, Susan, (2003b) 'Yanda 2001: Form and Strategy in a Chinese Anticrime Campaign', 36, *Australian and New Zealand Journal of Criminology*, 272–92.

Trevaskes, Susan, (2004) 'Propaganda Work in the Chinese Courts', 6, *Punishment and Society*, 5–21.

Trubek, David, (1972) 'Toward a Social Theory of Law: An Essay on the Study of Law and Development', 82, *The Yale Law Journal*, 1–50.

Trubek, David, Dezalay, Yves, Buchanan, Ruth and Davis, John, (1994) 'Global Restructuring and the Law: Studies of the Internationalization of Legal Fields and the Creation of Transnational Arenas', 44, *Case Western Reserve Law Review*, 407–98.

Tucker, Eric, (1984) 'The Law of Employers' Liability in Ontario 1861–1900: The Search for a Theory', 22, *Osgoode Hall Law Journal*, 213–80.

Turack, Daniel, (1999) 'The New Chinese Criminal Justice System', 7, *Cardozo Journal of International and Comparative Law*, 49–72.

Turk, Austin, (1989) 'Political Deviance and Popular Justice in China: Lessons for the West', in *Social Control in the People's Republic of China*, Troyer, R., Clark, J. and Rojek, D. (eds.), New York, Praeger, 34–42.

Turner, Karen, Gao, Hongjun and He, Weifang (eds.), (1994) *Meiguo Xuezhe Lun Zhongguo Falu Chuantong (Recent American Academic Writings on Traditional Chinese Law Selected Translations)*, Beijing, Zhongguo Zhengfa Daxue Chubanshe (China University of Politics and Law Press).

Unger, Roberto, (1976) *Law in Modern Society*, New York, The Free Press.

Van Hoecke, Mark and Warrington, Mark, (1998) 'Legal Cultures, Legal Paradigms and Legal Doctrine: Towards a New Model for Comparative Law', 47, *International and Comparative Law Quarterly*, 495–536.

von Senger, H., (2000) 'Ideology and Law-Making', in *Law-Making in the People's Republic of China*, Otto, Jan Michiel, Polak, Maurice V., Chen, Jianfu and Li, Yuwen (eds.), The Hague, Kluwer Law International, 41–54.

von Senger, Harro, (1985) 'Recent Developments in the Relations Between State and Party Norms in the People's Republic of China', in *The Scope of Power in China*, Schram, S.R. (ed.), Hong Kong, The Chinese University Press, 171–207.

Walder, Andrew, (1995) *The Waning of the Communist State: Economic Origins of Political Decline in China and Hungary*, Berkeley, University of California Press.

Wang, Chengbo, (1999) 'Gong'an Jiguan Mianlin de Shige Jinpo Wenti (Ten Urgent Problems Confronting Public Security Organs)', 1, *Gong'an Yanjiu* (*Public Security Studies*), 55–8.

Wang, Fang (ed.), (1993) *Mao Zedong Gong'an Gongzuo Lilun* (*Mao Zedong Public Security Work Theory*), Beijing, Qunzhong Chubanshe (Masses Press).

Wang, Faqiang, (1997) 'Tan Laodong Jiaoyang Zhidu de Cunfei (Discussing Preservation or Abolition of Re-education Through Labour)', 4, *Faxue Zazhi* (*Juridical Science Journal*), 32.

Wang, Feiling, (2005) *Organizing Through Division and Exclusion: China's Hukou System*, Stanford, Stanford University Press.

Wang, Gongfan, (1997) 'Cong Shehui Guanli Jizhi Shang Tantao Dangqian Xingshi Anjian Cengduo Yuanyin yu Gongzuo Duice (An Inquiry into the Reasons and Work Responses to the Increase in Criminal Cases up Till Now from the Base of Social Management Mechanisms)', in *Lun Zhongguo Tese de Gong'an* (*Discussion of Public Security with Chinese Characteristics*), Kang, Damin (ed.), Beijing, Qunzhong Chubanshe (Masses Press), 275–82.

Wang, Gongfan and Lu, Qingfu, (1994) 'Guanyu Ezhi Daodu Wailai Renkou Fanzui de Chuyi (Our Humble Opinion on Containing Crime by the Population who have Immigrated to the Capital from Outside)', in *Zhongguo Renmin Gong'an Daxue Xiaoqing Shizhounian Lunwen Xuanji* (*Collection of Essays to Celebrate the Tenth Anniversary of the Establishment of the China People's Public Security University*), Anon. (ed.), Beijing, Zhongguo Renmin Gong'an Daxue Chubanshe (China People's Public Security University Press), 130–8.

Wang, Hongshan, (1991) 'A Discussion of the Psychological Effect of Legal Punishment', in *Crime Trend in the 1990s and its Countermeasures of Prevention and Control*, Beijing, Chinese People's Public Security University Press (ed.), 107–16.

Wang, Huaian (ed.), (1989) *Zhongguo Renmin Gongheguo Falu Quanshu* (*Collection of Laws of the PRC*), Jilin, Jilin Renmin Chubanshe (Jilin People's Press).

Wang, Huaian *et al.* (eds.), (1993) *Zhongguo Renmin Gongheguo Falu Quanshu (Collection of Laws of the PRC*), Jilin, Jilin Renmin Chubanshe (Jilin People's Press).

Wang, Huanxin, (1989) 'Sifa Duli Shi Zhengzhi Tizhi Gaige Yunzuo Zhuangtai (Judicial Independence is a Component Part of Political System Reform)', *Faxue* (*Legal Studies*), reproduced from 9 January 1989, *Shijie Jingji Dabao* (*World Economic Herald*), 152.

Wang, Jiafu, (1995) 'Shehui Zhuyi Shichang Jingji Falu Zhidu Jianshe Wenti (Questions on Construction of a Socialist Market Economy Legal System)', in *Zhonggong Zhongyang Juban Falu Zhishi Jiangzuo Jishi (Record of the Course of Lectures on Legal Knowledge held by the CCP Central Committee*), Sifa Bu Fazhi Xuanquan Si (Ministry of Justice Legal System Propaganda Department) (ed.), Beijing, Falu Chubanshe (Law Press), 78–106.

Wang, Jiafu, Li, Buyun, Liu, Hainian, Liu, Han, Liang, Huixing and Xiao, Xianfu, (1996) 'Lun Yifa Zhiguo (Discussing Ruling the Country According to Law)', in *Yifa Zhiguo Jianshe Shehuizhuyi Fazhi Guojia* (*Ruling the Country According to Law Establishing a Socialist Nation Ruled According to Law*), Liu, Hainian, Li, Buyun and Li, Lin (eds.), Beijing, Zhongguo Fazhi Chubanshe (China Legal System Press), 6–19.

Wang, Jiancheng, (1992) 'Shourong Shencha Chulu Hezai (Where lies the way out for Detention for Investigation)', in *Xingshi Susong Fa de Xuigai yu Wanshan* (*Revision and Perfection of the Criminal Procedure Law*), Zhongguo Faxue Hui Susong Fa Yanjiu Hui (Procedure Law Association of the China Law Society) (ed.), Beijing, Zhongguo Zhengfa Daxue Chubanshe (China University of Politics and Law Press), 179–86.

Wang, Jiancheng, (2000) 'Qiangzhi Cuoshi (Coercive Measures)', in *Xingshi Susongfa Shishe Wenti Yanjiu (Research on the Issues in Implementation of the Criminal Procedure Law*), Chen, Guangzhong (ed.), Beijing, Zhongguo Falu Chubanshe (China Law Press), 78–99.

Wang, Jingtao and Zhou, Hong, (1993) 'Guanyu Jiaqiang Zhengfawei Gongzuo de Yidian Sikao (A Reflection on Strengthening the Work of the Political-Legal Committee)', 3, *Fanzui yu Duice* (*Crime and Countermeasures*), 9–12.

Wang, Kexian, (2002) 'Shourong Qiansong Zhidu Yingyu Feizhi (The System of Detention for Repatriation Should be Abolished)', *Guangxi Zhengfa Guanli Ganbu Xueyuan Bao* (*Journal of Guangxi Administrative Cadre Institute of Politics and Law*), 72–3.

Wang, Kexian, (2003a) 'Chajin Maiyin Piaochang de Xianjue Tiaojian (Preconditions for the Prohibition of Prostitution and Using Prostitutes)', *Zhongguo Lushi* (*Chinese Lawyer*), 77–8.

Wang, Kexian, (2003b) 'Shixi Chajin Maiyin Piaochang Cunzai de Jige Falu Wenti (An Exploratory Analysis of Several Existing Legal Problems on the Prohibition of Prostitution and Using Prostitutes)', 2006, www.wkxls.com/shownews.asp?newsid=145.

Wang, Mincan and Zhang, Shangyu (eds.), (1983) *Xingzheng Fa Gaiyao* (*Outline of Administrative Law*), Tianjin, Falu Chubanshe (Law Press).

Wang, Mingliang, (2004) *'Yanda' de Lixing Pingjia* (*An Appraisal of the Rationality of the 'Hard Strike'*), Beijing, Peking University Press.

Wang, Mingxin, (1993) *Gong'an Zhandouli Lun* (*Discussion of the Strike Force of the Public Security*), Beijing, Jingguan Jiaoyu Chubanshe (Police Officer's Education Press).

Wang, Shengjun (ed.), (1998) *Zhongguo Shehui Zhi'an Zonghe Zhili Nianjian, 1995–1996 (Yearbook of the Comprehensive Management of Public Order 1995–1996)*, Beijing, Falu Chubanshe (Law Press).

Wang, Shengjun (ed.), (2000) *Zhongguo Shehui Zhi'an Zonghe Zhili Nianjian, 1997–1998* (*Yearbook of the Comprehensive Management of Public Order 1997–1998*), Beijing, Falu Chubanshe (Law Press).

Wang, Shengzi, Li, Zhenyu, Zhang, Caigui and Zhang, Jincun, (2000) 'Guanyu Gong'an Minjing Canyu Feijingwu Huodong de Diaocha (Investigation on Pubic Security People's Police Being Involved in Non-Police-work Activities)', 1, *Gong'an Yanjiu (Public Security Studies)*, 21–4.

Wang, Shuilin, on behalf of Zhejiang Shen Gong'anting Keti Bianweihui, (Topic Editorial Committee of the Zhejiang Provincial Public Security Office), (1990) 'Zhejiangshen Xingshi Anjian Li'an Bushi Qingkuang de Diaocha yu Fenxi (Investigation and Analysis of the Situation of Inaccuracy in Filing Criminal Cases in Zhejiang Province)', in *Zhongguo Xianjieduan Fanzui Wenti Yanjiu (Lunwenji) (Study of the Problem of Crime in China in the New Era (Collection of Essays)*, Vol. 2, Yu, Lei (ed.), Beijing, Zhongguo Renmin Gong'an Daxue Chubanshe (China People's Public Security University Press), 577–91.

Wang, Xixin, (1993) 'Shourong Shencha Zhidu Ying yu Feichu (The System of Detention for Investigation Should be Abolished)', 3, *Zhongguo Faxue*, 110–12.

Wang, Xixin, (1998) 'Administrative Procedure Reforms in China's Rule of Law Context', 12, *Columbia Journal of Asian Law*, 251–77.

Wang, Xuezheng, (2001) 'Lun Woguo Xingzheng Susong he Xingzheng Fuyi Zhidu zhi Chuangxin (Discussing New Ideas in China's Administrative Litigation and Administrative Review Systems)', 102, *Zhongguo Faxue* (*Chinese Legal Science*), 67–74.

Wang, Yadong, Xia, Chenghua and Lei, Dongsheng, (1997) 'Gong'an Jiguan Yao Jiji Canyu Shehuizhuyi Jingshen Wenming Jianshe (Public Security Organs Must Actively Participate in Construction of Socialist Spiritual Civilization)', 1, *Gong'an Yanjiu* (*Public Security Studies*), 20–2.

Wang, Yong and Li, Jianhe, (1996) *Jingcha Xunluo Qinwulun* (*Discussion of Police Patrol Service*), Beijing, Zhongguo Renmin Gong'an Daxue Chubanshe (China People's Public Security University Press).

Wang, Yuming (ed.), (1993) *Mao Zedong Falu Sixiang Ku* (*Repository of Mao Zedong's Legal Thought*), Beijing, Zhongguo Zhengfa Daxue Chubanshe (China University of Politics and Law Press).

Wang, Zhenguang, (1992) 'Shenli Shourong Shencha Anjian zhi Qianjian (My Humble Opinion on Hearing Detention for Investigation Cases)', 4, *Fanzui yu Duice* (*Crime and Countermeasures*), 58–60.

Wang, Zhongfan, (1992) *Zhongguo Shehui Zhi'an Zonghe Zhili de Lilun yu Shijian (Theory and Practice of Comprehensive Management of Public Order in China)*, Beijing, Qunzhong Chubanshe (Masses Press).

Ward, Richard and Bracey, Dorothy, (1985) 'Police Training and Professionalism in the People's Republic of China', *The Police Chief*, 36–8.

Webb, Jen, Schirato, Tony and Danaher, Geoff, (2002) *Understanding Bourdieu*, London, Sage Publications.

Weber, Max, (1954) *Max Weber on Law in Economy and Society*, New York, Clarion.

Wei, Na, (2003) *Shequ Zuzhi yu Shequ Fazhan (Community Organisation and Community Development)*, Beijing, Hongqi Chubanshe (Red Flag Press).

Wei, Xiaopeng, (1998) 'Dui Laodong Jiaoyang Gongzuo de Diaocha (An Investigation of Re-education Through Labour Work)', 6, *Faxue Zazhi (Juridical Science Journal)*, 41–2.

Wen, Xuancai, (2000) 'Jingsheng Wenming Jianshe yu Shehui Xiandaihua (Construction of Spiritual Civilisation and the Modernisation of Society)', 64, *Changchun Shiwei Danxiao Xuebao (Journal of the Changchun Communist Party Institute)*, 8–11.

White, Lynn T., (1998) *Unstately Power: Local Causes of China's Intellectual, Legal and Governmental Reforms*, London, M.E. Sharpe.

Winkler, Edwin A., (1999) 'Describing Leninist Transitions', in *Transition from Communism in China: Institutional and Comparative Analyses*, Winkler, Edwin A. (ed.), London, Lynne Rienner Publishers, 3–48.

Wong, Kam, (1996) 'Police Powers and Control in the People's Republic of China: The History of Shoushen', 10, *Columbia Journal of Asian Law*, 367–90.

Wong, Kam, (2002) 'Policing in the People's Republic of China; The Road to Reform in the 1990s', 42, *British Journal of Criminology*, 281–316.

Wong, R. Bin, (1997) 'Confucian Agendas for Material and Ideological Control in Modern China', in *Culture & State in Chinese History: Conventions, Accommodations, and Critiques*, Huters, Theodore, Wong, R. Bin and Yu, Pauline (eds.), Stanford, Stanford University Press, 303–25.

Wright Mills, C., (1959) *The Sociological Imagination*, New York, Oxford University Press.

Wu, Dexing, (1999) 'Xingzheng Chengxu Fa Lun (Discussing Administrative Procedure Law)', in *Xingzheng Faxue Luncong (Administrative Law Review)*, Vol. 2, Luo, Haocai (ed.), Beijing, Falu Chubanshe (Law Press), 74–134.

Wu, Hongda Harry, (1992) *Laogai – The Chinese Gulag*, Ted Slingerland, (trans.), Boulder, Westview Press.

Wu, Qixiao (ed.), (1994) *Shilun Gong'an Jiguan de Zhengti Zuozhan he Kuaisu Fanying Nengli (Discussion of the Capacity of Public Security Organs for Waging Comprehensive Battles and for Rapid Response)*, Beijing, Zhongguo

Renming Gong'an Daxue Chubanshe (China People's Public Security Press).

Xi, Guoguang and Yu, Lei (eds.), (1996) *Zhongguo Renmin Shigao* (*Draft History of the Chinese People's Public Security*), Beijing, Jingguan Jiaoyu Chubanshe (Police Officers' Education Press).

Xia, Chongsu (ed.), (2001) *Laodong Jiaoyang Zhidu Gaige Wenti Yanjiu* (*Research on the Reform of Re-education Through Labour*), Beijing, Falu Chubanshe (Law Press).

Xiao, Jianguo, (2000) *Xiandai Shehui Zhi'an Fangfan* (*Contemporary Social Order Precautions*), Beijing, Falu Chubanshe (Law Press).

Xiao, Xun, (1989) 'Shilun Renmin Fayuan Shencha Juti Xingzheng Xingwei Hefaxing de Yuanze (Comments on the Principle of the People's Courts Investigating the Lawfulness of a Specific Administrative Act)', 4, *Zhongguo Faxue*, 30–6.

Xiao, Xun, (1994) *Zhonghua Renmin Gongheguo Guojia Peichang Fa de Lilun yu Shiyong Zhinan* (*Guide to the Theory and Application of the PRC State Compensation Law*), Beijing, Zhongguo Minzhu Falu Chubanshe (China Democracy and Law Press).

Xiao, Yang (ed.), (1996) *Zhongguo Xingshi Zhengce he Celue Wenti* (*Problems of China's Criminal Policy and Tactics*), Beijing, Falu Chubanshe (Law Press).

Xie, Chuanyu, (2000) *Zhi'an Xingzheng Cuoshi Tonglun* (*General Discussion of Public Security Administrative Measures*), Beijing, Zhongguo Renmin Gong'an Daxue Chubanshe (China People's Public Security University Press).

Xie, Chuanyu, (2002) 'Gong'an Paichusuo Minjing Jiben Yewu Kaoshi Fudao (Study Guide for the Basic Professional Work Test for Police Station Police Officers)', *Gong'an Jiaoyu* (*Public Security Education*), 50–2.

Xin, Chunying, (2002) 'Judicial Reform in China: A Mission that Could Not be Avoidable', XXIII, *Social Sciences in China*, 84–8.

Xin, Ren, (1993) 'China', in *Prostitution: An International Handbook on Trends, Problems and Policies*, Davis, Nanette (ed.), Westport, Greenwood Press, 87–107.

Xin, Ren, (1999) 'Prostitution and Economic Modernisation in China', 5, *Violence Against Women*, 1411–36.

Xing, Jie (ed.), (2002) *'Gong'an Jiguan Banli Laodong Jiaoyang Anjian Guiding' Lijie yu Shiyong* (*'Regulations on Public Security Organs Handling Re-education Through Labour Cases' Understanding and Application*), Beijing, Zhongguo Fanzheng Chubanshe (China Fangzheng Press).

Xinhua News Agency, (8 November 1998) 'Public Order "Still Grim" Says Parliamentarian', BBC Summary of World Broadcasts – Asia Pacific Stories.

Xinhua News Agency, (17 February 1999) 'Judiciary Reports Seven Million Cases Re-examined in Clean-up Campaign', BBC Summary of World Broadcast – Asian Pacific Stories.

Xinhua News Agency, (6 November 1999) 'Li Peng Rounds on Police Bullying of People', BBC Summary of World Broadcasts – Asia Pacific Stories.

Xinhua News Agency, (11 March 2000) 'Committee Meets to Discuss Measures to Maintain Public Security', BBC Summary of World Broadcasts – Asia Pacific Stories.

Xinhua News Agency, (29 June 2006) 'Former Navy Commander Stripped of Parliamentary Post', *Xinhua General News Service*.

Xiong, Xianguo, (2001) *Yifa 'Yanda'* (*'Strike Hard' According to the Law*), *Renmin Fayuan Bao* (*People's Court Daily*).

Xu, Anbiao, (1997) 'Guanyu Woguo Lifa Quanxian de Huafen (On the Division of the Boundaries of China's Legislation-making Powers)', in *Lifa Fa Yanjiu* (*Research on the Legislation Law*), Li, Buyun (ed.), Changsha, Hunan Renmin Chubanshe (Hunan People's Press), 80–93.

Xu, Changqi, (1994) 'Shehui Zhuyi Shichang Jingji Tiaojian Xia Ruhe Jianchi Renmin Jingcha Zongzhi de Ruogan Sikao (Several Reflections on How to Adhere to the Aims of the People's Police under the Conditions of the Market Economy)', in *Zhongguo Renmin Gong'an Daxue Xiaoqing Shi Zhou Nian Lunwen Xuanji* (*Selection of Essays for the Tenth Anniversary of the China People's Public Security University*), Beijing, Zhongguo Renmin Gong'an Daxue Chubanshe (China People's Public Security University Press), 299–305.

Xu, Chongde and Pi, Chunxie (eds.), (1991) *Xin Zhongguo Xingzheng Faxue Yanjiu Zhongshu 1949–1990* (*Complete Book of New China's Administrative Legal Studies*), Beijing, Falu Chubanshe (Law Press).

Xu, Songlin, (2001) 'Bao'an Chufen Ji Woguo Xingfa Zhidu de Wanshan (The Security Defence Punishment and Perfection of China's System of Criminal Law)', 23, *Xiandai Faxue* (*Modern Legal Science*), 131–5.

Xu, Weihua, (1996) *Shehui Zhi'an Zongghe Zhili Gongzuo Chutan* (*Preliminary Exploration of Comprehensive Management of Public Order Work*), Beijing, Renmin Fayuan Chubanshe (People's Court Press).

Xu, Yuansheng and Fang, Shiqiao, (1997) 'Lun Woguo Gong'an Gongzuo de Yi Da Tese – Laodong Jiaoyang Zhidu (Discussing a Major Characteristic of Our Country's Public Security Work – The System of Re-education Through Labour)', in *Lun Zhongguo Tese de Gong'an* (*Discussion of Public Security with Chinese Characteristics*), Kang, Damin (ed.), Beijing, Qunzhong Chubanshe (Masses Press), 30–46.

Xue, Dongsheng, (1996) 'Laodong Jiaoyang Bushu "Xingzheng Chufa Fa" Tiaozheng Fanwei (Re-education Through Labour is not Regulated Within the Scope of the "Administrative Punishments Law")', December, *Renmin Gong'an (People's Police)*, 35.

Yan, Cunsheng, (1996) 'Luelun Fazhi Guannian de Xiandaihua (Brief Discussion of Modernization of the Concept of the Legal System)', in *Fazhi Xiandaihua Yanjiu* (*Studies on Modernization of the Legal System*), Vol. 2,

Nanjing Normal University Legal System Modernisation Research Centre (ed.), Nanjing, Nanjing Normal University Press, 197–210.

Yan, Jiaqi, (1995) 'The Nature of Chinese Authoritarianism', in *Decision-Making in Deng's China: Perspectives from Insiders*, Hamrin, Carol Lee and Zhao, Suisheng (eds.), Armonk, New York, M.E. Sharpe, 3–14.

Yang, Chongxiao and Liu, Jinguo, (1990) 'Laodong Jiaoyang shi Yizhong Xingzheng Chufa (Re-education Through Labour is a Type of Administrative Punishment)', in *Laodong Jiaoyang Yanjiu Lunwen Xuanji (Re-education Through Labour Research, Selected Collection of Theses)*, Zhu, Hongde (ed.), Beijing, Qunzhong Chubanshe (Masses Press), 78–83.

Yang, Hongtai, (1996) 'Liang ci "Yanda" Douzheng de Bijiao yu Sikao (Comparison and Reflections on the Two "Hard Strike" Struggles)', 5, *Qingshaonian Fanzui Wenti (Issues on Juvenile Crime and Delinquency)*, 20–1, 17.

Yang, Jiejun, (2001) *Zouxiang Fazhi de Queshi Yanshuo: Fali, Xingzhengfa de Sikao (Putting into Words the Imperfections and Omissions on the Path to Rule by Law; A Reflection on Jurisprudence and Administrative Law)*, Beijing, Falu Chubanshe (Law Press).

Yang, Xiaojun, (1998) 'Shilun Xingzheng Qiangzhi Cuoshi yu Xingshi Qiangzhi Cuoshi de Chubie Ji Qi yu Xingzheng Susong de Guanxi (Tentative Discussion of the Distinction Between Administrative Coercive Measures and Criminal Coercive Measures and their Relationship to Administrative Litigation)', 3, *Gansu Zhengfa Xueyuan Xuebao (Journal of the Gansu Political-Legal College)*, 7–13, 23.

Yang, Xinhua, (1991) 'Shourong Shencha Cunzai de Wenti Ji Duice (Problems and Strategies of the Existence of Detention for Investigation)', 4, *Jiangxi Faxue (Jiangxi Legal Studies)*, 42.

Yang, Xuedong and Chen, Jiagang (eds.), (2004) *Lifa Tingzheng yu Difang Zhili Gaige (Legislative Hearings and Local Governance Reform)*, Beijing, Zhongyang Bianyi Chubanshe (Central Compilation & Translation Press).

Ye, Feng, (2000) 'The Development of Criminal Law in the PRC Since the Institution of the Reform and Opening Up Policy', in *Law-Making in the People's Republic of China*, Otto, Jan Michiel, Polak, Maurice V., Chen, Jianfu and Li, Yuwen (eds.), The Hague, Kluwer Law International, 205–14.

Yin, Kezhong, (1996) 'Dangqian Shehui Zhi'an Zonghe Zhili Cunzai de Zhuyao Wenti Ji Duice (Main Problems to date in the Comprehensive Managment of Social Order and their Countermeasures)', 1, *Zhengfa Xuekan (Journal of Political Science and Law)*, 1–6.

Yin, Shusheng and Li, Wencheng, (1997) 'Qunzhong Luxian shi Zhongguo Gong'an Gongzuo de Genben Tese (The Mass Line is a Basic Characteristic of Chinese Public Security Work)', in *Lun Zhongguo Tese de Gong'an* (*Discussion of Public Security with Chinese Characteristics*), Kang, Damin (ed.), Beijing, Qunzhong Chubanshe (Masses Press), 12–29.

Ying, Songnian (ed.), (1992a) *Xingzheng Fa yu Xingzheng Susong Fa Cidian* (*Dictionary of Administrative Law and Administrative Litigation Law*), Beijing, Zhongguo Zhengfa Daxue Chubanshe (China University of Politics and Law Press).

Ying, Songnian (ed.), (1992b) *Xingzheng Fa Zhuanti Jiangzuo* (*Series of Lectures on Specialist Topics in Administrative Law*), Beijing, Dongfang Chubanshe (Eastern Press).

Ying, Songnian (ed.), (1993) *Xingzheng Xingwei Fa: Zhongguo Xingzheng Fazhi Jianshi de Lilun yu Shijian* (*Administrative Action Law: Theory and Practice of the Construction of China's Administrative Legal System*), Beijing, Renmin Chubanshe (People's Press).

Ying, Songnian (ed.), (2001) *Xingzheng Chengxu Fa Lifa Yanjiu* (*Research on Legislation of the Administrative Procedure Law*), Hebei, Zhongguo Falu Chubanshe (China Law Press).

Ying, Songnian and Liu, Xin, (1996) *Zhongguo Chufa Fa Lilun yu Shiwu* (*Theory and Practical Tasks of China's Administrative Punishments Law*), Beijing, Zhongguo Shehui Chubanshe (China Society Press).

Ying, Songnian and Ma, Huaide, (1996) *Zhonghua Renmin Gongheguo Xingzheng Chufa Fa: Xuexi Fudao* (*Administrative Punishments Law of the PRC: Study Guide*), Beijing, Renmin Chubanshe (People's Press).

Ying, Songnian, Wang, Chengdong and Zhang, Xingxiang (eds.), (1999) *Xingzheng Fuyi Fa Lijie yu Shiyong* (*Application, Cases and Explanation of the Administrative Review Law*), Beijing, Zhongguo Minzhu Fazhi Chubanshe.

Young, Nam Cho, (2002) 'From "Rubber Stamps" to "Iron Stamps": The Emergence of Chinese Local People's Congresses as Supervisory Powerhouses', 171, *The China Quarterly*, 724–40.

Yu, Depeng, (2002) *Chengxiang Shehui: Cong Geli Zouxiang Kaifang* (*Urban and Rural Society: From Segregation Toward Openness*), Jinan, Shandong Renmin Chubanshe (Shandong People's Press).

Yu, Lei (ed.), (1992) *Dangdai Zhongguo de Gong'an Gongzuo* (*Public Security Work in Contemporary China*), Beijing, Dangdai Zhongguo Chubanshe (Contemporary China Press).

Yu, Lei (ed.), (1993) *Zhongguo Xian Jieduan Fanzui Wenti Yanjiu* (*Zongjuan*) (*Study of the Problem of Crime in China's New Era*) (*Central Volume*), Beijing, Zhongguo Renmin Gong'an Daxue Chubanshe (Chinese People's Public Security University Press).

Yu, Olivia and Zhang, Lening, (1999) 'The Under-recording of Crime by Police in China: A Case Study', 22, *Policing: An International Journal of Police Strategies and Management*, 252–63.

Yu, Wei, (1996) 'Bao'an Chufen Xingshi Lifahua (The Criminal Legislation of the Security Defence Punishment)', 79, *Faxue Pinglun* (*Law Review*), 9–17.

Yu, Xingzhong, (1989) 'Legal Pragmatism in the People's Repubic of China', *Journal of Chinese Law*, 29–51.

Zhai, Zhongdong, (2002) 'Bao'an Chufen Shiyong de Pingjing Ji Qi Jiejue (The Bottleneck on Application of Security Defence Punishments and its Resolution)', 17, *Faxue Luntan* (*Legal Forum*), 28–34.

Zhan, Wei, (2005) 'Zhongguo dui Maiyin Piaochang Renyuan Shourong Jiaoyu Zhidu de Yanjiu Baogao (Research Report on China's System of Detention for Education of Prostitutes and Clients of Prostitutes)', in *Xianzhi dui Renshen Ziyou de Xianzhi* (*To Refrain from the Restrictions on Personal Freedom*), Guo, Jian'an and Zheng, Xiaze (eds.), Beijing, Falu Chubanshe (Law Press), 416–70.

Zhan, Zhongle, (1997) 'Xingzheng Fa Jiben Lilun Yanjiu zhi Wojian – yi Pingheng lun Goujian Dangdai hua Zhongguo Xingzheng Faxue Tixi (My View on the Study of the Basic Theory of Administrative Law – Using Balance Theory to Establish a Contemporary Chinese Administrative Law Study System)', in *Xiandai Xingzhengfa de Pingheng Lilun* (*Balance Theory in Contemporary Administrative Law*), Luo, Haocai (ed.), Beijing, Beijing Daxue Chubanshe (Peking University Press), 105–15.

Zhang, Changgong, (1993) 'On the Management and Purity of the Police Force', in *Seminar on Police Management: A Paper Collection*, Office, Chinese People's Public Security University Foreign Affairs (ed.), Beijing, Chinese People's Public Security University Foreign Affairs Office, 14–17.

Zhang, Chengfeng, (1994) 'Jianshi Qiangda de Gong'an Duiwu Shouxian Bixu Henzhua Duiwu de Zhengguihua (In Order to Construct a Powerful Public Security Force We Must First Vigorously Promote its Regularised Development)', in *Zhongguo Renmin Gong'an Daxue Xiaoqing Shi Zhou Nian Lunwen Xuanji* (*Selection of Essays for the Tenth Anniversary of the China People's Public Security University*), Xiaoqing Chouban Bangongshi Xueshu Xiaozu (Anniversary Preparation Office Academic Small Group) (ed.), Beijing, Zhongguo Renmin Gongan Daxue Chubanshe (China People's Public Security Press), 275–80.

Zhang, Chong, (1990) 'Dui Laodong Jiaoyang Shenpi Chengxu de Tantao (Inquiry into the Procedure for Examination and Approval of Reeducation Through Labour)', in *Laodong Jiaoyang Yanjiu Lunwen Xuanji* (*Re-education Through Labour Research, Selected Collection of Theses*), Zhu, Hongde (ed.), Beijing, Qunzhong Chubanshe (Masses Press), 265–73.

Zhang, Chunhu, (1994) 'Jingli Qianshi (A Simple Explanation of Police Power)', in *Zhongguo Renmin Gong'an Daxue Xiaoqing Shi Zhou Nian*

Lunwen Xuanji (*Selection of Essays for the Tenth Anniversary of the China People's Public Security University*), Xiaoqing Chouban Bangongshi Xueshu Xiaozu (Anniversary Preparation Office Academic Small Group) (ed.), Beijing, Zhongguo Renmin Gongan Daxue Chubanshe (China People's Public Security Press), 345–54.

Zhang, Chunsheng, (1998) *The Development and Prospect of the Administrative Procedure Law of China*, International Symposium of Administrative Procedure Law and the 3rd East Asia Administrative Law Annual Meeting, Shanghai, 1–16.

Zhang, Chunsheng (ed.), (2000) *Zhonghua Renmin Gongheguo Lifa Fa Shiyi* (*Explanation of the PRC Legislation Law*), Beijing, Falu Chubanshe (Law Press).

Zhang, Dunli, (2000) 'Yi Wei Xuezhe dui Maiyin Piaochang Xianxiang de Yanjiu Baogao (Research Report of One Academic on the Phenomena of Prostitution and Using Prostitutes)', *Falu yu Shenghuo* (*Law and Life*), 20–1.

Zhang, Jianwei and Li, Zhongcheng, (1994) 'Lun Feichu Shourong Shencha (Discussing the Abolition of Detention for Investigation)', 3, *Zhongwai Faxue*, 55–9.

Zhang, Jun, (2004) 'Dui Jiedu Gongzuo de Tansuo yu Sikao (Exploration and Reflections on the Work of Giving up Drugs)', in *Jindu Wenti Yanjiu* (*Reserach on the Problem of Prohibiting Drugs*), Luo, Bingsen, Liang, Puyun and Yang, Hongping (eds.), Beijing, Zhongguo Renmin Gongan Daxue Chubanshe (China People's Public Security University Press), 435–8.

Zhang, Qingwu, (1990) 'Hukou Qianyi Zhengce Yanjiu (Study of Household Registration Migration Policy)', 1, *Gong'an Yanjiu* (*Public Security Studies*), 35–7.

Zhang, Qiong (ed.), (2002) *'Yanda' Zhengci de Lilun yu Shiwu* (*The Theory and Practice of the 'Hard Strike' Policy*), Beijing, Zhongguo Jiancha Chubanshe (China Procuratorate Press).

Zhang, Qiuhan (ed.), (1993) *Liuhai Anjian Falu Shiwu* (*Legal Workbook on Six Evils Cases*), Beijing, Zhongguo Zhengfa Daxue Chubanshe (China University of Politics and Law Press).

Zhang, Shanyu and Zhang, Shuyi (eds.), (1991) *Zouchu Digu de Zhongguo Xingzheng Faxue – Zhongguo Xingzheng Faxue Zongshu Yu Pingjia* (*The Underestimated Chinese Administrative Law Studies – Summary and Review of China's Administrative Law Studies*), Beijing, Zhongguo Zhengfa Daxue Chubanshe (China University of Politics and Law).

Zhang, Shencai, (2002) 'Qiantan Xidu Renyuan de Shehui Bangjiao (Brief Talk on Social Help and Rescue of Drug Users)', 71, *Gong'an Xuekan* (*Public Security Science Journal*), 25–7.

Zhang, Shiqi and Xu, Fanggen, (1994) 'Lun Wanshan Woguo Laodong Jioaoyang Zhidu (Discussing Perfecting My Country's Re-education

Through Labour System)', in *Xin Shiqi Gong'an Gongzuo Lilun yu Shijian Lunwenxuan* (*Selection of Essays on the Theory and Practice of Public Security Work in the New Era*), Yu, Lei (ed.), Beijing, Zhongguo Renmin Gong'an Daxue Chubanshe (China People's Public Security University Press), 703–12.

Zhang, Shufang and Guan, Baoying, (1992) 'Xingzheng Ziyou Cailiangquan Qiantan (Brief Exploration of Administrative Discretion)', 2, *Xingzheng Fa, Faxue Lunwenji* (*Administrative Law, Legal Studies Thesis Collection*), 191–3.

Zhang, Shusen, (1993) 'Dangdai Liudong Renkou Guanli Xianzhuang ji Duice (Current Situation and Countermeasures for Contemporary Management of the Floating Population)', *Fanzui Yu Duice (Crime and Countermeasures)*, 58–60.

Zhang, Shuyi, (1992) 'Examination of Several Controversial Issues in the Administrative Litigation Law (Draft)', 24, *Chinese Law and Government*, 47–53.

Zhang, Shuyi (ed.), (2000) *Xunqiu Xingzheng Susong Zhidu Fazhan de Liangxing Xunhuan* (*In Search of the Virtuous Cycle in Development of the System of Administrative Litigation*), Beijing, Zhongguo Zhengfa Daxue Chubanshe (China University of Politics and Law Press).

Zhang, Wei, (2002) 'Guanyu Shehui Zhi'an Zonghe Zhili de Lifa Wenti (On Legislation Problems with the Comprehensive Management of Public Order)', 23, *Dongyue Luncong* (*Dongyue Tribune*), 56–61.

Zhang, Xu, (1993) 'Lun Shoushen de Chulu yu Daibu de Gaige (Discussing the Way Out for Detention for Investigation and Reform of Arrest)', 2, *Xiandai Faxue* (*Modern Legal Science*), 20.

Zhang, Xuelei, (1996) 'Guanyu Laodong Jiaoyang Zhidu de Falu Sikao (Legal Reflections on the System of Re-education Through Labour)', in *Xingzheng Shenpan Yinan Wenti Xinlun* (*New Discussion of Difficult Problems of Administrative Adjudication*), Beijing, Zuigao Fayuan Chubanshe (Supreme People's Court Press), 30–44.

Zhang, Xueyun and Wang, Zhiqiang, (2000) 'Fazhihua: Shehui Zhi'an Zonghe Zhili de Biran Zouxiang (Legalization: The Inevitable Trend for the Comprehensive Management of Public Order)', 4, *Tianjin Shi Zhengfa Guanli Ganbu Xueyuan Xuebao*.

Zhang, Zhihui, (1991) 'Value Trend of Countermeasure Against Crime in the PRC in the 1990s, in *Crime Trend in the 1990s and its Countermeasures of Prevention and Control*, Chinese People's Public Security University (ed.), Beijing, 92–7.

Zhao, Bingzhi, (2001) 'Dui "Yanda" Zhong Jige Falu Guanxi de Sikao (Reflection on Several Legal Relationships in the "Hard Strike")', 9, *Renmin Jiancha* (*People's Procuratorate Monthly*).

Zhao, Bingzhi and Yu, Zhigang (eds.), (2000) *Dupin Fanzui* (*Drug Crimes*), Beijing, Zhongguo Renmin Gong'an Daxue Chubanshe (China People's Public Security University Press).

Zhao, Jisheng, (1991) 'Trends in Juvenile Delinquency in Recent Years in China and Thoughts on its Countermeasures', in *Crime Trend in the 1990s and its Countermeasures of Prevention and Control*, Chinese People's Public Security University (ed.), Beijing, 71–6.

Zhao, Zhenxiang (ed.), (1997) *Zhongguo Xin Xingfa Shilun yu Zuian* (*China's New Criminal Law: Explanation and Criminal Cases*), Beijing, Zhongguo Fangzhen Chubanshe (China Fangzhen Press).

Zheng, Mengwang, (2003) 'Guanyu Chajin Maiyin Piaochang Huodong de Lifa, Zhefa Sikao (Reflecting on Legislation and Enforcement in Banning Prostitution and Using Prostitutes)', 21, *Hebei Faxue* (*Hebei Law Science*), 94–7.

Zheng, Xinjun, (2000) 'Chuang Renmin Manyi Huodong de Shijian yu Sikao (Practice and Reflections on the Movement to Make the People Satisfied)', 1, *Gong'an Yanjiu* (*Public Security Studies*), 14–17.

Zhengci Falu Jiaoyanshi (Politics and Law Teaching and Research Office) (ed.), (1983) *Gong'an Gongzuo Gailun* (*Introduction to Public Security Work*), Zhongguo Xingshi Jingcha Xueyuan Chuanshe (China Criminal Police Institute Press).

Zhi'an Guanli Bianxie Zu (Public Order Management Editorial Committee) (ed.), (1992) *Zhi'an Guanli* (*Public Order Management*), Beijing, Qunzhong Chubanshe (Masses Press).

Zhonggong Zhongyang Wenxian Yanjiu Shi (Central Committee Documents Research Office) (ed.), (1992a) *Jianguo Yilai Zhongyao Wenxian Xuanbian 1949–1950* (*Selection of Important Documents Since the Establishment of the PRC 1949–1950*), Beijing, Zhongyang Wenxian Chubanshe (Central Documents Press).

Zhonggong Zhongyang Wenxian Yanjiu Shi (Central Committee Documents Research Office) (ed.), (1992b) *Jianguo Yilai Zhongyao Wenxian Xuanbian 1951* (*Selection of Important Documents Since the Establishment of the PRC 1951*), Beijing, Zhongyang Wenxian Chubanshe (Central Documents Press).

Zhonggong Zhongyang Wenxian Yanjiu Shi (Central Committee Documents Research Office) (ed.), (1992c) *Jianguo Yilai Zhongyao Wenxian Xuanbian 1952* (*Selection of Important Documents Since the Establishment of the PRC 1952*), Beijing, Zhongyang Wenxian Chubanshe (Central Documents Press).

Zhongguo Faxue Hui Susong Fa Yanjiu Hui (Procedure Law Association of the China Law Society) (ed.), (1992) *Xingshi Susongfa de Xiugai yu Wanshan* (*Revision and Perfection of the Criminal Procedure Law*), Beijing, Zhongguo Zhengfa Daxue Chubanshe (China Univeristy of Politics and Law Press).

Zhongguo Jingcha Xuehui (China Police Studies Society) (ed.), (2002) *Zhongguo Jingcha Fa Xue* (*Study of China's Police Law*), Beijing, Qunzhong Chubanshe (Masses Press).

Zhonghua Renmin Gong'an Bu (PRC People's Ministry of Public Security) (ed.), (1994) *Zhonghua Renmin Gongheguo Gong'an Guizhang Huibian 1957–1993* (*Collection of PRC Public Security Rules*), Beijing, Zhongguo Renmin Gong'an Daxue Chubanshe (PRC People's Public Security University).

Zhonghua Renmin Gongheguo Gong'an Bu (Ministry of Public Security of the PRC), (2005) *Zhonghua Renmin Gongheguo Jingcha Falu Quanshu: Guizhang Ji Guifanxing Wenjian Juan – Xiace* (*Encyclopedia of PRC Police Laws: Rules and Normative Documents Volume 2*), Beijing, Zhongguo Renmin Gong'an Daxue Chubanshe (China People's Public Security Press).

Zhou, Guangyang, (1999) 'Gong'an Jiguan Ruhe Shixian Yifa Xingzheng (How the Public Security Organs are to Realise Administration According to the Law)', 1, *Gong'an Yanjiu* (*Public Security Studies*), 33–6.

Zhou, Wei and Zhang, Jie, (1990) 'Guanyu Xingzheng Zhifa Wenti de Yantao (Discussion of Issues on Administrative Law Enforcement)', *Zhongguo Faxue*, 44–6.

Zhou, Yan, (1999) 'Woguo Laodong Jiaoyang Zhidu Gaige Chuyi (Proposals for Reform of My Country's Re-education Through Labour System)', 42, *Zhongguo Xingshifa Zazhi* (*China Criminal Science*), 21–7.

Zhou, Yongkang (ed.), (2005) *Zhonghua Renmin Gongheguo Jingcha Falu Quanshu* (*Encyclopedia of PRC Police Laws*), Beijing, Zhonghua Renmin Gong'an Daxue Chubanshe (Chinese People's Public Security University Press).

Zhou, Zhenxiang, (1997) *Zhongguo Xin Xingfa Shilun yu Zui'an* (*China's New Criminal Law: Explanation and Cases*), Zhongguo Fangzheng Chubanshe (China Fangzheng Press).

Zhu, Daren, (1996) 'Guanyu "Yanda" Douzheng de Xianshi Sikao (Reflecting on the Reality of the "Hard Strike" Struggle)', 4, *Gong'an Yanjiu* (*Public Security Studies*), 1–5.

Zhu, Fucheng, (1992) *Gong'an Xingzheng Zhifa Wenda* (*Questions and Answers on Public Security Administrative Enforcement*), Beijing, Jingguan Jiaoyu Chubanshe (Police Officer's Education Press).

Zhu, Guoxiong, (1996) 'Kuoda Xingzheng Susong Shouan Fanwei Chutan (Preliminary Exploration of Expanding the Scope of Receiving Cases in Administrative Litigation)', in *Xingzheng Shenpan Yinan Wenti Xinlun* (*New Discussion of Difficult Problems of Administrative Adjudication*), Beijing, Zuigao Fayuan Chubanshe (Supreme People's Court Press), 523–35.

Zhu, Hongde (ed.), (1990) *Laodong Jiaoyang Yanjiu Lunwen Xuanji* (*Re-education Through Labour Research, Selected Collection of Theses*), Beijing, Qunzhong Chubanshe (Masses Press).

Zhu, Jiang, (1999) 'Lun Laodong Jiaoyang de Lifa Wanshan (Discussing the Perfection of Legislation for Re-education Through Labour)', 1, *Gong'an Yanjiu* (*Public Security Studies*), 30–2, 58.

Zhu, Mingshan (ed.), (1994) *Zhongguo Shenpan Anli Yaolan* (*Anthology of Important Cases*), Beijing, Zhongguo Renmin Gong'an Daxue Chubanshe (China People's Public Security Press).

Zhu, Mingshan (ed.), (1998) *Renmin Fayuan Anlixuan* (*Selection of People's Court Cases*), Beijing, Shishi Chubanshe.

Zhu, Pingshan (ed.), (1991) *Zhi'an Guanli Chufa Tiaoli Jiaocheng* (*Teaching Materials on the Security Administrative Punishment Regulations*), Beijing, Qunzhong Chubanshe (Masses Press).

Zhu, Rongji, (1999) 'Renzhen Guanche Yifa Zhiguo Fanglue Qieshi Quanmian Tuijin Yifa Xingzheng (Diligently Implementing the General Plan of Ruling the Country According to Law is to Conscientiously and Comprehensively Advance Administration According to Law)', in *Yifa Xingzheng, Congyan Zhizheng, Jianshi Lianjie, Qinzheng, Wushi, Gaoxiao Zhengfu* (*Administration According to Law, Strictly Establish an Honest, Industrious, Pragmatic and Highly Efficient Government*), Guowuyuan Yifaxingzheng Gongzuo Huiyi (State Council Administration According to the Law Working Committee) (ed.), Beijing, Zhongguo Fazhi Chuanshe (China Legal System Press), 1–12.

Zhu, Weiqiu, (2000) *Zhongguo Minzhu Zhengzhi Faluhua Tanjiu* (*Exploration of the Legalisation of China's Democratic Policy*), Beijing, Zhongguo Zhengfa Daxue Chubanshe (China Politics and Law University Press).

Zhu, Xudong, (2001) 'Gaige Kaifang Yi Lai Maiyin Piaochang Wenti Yanjiu Zongshu (A Summary of the Research on the Problem of Prostitution and Using Prostitutes Since the Reform and Opening Up Policy)', 4, *Gong'an Yanjiu* (*Police Research*), 92–6.

Zuigao Renmin Fayuan (Supreme People's Court) (ed.), (1998) *Renmin Fayuan Anlixuan* (*Selection of Cases of the People's Courts*), Beijing, Shishi Chubanshe.

Zuigao Renmin Jianchayuan Jiansuo Jiancha Ting (ed.), (1992) *Laodong Jiaoyang Laodong Jiaoyang Jiancha Ciliao Fagui Leibian* (*Collection of Materials and Rules on the Category of Re-education Through Labour, Supervision of Re-education Through Labour*), Beijing, Zhongguo Jiancha Chubanshe (China Procuratorate Press).

INDEX